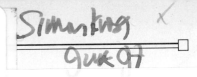

UNIVERSITY OF
GLOUCESTERSHIRE
at Cheltenham and Gloucester

The Irwin Series in Marketing

Gilbert A. Churchill, Jr., Consulting Editor
University of Wisconsin, Madison

Cases in Product Management

John A. Quelch
Sebastian S. Kresge Professor of Marketing
Graduate School of Business Administration
Harvard University

IRWIN

Chicago • Bogota • Boston • Buenos Aires • Caracas
London • Madrid • Mexico City • Sydney • Toronto

Senior sponsoring editor: Stephen M. Patterson
Editorial assistant: Christine Scheid
Marketing manager: Jim Lewis
Project editor: Karen J. Nelson
Production manager: Laurie Kersch
Designer: Heidi J. Baughman
Art coordinator: Heather Burbridge
Compositor: Bi-Comp, Inc.
Typeface: 10/12 Times Roman
Printer: R. R. Donnelley & Sons Company

Library of Congress Cataloging-in-Publication Data

Quelch, John A.
    Cases in product management / John A. Quelch.
        p.   cm. — (The Irwin series in marketing)
    Includes index.
    ISBN 0-256-16347-2
    1. Product management—Cases studies.   2. New products—Marketing—
Case studies.   I. Title.   II. Series.
    HF5415.15.Q45 1995
    658.5—dc20   94–14311

Printed in the United States of America
1 2 3 4 5 6 7 8 9 0 DO 1 0 9 8 7 6 5 4

Preface

Product management issues are increasingly critical to successful marketing management. Despite significant advances in marketing research methodologies, the new product failure rate remains high. Private label products continue to gain share at the expense of national brands in many categories. And the claim is now often heard that traditional marketing-driven brand management is no longer relevant in a world dominated by distributor power, multifunctional teamwork, and flat organizations. At the same time, the high acquisition prices frequently paid for consumer product companies emphasize the continuing value of brand equities developed and nurtured by successive product managers, often over many decades.

These and other important issues are addressed in the case studies presented in this compendium. The book should be of interest to instructors wishing to offer not only product management courses but also courses in marketing management and marketing strategy tailored to students contemplating careers in product management. The book may be used as a required supplement to a textbook or as the principal required text in conjunction with assigned readings.

Books are rarely the product of a single individual. Ideas, thoughts, and suggestions from many sources all contribute to ultimately shaping a final product. With casebooks, this is even more true. Cases would not be possible without close cooperation between industry and academia. In my own case, these relationships have been forged over many years and I am extremely grateful to those executives who have so generously shared with me and my associates their time, insights, and experiences. It is their "real-life" challenges in a diverse and increasingly competitive marketplace that I have attempted to capture in this compendium in order to provide a practical context for the understanding, learning, and application of sound managerial principles.

Cases demonstrate principles continuously defined, challenged, and refined in business school classrooms. For their thoughts and comments, I would like to extend my gratitude to my colleagues who have read through and taught these cases and so enriched them as learning vehicles. I also wish to thank three faculty colleagues for permitting me to use case studies they prepared. They are V. Kasturi Rangan (Harvard Business School), Paul W. Farris (University of Virginia), and N. Craig Smith (Georgetown University). In addition, my thanks goes to the Harvard Business School research associates who worked long and hard to gather and compile information and prepare drafts of the cases themselves. These include, Cynthia Bates, Neil Collins, Alice MacDonald Court, Tammy Bunn Hiller, Nathalie Laidler, Susan P. Smith, Melanie D. Spencer, John L. Teopaco, and Julie L. Yao.

Finally I wish to thank Steve Patterson and Christine Scheid at Richard D. Irwin for their enthusiasm and editorial support.

John Quelch
Boston, Massachusetts

About the Author

John A. Quelch is the Sebastian S. Kresge Professor of Marketing, Graduate School of Business Administration, Harvard University. He has served on the Harvard faculty since 1979. He currently teaches in the HBS International Senior Managers Program and also teaches the International Marketing Management course in the MBA program.

Professor Quelch has (co)authored eleven books including *Marketing Management* (Irwin, 1993), *Ethics in Marketing* (Irwin, 1992), *Global Marketing Management* (Addison-Wesley, 3rd ed., 1994), *Cases in Advertising and Promotion Management* (Irwin, 4th ed., 1994), *The Marketing Challenge of Europe 1992* (Addison-Wesley, 2nd ed., 1991), *How to Market to Consumers: Ten Ways to Win* (Wiley, 1989), *Sales Promotion Management* (Prentice-Hall, 1989), *Advertising and Promotion Management* (Krieger, 2nd ed., 1987), and *Cases in Consumer Behavior* (Prentice-Hall, 2nd ed., 1986). His numerous articles on marketing management topics have appeared in *Harvard Business Review, Sloan Management Review, Marketing Science, McKinsey Quarterly, Journal of Business Research, Journal of Consumer Marketing, Journal of Consumer Policy, Journal of Retailing,* and *Business Horizons.*

Professor Quelch has consulted to more than 25 Fortune 500 companies and has given seminars in over 20 countries. He serves as a nonexecutive director and chairman of the audit committee of both Reebok International Ltd. and WPP Group plc, the British marketing services company.

Professor Quelch graduated from Oxford University (B.A. and M.A.), University of Pennsylvania (M.B.A.), and Harvard University (M.S. and D.B.A.).

Contents

PART I   The Product Development Process

General Mills, Inc.: Yoplait Custard Style Yogurt (A)

In June 1980, Bruce Becker, director of New Business Development at Yoplait USA, a Consumer Foods Group subsidiary of General Mills, Inc., was deciding on how to proceed with a new product, Custard Style Yogurt. The product was the first in Yoplait's product line expansion program, and test results to date were encouraging. Yoplait's original product line had been introduced into 60 percent of the USA—the Midwest and West—during the previous two years, and had become the number two yogurt brand nationally. General Mills management was very pleased with Yoplait Original Style's success, but they were also eager to introduce new products to capitalize on Yoplait's momentum and to preempt competition.

Management attention was focused on Custard Style Yogurt, identified early on as the most promising line extension. Consumer product testing results had been positive, but Becker realized that he needed test market data for a more reliable measure of Custard Style's potential. He was considering the following options: a simulated test market, a "mini-market" test, and a regular test market. Given unlimited time, Becker would have considered doing all three, but under pressure to roll out Custard Style as soon as possible, he had to select one or two test approaches to conduct in sequence or at the same time. In preparing for any test, Becker knew that there were still several marketing issues that needed resolution such as Custard Style's positioning, pricing, and final product specifications.

Company Background

In 1928, James Ford Bell, president of the Washburn Crosby Company, incorporated several flour millers to form the world's largest grain processor, General Mills, Inc. Gold Medal Flour, General Mills' original prod-

---

This case was prepared by Research Assistant John L. Teopaco under the direction of Professor John A. Quelch as the basis for class discussion rather than to illustrate effective or ineffective handling of an administrative situation. Proprietary data have been disguised. Copyright © 1986 by the President and Fellows of Harvard College. Harvard Business School case 9–586–087.

uct, was still a major brand in 1980, but by then, General Mills had expanded into other consumer foods and nonfood categories.

Total company sales for fiscal year 1980 (ending May 25, 1980) were $4.17 billion with net earnings of $170.0 million. Fiscal 1980 was the fourteenth successive year of sales increase and the eighteenth consecutive year of gain in earnings. Advertising expenditures increased 13 percent in 1980 to $213.1 million.

General Mills comprised five major operating groups—Consumer Foods, Restaurants (e.g., Red Lobster Inns, York Steak Houses), Creative Products (e.g., Parker Brothers, Star Wars toys), Fashion (e.g., Izod/ Lacoste shirts, Monet jewelry), and Specialty Retailing (e.g., Pennsylvania House furniture). Consumer Foods was the largest group with 1980 sales of $2.2 billion and operating profits of $210.5 million (53 percent of total company sales and operating profits). The group marketed products such as Cheerios and Wheaties breakfast cereals, Nature Valley Granola Bars, Gold Medal Flour, Hamburger Helper Dinner Mixes, Betty Crocker Desserts, Gorton's Frozen Fish products, and Yoplait Yogurt.

Product Management at General Mills

General Mills established its product management system more than 20 years ago. Under this system, responsibility for every General Mills brand was assigned to a product manager. By placing one person in charge of a brand's overall performance in the marketplace, General Mills tried to ensure that every brand was managed as if it were a small company, rather than part of a large bureaucracy. It was the product manager's duty to be wholly knowledgeable about all issues involving his or her brand—from product ingredients to media planning.

General Mills recruited MBAs for its product management training program. They began as marketing assistants working under the supervision of a product manager. After about a year, they were promoted to assistant product manager. Approximately two years later, the successful assistant product manager was promoted to product manager.

General Mills took pride in several distinctive features of its product management system. The organization had fewer levels than most large consumer goods companies. Product managers reported to marketing directors (each responsible for a group of brands) who, in turn, reported to division general managers.[1] Unlike other packaged goods companies, General Mills did not have senior product managers or group product managers between the product managers and the marketing directors, nor

---

[1] There were six division general managers within the Consumer Foods operating group. Each division had its own marketing research organization, but shared an 800-person national sales force. In addition, division general managers did not control plants dedicated to manufacturing their products but, rather, purchased manufacturing services from the Packaged Foods Operations Division.

were there business unit managers between the marketing directors and division general managers. General Mills believed that a flat organizational structure and an emphasis on verbal rather than written communications promoted more efficient decision making and greater breadth of responsibility for entry-level managers.

A second distinctive feature of General Mills' product management system was the systematic rotation of junior marketing personnel not only among brands at different stages of development, but also across divisions. For example, a marketing assistant on Cheerios might be promoted to assistant product manager on new products, say Betty Crocker desserts, and later be reassigned to an established frozen foods brand. Career development was further helped by General Mills' mix of small and large brands. According to one marketing director:

> A small brand would have only one marketing assistant reporting to a product manager. He or she can take a cut at everything and develop considerable breadth. On a large brand, each of several marketing assistants might be given a specific functional responsibility on a six-month rotational basis. In this kind of job, an individual can develop depth of expertise.

General Mills felt that a series of assignments on diverse brands of varying sizes enriched the manager's learning experience and prepared him or her for general management.

Yoplait USA

In October 1977, General Mills acquired the rights to market Yoplait products in the USA from Sodima, a French dairy cooperative. General Mills was interested in entering the yogurt market, but without any dairy experience, the company decided to enter via acquisition instead of internal development. Sodima had been licensing its technology around the world since the late 1960s, and in the USA it began by licensing the rights to Yoplait Yogurt to Michigan Brand Cottage Cheese, a regional dairy company. The company sold Yoplait Original Style Yogurt in five flavors in Michigan, Indiana, and Ohio. Annual sales were about $10 million. Upon taking over the rights to the Yoplait name, General Mills also bought Michigan Brand's yogurt manufacturing plant.

General Mills integrated the Yoplait acquisition into its operations by forming Yoplait USA as a subsidiary of the Consumer Foods Group. At 33 years of age, Stephen Rothschild, formerly a marketing director in the New Business Division, was made president of Yoplait USA.[2] Rothschild believed that Yoplait required a nontraditional type of management. Yogurt was different from the standard General Mills product—it was refrigerated and had only a 30-day shelf life; Production could not build up

---

[2] General Mills typically maintained a New Business Division, investigating new product opportunities in categories in which the company did not yet compete.

inventory. This required greater coordination with Distribution and Sales and quick decision making in day-to-day operations.

Recruiting from various parts of the General Mills organization, Rothschild assembled an entrepreneurial management team of individuals who were looking for a challenge and who wanted to "do something different." As Bruce Becker observed, "The appeal was the opportunity to deal with the total business. The team was highly self-motivated. Being located in a building outside corporate headquarters, we built up a strong camaraderie. Sometimes, we spent weekends in the pilot plant making yogurt."

Exhibit 1 shows Yoplait USA's organizational structure in 1980. With a background in marketing research, Becker assumed responsibilities for new product development and marketing research. He had an assistant product manager who worked on new products. A three-person brand group managed regular style yogurt and, along with Becker's group, reported to the vice president of Marketing.

The Yogurt Market

Yogurt was produced by inoculating milk with bacteria. After multiplying in the milk, the bacteria consumed the milk's sugar lactose and replaced it

EXHIBIT 1   Yoplait USA Organizational Structure

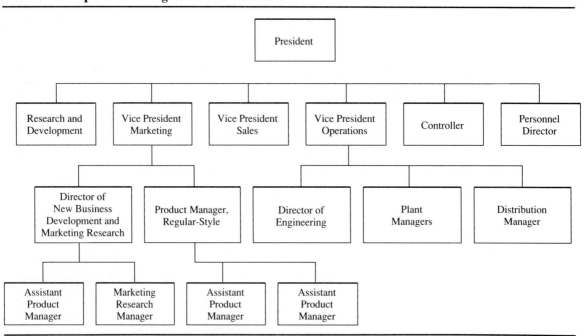

with acids. The acids curdled the milk, giving yogurt its thick consistency and tart flavor.

When General Mills began rolling out Yoplait regular style yogurt to the West Coast in late 1978, the yogurt market comprised three product segments: sundae-style (53 percent of yogurt volume), Swiss-style (37 percent), and plain (9 percent). Sundae-style yogurts such as Dannon contained fruit on the bottom of the cup which was stirred up prior to eating. Swiss-style contained fruit mixed in or blended throughout the yogurt, while plain yogurt contained no fruit. All three types had a thick consistency.

Yoplait Original Style Yogurt was all natural and had fruit mixed throughout. Yoplait was differentiated by its French origin (all other yogurts were American), its unique, reverse-cone, plastic package very different from the traditional, cylindrical, waxed paper cup, and most especially, by its creamy, smooth texture as opposed to the thicker consistency of sundae-style and Swiss-style yogurts. Yoplait also was less tart than other yogurts.

The total US refrigerated yogurt market in 1980 was estimated at 87 million cases (12 8-oz. cups/case) or $425 million in retail sales. This represented annual consumption of five cups per capita compared to 45 cups per capita in France. Unit volume had not changed from the previous year, but over the last 10 years category volume had increased at an average annual rate of 13 percent, roughly trebling since 1970. However, in 1980, 45 percent of Americans still had not tried yogurt and only 25 percent of households were buying yogurt in any two-month period. Ten percent of the population accounted for three-quarters of all yogurt consumption. Advertising media spending for yogurt in 1980 was estimated at $18 million.

The yogurt market was fragmented and highly regional, partly because regional dairies used surplus milk to manufacture either yogurt or cottage cheese. There was no nationally distributed brand in 1980 although Dannon, the number one brand with a 24 percent unit market share and availability in two-thirds of the country, was expected to be national within two years, along with Yoplait. Private labels, accounting for 26 percent of yogurt volume nationwide, made it difficult for new national brands to obtain shelf space without heavy dealing (especially in the East) and without convincing the trade that the total category would expand in size.

Exhibit 2 lists market shares and yogurt per capita consumption indexes (PCI) for key markets. In Southern California, Yoplait was the leading brand with a 25.2 percent market share followed by Knudsen with 20.6 percent and Jersey Maid with 11.3 percent. In metropolitan New York, on the other hand, Dannon was the leader with 41.0 percent of the market followed by Colombo with 12.6 percent and Breyers with 11.5 percent. Category development, as measured by a market's per capita consumption of yogurt relative to the national average, also varied greatly

---

EXHIBIT 2   Yogurt Per Capita Indexes (PCI) and Unit Market Shares (February/March 1980)

Market	Percent of US Population	PCI	Leading Brand's Market Shares
Southern California	6.4%	252	Yoplait—25.2% Knudsen—20.6 Jersey Maid—11.3 Johnston's—6.1 Private Label—27.7
Northern California	4.1	220	Yoplait—20.5 Knudsen—15.1 Crystal—5.8 Private Label—47.7
Pacific Northwest	3.4	132	Yoplait—19.5 Yami—10.4 Private Label—57.5
Minnesota/Iowa	3.0	55	Dannon—25.3 Yoplait—20.8 Slim 'n Trim—10.6 Gaymont—6.0 Private Label—0
Metropolitan Chicago	3.5	96	Dannon—54.8 Yoplait—18.9 Private Label—17.9
Metropolitan New York	7.1	192	Dannon—41.0 Colombo—12.6 Breyers—11.5 Light 'n Lively—9.3 La Yogurt—7.3 Private Label—9.1
Baltimore/Washington	3.4	82	Dannon—30.8 Breyers—10.2 Light 'n Lively—7.1 Private Label—40.4
Carolina/Virginia	6.6	40	Dannon—29.6 Light 'n Lively—18.6 Breyers—12.5 Pet—7.0 Private Label—27.1

by region. Southern California was highly developed with a 252 PCI whereas Carolina/Virginia was underdeveloped with a 40 PCI.

The yogurt market was expected to become highly competitive with the growing involvement of sophisticated marketers. Dannon was owned by Beatrice Foods, Breyers and Light 'n Lively by Kraft, Inc., and Borden yogurt by Borden, Inc. The market was becoming increasingly segmented as the various brands attempted to carve out market niches through a variety of product positionings. Dannon's strategy was to offer nutrition and value; Breyers was positioned as superior-tasting natural yogurt; Light 'n Lively also emphasized taste and naturalness, but was targeted at light users and nonusers of yogurt; Borden was positioned as the all-natural American yogurt and capitalized on the company's heritage as a dairy products leader; New Country claimed fewer calories and full taste. Yoplait regular style was positioned as a premium, all-natural French yogurt with a smooth, creamy texture. Johanna Farms had a strong presence in metropolitan New York with La Yogurt, a Yoplait-type product that emphasized superior taste, claiming that it was yogurt made the French way—all natural fruit blended with yogurt to produce a creamy, smooth texture. Exhibit 3 summarizes competitive positionings, advertising expenditures, and geographic coverage.

Competitors also differed in their distribution systems. Using a fleet of leased trucks, Dannon delivered its yogurt directly to supermarkets where the drivers stocked the shelves. Dannon's shelf life was limited to 17 days. Inventory control and shelf space management were, therefore, extremely important. However, some major supermarket chains, especially in the West, disliked store door delivery and wanted Dannon to ship to their refrigerated warehouses. Yoplait and most other yogurt producers, except for some regional dairies, shipped to chain warehouses rather than using store door delivery. Yoplait had experimented with store door delivery in Chicago, but the test proved uneconomical. The chains objected to the loss of control, there was union opposition, and out-of-stocks were frequent on the most popular flavors.

EXHIBIT 3 Yogurt Brands' Geographic Coverages, Positionings, and Media Expenditures (fiscal year 1980)

Brand	Parent Company	Percent US Coverage	Positioning/Strategy	Estimated Media Expenditures (000s)	Percent Change vs. Previous Year
Yoplait	General Mills, Inc.	60%	All-natural, premium quality, creamy French yogurt	$3,150	+90%
Dannon	Beatrice Foods	66	Nutrition/value reassurance	6,500	+110
Breyers	Kraft, Inc.	54	Superior-tasting, natural yogurt	2,800	+15
Light 'n Lively	Kraft, Inc.	48	Good taste, natural reassurance	2,700	+50
Borden	Borden, Inc.	45	Good-tasting, all-natural American yogurt/Borden heritage	660	+15
Knudsen	Knudsen Co.	14	Nutrition/taste/leadership	810	+15
Colombo	Colombo Co.	21	Production reassurance/all-natural	600	+50
La Yogurt	Johanna Farms	NA	Superior taste because of fruit and French recipe/natural reassurance	NA	NA

Consumer Attitudes and Usage

A Gallup national survey of yogurt users showed that the yogurt user group stopped growing in 1979—32 percent of adults had eaten refrigerated yogurt in the past four weeks, the same as in 1978. Little or no growth was anticipated in the near term because the number of people who expected to eat yogurt in the next four weeks grew only 2 percent:

	Among All Respondents		
	1977	*1978*	*1979*
Have eaten yogurt in past four weeks	28%	32%	32%
Expect to eat yogurt in next four weeks	32	36	38

Current users ate yogurt primarily for taste, followed by nutrition and dietary considerations. The biggest changes since the survey began in 1977 were the decreases in use for dietary reasons and as a lunch or meal substitute. This reflected the growing recognition of yogurt as a high-calorie product:

	Among Respondents Expecting to Use Yogurt in Next Four Weeks		
Reasons for Usage	*1977*	*1978*	*1979*
Like the taste	51%	57%	54%
Nutritious	21	17	21
Nonfattening/dietary	20	14	13
Eat for lunch/meal	12	5	4

In terms of usage occasion, yogurt continued to be eaten most often at lunchtime, but this occasion continued to decline significantly. "Evening snack" and "between meals" were the next most important usage occasions:

	Have Eaten Yogurt in Past Four Weeks and Intend to Use in Next Four Weeks		
Have Eaten Yogurt at:	*1977*	*1978*	*1979*
Lunchtime	62%	56%	51%
Evening snack	32	30	36
Between meals	31	34	34
Dessert	18	14	14
With dinner	12	14	12

Among those who ate yogurt at lunch, for the first time since 1977 more consumers ate yogurt with other foods than by itself:

	Among Respondents Who Ate Yogurt at Lunch		
Ate Yogurt:	*1977*	*1978*	*1979*
By itself	50%	46%	40%
With other foods	38	37	47

On a national basis, Dannon scored highest on unaided brand awareness, followed by Light 'n Lively and Yoplait. Yoplait moved up from fifth place in 1978, passing Breyers and Borden. In its two major markets, the Midwest and West, Yoplait had the second-highest unaided awareness:

	Unaided Brand Awareness—1979		
	US	*Midwest*	*West*
Yoplait	12%	28%	13%
Dannon	47	68	2
Light 'n Lively	13	11	0
Knudsen	6	0	28
Breyers	8	3	1

Dannon was the brand eaten most often on a national basis. No other brand was mentioned by more than 5 percent of respondents. Regionally, Yoplait was the second most frequently consumed brand in the Midwest, and third in the West:

	Brand Eaten Most Often—1979		
	US	*Midwest*	*West*
Yoplait	4%	8%	6%
Dannon	41	51	0
Light 'n Lively	3	1	0
Knudsen	5	0	21
Breyers	3	1	1
Lucerne	3	2	8

Respondents who were aware of both Yoplait and Dannon rated the two brands along several product attributes. Dannon was rated superior to Yoplait on nine attributes including overall quality, overall taste, and texture:

| | Percent Rating Excellent—1979[3] | |
	Yoplait	Dannon
Overall quality	17%	31%
Overall taste	17	35
Fruit flavor	17	37
Texture	14	28
Amount of fruit	13	23
Overall appearance	16	27
Appeal to entire family	8	21
Container	11	18
Value	10	18

A demographic analysis of respondents who indicated that they would be likely to eat yogurt in the next four weeks showed that the characteristics of those who would be relatively more inclined to eat yogurt were college educated, female, young (18–34 years) or old (63+ years), living in metropolitan areas in the West and East, and concerned with weight and diet. Children's usage declined from 1978 to 1979. In 1978, 32 percent of families with children reported child consumption of yogurt, versus 25 percent in 1979. The predominant usage occasions for children were as a between-meal and after-school snack (56 percent of yogurt-eating children) and as an evening snack (46 percent).

Yogurt Motivation Study

As a result of the unexpected decline in yogurt usage in 1979, General Mills conducted an in-depth qualitative research study involving 30 focus groups nationwide to identify the underlying motivations of yogurt usage. The major change that had taken place in the yogurt category was the shift from meal to snack as the primary usage occasion. This was a result of consumers realizing that fruit yogurt was high in calories and that yogurt was not filling enough to replace a meal. The shift toward a snack orientation resulted in a decline in consumption among both regular/traditional and new users of yogurt. Yogurt was increasingly viewed as a treat rather than a staple by the health and diet conscious and by ethnic traditional-

---

[3] Dannon's earlier market introduction meant that it had achieved a higher trial rate than Yoplait at the time of the Gallup survey.

ists. In its new role as a snack, yogurt was in competition with other snacks which were mostly shelf-stable, easier to keep in inventory in the home, and often cheaper.

The reduction in yogurt purchases by regular user households had a secondary effect among marginal users—members of regular user households for whom yogurt was not specifically purchased, but who, on occasion, ate the product because it was available. Marginal users' consumption declined with the reduction in yogurt inventory kept by regular users. Regular/traditional yogurt users continued to be an important market segment, but new users had passed them in number. New users were more likely to view yogurt consumption as an indulgence and treat it primarily as a snack. Total yogurt consumption was down because the volume accounted for by new users did not make up for the lost volume from regular/traditional users. The study forecast that long-term yogurt volume would erode substantially unless the category was able to reestablish a strong, heavy user base.

The shift to a snack orientation resulted in a proliferation of new, taste-oriented yogurts and taste improvements among existing brands. In spite of such efforts, hard-core nonusers were not expected to be converted. It was believed that they would always hold a negative taste perception for yogurt. However, improved flavor was expected to increase yogurt's appeal among children. Its foreign taste had dissuaded many children from eating yogurt. The study concluded that price would play a more important role in yogurt purchase behavior. As a meal, yogurt was inexpensive, but not as a snack.

In mature yogurt markets, consumers perceived Dannon as being synonymous with yogurt. The reason was not that Dannon was their regular brand, but that Dannon had been on the market the longest. Most yogurt users had tried the brand. Yoplait was perceived as a high-quality, premium-priced brand. Yoplait's primary positive attribute was its flavor; many preferred its less tart taste. But Yoplait's thinner consistency typically determined a consumer's acceptance or rejection of the brand. Many disliked it, but everyone considered the texture to be unique. The research indicated that Yoplait's thinner texture would continue to limit the scope of its appeal.

Yoplait USA Operations and Strategy

Yoplait had three yogurt plants in California, Michigan, and Texas. They made yogurt with freeze-dried yogurt cultures imported from France. Yogurt's production process began with raw milk in a base formula that was heat treated and inoculated with bacteria culture. The product was fermented in tanks and collected, and afterwards, fruit was added. The yogurt was packaged and refrigerated. Sodima worked closely with General Mills in developing Yoplait USA's technical expertise. A Sodima engineer worked at Yoplait USA for two years to help in product development.

At the time of the General Mills acquisition, Yoplait was sold through brokers, but by 1980, it was sold in almost all markets by the General Mills sales force who handled all Consumer Foods Group products. Stephen Rothschild had committed to four five-year goals when he assumed Yoplait USA's presidency: (1) national distribution, (2) $100 million in sales, (3) 20 percent market share, and (4) profitability. His first priority was to expand Yoplait Original Style to the entire country within three years, but he also identified early on that the major growth opportunity lay in additional product lines. To this end, the New Business Development Group was formed in July 1978. As a starting point, Yoplait USA looked to Sodima, who had many products, such as soft cheeses, refrigerated desserts, and different types of yogurt, for new product ideas.

Custard Style's Product Development

The New Business Development Group's charter was to make Yoplait USA a multiproduct company. The group decided initially to focus its new product exploration on the refrigerated yogurt category, including new forms of yogurt and yogurt-based products. Becker and his staff held idea generation sessions with their advertising agency and research and development personnel which resulted in 26 product concepts considered suitable for testing.

The first screening was a concept test (no actual products were presented to respondents) to measure the incremental volume that each potential new product would add to the existing Yoplait line. To pass the screening, a concept had to be in the top quartile in anticipated unit purchases for both the total Yoplait line and the test product line only. The concept also had to be in the top 50 percent in anticipated retail dollar sales for both the total Yoplait line and the new line only. Out of the 26 product concepts tested, 7 met these criteria. Based on further analysis of the results, the New Business Development Group decided to give top development priority to Custard Style.

The key issue in Custard Style's early development was defining the yogurt's consistency or texture. Yoplait USA started with prototypes similar to Sodima's set-style yogurt, which had a firm texture. But as Yoplait USA's R&D director said, "We had to Americanize the French product from ingredients, texture, and flavor standpoints." A completely new flavoring system had to be developed to meet US consumer tastes. In France, "natural identical" ingredients—artificial ingredients that had the same chemical structure as their natural counterparts—could legally be called "natural." In the US, an all-natural claim had to be based on truly natural or nonartificial ingredients.

Hundreds of prototypes were developed in the search for a viable set-style formula, including formulations with varying levels of fat, different types of fruit and fruit flavors, colors, mouthfeel, textures, and fermentation processes. The yogurt could be either fermented in vats or in individual cups. Vat fermentation required less capital investment, lower labor costs, and could be integrated more easily with current Yoplait operations, but it produced an inferior yogurt texture. Fermentation in the cup, the French method of set-style production, produced the proper custard-like texture. Custard Style Yogurt required a firm texture that produced a clean cut when sliced with a spoon. The texture had to be smooth and creamy, yet firm and thick like fine French custard. It could not be lumpy, gelatinous, or watery.

Due to the great number of prototypes developed, all could not be consumer tested. Members of the project team met in biweekly R&D review meetings and monthly new business review meetings. On these occasions, they sampled prototypes and used their collective judgment to screen and provide direction for future product development.

Aside from the product formulation, there were several other issues that had to be addressed, including packaging, size, positioning, and name. The team tackled these issues with the aid of consumer research. Focus group research indicated that the key appeal of the concept was its custardlike texture. The concept conveyed a smooth, creamy, thick, and rich-tasting yogurt. Anticipated usage varied among consumers—many expected the same usage as for other yogurts; some thought a dessert orientation more appropriate due to Custard Style's richness and creaminess; those with younger children indicated usage as a snack.

Marketing Issues

Concept testing and product prototype testing in focus groups had shown Custard Style Yogurt to be a potentially viable addition to the Yoplait line. Yoplait management, however, was still faced with several fundamental issues such as product positioning, name, packaging type, and size. The research pointed to the custardlike texture as a potential basis for positioning, but the New Business Development Group wondered whether texture, as opposed to taste, was sufficiently significant and communicable to be the key selling point.

There was also the question of whether the new yogurt should be positioned as a meal substitute, a snack, or a dessert. Some Yoplait executives argued that a new usage occasion positioning such as dessert might be more effective and help to increase category usage. A snack positioning was also being considered, offering Custard Style Yogurt as an alternative to snacks such as potato chips, cookies, and ice cream. Aside from usage occasion positionings, Becker and the advertising agency also were looking at the overall quality of Custard Style as a possible basis for positioning. Some of the positioning ideas included "the elegant/highest-quality yogurt—the Haagen-Dazs of yogurts"; "the superior-tasting yogurt—the gourmet's yogurt"; and "the yogurt for non-yogurt eaters."

When Yoplait regular style yogurt was first introduced in the USA, many consumers could not remember or pronounce the name, but they remembered the unique, conical, plastic cup. For Custard Style's packaging, Becker was faced with the decision of using the same Vercon (the name of the manufacturer) cup, capitalizing on its high recognition, or of using a different design such as a traditional straight cup to reduce cannibalization of regular style.

Becker also had to decide between a 4-oz. and a 6-oz. size. Most yogurt brands were sold in 8-oz. packages, while regular Yoplait was sold in a 6-oz. size, positioning it more as a snack than a meal substitute. Since Custard Style Yogurt was very filling, a 4-oz. size seemed adequate. A 4-oz. size, the standard serving size for pudding, would be compatible with a dessert positioning, and a small size would be a way to keep the unit price down. Finally, a 4-oz. size would be more appropriate for children and would reduce waste, an important point for Yoplait because its cup was not recappable with its aluminum foil cover. Tooling for a 4-oz. cup would require $75,000 in capital investment.

The New Business Development Group and the advertising agency were exploring two directions in developing a product name: linking the name to Yoplait and developing a name that was totally unrelated in sound or spelling to Yoplait, but used a "from the maker of Yoplait" tag. In exploring the first option, some of the names proposed so far were Yoclaire and Yofleur. Examples in the second category were Crème de Yogourt and Yogourt Classique. The term "custard style" could not be trademarked because it was too generic.

Becker and the R&D team members were also deciding on the appropriate fat level for Custard Style Yogurt. Regular Yoplait was a full-fat formulation. Full-fat provided a better eating experience. Low-fat (less than 2 percent fat) was lower in calories and healthier. Some project team members argued for the low-fat option to develop a further difference between Custard Style and regular Yoplait.

Concept Fulfillment Test

Faced with various alternative product formulations (low-fat vs. full-fat), positionings (dessert vs. snack), packages (Vercon vs. traditional) and sizes (4 oz. vs. 6 oz.), the New Business Development Group conducted a concept fulfillment test to determine which "mix" was the best for Custard Style Yogurt. Seven product/positioning/package/cup size "mixes"

**EXHIBIT 4 Concept Fulfillment Test
Custard Style Yogurt Concept Board**

**INTRODUCING NEW CUSTARD STYLE YOGURT FROM YOPLAIT—A NEW
KIND OF YOGURT MADE ESPECIALLY FOR DESSERT**

Now, you can have a delicious-tasting dessert with the richness and creaminess of the
  finest French custards, yet it has the lightness, nutrition, and lower calories of yogurt.
Yoplait Custard Style Yogurt has a unique texture that is firm, but smooth and
  creamy—just like custard—and it's blended throughout with 100% natural real fruit
  purée to give you the same delicious natural fruit taste in every spoonful.
It's available in strawberry, raspberry, blueberry, lemon, and plain.
Nothing artificial is added and it contains active yogurt cultures.
It comes in an individual 4-oz. cup that is just the right size for dessert. One cup contains
  only 120 calories and costs 35¢.

plus the regular Yoplait concept (as control) were developed for an in-home concept fulfillment test.[4]

Interviewers screened random supermarket shoppers for interest in purchasing one of the seven concepts based on exposure to a concept board such as that shown in Exhibit 4. They gave interested respondents two cups of the strawberry product corresponding to the concept for which they were screened. Three days later, the respondent was interviewed by phone. Results indicated that, on the basis of sales volume potential, the dessert/full-fat/traditional cup/4-oz. product mix (48.8 volume index) and the snack/full-fat/Vercon/6-oz. mix (47.2 volume index) were virtually tied as the top alternatives. In terms of delivered profit margins, the latter scored highest (60.4 delivered margin index) with the former (50.3 delivered margin index) taking second place. Two different package configurations, the regular Vercon cup and the traditional cup, were compared using the snack positioning, full-fat formulation and 4-oz. size. The Vercon cup scored significantly higher than the traditional cup.

---

[4] The regular Yoplait concept was tested in markets where it had not yet been
introduced, so there was no bias as a result of in-market experience.

The winning Custard Style alternative (snack positioning/full-fat product/Vercon cup/6-oz. size) was estimated to add 36 percent in incremental volume to the total Yoplait line. This was based on the assumption that Custard Style's volume relative to regular Yoplait's was the ratio of their volume indexes from the test: 47.2 Custard Style/66.7 regular Yoplait = 71 percent of regular Yoplait's volume. It was assumed further that Custard Style would have only 75 percent of regular Yoplait's distribution level, and that one-third of Custard Style's volume would be cannibalization of regular Yoplait's volume (or, two-thirds of Custard Style's volume would be incremental). This resulted in incremental volume from Custard Style equal to 36 percent of regular Yoplait volume (71 percent × 75 percent × ⅔). The study forecast further that, if Custard Style were introduced as the lead item in non-Yoplait markets, it would generate 17 percent more volume than Original Style. Custard Style seemed more likely than Original Style to attract light users and nonusers.

Diagnostic information from the test pointed to potential improvements for the winning Custard Style prototype—more fruit, sweeter, more natural, stronger fruit flavor, and more color. The product received high scores on texture attributes:

Product Attribute	Custard Style Satisfaction Level
Amount of fruit	30%
Naturalness of fruit taste	47
Strength of fruit flavor	49
Appearance	51
Color	54
Overall flavor	56
Sweetness/tartness	58
Calories	58
Texture/heaviness	63
Amount of product	72
Consistency	74
Smoothness/creaminess	76

Creative Group Interviews

Custard Style Yogurt's 36 percent incremental volume potential seemed quite promising to the new business group. Becker wanted some marketplace experience to confirm Custard Style's viability. He also needed further insights on possible positionings as a basis for developing advertising concepts. The New Business Development Group and the advertising agency decided to conduct group interviews with yogurt users and nonusers to aid in creative development. Respondents were shown headline descriptions and given product samples of Custard Style.

The interviews confirmed earlier research findings that texture was the main difference between Custard Style and other yogurts. The research showed, however, that yogurt nonusers would be difficult to convert. Several nonusers thought that the Custard Style Yogurt was bitter, sour, and tangy. However, some yogurt users thought that the product would appeal to members of their families who did not eat yogurt because Custard Style sounded less "yogurty." Custard Style's retail price (45¢) was a purchase barrier to the more casual users who bought the less-expensive store brands. On the other hand, many name brand (e.g., Dannon) yogurt users liked the Custard Style concept. The product was viewed as more dessert oriented than most yogurts because of its custard-like connotations. None of the respondents were concerned about the absence of fruit pieces—they were more concerned about a natural fruit taste. Yogurt users said the product tasted like yogurt with virtually no fruit flavor.

Volume Estimation Options

By June 1980, nearly two years after its formation, the New Business Development Group felt ready to test market Custard Style Yogurt. Concept testing and consumer evaluations had indicated the potential viability of the product, and management now wanted a more "scientific" sales volume estimate to help in planning production requirements. They also needed a reliable measure of Custard Style's cannibalization of regular Yoplait.

Becker's first decision was whether to conduct a test market simulation, such as BASES, before a field test market, or to go directly to a field test market. BASES, a sales estimation technique for new products, was a service offered by Burke Marketing Services, Inc. BASES's major advantages over a test market were its low cost ($29,000) and fast results (12 weeks). Other General Mills divisions had used BASES before but Yoplait USA had not. As Becker explained, "We weren't sure how relevant the Betty Crocker Division's experience with BASES was to a radically different category such as refrigerated yogurt. Also, we considered ourselves to be an entrepreneurial team. I wondered if we were researching ourselves to death. We were rolling out regular Yoplait quite successfully without a whole lot of industry data and primary research. Aside from that, the research we had done on Custard Style had consistently indicated that it was a winner. We had the unshakable belief that Custard Style was the way to go."

The BASES test that Yoplait was considering combined a concept test and a home-use test to provide year one and year two sales volume estimates. Finished commercials and packaging were not required. BASES allowed for simulation of the sales effects of key marketing variables before major resources were committed. The methodology required a shopping mall intercept of up to 300 shoppers in each of at least four geographically dispersed cities. Respondents were screened for purchase interest in the product concept. Test product was placed with interested respondents and their reactions were obtained through telephone call-back. Key after-use measures provided inputs to the BASES estimating model, including buying intentions, intended frequency and quantity of repurchase, price/value assessments, and other diagnostics. Secondary model inputs were provided by the client, including estimates of distribution build, media weights, trade and consumer promotion plans, size of the target market, and consumption indexes. The BASES model could evaluate alternative marketing scenarios by varying media weight, distribution build, and sales promotion expenditures, and by analyzing the impact of these adjustments on trial rates, repeat rates, total sales volume, and cannibalization.

BASES claimed advantages over other simulated test markets. First, it was less expensive than some because it did not require the use of a finished commercial for the test product. Second, it forecast sales volume rather than market share and was, therefore, more suitable for test products in new or underdeveloped categories. Third, the model was dynamic and could therefore take into account the timing of proposed marketing expenditures. BASES claimed that 35 percent of validated test cases forecast sales that were no more than 5 percent different from actual market results; another 31 percent of test cases had an error range of 5–10 percent.

If Becker decided on a field test of Custard Style, he had the option of a full-scale test market or a "mini-market." A full-scale test meant marketing the test product in two to four nationally representative markets through normal distribution channels with the General Mills sales force selling the test product to the trade. The results would have great credibility because the test would replicate actual roll-out conditions. He explained, "Ideally, yes, a full-scale test was the sophisticated thing to do. But, again, Yoplait USA was still a 'start-up' company. I didn't have much money for research; we were on a shoestring budget. A full-scale test market would cost $1,700,000 and would take a year to give a proper reading." Becker was also concerned about giving competition an opportunity to size up Yoplait's actions and to retaliate accordingly.

An alternative to a full-scale field test market was a mini-market test. The New Business Development Group was considering the La Crosse/Eau Claire market in western Wisconsin because it was close to General Mills headquarters in Minneapolis and it was already a strong Yoplait market which would permit a good measure of cannibalization. The area was upscale and had above-average quality stores and dairy sections. The group felt that the market would provide a "clean" reading of test results. A mini-market test had the advantage over BASES of true marketplace experience, and yet at $200,000, it cost significantly less than a full-scale test market. A mini-market test was limited in that trade reaction to Custard Style could not be evaluated since distribution was "forced" or controlled by the marketing research firm hired to administer the test. Given the extensive regional differences in the yogurt market, a La Crosse/Eau Claire test could not provide a national sales estimate for Custard Style or a nationally projectible estimate of regular Yoplait cannabilization. A mini-market test would take 20 weeks.

Conclusion

Bruce Becker had to decide what research step to take next—a BASES test, a full-scale test market, or a mini-market test. Aside from what was best from a market research standpoint, there were production considerations that bore on this decision. Yoplait's plants could not yet produce Custard Style Yogurt. All prototype production had been done in General Mills' R&D technical center. A full-scale test would require tooling up one of the existing Yoplait plants for Custard Style production whereas a mini-market test's more limited requirements could be accommodated by production at the General Mills' technical center where the pilot plant was one-tenth the scale of a full plant. Becker realized that capacity had to be managed properly in the scale-up from a pilot plant to full-scale production and that product quality had to be maintained in the scale-up process.

Becker continued to wrestle with the details of questions associated with Custard Style Yogurt's marketing mix. The snack positioning/Vercon cup/6-oz. size alternative in the concept fulfillment test seemed to be a convincing winner in terms of delivered margins, but the dessert positioning/traditional cup/4-oz. alternative was equally promising in terms of volume potential. In support of the latter, creative group interviews indicated that a major appeal of Custard Style was its "unyogurty" and dessert-like connotations.

Yoplait Custard Style Yogurt was the name favored by many Yoplait executives because custard accurately described the product's texture, and because the name built on the Yoplait brand name. On the other hand, a name such as Yoclaire gave the product a greater individual identity, and potentially could offer more incremental volume than a name that was shared with regular Yoplait.

Pricing was an area that had not been considered an issue. Custard Style Yogurt had the same basic cost structure as Original Style, and the New Business Development Group operated under the assumption that the Custard Style line would be priced the same as Yoplait Original Style. The most recent financial analysis, which assumed that Custard Style would be available in six flavors (strawberry, raspberry, blueberry, lemon, vanilla, and plain), and produced in two plants, showed that Custard Style had a delivered margin over variable costs comparable to Yoplait Original Style.

Becker had to decide whether to resolve these marketing program issues before the next phase of research and test one concept, or test several alternatives.

1-2 General Mills, Inc.: Yoplait Custard Style Yogurt (B)

Bruce Becker, director of New Business Development at Yoplait USA, decided in June 1980 to put new Yoplait Custard Style Yogurt in a 6-oz. Vercon cup into a "mini-market" test. Results were positive. The test showed that, on a national basis, total Yoplait volume would more than double (+107 percent) with the addition of Custard Style. To obtain a more nationally representative volume estimate, a BASES volume test was conducted next. The test forecast that total Yoplait volume would grow by 43 percent with Custard Style. Becker now was convinced that Yoplait Custard Style Yogurt was a winner, and ready for roll-out. However, details of the introductory marketing program still had to be decided along with the level of support that should be placed behind Custard Style, relative to Original Style Yogurt. In addition, some members of Yoplait management still favored putting Custard Style into a full-scale test market first before deciding on a national roll-out.

Mini-Market Test

By June 1980, Custard Style Yogurt had been in development for nearly two years. Numerous consumer tests had shown consistently that the product had high potential. When the time came for test market confirmation, the New Business Development Group was faced with a slim budget, production capacity limitations, and the pressure to introduce Yoplait's first new product as soon as possible. As a result, Bruce Becker

This case was prepared by Research Assistant John L. Teopaco under the supervision of Professor John A. Quelch as the basis for class discussion rather than to illustrate effective or ineffective handling of an administrative situation. Proprietary data have been disguised. Copyright © 1986 by the President and Fellows of Harvard College. Harvard Business School case 9–586–088.

opted for a mini-market test in the Eau Claire/La Crosse, Wisconsin, ADI market instead of a full-scale test market.[1]

The New Business Development Group realized that the results of a limited test market in Wisconsin could not be projected nationally because the US yogurt market was highly regional. On the other hand, the test was easily managed due to the small size of the market and its proximity to Minneapolis, the location of General Mills headquarters.

Methodology

The test involved 22 stores, lasted 20 weeks, and cost about $150,000. After a pretest audit to establish market shares and case movement, Yoplait Custard Style was placed in all the stores priced the same as Original Style at 49¢ per cup. Weekly store audits were conducted for sales and share information during the entire test period by an outside market research firm.

To supply the test market, approximately 200 12-cup cases per week were produced in a pilot plant at the General Mills R&D Technical Center. Becker commented:

The mini-market was very much a self-managed test. But with our limited production experience and capacity, we had to choose a test market that was close by because we would be shuttling product back and forth. We couldn't find a refrigerated warehouse to serve as an inventory drop-off, so we bought a walk-in cooler and installed it in a mini-warehouse. On some days, we drove the truck down ourselves.

Becker acknowledged the unsophisticated nature of the mini-market test. But in spite of the limitations, he and his staff attempted to make the results as valid as possible. Their objective was to replicate a realistic national marketing program.

Marketing Variables

The marketing support behind Custard Style consisted of radio and newspaper advertising, product sampling, and trade deals. Radio was used instead of television in order to control costs and minimize wasted impressions. Radio media weight was adjusted upwards to compensate for

---

[1] An Area of Dominant Influence (ADI) was a geographical market defined primarily by the range of VHF television signals.

the absence of television's visual dimension. A total of 500 gross rating points of radio advertising targeted at women over 18, and 12 newspaper insertions (6 each in Eau Claire and La Crosse newspapers) were used in the test. The advertising copy, known as the Fourchette campaign, emphasized the Frenchness, thickness, and everyday use of Yoplait Custard Style and had been selected over an execution that conveyed a more gourmet, dessert image. Exhibit 1 presents a newspaper advertisement from the campaign. The total media plan was the equivalent of a national spending plan of $5.7 million.

Product sampling was a major consumer promotion tactic used by Yoplait for generating trial. In the mini-market, Yoplait management followed Original Style's strategy of in-store consumer sampling in nine stores at an average of two days per store. Sampling took place during the first seven weeks of the test. Given a sampling cost of 48¢ per unit, the mini-market's national equivalent sampling plan was $800,000.

Three trade deals were offered during the test, each lasting six weeks. Average Custard Style volume in stores that accepted one or more deals was 52 percent higher than in those that accepted none. The test's national equivalent trade promotion plan was $900,000.

Share and Volume Results

The mini-market test forecast sustainable market shares of 23.1 percent for Custard Style, and 24.9 percent for Original Style. The addition of Custard Style resulted in a total Yoplait share of 48.0 percent, up 21.4 points from Yoplait Original Style's 26.6 percent pretest market share. Custard Style gained share mainly from Dannon, the number one brand, and Gaymont, a major regional brand. Exhibit 2 presents the mini-market test share and volume results.

Average category weekly sales, excluding sampling store volume during sampling weeks, increased 26 percent with the introduction of Custard Style. Yoplait Original Style volume increased 18 percent, while Dannon and Gaymont declined. In test market stores, an average of 6.8 (out of 10) flavors of Original Style and 5.3 (out of 6) flavors of Custard Style were on the shelves at the end of the test period.

Custard Style volume potential was calculated using the sustainable share estimates under two category volume scenarios—no change and a 26 percent category growth with Custard Style. The estimation procedure assumed national distribution of 80 percent ACV (all-commodity volume), similar to that achieved by Original Style Yogurt. With no category growth, Custard Style would deliver 87 percent of Original Style's current national volume potential, and 109 percent with category growth. Total Yoplait volume would be up to 227 percent of Original Style's national volume projection. See table at top of page 27. Exhibit 3 on page 26 details the volume estimation methodology.

EXHIBIT 1   Mini-Market Test Print Advertisement

EXHIBIT 2   **Mini-Market Test Share and Volume Results Share of Sales**

	Pretest	*Sustaining Estimate**	*Change from Pretest*
Yoplait Custard Style	—	23.1%	+23.1%
Yoplait Original Style	26.6%	24.9	− 1.7
Total Yoplait	26.6%	48.0%	+21.4%
Dannon	38.2%	21.8%	−16.4%
Gaymont	10.7	6.0	− 4.7
Old Home	10.8	10.7	− 0.1
Slim 'n Trim	10.9	9.2	− 1.7
All others	2.7	4.1	+ 1.4

* Average rolling four-week share for weeks 11–20 (after Custard Style sampling was completed).

Weekly Equivalent* Case Volume/Store

	Pretest	*Sustaining Weekly Volume*	*Percent Change vs. Pretest*
Yoplait Custard Style	—	12.1	
Yoplait Original Style	11.0	13.0	+ 18.2
Total Yoplait	11.0	25.1	+128.2
Dannon	15.8	11.4	− 27.9
Gaymont	4.4	3.1	− 29.6
Old Home	4.5	5.6	+ 24.4
Slim 'n Trim	4.5	4.8	+ 6.7
All Others	1.1	2.2	+100.0
Total Category	41.3	52.2	26.0%

* One equivalent case = 12 single-serving cups, 6 oz. or 8 oz.

EXHIBIT 3   **Mini-Market Volume Estimation Methodology (unadjusted)**

Custard Style

$$\text{Custard style national volume} = \frac{\dfrac{\text{Custard Style share in test market}}{\text{Yoplait share before test period}} \times \dfrac{\text{Test period category volume in test market}}{\text{Pretest category volume in test market}}}{} \times \text{Current Yoplait projected national volume}$$

A. Assuming no market growth

    Test period category volume = Pretest category volume

$$= \frac{23.1 \times \text{Test period category volume}}{26.6 \times \text{pretest category volume}} \times \text{Current Yoplait projected national volume}$$

    = .87 current Yoplait projected national volume

B. Assuming 26% market growth

    Test period category volume = 1.26 pretest category volume

$$= \frac{23.1 \times 1.26 \times \text{Pretest category volume}}{26.6 \times \text{Pretest category volume}} \times \text{Current Yoplait projected national volume}$$

    = 1.09 current Yoplait projected national volume

	Percent of Yoplait Original Style's National Volume Potential	
	Minimum (no market growth)	*Maximum (26% market growth)*
Yoplait Custard Style	87%	109%
Yoplait Original Style	94	118
Total Yoplait	181%	227%

Pretest plans assumed that, on the average, 75 percent of the Custard Style line would be in stock. In the test, 89 percent were stocked. Volume potential estimates were adjusted downward to reflect the pretest assumption. Exhibit 4 details the adjusted volume estimation methodology. On an adjusted basis, Custard Style volume would be 73 percent to 92 percent of Original Style's national potential, and total Yoplait volume would be 168 to 207 percent.

	Percent of Yoplait Original Style's National Volume Potential	
	Minimum (no market growth)	*Maximum (26% market growth)*
Yoplait Custard Style	73%	92%
Yoplait Original Style	95	115
Total Yoplait	168%	207%

Consumer Dynamics Study

In addition to the weekly store audit, a yogurt consumer dynamics study was conducted during the test. The research consisted of three waves of a supermarket intercept study, each conducted over three consecutive weekends (3–5 weeks, 9–11 weeks, and 15–17 weeks after the start of advertising). Interviewers, stationed in the yogurt section of each store, recorded consumers' yogurt purchases by brand. Each yogurt shopper was then asked questions about trial and repeat and future purchase interest. Waves 2 and 3 included a telephone follow-up interview of Yoplait Custard Style, Original Style, and Dannon purchasers. Respondents were asked questions on product likes, dislikes, and usage.

Custard Style trial among yogurt buyers increased with each wave of the study and by the third wave (35 percent) was approaching Original Style's trial level (36 percent) and that of all competitors except Dannon (63 percent). Exhibit 5 reports trial levels by wave. Repeat intention for

EXHIBIT 4 Mini-Market Volume Estimation Methodology (adjusted)

Custard Style

$$\text{Custard style national volume} = \frac{[(\%\text{ line adjustment})^{*}(\text{CS test market share})(\text{Market growth factor})(\text{Total market pretest})] + [(1 - \%\text{ line adjustment}^{\dagger})(\text{CS pretest share})(\text{Total market pretest})]}{(\text{Yoplait pretest share})(\text{Total market pretest})} \times \text{Current Yoplait projected national volume}$$

A. Assuming no market growth

Test period category volume = Pretest category volume

$$= \frac{(75/89)(23.1)(1.00)(\text{total market pretest}) + (14/89)(0)(\text{Total market pretest})}{26.6\ (\text{total market pretest})} \times \text{Current Yoplait projected national volume}$$

= .73 current Yoplait projected national volume

B. Assuming 26% market growth

Test period category volume = 1.26 × Pretest category volume

$$= \frac{(75/89)(23.1)(1.26)(\text{Total market pretest}) + (14/89)(0)(\text{Total market pretest})}{26.6\ (\text{Total market pretest})} \times \text{Current Yoplait projected national volume}$$

= .92 current Yoplait projected national volume

* Adjustment made for the percent of the Custard Style line in stock. In the test market 89 percent of Custard Style flavors were stocked on average. 75 percent of Custard Style flavors in stock was anticipated for national introduction. Yoplait Original Style percent flavors in stock for the test was equivalent to current national levels and, therefore, required no adjustment.

† Adjustment to reflect Yoplait regular performance if fewer Custard Style flavors stocked (75 vs. 89%).

**EXHIBIT 5   Mini-Market Consumer Dynamics Study
Yoplait Custard Style Trial**

	Percent of Yogurt Buyers		
	Wave 1	*Wave 2*	*Wave 3*
Yoplait Custard Style	25%	31%	35%
Yoplait Original Style	34	34	36
Dannon	68	66	63
Old Home	18	20	19
Gaymont	21	22	21

Custard Style nearly equaled Original Style's and Dannon's, and exceeded Gaymont's and Old Home's. The percentage of Custard Style triers who actually repeated consistently increased throughout the study; all depth of repeat categories (percent of triers who made 1 through 10 or more repeat purchases) showed steady growth, indicating strong consumer satisfaction.

Of those who used any Yoplait product, 20 percent were exclusive Custard Style users, 20 percent were exclusive Original Style users, and 60 percent used both. Custard Style users were primarily past buyers of Original Style and Dannon:

	Source of Custard Style Buyers as of Wave 3	
Past Buyers of:	*Trial*	*Repeat*
Yoplait	38%	41%
Dannon	33	27
Gaymont	4	5
Old Home	8	7
All other	17	21
	100%	100%

By Wave 3, 91 percent of Original Style and 63 percent of Dannon buyers had tried Custard Style, versus 35 percent of Gaymont and 37 percent of Old Home buyers.

The number of Custard Style units bought per buying occasion by repeaters (1.7) was about the same as the number of Original Style (1.6) and Dannon (1.8) units, but more than the number of Old Home (1.1) and Gaymont (1.1) units bought by these brands' repeaters. This suggested to Becker that Custard Style buyers were mainstream yogurt consumers. Of the total yogurt purchases made by Custard Style buyers, 70–80 percent were of Custard Style, about the same level as for Original Style and

Dannon. This indicated that Custard Style would not be merely a secondary brand among its consumers.

Among Custard Style acceptors, the most often mentioned reasons for repeat purchasing were "flavor" (33 percent), "natural fruit flavor" (23 percent), "firm, thick texture" (22 percent), and "smooth, creamy texture" (16 percent). Custard Style rejectors' most frequently mentioned reasons for not repeating were "too custardy/don't like custard" (21 percent), "too thick/too firm" (18 percent), "don't like texture" (18 percent) and "no fruit/no chunks of fruit" (16 percent). Acceptors indicated that they would eat Custard, Style on the same occasions as other yogurts:

	Breakfast	Lunch	Dinner	Morning Snack	Afternoon Snack	Evening Snack
Percent of Custard Style uses	14.1%	21.1%	9.7%	10.1%	22.4%	21.2%
Percent of other yogurt uses	15.3	23.3	8.6	9.2	21.9	21.9

No unusual competitive responses were observed during the mini-market test. Dannon was preoccupied with penetrating the West Coast market and with testing a new product of its own, Melangé, which appeared to be positioned against Original Style.

By any standards, the mini-market test results were encouraging. The estimated doubling of total Yoplait volume with the addition of Custard Style was considered by Becker and his group to be outstanding. Some Yoplait executives, however, were skeptical, claiming that the test results could not be used to project Custard Style's performance in regions with different market structures at different stages of yogurt market development. In short, the test was too localized. Management wanted national and regional estimates of Custard Style's volume potential, and its impact on Original Style's volume, before making a decision on Custard Style's introduction, and the associated plant investment. To address these concerns, a BASES simulated test market was conducted.

BASES Test

Methodology

The BASES test was conducted in 12 geographically dispersed cities, distributed equally among three regions.[2] Two hundred respondents were interviewed in each region. An additional 200 interviews were conducted

---

[2] East—Boston, Buffalo, Cleveland, Hartford; Midwest—Minneapolis, Chicago, St. Louis, Milwaukee; West—Los Angeles, San Francisco, Portland, Phoenix.

in Minneapolis/St. Paul to compare results with those of the La Crosse/ Eau Claire mini-market test. Respondents qualified if they were female heads of household at least 18 years old, and were the principal household shoppers. Current users and nonusers of yogurt were included in the sample.

Qualified respondents were shown a color print advertisement with a picture of the Custard Style product, a concept statement, and the price (53¢). They were asked questions on purchase intent, likes/dislikes of the concept, price/value evaluation, and past category usage. Respondents who indicated that they definitely or probably would buy Yoplait Custard Style Yogurt took home as many cups as they would buy at trial. (All flavors were available except for plain.) After two weeks, participants responded again to the same set of questions asked before the in-home use test.

In addition to the consumer test results, Yoplait provided the following inputs to the BASES volume estimation model: target market, consumption indexes for each city, seasonality indexes, year 1 distribution and out-of-stock estimates by flavor, and marketing expenditures for each quarter of the first two years following launch.

Marketing Variables

Three national spending plans were simulated by the BASES model: high (Plan A), medium (Plan B), and low (Plan C). Plan A assumed that Custard Style would be supported at 100 percent of the media spending level used in the Yoplait Original Style introductory plan. Plan B represented 50 percent of Original Style media spending while Plan C assumed a lower spending level. The plans assumed that two-thirds of expenditures would be made during the first half of any year, and that 70 percent of media spending would be on television advertising.

	Year 1 (000s)			Year 2 (000s)		
Promotion	*Plan A* *(high)*	*Plan B* *(medium)*	*Plan C* *(low)*	*Plan A* *(high)*	*Plan B* *(medium)*	*Plan C* *(low)*
Media	$ 9,200	$4,600	$3,700	$6,100	$3,050	$2,380
Consumer	2,300	700	700	—	—	—
Trade	1,000	700	700	1,250	950	920
Total	$12,500	$6,000	$5,100	$7,350	$4,000	$3,300

Volume Results

Yoplait management established, on the basis of economic analysis, two performance criteria for Custard Style: it had to provide at least 40 percent incremental volume to the total Yoplait line, and its sales volume had to be at least 60 percent of Original Style's under plan B.

The BASES results showed that with the medium plan, Custard Style would deliver 3.5 million cases (12-pack) in year 2. The BASES model forecast that total Yoplait volume would grow by 43 percent:

	Custard Style National Estimates		
	Plan A *(high)*	*Plan B* *(medium)*	*Plan C* *(low)*
Year 1 trial	14.9%	10.4%	9.1%
Repeat (measured)	38.7%	38.8%	38.6%
Year 1 volume (12-unit cases)	4.4 M	3.2 M	3.0 M
Year 2 volume	4.8 M	3.5 M	3.3 M
Year 2 percent incremental volume	57%	43%	41%

Custard Style volume seemed somewhat sensitive to spending. Under Plan A, at twice the media dollars of Plan B, year 2 volume was 34 percent higher, whereas under the low-spending Plan C, volume was only 5 percent lower than Plan B's.

Custard Style's performance varied by region. Sales were strongest in the West, although lower than Original Style's. The East showed larger than expected sales:

	Regional Volume Indexes—Plan B/Year 2			
	West	*Midwest*	*East*	*Total US*
Custard Style	180	88	120	100
Original Style	190	82	98	100

There was no significant regional variation in each flavor's expected share of year 1 Yoplait Custard Style volume. Average flavor splits were:

Strawberry	28%	Vanilla	25%
Raspberry	18	Plain	9
Blueberry	13	Lemon	7

Potential Steal

On a national basis, the BASES model estimated that 22 percent of Custard Style volume would be at the expense of Original Style. Regionally, potential steal varied widely with the Midwest showing the highest level (28 percent).

The greatest competitive source of Custard Style volume was Dannon (22 percent) in the East, Yoplait Original Style (28 percent) in the Midwest, and Knudsen (18 percent) in the West:

	Sources of Custard Style Volume			
	West	*Midwest*	*East*	*Total US*
Total new yogurt purchases	51%	51%	49%	50%
Steal from yogurt:	49	49	51	50
Dannon	8	15	22	15
Yoplait Original Style	13	28	14	22
Knudsen	18	0	0	6
All others	10	6	15	6

Comparison to Mini-Market

BASES estimates based on the responses of the 200 interviewees in Minneapolis/St. Paul, a similar competitive environment to La Crosse/Eau Claire, were very similar to those from the mini-market. Assuming 80 percent Custard Style ACV (all-commodity volume) distribution (Yoplait Original Style distribution level in the Twin Cities), BASES estimated Custard Style's volume at 97 percent of Original Style's. Assuming 90 percent ACV distribution, Custard Style volume was forecast at 110 percent of Original Style's. The mini-market test, which forecast 26 percent category growth following Custard Style's introduction, had estimated a Custard Style volume of 109 percent of Original Style's. This forecast was based on 89 percent of the line being stocked on average as observed in the mini-market.

Additional Findings

Exhibit 6 presents additional findings from the BASES interviews. After exposure to the concept, about 40 percent of the respondents said that they definitely or probably would buy Custard Style. Among triers, 68 percent expressed continued purchase intent. These purchase intent levels met the norms for successful, new refrigerated products. Custard Style's price/value rating (3.6 on a 5-pt. scale) equaled the refrigerated products' norm, while its "liking" rating (5.6 on a 9-pt. scale) was close to the norm (5.5).

Before trying Custard Style, taste/flavor (particularly the variety of flavors), texture/consistency (creamy, thick, smooth), and health/nutrition were the most frequently mentioned reasons for liking the concept. After use, taste and texture reasons again were cited most often, but few mentioned the health benefits of Custard Style. Taste was the most frequently mentioned reason for not liking Custard Style, both before and

---

EXHIBIT 6   Additional Findings from BASES Test

Purchase Intent—Percent "Definitely/Probably Would Buy"

	Total US	West	Midwest	East
Before use	41%	42%	39%	42%
After use	68	67	66	69

Norms: before use—40%; after use—65%

Price/Value—5-Point Scale

Before use	3.7	3.6	3.7	3.8
After use	3.6	3.6	3.5	3.7

Norm: after use—3.6

Liking Rating—9-Point Scale

Before use	5.2	5.3	5.1	5.2
After use	5.6	5.5	5.5	5.7

Norm: after use—5.5

Product vs. Expectations

Better than expected	58%	56%	54%	64%
About the same	28	29	28	25
Worse than expected	13	14	16	10
Don't know	1	1	2	1

---

after use. After trying the product, some commented on the absence of fruit pieces. Price was the second most often mentioned reason for disliking Custard Style before trial, but after use, its share of mentions was much lower.

Alternative Spending Levels

In addition to the three marketing spending levels used in the first BASES analysis, two additional sets of media and consumer promotion spending levels were simulated later. The objective was to determine the optimal allocation of incremental spending. One alternative plan (A Media/B Promotion) used the original Plan A's high-level media spending and Plan B's low-level consumer promotion spending. The other new plan (B Media/A Promotion) used low-level media and high-level promotion spending:

		A Media/B Promotion	*B Media/A Promotion*
Year 1:	Media	$9,200	$4,600
	Consumer promotion	700	2,300
Year 2:	Media	6,100	3,050
	Consumer promotion	0	0

For planning purposes, Yoplait management considered the original Plan B (B Media/B Promotion) as Custard Style's base support level. Based on this, the new simulation results indicated that incremental spending in consumer promotion was more efficient than incremental media spending. The B Media/A Promotion plan resulted in the lowest cost per incremental case:

Alternate Plans	*Incremental Spending vs. Plan B*	*Incremental Cases vs. Plan B*	*Cost per Incremental Case*
B Media/A Promotion	$1,600,000	455,000	$3.52
A Media/B Promotion	4,000,000	694,000	6.61
A Media/A Promotion	6,200,000	1,190,000	5.19

Exhibit 7 shows the performance results of Custard Style under the new alternate plans.

Copy Testing

The BASES test results confirmed the New Business Development Group's conclusion from the mini-market that Custard Style had high volume potential. They began preparation for the new product's launch by next developing and testing four television commercial executions: (1) Custard Style only with a Yoplait tag and no celebrity (police execution), (2) Custard Style only with a Yoplait tag and a celebrity (Sanford execution), (3) integrated Custard Style and Original Style without celebrities (secretaries execution), and (4) integrated Custard Style and Original Style with celebrities (Lasorda/Brothers execution). Several executives argued strongly that Custard Style advertising should be clearly distinguishable by consumers from the Original Style campaign.

Methodology

After a series of focus groups, a four-panel advertising copy test with 300 respondents per panel was conducted in nine geographically dispersed cities. In each panel, 150 respondents were selected from established

EXHIBIT 7 BASES Alternative Spending Plan Simulations

	Plan A Media/Plan B Promotion					Plan B Media/Plan A Promotion				
	West	Midwest	East	Remaining US	Total US	West	Midwest	East	Remaining US	Total US
Year 1 consumer volume (in cases of 12)	1,194M	315M	1,625M	270M	3,904M	1,015M	880M	1,445M	325M	3,665M
Year 2 consumer volume	1,206M	812M	1,940M	300M	4,258M	1,100M	855M	1,502M	401M	3,858M

	Plan B Media/Plan B Promotion					Plan A Media/Plan A Promotion				
	West	Midwest	East	Remaining US	Total US	West	Midwest	East	Remaining US	Total US
Year 1 consumer volume (in cases of 12)	940M	705M	1,305M	260M	3,210M	1,260M	935M	1,805M	400M	4,400M
Year 2 consumer volume	945M	720M	1,530M	320M	3,515M	1,290M	940M	2,105M	435M	4,770M

Yoplait West Coast markets which were also Knudsen yogurt markets, and 150 were selected from other established Yoplait markets which were also Dannon markets. Respondents were female shoppers, aged 18–60, who had purchased yogurt two or more times in the previous three months.

Each respondent viewed a prerecorded videotape which contained the following: the Yoplait Original Style Jack Klugman commercial (see Exhibit 8 at the end of the case),[3] a Knudsen (West Coast markets) or Dannon (all other markets) commercial and one of the four alternative Custard Style commercials. After viewing the tape, the respondent was asked about her likelihood of buying different brands of yogurt. From the responses, share scores were calculated and weighted according to each respondent's past category usage. Regional share scores were combined on the basis of each region's share of total category volume.

Finally, a subsample of 100 respondents per panel was re-exposed to the Custard Style test commercial, and asked a series of communication/comprehension diagnostic questions.

The four test commercials showed different people discovering the characteristics of Yoplait Custard Style. One focused on two female secretaries, a second on a group of police officers. A third featured baseball coach Tommy Lasorda and popular psychologist Dr. Joyce Brothers, while the fourth featured television personality Isabel Sanford. The Sanford commercial is shown in Exhibit 9 at the end of the case.

Results

Yoplait management had decided that the commercial that received the highest postviewing share would be recommended for introductory Custard Style copy. These criteria were to be applied separately to Knudsen markets and Dannon markets.

In both Knudsen and Dannon markets, the Isabel Sanford commercial scored highest.

	Custard Style Post Shares		
	Total US	*Knudsen Markets*	*Dannon Markets*
Sanford	21.8%	23.6%	21.0%
Secretaries	19.0	16.4	20.1
Lasorda/Brothers	18.7	18.6	19.5
Police	16.4	19.8	15.3

NOTE: The Sanford advertisement scored significantly better than the other executions at the 0.8 confidence level in Knudsen markets, and in aggregate, but not in Dannon markets.

---

[3] A series of celebrity spokesperson commercials which emphasized Yoplait's heritage as the yogurt of France.

| | Total Yoplait Post Shares | | |
Commercials	Total US	Knudsen Markets	Dannon Markets
Sanford	43.7%	48.7%	41.6%
Police	38.5	46.9	35.2
Secretaries	38.0	44.9	35.0
Lasorda/Brothers	37.0	44.9	33.7

NOTE: Sanford execution scored significantly higher (at 0.8 confidence internal) in total US and in Dannon markets, but not in Knudsen markets.

In general, diagnostic results for the four Custard Style commercials were very similar. Exhibit 10 shows communication results from the test. The Sanford and Police commercials (Custard Style–only executions) communicated best Custard Style's thickness. They were less effective than the integrated commercials in communicating that Custard Style was a new type/style of yogurt. The Custard Style–only commercials also deemphasized the product's "Frenchness." In the Knudsen markets, the Sanford commercial communicated "better taste" most effectively. Otherwise, there were no significant differences in the pulling power of the four executions between Knudsen and Dannon markets.

On brand recall, the Sanford commercial scored highest with 90 percent of respondents remembering the Yoplait Custard Style name (and variations). Brand recall was better for the Sanford commercial than for the other alternatives in both Knudsen and Dannon markets.

Conclusion

By February 1981, Becker and the New Business Development Group were ready to introduce Yoplait Custard Style Yogurt in six flavors. Consumer product testing, the mini-market test, and BASES test results all showed Custard Style to be a highly viable product that would not steal significantly from Original Style volume. In addition, they now believed they had a television commercial that could support strongly Custard Style's introduction.

As the national launch decision approached, there was increasing debate over where Custard Style should be rolled out first. In the BASES test, Custard Style sales were strongest in the West, but sales in the East were greater than expected (based on Original Style volume). Becker believed that Custard Style should be introduced first in markets such as the West, where Yoplait was strongest. But some executives contended that Custard Style provided an opportunity for establishing Yoplait in the East where it had been weak and unable to break Dannon's dominance. They advocated an Eastern introduction. A third alternative was to launch Custard Style as Yoplait's lead product in new markets such as

EXHIBIT 10   Custard Style Copy Test Communication Results

1. Main Idea—Percent Indicating

	Commercials			
	Sanford	*Lasorda/ Brothers*	*Secretaries*	*Police*
New type	16.4%	19.0%	21.5%	12.5%
Thicker	19.8	10.2	14.2	21.7
Frenchness	1.7	7.1	6.0	3.0

2. What's New or Different

	Sanford	*Lasorda/ Brothers*	*Secretaries*	*Police*
New style/type	7.4%	11.2%	12.8%	10.2%
Thicker	15.7	12.6	12.8	14.6
Frenchness/classy	11.8	13.9	13.2	12.2
Casting/type of people	4.1	6.8	2.6	3.1

3. Everything Seen or Heard

	Sanford	*Lasorda/ Brothers*	*Secretaries*	*Police*
Two types	13.7%	12.2%	14.8%	11.8%
Eat with fork (thick)	26.5	19.0	21.9	24.4
Casting (celebrities)	31.2	32.0	30.7	31.2
Fruit in yogurt	4.7	3.8	2.4	1.7

4. Advantages over Other Yogurts

	Sanford	*Lasorda/ Brothers*	*Secretaries*	*Police*
Two styles/better	11.1%	11.2%	13.2%	9.5%
Thicker/creamier	13.4	9.8	16.5	12.9

5. Brand Recall

	Sanford	*Lasorda/ Brothers*	*Secretaries*	*Police*
Yoplait Custard Style	87.2%	80.2%	82.4%	82.0%
Variations	3.0	2.4	2.1	2.0
Total	90.2%	82.6%	84.5%	84.0%

those in the West which neither Original Style Yoplait nor Dannon had yet penetrated.

As Becker considered these options, he wondered how the sales force and trade would react to each. The trade regarded yogurt as a difficult category to manage, given the proliferation of brands and flavors. In some areas of the country, continuous trade deals were almost mandatory to secure shelf space. At the same time, Yoplait's sales force and brokers had been under pressure to secure distribution for more Original Style flavors. Some Yoplait executives believed the sales force would welcome

Custard Style as "genuine product news." Others felt that the introduction of Custard Style would give them an excuse for not meeting flavor distribution goals for Original Style.

Another issue related to the roll-out plan was the appropriate balance of advertising and promotion support to be placed behind Custard Style and Original Style, particularly in those regions where both would be distributed. Becker believed Custard Style had the potential to be a major new product introduction. Since both Custard Style and Original Style would carry the Yoplait name and be sold in similar packages, he argued that the weight of support should be placed behind Custard Style and that this would maintain awareness and distribution of Original Style. The brand manager on Original Style argued against this approach. Indeed, he proposed that Custard Style, once launched, should be managed within his brand group as a line extension to ensure the integration of Custard Style and Original Style marketing programs.

Finally, Becker believed that although Custard Style offered significant, incremental volume potential, it should be priced the same as Original Style (54¢ suggested retail price). According to him, a price differential would cause consumer and sales force confusion, and be hard to explain to the trade. A member of the new business group felt, however, that Custard Style could be positioned as Yoplait's premium product, and priced higher than Original Style. He pointed to the limited steal level from Original Style as an indication that consumers perceived the two products differently.

Becker had to decide on an introductory program for Custard Style to recommend to Stephen Rothschild. He proposed Salt Lake City for the launch because it was an established market where Yoplait was the share leader (22 percent). Yoplait sales for fiscal year 1981 were up 32 percent over the previous year. The Salt Lake market was well managed and served by highly committed salespeople.

Becker's Salt Lake City marketing program was based on a national equivalent spending plan of $4.7 million consisting of the following:

Advertising	650 television GRPs (annual, in four flights) 50 radio GRPs (introductory) 3 full-page newspaper free-standing inserts with coupons	$3.2 million
Consumer Promotion	12 weeks of in-store trial demonstrations	0.9 million
Trade Promotion	7 weeks normal volume on introductory deal @ $.60 per case	0.6 million

Becker was confident that he could convince Rothschild and other key Yoplait executives that Custard Style was a major new product opportunity worthy of substantial investment.

EXHIBIT 8 **Yoplait Original Style Television Commercial**

ANNCR: The yogurt of France is called Yoplait.

Some Americans don't know about it... yet.

But what happens when Americans get their first taste of Yoplait...

they'll think...it's different...it's creamy, smooth,

all natural yogurt...with real fruit.

It's just amazing what happens when a real American gets a little taste of French culture.

JACK KLUGMAN: Ce Yogurt Yoplait est fantastique,

merveilleux , sensationnel, cremeux... (HE CONTINUES UNDER V.O. ANNCR)

ANNCR: Yoplait Yogurt. Get a little taste of French culture.
JACK KLUGMAN: ...naturel.

EXHIBIT 9   Isabel Sanford Custard Style Television Commercial

ANNCR: Yoplait, the yogurt of France introduces a second yogurt,

ISABEL: Custard style???

ANNCR: And when Americans get their first taste,

ISABEL: With a fork?

ANNCR: they'll think it's different.

ANNCR: Wholesome, with real fruit pureed throughout, but very different,

because new Yoplait Custard Style is thick.

ANNCR: So thick, you can eat it with

ISABEL: Un "fourchette!"

ANNCR: New Yoplait Custard Style, so thick you can eat it with a...

fourchette. But please, eat Yoplait original with a....

cuillere.

H.J. Heinz Co.: Plastic Bottle Ketchup (A)

In March 1983, Barbara Johnson, product manager on Heinz ketchup, was debating whether or not to launch ketchup in a new plastic bottle and, if so, what level of support to place behind the move. The new product had been in development for three years. Johnson commented: "I have to determine if the plastic bottle is truly a 'big idea' or just another line extension."

Company Background

H.J. Heinz Company was founded in 1869 on a packaging innovation: Henry Heinz packaged horseradish in clear glass jars. In fiscal year (FY) 1983 (ending April 30), the food manufacturer recorded sales of $3.7 billion and net income of $214.3 million. During the previous 10 years, sales had grown at an average annual rate of 12.7 percent, and earnings per share at 14.6 percent. In the United States, H.J. Heinz Co. consisted of five subsidiaries: Heinz USA, Star Kist Foods, Ore Ida Foods, Hubinger Co., and Weight Watchers International. Star Kist marketed tuna and pet foods (9-Lives), Ore-Ida frozen potato products, and Hubinger industrial corn sweeteners. Weight Watchers International promoted well-known weight-control programs. Heinz USA, the oldest subsidiary, employed 6,000 people and marketed such diverse products as ketchup, pickles, vinegar, baby foods, soups, ALBA dry beverage mixes, and foodservice products.

Heinz USA employed a 200-person sales force that covered the northeastern and north central regions. Salespeople were compensated on salary plus a bonus linked to two volume goals: a ketchup goal and a second goal covering all other products. Heinz used brokers in the South and West.

This case was written by Research Assistant John L. Teopaco under the direction of Professor John A. Quelch, as the basis for class discussion rather than to illustrate effective or ineffective handling of an administrative situation. Copyright © 1985 by the President and Fellows of Harvard College. Harvard Business School case 9–586–035.

Heinz had been selling ketchup for over a century. By FY 1983, it held a 45.6 percent share of retail ketchup volume and a 45.0 percent share of foodservice volume, making it the dominant competitor in the ketchup market. Heinz retail ketchup sales were $215 million and accounted for 30 percent of Heinz USA sales and 35 percent of profits; Heinz foodservice ketchup sales were $175 million.

Heinz manufactured ketchup at three plants, one of which had the world's fastest filling line for large-sized ketchup varieties. The company actively pursued technological innovations. In an early application of genetic engineering to a commercial food crop, Heinz researchers created a "super tomato" with a higher solid content and better acid balance specially suited for ketchup production.

Heinz USA's Product Management System

Exhibit 1 shows the organizational structure of Heinz USA's product management system. Prior to 1980, the divisions were aligned with the factories; each division marketed the products made in a single plant. In 1980, the divisions were restructured to provide a greater marketing orientation. The product management organization included 40–50 professionals. Product managers were responsible for individual brands (such as Heinz ketchup), and they reported to group product managers who, in turn, reported to the general managers. Each general manager was in charge of a major product group. The Packaged Goods general managers, for example, managed more cost-sensitive, trade/push-oriented products, so the two general managers in this area were heavily involved in manufacturing cost-control projects. In contrast, the Consumer Products general managers handled more pull-oriented products.

Heinz considered its product management system lean and flexible. The number of management layers above an individual depended upon the person's level of experience. In describing the system, one Heinz manager stated: "We need people who are independent, self-starting, see what needs to get done, ask the right questions, and do not need to have their hand held through the system." Because of the organization's leanness, it was not easy to rotate managers systematically from one type of brand to another. On the other hand, the nature of assignments—particularly the products under each general manager—were often changed according to an individual's experience and development needs.

The ketchup brand group consisted of an assistant product manager, two associate product managers, and a product manager reporting to a group product manager. The group met regularly with representatives of other functions including packaging, product development, purchasing, production planning, engineering, and sales planning.

EXHIBIT 1 Heinz USA Marketing Organization

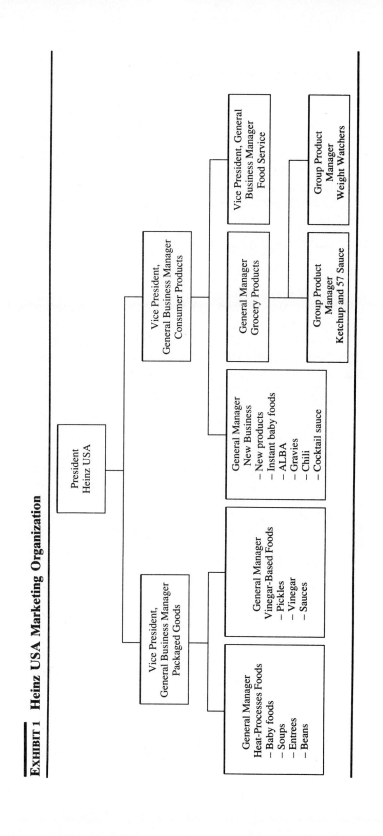

The Ketchup Market

Category Consumption

In FY 1983, US retail ketchup sales were 33.8 million (equivalent) cases[1] valued at $434 million in manufacturers' selling prices. Ketchup was the twenty-ninth largest dry grocery food category in the US, up from thirty-fifth in 1981. During the previous three years, retail ketchup volume had increased at an average annual rate of 3 percent. Increasing consumption of ketchup was believed to reflect life-style trends favoring quick, convenient meals, such as hamburgers. In addition, ketchup consumption was thought to be correlated negatively with the price of beef, which had fallen during each of the previous three years.

Major Competitors

Heinz, Hunt's, and Del Monte were the three major ketchup brands. Hunt's was owned by Esmark, Inc., and Del Monte by R. J. Reynolds, Inc. Hunt's ketchup sales accounted for 3 percent of Esmark's U.S. Foods Division sales while Del Monte ketchup sales made up 5 percent of R. J. Reynolds' Dry Grocery and Beverages Division sales. Hunt's and Del Monte employed their own sales forces to sell their products nationwide.

Heinz's 45.6 percent retail share of ketchup volume in 1983 compared to Hunt's 14.1 percent and Del Monte's 11.8 percent. Private-label, generic, and minor brands made up the remaining 28.5 percent. Heinz volume was up 23 percent over the 1979 level; it was the only major brand that had grown over the past four years. Exhibit 2 shows market shares by region for FY 1979–FY 1983. Heinz had increased its share during the previous five years, but in FY 1983 Heinz had lost half a share point to Hunt's and private-label brands. Market shares varied by region; Heinz was strongest in the Northeast with a 60.9 percent market share and weakest in the West and South.

Package Sizes

In 1983, the major manufacturers sold four sizes of ketchup: 14 oz., 24 oz., 32 oz., and 44 oz. Exhibit 3 shows industry volume mix by size over the previous 20 years. In 1964, only two sizes had been available, and the 14-oz. size accounted for two-thirds of the volume. By 1983, over 80 percent of ketchup sales were in sizes that had not existed 20 years earlier.

---

[1] One equivalent case = 24 14-oz. bottles, or 336 ounces.

EXHIBIT 2   Ketchup Brand Shares by Region

		FY 1979	FY 1980	FY 1981	FY 1982	FY 1983
Northeast	Heinz	52.9%	57.1%	59.8%	61.4%	60.9%
	Hunt's	10.1	8.9	8.3	7.8	7.0
	Del Monte	5.0	4.2	2.5	1.7	2.6
North Central	Heinz	44.2	45.6	45.4	46.1	47.6
	Hunt's	10.1	10.4	10.1	10.3	9.6
	Del Monte	16.3	13.9	15.0	13.3	12.9
South	Heinz	29.4	30.9	32.8	38.4	37.0
	Hunt's	27.9	26.0	25.2	21.5	23.6
	Del Monte	18.7	16.4	17.7	15.3	13.2
West	Heinz	33.6	34.9	36.5	37.4	36.8
	Hunt's	12.5	13.7	14.2	12.2	11.2
	Del Monte	25.5	22.4	23.3	23.7	21.7
Total US	Heinz	40.1	42.0	43.4	46.1	45.6
	Hunt's	16.2	15.7	15.5	13.8	14.1
	Del Monte	15.4	13.3	13.9	12.5	11.8

EXHIBIT 3   Size Mix of Ketchup Category Volume

	1964	1969	1974	1979	1980	1981	1982	1983
14 oz.	68%	48%	33%	23%	22%	20%	19%	17%
20 oz.	32	37	24	10	6	1	—	—
24 oz.	—	—	—	5	10	13	13	11
26 oz.	—	15	20	9	3	—	—	—
32 oz.	—	—	23	49	46	50	51	55
44 oz.	—	—	—	4	13	16	17	17
Total	100%	100%	100%	100%	100%	100%	100%	100%

Exhibit 4 shows the volume mix by size and by region for each major ketchup brand in 1983. For the three major brands, the bulk of their business was accounted for by the 32-oz. size. This size was even more important for Hunt's and Del Monte than for Heinz.

Pricing

Heinz was the highest-priced ketchup brand on all sizes in all regions (except for the 24-oz. size in the West, where Del Monte was priced higher by 1.7 percent). Exhibit 5 shows the major manufacturers' base selling prices and actual retail selling prices by region. Except on the 14-oz. size, Heinz's retail prices were between 1 percent and 9 percent

EXHIBIT 4   FY 1983 Volume Mix by Brand, Size, and Region

		14 oz.	*24 oz.*	*32 oz.*	*44 oz.*	*Total*
Northeast	Heinz	20%	14%	42%	23%	100%
	Hunt's	34	14	43	9	100
	Del Monte	19	12	69	—	100
North Central	Heinz	13	12	46	28	100
	Hunt's	10	8	64	18	100
	Del Monte	9	14	60	17	100
South	Heinz	17	9	49	25	100
	Hunt's	13	16	59	12	100
	Del Monte	18	16	56	9	100
West	Heinz	21	10	41	28	100
	Hunt's	18	11	59	12	100
	Del Monte	20	10	56	14	100
Total US	Heinz	18	12	45	25	100
	Hunt's	16	14	57	13	100
	Del Monte	13	11	63	13	100

higher than Hunt's and Del Monte's. Hunt's and Del Monte's average national retail prices differed by 3 percent to 6 percent across the different sizes. As Exhibit 5 shows, the trade was taking the lowest margin on the 32-oz. size, which accounted for 55 percent of industry volume. It was believed that the trade treated the dominant 32-oz. size as a "loss leader."

Heinz had taken its last price increase in early 1982, a uniform 5 percent raise across the entire product line. Hunt's and Del Monte had followed with the same dollar per case increase. With a 40 percent manufacturer's gross margin, Heinz executives were concerned that Heinz might be priced too high. Fearing that competition could cut prices and gain market share from Heinz, Heinz management had resolved to try not to take any more price increases in the near future.

Trade Promotion

Trade deals and allowances played a major role in ketchup marketing. A significant proportion of FY 1983 ketchup industry volume was sold on deal, as shown below:

	14 oz.	*24 oz.*	*32 oz.*	*44 oz.*
Percentage of size volume sold on deal	30%	40%	90%	60%
Deal rates as percentage of base selling prices	9	10	15	12

EXHIBIT 5 1983 Manufacturer Base* Selling Prices and Actual Retail Prices (per bottle)

		14 oz.		24 oz.		32 oz.		44 oz.	
		Manufacturer	Retail	Manufacturer	Retail	Manufacturer	Retail	Manufacturer	Retail
Northeast	Heinz	$.64	$.72	$1.05	$1.17	$1.34	$1.37	$1.78	$1.91
	Hunt's	.61	.69	.99	1.14	1.28	1.31	1.72	1.85
	Del Monte	.62	.72	1.03	1.08	1.29	1.25	NA	2.10
North Central	Heinz	.64	.73	1.04	1.19	1.32	1.33	1.77	1.84
	Hunt's	.61	.73	1.00	1.17	1.27	1.19	1.68	1.77
	Del Monte	.61	.74	1.01	1.09	1.29	1.26	1.70	1.78
South	Heinz	.64	.76	1.04	1.22	1.32	1.30	1.77	1.89
	Hunt's	.64	.75	1.01	1.16	1.29	1.21	1.72	1.89
	Del Monte	.62	.73	1.01	1.05	1.29	1.24	1.69	1.85
West	Heinz	.63	.79	1.04	1.25	1.32	1.39	1.75	1.96
	Hunt's	.60	.78	1.00	1.17	1.25	1.27	1.69	1.95
	Del Monte	.63	.80	1.06	1.15	1.31	1.35	1.67	1.89

* Before promotional allowances.

Distribution

Share of market was thought to be partially correlated with level of retail distribution. Heinz, the market leader, was in practically all food stores with at least one size (97 percent All Commodity Volume),[2] followed by Hunt's (84 percent ACV), and Del Monte (72 percent ACV). Exhibit 6 shows retail distribution during FY 1983 by brand and by size.

Heinz average sales per linear foot of grocery shelf space, $1,021 per year, were significantly higher than sales of other ketchup brands (Hunt's $539, Del Monte $619) as well as other condiments (mustard $336, salad dressings $372). In spite of this, Heinz's share of shelf space was often less than its share of sales.

Market Development

Ketchup market development varied by region for the category and the individual brands. In terms of category volume, the South was the most important, representing 35 percent of volume, followed by the northeast and north central regions with 25 percent each, and the West with 15 percent. Based on a region's per capita consumption of ketchup relative to the national average, ketchup was underconsumed in the West and moderately overconsumed in the north central and southern regions. Exhibit 7 shows category (CDI) and brand development indexes (BDI) by region. Heinz was highly developed in the northeastern region (124 BDI) and underdeveloped in the West (71 BDI). Hunt's and Del Monte's BDIs were significantly more unbalanced. Hunt's was significantly overconsumed in the South (178 BDI) and underconsumed in the Northeast (47 BDI) and West (55 BDI). Del Monte had only a 26 BDI in the Northeast, but had over 120 in the other regions.

Advertising

In FY 1983, ketchup category advertising totaled $18.6 million, up from $6.7 million just three years earlier. Heinz accounted for 86 percent of advertising spending. Exhibit 8 shows category spending and brand shares for FY 1980–FY 1983. Hunt's stepped up its advertising, moving from virtually no advertising in FY 1981 and FY 1982 to $2 million in FY 1983. Del Monte did the reverse, going from $2 million in FY 1981 to zero advertising in FY 1983.

Consumer Behavior

The average US household bought the equivalent of four 32-oz. bottles of ketchup per year. The most popular uses were for hamburgers, french fries, and hot dogs. Heinz market research showed that both incidence

---

[2] Stores representing 97 percent of total US grocery sales stocked at least one size of Heinz ketchup.

EXHIBIT 6   FY 1983 Average Retail Distribution (percent ACV)

	14 oz.	24 oz.	32 oz.	44 oz.
Heinz	96%	78%	88%	80%
Hunt's	69	35	71	35
Del Monte	52	40	59	27

EXHIBIT 7   Ketchup Category and Brand Development Indexes*

	National	Northeast	North Central	South	West
Category	100	94	111	109	79
Heinz	100	124	113	89	71
Hunt's	100	47	87	175	55
Del Monte	100	26	126	123	133
Annual per capita consumption of category	51 oz.	48 oz.	56 oz.	55 oz.	40 oz.

$$* \text{ Index } = \frac{\text{Consumption per capita in area}}{\text{Average consumption per capita nationally}}$$

EXHIBIT 8   Ketchup Category Advertising and Advertising Shares

	FY 80	FY 81	FY 82	FY 83
Category (millions)	$6.7	$10.5	$14.4	$18.6
Heinz share (percent)	82%	82%	97%	86%
Hunt's share (percent)	3	0	1	11
Del Monte share (percent)	13	19	2	0
Private label and all other share (percent)	2	0	0	3

and amount of ketchup use increased in 1983: 67 percent of households (vs. 65 percent in 1981) purchased ketchup in the previous four weeks, and they used an average of 32.3 ounces per month (vs. 30.8 ounces in 1981). Other key findings from Heinz market research showed that:

- 97 percent of US households used ketchup and 89 percent of all households used it at least once every week. However, level of use varied widely:

	Percent of Users	Percent of Consumption
Heavy users (33 oz./mo. or more)*	28%	54%
Medium users (17–32 oz./mo.)	39	34
Light users (16 oz./mo. or less)	33	12

* Heavy ketchup users consumed, on average, 67 ounces per month.

- Consumers used ketchup all year round. The volume consumed in the highest period, June–July, was only 14 percent higher than that consumed during the lowest period, October–January.
- Children, who made up 20 percent of the population, accounted for 30 percent of ketchup "eating occasions." Their volume per use was also greater partly due to waste in usage.

Exhibit 9 presents key tables from a 1983 national market survey conducted for Heinz by Market Facts. Brand loyalty for Heinz increased significantly between 1975 and 1983. Heinz was not as successful as Hunt's, however, in attracting heavy users. Most major brand purchasers selected the brand first, then the bottle size.

Exhibit 9 also reports ketchup user attitudes. Family acceptance and the "best flavor" were the most important product attributes. Heavy users were more likely to believe that ketchup brands were different, and they also paid closer attention to price.

New Product Introductions

During most of the 1970s, the ketchup industry focused on cost control rather than new product development. The 32-oz. size was the only new product, first introduced by Heinz in 1974. To streamline operations, Heinz closed four of its seven ketchup plants. Heinz enjoyed cost advantages over its competition due to quantity purchasing discounts on raw materials and low transportation costs. After the 32 oz. introduction in 1974, Heinz's new product development during the rest of the decade was focused on gravy and Weight Watchers products.

The late 1970s and early 1980s saw two major new product introductions: the 24-oz. and 44-oz. sizes. The 24-oz. size was introduced by Hunt's and Del Monte in October 1978 as a consolidation of the 20-oz. and 26-oz. sizes. Since, by that time, the 32-oz. size accounted for nearly one-half of category volume, three smaller sizes (14 oz., 20 oz., and 26 oz.) seemed excessive. Manufacturers believed that they would be unable to hold distribution for both 20-oz. and 26-oz. sizes. The 14-oz. bottle, used heavily in restaurants, was considered a "classic," so was left in the

EXHIBIT 9   Highlights of 1983 Market Facts Study on Ketchup Usage and Attitudes

1. Ketchup Brand Loyalty

	Percent Who Purchased Only One Brand in Past 3 Months	**Brand Purchased Exclusively**			
		Heinz	*Hunt's*	*Del Monte*	*Private Label, Generic, All Others*
1975	45%	23%	8%	8%	6%
1983	54	34	7	7	7

Percent of Respondents Who Buy This Brand Most Often, Who Bought No Other Brand in Past 3 Months

	Heinz	*Hunt's*	*Del Monte*	*Private Label*	*Generic*
1975	55%	34%	41%	42%	NA
1983	60	35	42	40	53%

2. Ketchup Brands Purchased Last by Usage Level

	Heavy Users	*Medium Users*	*Light Users*
Heinz	51%	53%	51%
Hunt's	21	18	14
Del Monte	12	14	18
Private label, generic, all others	16	15	17

3. Brand vs. Size Decision on Brand Purchased Last

	Heinz	*Hunt's*	*Del Monte*	*Private Label*
Selected brand first, then bottle size	88%	79%	81%	55%
Selected size first, then brand	12	21	19	45

4. Size Usage

	14 oz.	*24 oz.*	*32 oz.*	*44 oz.*
Purchased last	15%	13%	53%	12%
Purchased most often	15	16	52	12

5. Promotional Activity on Last Purchase

	Heinz	*Hunt's*	*Del Monte*	*Private Label*
Regular price	44%	46%	42%	62%
"On special," no coupon	23	30	31	28
"On special," with retailer coupon	1	1	2	—
Newspaper manufacturer coupon	22	17	18	5
Magazine/mail/on-pack coupon	9	5	6	4
On special display	18	19	21	17

(continued)

EXHIBIT 9 *(concluded)*

6. Importance of Ketchup Attributes

		Percent of Users Stating Attribute Is "Very Important"		
	Total	*Heavy Users*	*Medium Users*	*Light Users*
Whole family likes it	64%	70%	67%	57%
Best flavor	62	63	65	58
Good value for the money	56	59	58	53
Good to use on food at the table	54	60	56	48
Brand name I trust	50	50	53	47
Thick consistency	40	42	40	37

7. Attitudes toward Ketchup

	Percent Stating That They "Definitely/Generally Agree"		
	Heavy Users	*Medium Users*	*Light Users*
Brand Differentiation:			
Some brands are much thicker than others	74%	66%	59%
There's a lot of difference between ketchup brands	59	57	51
Most brands of ketchup taste the same	15	15	11
Brand Loyalty:			
I like to stick to one brand of ketchup	59	62	58
Price/Value:			
Some brands of ketchup cost more and are worth it	47	46	46
When buying ketchup, I pay close attention to the price	57	49	45
I usually buy whatever ketchup brand is on sale	22	22	19
Packaging:			
Would pay up to 20 cents more for ketchup in a plastic bottle than I would for a glass bottle	10	8	10
I like the idea of packing it in squeeze bottles	37	33	33
The convenience of squeezable packaging for ketchup makes it worth an extra 20 cents per bottle	12	10	11

line. Therefore, when introducing the 24-oz. size, Hunt's and Del Monte voluntarily deleted the 20-oz. and 26-oz. sizes in all regions. In January 1979, Heinz followed with its 24-oz. introduction in the South and West. Concurrently, the company also introduced a new 44-oz., keg-shaped, glass bottle in the same regions.

The Heinz 32-oz. bottle introduced in 1974 was the first ketchup container with a keg design. Heinz 44 oz. was also a keg. The keg was rounder, squatter, and shaped more like a barrel than the classic cylindrical bottle; it also had a ring or "ear" for gripping. After its simultaneous introduction with the 24-oz. size in January 1979, the 44 oz. was rolled out into the rest of the country by April 1979, taking only four months to reach 70 percent ACV. In its high BDI northern markets, Heinz temporarily gained distribution for five sizes (the 44 oz. and the existing line). In these well-developed Heinz markets, Heinz was able to retain both the 20-oz. and 26-oz. sizes in distribution for a while. Since it was relatively easy to procure the necessary packaging materials and to adjust production lines, Hunt's and Del Monte followed with their own 44-oz. sizes about eight months later. Hunt's and Del Monte captured only about a quarter of the 44-oz. market, however.

Heinz introduced the 24-oz. size in its low BDI markets first, partly to facilitate the 44-oz. introduction in those areas. In these markets, Heinz managers believed that they had to delete the 20-oz. and 26-oz. items (and replace them with the 24 oz.) in order to make shelf space for the 44 oz. This was not thought to be the case in high BDI markets.

Although Heinz was two to three months behind Hunt's and Del Monte in the 24-oz. introduction in the South and West, Heinz nevertheless came to dominate this size segment. By 1983, Heinz 24 oz. had captured 5.3 percent of the ketchup market versus Hunt's 2.0 percent and Del Monte's 1.2 percent. Exhibit 10 shows market shares by size for FY 1979–FY 1983. Heinz 24-oz. distribution built rapidly, growing from 50 percent ACV in FY 1979 to 80 percent ACV in FY 1981. Hunt's 24-oz. distribution declined from 55 percent ACV in FY 1979 to 35 percent ACV in FY 1983; Del Monte's equivalent distribution levels were 57 percent and 38 percent. Exhibit 11 shows retail distribution by size at the end of fiscal years 1979–1983.

Heinz's introduction of the 24-oz. and 44-oz. sizes was relatively easy to implement. No new capacity was required because the 44-oz. bottle could be run on the 32-oz. line, and the 24 oz. could be run on the old 20-oz. and 26-oz. lines. The sales force had no difficulty selling-in to the trade because they did not have to obtain incremental shelf space—two new items were traded for two existing items. The only additional promotional support was an introductory $1.00 per case trade allowance and a cents-off coupon promotion for each of the two new sizes in Sunday free-standing inserts (FSIs). There was no incremental advertising spending,

EXHIBIT 10   US Ketchup Market Shares by Size

	FY 1979			FY 1980			FY 1981			FY 1982			FY 1983		
	Heinz	Hunt's	Del Monte	Heinz	Hunt's	Del Monte	Heinz	Hunt's	Del Monte	Heinz	Hunt's	Del Monte	Heinz	Hunt's	Del Monte
14 oz.	8.2%	3.2%	2.8%	8.2%	3.1%	3.0%	8.8%	2.6%	2.6%	8.6%	2.5%	2.3%	8.0%	2.3%	1.4%
20 oz.	4.3	2.0	1.5	2.6	.5	.2	.1	.1	—	6.2	2.2	1.6	5.3	2.0	1.2
24 oz.	1.7	1.3	1.9	3.7	2.7	2.7	6.7	2.0	2.4	—	—	—	—	—	—
26 oz.	4.0	.8	1.5	1.4	.3	.1	—	—	—	—	—	—	—	—	—
32 oz.	19.5	8.9	6.3	15.8	7.4	6.2	17.4	8.1	6.6	19.3	7.2	6.4	20.5	8.1	6.9
44 oz.	2.4	—	—	10.3	1.7	—	10.5	2.7	1.9	12.0	2.0	1.9	11.7	1.8	1.4

EXHIBIT 11   Ketchup Retail Distribution (% ACV)—End of Fiscal Year

	FY 1979			FY 1980			FY 1981			FY 1982			FY 1983		
	Heinz	Hunt's	Del Monte	Heinz	Hunt's	Del Monte	Heinz	Hunt's	Del Monte	Heinz	Hunt's	Del Monte	Heinz	Hunt's	Del Monte
14 oz.	95%	70%	66%	95%	65%	62%	95%	62%	58%	95%	58%	54%	96%	79%*	51%
20 oz.	34	24	16	26	3	1	80	42	48	78	36	42	78	35	38
24 oz.	50	55	57	70	52	59	—	—	—	—	—	—	—	—	—
26 oz.	33	13	15	21	3	1	—	—	—	—	—	—	—	—	—
32 oz.	86	68	57	87	71	59	87	71	55	87	69	54	89	69	62
44 oz.	59	—	—	75	45	—	78	40	29	79	37	28	81	32	27

* Increased distribution of Hunt's 14 oz. in FY 1983 was partly due to its introduction of a no-salt ketchup in that bottle size.

and the advertising did not focus on the new packages. They were not considered newsworthy enough.

The 1980s: A Period of Aggressive Marketing

The early 1980s were a period of aggressive marketing by the major brands. During this time, Heinz concentrated its efforts in the South. Exhibit 12 shows Heinz ketchup marketing spending per case for the total United States and the South for FY 1979–FY 1983. Heinz increased total national spending per case during this period by 92 percent, and spending in the South by 147 percent. Aside from increasing advertising spending, Heinz used more competitive, comparison copy. The ads featured side-by-side demonstrations of Heinz and other national brands, pointing out Heinz's thicker consistency. Exhibit 13 presents a Heinz TV commercial used in this campaign.

In 1982, Hunt's challenged the validity of this commercial in a complaint filed with the National Advertising Division (NAD) of the Council of Better Business Bureaus. Hunt's complained that the demonstrations were not related to normal use, and that the differences did not reflect true thickness. Heinz countered by arguing that resistance to separation was relevant to evaluating thickness, and they also provided blind, paired comparison test results that showed preference for Heinz over Hunt's and Del Monte. The NAD concluded that the Heinz claims were substantiated.

In 1983, Hunt's and Del Monte reformulated their ketchup to improve taste and consistency. Spices were added to improve the taste, and each company invested about $1.5 million in homogenization, a process that

EXHIBIT 12   Heinz Ketchup Marketing Spending per Equivalent Case

	FY 79	*FY 80*	*FY 81*	*FY 82*	*FY 83*
Total US:					
Trade promotion	$ .75	$1.20	$1.06	$1.09	$1.20
Consumer promotion	.30	.35	.22	.24	.42
Advertising	.33	.42	.55	.90	1.01
Total	$1.38	$1.97	$1.83	$2.23	$2.63
South:					
Trade promotion	$ .83	$1.25	$1.14	$1.21	$1.43
Consumer promotion	.38	.55	.53	.57	1.06
Advertising	.37	.49	.76	1.20	1.42
Total	$1.58	$2.29	$2.43	$2.98	$3.91

Part I   The Product Development Process

EXHIBIT 13   1982 Heinz Ketchup TV Commercial

EXHIBIT 13   1982 Heinz Ketchup TV Commercial

LEO BURNETT COMPANY, INC.   H.J. HEINZ
AS FILMED AND RECORDED(8/82)   "New Southern Plate Test/32 Oz." :30   HZHK 1330

1. PULLUP (Anncr VO): If I take some Heinz Ketchup at the start of your meal...

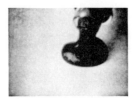

2. and put it right here...

3. and put this Hunt's Ketchup right here...

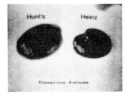

4. something amazing happens before you're half through.

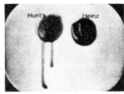

5. See the difference? We challenged the competition and they ran.

6. Heinz ketchup is thicker and Heinz is never thin on flavor.

7. Now which one would you rather have on your hamburger?

8. Heinz.

9. America's thickest, best-tasting ketchup.

produced a product almost as thick as Heinz's.[3] As a result, Heinz could no longer run its comparison advertising campaign. In addition, homogenization improved Hunt's and Del Monte's variable cost per bottle.

As a result, Heinz lost half a point in national market share, and 1.4 points in the South between FY 1982 and FY 1983. Heinz counterattacked with a new television advertising campaign that stressed Heinz's taste superiority and greater popularity, claiming that it was the consumer's 3 to 1 choice over any other brand. Exhibit 14 shows a commercial from this campaign. Heinz also added extra trade deals and coupon drops in the South. Overall, however, the counterattack proved to be ineffective in fighting off Hunt's offensive. In addition, Del Monte and private label brands benefited as the two major brands competed head-to-head.

[3] Homogenization processed tomatoes into very small pieces that did not coagulate, thereby producing a higher solid yield. Heinz already used this process.

EXHIBIT 14   1983 Heinz Ketchup TV Commercial

LEO BURNETT COMPANY, INC.   H.J. HEINZ CO.
AS FILMED AND RECORDED (8/83)   "RETORT II/PARITY :CC"   HZHK3780

1. WOMAN: I decided to test Heinz ketchup myself.

2. To see why more folks choose it.

3. You know what happened?

4. Heinz didn't run.

5. Then I tasted Heinz. Because, to me, that's proof.

6. One taste and I knew which ketchup I liked best.

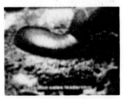

7. (Anncr VO): Unbeatably thick, rich Heinz is America's three to one choice over any other single ketchup. Taste it for yourself.

8. WOMAN: No contest!

9. (Anncr VO): Heinz. America's favorite for thick, rich ketchup.

Hunt's aggressiveness, and word from packaging suppliers that plastic technology applicable to ketchup packaging was being developed, stimulated Heinz to pursue aggressively the development of a plastic bottle. Heinz had a tradition of packaging innovation—they had been first to market the 32-oz. size and the 44-oz. keg-design bottle—and wanted to be first with a plastic bottle ketchup.

The Plastic Bottle Development

In describing Heinz's attitude toward new product development, Barbara Johnson noted: "We've found that the best way to be a leader is not to act like a leader, but to be hungry, always looking for new products." Heinz first started investigating plastic packaging 15 years earlier, but not until 1980 did they contact suppliers to begin developmental work. Heinz eventually signed an exclusive agreement with American Can Co. to develop a commercially feasible technology for producing the plastic for bottling ketchup. The plastic had to form a barrier such that the plastic resins could not affect the flavor of the ketchup and oxygen could not penetrate the walls of the bottle. In addition, the plastic had to be resistant to the boiling temperature of the ketchup as it was inserted into the bottles during production.

Early in the product in 1980, only three departments at Heinz (marketing, packaging, and purchasing) were involved. Heinz did not tell suppliers of the required manufacturing equipment the full nature of the project. Heinz engineers bought parts piecemeal and made some of the equipment themselves. Company management was willing to trade slower progress for maximum secrecy. As the project showed greater viability, more Heinz departments were brought in. The project turned out to be so technically complex that management formed a task force to provide the necessary close working relationship among the various functions of purchasing, packaging, engineering, manufacturing, operations, and marketing.

Heinz's expertise with can and glass production lines was of modest value in developing a plastic line. On a glass line, for example, the weight of the bottles held them in position. Plastic bottles, however, were light and had to be secured. In addition, plastic bottles required different lubricants, a different type of glue for the labels, and special handling as they became pliable with heat. In developing a new production line, including a new bottle filling process, Heinz borrowed technology from liquid detergent manufacturers. The company spent over $2 million in three years to develop its proprietary plastic packaging process.

Heinz's prototype plastic line was a converted glass line—converted at a $1 million cost. However, the line was slower than a new line designed specifically for plastic, and higher speeds were necessary to improve profitability.

The prototype plastic bottle offered ketchup users several benefits: it was lightweight, shatterproof, squeezable for better access and portion control, and had a convenient, nonremovable flip-top cap.[4] Unlike glass bottles, however, the plastic bottle had to be refrigerated after opening.[5] The plastic flip-top cap allowed greater air inflow than the lug-style metal closure used on the glass bottle, which provided a tighter seal. Refrigeration was necessary to retard the ketchup's oxidation, the chemical reaction of the ketchup with oxygen which resulted in the dark residue that formed around the seal. Although shatterproof, the plastic bottle was

---

[4] The squeezable and flip-top cap features could be applied to smaller bottles, but not to keg-design bottles.

[5] Over 80 percent of ketchup-using households kept glass bottles in the refrigerator after opening. The plastic bottle, if introduced, would have to carry a label instruction to refrigerate upon opening.

EXHIBIT 15   Heinz Ketchup Cost Structures (per bottle)

	14-oz. Glass	24-oz. Glass	28-oz. Plastic	32-oz. Glass	44-oz. Glass	64-oz. Plastic
Ingredients	$.156	$.267	$.314	$.356	$ .496	$ .712
Bottle and case	.051	.118	.321	.219	.282	.696
Cap	.029	.029	.050	.035	.035	.063
Label	.079	.091	.044	.010	.010	.098
Labor and overhead	.027	.050	.077	.060	.083	.183
Distribution	.042	.062	.096	.098	.123	.228
Total	$.384	$.617	$.902	$.778	$1.029	$1.980

breakable—another potential drawback since consumers might mistakenly assume that all plastic containers were unbreakable. Refrigeration added to the problem since the plastic (polypropylene) became brittle with cooling.[6]

Heinz managers were confident that the plastic bottle delivered significant consumer benefits, but they were not sure which size(s) was right. Should they start with an existing size or create a new size for plastic? The ketchup brand group planned a consumer testing program of various package sizes, primarily 64 oz. and 28 oz. Johnson and her group started with the 64-oz. size (5⅜″ wide × 4″ deep × 10¾″ tall) because plastic's shatterproof and lightweight attributes would be most beneficial in a large size. The plastic 64-oz. container offered 20 ounces more ketchup than the 44-oz. glass bottle but, when full, both packages weighed the same. In addition, the category trend was towards larger sizes, as evidenced by the success of Heinz 44-oz. ketchup.

As an alternative, the brand group originally considered a 32-oz. plastic bottle. But in order to attain a lower price point, a 28-oz. size (4⅛″ wide × 2⅛″ deep × 10⅜″ tall) was pursued instead. The plastic bottle cost significantly more than a glass container of equivalent size. Exhibit 15 shows a cost comparison of the 28-oz. plastic, 32-oz. glass, and 64-oz. plastic bottles.

Unbranded Home-Use Tests

September 1981: 64-oz. Plastic and 64-oz. Glass
The first in a series of product tests of the plastic bottle used a 64-oz. size. Sixty-four-oz. plastic and glass prototypes, with no brand names, were consumer tested in two monadic (separate, single product exposure as

---

[6] One of 10 bottles, if full and dropped from counter height after refrigeration, would break.

opposed to paired comparison) home-use tests. The samples consisted of regular users of 44-oz. ketchup. Both products scored comparably on ketchup ratings, including overall flavor, spiciness, sweetness, consistency, pourability, and color; at least 80 percent of respondents said that both products were "about right" on each of these attributes. On overall ketchup evaluation, both products received an 82 rating (on a 100-point scale). This compared with an 83 rating that the existing 44-oz. glass package had received in a previous test.

Exhibit 16 presents results of the package ratings. On overall package evaluation, the plastic bottle received a 78 rating versus 70 for glass.

EXHIBIT 16   Results of Monadic Home-Use Tests

	September 1981*		Previous Test†
	64-oz. Plastic (N = 300)	*64-oz. Glass (N = 540)*	*44-oz. Glass (N = 394)*
Package Rating‡	78	70	84
Visual Appearance			
Very attractive	12%	14%	18%
Somewhat attractive	36	41	37
Neither attractive nor unattractive	37	35	41
Somewhat unattractive	14	9	3
Very attractive	1	1	1
Ease of Handling by Adults (vs. 44 oz.)			
Much easier	11%	5%	9%
Somewhat easier	18	5	8
About the same	41	38	63
Somewhat harder	25	36	15
Much harder	3	14	3
Ease of Handling by Children (vs. 44 oz.)§			
Much easier	10%	2%	8%
Somewhat easier	10	2	5
About the same	20	18	33
Somewhat harder	29	27	26
Much harder	21	37	13

* The research was designed as two monadic home-use tests—one for the 64-oz. plastic and the other for the 64-oz. glass. Qualified respondents were recruited in shopping malls if they said they bought the 44-oz. ketchup size most often. They were given one 64-oz. bottle (plastic or glass) to use in their home for two weeks. After the usage period, telephone interviews were completed from a central research facility.

† Qualified respondents in this test bought the 32-oz. size most often.

‡ 100 = perfect, 90 = excellent, 80 = like very much . . . 20 = dislike very much, 10 = terrible, 0 = worst possible.

§ Among households with children.

Plastic's 78 rating, however, was significantly lower than the 84 rating that 44-oz. glass had received in the earlier test.

On unpriced purchase intent, the 64-oz. plastic product scored higher than its glass counterpart on the "definitely buy" measure. However, compared to the previous test's 49 percent "definitely buy" score for 44-oz. glass, plastic's 40 percent purchase score was significantly lower. When the 64-oz. products were priced at $2.39, both received similar scores, but when both were priced at parity with 44-oz. glass on a per-ounce basis, plastic received a significantly higher purchase-intent score than 64-oz. glass. Respondents who tested the 64-oz. glass were asked their purchase interest in plastic, and the reverse was asked of those who tested plastic. Purchase intent was significantly higher for plastic among glass users (see Exhibit 17).

October 1982: 28-oz. Plastic

Encouraged by consumer testing results of the 64-oz. plastic bottle, the brand group decided to develop and test a squeezable, 28-oz. plastic prototype. (The 64-oz. plastic package was not designed to be squeezable; it was too bulky and did not have a flip-top cap with a narrow nozzle.) In this test, 180-day-old product was used.[7]

The ketchup in the 28-oz. squeezable bottle received an 80.2 rating compared to "Benchmark Ketchup's" 81.5 rating. "Benchmark Ketchup" was a standard formulation that Heinz management used as a control for regular testing of factory production. The 28-oz. product received uniformly high scores on overall flavor, spiciness, sweetness, pourability, and color. At least 80 percent of respondents rated the ketchup as being "about right" on these attributes.

Exhibit 18 presents results of the package ratings. On the 100-point overall rating scale, the 28-oz. package received an 84.4 rating. The bottle used in this test had a nonremovable flip-top cap. This prevented consumers from refilling the plastic bottle with ketchup from less expensive glass bottles. Aside from a removable cap's potentially adverse effect on plastic bottle sales, Heinz management was also concerned about the hygiene risk associated with consumers' refilling ketchup bottles. Since the test bottle's flip-top was nonremovable, respondents were questioned on how this feature would affect their purchase behavior. Sixty-three percent said it made no difference, while 20 percent said that they would be less likely to purchase; 25 percent said that they tried to remove the cap.

---

[7] The ketchup had been in the plastic bottles used in the test for 180 days. Once produced, a bottle of Heinz ketchup had a two-year life but would normally be fully consumed six months after it left the plant.

EXHIBIT 17 Purchase Intent: 64-oz. Plastic and Glass

	Unpriced		Priced @ $2.39		Same Price/oz. as 44 oz.		For Plastic/ Glass Testers (N = 540)	For Glass/ Plastic Testers (N = 300)
	Plastic (N = 300)	Glass (N = 540)	Plastic (N = 300)	Glass (N = 540)	Plastic (N = 300)	Glass (N = 540)		
Definitely buy	40%	34%	24%	22%	47%	39%	27%	9%
Probably buy	44	39	53	50	34	31	47	39
Probably not buy	13	18	19	19	13	22	18	36
Definitely not buy	3	9	3	8	5	8	8	16

EXHIBIT 18   October 1982 Home-Use Test:*
28-oz. Plastic

	Package Ratings (N = 200)
Average rating†—bottle	84.4
Difficulty with label instructions	
Yes	3%
No	97
Trouble with cap	
Yes, opening	4%
Yes, closing	2
Yes, using	3
No trouble with cap	93
Problems with seal	
Yes	10%
No	90
Item used to break seal	
Toothpick	7%
Knife	27
Fork	16
Other	33
Try to remove cap	
Yes	25%
No	74
Effect of cap on purchase	
More likely to purchase	17%
Less likely to purchase	20
No difference	63

* Respondents who had purchased ketchup (any size) in the previous 30 days.

† 100 = perfect, 90 = excellent, 80 = like very much . . . 20 = disklike very much, 10 = terrible, 0 = worst possible.

Three purchase-intent scenarios were tested with the following results:

	Purchase Intent: 28-oz. Plastic (N = 200)		
	Unpriced	*Priced @ $1.59*	*If Filled with Heinz*
Definitely buy	31%	20%	37%
Probably buy	52	51	43
Probably not buy	13	18	14
Definitely not buy	3	8	7

When asked to choose between a $1.59 28-oz. Heinz plastic bottle and a $1.32 Heinz 32-oz. glass bottle, 55 percent chose the latter, 40 percent the former.

Among the 83 percent of respondents who would definitely or probably buy the 28-oz. plastic bottle (unpriced), 13 percent said that they would buy the plastic bottle in addition to an existing ketchup size that they currently used, while 83 percent said that the plastic container would be used as a replacement, primarily for the 32-oz. bottle:

Size Would Replace (base-positive purchase interest, N = 164)				
14 oz.	*24 oz.*	*32 oz.*	*44 oz.*	*Other/Don't Know*
11%	10%	43%	7%	37%

When asked what they liked about the 28-oz. plastic bottle, respondents most frequently mentioned "unbreakable," "squeezable," "easy to handle," and the "flip-top cap." One-third of respondents voiced dislikes about the plastic bottle although there was no one predominant complaint. Some of the more frequently mentioned concerns were "too large to store" and "bottom was too large." At least 85 percent of respondents stored the plastic bottle in the refrigerator after opening. Nineteen percent agreed strongly with the statement, "Plastic squeeze containers are somewhat more expensive, but they're worth it."

"More Expensive, but Worth It" (base-total respondents, N = 200)				
Strongly Agree	*Somewhat Agree*	*Neither Agree nor Disagree*	*Somewhat Disagree*	*Strongly Disagree*
19%	43%	20%	13%	5%

Conclusion

Barbara Johnson felt positive about the ketchup plastic bottle. The package received good scores in tests, and it would be the first lightweight, shatterproof, and for the 28 oz., squeezable ketchup bottle. Johnson wondered, however, if consumers would perceive it as a major innovation. After all, it was still the same product—ketchup. But in addition to the marketing research results, Johnson also knew that mustard in squeezable plastic containers, which was priced higher per ounce than mustard in glass containers, now accounted for 18 percent of retail volume.

H.J. Heinz Co.: Plastic Bottle Ketchup (B)

Barbara Johnson and the ketchup brand group considered the home-use test results of the plastic bottle sufficiently positive to recommend further testing in the Laboratory Test Market (LTM). The LTM was the Yankelovich, Skelly and White, Inc., test market simulation technique for estimating the sales volume potential of new products. It was faster and less expensive than a field test market. Exhibit 1 describes the LTM research procedure.

Laboratory Test Market Study

The LTM study was conducted in two cities—New York, a high BDI market for Heinz ketchup, and Dallas, a low BDI market. Both 28-oz. and 64-oz. plastic sizes were tested. The 28-oz. bottle was tested under two price levels, $1.49 and $1.59; each pricing scenario comprised one experimental cell. The 64-oz. plastic, priced at $2.81, was offered in the test in combination with the 28-oz. plastic, priced at $1.59—this comprised the third experimental cell. A fourth cell, made up of the existing Heinz glass line, was used as a control. In all three experimental cells, the plastic product(s) replaced the 24-oz. glass product in the Heinz ketchup line.

	Sample Size (N)	
Cell Description	*New York*	*Dallas*
1. Control—existing Heinz glass line	202	199
2. 28-oz. plastic @ $1.59 replacing 24-oz. glass	155	161
3. 28-oz. plastic @ $1.49 replacing 24-oz. glass	155	158
4. 28-oz. plastic @ $1.59 and 64-oz. plastic @ $2.81 replacing 24-oz. glass	204	210

This case was written by Research Assistant John L. Teopaco under the direction of Professor John A. Quelch as the basis for class discussion rather than to illustrate either effective or ineffective handling of an administrative situation. Copyright © 1985 by the President and Fellows of Harvard College. Harvard Business School case 9–586–036.

Exhibit 1   Laboratory Test Market Research Design for Heinz Ketchup

Female heads of household with family incomes of $15,000 or more participated in the study. Respondents were divided into a control cell and three experimental cells. Respondents in the control cell (N = 401) were exposed to the current Heinz glass product line only. Respondents in one experimental cell (N = 316) were exposed to the Heinz line with the 28-oz. plastic at $1.59 whereas respondents in the second experimental cell (N = 313) were exposed to the 28-oz. plastic priced at $1.49. Respondents in the third experimental cell were exposed to the 28-oz. at $1.59 *and* the 64-oz. plastic at $2.81. In all experimental cells, the plastic product(s) replaced the 24-oz. glass in the Heinz line. These steps were followed:

1. Respondents viewed TV commercials (in the context of a film) featuring the appropriate Heinz product for their cell along with other nonketchup commercials.
2. Respondents proceeded to the laboratory store, which stimulated a supermarket. Heinz ketchup was shelved in the ketchup section along with competitive products—all priced. Participants were given 50¢ "seed money" toward the purchase of any ketchup item, which included Heinz, Hunt's, Del Monte, and a store brand (14 oz., 24 oz., 32 oz., and 44 oz.).
3. A Selected sample of buyers of the plastic bottle and nonbuyers broke into separate focus group discussions that probed their reasons for purchase or nonpurchase as well as their attitudes and behavior with respect to ketchup usage.
4. Participants used their purchased products at home under normal usage conditions. They were not informed that there would be a follow-up interview.
5. Three weeks later, all purchasers were interviewed by telephone to determine reactions to the product, satisfaction, and repurchase intentions.
6. Among users of the Heinz plastic bottle, two additional interviews, three weeks apart, were conducted to provide additional opportunities (sales waves) for them to repurchase and to obtain additional usage data.

The LTM technique forecasted sales for a new entry on an ongoing basis—after the introductory effort was complete and the market had stabilized. The estimating model used LTM data on trial, repeat, and rate of projected use and incorporated the marketing plan's level of spending for advertising and consumer promotion and anticipated level of distribution. Empirically determined corrective factors were applied to adjust for the exaggerated trial rates of the laboratory, including: "the Laboratory Factor"—a downward correction for the test's novelty effect; "the Clout Factor"—a downward correction for the heightened awareness and controlled distribution of the product.

In forecasting sales, the LTM model assumed two alternative spending plans for cells 2 and 3. The base plan of $4.2 million consisted of $2.7 million in advertising and $1.5 million in consumer promotion; the $7.4-million high-spending plan consisted of $4.1 million in advertising and $3.3 million in consumer promotion. Trade promotion was not a variable in the LTM estimating model. Exhibit 2 presents the sales estimates for 28-oz. plastic nationally and for each test market under a solo introduction. All pricing and spending scenarios resulted in incremental Heinz volume, ranging from +5.5 percent to +11.5 percent on a national basis, and in incremental category volume of +2.5 percent to +5.5 per-

EXHIBIT 2   28-oz. Plastic LTM Sales Estimate

	National Projection			
	$1.59 Price		$1.49 Price	
	$4.2MM Plan	*$7.4MM Plan*	*$4.2MM Plan*	*$7.4MM Plan*
Incremental* Heinz case volume				
Percent	+5.5%	+8.5%	+7.5%	+11.5%
Cases (equivalent)	+836,000	+1,292,000	+1,140,000	+1,748,000
New total Heinz case volume	16.04MM	16.49MM	16.34MM	16.95MM
Heinz plastic case volume				
Percent	12.5%	16.5%	17.5%	22.5%
Cases (equivalent)	2,005,000	2,721,000	2,860,000	3,813,000

* Base: Fiscal year 1982 Heinz sales.
     Total units = 15.2MM cases.
     Market share = 46.1%.

	New York			
	$1.59 Price		$1.49 Price	
	$4.2MM Plan	*$7.4MM Plan*	*$4.2MM Plan*	*$7.4MM Plan*
Incremental* Heinz case volume				
Percent	+4.5%	+7.0%	+7.5%	+11.5%
Cases	+72,000	+112,000	+120,000	+185,000
New total Heinz case volume	1.677MM	1.717MM	1.725MM	1.790MM
Plastic as percent of total Heinz volume	12.5%	15.5%	17.5%	22.5%

* Base: Fiscal year 1982 Heinz sales.
     Total units = 1.605MM cases.
     Market share = 71.6%.

	Dallas			
	$1.59 Price		$1.49 Price	
	$4.2MM Plan	*$7.4MM Plan*	*$4.2MM Plan*	*$7.4MM Plan*
Incremental* Heinz case volume				
Percent	+6.5%	+9.5%	+7.0%	+10.5%
Cases	+28,000	+40,000	+29,000	+45,000
New total Heinz case volume	454,000	466,000	455,000	471,000
Plastic as percent of total Heinz volume	15.5%	19.5%	17.5%	22.5%

* Base: Fiscal year 1982 Heinz sales.
     Total units = 426,000 cases.
     Market share = 35.7%.

cent. The sales volume estimate for 28-oz. plastic ranged from 2,005,000 (equivalent) cases to 3,813,000 cases. Both test markets showed the same pattern as the national projection: the 28-oz. plastic generated incremental Heinz volume under all scenarios, and higher spending resulted in greater incremental volume.

The sales forecast for cell 4 used a single base spending plan of $8.2 million to support both products, $4.8 million in advertising and $3.4 million in consumer promotion. Exhibit 3 presents sales estimates for 28-oz. and 64-oz. plastic nationally and for each test market. The dual introduction resulted in a total plastic volume of 3,380,000 cases, and produced 8.5 percent incremental volume for the total Heinz line. The New York and Dallas test markets showed incremental Heinz volume of 7 percent and 10 percent, respectively.

Exhibit 4 reports the percentages of respondents who tried a Heinz ketchup product for each test cell. All experimental cells recorded a higher Heinz purchase level than the control cell with an all-glass line.

EXHIBIT 3   LTM Sales Estimate

	28 oz. @ $1.59/64 oz. @ $2.81 $8.2MM Plan		
	National Projection	*New York*	*Dallas*
Incremental Heinz case volume			
Percent	+8.5%*	+7.0%†	+10.0%‡
Cases (equivalent)	+1,292,000	+112,000	+42,600
New total Heinz case volume	16.49MM	1.717MM	468,600
Heinz plastic case volume			
Percent of total Heinz	20.5%	17.5%	22.5%
Cases (equivalent)	3,380,000	300,475	105,435

* Base: Fiscal year 1982 Heinz sales = 15.2MM cases; market share = 46.1%.

† Base: Fiscal year 1982 Heinz sales = 1.605MM cases; market share = 71.6%.

‡ Base: Fiscal year 1982 Heinz sales = 426,000 cases; market share = 35.7%.

EXHIBIT 4   LTM Purchase Levels for Heinz Ketchup Line—New York and Dallas Combined

	Percent of Respondents Who Purchased a Heinz Ketchup Product		
Cell	*Total*	*Current Heinz Franchise**	*Competitive Brand Users*
1. Control—current glass line	39%	53%	23%
2. 28 oz. @ $1.59	51	53	47
3. 28 oz. @ $1.49	58	62	52
4. 28 oz. @ $1.59 + 64 oz. @ $2.81	50	52	47

* Base: Respondents who said they bought Heinz most often; 61 percent of sample after BDI weighting.

Comparing the results for cells 2 and 3, the 10¢ price differential depressed Heinz trials, especially among competitive brand users.

Exhibit 5 presents the Heinz purchase levels broken down according to the package size bought. The 28-oz. plastic captured the largest share in all experimental cells, including the fourth, which offered both the 28-oz. and 64-oz. plastic sizes.

Purchasers of the plastic bottle were called back three times (each three weeks apart) to place reorders. The higher-priced ($1.59) 28-oz. plastic registered the highest percentage of users who reordered over the three sales waves. All three experimental cells showed a drop in reorder level between the first and second opportunities.

	28-oz. Plastic		
	$1.59 (N = 226)	*$1.49 (N = 131)*	*64-oz. Plastic (N = 128)*
Reordered (net)	48%	43%	46%
1st opportunity	36	31	28
2nd opportunity	12	9	8
3rd opportunity	10	16	17

Exhibit 6 presents other major findings from the LTM study, including user profiles, level of satisfaction, repurchase intent, and frequency of use. In general, the new plastic bottle seemed to have broad appeal.

Marketing Program Development
If she decided to introduce the plastic bottle nationally, Johnson had several marketing and manufacturing issues to address.

EXHIBIT 5   LTM Purchase Levels for Heinz according to Package Size—New York and Dallas Combined

	Cell			
Size Bought	*Current Glass Line (N = 401)*	*28 oz. at $1.59 (N = 316)*	*28 oz. at $1.49 (N = 313)*	*28 oz. at $1.59 and 64 oz. at $2.81 (N = 414)*
14 oz.	16%	6%	5%	6%
24 oz.	4	NA	NA	NA
32 oz.	15	3	1	2
44 oz.	2	3	3	—
28 oz.	NA	40	50	36
64 oz.	NA	NA	NA	8

Note: Column totals not consistent with *Exhibit 4* due to rounding.

EXHIBIT 6   Selected Findings from the LTM Study

---

1. **Profile of Heinz Purchasers—Frequency of Using Ketchup**

			Purchased Heinz Plastic		
	Total	*Current Heinz Franchise*	*28 oz. @ $1.59*	*28 oz. @ $1.49*	*64 oz.*
Used ketchup at least four times/week	36%	40%	54%	40%	39%

2. **Profile of Heinz Purchasers—Size Usually Purchased (SUP)**

			Purchased Heinz Plastic		
	SUP Total	*SUP–Current Heinz Franchise*	*28 oz. @ $1.59*	*28 oz. @ $1.49*	*64 oz.*
14 oz.	16%	14%	7%	12%	1%
24 oz.	22	22	23	21	10
32 oz.	44	43	48	41	51
44 oz.	18	21	22	26	38

3. Currently, 29 percent of households used ketchup four or more times a week. Thirty-nine percent of those who chose 28-oz. plastic and 52 percent of those who chose 64-oz. plastic said they used ketchup at least four times a week.
4. Eighty-nine percent of 28-oz. triers and 85 percent of 64-oz. users were "completely satisfied" with the product.
5. Sixty-six percent of 28-oz. triers and 75 percent of 64-oz. triers said that they "definitely will rebuy" the product.
6. Fifty-three percent of 28-oz. triers and 40 percent of 64-oz. triers said that they "will buy Heinz Ketchup in plastic bottles only."

Timing and Place

Johnson wanted to introduce initially only the 28-oz. squeezable bottle. Some of her colleagues, citing the research results and the LTM study, advocated introducing the 28-oz. and 64-oz. plastic at the same time. Production and Sales, however, had strong reservations about this strategy. The sales department preferred to go with the 28 oz. now, followed by the 64 oz. later. Some executives even suggested reviving and introducing a 32-oz. plastic, instead of either 28 oz. or 64 oz., to replace the 32-oz. glass. Aside from the sequencing issue, Johnson also had to decide where to introduce the 28-oz. and/or 64-oz. sizes first. Should she recommend rolling out first to weak Heinz regions, or to well-developed markets?

Marketing Support

Johnson had to decide on the nature and level of marketing support for a plastic bottle introduction. Was the plastic bottle a revolutionary, breakthrough product, or was it just another line extension? She wondered whether the introduction warranted advertising that focused solely on the new plastic bottle. Advertising a new ketchup package would be a first for Heinz. Johnson also had to decide on the amount of spending that she should recommend. Should she ask for incremental marketing funds from management, or should she just reallocate dollars from the FY 1984 advertising and promotion budget for the Heinz ketchup line (assuming no new product introduction) of $43 million? A reallocation would probably mean cutting base advertising and consumer promotions on existing sizes. An additional consideration was making room for the plastic bottle on the promotion calendar. One proposal was to reduce the number of trade promotions on 32-oz. glass from four to three per year, and another was to withdraw all promotional support from the 24 oz.-size.

Trade Acceptance

The ketchup category was already highly segmented by size, and as Johnson explained, "It's hard to find another product category where the major brands each have four, and potentially, five, sizes of the same product." Advocates of the 32-oz. plastic size mentioned the potential trade resistance to allocating incremental shelf space to a new 28-oz. size. Heinz management was equally concerned about losing 24 oz. distribution as a result of a 28 oz. introduction. Johnson was also concerned about what case size should be used for 28-oz. plastic. Johnson believed that a 24-pack, rather than the 12-pack now used for 32-oz. glass, would help ensure against stockouts. Should there be a special sales incentive for the Heinz and broker sales forces? Heinz normally did not offer such incentives for a new size introduction.

Pricing

For the 28-oz. plastic bottle, Johnson favored a base selling price to the trade of $1.30, and a suggested retail price of $1.59, giving the trade an 18 percent gross margin. There was the issue, however, of what margin the trade would actually take. Heinz had a base selling price of $1.32 and a suggested retail price of $1.59 on the 32-oz. glass, yet the trade gave it an everyday price of $1.34 and a deal price of $1.09–$1.19. In evaluating what base selling price to choose, Johnson assumed that the trade would want to take a higher margin on the 28-oz. plastic than it did on the 32-oz. glass.

Members of the brand group who advocated a 64 oz. introduction recommended a discount pricing strategy to provide consumers an economic incentive to purchase this new large size. They recommended a base selling price per bottle of $2.57, and a suggested retail price of $2.99, giving the trade a 14 percent gross margin. At this level, the base price per ounce of 64-oz. plastic (4.016¢) would be the lowest in the Heinz line, 5 percent less than for the 44-oz. glass bottle (4.227¢/oz.).

In addition to the marketing program, Johnson was concerned about how competition would respond. The word was that Hunt's was collaborating with Owens-Illinois, and private label manufacturers with Continental Can, to develop their plastic packaging.

Johnson also had to grapple with the manufacturing issues surrounding the new plastic bottle technology. The only plastic bottle line that would be available for the introductory year was the converted glass line with a first-year capacity of 900,000 cases (24–28 oz. pack). However, the line was untested under full production conditions, and the consumer demand for Heinz ketchup in plastic bottles was uncertain. A single new line, designed specifically for plastic, required a capital investment of $2–$3 million, a one-year lead time, and would provide an annual capacity of 2 million cases of the 28-oz. bottle. Depending on product needs, the converted line could continue to fill plastic bottles, and it could be adjusted for either 28 oz. or 64 oz. production.

After analyzing the situation, Barbara Johnson was convinced that Heinz should introduce the 28-oz. size first. She developed the following program for the introduction using a national equivalent advertising and promotion budget of $6.1 million.

Advertising:	740 annual GRPs of TV advertising (beginning in September 1983)	$2.7 million
Consumer Promotion:	October 1983 25¢ FSI coupon, February 1984 20¢ FSI coupon, Buy-two-get-one-free refund offer	$1.5 million
Trade Promotion:	Standard two-month introductory allowance @ 9% of base price[1] plus $1 stocking allowance	$1.9 million[2]

[1] Normal deal rate on 32 oz. at that time was 15 percent.

[2] Assumed 50 percent of first-year cases sold on deal.

Feeling confident about her decision, Johnson prepared to present her recommendations to the General Manager–Grocery Products in the first week of July.

Warner-Lambert Ireland: Niconil

Declan Dixon, director of marketing for Warner-Lambert Ireland (WLI), examined two very different sales forecasts as he considered the upcoming launch of Niconil®, scheduled for January 1990. Niconil was an innovative new product that promised to help the thousands of smokers who attempted to quit smoking each year. More commonly known simply as "the patch," Niconil was a transdermal skin patch that gradually released nicotine into the bloodstream to alleviate the physical symptoms of nicotine withdrawal.

Now in October of 1989, Dixon and his staff had to decide several key aspects of the product launch. There were different opinions about how Niconil should be priced and in what quantities it would sell. Pricing decisions would directly impact product profitability, as well as sales volume, and accurate sales forecasts were vital to planning adequate production capacity. Finally, the product team needed to reach consensus on the Niconil communications campaign to meet advertising deadlines and to ensure an integrated product launch.

Company Background

Warner-Lambert was an international pharmaceutical and consumer products company with over $4 billion in worldwide revenues expected in 1989. Warner-Lambert consumer products (50 percent of worldwide sales) included such brands as Dentyne chewing gum, Listerine mouthwash, and Hall's cough drops. Its pharmaceutical products, marketed through the Parke Davis division, included drugs for treating a wide variety of ailments including heart disease and bronchial disorders.

Warner-Lambert's Irish subsidiary was expected to generate £30 million in sales revenues in 1989:[1] £22 million from exports of manufactured products to other Warner-Lambert subsidiaries in Europe and £4 million

Research Associate Susan P. Smith prepared this case under the supervision of Professor John A. Quelch as the basis for class discussion rather than to illustrate effective or ineffective handling of an administrative situation. Copyright © 1992 by the President and Fellows of Harvard College. Harvard Business School case 9–593–008.

[1] In 1989, one Irish pound was equivalent to US$1.58.

each from pharmaceutical and consumer products sales within Ireland. The Irish drug market was estimated at £155 million (in manufacturer sales) in 1989. Warner-Lambert was the sixteenth largest pharmaceutical company in worldwide revenues; in Ireland, it ranked sixth.

Dixon was confident that WLI's position in the Irish market would ensure market acceptance of Niconil. The Parke Davis division had launched two new drugs successfully within the past nine months: Dilzem, a treatment for heart disease, and Accupro, a blood pressure medication. The momentum was expected to continue. The Irish market would be the first country launch for Niconil and thus serve as a test market for all of Warner-Lambert. The companywide significance of the Niconil launch was not lost on Dixon as he pondered the marketing decisions before him.

Smoking in the Republic of Ireland

Almost £600 million would by spent by Irish smokers on 300 million packs of cigarettes in 1989; this included government revenues from the tobacco sales tax of £441 million. Of 3.5 million Irish citizens, 30 percent of the 2.5 million adults smoked cigarettes (compared to 40 percent of adults in continental Europe and 20 percent in the United States).[2] The number of smokers in Ireland had peaked in the late 1970s and had been declining steadily since. Table A presents data from a 1989 survey that WLI had commissioned in 1989 of a demographically balanced sample of 1,400 randomly chosen Irish adults. Table B shows the numbers of cigarettes smoked by Irish smokers; the average was 16.5 cigarettes.

Media coverage on the dangers of smoking, antismoking campaigns from public health organizations such as the Irish Cancer Society, and a mounting array of legislation restricting tobacco advertising put pressure on Irish smokers to quit. Promotional discounts and coupons for tobacco products were prohibited, and tobacco advertising was banned not only on television and radio, but also on billboards. Print advertising was allowed only if 10 percent of the ad space was devoted to warnings on the health risks of smoking. Exhibit 1 shows a sample cigarette advertisement from an Irish magazine.

Smoking as an Addiction

Cigarettes and other forms of tobacco contained nicotine, a substance that induced addictive behavior. Smokers first developed a tolerance for nicotine and then, over time, needed to increase cigarette consumption to

---

[2] *Adults* were defined as those over the age of 15, and *smokers* as those who smoked at least one cigarette per day.

**TABLE A   Incidence of Cigarette Smoking
in Ireland (1988–1989)**

Of adult population (16 and over)	30%	(100%)
By gender		
Men	32	(50)
Women	27	(50)
By age		
16–24	27	(17)
25–34	38	(14)
35–44	29	(12)
45–54	29	(9)
55+	27	(19)
By occupation		
White collar	24	(25)
Skilled working class	33	(30)
Semi- and unskilled	38	(29)
Farming	23	(17)

NOTE: To be read (for example): 27 percent of Irish citizens aged 16–24 smoked and this age group represented 17 percent of the population.

**TABLE B   Number of
Cigarettes
Smoked Daily in
Ireland (based
on 400 smokers
in a 1989 survey
of 1,400 citizens)**

More than 20	16%
15–20	42
10–14	23
5–9	12
Less than 5	4
Unsure	3

---

maintain a steady, elevated blood level of nicotine. Smokers became progressively dependent on nicotine and suffered withdrawal symptoms if they stopped smoking. A craving for tobacco was characterized by physical symptoms such as decreased heart rate and a drop in blood pressure, and later could include symptoms like faintness, headaches, cold sweats, intestinal cramps, nausea, and vomiting. The smoking habit also had a psychological component stemming from the ritualistic aspects of smoking behavior, such as smoking after meals or in times of stress.

Since the 1950s, the ill effects of smoking had been researched and identified. Smoking was widely recognized as posing a serious health

EXHIBIT 1   Cigarette Advertisement from an Irish Magazine

threat. While nicotine was the substance within the cigarette that caused addiction, it was the tar accompanying the nicotine that made smoking so dangerous. Specifically, smoking was a primary risk factor for ischaemic heart disease, lung cancer, and chronic pulmonary diseases. Other potential dangers resulting from prolonged smoking included bronchitis, emphysema, chronic sinusitis, peptic ulcer disease, and for pregnant women, damage to the fetus.

Once smoking was recognized as a health risk, the development and use of a variety of smoking cessation techniques began. In *aversion therapy*, the smoker was discouraged from smoking by pairing an aversive event such as electric shock or a nausea-inducing agent with the smoking behavior, in an attempt to break the cycle of gratification. While aversion therapy was successful in the short term, it did not prove a lasting solution as the old smoking behavior would often be resumed. Aversion therapy was now used infrequently. *Behavioral self-monitoring* required the smoker to develop an awareness of the stimuli that triggered the desire to smoke and then to systematically eliminate the smoking behavior in specific situations by neutralizing those stimuli. For example, the smoker could learn to avoid particular situations or to adopt a replacement activity such as chewing gum. This method was successful in some cases but demanded a high degree of self-control. While behavioral methods were useful in addressing the psychological component of smoking addiction, they did not address the physical aspect of nicotine addiction that proved an insurmountable obstacle to many who attempted to quit.

Niconil

Warner-Lambert's Niconil would be the first product to offer a complete solution for smoking cessation, addressing both the physical and psychological aspects of nicotine addiction. The physical product was a circular adhesive patch, 2.5 inches in diameter and containing 30mg of nicotine gel. Each patch was individually wrapped in a sealed, tear-resistant packet. The patch was applied to the skin, usually on the upper arm, and the nicotine was absorbed into the bloodstream to produce a steady level of nicotine that blunted the smoker's physical craving. Thirty milligrams of nicotine provided the equivalent of 20 cigarettes, without the cigarettes' damaging tar. A single patch was applied once a day every morning for two to six weeks, depending on the smoker. The average smoker was able to quit successfully (abstaining from cigarettes for a period of six months or longer) after three to four weeks.

In clinical trials, the Niconil patch alone had proven effective in helping smokers to quit. A WLI study showed that 47.5 percent of subjects using the nicotine patch abstained from smoking for a period of three months or longer versus 15 percent for subjects using a placebo patch. Among the remaining 52.5 percent who did not stop completely, there was a marked reduction in the number of cigarettes smoked. A similar study in the United States demonstrated an abstinence rate of 31.5 percent with the Niconil patch versus 14 percent for those with a placebo patch. The single most important success factor in Niconil effectiveness, however, was the smoker's motivation to quit. "Committed quitters" were the most likely to quit smoking successfully using Niconil or any other smoking cessation method.

There were some side effects associated with use of the Niconil patch, including skin irritation, sleep disturbances, and nausea. Skin irritation was by far the most prevalent side effect, affecting 30 percent of patch users in one study. This skin irritation was not seen as a major obstacle to sales as many study participants viewed their irritated skin areas as "badges of merit" that indicated their committment to quitting smoking. WLI recommended placement of the patch on alternating skin areas to mitigate the problem. Future reformulations of the nicotine gel in the patch were expected to eliminate the problem entirely.

Niconil had been developed in 1985 by two scientists at Trinity College in Dublin working with Elan Corporation, an Irish pharmaceutical company specializing in transdermal drug delivery systems. Elan had entered into a joint venture with WLI to market other Elan transdermal products: Dilzem and Theolan, a respiratory medication. In 1987 Elan agreed to add Niconil to the joint venture. Warner-Lambert planned to market the product worldwide through its subsidiaries with Elan earning a royalty on cost of goods sold.[3]

Ireland was the first country to approve the Niconil patch. In late 1989 the Irish National Drugs Advisory Board authorized national distribution of Niconil, but stipulated that it could be sold by prescription only. This meant that Niconil, as a prescription product, could not be advertised directly to the Irish consumer.

Health Care in Ireland

Ireland's General Medical Service (GMS) provided health care to all Irish citizens. Sixty-four percent of the population received free hospital care through the GMS, but were required to pay for doctors' visits, which averaged £15 each, and for drugs, which were priced lower in Ireland than the average in the European Economic Community. The remaining 36 percent of the population qualified as either low-income or chronic-condition patients and received free health care though the GMS. For these

---

[3] A royalty of 3 percent on cost of goods sold was typical for such joint ventures.

patients, hospital care, doctors' visits, and many drugs were obtained without fee or copayment. Drugs paid for by the GMS were classified as "reimbursable"; approximately 70 percent of all drugs were reimbursable in 1989. Niconil had not qualified as a reimbursable drug; though WLI was lobbying to change its status, the immediate outlook was not hopeful.[4]

Support Program

While the patch addressed the physical craving for nicotine, Dixon and his team had decided to develop a supplementary support program to address the smoker's psychological addiction. The support program included several components in a neatly packaged box which aimed to ease the smoker's personal and social dependence on cigarettes. A booklet explained how to change behavior and contained tips on quitting. Bound into the booklet was a personal "contract" on which the smoker could list his or her reasons for quitting and plans for celebrating successful abstinence. There was a diary which enabled the smoker to record patterns of smoking behavior prior to quitting and which offered inspirational suggestions for each day of the program. Finally, an audio-tape included instruction in four relaxation methods which the smoker could practice in place of cigarette smoking. The relaxation exercises were narrated by Professor Anthony Clare, a well-known Irish psychiatrist who hosted a regular television program on the BBC. The tape also contained an emergency help section to assist the individual in overcoming sudden episodes of craving. A special toll-free telephone number to WLI served as a hot line to address customer questions and problems. Sample pages from the Niconil support program are presented in Exhibit 2.

While studies had not yet measured the impact of the support program on abstinence rates, it was believed that combined use of the support program and the patch could only increase Niconil's success. It had proven necessary to package the Niconil support program separately from the patch to speed approval of the patch by the Irish National Drug Board. A combined package would have required approval of the complete program, including the audio-tape, which would have prolonged the process significantly. If separate, the support program could be sold without a prescription and advertised directly to the consumer. Development of the support program had cost £3,000. WLI planned an initial production run of 10,000 units at a variable cost of £3.50 per unit.

---

[4] None of the products in the smoking cessation aid market was reimbursable through the GMS. Reimbursable items excluded prescriptions for simple drugs such as mild painkillers and cough and cold remedies.

EXHIBIT 2 Sample Pages from Niconil Support Program

The first step

Fill in the contract in your own words. Write down all the reasons that are most important to you for beating the smoking habit.

Then write down how your life will be better and more enjoyable without the smoking habit.

Finally, write down how you will reward yourself for your courage and hard work. You will deserve something very special.

Choose the day

Decide when to stop and put a ring round that date on your calendar.

Try to find a time when you are not going to be under pressure for a few days. The start of a holiday is good for two reasons. You will not have the stress of work and you will be free to change your routine.

Countdown

1. In the days leading up to your stop date see if you can get your partner or a friend to stop smoking along with you.

2. Ask a local charity to sponsor you or join a non-smoking group. Having other people to talk to who have kicked the habit can be a lifeline when your willpower gets shaky. They will know and understand what you are going through. Your doctor will be able to tell you what groups are running in your area.

3. The evening before your stop date, throw away **all** your cigarettes and get rid of your lighters and ashtrays. You will not need them again.

4. Read over your smoker's diary entries. Know your habit.
   - What are the most dangerous times?
   - Where are the most dangerous places?
   - What are the most dangerous situations?
   - Who do I usually smoke with?

CONTRACT

1. I, ...,
   HAVE STOPPED SMOKING BECAUSE I WANT:

2. **MY LIFE WILL BE BETTER WHEN I AM FREE OF SMOKING BECAUSE:**

3. **AFTER BEATING SMOKING FOR A MONTH I WILL CELEBRATE BY:**

SIGNED:

DATE:

COUNT DOWN TO D-DAY   DAY 1

Cigarette	Time of day?	Where were you?	Who were you with?	What were you doing?	How did you feel?
1					
2					
3					
4					
5					

WEEK ONE   *THE WINNER'S DIARY*

DAY

1. Today is the greatest challenge. If you succeed today, tomorrow will be easier. You can do it.

2. Well done. The first 24 hours are over. Your lungs have had their first real rest for years.

3. Remember: smoking is for losers. If you find yourself getting tense, use your relaxation tape.

4. Read your contract again. See how much better life is getting now that you are freeing yourself from this unpleasant addiction.

5. Your body says "thank you". It's feeling fitter already.

6. Don't forget to distract yourself at key cigarette times.

7. Well done. You're through your first week. Give yourself a treat. Go out for a meal or buy yourself something you've always wanted.

The support program could serve a variety of purposes. Several WLI executives felt that the support program should be sold separately from the nicotine patches. They considered the support program a stand-alone product that could realize substantial revenues on its own, as well as generating sales of the Niconil patches. Supporting this position, a pricing study completed in 1989 found that the highest mean price volunteered for a 14-day supply of the patches and the support program combined was £27.50, and for the patches alone, £22.00. The highest mean price for the support program alone was £8.50, suggesting a relatively high perceived utility of this component among potential consumers. There was a risk, however, that consumers might purchase the Niconil support program either instead of the patches, or as an accompaniment to other smoking cessation products, thus limiting sales of the Niconil patches.

Another group of executives saw the support program as a value-added point of difference that could stimulate Niconil patch sales. This group favored wide distribution of the support programs, free of charge, to potential Niconil customers. A third group of WLI executives argued that the support program was an integral component of the Niconil product which would enhance the total package by addressing the psychological aspects of nicotine addiction and improve the product's success rate, thereby increasing its sales potential. As such, these executives believed that the support program should be passed on only to those purchasing Niconil patches, at no additional cost.

Two options, not necessarily mutually exclusive, were under consideration for the distribution of the support programs. One option was to distribute them through doctors prescribing Niconil. A doctor could present the program to the patient during the office visit as he or she issued the Niconil prescription, reinforcing the counseling role of the doctor in the Niconil treatment. Supplying the GPs with support programs could also serve to promote Niconil in the medical community. A second option was to distribute the support programs through the pharmacies, where customers could receive the support programs when they purchased the Niconil patches. A disadvantage of this option was that a customer might receive additional support programs each time he or she purchased another package of Niconil. However, these duplicates might be passed on to other potential consumers and thus become an informal advertising vehicle for Niconil.

Pricing

Because all potential Niconil customers would pay for the product personally, pricing was a critical component of the Niconil marketing strategy. Management debated how many patches to include in a single package and at what price to sell each package. In test trials, the average smoker succeeded in quitting with Niconil in three to four weeks (i.e., 21 to 28 patches); others needed as long as six weeks.[5]

As Niconil was essentially a tobacco substitute, cigarettes provided a logical model for considering various packaging and pricing options. The average Irish smoker purchased a pack of cigarettes daily, often when buying the morning newspaper. Fewer than 5 percent of all cigarettes were sold in cartons.[6] Because the Irish smoker rarely purchased a multi-week cigarette supply at once, he or she was thought likely to compare the cost of cigarette purchases with the cost of a multi-week supply of Niconil. WLI thus favored packaging just a 7-day supply of patches in each unit. However, Warner-Lambert subsidiaries in continental Europe, where carton purchases were more popular, wanted to include a six-week supply of patches in each package if and when they launched Niconil. Managers at Warner-Lambert's international division wanted to standardize packaging as much as possible across its subsidiaries and suggested as a compromise a 14-day supply per package.

Following the cigarette model, two pricing schemes had been proposed. The first proposal was to price Niconil on a par with cigarettes. The average Irish smoker smoked 16.5 cigarettes per day and the expected retail price in 1990 for a pack of cigarettes was £2.25. WLI's variable cost of goods for a 14-day supply of Niconil was £12.00.[7] Pharmacies generally added a 50 percent retail markup to the price at which they purchased the product from WLI. A value-added tax of 25 percent of the retail price was included in the proposed price to the consumer of £32.00 for a 14-day supply. In addition, the consumer paid a £1.00 dispensing fee per prescription.

Under the second pricing proposal, Niconil would be priced at a premium to cigarettes. Proponents argued that if the Niconil program were successful, it would be a permanent replacement for cigarettes and its cost would be far outweighed by the money saved on cigarettes. The proposed price to the consumer under this option was £60.00 for a 14-day supply.

Competition

Few products would compete directly with Niconil in the smoking cessation market in Ireland. Two small niche products were Accudrop and Nicobrevin, both available without a prescription. Accudrop was a nasal

---

[5] Smokers were advised not to use the patch on a regular basis beyond three months. If still unsuccessful in quitting, they could resume use of the patch after stopping for at least a month.

[6] A carton of cigarettes contained 20 individual packs of cigarettes; each pack contained 20 cigarettes.

[7] This cost of goods included Elan's royalty.

spray that smokers applied to the cigarette filter to trap tar and nicotine, resulting in cleaner smoke. Anticipated 1990 manufacturer sales for Accu-drop were £5,000. Nicobrevin, a product from the UK, was a time-release capsule that eased smoking withdrawal symptoms. Anticipated 1990 manufacturer's sales for Nicobrevin were £75,000.

The most significant competitive product was Nicorette, the only nicotine-replacement product currently available. Marketed in Ireland by Lundbeck, Nicorette was a chewing gum that released nicotine into the body as the smoker chewed the gum. Because chewing gum in public was not socially acceptable among Irish adults, the product had never achieved strong sales, especially given that its efficacy relied on steady, intensive chewing. A second sales deterrent had been the association of Nicorette with side effects such as mouth cancer and irritation of the linings of the mouth and stomach.

Nicorette was sold in 10-day supplies, available in two dosages: 2 mg and 4 mg. Smokers would chew the 2 mg Nicorette initially, and switch to the 4 mg gum after two weeks if needed. In a 1982 study, 47 percent of Nicorette users quit smoking versus 21 percent for placebo users. A long-term follow up study in 1989, however, indicated that only 10 percent more Nicorette patients had ceased smoking compared to placebo users. The average daily treatment cost to Nicorette customers was £0.65 per day for the 2 mg gum and £1.00 per day for the 4 mg gum. Nicorette, like Niconil, was available at pharmacies by prescription only, so advertising had been limited to medical journals. Anticipated 1990 manufacturer sales of Nicorette were £170,000; however, the brand had not been advertised in three years.

Forecasting

Although Nicorette was not considered a successful product, WLI was confident that Niconil, with its less intrusive nicotine delivery system and fewer side effects, would capture a dominant position in the smoking cessation market and ultimately increase the demand for smoking cessation products. Precise sales expectations for Niconil were difficult to formulate, however, and two different methods had been suggested.

The first method assumed that the percentage of smokers in the adult population (30 percent in 1990) would drop by one percentage point per year through 1994. An estimated 10 percent of smokers attempted to quit smoking each year, and 10 percent of that number purchased some type of smoking cessation product. WLI believed that Niconil could capture half of these "committed quitters" in the first year, selling therefore to 5 percent of those who tried to give up smoking in 1990. Further, they hoped to increase this share by 1 percent per year, up to 9 percent in 1994. Having estimated the number of customers who would purchase an initial two-week supply of Niconil, WLI managers then had to calculate the total number of units purchased. Based on experience in test trials, WLI anticipated that 60 percent of first-time Niconil customers would purchase a second two-week supply. Of that number, 20 percent would purchase a third two-week supply. About 75 percent of smokers completed the program within six weeks.

A more aggressive forecast could be based on WLI's 1989 survey. Of the 30 percent of respondents who were smokers, 54 percent indicated that they would like to give up smoking, and 30 percent expressed interest in the nicotine patch. More relevant, 17 percent of smokers indicated that they were likely to go to the doctor and pay for such a patch, though a specific purchase price was not included in the question. A rule of thumb in interpreting likelihood-of-purchase data was to divide this percentage by three to achieve a more likely estimate of actual purchasers. Once the number of Niconil customers was calculated, the 100/60/20 percent model used above could then be applied to compute the total expected unit sales.

Production

Under the terms of the joint venture with Elan and using current manufacturing technology, production capacity would be 1,000 units (of 14-day supply packages) per month in the first quarter of 1990, ramping up to 2,000 units per month by year-end. WLI had the option to purchase a new, more efficient machine that could produce 14,000 units per month and reduce WLI's variable cost on each unit by 10 percent. In addition, if WLI purchased the new machine and Niconil was launched in continental Europe, WLI could export some of its production to the European subsidiaries, further expanding its role as a supplier to Warner-Lambert Europe. WLI would earn a margin of £2.00 per unit on Niconil that it sold through this channel.[8] Estimated annual unit sales, assuming a launch of Niconil

TABLE C	Estimated Unit Sales of Niconil in Western Europe
Year 1	100,000 units
Year 2	125,000 units
Year 3	150,000 units
Year 4	175,000 units
Year 5	200,000 units

---

[8] Warner-Lambert's European subsidiaries were likely to consider purchasing this new machine themselves as well.

throughout Western Europe, are listed in Table C. Warner-Lambert management aimed to recoup any capital investments within five years; the Niconil machine would cost £1.2 million and could be on-line within nine months.

Marketing Prescription Products

Prescription products included all pharmaceutical items deemed by the Irish government to require the professional expertise of the medical community to guide consumer usage.[9] Before a customer could purchase a prescription product, he or she first had to visit a doctor and obtain a written prescription which specified that product. The customer could then take the written prescription to one of Ireland's 1,132 pharmacies and purchase the product.

The prescription nature of Niconil thus created marketing challenges. A potential Niconil customer first had to make an appointment with a doctor for an office visit to obtain the necessary prescription. Next, the doctor had to agree to prescribe Niconil to the patient to help him or her to quit smoking. Only then could the customer go to the pharmacy and purchase Niconil. This two-step purchase process required WLI to address two separate audiences in marketing Niconil: the Irish smokers who would eventually use Niconil and the Irish doctors who first had to prescribe it to patients.

Niconil's potential customers were the 10 percent of Irish smokers who attempted to give up smoking each year (2 percent of the total Irish population). Market research had shown that those most likely to purchase Niconil were aged 35–44 and in either white-collar or skilled occupations (18 percent of Irish smokers). Smokers under the age of 35 tended to see themselves as "bullet proof"; because most were not yet experiencing the negative health effects of smoking, it was difficult to persuade them to quit. Upper-income, better-educated smokers found less tolerance for smoking among their peers and thus felt greater pressure to quit. Research had also indicated that women were 25 percent more likely to try Niconil as they tended to be more concerned with their health and thus more often visited the doctors from whom they could learn about Niconil and obtain the necessary prescription.

The most likely prescribers of Niconil would be the 2,000 general practitioners (GPs) in Ireland. The average GP saw 15 patients per day

---

[9] Drugs and other pharmaceutical products that did not require a written prescription from a doctor were called "over-the-counter" or OTC drugs.

and 8 out of 10 general office visits resulted in the GPs' writing prescriptions for patients. Although 10 percent of Irish doctors smoked, virtually all recognized the dangers of smoking and rarely smoked in front of patients. A *Modern Medicine* survey of 780 Irish GPs indicated that 63 percent formally gathered smoking data from their patients. GPs acknowledged the health risk that smoking posed to patient health, but they were usually reluctant to pressure a patient to quit unless the smoker was highly motivated. Unsolicited pressure to quit could meet with patient resistance and result, in some cases, in a doctor losing a patient and the associated revenues from patient visits. Smoking cessation was not currently a lucrative treatment area for GPs. Most would spend no longer than 15 minutes discussing smoking with their patients. To the few patients who asked for advice on how to quit smoking, 92 percent of GPs would offer "firm, clear-cut advice." Fewer than 15 percent would recommend formal counseling, drug therapy, or other assistance. GPs were not enthusiastic about Nicorette due to poor results and the incidence of side effects.

WLI was confident that Niconil would find an enthusiastic audience among Irish GPs. As a complete program with both physical and psychological components, Niconil offered a unique solution. In addition, the doctor would assume a significant counseling role in the Niconil treatment. It was anticipated that the GP would initially prescribe a 14-day supply of Niconil to the patient. At the end of the two-week period, the patient would hopefully return to the doctor for counseling and an additional prescription, if needed.

Marketing Communications

WLI intended to position Niconil as *a complete system that was a more acceptable alternative to existing nicotine replacement therapy for the purpose of smoking cessation*. Niconil would be the only smoking cessation product to address both the physical dimension of nicotine addiction through the patch, and the psychological dimension through the support program. Compared to Nicorette gum, Niconil offered a more acceptable delivery system (Niconil's transdermal system vs. Nicorette's oral system) and fewer, less severe side effects. WLI planned to promote these aspects of the product through a comprehensive marketing program. The Niconil launch marketing budget, detailed in Exhibit 3, followed the Warner-Lambert standard for new drug launches. Several WLI executives felt that this standard was inadequate for the more consumer-oriented Niconil, and pressed for increased communications spending.

EXHIBIT 3 Niconil First Year Marketing Budget (£ 000)

Advertising	
Ad creation	£ 4
Media advertising	28
Total advertising	32
Promotion	
Development of support program	3
Production of support programs	35
Training/promotional materials	44
Direct mailing to GPs	2
Total promotion	84
Public relations	
Launch symposium	5
Roundtable meeting	2
Press release/materials	1
Total public relations	8
Market research	3
Sales force allocation	23
Product management allocation	50
Total budget	£200

EXHIBIT 4 1990 Niconil Media Advertising Schedule

Publication	Frequency	Circulation	Cost/1,000	Placements
Irish Medical Times	Weekly	5,200	£154	13
Irish Medical News	Weekly	5,100	137	11
Modern Medicine	Monthly	3,700	176	5

Advertising

Because Irish regulations prohibited the advertising of prescription products directly to the consumer, Niconil advertising was limited to media targeting the professional medical community. Three major publications targeted this audience: *Irish Medical Times, Irish Medical News,* and *Modern Medicine.* WLI planned to advertise moderately in the first year to raise awareness of Niconil in the medical community. After that it was hoped that the initial momentum could be maintained through strong public relations efforts and personal testimony to the product's efficacy. Exhibit 4 summarizes the proposed 1990 media advertising schedule for Niconil.

WLI's advertising agency had designed a distinctive logo for Niconil that would be used on all packaging and collateral materials such as "No Smoking" placards. These would feature the Niconil logo and be distributed to doctors' offices, hospitals, and pharmacies to promote the product. Ideally, the logo would become sufficiently well recognized that it could be used eventually on a stand-alone basis to represent Niconil to the end consumer without the brand name. This would allow some flexibility in circumventing Irish advertising restrictions to reach the end consumer. Sample logos and packaging are illustrated in Exhibit 5. The agency had also developed four concepts for a Niconil advertisement, which are summarized in Exhibits 6A–D.

Direct Mail

A direct mail campaign to Ireland's 2,000 GPs was planned in conjunction with the Niconil product announcement. Two weeks prior to launch, an introductory letter would be mailed with a color photo of the product, a reply card offering a support program, and additional product information. The support programs would be mailed in response to the reply cards, arriving just prior to the launch. A response rate of at least 50 percent was anticipated based on past direct mail campaigns.

Public Relations

The formal Niconil product announcement was scheduled to occur in Dublin at a professional event that WLI had dubbed the "Smoking Cessation Institute Symposium." The symposium would be chaired by Professor Anthony Clare, the narrator of the Niconil audio-tape; Professor Hickey, an expert in preventive cardiology; and Professors Masterson and J. Kelly from Elan Corporation. Open to members of the medical profession and media, the event was intended to focus attention on the dangers of smoking and to highlight Niconil as a ground-breaking product designed to address this health hazard.

WLI had sought endorsements from both the Irish Cancer Society and the Irish Heart Foundation, two national health organizations that actively advocated smoking cessation. Because both nonprofit institutions relied on donations for financing and were concerned that a specific product endorsement would jeopardize their tax-exempt status, they refused to endorse Niconil directly. Representatives from each institution had, however, stated their intention to attend the launch symposium.

In advance of the symposium, a press release and supporting materials would be distributed to the media. Emphasis would be placed on the

EXHIBIT 5   Sample Niconil Logo and Packaging

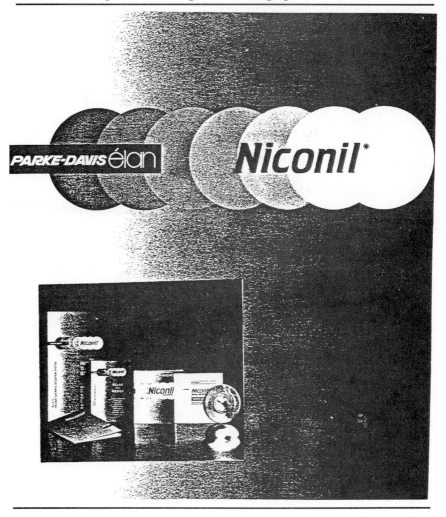

EXHIBIT 6A   Niconil Advertising Concept (A)

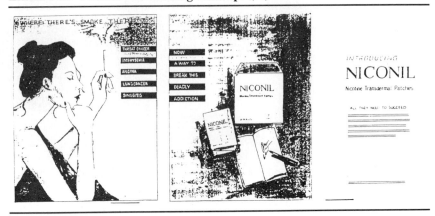

EXHIBIT 6B   Niconil Advertising Concept (B)

EXHIBIT 6C   Niconil Advertising Concept (C)

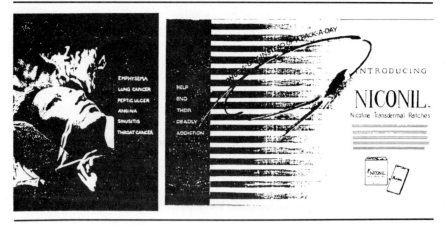

EXHIBIT 6D   Niconil Advertising Concept (D)

role that Niconil would play in disease prevention. It would also be noted that Niconil had been developed and manufactured locally and had the potential for worldwide sales. Other planned public relations activities included a round-table dinner for prominent opinion leaders in the medical community. Publicity in the media was planned to coincide with key "commitment to change" times such as New Year's and Lent.[10]

---

[10] Lent was an annual penitential period during spring of the Roman Catholic religious calendar that was still observed by many of the 95 percent of the Irish who were Roman Catholic.

Sales Strategy

WLI Ireland had a sales force of 16 representatives, whose average annual salary, bonus, and benefits amounted to £25,000 in 1988. They focused their selling efforts on 1,600 Irish GPs who were most accessible geographically and most amenable to pharmaceutical sales visits. The sales staff was divided into three selling teams of four to six representatives. Each team sold separate product lines to the same 1,600 GPs. The team that would represent Niconil was already selling three other drugs from Elan Corporation that were marketed by WLI as part of their joint venture. These four salespeople would add Niconil to their existing product lines. Sales training on Niconil would take place one month prior to the product launch.

The pharmaceutical salesperson's challenge was to maintain the attention of each GP long enough to discuss each item in his or her product line. Because Niconil was expected to be of great interest to GPs, the salespeople were keen to present Niconil first during the sales visit, followed by the less exciting products. Normally, a new product would receive this up-front positioning. However, Dixon argued that Niconil should be presented last during the sales call to maximize the time that a salesperson spent with each GP and to prevent the sales time devoted to the other three Elan products from being cannibalized by Niconil. Based on revenue projections for all four products, salespeople would be instructed to spend no more than 15 percent of their sales call time on Niconil. On average, each WLI salesperson called on six to seven doctors per day. The goal was for each sales team to call on the 1,600 targeted GPs once every three months. In the case of Niconil, all 16 salespeople would present the new brand during their calls for six weeks after launch.

Critical Decisions

With just three months to go before the launch of Niconil, Dixon felt he had to comply with the international division's suggestion to include a 14-day supply of patches in each Niconil package, but he debated whether to price the product on a par with or at a premium to cigarettes. Equally important, he had to decide which sales forecast was more accurate so that he could plan production capacity. And finally, he needed to make decisions on the communications program: which advertising concept would be the most effective, what other efforts could be made to enhance product acceptance, and whether the current budget was adequate to support Warner-Lambert's first national launch of such an innovative product.

Procter & Gamble Company: Lenor Refill Package

In July 1987, Kathy Stadler, assistant brand manager for Lenor—Procter & Gamble GmbH's (P&G Germany) profitable fabric softener brand—was preparing for an upper-level management meeting to discuss a proposal for the national launch of a Lenor refill package. The refill package represented an innovative solution to West Germany's growing environmental concerns by promising to reduce by 85 percent the packaging materials used in Lenor's standard plastic container. Management hoped that this line extension would help stem Lenor's eroding sales volume and market share.

Stadler recalled a memo written two years earlier by Rolf Kunisch, the general manager for P&G Germany, in which he advocated "moving the company's attitudes from defensive thinking in environmental terms toward proactive and successful approaches." While Stadler felt that the Lenor refill package met this mandate, she was uncertain about the consumer response. Stadler knew that the refill package would not address many German consumers' concerns that fabric softeners were "superfluous" products. A "biodegradable" version of Lenor still needed three years of development. The refill package seemed to offer an interim response to consumers. Would the public hail it as an attempt to protect the environment? Or would they view it as an effort to avoid addressing the public's underlying concern with Lenor's product formula?

Stadler's brand manager, Leonard Phillippe, felt that an aggressive promotion of an existing concentrated formula of Lenor, which used less packaging materials than the more popular, fully diluted version, would be less risky than the refill package introduction. Stadler, however, believed that this strategy would not stem Lenor's eroding sales volume. Nevertheless, she knew that both options would be hotly debated at the forthcoming meeting with Rolf Kunisch.

Julie L. Yao, MBA 91, prepared this case under the supervision of Professors John A. Quelch and Minette E. Drumwright as the basis for class discussion rather than to illustrate either effective or ineffective handling of an administrative situation. Certain data and names have been disguised. Copyright © 1991 by the President and Fellows of Harvard College. Harvard Business School case 9–592–016.

THE PROCTER & GAMBLE COMPANY

In 1987,[1] the Procter & Gamble Company (P&G), a leading consumer products company, had more than $13.7 billion in assets, generated $17 billion in worldwide revenues, and delivered $617 million in pretax earnings. P&G sold products in 125 countries, marketing more than 100 brands of laundry, household cleaning, personal care, food, and beverage products. International operations, which included Europe, South America, and Asia, accounted for over 30 percent of P&G's 1987 sales and earnings. In 1987, international sales grew 38 percent, almost five times as much as US domestic sales.

P&G had a long-standing reputation for superior products, marketing expertise, talented employees, conservative management, and high integrity in its business dealings. A strong corporate culture pervaded the firm. The 1987 annual report stated the company's philosophy as follows:

> We will provide products of superior quality and value that best fill the needs of the world's consumers. We will achieve that purpose through an organization and a working environment which attracts the finest people; fully develops and challenges our individual talents; encourages our free and spirited collaboration to drive the business ahead; and maintains the Company's historic principles of integrity and doing the right thing. Through the successful pursuit of our commitment, we expect our brands to achieve leadership share and profit positions and that, as a result, our business, our people, our shareholders, and the communities in which we live and work will prosper.

To develop these superior products, P&G relied on continual product development. In 1987, more than 3.3 percent of its revenues were spent on research. In addition, P&G believed in extensive product and market testing. P&G frequently took two to three years to test a new product and its marketing strategy before a major launch.

Procter & Gamble GmbH

Procter & Gamble GmbH was established in 1960 following the acquisition of a local detergent manufacturer. By 1987, P&G Germany generated DM 1,037 million in revenues.[2] P&G Germany sold more than 30 brands, including Ariel, a top-selling detergent, and Lenor, West Germany's leading fabric softener. Seventy-seven percent of its revenues and 60 percent

---

[1] P&G operated on a July 1 to June 30 fiscal year basis; at the time of this case, P&G had just entered its 1988 fiscal year. Unless otherwise specified, all P&G company data are on a fiscal year basis.

[2] One US dollar was equivalent to 1.9 deutschmarks (DM).

of its earnings came from the Laundry and Cleaning Division, which included detergents, cleaners, and fabric softener.

P&G Germany's 6,700-person subsidiary comprised four divisions: Laundry and Cleaning, Paper, Beverages, and Health and Beauty Care. Each division had Sales, Finance, Manufacturing, and Product Development organizations. Every major P&G Germany product also had its own brand management team, which developed and implemented the brand's marketing strategy against sales and profit targets approved by top management. A brand team generally consisted of a brand manager, an assistant brand manager, and one or two brand assistants, who all worked closely with the division's other departments as well as with staff groups specializing in advertising services, management information systems, and personnel.

A 320-person sales force marketed P&G Germany products to the retail trade. Key account managers called on the headquarters of the large retail grocery chains year-round, while field salespeople serviced independent stores as well as chain outlets.

P&G Germany manufactured most of its products locally. While some production was outsourced, P&G Germany generally preferred to manufacture its own products to ensure the highest level of quality control.

THE FABRIC SOFTENER INDUSTRY

Fabric softener products first appeared during the 1950s to combat the perceived harsh effects of detergents; when added to the wash, fabric softener produced soft, scented, and static-free clothes. It was particularly popular in Europe where hard water washing conditions were common. In 1987, consumers could purchase fabric softener in one of three forms: a diluted liquid; a concentrated liquid, three times stronger than the dilute; and woven sheets which were used during machine drying. The regular user's average purchase cycle was two months. Dosage varied according to the type and volume of laundry, but an average washload required 100 milliliters of dilute or 35 ml of concentrate.

Fabric softener liquids combined 5 percent softening ingredients, called cationic tensides, with 95 percent water. Fabric softener concentrates included 15 percent softening ingredients. Fabric softeners were packaged in hard, high-density polyethylene plastic containers. Users added liquid fabric softener during a washing machine's wash cycle or poured it into a convenient special dispenser built into the machine before the start of the wash.

Like many other household chemical products, fabric softeners, with 2 percent inert nonbiodegradable ingredients, were considered by some environmentally conscious consumers to be unnecessary. An increasing number of consumers believed that a buildup of nonbiodegradable chemicals could affect their water supply and that the benefit delivered by fabric softeners was superfluous. P&G and its competitors were working on the development of totally biodegradable fabric softeners, but it was thought unlikely that such products would be brought to market before 1991.

Environmental Concern

During the 1980s, public anxiety about environmental problems escalated in Europe. A 1986 survey of 11,800 Western European consumers revealed that 72 percent were "somewhat" or "very" concerned about ecological problems such as acid rain, toxic waste, landfill capacity, and the greenhouse effect. The media attributed these growing concerns to Europe's high population density, its centuries-old exploitation of natural resources, and the impact on public awareness of the Chernobyl nuclear power plant accident in the former Soviet Union.[3]

West German attitudes were consistently "greener" than those of neighboring countries. In 1987, an opinion pool entitled "Sorrows of the Nation" found that 53 percent of West Germans surveyed were concerned with the protection of the environment, up from 16 percent four years earlier. Concern for the environment ranked as their second most common concern, behind unemployment. Environmental issues also affected the German political arena, as evidenced by the rising popularity of the pro-environment Green Party.

A 1987 opinion pool showed that 47 percent of German households agreed that they used fewer environmentally problematic goods than previously, versus 21 percent who agreed with the same statement in 1985. Both consumer awareness of environmental issues and the percentage of consumers claiming a willingness to pay more for environmentally friendly packaging had increased. In practice, however, consumers traded off price against environmental safety; there was a limit to the price premium they were prepared to pay. In addition, many consumers indicated that they were not willing to give up product quality for the environment. Nevertheless, environmentally uncontroversial products such as phosphate-free detergents had become increasingly popular.

In 1984, a West German federal government agency publicly denounced allegedly environmentally harmful products, including P&G Germany's laundry booster, Top Job. A consumer boycott to force the removal of these products from the market caused Top Job's sales volume

---

[3] A. Hussein, *Eco-Labels: Product Management in a Greener Europe* (Environmental Data Services, Ltd., Finsbury Business Center), p. 53.

to drop by 50 percent in the following year. In 1986, the government passed the Waste Avoidance, Utilization, and Disposal Act, which gave authorities the power to restrict or even ban materials with problematic toxicity or waste volume.

The West German government also supported a nationwide eco-labeling initiative, called the Blue Angel program, to promote environmentally compatible products through labeling. By 1987, more than 2,000 products in 50 categories bore the Blue Angel seal; fabric softener products had never qualified. By 1987, the Blue Angel seal was recognized by 80 percent of West German consumers.[4] Industry experts believed that products "blessed" with the Blue Angel seal enjoyed increased sales of up to 10 percent.

Though public and media attention centered more on a product's contents and less on its packaging, the issue of solid waste reduction was rapidly capturing the German public's attention. Land was scarce; West Germany burned 34 percent of its trash, compared to only 3 percent in the United States. In some German communities, there was a social stigma associated with a household's use of larger trash bins. About 20 percent of municipalities charged citizens for garbage collection based on volume. By 1985, West Germans recycled more than one-third of their paper, glass, and aluminum waste; however, plastic recycling was limited. Focus group research indicated consumers would be receptive to products with reduced packaging.

Market Size and Trends

The average West German homemaker used eight different products, such as bleach and fabric softener, for washing and cleaning. The German fabric softener consumer enjoyed "fresh" clothes, which combined the characteristics of a soft touch, "clean" smell, and bright appearance. A 1986 P&G Germany market research study concluded that fabric softener usage and dosage were relatively uniform across all age groups, irrespective of brand. Fabric softener users, however, spent more effort on pretreating and prewashing their laundry than nonusers.

In 1987, West Germany was the largest fabric softener market in Europe, with retail sales totaling DM 346 million ($182 million), compared with almost $1 billion in the US market, with a population four times West Germany's. Although the value of retail sales had increased due to price rises, market volume had fallen from a peak of 18,200 MSUs in 1983 to

---

[4] Lori K. Carswell, *Environmental Labeling in the United States: Background Research, Issues and Recommendations*, Draft Report, Applied Decision Analysis, 1989, p. 10.

16,700 MSUs in 1987.[5] Forecasters predicted further volume decreases of 1 to 3 percent per year.

Research had shown that this decline was attributed to a shrinking base of fabric softener users. Table A shows usage trends from periodic diary studies:[6]

TABLE A   Fabric Softener Usage Trends (percentage surveyed)

	1982	1984	1986
Fabric softener users	89%	84%	72%
Total wash loads softened*	72	67	57
Wash loads softened among users†	75	73	74

* Percentage of all wash loads recorded in diary study that had fabric softener added.
† Among fabric softener users, average percentage of wash loads per user that had fabric softener added.

Results from a 1986 telephone survey found that many consumers had ceased using fabric softener due to environmental concerns highlighted by the news media. Research revealed that West German consumers were more concerned about the environmental effects of using supplementary household products such as fabric softener than consumers in other West European countries. Exhibit 1 presents key results from this study.

Competition

In 1987, four competitors sold 78 percent of the volume in the West German fabric softener market.[7] P&G Germany's Lenor led the market with a 37 percent volume share, followed by Colgate-Palmolive's Softlan (20 percent), Unilever's Kuschelweich (Snuggle) (13 percent), and Henkel's Vernel (8 percent). Generic and private-label brands accounted for the remaining 22 percent of the market.

All four multinationals sold their fabric softener brands throughout Western Europe. Each competitor promoted similar product benefits: freshness, softness, ease of ironing, and elimination of static cling.

---

[5] An MSU, or thousand statistical units, was a standardized P&G measure that permitted comparison of products on the basis of an equal number of uses. Consequently, a 1-liter bottle of 4:1 Lenor concentrate and a 4-liter bottle of Lenor dilute were equivalent on an MSU basis because both gave the consumer the same number of uses. Costs and unit volumes are presented per SU (abbreviation for statistical unit) for comparison purposes.

[6] Each participant was asked to keep a diary of his or her usage habits during a two-week time period, from which results were tabulated.

[7] All market share figures were based on statistical unit (MSUs) volume.

EXHIBIT 1   Selected Results from Fabric Softener Usage Monitoring Studies

	June 1985	*February 1986*
Percentage of respondents who were:		
Fabric softener users*	60.0%	60.0%
Nonusers	40.0	40.0
Homemakers aware that fabric softener allegedly harms the environment:		
Fabric softener users	55.0%	74.0%
Nonusers	66.0	70.0
Fabric softener users claiming to:†		
Use less fabric softener per load	18.0%	24.0%
Soften fewer loads	16.0	14.0
Total (unduplicated)	26.0	27.0
Reasons nonusers never used/stopped using fabric softener:		
Environmental reasons	42.0%	48.0%
Softness dissatisfaction	26.0	13.0
Effects on skin	29.0	23.0
Drying on clothesline	20.0	29.0

* Fabric softener users had used the product at least once in the previous three months before the interview; nonusers had not.
† Seventy-two percent of the users who used less softener or softened fewer loads claimed to be doing so for environmental reasons.

Lenor's distinctive, 4-liter blue container appeared in the mid-1970s and quickly became the standard package size and shape imitated by competitors. By 1987, all brands were sold in both diluted and concentrated formulas, in 4-liter and 1-liter sizes, respectively. In addition, in 1987 Henkel and P&G introduced dryer sheets, which accounted for less than 1 percent of market volume. All brands were broadly distributed throughout the retail trade.

Vernel followed a low-budget advertising strategy. Softlan, on the other hand, was aggressively advertised through the media. Kuschelweich gained high consumer awareness through its "stuffed bear" advertising mascot. Lenor emphasized its "Aprilfrisch" scent. In newspaper and handbill copy, Lenor led in share of fabric softener features in retail newspaper ads and handbills (42 percent for May/June 1987), followed by Softlan (21 percent), Kuschelweich (15 percent), and Vernel (5 percent).[8]

The materials cost for each brand varied due to different chemical formulations. Table B shows selected relative costs and pricing for the top four brands of diluted fabric softener in 1987.

---

[8] Feature share, calculated from a survey of 200 West German newspapers and 2,000 grocery handbills, represented the percentage of times a particular brand was featured in retail trade promotions for fabric softeners.

TABLE B **1987 Indexed Costs and Prices for Leading German Fabric Softener Brands**

	P&G	*Colgate*	*Lever*	*Henkel*
Brand name	Lenor	Softlan	Kuschelweich	Vernel
Packaging	100	106	106	106
Chemicals	100	85	93	92
Media expenses	100	136	85	40
Total costs	100	105	94	82
Recommended retail price	100	87	88	85

NOTE: The index is based on a 4-liter package of dilute.

Consumers perceived little differentiation among fabric softener brands except on the basis of price and scent. Consequently, fabric softener brands were frequently involved in price and promotion wars to defend or capture market share, which depressed manufacturer and trade margins. For example, the average profit margin realized by retailers on Lenor declined from 12.7 percent in 1984 to 2.5 percent in 1986.

Henkel, a prominent German household products company with 1987 sales of DM 9.9 billion, rapidly imitated innovative product ideas and marketed them globally. Henkel also strongly emphasized environmental protection, spending nearly 25 percent of its DM 285 million research budget on this issue in 1987. Colgate-Palmolive (DM 10.6 billion in 1987 sales) and Unilever (DM 57 billion) devoted less than 2 percent of their revenues to R&D.

In early 1987, Henkel acquired Lesieur-Cotelle S.A., a French detergent manufacturer that produced Minidou, a fabric softener concentrate that since the early 1980s had been sold in 250-ml flat plastic pouches. Minidou users emptied the pouch's contents into any 1-liter container and then diluted the concentrate with water. Some P&G executives suspected that Henkel might try either to extend the successful Minidou concept, which had captured 29 percent of the French market by 1987, to other markets or to license the use of the technology of Colgate-Palmolive, which was pursuing lower-cost packaging alternatives.

Distribution

Fabric softener was sold through West Germany's highly concentrated retail market; five major chains together controlled more than 75 percent of total grocery sales (DM 127 billion in 1987). Manufacturers sold their products through several classes of trade: mass merchandisers (more than 53,800 sq. ft. in size), hypermarkets (16,100–53,800 sq. ft.), supermarkets

(8,600–16,100 sq. ft.), convenience stores (under 8,600 sq. ft.), and discounters (various sizes). West German consumers shopped for fabric softener in all types of stores, although it was less likely than other grocery items to be purchased in convenience stores.

Fierce competition meant that grocery retailers achieved total after-tax profit margins of only 1 percent to 1.5 percent. Because they focused increasingly on the direct product profitability (DPP) of their stock per linear foot of shelf space, retailers were especially keen on high-margin, space-efficient products with rapid turnover. The emphasis placed on DPP resulted in a selective product assortment; only the large mass merchandisers and hypermarkets maintained a complete selection of brands and package sizes for any product category. Supermarkets kept a full range of brand names, but with limited size selection, whereas convenience stores and discounters sold only one or two brands. All classes of trade, except for convenience stores, also sold their own private-label brands in many high-turnover categories.

Every August, manufacturer account representatives negotiated with each major retailer the following year's major target purchase levels, volume discounts, and new-product listing agreements. Manufacturers needed a retailer's listing for each new product, even for product line extensions; individual retail stores could purchase products only from their chain headquarters' approved list. Although manufacturers could introduce new products throughout the year, listing agreements were easier to obtain during the August meetings. Approved products generally reached store shelves within two weeks of an order being placed. In addition to account representatives, each manufacturer also had field salespeople who serviced individual stores, both chain owned and independents, by taking stock orders, suggesting shelf arrangements, and implementing local sales promotions.

To minimize handling and reshelving costs, many retail stores sought to display products in their original shipping cartons and stressed convenient packaging to the manufacturers. A set of product packaging guidelines, known as the "10 commandments," was developed by a retail trade association for manufacturers. These guidelines defined the dimensions, weight, and appearance of the shipping cartons that retailers preferred. Few products met all 10 guidelines.

Advertising and Promotion

In 1987, most television advertising reached German consumers via the two state-run national channels. Each September, manufacturers reapplied for time slots; the television stations then allocated specific commercial spots to each firm for the upcoming year. P&G Germany would then allocate the time slots it had been granted among its brands.

Regulations limited the consumer promotions that West German manufacturers could use. Coupons and refund offers were not permitted; the value of on-pack and in-pack premiums (gifts attached to or included in product packages) could not exceed DM 0.30 in value. Bonus packs, which gave consumers extra volume of product for the same price, were difficult to implement on liquid products such as Lenor. Price packs (products with a lower-than-normal recommended retail price preprinted on the package) were allowed but were rarely used due to trade opposition. Some manufacturers did run sweepstakes and contests, although they were tightly regulated by government agencies.

Volume discounts and trade promotion allowances for each product were traditionally negotiated with individual retailers. P&G Germany instituted account-specific promotion plans based on total sales volume rather than the sales of each brand. This approach was considered more effective in building trade relationships because it gave retailers more flexibility in what they promoted.

LENOR FABRIC SOFTENER

Lenor, launched in West Germany in 1963, was the first nationally marketed brand of fabric softener. By 1987, Lenor had achieved 98 percent store penetration. More than half of Lenor's total volume was sold through mass merchandisers, as indicated in Exhibit 2. Sales revenue and unit volume in 1987 were DM 180 million and 6,200 MSUs, respectively.

At first, Lenor was sold as a specialty item in small, 500-ml containers, at a price nearly 10 times higher than the 1987 inflation-adjusted price for the same quantity. In 1965, P&G Germany broadened Lenor's appeal by lowering its price and developing a highly successful advertising campaign that remained in use for the following 18 years.

EXHIBIT 2   Lenor Sales Volume by Store Type in 1987

Store Type (by size)	Number of Stores	Number of Stores (%)	Grocery Market Turnover* (billion DM)	Market Turnover (%)	Lenor Volume Breakdown†	
					4-Liter Dilute	1-Liter Concentrate
Mass merchandisers	412	0.6%	17.2	13.6%	62.0%	36.0%
Hypermarkets	1,195	1.6	17.2	13.6	20.0	20.0
Supermarkets	2,542	3.5	18.6	14.7	9.0	13.0
Convenience stores	64,409	88.2	59.9	47.3	6.0	16.0
Discounters	4,442	6.1	13.8	10.9	3.0	14.0
Total	73,000	100.0%	126.7	100.0%	100.0%	100.0%

* Market turnover is defined as sales volume times retail value. 1.9 DM = US$1
† Percentages are based on statistical unit volume for the first six months of 1987.

TABLE C   Percentage Breakdown of Advertising and Sales Budget

	Dilute 1986	Dilute 1987	CT 1986	CT 1987
Media	20%	23%	20%	21%
Consumer promotion	4	1	1	1
Trade promotion	74	74	77	75
Indirect brand support	2	2	2	2
Total	100%	100%	100%	100%

The 1-liter Lenor concentrate (Lenor CT) joined Lenor dilute on retail shelves in 1983. By 1987, 30 percent of Lenor's volume was sold in this 3:1 concentrated form. The package cap doubled as a measuring cup which the consumer could use to determine how much liquid to add, in undiluted form, to the wash. Brand management believed that some fabric softener users regarded the concentrate's performance as inferior to the dilute's, although laboratory tests demonstrated no difference in efficacy. These users questioned whether "so little could perform as well." One P&G executive explained, "Although the concentrate is less awkward to carry home from the store, many consumers are wedded to the 4-liter package." Advertising for Lenor concentrate stressed the number of wash loads that could be softened with the contents of the small, one-liter package. Dryer sheets, introduced in the spring of 1987, sold to a limited market (0.4 percent of Lenor's 1987 sales volume) because 75 percent of West German households line-dried their laundry rather than using electric clothes dryers.

P&G Germany promoted Lenor heavily to the retail trade and consumers, spending 25 percent of the product's yearly manufacturer's sales on television and radio advertising, consumer promotions, trade promotions, and indirect brand support.[9] Table C indicates the percentage breakdowns of Lenor's advertising and promotion expenses for 1986 and 1987. Approximately 30 percent of the brand's total marketing budget was allocated to the concentrate.

In 1987, liquid Lenor was available in the package sizes and prices shown in Exhibit 3. Recommended retail prices were at least 10 percent higher than those of its competitors. However, Lenor was a popular loss leader among retailers.[10] Ninety percent of Lenor dilute volume and 25

---

[9] Indirect brand support included development costs for advertisements and commercials, production expenses associated with store displays, and other expenses incurred for consumer and trade promotions.

[10] Loss leaders (products retailers sold at prices below cost to attract consumers) were usually popular brands in frequently purchased product categories.

EXHIBIT 3 Lenor Liquid Package Sizes and Prices, 1987

Formulation	Size	Number of Units per Case	Number of Statistical Units per Case*	Suggested Retail Price (DM)	Average Feature Price (DM)	Suggested Retail Price Per SU (DM)	Average Feature Price Per SU (DM)	Percent Lenor Sales Volume
Dilute	4 liter	4	0.68	5.53	4.64	32.53	27.29	70%
Concentrate (3:1)	1 liter	16	2.01	4.75	4.08	37.81	32.48	30

* Statistical units (SUs) convert different sizes and products to an equivalent use basis. Thus, two items with the same number of SU will deliver an equivalent number of uses to the consumer.

108

percent of concentrate volume were sold by retailers at feature prices in 1987.

Between 1984 and 1986, Lenor's sales volume had declined by 7.5 percent annually, with an actual loss of more than 1,000 MSUs. Sales volume in 1988 was predicted to decline similarly if nothing was done to revive the brand. Brand management attributed this loss to increasingly aggressive competitive price promotion, which eroded Lenor's market share, and to a shrinking market due to unfavorable consumer sentiment. Lenor brand management had to develop a marketing strategy that would combat Lenor's eroding sales and market share in the face of consumers' increasing environmental concerns.

LENOR'S STRATEGIC OPTIONS

Stadler reviewed the strategic options her brand management team had developed in the last few months.

Relaunch the 3:1 Concentrate

One option explored was the aggressive relaunch of Lenor concentrate, promoting waste reduction benefits similar to those of a refill package. The 1-liter concentrate used approximately 45 percent less packaging materials than the 4-liter bottle on an equivalent use basis. Lenor's 1988 advertising and promotion budget (DM 45.2 million) could be increased by DM 2.9 million and be reallocated so that 40 percent would be spent on the dilute and 60 percent on the concentrate. Brand management estimated that this change would increase the concentrate's sales by 780 MSUs, 400 MSUs of which would result from cannibalization of the dilute. The finance department felt that the cannibalization rate would be even higher, with up to 480 MSUs of lost dilute sales.

The Lenor Refill Package

A second option was introducing a new, more potent form of Lenor concentrate in a refill package. With the 4-from-1 concentrate, consumers would pour one liter of the concentrate into an empty 4-liter Lenor dilute bottle at home and add three liters of water to produce the original Lenor dilute formula. The Lenor brand group believed that the waste reduction benefits gained both from packaging reduction and bottle reuse would appeal to environmentally conscious consumers. The refill idea was not new to West Germans; many shoppers purchased milk packaged in flat plastic bags that were then slotted inside a permanent container at home. Stadler also felt that "German consumers were ready to bear the extra trouble associated with refilling to help their environment."

Preliminary Research

In the fall of 1986, P&G conducted two focus group interviews of 8 to 12 fabric softener users to explore their attitudes toward a refill concept and determine how to market such a product. Several users expressed interest in trying a refill product that they felt would reduce waste through container reuse. When asked how they would sell this idea to their neighbors, many said they would stress waste reduction.

Next, a consumer panel test explored the acceptance of specific refill package ideas. Participants used different types of trial refill Lenor packages for four weeks, and afterwards answered a survey about their likes, dislikes, and purchase intentions. From the results, researchers concluded that the refill concept had significant business-building potential.

Package Design

In the spring of 1987, P&G Germany explored two specific refill package options. Technical researchers suggested two designs: (1) a laminated cardboard carton, similar in design to a milk carton, and (2) a stand-alone, soft plastic package, known as a "doypack" pouch, already used in West Germany to sell single servings of fruit juice. The technical staff believed that they could expand the size of this package to hold fabric softener concentrate.

In March 1987, P&G Germany tested these refill options in a consumer panel test. Participants were asked to test one of two package designs for Lenor concentrate: a one-liter laminated "milk" carton and a one liter doypack pouch. Users rated the laminated carton highest for its environmental compatibility, ease of use, and convenience; the doypack pouch ratings followed closely behind. Messiness was also a significant factor in preference for either package; participants who spilled the product when transferring it into the larger container rated both packages lower in terms of handling. Exhibit 4 summarizes the test results.

Laminated Cartons versus Doypack Pouches

Brand management investigated further the advantages and disadvantages of the two refill package designs. Both designs promised the same 85 percent reduction in package materials volume. In either case, P&G Germany had no facility that could produce the new packaging and would therefore need to hire subcontractors to meet a September launch date. This posed additional costs and risks. P&G Germany had not worked with any of the potential packaging suppliers before; consequently, Lenor's management did not have firsthand experience with their reliability in terms of delivery or quality. In addition, Lenor's product development

EXHIBIT 4   Consumer Panel Results: March 1987

	1-Liter Carton	1-Liter Doypack
Number of users	205	205
Participants who would buy the alternative regularly at 4.98 DM	53%	49%
Favorable/unfavorable comments on handling	88%/33%	88%/41%
Percentage of reused containers that were "smeary" after transfer	10%	28%
Packaging ratings		
Ease of opening	57%	52%
Transferability of product	63	46
Environmental friendliness	74	65
Ease of disposal	79	75
Incidence of spillage	8	25

group felt that there might be future capacity problems, since none of the potential subcontractors had ever handled the quantity of product P&G Germany was asking for.

Laminated Cartons.   Laminated carton technology had existed for 20 years. The cartons rarely leaked and consumers spilled a minimum of product during refill tests. Retailers could easily display the rigid carton on their shelves; the product would not require a customized shipping case. Each case would hold 10 1-liter cartons of Lenor.

West German safety regulations, focusing on the potential for accidental misuse of products, strongly discouraged packaging nonfood substances in containers generally used for food items. Consequently, P&G Germany ran some risk of government intervention if it used the laminated carton for its refill package. In addition, although the general public considered the carton as environmentally friendly, environmental experts regarded the wax-coated cardboard material as difficult to recycle.

Doypack Pouch.   Adapting the doypack pouch to Lenor's requirements proved difficult; the largest pouch size previously produced was 500 ml, half the size needed for Lenor. The first prototypes leaked and more than 10 percent of the packages burst when dropped. Lenor's product development group felt optimistic, however, that these issues would be resolved within two months. Furthermore, a product-handling test in June 1987 revealed spillage difficulties. Participants in studio tests were asked to open the pouch and pour its contents into a 4-liter Lenor container. Although the least spillage occurred after the doypack's entire top was cut off with scissors, researchers found that users preferred to clip off only a

EXHIBIT 5   Case of Doypack Refill Pouches

corner of the package top. Lenor's brand management was concerned that the refill package would prove to be too messy for many consumers.

P&G Germany would need to produce customized shipping containers that would display the product attractively while following the stringent criteria determined by retailers. Pictures of the doypack and the proposed case design are presented in Exhibit 5.

Comparative Production Costs.   The laminated carton and doypack pouch would achieve respectively 5 percent and 14 percent cost savings per SU over Lenor dilute, due to reduced package materials and lower delivery costs. Exhibit 6 shows a detailed cost breakdown for the proposed and existing Lenor product line. Lenor's allocated fixed costs were approximately DM 68 million per year.[11] The first 400 MSUs would cost an extra 33 percent and 41 percent for the carton and doypack, respectively.

Pricing.   Exhibit 7 shows the breakdown of 1987 proposed prices and trade margins for the Lenor product line. Brand management wanted the suggested retail price for the refill package to be at least DM 1.5/SU lower than that for the 4-liter dilute to reflect packaging cost savings. This would provide the price incentive needed to motivate consumers to buy the refill packs. The savings were 5 percent of manufacturer's list price.

---

[11] Fixed costs included general sales/marketing, administrative, and distribution costs (80 percent of total), fixed manufacturing (17 percent), and product research and development costs (3 percent).

EXHIBIT 6   1988 Breakdown of Direct Materials and Manufacturing Costs (DM per statistical unit)

	1-Liter Carton*	1-Liter Doypack*	4-Liter Dilute	1-Liter Concentrate
Fabric softener chemicals	DM4.60	DM4.60	DM4.69	DM4.77
Packaging materials	1.84	1.82	3.40	2.72
Manufacturing	3.33	3.19	2.93	2.60
Delivery	0.86	0.76	1.79	1.01
Contractor expense	1.52	0.65	—	—
Total direct costs (DM)	12.15	11.02	12.81	11.10
Cost index (Lenor dilute = 100)	95	86	100	87
SU per container	0.17	0.17	0.17	0.126
Total costs per container (DM)	2.06	1.87	2.18	1.40

* P&G Germany expected that the first 400 MSU produced would cost 33 percent and 41 percent more for the carton and doypack, respectively, due to initial start-up costs.

EXHIBIT 7   1988 Proposed Retail Price and Trade Margins

	1-Liter Refill	4-Liter Dilute	1-Liter Concentrate
Expected retail price (DM)	5.49	5.79	4.89
Expected retail margin	9%	0%	9%
Manufacturer's selling price (DM)	5.04	5.79	4.49
SU per container	0.17	0.17	0.126
Retail revenues (DM/SU)	32.29	34.06	38.81
Manufacturer's revenues (DM/SU)	29.65	34.06	35.64

Volume Forecasts.   The brand group forecast a 1988 sales volume of 1,500 MSU for the refill pouch; however, the team predicted that 60 percent of the refill package sales would come from cannibalization of existing Lenor sales. The finance department was less optimistic, forecasting an 80 percent cannibalization rate and a sales volume of 750 MSUs, resulting in only a 150 MSU net increase in total sales. For the launch, P&G would need 400 MSUs to stock 70 percent of West Germany's retail chain stores.

Promotion and Advertising.   Brand management proposed a 6.5 percent increase over its original 1988 advertising and promotion budget, with DM 6.5 million to be allocated specifically to the refill package relaunch. At estimated refill sales of 1,500 MSUs, this budget equaled DM 4.31/SU.

TABLE D   Alternative 1988 Advertising and Promotion Budgets

	Without Launch	*With Launch*	*Difference*
Media	DM 10,849	DM 12,227	DM 1,378
Consumer promotion	1,957	1,976	19
Trade promotion	29,830	31,350	1,520
Indirect brand support	2,546	2,565	19
Total	45,182	48,118	2,936

Table D breaks down the Lenor marketing budget with and without the refill package introduction.

The Lenor brand group proposed to focus all Lenor advertising on the refill package for the first three months after launch. P&G Germany's advertising agency developed and tested two commercials called *Splish-Splash* and *Perspectives*, based on the doypack pouch option (see Exhibits 8 and 9). *Splish-Splash* and *Perspectives* achieved unaided recall ratings of 37 percent and 47 percent, respectively, exceeding P&G Germany's 35 percent average unaided recall score for acceptable new copy.[12] Product labeling would highlight the environmental benefits of the packaging, in particular the 85 percent volume reduction in packaging materials, and would carry the phrase *refill pack*. Stadler hoped that the refill package would qualify for a Blue Angel label, which could help increase Lenor's sales, but felt uncertain that the improved packaging alone would gain the Blue Angel program's endorsement.

Proposed sales literature emphasized reductions in the retailer's warehousing (48 percent less), transportation (72 percent), and handling costs (70 percent) compared with the 4-liter Lenor dilute. The case container designs for both the carton and the doypack met 8 of the trade's 10 commandments, more than did any existing P&G Germany product. Finally, brand management felt that the opportunity to realize higher retail margins than could currently be obtained on the heavily promoted 4-liter dilute (9 percent vs. 0 percent) would also appeal to the trade.[13]

---

[12] Day-after recall testing measured communication effectiveness. Consumers who had watched television at the time when a test commercial spot was being shown were interviewed by telephone the following day. Unaided recall occurred when a consumer remembered the brand and message content of the test commercial without prompting. Aided recall involved prompting.

[13] Retail trade margins of 0 percent were due to the frequent use of the Lenor 4-liter dilute as a loss leader. Retail margins on Lenor sold at feature prices were often negative.

An Integrated Marketing Option

As Stadler pondered the pros and cons for the refill package, Daniel Knower, the assistant brand manager for Vizir, P&G Germany's liquid detergent brand, stopped by her office to discuss a new marketing concept he wanted to pursue. He said, ''You know, we are struggling with the same environmental issues. I think that this refill concept is great, and could be expanded to other brands, such as Vizir. We could market the products more efficiently under a new brand name, such as *Eco-pak*. Advertising copy could focus on the refill package as a product form that spanned multiple brands—Lenor, Vizir, and other liquid products.'' Realistically, both Stadler and Knower speculated that the manufacturing complications, larger marketing scope, and increased coordination associated with such a strategy would add at least three months to the Lenor refill package's September introduction date. However, both felt that the idea merited discussion with their respective brand managers.

EXHIBIT 8   Advertising Copy for Lenor Pouch:
Splish-Splash **Commercial**

(Music begins, with young male and female dancers, brightly dressed,
   dancing while holding Lenor containers and the Lenor pouch)

Singing to the 1960s tune *Splish-Splash*:

Splish, Splash,
We're up-to-date,
Use Lenor in the refill pouch.

Just take your empty bottle,
Refilling is not difficult.
Just add water.

Splish, Splash,
You feel it immediately,
Everything April-fresh and soft.
New Lenor in the
Environmentally safe refill pouch.

Splish, Splash,
The pouch is great,
Makes itself really small for the garbage.

Splish, Splash,
Be up-to-date,
Use Lenor in the refill pouch.

EXHIBIT 9 Storyboard for *Perspectives* Commercial

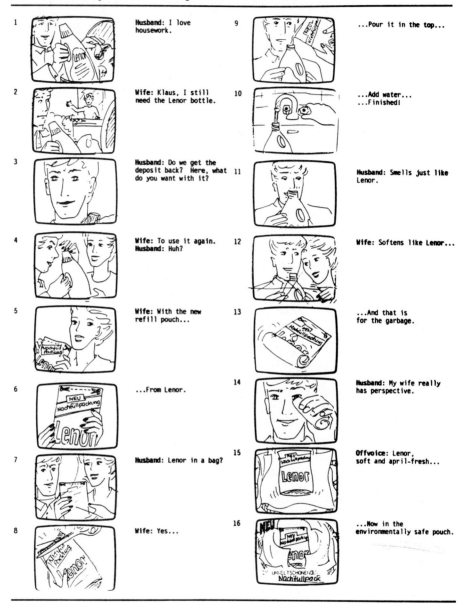

1. Husband: I love housework.

2. Wife: Klaus, I still need the Lenor bottle.

3. Husband: Do we get the deposit back? Here, what do you want with it?

4. Wife: To use it again. Husband: Huh?

5. Wife: With the new refill pouch...

6. ...From Lenor.

7. Husband: Lenor in a bag?

8. Wife: Yes...

9. ...Pour it in the top...

10. ...Add water... ...Finished!

11. Husband: Smells just like Lenor.

12. Wife: Softens like Lenor...

13. ...And that is for the garbage.

14. Husband: My wife really has perspective.

15. Offvoice: Lenor, soft and april-fresh...

16. ...Now in the environmentally safe pouch.

CONCLUSION

At the next day's meeting, Rolf Kunisch discussed several issues with the Lenor brand management team. First was the possibility that any effort P&G made to address environmental issues could backfire. The Public Relations Department had warned of "waking a sleeping dog." P&G had many highly visible products that might attract opposition from environmentalists. Although the Lenor refill package might raise the firm's profile as an environmentally conscious corporate citizen, it might also draw attention to other P&G products for which environmental and cost-effective improvements were not readily available.

Kunisch was also concerned about the rapidity with which brand management had developed the refill package proposal. Had the product been tested enough? Were there hidden issues that might have been missed in the rush to launch? Was there really an urgent need for action? No other German consumer goods company had addressed environmental issues through innovative packaging. With such a novel and relatively untested idea, what risks would P&G Germany run as the first to market?

Several other P&G country managers in Europe had scoffed at the "crazy German ideas about the environment," seeing little applicability of the refill-package idea to their own markets. Kunisch wondered if P&G Europe headquarters would also conclude that P&G Germany was over-reacting to the environmental concerns of some West Germany consumers. Stadler left the meeting, uncertain of the final outcome for the refill package's future.

After the meeting, Lenor's brand manager, Phillippe, asked Stadler to prepare a revised set of recommendations for Lenor, addressing some of Kunisch's concerns. Stadler continued to be positive about the new packaging concept; however, she realized that the internal sell would be tougher than she had anticipated.

Chemical Bank: The Pronto System

In September 1983 Graham Parker and Ronald Lacey, both vice presidents of Chemical Bank, met on the twenty-third floor of the New York headquarters to discuss Chemical's Pronto home banking system. Parker had worked on the Pronto system for almost three years within the Electronic Banking Division, helping to develop the software and subsequently supervising the implementation of a pilot test. His immediate concerns were how to market Pronto successfully to other banks as a franchise and how to develop Pronto so that it would be even more attractive to potential licensees.

Lacey was responsible for the forthcoming market introduction of Pronto in New York City. The Financial Services Group within the Metropolitan Banking Division for which he worked was, in effect, the first of Parker's licensees to launch Pronto commercially. With the launch just a few weeks away, Lacey and Parker—as they had done many times during the past year—reviewed the challenges and opportunities facing them.

Banking in the 1980s

Chemical Bank, headquartered in New York City, was the nation's sixth-largest bank in 1982 with assets of over $50 billion. Known for its aggressive new-product development, Chemical provided a full range of commercial banking services to corporate and retail customers. Over one million households in New York City held accounts at one of its 250 retail branches. Chemical's retail banking penetration was second only to that of Citibank, which held accounts for about 1,500,000 New York City households.

Chemical competed in an increasingly turbulent banking environment. Deregulation, particularly the removal of ceilings on the interest rates that banks could charge and the relaxation of interest banking restrictions, had heightened competition among banks for consumer deposits. Moreover, the competitive arena had broadened to include various less-regulated, nationally known institutions. These included stock brokerage firms such as Merrill Lynch, which had pioneered the introduction

Professor John A. Quelch prepared this case as the basis for class discussion rather than to illustrate effective or ineffective handling of an administrative situation. Names and certain data have been disguised. Copyright © 1984 by the President and Fellows of Harvard College. Harvard Business School case 9–584–089.

of money market accounts against which consumers could write checks. In the longer term, national retailers, such as Sears, Roebuck & Co. and J.C. Penney, were thought likely to take advantage of their national bases of credit card customers to offer a full range of financial services nationwide.

Partly because of increased competition from outside the traditional banking industry, deposit growth rates in commercial banks for both corporate and retail customers were declining. However, deposits by individual consumers (58 percent of the total in 1980) represented an increasing percentage of total deposits. Industry analysts pointed out that 96 percent of US households had a relationship with a bank and that banks enjoyed a level of trust with many consumers that other institutions could not match.

Banks responded to these trends by improving services, by broadening product lines, and by attempting to reduce costs. The retail banking industry was both labor-intensive and paper-intensive. In 1980, 1.5 million employees processed 47.7 billion items at an average cost of 37 cents. To reduce costs, many banks took one or more of the following steps:

- Provided tellers with on-line terminals to access customer records, permitting faster balance checking and improved customer service.
- Automated the back offices of branches to reduce paper processing, improve account record keeping, and cut the number of account errors and adjustments.
- Subcontracted the processing of checks and credit card transactions to other banks and financial service firms such as American Express, which operated automated clearinghouses. Having invested in the facilities required to process high volumes of transactions at minimal cost, these clearinghouses were able to charge their bank customers less than the per-unit cost if each ran its own dedicated processing operation.
- Developed on-line cash management systems for corporate customers, permitting them to move cash among accounts within a single bank and among accounts held at several participating banks. Chemical had pioneered corporate cash management with the development of software for its BankLink system, introduced in 1977. By 1983 the BankLink system had been franchised to 65 other banks, a quarter of all those that offered a cash management system in the United States.[1]

---

[1] The Financial Services Group within the Metropolitan Banking Division for which Lacey worked marketed the corporate cash management system together with payroll management systems and, most recently, Pronto, to Chemical's own corporate and retail customers. The Electronic Banking Division for which Parker worked marketed all of these products to other banks.

- Introduced automated teller machines (ATMs), which reduced labor costs and the pressure on tellers, permitted banks to offer uniform service around the clock, and enabled banks to expand their market reach for much less than the cost of building new branches. One study forecast that there would be 62,000 ATMs attached to bank branches or in remote locations by 1986. The same study estimated that unit transaction processing costs for an ATM (processing 6,000 transactions monthly) versus a human teller were 54 percent less in 1982 and would be 63 percent less by 1986.
- Offered a telephone-bill-paying service to retail customers. The number of banks providing this service was forecast to grow from 425 in 1983 to 2,000 by 1985. However, an average of only 3 percent of retail banking customers were using the service where it was available. Some industry analysts attributed this to insufficient marketing; others attributed it to the fact that consumers using the service had no visual record of their transactions until they received their monthly statements.

Home Banking

Electronic home banking systems permitted consumers to execute various banking tasks, including balance inquiry, interaccount funds transfer, and bill paying from the comfort of their homes. Compared with the approaches listed above, the cost savings and service improvements associated with home banking were seen by most analysts as further in the future. These benefits included the following:

- The elimination of the "float" that customers received when writing paper checks.
- The lower cost of processing a customer's electronic bill payment than of processing a paper check.
- The lower cost of sending the customer an electronic statement rather than printing and mailing one.
- The lower cost of advertising new services to customers by reaching them through electronic ads on the home banking system.
- The ability of banks offering home banking to serve their customers with fewer branch offices.
- The increased revenues from customers attracted from other banks by the availability of a competitive home banking service.

One industry study estimated that, by 1985, 250 banks would be providing home banking services to 1,250,000 accounts, displacing 105 million paper-based transactions each year. This figure, however, represented less than half of one percent of the total paper-based transactions forecast for 1985. Higher percentages of transactions were expected to be displaced by ATMs (3.9 percent) and automated clearinghouses (2.4 percent) and telephone bill payment (0.6 percent).

The study indicated that a home banking bill-payment system would reduce costs for the payer, the biller, and the bank. The cost of postage, envelopes, and paper checks would be eliminated for the payer. The biller would incur no bank deposit charge, would lose less on float, and would avoid the problem of bounced checks. The study estimated that the bank's costs of processing a check were 9 percent less using home banking in 1983 and would be 47 percent less by 1986.

In September 1983 about 45 US banks experimented with home banking. The only commercially available home banking service in the United States, however, was available to subscribers of Compuserve, a national computer information network. At a cost of $4 per month[2] over and above the $5 monthly Compuserve fee, a consumer with a home computer, telephone, and modem[3] could conduct simple banking transactions such as balance inquiry and account transfers with any of four participating banks. These banks were medium-sized and included the First Tennessee Bank in Knoxville, Tennessee, and the Huntington National Bank in Columbus, Ohio.

Among the leading banks in the nation, Chemical and Citibank had invested heavily in developing software for their home banking systems. Both had recently completed extensive pilot tests. The range of services offered on Chemical's Pronto system is summarized in Exhibit 1. Chemical began licensing Pronto to other banks that were not interested in developing their own systems either individually or as a joint venture. Citibank apparently had no such intention. Noting Citibank's aggressive nationwide marketing of credit cards, traveler's checks, and money market funds, some industry analysts believed that Citibank viewed its Homebase home banking system as a vehicle to build a national base of Citibank checking account customers. These analysts further forecast that no more than 10 banks would independently develop their own software.

The software had to be tailored to fit each home computer. Parker explained, "The Pronto software grabs the menus we send down and stores them in your computer's memory. When you return to a menu during a home banking session, it appears on the screen much faster."

Another technology for delivering home banking services was videotex, which could link a consumer's home television set to a central

---

[2] Additional telephone connect time charges were also incurred when the consumer accessed the home banking network.

[3] A modem converted computer signals into tones that traveled over telephone lines.

EXHIBIT 1   Services Provided to Pronto Consumers

Balance Inquiry
- Daily balances of all accounts (including Chemical credit card and money market accounts).
- Details of check activity (for example, to establish whether or not a particular check has cleared).

Electronic Statements
- Statements on-line before mailing.
- Available for current month and previous month.

Funds Transfer
- Shifts funds between accounts.
- Cash advances from revolving credit accounts.

Bill Paying
- Bills paid directly from accounts without writing checks.
- Payments recorded directly into home budgets.
- Value-dated payments, up to 90 days in advance.
- Recurring bills paid automatically.
- Payments can be renewed, changed, or canceled until they are made.

Electronic Checkbook
- Records checks as written.
- Monitors dates that checks clear.
- Checks recorded directly into home budget.
- Information concerning checks stored for printed monthly statements.

Home Budgeting
- Organizes income and expenditures in 50 categories.
- As many as five separate budgets.
- Multiple entries.
- Instant totals for any budget.
- Monthly summary of budget activity with regular monthly statement.
- Categorizes tax-deductible items as they occur.

Electronic Mail
- Permits user to send messages to other Pronto users.
- Customer can add accounts and ask the bank questions (and receive a reply from the customer service agent within 24 hours).

---

computer via the telephone (or cable in households with cable television) and a videotex terminal (costing about $600 in 1983). The consumer interacted with a videotex system either by punching a hand-held keypad or by typing on a full alphanumeric keyboard.

Unlike information networks such as Compuserve, which transmitted only black-and-white text, videotex data pages were in color and included graphics. The videotex terminal was necessary to decode the color and graphics signals relayed by the videotex central computer, tasks that a standard home computer could not perform. However, software packages costing $100, which would convert home computers with modems to videotex terminals, were under development.

By September 1983 over 25 videotex field trials were in progress in the United States. Banks and other financial institutions, such as Merrill Lynch, were involved as partners in most of these experiments along with communications companies such as Time, Inc., Knight-Ridder Newspapers, and Times-Mirror; network providers such as AT&T; and national retailers such as Sears, Roebuck, and Federated Department Stores. In one such field trial in Ridgewood, New Jersey, funded by AT&T and CBS, AT&T provided the computer facilities and home terminals. CBS provided various information services, including continuously updated news, weather, sports, education, games, advertising, and teleshopping. A home banking service was provided by ADP Telephone Computing Service, Inc., a division of Automatic Data Processing, and the Treasurer, a consortium of New Jersey banks. The service included balance inquiry, funds transfer, and bill-payment capabilities.

Banks participating in videotex experiments assumed the role of information suppliers and financial partners rather than system operators. The financial arrangements governing the relationships between home banking suppliers and system operators in commercial videotex systems were yet to be determined.[4]

Research Studies on Home Banking

Besides their in-house research, Parker and his colleagues had the benefit of two research studies conducted during 1982 by Booz, Allen and Hamilton (BAH) and by Reymer Gersin Associates.

The BAH study estimated that between 16 million (worst case) and 29 million (best case) of the 106 million households in the United States in 1995 would be users of home information services (HIS) and that, of these, 40 percent definitely would pay and 49 percent were somewhat likely to pay. Regarding home banking, the BAH study concluded that 75 percent of HIS users would have a "high propensity" to pay $2.50 per month for a home banking and bill-paying service; at $7.50 and $15.00, the numbers interested dropped to 60 percent and 25 percent, respectively. A home banking service including bill paying was one of two services registering the highest interest among respondents, the other being an entertainment-ticket-ordering service. Among those interested in the home banking service, a majority preferred a flat monthly rate to a monthly charge dependent upon level of use. According to BAH estimates, by

---

[4] For further information on the videotex industry, see Caroline Brainard and George S. Yip, "Note on the Consumer Videotex Industry," HBS case 9-584-029.

1995 home banking might replace between 5 percent (worst case) and 14 percent (best case) of personal check volume.

In 1982 Reymer Gersin Associates surveyed over 6,000 consumers to establish the appeal of different videotex services and the prices that consumers would willingly pay for them. The total sample was split into five groups of 1,240 respondents spread among 14 markets. The price per service presented to respondents before they were asked to express their level of interest in a standard set of videotex services varied across each of the five groups from no charge to $16 a month. The study identified six segments of respondents differing not only in their enthusiasm about videotex (from "all-around enthusiasts" to "anti-videotexers") but also in their interest in different services. Some consumers expressed more interest or exclusive interest in information-oriented services but not in transaction services. These segments were named "information-oriented enthusiasts" and "information onlies." As a result, the study recommended that videotex system operators allow customers to choose their own combinations of services, while requiring them to take at least two services, each priced at $12 a month.

Exhibit 2 shows the percentage of respondents in total and in the six segments who would purchase each of six videotex services at various prices. Consumers who favored transaction services appeared to be less price sensitive than those who favored information services. Interest in home banking appeared to be particularly strong. The survey also asked respondents whether they agreed or disagreed with several statements about home banking. The results appear in Exhibit 3. In addition, interest in home banking was greater among those respondents who subscribed to pay cable services, those who frequently used ATMs and credit cards, those who wrote more checks, those who spent more on monthly telephone bills, those who more often purchased by mail order, and those who owned or intended to buy a personal computer and/or video game equipment.

Chemical's Consumer Research on Pronto

The Field Trial

Chemical's consumer research program began in February 1982, when a field trial of Pronto was initiated. The pilot program had the following objectives:

- Identify potential market segments.
- Determine user preferences for services offered within the Pronto package.

EXHIBIT 2 Members of Six Videotex Segments Who Would Order Videotex Services at Different Prices (%)

Total Respondents

Segments	Free	$4/mo.	$8/mo.	$12/mo.	$16/mo.
Pay Services					
News service	100%	100%	100%	100%	100%
	64	43	37	32	26
Special interest information	55	39	32	28	24
Electronic mail	50	24	20	15	13
Home banking	31	16	13	11	8
Free Services					
Shopping guide	62	54	51	46	45
Shopping at home	47	48	46	42	44
Monthly revenue generated/HH*	0	$7	$10	$15	$20

All-Around Enthusiasts

Segments	Free	$4/mo.	$16/mo.
Pay Services			
News service	31%	20%	9%
	95	93	82
Special interest information	90	76	48
Electronic mail	76	53	50
Home banking	45	36	25
Free Services			
Shopping guide	93	94	86
Shopping at home	80	90	84
Monthly revenue generated/HH*	0	$10	$33

Transaction-Oriented Enthusiasts

Segments	Free	$4/mo.	$16/mo.
Pay Services			
News service	8%	14%	15%
	68	49	47
Special interest information	39	26	15
Electronic mail	9	14	11
Home banking	95	96	90
Free Services			
Shopping guide	92	99	96
Shopping at home	88	97	97
Monthly revenue generated/HH*	0	$7	$25

Information-Oriented Enthusiasts

Segments	Free	$4/mo.	$16/mo.
Pay Services			
News service	16%	6%	2%
	100	100	100
Special interest information	97	77	73
Electronic mail	83	66	54
Home banking	79	38	35
Free Services			
Shopping guide	90	93	76
Shopping at home	76	85	88
Monthly revenue generated/HH*	0	$6	$40

Transaction Onlies

Segments	Free	$4/mo.	$16/mo.
Pay Services			
News service	5%	10%	14%
	21	13	13
Special interest information	6	1	0
Electronic mail	1	4	4
Home banking	53	42	28
Free Services			
Shopping guide	40	45	63
Shopping at home	21	45	63
Monthly revenue generated/HH*	0	$10	$17

Information Onlies

Segments	Free	$4/mo.	$16/mo.
Pay Services			
News service	6%	4%	2%
	95	88	80
Special interest information	60	36	35
Electronic mail	24	15	24
Home banking	20	6	16
Free Services			
Shopping guide	58	38	35
Shopping at home	8	9	0
Monthly revenue generated/HH*	0	$4	$30

Anti-Videotexers

Segments	Free	$4/mo.	$16/mo.
Pay Services			
News service	34%	43%	56%
	20	14	14
Special interest information	13	6	7
Electronic mail	5	4	3
Home banking	9	3	2
Free Services			
Shopping guide	18	14	19
Shopping at home	5	11	16
Monthly revenue generated/HH*	0	$5	$17

SOURCE: Reymer Gersin Associates.

NOTE: To be read, for example, "Among the 1,240 respondents who were offered all pay services free, 95 percent of the group that was offered all pay services free) would obtain the news service. The monthly revenue generated for the average household in this group would be zero since all services were free."

* HH signifies per household.

EXHIBIT 3 Reasons for Getting or Not Getting Home Banking: Average Rating Summary by Segment

Disagree a Lot — 1.0 Agree a Lot — 6.0

How Do You Feel about the Following Statements?	Total Sample	All-Around Videotex Enthusiasts	Transaction-Oriented Videotex Enthusiasts	Information-Oriented Videotex Enthusiasts	Transaction Onlies	Information Onlies	Anti-Videotexers
Having banking at home isn't worth it because I'll still have to go to the bank in person to get cash.	3.9	3.0	2.9	3.3	3.9	4.9	4.5
I want banking at home because it'll be easier than paying bills by writing checks and mailing them.	3.5	4.6	5.0	3.9	4.1	2.6	2.7
I'm so used to paying my bills the way I do now that I'll never switch to banking at home.	3.6	2.4	2.0	3.9	3.5	3.9	4.4
I'll never take a chance paying bills at home because something might go wrong with it and the bills might not get paid.	3.6	2.8	2.5	3.3	3.7	4.0	4.2
I'll never bank or shop at home because I prefer dealing face-to-face with a person rather than with a machine.	3.5	2.4	2.3	2.9	3.3	3.9	4.3
I want banking at home because it won't let me bounce a check; it won't pay bills unless there's enough money or credit in my account.	3.3	4.2	4.5	3.7	3.1	2.6	2.7
I'll enjoy shopping and banking at home because I have such a busy life; I don't always have time to shop or bank in person.	3.1	4.5	4.4	3.9	3.4	2.0	2.3
Banking at home will help me keep better track of my checking, savings, and charge accounts, since right now I'm never sure what my balances are.	2.7	3.8	4.1	2.7	2.8	2.0	2.1
I often forget to pay bills on time, so I'll worry less with banking at home paying bills for me on time automatically.	2.4	3.5	3.5	2.8	2.5	2.0	1.8

SOURCE: Reymer Gersin Associates.

NOTE: Average ratings calculated only among those who had an opinion.

- Monitor customer usage to identify problem areas, help develop staffing requirements, and project operating costs.
- Develop positions on marketing issues including pricing, promotion, and product development.
- Gain operational experience relating to maintaining and upgrading applications software, the Tandem operating system, and the interfaces between the bank's mainframe accounting systems and Pronto.

Four hundred prospective participants were identified from among a random sample of 23,000 existing Chemical checking account customers. The criteria for participation included having a modular telephone jack in the same room as a working television, having some interest in home banking, and not owning a personal computer. The 200 households in the final test sample received an Atari 400 computer on loan as well as three video games. (At the time, IBM and Apple were seen as more involved in the business end of the personal computer market. Atari had the largest market share in the consumer segment of the market.) They were also mailed a welcoming letter, brochures and information on Pronto and on how to use the system, and a list of 300 merchants to whom electronic payments could be made through Pronto. Half the participants were aged 25 to 34, and half had completed a four-year degree. Their average household income was $34,500, and their average household size was 2.6 members. Fifty percent of the participants had used a computer terminal before the Pronto trial.

In July 1982 three focus groups were held in New York with heavy, moderate, and light field trial users of Pronto. The purpose was to assess the participants' attitudes toward Pronto, to identify concerns, and to explore posttrial purchase intentions. Group members indicated that they had participated either because they were interested in home banking or because the pilot test provided them with an opportunity to practice with a personal computer at no expense. Few respondents participated in order to change their banking behavior, but one claimed, "I feel a closeness with the bank now, that I probably wouldn't have if I didn't have the system."

In September 1982 a telephone survey of field trial participants was conducted to assess their attitudes toward the system and to determine their reasons for and methods of using Pronto services. A high percentage of respondents stated that they "regularly accessed" the balance inquiry service. The bill-paying and electronic checkbook services also scored high, followed by the electronic statement, funds transfer, and home budgeting services.

Although the home budgeting service was widely viewed as "hard to understand," many respondents also expressed concerns over the bill-paying service. The principal concern was that the service did not permit payments to be electronically transferred instantly to the account of the payee; time still had to be allowed for a transfer on paper to occur through Chemical headquarters. Other concerns were that the number of merchants was too limited, that it took Chemical too long to approve an additional merchant account suggested by a customer, and that the current system for scheduling multiple payments to a single merchant was cumbersome.

Respondents suggested that the instruction manual could be made clearer, that more "help" screens could be provided for new users, and that a test program could be provided for new users to practice on. Some of the more experienced users complained that they could not take shortcuts through the system to access more quickly the screens they required and that the time lag between transaction entry and execution was too long. As one respondent put it, "Pronto implies speed, but this system doesn't deliver."

Respondents were also tested on their price sensitivity and willingness to pay for Pronto once the pilot test ended. Sixty-five percent were willing to pay $8 per month, 43 percent would pay $12, and 33 percent would pay $16. Regarding the personal computer and modem, 25 percent said $300 was the maximum price that they would willingly pay Chemical, 40 percent said $400, and 33 percent said $500. Half the respondents preferred to purchase this equipment through a retailer rather than through a bank even if they could receive it in lieu of interest on a high-balance deposit account. Management concluded from these and other comments that consumers who already owned personal computers would be less price sensitive regarding monthly usage fees.

The research program also included the collection and analysis of Pronto usage data from participants in the field trial. The findings were as follows:

- In June a daily average of 27 participants accessed Pronto. In December the average was 16.
- Throughout the trial period, Pronto users accessed an average of 25 screens per session. In June users spent 1.21 minutes per screen. In December they spent 0.35 minutes per screen.
- In a typical session before September, participants accessed three Pronto services. After September they typically accessed two.
- The most popular time for sessions was after work on weekdays. The lowest number of sessions occurred on Saturdays and Sundays.
- An average of four bills was paid during any session that included bill paying.

By the end of April 1983, one-third of the original pilot participants had already ceased using the system (10 households had moved). Another one-third had used Pronto at least 10 times in the previous 90 days, and the other one-third had used the system 1 to 9 times during the same period. Among the group of more frequent users, 60 percent were between the ages of 25 and 34, and 75 percent were men. Although households with annual incomes over $50,000 represented almost one-third of Pronto's pilot users, they accounted for only 15 percent of those who were positive about the existing Pronto system.

In April 1983 the pilot test ended. The participants received a letter giving them the option of continuing to receive Pronto at $8 a month and a payment of $240 for the computer, modem, and games.

One-half of the pilot households discontinued the service. A telephone survey of these households revealed that 78 percent were, in fact, very or somewhat satisfied with Pronto, and only 17 percent expressed operational concerns about the system, primarily that the computer was too slow. Reasons for discontinuing the service are summarized in Exhibit 4. Although the most frequent objection was the price of the Atari computer, several households stated that their banking needs were not sufficiently complex to justify paying for Pronto, while some regarded transactions via Pronto as no easier than writing checks. Interestingly, 70

EXHIBIT 4   Reasons for Dropping Pronto Service among Pilot Users

Reasons for Dropping Pronto Service	Percent Citing as Very Important	Percent Citing as Primary	Comments: To Continue with Pronto, What Changes Do We Need to Make?	
Atari too expensive	52%	22%	9%	Mention lower computer cost
			9	Want it free
			7	Want a rental option
Monthly service charge too high	33	7	13	Want a lower monthly charge
Atari too awkward	39	15		
Atari too limited but would be interested if another were used.	50	13	17	Want more powerful computer
			33	Want to be compatible with other systems
Home banking services are not timely enough	46	4	11	Want more merchants
			17	Want quicker access time
			7	Speed up bill payment time
I did not find electronic banking useful	28	4		
Chemical bank is not my principal bank	7	4		
Pronto services are too limited	54	15	11	Want more merchants
			7	Want more noncredit service
Pronto is too difficult to use	22	4	7	Want it easier to use
			17	Want a single ledger or sole record-keeping device

percent of the households that discontinued the service expected to buy a similar home banking service within two years; only one respondent expected never to purchase such a service.

Respondents were asked to name their single most important selection criterion in deciding to use a service such as Pronto. The results follow:

Price	20%
Variety of services	26
Reputation/experience	9
Ease of use	24
Services save time	17

Additional Research

In February and March 1983, two waves of three focus groups each were conducted in New York City by Lacey's group. Two group discussions were held with Atari home computer owners, two with Apple and IBM home computer owners, and two with nonowners of home computers. Group members were exposed to each of the five advertising concepts that management was considering for Pronto's introduction promotional campaign in New York City. The five concepts were as follows:

- Introducing Pronto, the 24-hour money management system.
- Pronto is the computer that makes banking more human.
- With pronto, you can do your banking at home, 24 hours a day.
- You're the only one with a key to pronto.
- Pronto, state-of-the-art banking

Participants were shown a storyboard and a description of each concept. The descriptions are presented in Exhibit 5. The preferences of the focus groups' participants are reported in Table A.

Besides testing participants' reactions to the five advertising concepts, the focus groups were also used to elicit reactions to Pronto and to various pricing options following a demonstration of the system. Although the proposed $8-per-month fixed fee was regarded as reasonable, some participants expressed skepticism as to how long the fee would remain at $8. Those not owning a personal computer saw the cost of both the computer and modem along with the likely decline in personal computer prices and changes in technology as major barriers to adoption. Several thought, however, that the availability of Pronto might tip the scales and prompt them to buy personal computers. The participants enthusiastically supported the idea that Chemical Bank might provide

EXHIBIT 5 Texts of Five Pronto Advertising Concepts

1. Introducing Pronto, the 24-Hour Money Management System

Pronto takes the mystery out of banking. Using Pronto and your computer, you can be on-line with Chemical—24 hours a day. You'll know everything you need to know about all your accounts—checking, savings, money market, Mastercard, and Visa, and more. Pronto gives you an incredible amount of detail on every aspect of your various accounts.

Pronto's bill-paying service lets you arrange for payments of piles of bills in minutes, scheduling them for up to 90 days in advance.

You can also use balance inquiry to get daily, up-to-date reports on all your balances—by account.

You can watch your accounts—see when deposited funds are in float and when they have cleared. And you won't have to guess about how long it takes for that check you wrote to clear—Pronto keeps track of the dates checks clear and keeps track of those that are outstanding. For Mastercard and Visa, you can see the amount you owe and your credit availability, on a daily basis.

Pronto does the work for you automatically and is the perfect complement to your regular Chemical services—the bank branches and cash machines.

2. Pronto Is the Computer That Makes Banking More Human

With Pronto's home banking system, you don't have to know anything about computer programming. It's easy and practical to use because when you "sign on" to Pronto, instructions appear on your television screen. They tell you how to select the services you need and how to use them. You just pick numbers from the list and fill in the blanks.

It's like having your own personal bank branch at your fingertips.

You'll feel closer to the bank because it's easy for you to keep in touch with your money. You can even send electronic messages to your friends who have Pronto.

Instead of just being another customer at your branch, you'll have a close, personal link between you and Chemical.

3. With Pronto, You Can Do Your Banking at Home, 24 Hours a Day

Pronto offers you the convenience of doing most of your banking transactions at any time—in the privacy of your own home. Whenever you want to, without leaving home, you can pay bills, get daily balances in your accounts, keep an electronic checkbook, find out which checks have cleared, transfer funds from one account to another, and organize and review your expenses through the home budgeting service.

You can even send electronic messages to the bank when you have inquiries about your accounts, and Pronto will give you a quick answer. Having Pronto is like having the branch open in your own home—24 hours a day.

4. You're the Only One with a Key to Pronto

Financial transactions are a private matter. Pronto was designed with several layers of security to ensure that only *you* can perform transactions or see information regarding your accounts.

Each user selects his or her own security codes in addition to the one assigned by the bank. Pronto will not deliver information or perform transactions without confirming these codes.

Another Pronto security feature is transactions verification. Pronto verifies every transaction you request to make sure that the information is correct. Once the information is verified, you get a reference number for each transaction.

5. Pronto, State-of-the-Art Banking

Now you can participate in not only the computer revolution but in the banking revolution, too, by subscribing to Chemical's new electronic banking system, Pronto.

Today with your computer, you can play games such as Pac Man, do programming, and enjoy lots of other educational programs.

Pronto expands the uses of your computer. It's a dynamic system built to move with the technology of the future. With the Pronto system, you can bank in an entirely new way—pay bills electronically, check all your account balances, see statements, and more—24 hours a day. You can even send electronic messages to your friends who have Pronto.

TABLE A   Focus Group Results: Pronto Concept References

| | Number of Focus Group Participants Who . . . | | | | | |
| | Ranked First | | Ranked Second | | Ranked Third | |
Concept	Feb.	March	Feb.	March	Feb.	March
Money management system	12	17	6	3	1	0
Banking more human	8	7	9	8	2	7
24 hours a day	7	4	5	15	3	3
Key to Pronto	3	2	8	2	10	5
State-of-the-art	0	1	2	3	14	10

modems to consumers who purchased a certificate of deposit or maintained a mininum checking account balance.

The comments of focus group participants confirmed management's belief that the convenience of home banking and the 24-hour access to a consumer's financial status were Pronto's principal benefits. The system would also help consumers to organize their financial records better and could be a status symbol. However, some additional questions were raised:

- What if I have accounts at different branches of Chemical?
- Will someone train me to use the system?
- What if someone, somehow obtains my ID numbers and tries to wipe me out?
- How many banking transactions do I need to do to make it worthwhile?
- Can I store the information in my home computer or print a hard copy?
- Will I receive a paper record of my transactions? What if I make an error?
- How far back can I call up my banking information?
- Does the telephone line have to be tied up when I am using the system? (AT&T and others were close to completing the technology to provide a telephone line with simultaneous dual-call capacity.)

The participants' principal fears concerned confidentiality, security, and computer theft. Several consumers pointed out that, since not all checks could be paid electronically, dual paper and electronic checkbooks would have to be maintained.[5] Others noted that the convenience

---

[5] Only 300 merchants had agreed to accept electronic payments.

of home banking was limited by the necessity of visiting their banks to obtain cash.

Pronto Licensing Efforts

Because it had successfully franchised the BankLink cash management system, Chemical decided early on to license Pronto to other banks. Thus, the software was designed to be adaptable, with minimal additional programming, to the product lines and procedures of other banks. Parker estimated that three to six person-months would be required to develop the necessary programming interfaces for a particular licensee bank, depending on the size and complexity of its operations.

By September 1983 seven banks, including Crocker National in California, the twelfth-largest in assets in the United States, had made commitments to purchase Pronto. Some signed licensing agreements for defensive reasons, viewing it as a cheaper means of staking a position in the home banking arena rather than investing in the development of their own systems. Other licensees viewed Pronto as a vehicle to build their market shares. Parker was uncertain whether large, medium, or small banks would be the most promising licensees, and whether banks with well-developed retail branch and ATM networks would be better or worse prospects than those banks with weaker retail positions that might see home banking as a means of regaining market share.

The terms of the licensing agreement permitted the licensee to offer Pronto as its own home banking system, although the name *Pronto* had to be used, and the logo had to be presented in a prescribed manner. No minimum commitment of expenditures to marketing Pronto was required. Licensees received all present and future Pronto home banking software developed by Chemical and access to Chemical's cumulative expertise in marketing Pronto and knowledge of the videotex industry. Chemical also provided technical assistance to develop the necessary interfaces between Pronto and the licensee bank's systems along with some marketing consulting assistance. Parker hoped that, as more and more banks signed up, Chemical would be able to reduce the level of assistance that it was agreeing to provide.

Parker developed two pricing schedules for potential licensee banks interested in conducting pilot tests of Pronto over a two-year period with a maximum of 200 customers. If a licensee wished to process its electronic home banking transactions internally, Pronto was available for a signing fee of $100,000 plus $10,000 annually for software support plus $1 per month per home banking customer. Alternatively, if the bank wished Chemical to process these transactions, the signing fee was $25,000 while the processing fee was $1,500 per month plus $4 per month per home banking customer. These rates applied only to pilot tests; Chemical executives had not yet settled on a pricing structure for full-fledged systems. The pilot-test licensing agreement contained a clause permitting Chemical to raise fees as new services requiring additional software development were incorporated into Pronto.

Some executives of the Electronic Banking Division believed that licensing might not be the best marketing strategy. As one commented, "We have developed a leading-edge product. We should take it to the nation ourselves as Citibank is going to do with Homebase, and not give half the profits away by licensing the system to banks that may not aggressively market it." This argument was bolstered by the fact that only seven banks had signed commitments, although efforts to secure licensing agreements had been in progress for almost two years. Parker believed that many bankers did not view home banking as an urgent issue. Knowing that they would always be able to obtain a franchise from Chemical or one of its competitors, they saw no need to make an immediate commitment. Reinforcing this conservatism was the estimated cost of $250,000 to $500,000, exclusive of marketing expenditures, to organize and launch a commercially viable system. In addition, industry analysts believed that the implementation of a home banking system would result in higher per transaction costs until between 5 percent and 10 percent of a bank's customers regularly used the system.

Parker was preoccupied with how to increase the number of banks signing licensing agreements. He believed that he had to develop ways to demonstrate Chemical's long-term commitment to home banking. He knew that much would depend upon Chemical's success in launching Pronto to its own retail customers in the fourth quarter of 1983. Several banks were awaiting the preliminary results of this launch. Other banks indicated their willingness to sign licensing agreements but only if they received exclusive rights to Pronto within their market areas. Parker saw several disadvantages to such an arrangement but wondered whether he should consider it and, if so, how geographical exclusivity should change the other terms of the licensing agreement.

Future Pronto Product Development

Since the launch of the pilot field trial, Parker's group of 35 programmers had been working to upgrade Pronto. (This programming staff also worked on BankLink. About half of the staff worked principally on Pronto.) In response to concerns highlighted during the focus groups, the security system had been improved. Each subscriber had to type two passwords to gain access to his or her account information and to make transactions. In addition, a second level of security was encoded in the software that was not even known to the valid user, such that a thief could not readily use a stolen or copied home banking disk to access an account.

The programming team had also worked on improving the user-friendliness of the software. Both the bill-paying service and the home budgeting service had been revised although, subsequently, the use of the latter had not increased. In improving these services, Parker commented that he and his programmers frequently faced the problem of trading off the need for completeness with the desire to avoid complexity. Efforts were also made to adapt Pronto's software so that it could be used by owners of IBM, Apple, and Commodore home computers, as well as Atari models. By September this task was completed for IBM and Apple, but the introduction of new home computers would probably require continuing effort in this area.

Parker believed that home banking services, such as Pronto and Homebase, would come under increasing pressure from videotex system operators offering a full package of services of which home banking was but one. For example, Knight-Ridder's Viewtron system, scheduled to be launched commercially in southern Florida by the end of 1983, offered various transaction services including teleshopping, telebanking, and airline, entertainment, and restaurant reservations, as well as news- and education-oriented information services. Viewtron reached the consumer in alphageometric format with colorful graphics, whereas Pronto used the simpler alphanumeric format that was satisfactory for home banking but was lacking in other applications.

Parker ruled out reprogramming Pronto in alphageometric format, especially since the videotex decoder that a consumer would then have to buy cost at least six times that of the modem required by the current technology. Parker, however, believed that one or more services would have to be added to Pronto in 1984. There were two reasons for this conviction. First, the focus groups suggested that once consumers mastered home banking, they wanted and expected more for their monthly fees. Parker believed that such feelings would be especially strong among consumers who bought home computers primarily to use the Pronto home banking system. Second, Parker believed that both existing and prospective Pronto licensees were waiting to see whether Chemical would be able to further develop Pronto. Even existing licensees could defect to competitive systems if they were not satisfied. Parker estimated that the research and development investment needed to create a comprehensive package of transaction and information services was $12 million, equivalent to Chemical's investment in Pronto to date.

Some of Parker's colleagues advised him that Pronto should stick to home banking alone or, at most, add other financial services such as financial tips, investment advice, tax planning and preparation information, portfolio management, and discount stock brokerage, which they believed would be especially appealing to Pronto's potential licensees.

Parker knew that transaction services, such as stock trading and teleshopping, were more expensive and complex to develop and operate than one-way information services such as the delivery of news. Development costs would be lower and Chemical's merchant customers less annoyed if the bank added a teleshopping service via a gateway link to perhaps, Sears, Roebuck & Co. However, in such a situation, consumers would not be able to pay for purchases directly from their bank accounts and have the transactions immediately recorded in their Pronto files. Besides, if Pronto added services using the gateway approach, it would earn considerably less than if it was able to earn money on the transaction processing and credit authorization as well. In fact, Pronto would earn only the equivalent of a finder's fee and would risk loss of control and a blurring of its overall image.

Parker hesitated to add services that required frequent updating and that were therefore costly to provide (such as weather) and information services that few consumers were willing to pay much for, being used to obtaining them for free.

The Pronto Launch in New York City

Pronto was scheduled to be offered to Chemical customers in New York City at the end of September. A two-month advertising blitz was planned during October and November to build awareness and knowledge of the Pronto system. The campaign targeted college-educated professionals aged 25 to 49 with household incomes over $30,000. As indicated in Exhibit 6, the media plan called for print and television advertising at a cost of $760,000. The schedule attempted to maximize reach to target group members who would be exposed to a Pronto advertisement at least three times during the campaign (see Table B).

The proposed campaign would deliver 62 million impressions at a cost per thousand of $12.24. (A sample print advertisement is presented in Exhibit 7.) Looking ahead to 1984, Lacey tentatively budgeted $1 million for advertising for the entire year.

Besides the introductory advertising campaign, display centers demonstrating the system were to be installed initially in 15 of Chemical's

TABLE B   Advertising Agency's Reach and Frequency Estimates

	Target Group Reach	Average Frequency	Target Gross Rating Points	Reach to Those Exposed at Least Three Times
Print	81%	4.5 times	365	51%
Television	83	3.4	282	41

EXHIBIT 6 Media Schedule for Pronto New York Introduction Advertising Campaign

Week Beginning Monday

	August	September				October					November		
	29	5	12	19	26	3	10	17	24	31	7	14	21
Newspapers													
New York Times				X	X	X	X	X	X		X	X	X
Wall Street Journal (Eastern edition)			X	X	X	X	X	X	X				
Consumer Magazines (full page)													
Business Week (NY metro)				◄────	X ────►			◄────	X				X
Fortune (NY metro)				◄────	────►			◄────	────►	────►			────►
Money (NY metro)				◄────	────►				◄────	────►			────►
National Geographic (NY metro)					X				X			X	
New York				X	X	X		X	X				
NYT Magazine (national)						X				X	X		
Newsweek (NY metro)					X	X	X		◄────	────►		X	X
Signature (NY metro)						X		X		X			
Time (NY metro)				◄────	X ────►	X		X	◄────	X ────►		X	────►
Computer Magazines (full page)													
Antic	◄────	─────	─────	─────	────►								
Atari Connection					◄────	─────	─────	─────	────►				
Local Cable TV (30-second spots)													
CNN (Cable News Network)				◄────	─────	─────	─────	────►					
ESPN (Entertainment and Sports Programming Network)									◄────	─────	─────	─────	────►
Spot TV (30-second spots)													
AM, early and late news, prime time					◄────	─────	─────	─────	────►				

EXHIBIT 7   Pronto Magazine Advertisement

CHEMICAL WOULD LIKE TO OPEN A BRANCH IN YOUR LIVING ROOM.

At Chemical, we've figured out a way to provide banking with all the comforts of home.

ANNOUNCING PRONTO. THE HOME BANKING SYSTEM.

Simply stated, Pronto offers money management and banking services 24 hours a day at home. At your convenience. Not ours.

In fact, with the help of your personal computer, TV and telephone, you'll be able to do most of your banking without ever entering the bank.

For example, with Pronto, you can check your balance. Or check which checks or deposits have cleared. And automatically reconcile your checkbook.

Pay bills to over 350 different merchants and services. Without writing a check or buying a stamp. Or transfer money from one account to another.

There's also a feature called electronic mail. It can answer all your banking questions by putting you in direct contact with our Customer Service staff.

What's more, Pronto's budgeting system allows you to plan and control your finances while keeping track of all your expenses.

And no matter what kind of business you conduct on Pronto, it's strictly your business. You'll be the only one with access to your financial information.

CALL US OR COME IN. FOR A DEMONSTRATION.

To see the new Pronto system in action, come to one of the Chemical Bank locations listed at the bottom of this ad. Or call us toll free at 1-800-782-1000.

Just think, this might be the last time we'll ask you to leave home to go to the bank.

Pronto
THE HOME BANKING SYSTEM FROM CHEMICAL BANK.

MANHATTAN: 100 World Trade Ctr., 756 B'way, 2 Penn Plaza, 277 Park Ave., 1350 Ave. of the Americas, 377 Madison Ave., 11 W. 51st St., 622 W. 168th St. **LONG ISLAND:** 410 Northern Blvd., Great Neck, 350 Main St., Huntington, 10 N. Village Ave., Rockville Centre. **QUEENS:** 107-36 71st Ave., Forest Hills **BKLYN:** 50 Court St. **WESTCHESTER:** 676 White Plains Rd., Eastchester, 222 Mamaroneck Ave., White Plains

largest branches throughout the metropolitan area. These branches together served about 150,000 retail banking customers. Each display booth (see Exhibit 8) cost about $15,000 installed; a one-screen minicenter cost $5,000. These display centers were to be staffed by specially trained sales coordinators who would demonstrate Pronto, answer customer questions, and distribute brochures. Lacey planned to hire initially 20 sales coordinators for a six-month probationary period at a monthly salary of $1,500. He believed that additional sales help could be obtained from an outside agency when needed at $10 per hour. Besides placing display centers in the branches, Lacey was also considering approaching Bloomingdale's electronics department, Computerland, and Crazy

EXHIBIT 8   Pronto Display Center

Eddie's (an electronics discount chain) to place Pronto display centers in their high-traffic stores. He thought that Pronto could be sold when a customer purchased a home computer. He was uncertain, however, whether to offer these retailers Chemical sales coordinators to staff the display centers, a cooperative advertising program, or a straight commission of, perhaps, $15 on each Pronto sale.

Lacey knew that he had to stimulate the enthusiasm of the branch managers and employees besides recruiting and training the right type of sales coordinator. Accordingly, he planned to encourage the branches to identify the customers who matched the Pronto target market profile and to invite them to cocktail parties at which Pronto would be demonstrated by a sales coordinator. The cost of holding such an event outside of regular banking hours attended by 30 people would be about $250. Lacey was also considering a recognition program for branch personnel other than the sales coordinators to motivate them to identify Pronto prospects and close sales.

Lacey had decided to develop three brochures describing Pronto in varying degrees of detail that would be available to consumers according to their degree of interest in the system. He had initially ordered 75,000 fliers at 7 cents each, 75,000 six-page brochures at 57 cents each, and 35,000 brochures costing $3.00, each of which contained application forms and a starter kit. (A short application form was available to current Chemical customers. Non-Chemical customers had to complete a longer application form.) Lacey estimated that 25 percent of the retail customers visiting the 15 branches might pick up a flier and that 5 percent might be seriously interested enough to justify being given the application form. (Lacey had originally hoped to have customers complete application forms in the branches after they visited the display booths. However, logistical constraints plus the fact that many customers did not carry with them all the information necessary to complete the application form prevented this approach. The application form took about 15 minutes to complete.) In addition, depending upon their levels of interest, consumers would be mailed either a brochure or a starter kit after calling the 800 number listed in Pronto's advertising.

Lacey had set the price of Pronto service at $12.00 per month, plus normal banking charges. He estimated the monthly cost of providing Pronto, exclusive of marketing expenditures, at $10 per customer during the first year. Pronto subscribers could purchase a modem from Chemical for $75. Four hundred merchants (who collectively accounted for 70 percent of all bills mailed to consumers in the United States) had agreed to participate in the bill-paying service. (All home banking bill-paying services except Pronto's required subscribers to allow five days from the date they authorized withdrawals from their accounts to pay bills. By September 1983 Chemical had arranged for about 200 merchants to be listed as "instant pay" or "one-day pay.")

Lacey hoped that this marketing program would generate 2,000 sub-scribers by year-end and at least 15,000 by the end of 1984. He was uncertain how many home computers there were in New York City but estimated the number in September 1983 at 225,000, based on a list of Atari owners drawn from warranty cards. (By the end of 1984 industry analysts estimated that there would be over 600,000 home computers in New York City.) Because software permitting IBM, Apple, and Commo-dore owners to access Pronto would be available by early November, Lacey believed that he would then be able to appeal to 90 percent of all home computer owners.

Lacey had been informed by Chemical operations executives that the bank's Tandem computer could handle 300 consumers accessing Pronto at the same time before delays in response time or a computer breakdown would occur. Lacey estimated that the average Chemical retail banking customer would use the system for home banking for two hours during the first week, falling to half an hour by the end of the fourth week. (The average Chemical retail banking customer wrote about 120 checks each year, inquired about his or her balance 20 times, and made 30 transfers between savings and checking accounts.) Installing a second Tandem computer equivalent in capacity to the first would cost about $250,000.

Assuming the Pronto introduction proved successful, Lacey believed that an adaptation of Pronto targeted at small businesses with annual sales of $2 million to $5 million should be considered for 1984. This system would incorporate additional features such as a preauthorized line of credit that could be drawn down on Pronto, discount brokerage service, Treasury bill and certificate of deposit rate information, a general ledger, and consolidated monthly and year-end statements. Customers would be charged according to usage rather than a flat monthly fee.

Product Positioning

3-1 Suzuki Samurai

In June 1985, Leonard Pearlstein, president and CEO of keye/donna/ pearlstein advertising agency, and his colleagues were finalizing the presentation that they would make the next day to Douglas Mazza, vice president and general manager of American Suzuki Motor Corporation (ASMC). Pearlstein's agency was competing with a half-dozen other advertising firms to represent Suzuki's new entrant into the US automobile market, the Suzuki Samurai. Mazza had asked each agency the question: "How do you feel this vehicle should be positioned?" He had given keye/ donna/pearlstein eight days to prepare an answer.

Company Background

Suzuki Loom Works, a privately owned loom manufacturing company, was founded in 1909 in Hamamatsu, Japan, by Michio Suzuki. In 1952, the company began manufacturing and marketing a 2-cycle, 36 cubic centimeter (cc) motorcycle, which became so popular that in 1954 the company introduced a second motorcycle and changed its name to Suzuki Motor Company, Ltd. (Suzuki).

During the late 1950s, lightweight vehicle sales boomed in Japan. Suzuki's motorcycle business grew, and in 1959 it introduced a lightweight van. The van's success encouraged Suzuki to develop lightweight cars and trucks. In 1961, it introduced its first production car, the "Suzulight," the first Japanese car with a 2-stroke engine.

In 1964 Suzuki began exporting motorcycles to the United States, where it established a wholly owned subsidiary, US Suzuki Motor Company, Ltd., to serve as the exclusive importer and distributor of Suzuki motorcycles. Suzuki quickly established itself as a major brand in the US motorcycle industry.

By 1965, Suzuki's product line included motorcycles, automobiles, motorized wheelchairs, outboard motors, general-purpose engines, generators, water pumps, and prefabricated houses. The company concentrated, however, on producing and marketing lightweight vehicles. Until

Research Assistant Tammy Bunn Hiller prepared this case under the supervision of Professor John A. Quelch as the basis for class discussion rather than to illustrate either effective or ineffective handling of an administrative situation. Copyright © 1988 by the President and Fellows of Harvard College. Harvard Business School case 9–589–028.

1979, Suzuki cars and trucks were sold only in Japan, where they were popular as economical transportation. In 1979 Suzuki automobiles were introduced into foreign markets, and by 1984 they were available in over 100 countries and Hawaii.

In 1983, General Motors (GM) purchased 5 percent of Suzuki and helped the company develop a subcompact car for the US market. The car, named the Chevrolet Sprint, was introduced on the West Coast in mid-1984 and was sold exclusively by Chevrolet dealers. The Sprint was Suzuki's first entry into the continental US automobile market. The Sprint was subject to Japan's "voluntary" restraint agreement (VRA) on car shipments to the United States. The VRA, in place since 1981, limited the number of cars that each Japanese automobile manufacturer could ship to the United States in a given year. In 1984, Suzuki's total VRA quota of 17,000 cars went to GM as Sprints. GM quickly sold out of its allotment even though Sprint's distribution was limited to its West Coast dealers.

American Suzuki Motor Corporation (ASMC)

GM's success with Sprint showed Suzuki that a market existed for its cars in the continental United States. Suzuki, which called itself "the always something different car company," planned to introduce several unique vehicles into the US market over time. Suzuki had no guarantee, however, that GM would be willing to market the vehicles. Therefore, Suzuki decided to establish its own presence in the US automobile industry.

Japan's VRA quotas made it impossible for Suzuki to export any cars other than the Sprint to the United States in the foreseeable future. Consequently, in 1985, Suzuki and GM began negotiations with the Canadian government to build a plant in Ontario that could produce approximately 200,000 subcompact cars per year. Suzuki management expected the plant to be on-line by early 1989, and the company could then begin selling cars in the United States under its own name.

Market forces, however, made Suzuki loath to wait until 1989. In 1984, Japanese imports achieved a record 17.7 percent share of US new-car and truck sales. Based on first-quarter sales, industry experts predicted that Japanese imports would command a 19.2 percent share of the US market in 1985. Total US automobile sales were expected to grow by 10 percent in 1985, and this rapid growth made dealers optimistic and willing to invest money in new car lines, especially Japanese brands.

In addition, two other car companies, Hyundai Motor Company of South Korea and Zavodi Crvena Zastava (Yugo) of Yugoslavia, were expected to enter the US car market in 1986. Suzuki managers believed that brand clutter might limit their success if they waited until 1989 to introduce the Suzuki name into the continental United States.

Suzuki management was convinced that the time was right to enter the continental United States and that Suzuki had the right product to do so, the SJ413. Its forerunner, the SJ410, was a mini-4-wheel drive off-road vehicle with a 1,000 cc engine that Suzuki had introduced in 1960. By 1985, the SJ410 was sold in 102 countries and Hawaii. In 1985, Suzuki introduced the SJ413, an upgraded model that featured a 1,324 cc engine and was designed with the US market specifically in mind. The SJ413 was more powerful and more comfortable than the SJ410. The upsizing of Suzuki's vehicle, combined with the downsizing of US consumer automobile preferences, made the SJ413 a viable continental US product.

If the SJ413 was imported without a back seat, the US government classified it as a truck, for customs purposes. Trucks were not subject to Japanese VRA quotas; instead, they were subject to a 25 percent tariff versus a 2.5 percent tariff on cars. The tariff was high, but Suzuki management believed that it was worth paying.

On May 10, 1985, Suzuki hired Douglas Mazza to organize and head its new subsidiary, ASMC. Mazza was charged with developing a Suzuki dealer network to begin selling the SJ413 by November 1985. He was also responsible for creating the marketing plan for the SJ413, which would be named the Suzuki Samurai in the United States, as it was in Canada. Suzuki planned to market two versions of the Samurai in the United States, a convertible and a hardtop.

Samurai Dealer Network

Mazza's goal was to establish ASMC as a major car company in the United States. To achieve this goal, he believed that he had to convince prospective dealers to build separate showrooms for the Samurai. If ASMC allowed a dealer merely to display the vehicle in an existing showroom, the dealer would invest little in the Samurai, monetarily or emotionally, and probably would sell only a few Samurais each month. Low Samurai sales per dealer and lack of facility and management commitment could jeopardize Suzuki's plan to introduce other cars into the United States starting in 1989.

Therefore, Mazza drafted a dealer agreement that required prospective Samurai dealers to build an exclusive sales facility for the Samurai. The facility had to include a showroom, sales offices, and a customer waiting and accessory display area. Service and parts could share a facility with a dealer's other car lines, but a minimum of two service stalls had to be dedicated to Suzuki and operated by Suzuki-trained mechanics. Furthermore, Suzuki dealerships had to display required signs outside the sales office and in the service stalls. A minimum of three salespeople, two service technicians, one general manager, and one general office clerk had to be dedicated to the Suzuki dealership.

The prospectus also explained that, as the product line grew, dealer requirements would expand to include a full, exclusive facility complete with attached parts and service. This up-front expansion plan was a first in the industry and was based on the belief that quick dealer profitability would be key to success—as a dealer's sales opportunities grew, so too would the financial commitment and overhead.

ASMC's planned suggested retail price for the basic Samurai was $5,995. The planned dealer invoice price was $5,095, only 7.5 percent higher than AMC's own landed cost for the vehicle. ASMC planned to offer about 50 dealer-installed options, the sale of which would boost a dealer's average unit profit. Mazza estimated that each dealership would need to sell approximately 30 Samurais per month to cover its monthly operating costs plus the finance charges on its initial investment.

To attract good dealers, Mazza knew that he must make the opportunity match the investment requirements. He therefore planned to limit the number of Samurai dealers so that ASMC could guarantee a minimum supply of 37 units per month to each one. Thus each dealership could earn a profit every month if it sold its total allotment. Suzuki had set Mazza the goal of selling 6,000 Samurais in the first six months of US distribution, but Mazza and his new management team convinced the Japanese management that the US opportunity was far greater. Suzuki raised its commitment to ASMC to 10,500 vehicles for the same time period. Consequently, Mazza decided to limit his initial dealer network to no more than 47 dealers. This small network implied rolling out the Samurai in only two or three states in November 1985. Mazza chose to introduce the Samurai into California, the nation's largest automobile market, and Florida and Georgia, where Japanese import sales were higher than the US average.

Before Mazza could enlist dealers, he had to decide how to position the Samurai to consumers. The position he chose would help define the vehicle's target market which, in turn, would influence ASMC's preferred dealer locations. By combining car registration data and census information, the concentration of owners of imported vehicles or owners of sports utility vehicles, for example, could be pinpointed by zip code. Dealerships could be selected with trading areas that encompassed zip codes with high concentrations of households that fell into Suzuki's target market.

Samurai Positioning

The keye/donna/pearlstein advertising agency had no experience in developing campaigns for automobiles. This appealed to Mazza, because he believed that a fresh approach was needed for his company's new product. After accepting Mazza's offer to compete for the Samurai account, Pearlstein and his associates quickly scanned automobile advertising of other manufacturers. They concluded that industry practice was to position vehicles according to their physical characteristics as, for example, subcompact cars versus compact cars versus luxury sedans. Most advertising was feature/benefit- or price-oriented. A typical ad noted that a vehicle was of a specific type and emphasized differentiating features and/or superior value for the money.

If they followed industry practice, Pearlstein's group had three options for positioning the Samurai based on its physical characteristics—as a compact sport utility vehicle, as a compact pickup truck, or as a subcompact car.

Exhibit 1 shows pictures of the Samurai. The most obvious position for the Samurai was as a sport utility vehicle. It looked like a "mini-Jeep," had 4-wheel drive capability, and was designed to drive well off-road. Such a position would be consistent with the Samurai's heritage and its positioning in the 102 countries where the SJ410 and SJ413 were sold. Foreign owners praised the Samurai's reliability, ability to go places where larger vehicles could not, and ease of repair.

The Samurai's size and price distinguished it from all other sport utility vehicles sold in the United States in 1985. The Samurai was smaller and lighter than the other vehicles, and its $5,995 suggested retail price was well below the other vehicles' $10,000 to $13,000 price range.

Pearlstein believed that if the Samurai were positioned as a sport utility vehicle, it should be advertised as a "tough little cheap Jeep." Advertising copy would show the Samurai in off-road wilderness situations, squeezing through places where bigger sport utility vehicles could not go. Ads would also emphasize that the Samurai cost only half the price of an average Jeep.

Pearlstein was unsure, however, whether a compact sport utility positioning could generate the sales volume that Mazza envisioned for the Samurai. The market for sport utility vehicles was relatively small. As Exhibit 2 shows, total 1984 compact sport utility vehicles sales in the United States were less than 3 percent of total automobile industry sales. Mazza's goal was to build annual US Samurai sales to 30,000 units within two years of the vehicle's introduction. To achieve this objective, annual Samurai sales would have to exceed the combined 1984 sales of all imported compact sport utility vehicles.

The second option, positioning the Samurai as a compact pickup truck, would tap a market that was two and one-half times the size of that for compact sport utility vehicles. Moreover, Japanese import trucks sold well in the United States, accounting for 54 percent of total 1984 compact pickup truck sales. The Samurai could be used as a truck when purchased without a back seat or when its back seat was folded up. Therefore, positioning it as a truck seemed feasible.

ASMC set the Samurai's suggested retail price at $5,995 in order to price it comparably with Japanese import compact pickup trucks, which had a high level of US consumer acceptance. Therefore, in Pearlstein's

---
Exhibit 1   Samurai Convertible and Hardtop

---

view, if advertised as a truck, the Samurai's price would not be emphasized but mentioned only to indicate parity with other truck prices. Advertising copy would probably be serious, practical, male-targeted, and designed to portray the Samurai as a tough truck.

The third option, to position the Samurai as a subcompact car, would open up the largest of the three possible markets. Although the Suzuki SJ413 was not positioned as a car in Europe, a trend was developing in which professionals, especially doctors and lawyers, drove their SJ413s to their offices in the city and left their Mercedeses at home. Similarly, in the United States, especially in California, sport utility vehicles were

EXHIBIT 2   US Automobile Industry Unit Sales

Make	1984 Unit Sales	Projected 1985 Unit Sales
Compact Sport Utility Vehicles		
Suzuki SJ410 (Hawaii)	2,124	2,500
Mitsubishi Montero	2,690	2,800
Toyota 4Runner	9,181	19,300
Toyota Landcruiser	4,170	4,400
Isuzu Trooper	6,935	25,400
Total Japanese import	25,100	54,400
Ford Bronco II	98,446	104,500
GM Chevrolet S10 Blazer/GMC S15 Jimmy	175,177	225,200
Jeep CJ/YJ series	41,627	40,100
Jeep Cherokee/Wagoneer	84,352	113,900
Total domestic	399,710	438,700
Total compact sport utility	424,810	538,100
Compact Pickup Trucks		
Mitsubishi P/U	11,102	21,900
Toyota P/U	144,675	171,500
Nissan P/U	140,864	188,700
Mazda P/U	115,303	114,600
Isuzu P/U	32,372	46,200
Total Japanese import P/U 2WD	444,316	542,900
Jeep Comanche P/U	0	3,800
Ford Ranger P/U	173,959	185,800
Chevy/GMC S10/S15 P/U	181,692	200,200
Dodge Ram 50 P/U	37,356	56,100
Total domestic P/U 2WD	393,007	445,900
Total compact P/U truck 2WD	837,323	988,800
Mitsubishi P/U 4×4	2,156	1,900
Toyota P/U 4×4	81,904	101,400
Nissan P/U 4×4	51,082	65,400
Isuzu P/U 4×4	3,537	4,900
Total Japanese import P/U 4×4	138,679	173,600
Jeep Comanche 4×4	0	4,800
Ford Ranger 4×4	48,110	56,400
Chevy/GMC S10/S15 4×4	47,409	51,200
Dodge Ram 50 P/U 4×4	12,499	12,500
Total domestic P/U 4×4	108,018	124,900
Total compact P/U truck 4×4	246,697	298,500
Total Japanese import P/U 2WD and 4×4	582,995	716,500
Total domestic P/U 2WD and 4×4	501,025	570,800
Total compact P/U 2WD and 4×4	1,084,020	1,287,300

(*continued*)

EXHIBIT 2   *(concluded)*

Make	1984 Unit Sales	Projected 1985 Unit Sales
Subcompact Cars		
Toyota Starlet	781	0
Toyota Tercel	107,185	95,400
Toyota Corolla	156,249	173,900
Nissan Sentra	194,092	225,700
Nissan Pulsar	39,470	51,400
Mitsubishi Mirage	2,354	12,400
Honda Civic	173,561	196,800
Mazda 323/GLC	43,641	60,000
Isuzu I-Mark	4,822	13,000
Total Japanese import	722,155	828,600
Volkswagen Rabbit/Golf	85,153	71,300
Chevrolet Spectrum	1,646	51,700
Chevrolet Sprint	9,464	29,700
Dodge/Plymouth Colt	82,402	96,100
Total domestic	944,668	1,112,900
Total subcompact	1,752,248	2,016,095
Total Car and Truck		
Total Japanese car	1,846,398	2,139,500
Total Japanese truck	664,813	849,800
Total Japanese car and truck	2,511,211	2,989,300
Total industry car	10,128,318	10,888,600
Total industry truck	4,048,998	4,675,200
Total industry car and truck	14,177,316	15,563,800

Note: Sums of individual vehicle makes do not always equal totals and subtotals since only the top-selling makes are listed.

SOURCE: R. L. Polk & Company market area report.

---

sometimes driven in town, although none had hitherto been positioned as a car.

The Samurai boasted an average 28 miles per gallon in combined city and highway driving, was priced lower than many subcompact cars, and offered more versatility. Therefore, it could reasonably be considered by those who were shopping for an economy car. If positioned against subcompact cars, Pearlstein believed that Samurai advertising copy should emphasize the vehicle's looks. The message to consumers would be "Why buy a Toyota Tercel or a Nissan Sentra when, with the same amount of money, you can buy a much cuter vehicle, the Samurai?"

However, the vehicle might not meet consumers' expectations if it was positioned as a car. Because the Samurai was built on a truck platform, its ride was stiffer and less comfortable than even the least-expensive subcompact.

Market Research

Pearlstein defined positioning as "the unique way we want prospects to think about a product." Before choosing a position for the Samurai, he asked Don Popielarz, director of research and planning, to conduct research in order to gain a thorough understanding of not only the attributes that prospective buyers ascribed to the Samurai versus other vehicles but also the profile and characteristics of potential buyers. This information would help Pearlstein decide how to position the vehicle. Then his team could develop advertising copy and choose the media that would be most efficient in delivering the Samurai's message to its consumer target.

Popielarz started by reviewing the latest research available from outside sources. A demographic segmentation study conducted by J. D. Power and Associates divided new-car buyers into demographic segments based on the size/style of the car that was purchased. The "basic small-car" segment included cars such as the Chevrolet Sprint, Ford Escort, Honda Civic, Toyota Tercel, and Mazda 323. Most (54 percent) of the car purchasers in this segment were men, but only 43 percent of the principal drivers were male. The median age of the buyers was 38. The average domestic car buyer was 41, while the average imports car buyer was 36. Sixty percent of the car buyers were married; over one-third had executive/professional/technical careers, and 43 percent were college graduates. The median household size was 2.69 people, and the median household income was $34,240.

From a survey conducted by *Newsweek* for use by pickup truck and sport utility vehicle manufacturers, Popielarz learned how consumers perceived sport utility vehicles versus pickup trucks. Consumers were asked to rate 29 vehicle features of domestic and imported pickup trucks and sport utility vehicles. The features were aggregated into seven factors that were then plotted on two-dimension perceptual maps. The seven factors were everyday driving, off-road/snow driving, passenger comfort, quality/durability, styling, capacity, and gas mileage. Exhibit 3 lists the vehicle features that made up each of the seven factors. Exhibits 4–7 show four maps that summarize consumers' perceptions of pickup trucks versus sport utility vehicles on the seven factors.

After reviewing research from outside sources, Popielarz studied a survey that Suzuki had recently conducted in Canada, where it sold approximately 4,000 Samurais in 1984. Suzuki randomly surveyed 374 Canadian Samurai owners. The majority (75 percent) of the Samurai buyers

EXHIBIT 3 *Newsweek* **Study: Factors and the Features That Constitute Them**

Factor	Feature
Everyday driving	For highway driving
	Acceleration/power
	Riding comfort
	Ease of handling
	Quietness
	Maneuverability in traffic
	For long-distance vacations
	Safety features
	Seating comfort
	Towing capacity
Passenger comfort	Passenger seating capacity
	As a family vehicle
	Interior roominess
	For long-distance vacations
	Seating comfort
	Level of luxury
	Riding comfort
Quality/durability	Quality of workmanship
	Durability/reliability
	Quality of materials
	Tough, rugged
Styling	Interior styling
	Exterior styling
	Design of instrument panel
	Level of luxury
	Ground clearance
Off-road/snow driving	Off-road capability
	For driving in snow
	Ground clearance
	Fun to drive
	Tough, rugged
Capacity	Ability to carry large items
	Cargo capacity
	Towing capacity
Gas mileage	Gas mileage/fuel economy

EXHIBIT 4   Perceptual Map from *Newsweek* Study: Off-Road/Snow Driving versus Everyday Driving

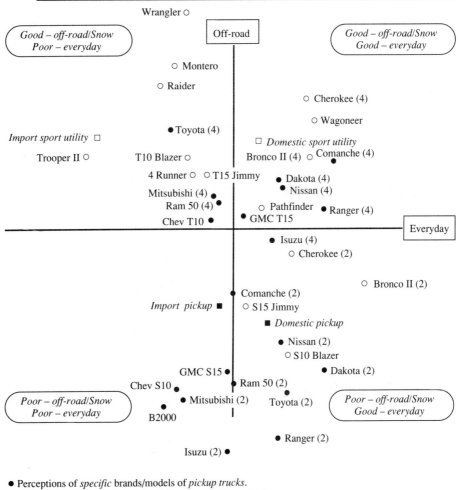

• Perceptions of *specific* brands/models of *pickup trucks.*
○ Perceptions of *specific* brands/models of *sport utility vehicles.*
■ Perceptions of the *category of pickup trucks.*
□ Perceptions of the *category of sport utility vehicles.*

EXHIBIT 5 Perceptual Map from *Newsweek* Study: Passenger Comfort versus Styling

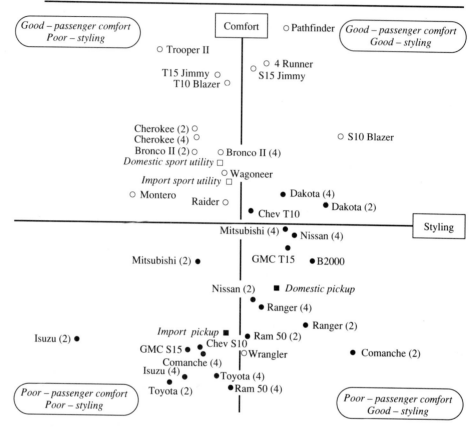

• Perceptions of *specific* brands/models of *pickup trucks*.
○ Perceptions of *specific* brands/models of *sport utility vehicles*.
■ Perceptions of the *category of pickup trucks*.
□ Perceptions of the *category of sport utility vehicles*.

Exhibit 6   Perceptual Map from *Newsweek* Study: Gas Mileage versus Everyday Driving

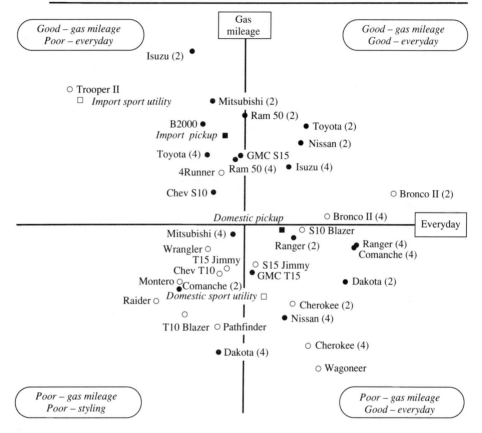

- Perceptions of *specific* brands/models of *pickup trucks.*
○ Perceptions of *specific* brands/models of *sport utility vehicles.*
■ Perceptions of the *category of pickup trucks.*
□ Perceptions of the *category of sport utility vehicles.*

EXHIBIT 7   Perceptual Map from *Newsweek* Study: Quality/Durability versus Passenger Comfort

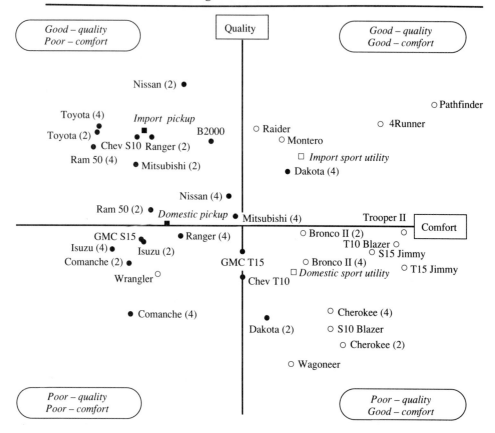

● Perceptions of *specific* brands/models of *pickup trucks*.
○ Perceptions of *specific* brands/models of *sport utility vehicles*.
■ Perceptions of the *category of pickup trucks*.
□ Perceptions of the *category of sport utility vehicles*.

were male, and 62 percent were between the ages of 18 and 34. The average age of the buyers was 33. The most frequently mentioned occupation was a skilled tradesperson (32 percent). Only 21 percent were college graduates, and only 1 percent were currently students. Fifty-one percent of the buyers lived in two-person households, and the average household income was $43,800.

When asked ''When you hear the name Suzuki, what do you think of?'' 40 percent of the Samurai owners responded ''motorcycle.'' Other answers included 4×4/4-wheel drive (23 percent), Jeep (16 percent), Japanese product/efficiency (14 percent), quality/well-made (11 percent), dependable/reliable (10 percent), versatility/work/play/goes anywhere (10 percent), small (9 percent), pleasure vehicle/fun (8 percent), my car (7 percent), and economical (6 percent). When the owners were asked to describe the Samurai using only one word or phrase, the word most often mentioned was "fun." Exhibit 8 lists all the words that were volunteered by five or more owners.

As Exhibit 9 shows, design/appearance was mentioned most frequently by owners as their main reason for purchasing the Samurai. When asked "Before making your purchase, what other automobiles did you consider?" 29 percent mentioned various models of Jeep. Other vehicles mentioned included Ford Bronco and Ranger (24 percent), GMC Chevrolet Jimmy (7 percent), GM Chevrolet 5-10 Blazer (8 percent), Toyota 4×4 pickup truck and Landcruiser (12 percent), and Nissan 4×4 pickup truck (4 percent). No other model was mentioned by as many as 4 percent of the respondents. When asked why they selected the Samurai over their "first alternative" vehicle, the overwhelming response was economy/value (59 percent) followed by design/appearance (29 percent).

Popielarz was unsure how to interpret the data from the Canadian study, given climatic and cultural differences between the United States

---

EXHIBIT 8   Canadian Samurai Buyer Survey: Suzuki Samurai One Word/ Phrase Description

Word/Phrase Mentioned	Number of Mentions
Fun	41
Jeep	15
Great	13
Goes everywhere	11
Good	11
Economical	10
Practical	9
Reliable	8
All-terrain	7
Fantastic	7
Pleasure	7
Tough	7
4-wheel drive	6
4×4	5
Sporty	5
Versatile	5

Note: Samurai buyers were asked, "If you had to describe the Suzuki Samurai using only one word or phrase, what would you say about it?"

EXHIBIT 9 Canadian Samurai Buyer Survey: Reasons for Purchasing Samurai

Main Reason for Purchasing	Percent Mentioning
Design/appearance (net)	64%
4×4/4-wheel drive/jeep	39
Appearance/good-looking/sporty-looking	22
Convertible	19
Size/small/compact	8
Economy/value (net)	55
Economy/economical	18
Good mileage/fuel saving	18
Cost/reasonable price	18
Inexpensive/low price	10
Performance (net)	51
Traction/can go anywhere	19
All-season vehicle/functional	17
Fun/fun to drive	11
Ease of driving/handling/parking	7
Reliable/service (net)	19
Dependable/reliable	13
Quality/well-made/good	7
Need for jeep/second vehicle	8
Suits my life-style/needs/I like it	5

Note: Samurai buyers were asked, "What are your main reasons for purchasing this vehicle?"

and Canada. Furthermore, the Samurai was positioned as a rugged utility vehicle in Canada, where it was priced higher than was planned in the United States. In Canada, the Samurai was priced similar to the least-expensive sport utility vehicles and substantially higher than both light trucks and subcompact cars.

Fortunately, there was one continental US market where Suzuki SJ410s were being sold, albeit unauthorized by Suzuki. In Florida, a "gray market" existed for Suzuki SJ410s. Since 1984, approximately 3,000 had been sold there by dealers who imported them from other Suzuki markets, including Puerto Rico, Guam, the US Virgin Islands, and Panama.

Popielarz and Tim O'Mara, one of the agency's account supervisors, decided to conduct face-to-face interviews with five sales managers and sales representatives at three Florida dealerships that sold SJ410s. They asked the salespeople four questions. The first question was "Who is the buyer?" The dealers said the SJ410 buyer was young, on average between 18 and 30 years old, often single, often a first-time car buyer, and often a student. Young women seemed to like the vehicle, and many sales involved fathers buying SJ410s for their children. Additionally, there was an important secondary buyer group comprising people over 30, both single and married, who bought the Suzuki to use as a third or fourth vehicle.

The second question, "What does the buyer see as competition?" elicited a unanimous response from the dealers. There was no direct competition. Indirect competition included 4-wheel drive vehicles, small cars, and convertibles. The SJ410 was less expensive than other convertibles and 4-wheel drive vehicles, however, and was more "fun and (had more) style than small cars."

"Why does the buyer want this vehicle?" was the third question the dealers addressed. The "most fun for the dollars" was usually mentioned. As one sales manager stated, "I don't see too many people driving down the road in Chevettes and having a blast." Other replies included convertible top; versatility; utility; gas mileage; durability; cute and unique; handles in rain, snow, and off-road; and great for fishing, camping, and skiing.

The final question, "How are they selling?" prompted smiles from the salespeople, who typically responded, "People were just lining up to get them. Just couldn't get enough of them in." The SJ410s sold for an average price of $8,500 at the three dealerships.

One of the dealerships, King Motors in Fort Lauderdale, routinely surveyed its automobile buyers. The dealership had surveys completed by 150 recent Suzuki SJ410 buyers, which it allowed Popielarz and O'Mara to study. The vehicle buyer filled out the questionnaire; however, in many instances, the buyer was not the ultimate driver. Information on age was incomplete, but of those who gave their age, 56 percent of the buyers were between 18 and 30; the rest were over 30. One-third of the purchasers were women.

Exhibit 10 tabulates the King Motors survey responses. The majority of buyers learned about the Suzuki through word of mouth or seeing it when driving by the dealership. Most buyers came to King Motors planning to buy the Suzuki rather than the AMC Jeep line, which was also sold there. Fewer than half of the buyers considered buying another vehicle but when other automobiles were considered, they included both new and used Jeeps, small imported cars, and large used American convertibles.

Four-wheel drive was not the principal feature generating interest in the Suzuki. Only 45 percent of the men and 32 percent of the women surveyed said that it was an important factor in their purchase decision. The attributes that buyers rated as most important were price and the fact that it was a convertible model.

Popielarz knew that the Florida buyers who participated in the survey might not be typical of the kinds of people who would buy the Samurai once it was introduced nationwide. He did believe, however, that the survey results gave clues about who the early adopters were likely to be.

EXHIBIT 10   King Motors' Suzuki SJ410 Buyer Survey

	Total	*Total Men*	*Total Women*
Where heard about Suzuki			
Word of mouth	41%	41%	42%
Dealer location	30	36	22
Ft. Lauderdale newspaper	20	17	24
Radio	6	5	7
Pompano Shopper	3	1	5
Came to dealer to see			
Suzuki	76	75	77
AMC Jeep	17	21	14
Encore	1	0	2
Alliance	0	0	0
Wagoneer	0	0	0
Other	5	4	7
Considered other vehicle			
Yes	40	42	37
No	60	58	63
Considered AMC Jeep first			
Yes	28	30	25
No	72	70	75
Important purchase factors			
Price	76	72	80
Convertible	62	59	66
Gas mileage	46	46	45
4-wheel drive	40	45	32
Size of vehicle	39	37	41
Color	22	26	18
Driving and handling	20	22	16
Other	7	9	5

After interviewing the Florida dealers, Popielarz and O'Mara conducted focus group interviews in California with a group of women aged 25 to 33, a group of men aged 18 to 24, and another group of men aged 25 to 35. All of the participants were actively shopping for a new vehicle that was either a sport utility vehicle, a subcompact car, or an imported pickup truck. All had visited at least one dealer showroom within the previous two months.

During the sessions, focus group members viewed pictures of both the convertible and hardtop Samurais that would be sold in the United States, pictures of a variety of people who might drive the Samurai, a five-minute videotape showing the Samurai in action, and pictures of several vehicles with which the Samurai might compete. Respondents reacted favorably to the Samurai's appearance, describing it as "cute," "neat," and "fun." The Samurai's size invoked mixed reactions. Some believed its size would add to its drivability and maneuverability; they said it looked easy to drive around town and in the country. For others, especially those with children or pets, the small size was a drawback. Also, those who planned rugged off-road use said the Samurai was too small.

Group members who needed occasional 4-wheel drive capability readily accepted the Samurai as a viable alternative to other 4-wheel drive vehicles. Those people who did not need the 4-wheel drive feature said that it did not reduce their acceptance of the vehicle.

Some people said that the Samurai was exactly what they were looking for in a vehicle. They saw it as a symbol of their independence to do something different and their practicality to drive a versatile vehicle. Interest in the Samurai among focus group members appeared to be linked more to attitude than to age. When asked to choose potential Samurai buyers from the pictures that were shown to them, the interviewees chose the younger, more active people.

Most of the interviewees recognized the Suzuki name and associated it with motorcycles or the attributes of the Japanese manufacturers, that is, higher quality and better engineering than the domestic competition. Their price expectations were between $8,000 and $12,000, significantly higher than the planned $5,995 price tag. They were quite knowledgeable, however, about the prices of the competitive vehicles discussed. When told the Samurai's actual price, most people expressed surprise and pleasure. A few expressed suspicion about the vehicle's quality at that price.

Conclusions

Popielarz and O'Mara reviewed the market research findings with Pearlstein and Spike Bragg, the agency's executive vice president. They concluded that any young or young-at-heart person considering the purchase of a small car, small truck, or sport utility vehicle was a prospect for the Samurai. Suzuki should avoid positioning the Samurai as a specific type of vehicle so as not to exclude large groups of potential buyers.

Furthermore, they reasoned that Suzuki should not "overdefine" the vehicle. The Samurai appeared to represent different things to different people. Therefore, Suzuki should try to develop a position with broad enough appeal to attract a wide range of consumers so that each person could define the Samurai in his or her own way and rationalize the purchase decision in his or her own terms. Moreover, the ad agency thought that if each consumer was allowed to personally define the Samurai, this would lead to greater congruence between the vehicle's promise and its delivery than if Suzuki tried to tell consumers what the Samurai was.

Bragg suggested that the Samurai be positioned as "the alternative to small-car boredom." He reasoned that sport utility buyers could be attracted to the Samurai just by looking at the vehicle but that small-car buyers would need to be told that the Samurai was a fun alternative to dull automobiles. Furthermore, he believed that many purchasers of small trucks were buying them to use as cars because compact import pickup trucks were less expensive than import subcompact cars and offered more versatility. An "alternative to small-car-boredom" positioning could, therefore, attract buyers from all three vehicle segments.

Pearlstein liked Bragg's idea but expanded on it. He thought that the Samurai should be positioned as the "antidote to traditional transportation." It was important that the Samurai not be labeled as any type of vehicle. No ads should refer to it as a car, truck, or sport utility vehicle.

FINAL PREPARATIONS FOR PRESENTATION TO MAZZA

Pearlstein and his associates had to present their positioning recommendations to Mazza the following day. Although Mazza had not asked to be shown any creative execution of the position, the four men had developed copy that they believed would help to explain the "antidote-to-traditional-transportation" position that they had chosen. Exhibits 11 through 16 show examples of their proposed advertising copy.

Mazza had told Pearlstein that he planned to spend $2.5 million on advertising and promotion during the first six months after the Samurai's introduction. For 1985, estimated Jeep advertising was $40 million for the American market. Industry experts expected total 1985 car, truck, and sport utility vehicle advertising expenditures in the United States to approximate $4.25 billion. Traditionally, automobile manufacturers spent between $200 and $400 per vehicle on advertising and up to an additional $500 per vehicle on incentives such as rebates and extended warranties.

Pearlstein and his group had to recommend how the Samurai's advertising budget should be spent. A typical automobile manufacturer spent 77 percent of its advertising dollars on television ads, 10 percent on radio commercials to add frequency to the television schedule, 10 percent on print ads, and 3 percent on highway billboards. The print ads were to run in both general-interest magazines and enthusiast magazines—depending on the vehicle's positioning as a car, truck, or sport utility vehicle.

Pearlstein addressed his colleagues:

> If we are to win the ASMC account, tomorrow we must sell our Samurai positioning strategy to Mazza. To sell it to him, we must be convinced that it is the best positioning for the Samurai. Let's now discuss the pros and cons of the "unposition" we are proposing versus the three options we originally considered. We must be able to back up our positioning recommendation with sound market research data. We must address any risks associated with our recommended positioning. Finally, we must develop a recommendation on how to spend the $2.5 million six-month advertising budget. We should discuss how our budget allocation recommendations would vary according to the positioning strategy chosen.

EXHIBIT 11   **"End of Dull" Proposed Print Ad**

The end of dull.
The start of Suzuki.

Introducing the Suzuki Samurai.™ The end of dull, point and steer, econo-box
driving. The start of 4x4 versatility in a new compact size all its own, convertible or
hard top. With a nifty 1.3 liter, SOHC, 4-cylinder engine, 5-speed stick, and room for four.
The price? Low. The place? Where there's never a dull moment. Your Suzuki
automotive dealer. See him for a Samurai test drive today.

EXHIBIT 12 "Dull Barrier" Proposed Print Ad

Stop suffering the heartbreak of econo-box boredom. Get quick relief where there's never a dull moment. Your Suzuki auto dealer.

Take one test drive in a Suzuki Samurai™ and you, too, will break the dull barrier. The Samurai handles differently than an ordinary passenger car. Avoid sharp turns and abrupt maneuvers, and always wear your seat belt. For specific details, read your owner's manual.

SUZUKI SAMURAI BREAKS

THE DULL BARRIER

(DEALER NAME)

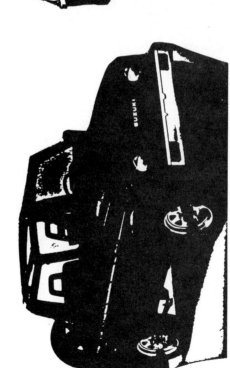

167

EXHIBIT 14   Copy for Proposed Television Ad

Setting:	A road leading from awesome mountains.
Atmosphere:	Dawn. Mysterious electrical storm flashes over the mountains. Something is about to happen. Something strange or wondrous.
What happens:	We see headlights approaching camera. From the dramatic music and overblown announcer, whatever's coming must be magnificent. Then the little Suzuki drives by at a casual speed. People inside wave to camera, giggle, car drives out of frame. Camera does double take, then watches car drive away.
(Dramatic music begins)	
Voice over:	"Prepare for the most extraordinary event of your lifetime . . ."
(Music builds)	
	"An event that will forever alter the course of mankind and womankind . . ."
(Music builds)	
	"The next major turning point in the history of all civilization."
(Music crescendos, then stops) (Beep, beep)	
People in the car:	"Hi!"
(Music continues)	
Voice over:	"Introducing the new Suzuki Samurai 4×4."
(Fades)	"The beginning of the universe was dull by comparison . . . The discovery of fire pales in significance."
(Live announcer dealer tag)	

EXHIBIT 15 Storyboard for Proposed "Dull Barrier" Television Ad

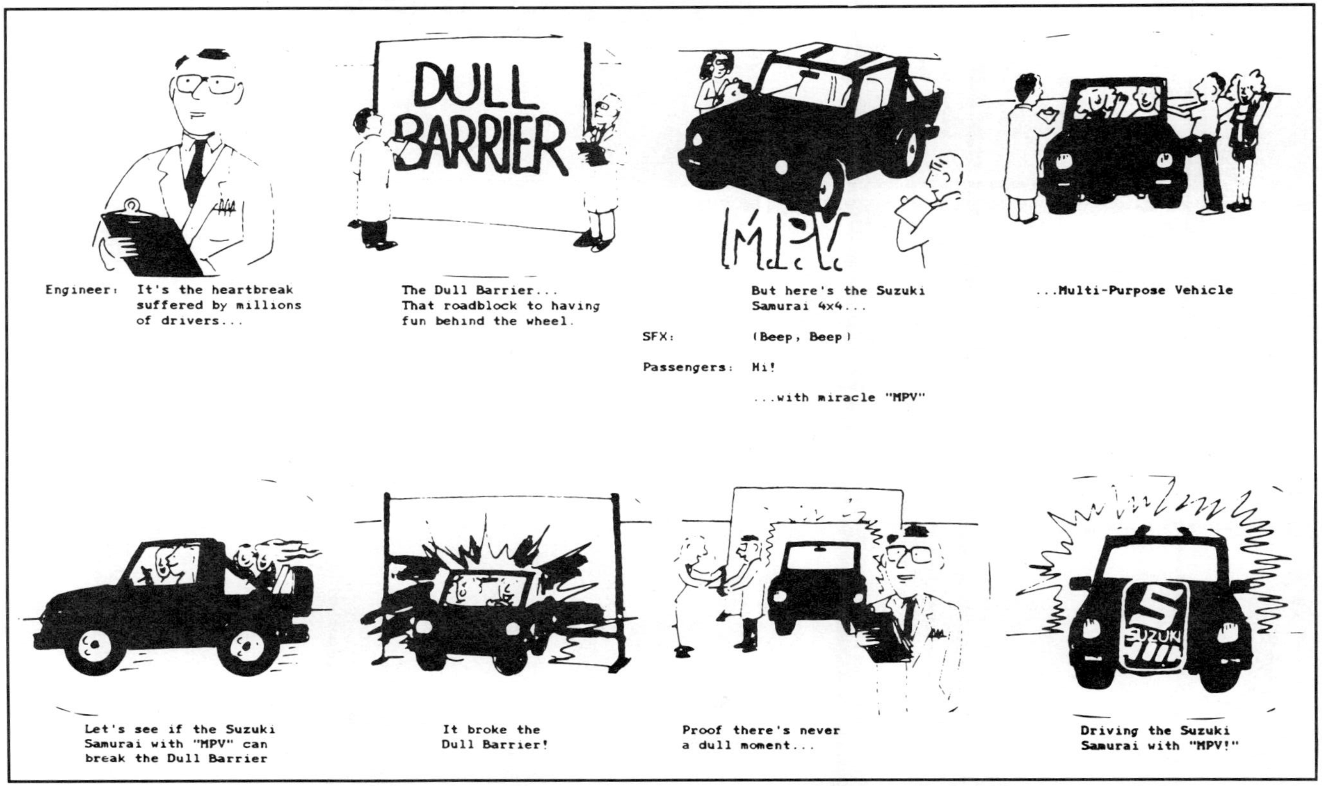
DULL BARRIER
MPV
Engineer: It's the heartbreak suffered by millions of drivers...
The Dull Barrier... That roadblock to having fun behind the wheel.
But here's the Suzuki Samurai 4x4...
SFX: (Beep, Beep)
Passengers: Hi!
...with miracle "MPV"
...Multi-Purpose Vehicle
Let's see if the Suzuki Samurai with "MPV" can break the Dull Barrier
It broke the Dull Barrier!
Proof there's never a dull moment...
SUZUKI
Driving the Suzuki Samurai with "MPV!"

EXHIBIT 16 Storyboard for Proposed "Amusement Park" Television Ad

Colgate-Palmolive Company: The Precision Toothbrush

In August 1992, Colgate-Palmolive (CP) was poised to launch a new toothbrush in the US, tentatively named Colgate Precision. CP's Oral Care division had been developing this technologically superior toothbrush for over three years but now faced a highly competitive market with substantial new product activity.

Susan Steinberg, Precision product manager, had managed the entire new product development process and now had to recommend positioning, branding, and communication strategies to division general manager Nigel Burton.

Company Background

With 1991 sales of $6.06 billion and a gross profit of $2.76 billion, CP was a global leader in household and personal care products. Total worldwide research and development expenditures for 1991 were $114 million and media advertising expenditures totalled $428 million.

CP's five year plan for 1991 to 1995 emphasized new product launches and entry into new geographic markets, along with improved efficiencies in manufacturing and distribution and a continuing focus on core consumer products. In 1991, $243 million was spent to upgrade 25 of CP's 91 manufacturing plants, 275 new products were introduced worldwide, several strategic acquisitions (e.g., the Mennen men's toiletries company, completed in 1992) were completed, and manufacturing began in China and Eastern Europe. Mr. Reuben Mark, CP's CEO since 1984, had been

Research Associate Nathalie Laidler prepared this case under the supervision of Professor John A. Quelch as the basis for class discussion rather than to illustrate either the effective or ineffective handling of an administrative situation. Proprietary data have been disguised. Copyright © 1993 by the President and Fellows of Harvard College. Harvard Business School case 9–593–064.

widely praised for his leadership in transforming a "sleepy and inefficient" company into a lean and profitable one. Since 1985, gross margins had climbed from 39 percent to 45 percent while annual volume growth since 1986 had averaged 5 percent. Although international sales remained CP's strong suit, accounting for 64 percent of sales and 67 percent of profits in 1991, the company faced tough competition in international markets from Procter & Gamble, Unilever, Nestle's L'Oreal division, Henkel of Germany, and Kao of Japan.

Colgate-Palmolive's Oral Care Business

In 1991, CP held 43 percent of the world toothpaste market and 16 percent of the world toothbrush market. Other oral care products included dental floss and mouth rinses. A team of 170 CP researchers worked on new technologies for oral care products, and in 1991 new products launched in the US market included Colgate Baking Soda toothpaste and the Colgate Angle and Wild Ones toothbrushes.

In 1991, worldwide sales of CP's oral care products increased 12 percent to $1.3 billion, accounting for 22 percent of CP's total sales. CP's US toothbrush sales in 1991 reached $77 million with operating profits of $9.8 million. Toothbrushes represented 19 percent of CP's US Oral Care division sales and profits and CP held the number one position in the US retail toothbrush market with a 23.3 percent volume share.

Exhibit 1 presents operating statements for CP's US toothbrush business since 1989. CP offered two lines of toothbrushes in 1991, the Colgate Classic and the Colgate Plus. Colgate Classic was positioned in the "value" segment and was CP's original entry in the toothbrush market while Colgate Plus was positioned as a higher quality product in the "professional" segment.

The US Toothbrush Market

As early as 3000 BC, ancient Egyptians used toothbrushes fashioned from twigs. In the twentieth century, a major design advance occurred in 1938 with the launch of Dr. West's Miracle Tuft Toothbrush, the first nylon-bristle brush. In the late 1940s, Oral-B began selling a soft-bristle brush which was better for the gums and, in 1961, Broxodent launched the first electric toothbrush.[1] Until the late 1970s, toothbrushes were widely viewed by consumers as a commodity and were purchased primarily on price. More recently, new product launches had increased and perfor-

---

[1] As of 1991, electric toothbrushes were used by only 6 percent of US households.

EXHIBIT 1   **Income Statements for Colgate-Palmolive Toothbrushes: 1989–1992**

	1989		1990		1991		1992E	
Unit sales (000s)	55,296		63,576		70,560		78,336	
Net sales ($000s)	$43,854	(100%)	$57,248	(100%)	$77,001	(100%)	$91,611	(100%)
Cost of sales	23,988	(55)	28,190	(49)	36,827	(48)	44,846	(49)
Total fixed overhead	4,429	(11)	6,304	(11)	10,007	(13)	11,423	(12)
Total advertising								
Media	3,667	(8)	6,988	(12)	8,761	(11)	9,623	(11)
Consumer promotions	4,541	(10)	5,893	(10)	5,286	(7)	6,978	(8)
Trade promotions	3,458	(8)	4,134	(7)	6,287	(8)	7,457	(8)
Operating profit	3,744	(9)	5,739	(10)	9,833	(13)	11,284	(12)

SOURCE: Company records.

mance benefits had become increasingly important purchase criteria. Exhibit 2 summarizes new product introductions in the category since 1980.

In 1991, the US oral care market was $2.9 billion in retail sales and had grown at an annual rate of 6.1 percent since 1986. Toothpaste accounted for 46 percent of this market, mouth rinses 24 percent, toothbrushes 15.5 percent ($453 million in retail sales), with dental floss and other products making up the remainder. Dollar sales of toothbrushes had grown at an average rate of 9.3 percent per annum since 1987, but, in 1992, they increased by 21 percent in value and 18 percent in volume, due to the introduction of 47 new products and line extensions during 1991–92. In the same period, media support increased by 49 percent and consumer coupon circulation by 48 percent. Consumers took more interest in the category and increased their purchase frequency. The trade, for whom toothbrushes represented a profitable, high-margin business, responded by increasing in-store promotional support and advertising features. Dollar growth exceeded volume growth due to the emergence of a super-premium subcategory of toothbrushes partly offset by downward pressure on average retail prices in mass merchandiser channels and because of growth in the sales of private label toothbrushes. Unit sales growth in 1993, however, was projected to be slower due to a buildup in household inventories of toothbrushes in 1992 as a result of increased sampling of free brushes through dentists and an abnormally high number of "two-for-one" consumer promotions.

Product Segments

In the 1980s, industry executives divided the toothbrush category into two segments: value and professional. Many consumers traded up to professional, higher-priced toothbrushes with a resulting erosion of the

---
EXHIBIT 2 Chronology of Toothbrush Innovations in the US

Date	New Product Introductions	Main Feature
1950s	Oral-B Classic	Traditional square head
1977	Johnson & Johnson Reach	First angled handle
1985	Colgate Plus	First diamond-shaped head
1986	Lever Bros. Aim	Slightly longer handle
1988	Johnson & Johnson Prevent	Aids brushing at 45° angle.
	Colgate Plus Sensitive Gums	Softer bristles
1989	Pepsodent	"Commodity" brush
	Oral-B Ultra	Improved handle
1990	J&J Neon Reach	Neon-colored handle
	Oral-B Art Series	Cosmetic feature
1991	Colgate Plus Angle Handle	Diamond-shaped and angled handle
	Colgate Plus Wild Ones	Cosmetic feature
	J&J Advanced Reach Design	Rubber-ridged, nonslip handle
	Oral-B Indicator	Bristles change color
	Aquafresh Flex	Flexible handle neck
	Pfizer Plax	Groove for thumb
1992	Crest Complete	Rippled bristles
	Colgate Precision	Triple-action bristles

SOURCE: Company records.

value segment despite growth in private label sales. The late 1980s saw the emergence of super-premium brushes (priced above $2.00). By 1992, super-premium brushes, with retail prices between $2.29 and $2.89, accounted for 35 percent of unit volume and 46 percent of dollar sales. Professional brushes, priced between $1.59 and $2.09, accounted for a corresponding 41 percent and 42 percent, and value brushes, priced on average at $1.29, accounted for 24 percent and 12 percent.

In 1992, three players dominated the US toothbrush market overall; Colgate-Palmolive and Johnson & Johnson, whose brushes were positioned in the professional segment; and Oral-B, whose brushes were positioned in the super-premium segment. New entrants in the early 1990s included Procter & Gamble and Smithkline Beecham who had positioned their new product launches in the super-premium segment. Table A profiles the principal new products offered in the super-premium toothbrush segment in 1992.

Toothbrushes differed further by bristle type (firm, medium, soft, and extra soft) and by head size (full/adult, compact, and child/youth). Firm bristle brushes accounted for 8 percent of toothbrushes sold but were declining at 13 percent a year. Medium bristle brushes accounted for 39 percent and were declining at 4 percent a year. Soft bristle brushes held a

Major New Products in the Super-Premium Toothbrush Segment

Product/ Manufacturer	Feature	Benefit	Reason	Tag-line	Launch date	No. of SKUs
Oral-B Indicator Oral-B (Gillette)	Indicator bristles	Tells you when to change toothbrush	Blue band fades halfway; dental heritage	The brand more dentists use	7/91	4 adult
Reach Advanced Design Johnson & Johnson	Angled neck; raised rubber ridges on handle	Cleans in even the hardest-to-reach places	Slimmed down, tapered head	Feel the difference	8/91	3 adult
Crest Complete Procter & Gamble	Rippled bristle design. Handle with rubber grip	Reaches between teeth like a dental tool	Rippled end-rounded bristles	Only Crest could make a brush this complete	8/91 (test) 9/92 (national)	10 adult
Aquafresh Flex Smithkline Beecham	Pressure sensitive, flexible neck linking brush and handle	Prevents gum irritation	Flexes as you brush	For gentle dental care	8/91 (Flex) 9/92 (line extension)	6 adult 1 child

48 percent market share and were growing at 7 percent per year. Extra-soft bristle brushes held only a 5 percent share but were growing even more rapidly. Sixty-nine percent of toothbrushes were sold with adult, full-sized heads, 17 percent had compact heads, and 13 percent had child/youth sized heads.

In the late 1980s, many new toothbrushes were introduced on the basis of aesthetic rather than functional features. The children's segment in particular had seen a variety of new products. For example, in 1988 and 1989 new toothbrushes targeting children featured sparkling handles, Bugs Bunny and other characters, and glow-in-the-dark handles. By 1991, however, new product introductions were again focused on technical performance improvements such as greater plaque removal and ease of use.

Consumer Behavior

CP's consumer research indicated that consumers of the baby boom generation (adults born in the 1940s, 1950s, and early 1960s) were becoming more concerned about the health of their gums as opposed to cavity prevention and were willing to pay a premium for new products addressing this issue. CP estimated that 82 percent of toothbrush purchases were unplanned and research showed that consumers were relatively unfamiliar with toothbrush prices. Although consumers were willing to experiment with new toothbrushes, they replaced their brushes on average only once every 7.5 months in 1991 (versus 8.6 months in 1990) while dental professionals recommended replacement every three months. Due to the prevalence of "two-for-one" offers, purchase frequency lagged replacement frequency with consumers purchasing toothbrushes once every 11.6 months in 1991 (up from 12.4 months in 1990 and estimated at 9.7 months for 1992).[2] Unlike toothpaste, toothbrushes were not typically shared by members of the same household.

Most consumers agreed that toothbrushes were as important as toothpaste to effective oral hygiene and that the primary role of a toothbrush was to remove food particles; plaque removal and gum stimulation were considered secondary. Proper brushing was seen as key to the prevention of most dental problems. According to CP research, 45 percent of consumers brushed before breakfast, 57 percent after breakfast, 28 percent after lunch, 24 percent after dinner, and 71 percent before bed. Forty-eight percent of consumers claimed to change their brush at least every three months; the trigger to purchase a new brush for 70 percent of them was when their toothbrush bristles became visibly worn. Eleven percent decided to switch to a new brush after seeing their dentists and only 3 percent admitted to purchasing on impulse.[3] Sixty-five percent of consumers had more than one toothbrush, 24 percent kept a toothbrush at work, and 54 percent had a special toothbrush for traveling.

Brand choice was based on features, comfort, and professional recommendations. Exhibit 3 summarizes the main reasons why consumers used specific brands. Consumers chose a brush to fit their individual needs: size and shape of the mouth, sensitivity of gums, and personal brushing style. The handle, bristles, and head shape were perceived to be the most important physical features of a toothbrush.

Consumers differed in the intensity of their involvement in oral hygiene. Table B summarizes the buying behavior of the three groups. Therapeutic brushers aimed to avoid oral care problems while cosmetic brushers emphasized preventing bad breath and/or ensuring white teeth. Uninvolved consumers were not motivated and adjusted their behavior only when confronted by oral hygiene problems.

---

[2] In 1992, consumers purchased toothbrushes more frequently than in 1991.

[3] Dentists played a significant role, both as a source of information on proper brushing techniques and as a distributor of toothbrushes. At any time, one in four consumers was using a toothbrush given to them by a dentist.

EXHIBIT 3   Brand Decision Factors for Consumers

Main Reasons for Using a Brand	Percent of Consumers
Fits most comfortably in my mouth	63%
Best for getting at hard-to-reach places	52
The bristles are the right softness	46
The bristles are the right firmness	36
Toothbrush my dentist recommends	35
Important part of my oral care regimen	30

NOTE: Respondents could check multiple items.
SOURCE: Company records.

TABLE B   Consumer Segmentation of Toothbrush Users

Involved Oral Health Consumers—Therapeutic Brushers (46% of adults)	Involved Oral Health Consumers—Cosmetic Brushers (21% of adults)	Uninvolved Oral Health Consumers (33% of adults)
Differentiate among products; search out functionally effective products	Search for products that effectively deliver cosmetic benefits	View products as the same; lack of interest in product category
Buy and use products for themselves	Buy and use products for themselves	Buy and use products for all family members
85% brush at least twice a day, 62% use a professional brush, and 54% floss regularly	85% brush twice a day, 81% use mouthwash, 54% use breath fresheners, 69% floss, 54% use a professional brush	20% brush once a day or less, 28% use only regular toothbrushes, 54% floss, and 66% use mouthwash
Major toothbrush brands used are Oral-B Angle and Oral-B Regular followed by Colgate Plus and Reach	Major toothbrush brands used are Colgate Classic and Oral-B Regular followed by Colgate Plus and Oral-B Angle	Major toothbrush brands used are Colgate Classic and Oral-B Regular followed by Colgate Plus and Reach

Competition

Exhibit 4 lists the major brands and product prices for each of the three toothbrush product segments. Exhibit 5 shows the number and type of stockkeeping units (SKUs) for each major brand and Exhibits 6 and 7 summarize market shares over time and by class of trade. Major competitor brands in the super-premium segment included Oral-B, Reach Advanced Design, Crest Complete, and Aquafresh Flex.

EXHIBIT 4   Toothbrush Brand Prices: 1992

	Manufacturer's List Price	Manufacturer's Net Price	Average Retail Selling Price (food channel)
Super-premium			
Oral-B Indicator	$2.13	$1.92	$2.65
Oral-B Regular	1.85	1.78	2.51
Crest Complete	1.67	1.67	2.40
Reach Advanced	1.75	1.66	2.38
Aquafresh Flex	1.85	1.61	2.32
Professional			
Colgate Plus	1.42	1.35	2.00
Reach Regular	1.37	1.30	2.01
Pepsodent Professional	1.20	1.08	1.88
Value			
Colgate Classic	0.69	0.69	1.22
Pepsodent Regular	0.91	0.48	1.25

NOTE: Net price was the effective manufacturer's price to retailers after a variety of discounts.
SOURCE: Company records.

EXHIBIT 5   Principal Toothbrush Brand Product Lines: August 1992

	Number of Stockkeeping Units	
Brand	Adult	Child/Teen
Colgate	28	8
Oral-B	16	5
Reach	14	4
Crest Complete	10	0
Aquafresh Flex	6	1
Lever	7	2
Plax	2	1
Total	83	21

SOURCE: Company records.

Oral-B (owned by Gillette) had been the market leader since the 1960s. In 1991, it held a 23.1 percent volume market share and a 30.7 percent value share of US retail sales with 27 SKUs. Oral-B relied heavily on professional endorsements and was known as "the dentist's toothbrush." In July 1991, Oral-B launched the Indicator brush, priced at a 15 percent premium to its other brushes. The Indicator brush had a patch of

EXHIBIT 6 **Principal Toothbrush Brand Unit and Dollar Market Shares: 1989–1992E**

Brand	1989 Volume (%)	1989 $ Share (%)	1990 Volume (%)	1990 $ Share (%)	1991 Volume (%)	1991 $ Share (%)	1992E Volume (%)	1992E $ Share (%)
Colgate								
Plus	12.0%	12.6%	13.7%	15.2%	16.9%	18.5%	17.3%	18.5%
Classic	8.5	6.6	8.1	6.2	6.4	4.9	4.9	2.9
Total	20.5	19.2	21.8	21.4	23.3	23.4	22.2	21.4
Oral-B								
Oral-B Indicator	0.0	0.0	0.0	0.0	1.0	1.3	3.7	4.9
Total	24.0	31.7	24.5	32.6	23.1	30.7	19.8	26.2
J&J								
Reach	18.1	20.5	18.2	20.0	18.5	20.9	19.2	21.0
Reach Advanced Design	0.0	0.0	0.0	0.0	0.7	0.9	4.0	5.2
Prevent	2.5	2.7	1.6	1.9	0.7	1.1	0.2	0.1
Total	20.6	23.2	19.8	21.9	19.4	21.8	19.4	21.1
Lever	10.5	10.4	9.8	9.0	7.2	6.6	5.0	4.0
Crest	0.0	0.0	0.0	0.0	0.0	0.0	2.0	2.6
Aqua-Fresh	0.0	0.0	0.0	0.0	0.9	1.1	4.6	5.7
Butler	NA	NA	NA	NA	2.0	2.4	2.0	2.2
Private label	NA	NA	NA	NA	11.2	5.9	11.5	6.1

NOTE: NA = not available.
SOURCE: Company records.

EXHIBIT 7 **Principal Toothbrush Brand Unit and Dollar Market Shares by Class of Trade: 1991**

	Food Volume (%)	Food $ Share (%)	Drug Volume (%)	Drug $ Share (%)	Mass Volume (%)	Mass $ Share (%)
Colgate						
Plus	18.9%	21.3%	9.6%	11.4%	29.3%	31.4%
Classic	7.0	4.8	4.5	3.7	3.9	3.2
Total	25.9	26.1	14.1	15.1	33.2	34.6
Oral-B						
Oral-B Indicator	0.9	1.1	1.0	1.5	0.7	0.9
Total	20.5	28.2	25.1	34.1	22.4	27.6
J&J						
Reach	22.3	23.8	14.3	16.6	18.3	20.7
Reach Advanced Design	1.2	N/A	0.3	0.4	0.3	0.4
Prevent	0.8	1.2	0.8	0.9	0.5	0.6
Total	23.2	25.0	15.1	17.5	18.8	21.4
Lever	9.1	8.9	5.8	5.6	6.3	7.4
Crest (TX test market)	5.1	6.5	0.0	0.0	0.0	N/A
Aqua-Fresh	4.9	N/A	0.4	0.5	0.3	0.5
Butler	1.3	2.0	3.5	6.6	0.5	0.9
Private label	10.7	5.5	17.4	10.6	4.4	2.4

SOURCE: Company records.

blue bristles that faded to white when it was time for replacement (usually after two to three months). In 1992, consumer promotions were expected to cost $4.5 million (5 percent of sales) and include $1.00-off coupons, "buy-one-get-one-free" offers, and $2.00 mail-in refunds. Media expenditures for 1992 were estimated at $11.2 million (12.7 percent of sales). Television commercials would continue to feature "Rob the dentist" using the Oral-B Indicator product. In 1991, Oral-B's operating margin on toothbrushes, after advertising and promotion costs, was estimated to be approximately 20 percent of factory sales.

In 1992, Oral-B announced that it would restage its dental floss, roll out a new mouthwash, and possibly introduce a specialty toothpaste. Oral-B management stated that "to be a leader in the oral care category, we must compete in all areas of oral care."[4]

Johnson & Johnson (J&J) entered the US toothbrush market in the 1970s with the Reach brand, which in 1991 comprised 18 SKUs. In 1988, J&J introduced a second product line under the brand name Prevent, a brush with a beveled handle to help consumers brush at a 45 percent angle, the recommended brushing technique. This product, however, was being phased out by 1992. In 1991, J&J ranked third in the US retail toothbrush market with a 19.4 percent volume share and a 21.8 percent value share. The Reach line was positioned as the toothbrush that enabled consumers to brush in even the hardest-to-reach-places, thereby increasing the efficiency of brushing. New products included Glow Reach (1990) and Advanced Design Reach (1991), which offered tapered heads, angled necks, and unique nonslip handles. Reach Between, to be launched in September of 1992, had an angled neck and rippled bristles that targeted the areas between the teeth. Consumer promotions in 1992 were estimated at $4.6 million (8.6 percent of sales) and included 60-cent coupons, $1.00 refunds by mail, and "buy-two-get-one-free" offers. Media expenditures were expected to reach $17.1 million (31.7 percent of sales) with a heavy reliance on television commercials. Johnson & Johnson's expected 1992 operating margin on toothbrushes, after advertising and promotion costs, was 8.4% of factory sales.

Procter & Gamble (P&G) was the most recent entrant in the toothbrush market with Crest Complete, an extension of the company's toothpaste brand name, Crest. Based on successful test markets in Houston and San Antonio from August 1991 to August 1992, P&G was expected to launch Crest Complete nationally in September 1992. The brush had captured a 13 percent value share in test markets and was expected to reach similar total market share levels in its first year after full launch. The product had long rippled bristles of different lengths, designed to reach between the teeth. Crest Complete claimed to have "the ability to reach between the teeth up to 37 percent farther than leading flat brushes." It

---

[4] *Brandweek*, Oct. 12, 1992.

was expected to be introduced at a manufacturer's list price to retailers of $1.67 and capture a 2.0 percent volume share and a 2.6 percent value share of the US retail market by the end of 1992. Consumer promotions already announced included 55-cent coupons and $1.99 refunds on toothbrushes purchased from floor stands. Media expenditures for the last quarter of 1992 were estimated at $6.4 million; television commercials would carry the theme, "Teeth aren't flat, so why is your brush?"

Smithkline Beecham entered the US toothbrush market in August 1991 with Aquafresh Flex, an extension of the company's toothpaste brand. Aquafresh Flex toothbrushes had flexible handles that allowed for gentle brushing. By the end of 1991, Aquafresh Flex held a 0.9 percent share by volume and 1.1 percent by value of the US retail market with 6 SKUs. In September 1992, the line was expected to expand to include two adult compact heads and one child brush. The 1992 promotion plan, estimated at $4.6 million (25 percent of sales), included $1.99 mail refunds, "buy-two-get-one-free" offers, toothbrush on-pack with toothpaste and a self-liquidating premium offer of towels. Media expenditures at $10 million (almost 50 percent of sales) included television commercials that showed the product brushing a tomato without damaging it to demonstrate the "flexibility and gentleness" of the brush. Smithkline Beecham was expected to make an operating loss on toothbrushes in 1992.

Other competitors included *Lever, Pfizer, and Sunstar.* In 1991, Lever offered three lines of toothbrushes: Aim; Pepsodent Professional with 5 SKUs; and Pepsodent Regular with 4 SKUs. Combined, Lever held a 7.2 percent volume and 6.6 percent value share of the US retail market in 1991. Lever's products were sold primarily in the value segment and the company did not have a track record of innovation in the category. Pfizer entered the market in June 1991 with its Plax brush which had a special groove for the thumb; it had captured 1.8 percent of the retail market by year end. Sunstar, with its Butler brand, held 2 percent of the retail market in 1992 but 19 percent of the $45 million in toothbrushes distributed through dentists.

Advertising and Promotion

In the toothpaste category, it was hard to increase primary demand, so new products tended to steal sales from existing products. In the case of toothbrushes, however, increased advertising and promotion enhanced the category's visibility, which, in turn, seemed to fuel consumer demand.

As the pace of new product introductions quickened in the late 1980s, the advertising media expenditures needed to launch a new toothbrush rose: Johnson & Johnson spent $8 million in media support to introduce its new Reach brush; Oral-B spent $10 million to launch its Indicator brush; and Procter & Gamble was expected to support its Crest Complete brush with $15 million in media expenditures. Total media spending for the category, primarily on television advertising, was estimated to total $55 million in 1992 and $70 million in 1993. Exhibit 8 shows media expenditures and shares of voice for the main toothbrush brands. Exhibit 9 summarizes the main message in each brand's commercials and Exhibit 10 summarizes the copy strategy of Colgate Plus's television commercials over time. Advertising and promotion expenditures for Colgate toothbrushes are given in Exhibit 11.

Growing competition also increased the frequency and value of consumer promotion events. In 1992, 8 percent of all brushes reached consumers either free with toothpaste (as on-pack or mail-in premiums) or free with another toothbrush (buy-one-get-one-free offers). The number of coupon events for toothbrushes increased from 10 in 1990 to 33 in 1992.

EXHIBIT 8   Principal Toothbrush Media Advertising Expenditures and Shares of Voice: 1991–1992E

	1991		1992E	
	Media $M	*Share Voice(%)*	*Media $M*	*Share Voice(%)*
Colgate Plus	$ 7.0	19%	$ 8.0	15%
Reach	15.5	42	17.1	31
Oral-B	10.2	27	11.2	20
Crest Complete	0.4	1	6.4	12
Aquafresh Flex	0.4	1	10.0	18
Pfizer Plax	2.3	6	2.2	4

SOURCE: Company records.

EXHIBIT 9   Television and Advertising Copy Strategies and Executions for Competitor Toothbrush Brands: 1991

Product	*Message*	*Tag-Line*	*Execution*
Crest Complete	Has rippled bristles to reach between teeth (37% further than a flat bristled brush)	"Only Crest could make a brush this complete"	Visual comparison of Crest Complete versus a dental tool
Aquafresh Flex	Has a flexible neck that is gentle on the gums	"For gentle dental care"	Spokesperson/demonstration
Advanced Design Reach	Features a new head/handle design	"Advanced Design Reach"	Visual demonstration of product design with cartoon character
Oral-B Indicator	Will tell you when to change your toothbrush	"The brand more dentists use"	Testimonial with demonstration
Plax	Is especially designed to remove plaque	"The new Plax, plaque removing toothbrush"	Computer graphic display of product design

SOURCE: Company records.

EXHIBIT 10 **Colgate Plus Television Advertising Copy Strategies and Execution: 1985–1992**

Date	Marketing Situation	Colgate Copy Platform	Execution	Tag-line
1985–1986	First toothbrush with diamond-shaped head; first professional toothbrush from a leading oral care company	Unique head; scientific/technical tone; comfort and efficacy	Product depicted as a hero	"Shaped to keep your whole mouth in shape"
1987–1990	Aim enters market, spurring increased competition. Colgate Plus market share suffers	Diamond shaped head; evolution of comfort/efficacy; lighter contemporary tone; implied superiority; emphasizes visual differences	"Odd looking" toothbrush character introduced in bathroom setting	"Odd looking, super-cleaning, comfy feeling toothbrush"
1991	Need to reenergize Colgate advertising copy given long duration of "odd looking" campaign	Diamond shape fits mouth and removes plaque from hard-to-reach places	The "odd looking" character in a dental chair; implied dental recommendation	"Because your smile was meant to last a lifetime"
1992	Increased competitive activity and consequent need for harder-hitting copy	Plaque focus; efficacy message	"Armed to the teeth" execution where the bristles are soldiers	"In the fight against plaque, it's a Plus"

SOURCE: Company records.

EXHIBIT 11 **Advertising and Promotion Expenditures for Colgate-Palmolive Toothbrushes: 1989–1992E ($000s)**

	1989		1990		1991		1992E	
Media*	$ 3,667	(31%)	$ 6,988	(41%)	$ 8,761	(43%)	$ 9,623	(40%)
Consumer promotions	4,541	(39)	5,893	(35)	5,286	(26)	6,978	(29)
Trade promotions	3,485	(30)	4,134	(24)	6,287	(31)	7,457	(31)
Total advertising	11,693	(100)	17,015	(100)	20,334	(100)	24,058	(100)

* Includes Working media expenditures; production and operating costs; and dental professional advertising.
SOURCE: Company records.

In the same period, the average toothbrush coupon value increased from $0.25 to $0.75.

Retail advertising features and in-store displays increased toothbrush sales. A typical CP toothbrush display increased sales by 90 percent over a normal shelf facing. When Colgate toothbrushes were combined with Colgate toothpaste in a single display, toothbrush sales increased by 170 percent. The importance of point-of-purchase displays and the variety of items, bristle qualities, and handle colors in each manufacturer's line led each to develop a variety of racks and display units for different classes of trade. CP, for example, had four display systems: Counter Tops, containing 24 to 36 brushes; Floor Stands, 72 brushes; Side Wings (used by mass merchandisers), 144 to 288 brushes; and Waterfall displays, 288 to 576 brushes. Exhibit 12 illustrates these display racks. In 1991, the percentages of special Colgate displays accounted for by each type were 10, 50, 25, and 15 percent respectively.

The CP toothbrush line held 25 to 40 percent of the category shelf space in most stores. To maximize retail sales, CP salespeople tried to locate the Colgate line in the middle of the category shelf space, between the Reach and the Oral-B product lines.

Distribution

In 1987, traditional food stores sold 75 percent of oral care products, but by 1992 they accounted for only 43 percent of toothbrush sales and 47 percent of toothpaste sales. Mass merchandisers gained share due to increased in-store promotional support. Partly in response and partly because of the increasing number of SKUs, food stores began to expand shelf space devoted to oral care products. Exhibit 13 summarizes toothbrush retail distribution trends by volume and value.

Though purchased too infrequently to be used as a traffic builder, toothbrushes provided retailers with an average margin between 25 percent and 35 percent, twice that for toothpaste. As a result, many retailers were more receptive to adding new toothbrush products than new varieties of toothpaste. In considering which brands to stock and feature, trade buyers evaluated advertising and promotion support and each manufacturer's track record in the category. Between October 1991 and February 1992, the average number of toothbrush SKUs had increased from 31 to 35 for mass merchandisers, from 27 to 34 for drug stores, and from 30 to 35 for food outlets. In September 1992, the average number of brands carried by these three classes of trade were 10, 12, and 8 respectively. Shelf space devoted to toothbrushes had also increased. K Mart, for example, had increased per store shelf space for toothbrushes from 2 to 7.5 feet in two years. Retail sales remained fragmented with 60 percent of sales derived from 40 percent of the SKUs.

In 1992, 22 percent of all toothbrushes were expected to be distributed to consumers by dentists. With a dedicated sales force, Oral-B dominated this market segment. Manufacturer margins on toothbrush sales through dentists were less than half those achieved through normal retail distribution. Exhibit 14 summarizes competitors' shares in this segment of the market.

EXHIBIT 12   Colgate Toothbrush Point-of-Sales Display Racks

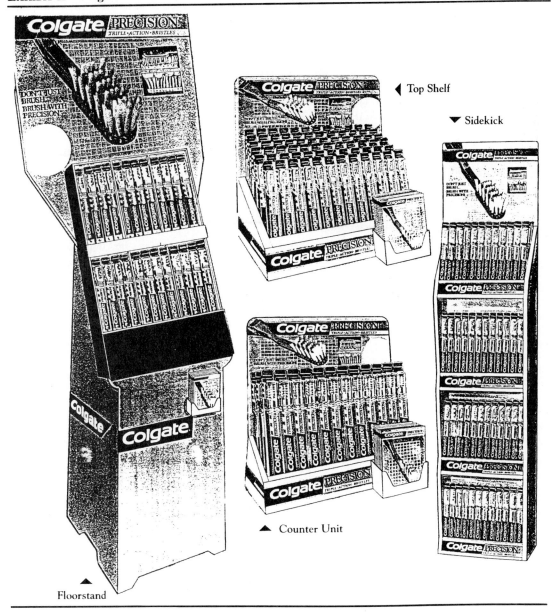

◀ Top Shelf

▼ Sidekick

▲ Counter Unit

▲
Floorstand

EXHIBIT 13   Retail Toothbrush Sales: 1989–1992 (estimated)

	1989		1990		1991		1992 (estimated)	
	Units M	*$ M*	*Units M*	*$ M*	*Units M*	*$ M*	*Units M*	*$ M*
Food stores	110 (45%)	175 (47%)	107 (44%)	175 (44%)	110 (42%)	192 (42%)	128 (42%)	236 (43%)
Drug stores	77 (32)	123 (33)	74 (31)	131 (33)	77 (29)	148 (33)	88 (29)	168 (31)
Mass merchandisers	46 (19)	61 (17)	44 (18)	69 (18)	54 (21)	89 (20)	68 (21)	114 (21)
Military	4 (2)	5 (1)	5 (2)	5 (1)	5 (2)	5 (1)	5 (2)	6 (1)
Club stores	3 (1)	4 (1)	9 (4)	11 (3)	12 (5)	15 (3)	15 (5)	19 (3)
Other	3 (1)	4 (1)	3 (1)	4 (1)	3 (1)	4 (1)	3 (1)	4 (1)

SOURCE: Company records.

EXHIBIT 14   US Professional Dental Market for Toothbrushes: Competitor Market Shares, 1991–1992 (estimated)

	1991		1992 (estimated)	
Brand (parent company)	*$ Millions*	*Market Share (%)*	*$ Millions*	*Market Share (%)*
Oral-B (Gillette)	$14.3	34.0%	$14.3	31.8%
Butler (Sunstar)	8.5	20.2	8.5	18.9
Colgate (CP)	6.7	16.1	8.3	18.4
Reach (J&J)	4.0	9.5	4.0	8.9
Pycopy (Block)	3.4	8.1	3.4	7.6
Aquafresh Flex (Beecham)	0.0	0.0	0.4	0.9
Crest Complete (P&G)	0.0	0.0	0.8	1.7
Other	5.1	12.1	5.4	11.9
Total	42.0		45.0	

NOTE: Aquafresh Flex and Crest Complete were not launched until 1992.
SOURCE: Company records.

The Precision Marketing Mix

Product Design and Testing

The Precision toothbrush was a technical innovation. In laboratory experiments, researchers used infrared motion analysis to track consumers' brushing movements and consequent levels of plaque removal. With this knowledge and through computer-aided design, CP developed a unique brush with bristles of three different lengths and orientations (see Exhibit 15). The longer outer bristles cleaned around the gum line, the long inner bristles cleaned between teeth, and the shorter bristles cleaned the teeth surfaces. The result was a triple-action brushing effect. In initial clinical tests, the brush achieved an average 35 percent increase in plaque removal compared to other leading toothbrushes, specifically Reach and

EXHIBIT 15   Reproductions of the Colgate Precision Toothbrush

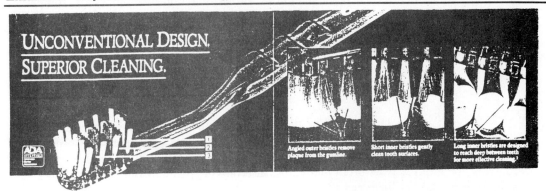

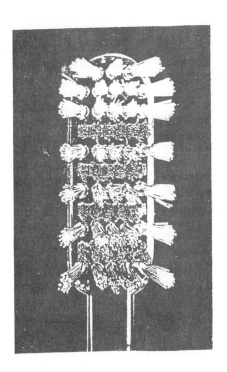

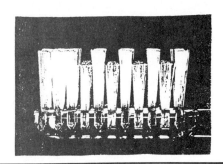

Oral-B. At the gum line and between the teeth, the brush was even more effective, achieving double the plaque removal scores of competitor brushes.

In 1989, CP had established a task force comprising executives from R&D and Marketing, dental professionals, and outside consultants. Its mission was to "develop a superior, technical, plaque removing device." The entire research and development process was managed from start to finish by Steinberg. The task force had five goals:

- Understanding the varying techniques consumers used when brushing their teeth. Researchers later concluded that brushing usually did a good job of removing plaque from teeth surfaces but was often ineffective at removing plaque from the gum line and between the teeth.
- Testing the between-teeth access of different toothbrush designs. The tests revealed that CP's new design was superior to both Oral-B and Reach in accessing front and back teeth using either horizontal or vertical brushing.
- Establishing an index to score clinical plaque removal efficacy at the gum line and between teeth. In tests, a disclosing solution was used to reveal the otherwise colorless plaque and each tooth was divided into nine specific areas. Presence of plaque was measured on each tooth area; the percentages of tooth areas affected by plaque pre- and postusage of different brushes were then calculated.
- Creating a bristle configuration and handle design offering maximum plaque removing efficacy. Three similar designs evolved from the above research, all incorporating bristles of different lengths that would allow freer movement of each individual tuft of bristles and thereby enable different bristle tufts to target different areas of the mouth. Clinical trials established that the new product removed an average 35 percent more plaque than other leading brushes and therefore helped to reduce the probability of gum disease.
- Determining, through clinical and consumer research, the efficacy and acceptance of the new toothbrush design. Extensive consumer research was carried out over a period of 18 months to test product design and characteristics, marketing concept, and competitive strengths. In addition, dental professional focus groups and product usage tests were conducted to determine the overall acceptance of Precision.

In July 1992, CP senior management decided to launch Precision early in 1993. It was decided that Precision would be priced within the super-premium segment and distributed through the same channels as

Colgate Plus. However, the decision as to how to position the product and the corresponding branding and communications strategies remained to be finalized.

Positioning

Precision was developed with the objective of creating the best brush possible and as such, it was a top of the range, super-premium product. It could be positioned as a niche product to be targeted at consumers concerned about gum disease. As such, it could command a 15 percent price premium over Oral-B and would be expected to capture 3 percent of the US toothbrush market by the end of the first year following its launch. Alternatively, Precision could be positioned as a mainstream brush, with the broader appeal of being the most effective brush available on the market. It was estimated that, as a mainstream product, Precision could capture 10 percent of the market by the end of the first year. Steinberg developed a marketing mix and financial projections for both scenarios and this information is summarized in Table C. Her assumptions and

TABLE C   Alternative Positioning Scenarios for Precision

	Precision as a Niche Product	*Precision as a Mainstream Product*
Planned capacity unit volume	Year 1 = 13 MM units Year 2 = 20 MM units	Year 1 = 42 MM units Year 2 = 59 MM units
Investment in capacity, where year 2 figures are for additional capacity	Year 1 = $3.250 M Year 2 = 1.300 M	Year 1 = $9.400 M Year 2 = 3.100 M
Manufacturer per unit cost: Years 1 and 2	$0.66	$0.64
Manufacturer price	$2.02	$1.76
Suggested retail price	2.89	2.49
Advertising: Year 1 Year 2	$5 Million 5 Million	$15 Million 12 Million
Consumer Promotions: Year 1 Year 2	4.6 Million 4 Million	13 Million 10 Million
Trade Promotions: Year 1 Year 2	1.6 Million 2.7 Million	4.8 Million 7 Million

Number of SKUs:
  Brushes
  Colors
	
	4 adult
	6 colors
		
		6 adult/1 child
		6 colors

Source of sales:
  Percent cannibalization from
    Classic
	
	5%
		
		10%

Percent cannibalization from Plus	30	50
Percent from competitors	60	30
Percent new demand	5	10

calculations behind the niche and mainstream positioning scenarios were as follows:

Volumes

Steinberg believed that with a niche positioning, Precision retail sales would represent 3 percent volume share of the toothbrush market in Year 1 and 5 percent in Year 2. With a mainstream positioning, these volume shares would be 10 percent in Year 1 and 14.7 percent in Year 2. Total category unit volumes were estimated at 268 million in 1993 and 300 million in 1994. The following table outlines how these unit volumes would reach the consumer:

	Niche Positioning Strategy	*Mainstream Positioning Strategy*
No. of units retail	Year 1 = 8 MM, Year 2 = 15 MM	Year 1 = 27 MM, Year 2 = 44 MM
No. of units consumer promotion sampling	Year 1 and 2 = 2 MM	Year 1 and 2 = 7 MM
No. of units through professionals	Year 1 and 2 = 3 MM	Year 1 and 2 = 8 MM

Capacity and Investment Costs

Three types of equipment were required to manufacture the Precision brush: tufters; handle molds; and packaging machinery. The following table gives the cost, depreciation period, and annual capacity for each class of equipment.

	Investment Cost	*Annual Capacity*	*Depreciation time*
Tufters	$500,000	3 MM units	15 years
Handle molds	$300,000	7 MM units	5 years
Packaging	$150,000	40 MM units	5 years

Production Costs and Pricing

Production was subcontracted to Anchor Brush, who also manufactured CP's Plus line of toothbrushes. Production costs included warehousing and transport costs. Under a niche-positioning strategy, Steinberg decided that CP would establish a factory list price to the trade of $2.13, a premium over Oral-B regular and at parity with Oral-B Indicator. The mainstream strategy price would be $1.85, at parity with Oral-B regular. In practice, however, almost all sales to the trade were made at a discount of approximately 5 percent. Eighty percent of sales through dental professionals would be priced at $0.79 per unit; the remainder would be sold at $0.95.

Positioning Precision as a mainstream toothbrush raised concerns about the possible cannibalization of Colgate Plus and about pressure on production schedules that had been developed for a niche positioning. Production capacity increases required 10 months lead time and switching to a mainstream positioning could result in inadequate supply of product. Some executives argued that unsatisfied demand could create the perception of a "hot" product but others felt that the problems associated with allocating limited supplies among trade customers should be avoided if possible. They argued for an initial niche positioning, which could later be broadened to a mainstream positioning as additional capacity came on line.

The positioning decision had important implications for the appropriate shelf location of Precision. Steinberg believed that the best location for Precision on the retail shelves would be between the Colgate Plus and Oral-B product lines, with the Colgate Classic product line on the other side of Colgate Plus. She wondered, however, if mainstream Precision could be located separately from the other Colgate lines, close by competitive super-premium toothbrushes such as Aquafresh Flex and Crest Complete. If Precision was positioned as a niche product, with four SKUs, it was unlikely that any existing SKUs would be dropped. However, positioning Precision as a mainstream product, with seven SKUs, would probably require dropping one or more existing SKUs such as a slow-moving children's brush from the Plus line.

Steinberg also believed that the positioning decision would impact distribution and percentage of sales by class of trade. Specifically, she reasoned that Precision positioned as a niche product would be carried primarily by food and drug stores. Under a mainstream launch scenario, a relatively greater proportion of sales would occur through mass merchandisers and club stores.

Branding

At the time consumer concept tests were carried out by the task force, name tests were also conducted among those consumers positively disposed toward the concept. Alternative names tested included Colgate Precision, Colgate System III, Colgate Advantage, Colgate 1.2.3, Colgate Contour, Colgate Sensation, and Colgate Probe. The Colgate Precision name was found to be appropriate by 49 percent of concept acceptors and appealing by 31 percent.

CP executives had not yet decided the relative prominence of the Precision and Colgate names on the package and in advertising. They debated whether the brush should be known as "Colgate Precision" or as

"Precision by Colgate." Executives who believed that the product represented "big news" in the category argued that the product could stand alone and that the Precision brand name should be emphasized. Stressing Precision as opposed to Colgate would, it was argued, limit the extent of cannibalization of Colgate Plus. It was estimated, both under the mainstream and niche-positioning scenarios, that cannibalization figures for Colgate Plus would increase by 20 percent if the Colgate brand name was stressed but remain unchanged if the Precision brand name was stressed. On the other hand, if the Colgate brand name was stressed, the product would likely break even in the first year, compared to a payback period of three years if the Precision brand name was stressed. In addition, CP's stated corporate strategy was to build on the Colgate brand equity.

Communication and Promotion

Once the basic product design was established, four concept tests, conducted among 400 adult professional brush users (Colgate Plus, Reach, and Oral-B users) 18 to 54 years of age, were run during 1990–91. Consumers were exposed to various product claims in prototype print advertisements and then asked about the likelihood that they would purchase the product (see Exhibit 16 for copies of the advertisements). The results of these tests are summarized in Exhibit 17 and indicate that a claim that the toothbrush would prevent gum disease motivated the greatest purchase intent among test consumers. Additional consumer research, including in-home usage tests, revealed that 55 percent of test consumers found Precision to be very different from their current toothbrushes and 77 percent claimed that Precision was much more effective than their current toothbrush.

Precision's unique design could remove more plaque from teeth than the other leading toothbrushes on the market. However, the brush looked unusual and test participants sometimes had mixed first impressions. A further problem was that the benefit of reduced gum disease from extra plaque removal was difficult to translate into a message with broad consumer appeal since few consumers acknowledged that they might have gum disease. Steinberg believed that Precision was the best brush for people who cared about what they put in their mouths but was still searching for the right superiority claim.

Consumer research revealed that, the more test consumers were told about Precision and how it worked, the greater their enthusiasm for the product. Precision created such a unique feel in the mouth when used that consumers often said "you can really feel it working." Once tried, consumer intent to purchase rose dramatically and Steinberg therefore concluded that sampling would be critical to Precision's success.

There was considerable debate over the CP toothbrush advertising and promotion budget, which amounted to $24.1 million in 1992, with $9.6

EXHIBIT 16   Copies of the Advertisements Used in the Consumer Concept Tests

Introducing a New Toothbrush from Colgate

This New Toothbrush Removes More Plaque Than The Leading Toothbrushes

Your current toothbrush may not be removing enough sticky bacterial plaque that is harmful to your teeth. This new toothbrush is clinically proven to remove more plaque than the leading toothbrushes because it's designed to clean plaque from those hard-to-reach trouble spots.

It's the unique brush design that allows this toothbrush to remove so much plaque. Short, tightly packed bristles sweep away plaque from the surfaces of your teeth. At the same time, long angled bristles search out and remove plaque between teeth, in crevices, and at the gum line. No other toothbrush is designed to remove plaque like this.

So you can remove more plaque than ever before.

INTRODUCING **Colgate** *1·2·3.*
DESIGNED TO BE THE BEST TOOTHBRUSH
FOR PREVENTING GUM DISEASE
BECAUSE IT REMOVES MORE PLAQUE—
35% MORE THAN REACH OR ORAL B.

"35% More Plaque/Prevent Gum Disease"

INTRODUCING
THE **Colgate** *SYSTEM III TOOTHBRUSH.*
DESIGNED TO HELP STOP GUM DISEASE
BEFORE IT STARTS BECAUSE IT REMOVES
MORE PLAQUE—35% MORE THAN
REACH OR ORAL B.

"GUM DISEASE ONLY"

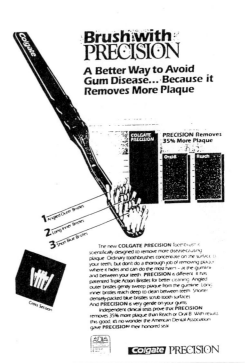

Brush with PRECISION

A Better Way to Avoid Gum Disease... Because it Removes More Plaque

---

EXHIBIT 17   Summary of Consumer Concept Test Results

Concept Test 1

	Plaque Remover	*Healthier Gums*	*Trouble Spots*
Probably would buy	69%	68%	66%
Definitely would buy	15	15	10

Concept Test 2

	35 Percent More Plaque Removal, Prevent Gum Disease	*35 Percent More Plaque Removal*	*Prevent Gum Disease*	*Feel the Difference*
Probably would buy	80%	71%	74%	68%
Definitely would buy	19	19	18	14

Concept Test 3

	Gum Disease/ Replacement	*Gum Disease Only*	*Replacement Message*	*Trouble Spots*
Probably would buy	63%	72%	62%	66%
Definitely would buy	13	16	11	14

Concept Test 4

	No Price Given, Prevent Gum Disease	*20 Percent Price Premium to Oral-B, Prevent Gum Disease*
Probably would buy	87%	61%
Definitely would buy	29	19

NOTE: "Definitely would buy" is a subset of "probably would buy."
SOURCE: Company records.

million in advertising, and $14.4 million in consumer and trade promotion. Some executives thought the budget should remain level as a percentage of sales in 1993 and be allocated among Classic, Plus, and Precision. Others believed it should be increased substantially to support the Precision launch with no reduction in planned support for Classic and Plus. One proposal consistent with a niche positioning for Precision was to increase total CP category spending by $11.2 million and to allocate this to the Precision launch. However, Steinberg believed that this was not enough to permit Precision to reach its full sales potential. She argued for an 80 percent increase in CP category spending in 1993, with fully 75 percent of all advertising dollars assigned to Precision and 25 percent to Plus. However, the Colgate Plus product manager, John Phillips, argued that Plus was the bread-and-butter of CP's toothbrush line and claimed that his mainstream brand should receive more rather than less support if Precision was launched. He argued that continued support of Plus was essential to defend its market position against competition.

Consumer promotions were planned to induce trial. Steinberg was considering several consumer promotions to back the launch: a free 5-oz. tube of Colgate toothpaste (retail value of $1.89) with the purchase of a Precision brush in strong competitive markets; and a 50%-off offer on any size of Colgate toothpaste (up to a value of $1.00) in conjunction with a 50-cent coupon on the Precision brush in strong Colgate markets. The cost of this promotion was estimated at $4 million and Steinberg believed it should be used as part of the launch program for a mainstream positioning strategy. The Colgate Plus product manager pressed for trade deals to load the trade in advance of the Precision launch. He believed that the trade would be unlikely to support two Colgate brushes at any one time. However, Steinberg believed that the launch of Precision would enable CP to increase its overall share of trade advertising features and special displays in the toothpaste category.

Another important tactic was to use dentists to sample consumers since professional endorsements were believed important to establishing the credibility of a new toothbrush. Steinberg believed that, under the niche scenario, 3 million Precision brushes could be channeled through dental professionals in the first year after the launch versus 8 million under the mainstream scenario.

Conclusion

Steinberg believed that Precision was more than a niche product or simple line extension and that the proven benefits to consumers represented a technological breakthrough. She wondered how Precision should be positioned, branded, and communicated to consumers, as well as what the advertising and promotion budget should be and how it should be broken down. Steinberg had to develop a marketing mix and profit and loss pro forma that would enable Precision to reach its full potential, yet also be acceptable to Burton and her colleagues, particularly the Colgate Plus product manager.

Procter & Gamble Company (A)

In November 1981, Chris Wright, associate advertising manager of the Packaged Soap & Detergent Division (PS&D) of the Procter & Gamble Company (P&G) was evaluating how the division could increase volume of its light-duty liquid detergents (LDLs).[1] The excellent growth of Dawn dishwashing liquid since its national introduction in 1976 meant that P&G now manufactured and sold three leading LDL brands, holding a 42 percent share (by weight) of the industry's $850 million in factory sales.

Based on input from the three LDL brand managers who reported to him, as well as his own knowledge of the LDL category, Wright believed there were three major opportunities for volume growth: (1) the introduction of a new brand, (2) a product improvement on an existing brand, and/or (3) increased marketing expenditures on existing brands. In preparation for an upcoming meeting with Bruce Demill, PS&D advertising manager, Wright began evaluating the volume and profit potential of the three options.

Company Background

In 1837 William Procter and James Gamble formed a partnership in Cincinnati, Ohio, so that they could buy more efficiently the animal fats essential to the manufacture of their respective products—candles and soaps. The Procter & Gamble Company emerged from this partnership and quickly gained a reputation as a highly principled manufacturer of quality goods. As James Gamble said: "If you cannot make pure goods and full weight, go to something else that is honest, even if it is breaking stone."

Research Associate Alice MacDonald Court prepared this case under the direction of Professor John A. Quelch as the basis for class discussion rather than to illustrate either effective or ineffective handling of an administrative situation. Names and proprietary data have been disguised, but all essential relationships have been preserved. Copyright © 1983 by the President and Fellows of Harvard College. Harvard Business School case 9–584–047.

[1] LDLs are defined as all mild liquid soaps and detergents designed primarily for washing dishes.

EXHIBIT 1   Consolidated Statement of Earnings ($ in millions except per share amounts)

	Fiscal Year Ending June 30	
	1981	*1980*
Income		
Net sales	$11,416	$10,772
Interest and other income	83	52
	11,499	10,824
Costs and expenses		
Cost of products sold	7,854	7,471
Marketing, administrative, and other expenses	2,361	2,178
Interest expense	98	97
	10,313	9,746
Earnings from operations before income taxes	1,186	1,078
Income taxes	518	438
Net earnings from operations (before extraordinary charge)	668	640
Extraordinary charge: costs associated with the suspension of sale of Rely tampons (less applicable tax relief of $58)	(75)	—
Net earnings	$ 593	$ 640
Per common share		
Net earnings from operations	$8.08	$7.74
Extraordinary charge	(.91)	—
Net earnings	$7.17	$7.74
Average shares outstanding 1981—82,720,858 1980—82,659,861		
Dividends	$3.80	$3.40

SOURCE: Company records.

In 1890 the Procter & Gamble Company was incorporated with a capital stock value of $4,500,000. This capital allowed P&G to build additional plants, buy new equipment, and develop and introduce new products. Sales volume more than doubled every 10 years following incorporation, largely as a result of new-product introductions. By 1981 P&G operated in 26 countries and sales totaled $11.4 billion, of which 70 percent were made in the United States (see Exhibit 1). P&G manufactured 90 consumer and industrial products in the United States and sold the leading brand in 14 of the 24 consumer-product categories in which the company competed (see Exhibit 2). One or more of P&G's products were used in 95 percent of US homes—a penetration unequaled by any other manufacturer. P&G had historically grown both by developing products

EXHIBIT 2 **Established US Brands by Product Category, 1981**

A. Consumer

Laundry and Cleaning	*Food*	*Personal Care*
All Fabric Bleach Biz (1967)*	**Coffee** #1—Folgers (vacuum packed and instant, 1963; flaked, 1977) Instant High Point (1975)	**Bar Soaps** Camay (1927) Coast (1974) #1—Ivory (1879) Kirk's (1930) Lava (1928) Safeguard (1963) Zest (1952)
Cleaners and Cleansers #1—Comet (1956)† Comet Liquid (1976) Mr. Clean (1958) Spic and Span (1945) Top Job (1963)	**Oil/Shortening** #1—Crisco (shortening, 1911) Crisco (oil, 1960) Fluffo (shortening, 1953) Puritan Oil (1976)	**Deodorants/Antiperspirants** Secret (1956) Sure (1972)
Detergents/Soaps Bold 3 (1976) Cheer (1950) Dash (1954) Dreft (1933) Era (1972) Gain (1966) Ivory Snow (1930) Oxydol (1952) Solo (1979) #1—Tide (1946)	**Orange Juice and Other Citrus Products** Citrus Hill **Peanut Butter** #1—Jif (1956) **Potato Chips** Pringles (1968)	**Disposable Diapers** #1—Pampers (1961) Luvs (1976) **Disposable Incontinent Briefs** Attends (1978)

Mouthwash
Scope (1965)

Paper Tissue Products
Charmin (bathroom, 1957)
#1—Puffs (facial, 1960)
White Cloud (bathroom, 1958)

Paper Towels
#1—Bounty (1956)

Prescription Drugs

Shampoos
Head & Shoulders (1961)
Pert (1979)
Prell (1946)

Dishwashing Detergents
Cascade (1955)
Dawn (1972)
#1—Ivory Liquid (1957)
Joy (1949)

Fabric Softeners
Bounce (1972)
#1—Downy (1960)

Soft Drinks
Crush (1980)
Hires Root Beer (1980)
Sun-Drop (1980)

Prepared Mixes
#1—Duncan Hines (cake, 1956;
brownie, 1956; snack cake,
1974; pudding recipe cake,
1977; cookie, 1978; bran
muffin, 1979)

Hand and Body Lotion
Wondra (1977)

Home Permanent
#1—Lilt (1949)

Toothpastes
#1—Crest (1955)
Gleem (1952)

B. Industrial

Finished Industrial Goods

All-purpose cleaning products
Floor and hard-surface cleaning products
Pot and pan washing products
Cleansers

Commercial laundry products
Coin-vended laundry products
Hand-washing products
Institutional bar soaps

Coffee
Shortenings and oils
Surgical drapes and gowns

Unfinished Industrial Goods

Animal feed ingredients
Cellulose pulp
Fatty acids
Fatty alcohols
Glycerine
Methyl esters

NOTE: Test-market brands have been excluded.

* The date the brand became part of the P&G line is in parentheses.

† Leading brand in the category is marked #1.

internally and by acquiring companies to which P&G's technological expertise was applied.[2]

P&G executives attributed the company's success in the marketplace to a variety of factors: (1) dedicated and talented human resources, (2) a reputation for honesty that won the trust and respect of its suppliers and customers, (3) prudent and conservative management that encouraged thorough analysis prior to decision making, (4) innovative products offering superior benefits at competitive prices, and (5) substantial marketing expertise. The following quotes from company executives and outside analysts emphasize these factors:

> If you leave the company [P&G] its money, its buildings, and its brands, but take away its people, the business will be in real jeopardy; but if you take away the money, the buildings, and the brands, but leave the people here, we will build a comparable new business in as little as a decade.
>
> —Richard R. Deupree
> Chairman of the board, P&G, 1948–1958

> Our predecessors were wise enough to know that profitability and growth go hand in hand with fair treatment of employees, of customers, of consumers, and of the communities in which we operate.[3]
>
> —Edward G. Harness
> Chairman of the board, P&G, 1974–1981

> There is no potential business gain, no matter how great, which can be used to justify a dishonest act. The ends cannot justify the means because unethical means, in and of themselves, can and will destroy an organization . . . The total dedication to integrity in every aspect of the business, and the restless, driving spirit of exploration have already been vital to the company's past and are critical to the company's future.
>
> —Owen B. Butler
> Chairman of the board, P&G, 1981–

> Key to Procter & Gamble's continued growth is the importance we attach to research and development . . . If anything, research and development will take on even greater importance to us in the future.
>
> —John Smale
> President, P&G, 1981–

> Disciplined and consistent, P&G people plan, minimize risk, and adhere to proven principles.
>
> —Ogilvy and Mather
> (advertising agency)

---

[2] P&G acquired the Duncan Hines Companies (prepared cake, cookie, and muffin mixes) in 1956; Charmin Paper Mills (toilet and facial tissues, paper towels, and paper napkins) in 1957; the Folger Coffee Company (ground, flaked, and instant coffee) in 1963; the Crush Companies (Crush, Sun-Drop, and Hires Root Beer soft drinks) in 1980; the Ben Hill Griffin Citrus Company (concentrated fruit juices) in 1981; and Morton Norwich (pharmaceuticals) in 1982.

[3] As quoted by Oscar Schisgall in *Eyes on Tomorrow* (Chicago: J. G. Ferguson Publishing, 1981). All other quotations are drawn from P&G recruitment literature.

The secret, in a word, is thoroughness. P&G manages every element of its business with a painstaking precision that most organizations fail to approach.

—Fortune

Company Organization

The company comprised eight major operating divisions organized by type of product: Packaged Soap & Detergents, Bar Soap and Household Cleaning Products, Toilet Goods, Paper Products, Food Products, Coffee, Food Service and Lodging Products, and Special Products. As Exhibit 3 shows, each division had its own brand management (called advertising), and its own sales, finance, manufacturing, and product development line management groups. These groups reported directly to the division manager, typically a vice president who held overall profit and loss responsibility. The divisions used centralized corporate staff groups for advertising services,[4] distribution, and purchasing.

The advertising department was formed in 1930 when P&G initiated its brand management system. This system allowed P&G to market aggressively several brands in the same product category by assigning the marketing responsibility for each brand to a single brand manager. He or she led a brand group that included an assistant brand manager and, depending on the dollar volume and marketing complexity of the product, one or two brand assistants. This group planned, developed, and directed the total marketing effort for its brand. It was expected to manage aggressively the marketing of the brand and to know more about the brand's business than anyone else in the organization.

One of the most important responsibilities of the brand group was the development of the annual marketing plan, which established volume objectives, marketing support levels, strategies, and tactics for the coming year. This plan took approximately three months to develop. It reflected substantial analysis of previous business results by the brand group. Additionally, the brand group solicited input from 6 to 12 internal staff departments and an outside advertising agency. Then it recommended a marketing plan, which was reviewed by three levels of management: the associate advertising manager, the advertising manager, and the division general manager. Since the planning process established the marketing plans and volume expectations for the coming year, it was regarded as a key determinant of brand progress. In addition, this process offered the brand groups substantial opportunity to interact with upper management. (Details of the planning process are presented in Exhibit 4.)

---

[4] Advertising services included the following specialized staff departments: TV commercial production, media, copy services, art and package design, market research, field advertising, marketing systems and computer services, and promotion and marketing services.

EXHIBIT 3   Divisional Line Management Organization

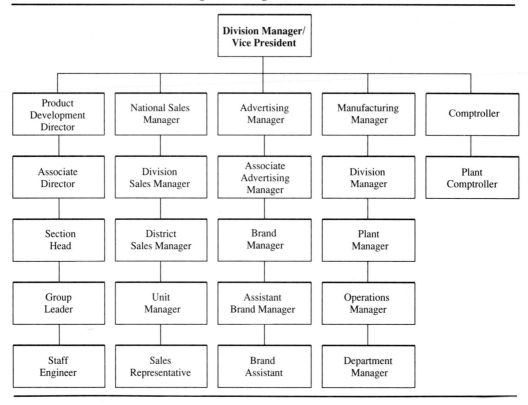

Promotion was based entirely on performance, and all promotions were from within the organization. Brand managers were evaluated on their ability to build brand business and to develop their people. A brand manager who demonstrated excellent management ability was promoted to associate advertising manager (see Exhibit 3). Associate advertising managers used the skills they had developed as brand managers to guide the marketing efforts of several brands within a division, as well as to further the development of their brand managers. Associates also became involved in broader divisional and corporate issues. For example, the associate responsible for coordinating division personnel policy would evaluate future personnel needs, coordinate recruitment efforts, ensure consistent evaluation methods, analyze training needs, develop a training budget, and work with the personnel department to implement training programs.

Each associate advertising manager reported to an advertising manager, who was responsible for the total marketing effort of all of a division's brands. The advertising manager played a significant role in the

EXHIBIT 4 Marketing Plan Development Process

Appropriate Number of Weeks before Plan Approved	Activity or Event	Purpose
12	**Business Review** Assistant brand manager thoroughly reviews brand's and major competition's past 12-month shipment and share results by region, size, and form. Key lessons learned and indicated actions for the brand are developed by analyzing influences on brand share, including advertising copy, media weight, promotion, trade merchandising (display, co-op advertising, and temporary price reduction), pricing, and distribution.	To determine what elements of the marketing mix are affecting the brand's business and to develop clear guidelines and actions to improve business results.
8	**Competitive Forecast** Brand group forecasts competitive volume and marketing expenditures for coming year, using input from Sales and advertising agency.	To allow brands to gauge level of expenditures necessary to compete effectively.
6	**Preliminary Forecast** Brand manager forecasts brand's volume and share for the coming year, and preliminarily recommends advertising and promotion expenditures.	To allow division and P&G management to preliminarily forecast total P&G volume, expenditures, and profits for the coming year, and the brand to get preliminary agreement to volume objectives and marketing plans.
4	**Promotion Review** Brand assistant thoroughly reviews results of past 12-month promotion plan by region, event, promoted size, and total brand. The document incorporates Sales's comments, competitive brand activity, and available research to explain possible reasons for success and failure. Plan includes broadscale effort and testing activities.	To gain preliminary agreement from Advertising and Sales management to the proposed promotion plan for the coming year.
4	**Media Plan** Advertising agency develops detailed media plan, working with brand manager and assistant brand manager. Plan includes broadscale media effort and testing activities.	To develop media plan for inclusion in budget proposal.
1	**Budget Proposal** Brand group prepares document detailing proposed volume, share, and marketing plan for coming year. Marketing plan includes detailed media and promotion plans, both broadscale effort and testing activities.	To provide a written record of the proposed plan.
0 (March)	**Budget Meeting** Brand group and advertising agency present the proposed plan to P&G management. The plan can either be approved in full, conditionally accepted provided certain issues raised in the meeting are addressed, or not approved.	To gain management input and agreement to the proposed plans.

general management of the division, as he or she was responsible for approving the brand group's recommendations for volume objectives, marketing plans, and expenditures. In addition, the advertising manager had responsibility for approving each brand's advertising plans, as recommended by its brand group and its advertising agency.[5] All new advertising required the approval of the associate advertising manager and the advertising manager, while significant changes in advertising direction required division manager approval.

Historically, brands competing in the same product category were assigned to different associate advertising managers within a division to ensure maximum interbrand competition. Each of the associates promoted the interests of his or her own brand to the advertising manager, who then coordinated the most effective and efficient use of limited divisional resources. In the fall of 1981, however, the PS&D Division was reorganized; each associate advertising manager became responsible for all the brands within a single product category, as shown in Exhibit 5. This change focused authority for key decisions within category groups (e.g., LDLs) at the associate advertising manager level, thus allowing the advertising manager to spend more time on divisional issues. The brand manager promoted the interests of his or her brand, while the associate advertising manager assumed responsibility for building the business of all P&G brands in his or her category.

Advertising's Relations with Other Line Departments

The brand groups worked closely with the following four line departments in both the development and the implementation of their marketing plans.

Sales

P&G's consumer divisions employed 2,310 sales representatives and 574 sales managers, who serviced an estimated 40 percent of grocery, drug, and mass merchandise retail and wholesale outlets, accounting for an estimated 80 percent of all grocery and health and beauty aid sales volume.[6] The PS&D Division employed 408 sales representatives and 102 sales managers, who serviced 27 percent of grocery outlets accounting for 75 percent of grocery sales volume. The PS&D sales force did not directly

---

[5] P&G retained 10 leading advertising agencies to work with the brand groups on advertising issues, of which 7 worked on the PS&D Division's products. Each LDL was handled by a separate agency. P&G's relationship with most of its agencies was long-standing, and many of the brands had been handled by the same agency since their introduction.

[6] Small convenience and corner stores accounted for most of the remaining 60 percent of retail outlets. P&G did not directly service these stores, as they accounted for only 20 percent of all commodity volume. These stores could, however, obtain P&G products through wholesalers.

EXHIBIT 5 PS&D Division Organization Chart, Fall 1981

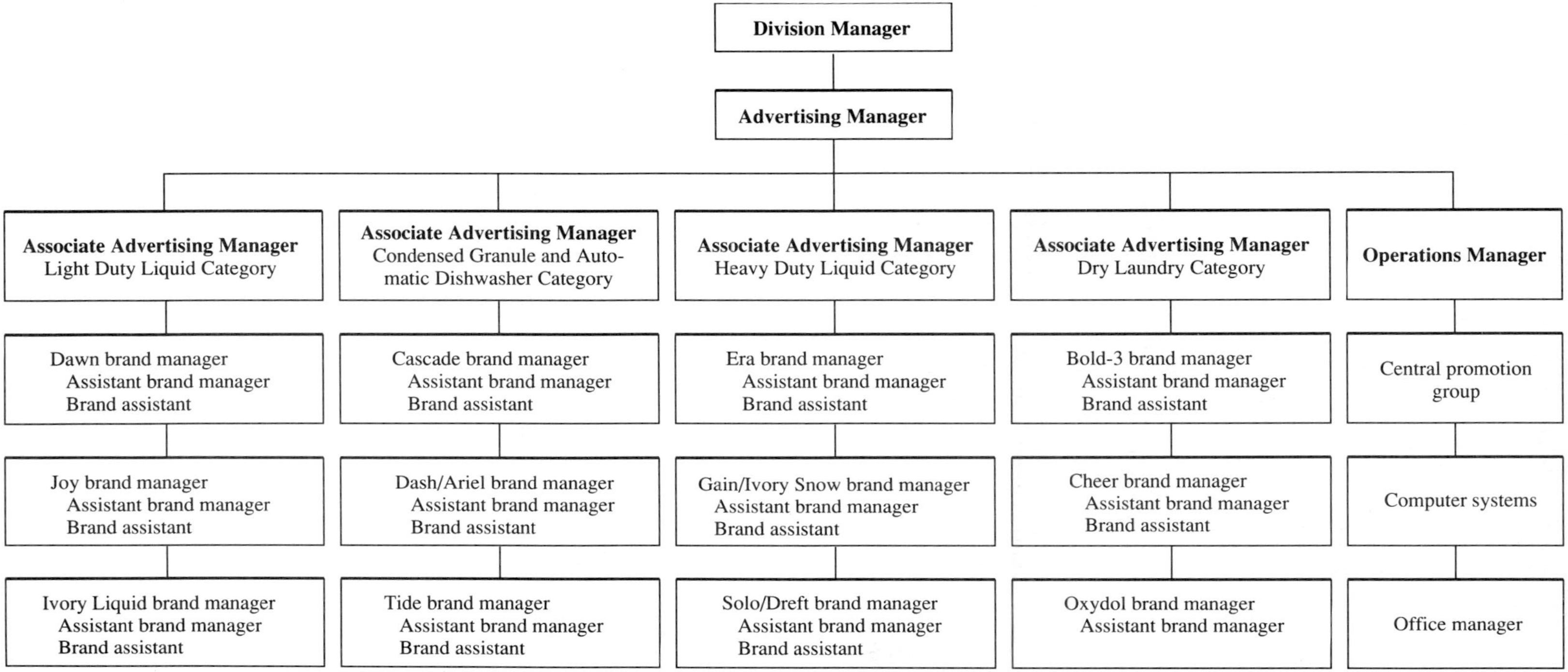

Division Manager

Advertising Manager

- **Associate Advertising Manager**
  Light Duty Liquid Category

  - Dawn brand manager
    Assistant brand manager
    Brand assistant

  - Joy brand manager
    Assistant brand manager
    Brand assistant

  - Ivory Liquid brand manager
    Assistant brand manager
    Brand assistant

- **Associate Advertising Manager**
  Condensed Granule and Auto-matic Dishwasher Category

  - Cascade brand manager
    Assistant brand manager
    Brand assistant

  - Dash/Ariel brand manager
    Assistant brand manager
    Brand assistant

  - Tide brand manager
    Assistant brand manager
    Brand assistant

- **Associate Advertising Manager**
  Heavy Duty Liquid Category

  - Era brand manager
    Assistant brand manager
    Brand assistant

  - Gain/Ivory Snow brand manager
    Assistant brand manager
    Brand assistant

  - Solo/Dreft brand manager
    Assistant brand manager
    Brand assistant

- **Associate Advertising Manager**
  Dry Laundry Category

  - Bold-3 brand manager
    Assistant brand manager
    Brand assistant

  - Cheer brand manager
    Assistant brand manager
    Brand assistant

  - Oxydol brand manager
    Assistant brand manager

- **Operations Manager**

  - Central promotion group

  - Computer systems

  - Office manager

service drug and mass merchandise outlets because of their modest sales potential.

P&G sales representatives were well trained and regarded by the trade as consistently professional. Richard Penner, district sales manager, said:

> Our sales representatives must be experts and professionals in their field. Our customers know that our sales representatives are well-trained professionals whose objective is not only to sell a good, quality product, but whose expertise can show them how to improve overall productivity; people who will bring them business-building merchandising ideas for the next feature or drive, which will reach present as well as new customers, thus increasing overall turnover and profit for the store.

The brand groups and sales force frequently interacted. While the brand group managed categories and brands, the sales force managed markets and accounts. As such, the sales force provided important perspective and counsel on trade and consumer promotion acceptance, stock requirements to support promotions, competitive pricing and promotion activity, and new-product activity. Each brand group worked closely with the sales force to develop the optimal sales promotion plan for its brand together with appropriate merchandising aids. An understanding of the sales function was considered so important to successful marketing planning that each brand assistant was trained as a sales representative and spent three to five months in the field sales force.

Product Development Department (PDD)

Since superior product performance was key to the success of P&G products, each brand group worked closely with PDD to ensure continued improvement of its brand's quality. Fifteen professionals worked exclusively on research and development for LDLs. The PDD continually strove to upgrade product quality or explore new-product formulations. If a potential new product was developed, it was extensively tested in consumer and laboratory tests before any test marketing began.

In 1981 P&G spent $200 million on research and development. This spending supported the efforts of about 3,500 employees. Approximately 1,200 were professionally trained staff, and nearly one-third of these held doctoral degrees. P&G had six major research centers, four of which were located in the United States. The PS&D Division spent $30 million on research and development in 1981, which supported the efforts of about 500 employees.

Manufacturing Department

P&G operated 40 manufacturing plants in 24 states. The PS&D Division utilized 10 of these facilities to manufacture its products. The brand group provided the manufacturing department with detailed brand volume estimates (by month, size, and form/flavor) to facilitate efficient production, as well as five-year volume-based forecasts for capacity planning. In addition, the brand group discussed promotions requiring label or packaging changes with manufacturing to determine the most efficient production methods. Manufacturing informed brand groups about ongoing manufacturing costs and provided potential cost-savings ideas. Interaction between the advertising and manufacturing departments was particularly frequent during any new-product development process and included discussions on manufacturing requirements, custom-packaging options for test markets, and critical paths for production.

Finance Department

P&G's finance department was divided into three major functional areas: divisional financial/cost analysis, treasury, and taxation. Both treasury and taxation were centralized groups, while financial/cost analysis was divisionalized and reported to the division manager (see Exhibit 3). Based on volume and marketing expenditure forecasts provided by the brand groups, financial/cost analysts developed and fed back brand profit and pricing analyses as well as profit and rate-of-return forecasts on new products and promotions. This information was key in helping the brand groups to recommend action that would maximize volume and profit growth.

Advertising Services Department

Within the department, there were nine staff groups that serviced the advertising department. These were market research, art and package design, TV commercial production, media, copy services, field advertising, marketing systems and computer services, promotion and marketing services, and advertising personnel.

P&G's extraordinary depth of staff resources was considered a key competitive advantage. For example, P&G invested an average of $20 million annually on consumer and market research,[7] 10 percent of which was spent on PS&D Division projects. PS&D market research included the following:

1. Market analysis, including bimonthly syndicated market data purchased from A. C. Nielsen Co.,[8] as well as selected data purchased from Nielsen, Selling Areas Marketing, Inc. (SAMI), and other suppliers for test markets.

---

[7] This $20 million was part of the $200 million the company spent on research and development.

[8] The A. C. Nielsen package that the LDL brands purchased included data on retail shelf movement and share, distribution penetration, retailer feature advertising, special displays, regular and feature prices, out-of-stocks, retail inventories, and percent of brands sold in special packs.

2. Consumer research, including studies to
   a. Monitor how consumers used products and track consumer usage of, attitude toward, and image of P&G and competitive brands.
   b. Test the performance of current products and possible product modifications under in-home usage conditions.
   c. Evaluate the advertising, packaging, promotion, and pricing of P&G brands; also, to evaluate the potential of new-product ideas, using such techniques as concept research and simulated test markets.

The major strength of P&G's consumer research was the quality of interviewing and consistent methodology among projects. This provided large databases of comparable research over several years from which P&G could establish norms and accurately track changing consumer perceptions and habits. Only a limited amount of the research was actually conducted by P&G employees; most was conducted by outside suppliers, but was closely supervised by P&G market researchers.

Light-Duty Liquid Detergents

During the 1940s, most US consumers used powdered laundry detergents to wash their dishes. Research indicated, however, that consumers found these detergents harsh on hands. In response to these concerns, P&G designed a mild, light-duty liquid in 1949. By 1981, the LDL industry recorded factory sales of $850 million and volume of 59 million cases.[9] The average US consumer had 1.5 LDL brands at home at any one time, used 0.6 fluid ounces of product per sinkful of dishes, and washed an average of 12 sinksful each week. The average purchase cycle was three to four weeks, and an average household would use over one case of product each year. As Table A shows, the most popular sizes in the category were 32 oz. and 22 oz.

TABLE A   Sizes of Dishwashing Liquid Used in Past Seven Days

	48 oz.	*33 oz.*	*22 oz.*	*12 oz.*
Percent of Respondents	13%	30%	42%	15%

SOURCE: Company research.

[9] Volume is measured in P&G statistical cases, each containing 310 ounces.

Table B suggests that increases in LDL consumption, resulting from the growing number of US households,[10] were partly offset by increased penetration of automatic dishwashers (ADWs), as ADW households used one-half as much LDL as non-ADW households.[11] Based on these trends, the LDL brand groups projected category volume growth of 1 percent per year over the next five years.

TABLE B   US LDL Market Influences

	1960	*1970*	*1980*	*1990**
LDL household penetration	53%	83%	90%	92%
ADW household penetration	5%	18%	36%	44%
Total households (millions)	53	63	79	91

* Company estimates.

LDLs could be conceptually divided on the basis of product benefit into three major segments: (1) the performance segment (35 percent of category volume) provided primarily a cleaning benefit; (2) the mildness segment (37 percent of category volume) provided primarily the benefit of being gentle to hands; and (3) the price segment (28 percent of category volume) whose primary benefit was low cost.[12]

As Exhibit 6 indicates, the performance segment had experienced the greatest growth in the past 10 years. Some LDL brand managers expected the performance segment to continue to grow at the expense of the mildness segment, since market research indicated that more consumers rated performance attributes (such as grease cutting and long-lasting suds) as the most important (see Exhibit 7). The price segment had been in decline, but was expected to stabilize at its current share level due to increasing consumer price sensitivity resulting from the depressed state of the economy. LDL brand managers did not expect this segment to grow because most price brands were not a good value, requiring two or three times as much volume to create the same amount of suds as a premium brand. P&G's Ivory Liquid, the market leader, used this comparison in its advertising to persuade consumers that Ivory was a better value.

The LDL market was relatively stable, with one new premium brand introduced every two and one-half years and an average of two price

---

[10] Household growth was a better indicator of LDL volume than population growth (research indicated LDL household consumption varied only slightly with the number of people in the household).

[11] ADW households still used LDLs for pots and pans and small cleanups.

[12] Price brands were sold to retailers for an average of $7.50 per statistical case versus $17.00 per statistical case for the premium-priced mildness and performance brands.

EXHIBIT 6   LDL Market Historic Growth Trends and Projections

Fiscal Year Ending June 30	Volume (millions cases)	Percent of Category Volume		
		Mildness	Performance	Price
A. Actual				
1973	56.4	44%	19%	37%
1974	57.0	45	20	35
1975	56.4	44	21	35
1976	56.8	43	22	35
1977	56.1	40	28	32
1978	57.8	40	30	30
1979	57.0	39	32	29
1980	58.7	38	33	29
1981	59.0	37	35	28
B. Projected				
1982	59.4	37%	35%	28%
1983	59.8	36	35	29
1984	60.1	36	35	29
1985	60.8	35	36	29
1986	61.1	35	36	29

NOTE: Classification and projections were based on collective brand manager judgment.
SOURCE: Company records.

EXHIBIT 7   Attribute Importance Ratings

Attribute*	Percent of Respondents							Average Rating
	6	5	4	3	2	1	No Answer	
Makes dishes shine	64%	16%	7%	6%	2%	2%	3%	5.3%
Pleasant odor or perfume	40	17	11	10	7	10	5	4.2
Don't have to use much	70	13	6	5	1	2	3	5.5
Doesn't make skin rough	65	12	7	5	4	3	4	5.0
Is low-priced	50	19	10	9	3	4	5	5.0
Good for handwashing laundry	29	14	9	11	9	23	5	3.7
Does a good job on pots and pans	75	13	4	2	1	1	4	5.6
Does not spot or streak glasses or dishes	67	15	8	3	2	2	3	5.4
Is mild to hands	68	13	5	5	3	3	3	5.2
Makes long-lasting suds	83	12	7	2	2	2	2	5.5
Cuts grease	87	6	2	1	—	1	3	5.8
Is economical to use	72	13	6	4	1	1	3	5.5
Soaks off baked-on or burnt-on food	60	17	7	5	2	4	5	5.2
Good for tough cleaning jobs	52	13	8	9	4	9	5	4.8

* Respondents were asked to rate the importance to them of LDL attributes on a 6-point scale, with 6 being "want the most" and 1 being "want the least." To be read, for example: 64% of respondents claimed "Makes dishes shine" as one of the attributes they wanted most in a dishwashing liquid, while 2 percent of respondents claimed this attribute as the one they wanted least.
SOURCE: Company research.

EXHIBIT 8   LDL Market Shares by Brand and Company (shares of statistical cases)

Brand	Segment	Share of Market		
		1961	*1971*	*1981*
P&G				
Joy	Performance	14.9%	12.0%	12.1%
Ivory	Mildness	17.5	14.9	15.5
Dawn	Performance	—	—	14.1
Thrill*	Mildness/performance	—	2.9	—
		32.4	29.8	41.7
Lever Brothers				
Lux	Mildness	17.3	7.3	3.1
Dove	Mildness	—	4.8	3.1
Sunlight	Performance	—	—	0.7
All others	Price	5.9	1.0	—
		23.2	13.1	6.9
Colgate-Palmolive				
Palmolive Liquid	Mildness	—	11.7	11.8
Dermassage	Mildness	—	—	3.5
All others	Price/performance	5.5	9.6	8.3
		5.5	21.3	23.6
All other LDLs	Mainly price/generics and private labels	38.9	35.8	27.8
Total LDLs		100.0%	100.0%	100.0%

* Thrill was introduced by P&G in 1969. The brand ultimately proved not to provide a needed product benefit and was discontinued in 1975 because of faltering volume.
SOURCE: Company records.

brands introduced and discontinued per year. As Exhibit 8 shows, three companies sold almost 75 percent of LDLs, with P&G holding a 42 percent share[13] of the market, Colgate-Palmolive Company a 24 percent share, and Lever Brothers, the US subsidiary of Unilever, a 7 percent share.[14] The remaining 27 percent of the market consisted mainly of generic and private-label brands.

As shown in Exhibit 9, marketing expenditures including advertising and promotion typically represented 20 percent of the sales of an established LDL brand.

---

[13] *Share of market* is defined as share of statistical case volume.
[14] In 1981 Colgate-Palmolive's US sales were $5.3 billion, and Lever Brothers' US sales were $2.1 billion.

**EXHIBIT 9 Cost Structure for an
Established LDL Brand**

Cost of goods	51%
Distribution	7
Selling and general administration	10
Marketing expenditures	20*
Profit	12
Total	100%

* Includes advertising, trade, and consumer promotion expenditures.
SOURCE: Company records.

Total advertising and promotion spending in the category in 1981 was $150 million, over half of which was spent by the P&G LDLs, the balance being spent primarily by Lever and Colgate-Palmolive.

Slightly over half of the marketing budgets of P&G LDLs was allocated to advertising, versus only about 40 percent for both Colgate and Lever LDLs. Colgate and Lever sold an estimated 75 percent of their LDL volume to the trade on deal, compared with about half for P&G. Both Lever and Colgate had introduced a single new brand in the past 10 years. Dermassage, introduced in 1974 by Colgate, offered a similar benefit to Ivory: mildness to hands. The brand held only a 2 percent share in 1981. Sunlight, introduced by Lever into Phoenix (test market) in 1980, offered benefits similar to Joy, as a good-cleaning, lemon-fresh LDL. The brand had achieved a 10 percent share in the test region after 12 months.

Procter & Gamble's LDL Brands

P&G's three brands in the LDL category (Ivory Liquid, Joy, and Dawn) together accounted for 30 percent of the dollar sales volume and profit of the PS&D Division. While each of the three brands was a different formulation that offered a distinct benefit to appeal to separate consumer needs, all were marketed similarly. All three brands were sized and priced in line with major premium-priced competition (see Table C). Price increases occurred, on average, every 18 months.

In general, brand managers spent over half of each LDL's marketing budget on advertising, of which 85–90 percent was spent on television media and commercial production, and the balance on print. Brands typically held four to six major promotion events each year, each lasting four weeks. Promotions primarily included coupons, price packs, bonus packs, and trade allowances. Consumer promotions typically accounted for at least 75 percent of promotion dollars, while trade allowances made up the balance.

TABLE C   Ivory, Dawn, and Joy Pricing

| | | Manufacturer's | | |
| | | Carload *Case Price* | Carload *Item Price* | Average *Retail Price* |
Size	*Items per Case*			
48 oz.	9	$22.77	$2.53	$2.99
32 oz.	12	21.24	1.77	2.04
22 oz.	16	19.20	1.20	1.46
12 oz.	24	16.08	0.67	0.84

EXHIBIT 10   LDL User/Nonuser Attribute Association (%)

| | Usual Brand* | | | | | | | | | |
| | Ivory Liquid | | Joy | | Dawn | | Palmolive | | Price Brands | |
Attribute	*Yes*	*No*	*Yes*	*No*	*Yes*	*No*	*Yes*	*No*	*Yes*	*No*
Best for mildness	89%	51%	53%	12%	41%	7%	71%	27%	13%	2%
Best overall for getting dishes clean	64	9	78	14	88	15	61	5	18	1
Best for cutting grease	41	6	49	7	96	45	35	4	16	1
Best for removing tough, cooked-on foods	47	7	55	10	88	28	41	6	19	2
Best for leaving dishes shiny	44	10	81	45	59	5	40	4	14	1
Gives the best value for your money	74	24	60	4	65	6	55	5	40	7
Makes the longest-lasting suds	79	29	60	10	67	11	50	5	12	1
Has the most pleasant fragrance	43	11	64	35	39	9	35	11	14	1

NOTE: Respondents were asked to indicate which one brand was best described by each attribute phrase. To be read, for example: 89 percent of respondents who claimed Ivory Liquid as their usual brand indicated that it was best for being mild to your hands; 51 percent of people who did not claim Ivory Liquid as their usual brand indicated it was best for being mild to your hands.
* A *brand user* was defined as a respondent who reported that brand as the usual brand used over the previous three-month period.
SOURCE: Company research.

P&G's LDL brands held strongly established market positions, as company research results reported in Exhibit 10 reveal. Neither Ivory Liquid nor Dawn had changed its basic product benefits or basic advertising claims since introduction. Joy, however, had undergone two basic changes. It was first introduced as a performance brand, but during the 1980s, as the mildness segment of the market began to grow, it was restaged with a mildness benefit. By the 1970s, Ivory Liquid was clearly established as the major mildness brand; as research revealed that a consumer need existed for a good cleaning brand, Joy was reformulated to provide a performance benefit and restaged.

Each brand's individual market position is discussed here:

Ivory Liquid. The product was introduced in 1957 as an excellent dish-washing liquid that provided the additional benefit of hand care. Its mildness positioning was supported by the heritage of Ivory bar soap, a patented mildness formula, and unique product aesthetics (its creamy-white color and mild scent). In 1981 it was the leading brand, with a market share of 15.5 percent. Although Ivory's share had declined slightly over the previous five years, it was expected to remain stable over the next five years. Ivory's advertising copy featured a mother/daughter comparison to demonstrate its benefit of "young-looking hands." In 1968 the brand added a value claim stressing the fact that Ivory washed more dishes per penny of product than price brands because of its higher-sudsing formula. During 1981 Ivory allocated two-thirds of its advertising budget to the mildness message and the remaining one-third to the value advertising copy. (Television advertising storyboards for these two campaigns are presented as Exhibits 11 and 12.) The brand was perceived by consumers as the mildest and highest-sudsing brand and had the highest ever-tried level in the category. For this reason, the principal objective of Ivory's consumer promotions was to encourage continuity of purchase rather than to stimulate trial.

Dawn. The product was introduced in 1976 as a performance brand. In two years, it rose to the no. 2 position in the LDL category, and by 1981 it held a 14.1 percent market share. Dawn captured about 70 percent of its volume from non-P&G brands, with the remaining 30 percent cannibalized equally from Ivory Liquid and Joy. Dawn's rapid growth was attributed to its unique position as the superior grease-cutting LDL in the category—a claim that was supported by its patented formula, which consumer research proved cut grease better than other formulas. The advertising claim "Dawn takes grease out of your way" was supported by a powerful product demonstration, as shown in Exhibit 13. Consumer research (reported in Exhibit 14) indicated that Dawn had the highest conversion rate of all the P&G LDL brands.[15] Dawn's promotion plan emphasized trial, with most of the budget allocated to consumer coupons. Its share was projected to increase to 16.5 percent over the next five years. It was expected to take over the leading share position from Ivory by 1985.

Joy. The product, introduced in 1949, was P&G's first LDL. Since 1970, it had been formulated to provide a performance benefit, and it was positioned in advertising to deliver "beautiful dishes that get noticed and appreciated." Joy's lemon-based formula, lemon fragrance, and yellow package supported this image. Joy's advertising (see Exhibit 15) claimed

---

[15] The conversion rate was the number of people citing a brand as their usual brand divided by total triers of the brand.

EXHIBIT 11   Ivory Liquid's TV Storyboard "Mildness" Message, 1981

COMPTON ADVERTISING, INC.
625 Madison Avenue, New York, N.Y. 10022
Telephone: PLaza 4-1100

CLIENT: PROCTER & GAMBLE CO.
PRODUCT: IVORY LIQUID
TITLE: "STOKES"
COMML. #   PGIL 5713   TIMING: 30 SECONDS
DATE: 10/22/80

1. (SFX: MUSIC)
   ANNCR: (VO) Can you pick Jean Stokes' hands from her two daughters?

2. LISA: Mom's hands are as young-looking as ours!

3. KATHY: We sing together for charity --

4. MOM: Strictly amateur -- but your hands get noticed.

5. ANNCR: (VO) And Jean does a lot of dishes. What's her secret?

6. LISA: Ivory Liquid!
   MOM: And I've told my girls how mild it is.

7. ANNCR: (VO) Lab tests show Ivory Liquid's

8. mildest of all leading brands.

9. And nothing gets dishes cleaner.

10. LISA: I'm going to stay with Ivory Liquid.

11. GROUP SINGS: Ivory Liquid.

12. ANNCR: (VO) Because young-looking hands are worth holding on to.

that it "cleans dishes right down to the shine and isn't that a nice reflection on you." As Exhibit 10 indicates, although Joy's image in the marketplace was good by category standards, it was not as strong as Ivory Liquid or Dawn. In addition, it had the lowest trial level of P&G's three LDLs. As a result, its promotion plan was trial-oriented, with particular emphasis on couponing. Joy's share of 12.1 percent was expected to increase by only 1 percent per year over the next five years.

Exhibit 12   Ivory Liquid's TV Storyboard "Value" Message, 1981

COMPTON ADVERTISING, INC.
625 Madison Avenue, New York, N.Y. 10022
Telephone: PLaza 4-1100

CLIENT: PROCTER & GAMBLE CO.
PRODUCT: IVORY LIQUID
TITLE: "THE KIPPERS"
COMML. #   PGIL 5573   TIMING: 30 SECONDS
DATE: 4/1/80

1. ANNCR: (VO) Is the Kippers' "bargain" brand a better buy than mild Ivory Liquid? Let's see...

2. INT: Let's test your brand against Ivory Liquid with a penny's worth of each.

3. Let's wash some dishes.

4. How are your suds? BOB: I don't have any suds now.

5. INT: How about the Ivory Liquid Mrs. Kipper? BEV: I still have a tubful.

6. INT: Let's scoop some up and compare.

7. Okay what happened? BEV: I did a lot more dishes.

8. What I thought was a bargain isn't really a bargain at all. INT: What's the bargain?

9. INT: What's the bargain? BEV: Ivory is the bargain.

10. It's gentle to my hands, and I can save money.

11. ANNCR: (VO) You don't have to give up

12. mild Ivory Liquid to save money.

EXHIBIT 13   1981 Dawn Advertising Storyboard

B&B

BENTON & BOWLES
909 THIRD AVENUE
NEW YORK, N.Y.
(212) 758-6200

Client: PROCTER & GAMBLE CO.
Product: DAWN
Length: 45 SECONDS (PGDN 6105)
Title: "SLEEPOVER REV/FP"

1. (SFX: KIDS TALKING)
   MOM: Lasagna? For breakfast? DAUGHTER: Oh,
   Mom! FRIEND: It's a
   slumber party!

2. MOM: O.K. But you <u>will</u>
   clean up.

3. DAUGHTER: All that
   grease! Yuck!!! Gross!

4. MOM: No, Dawn.

5. DAUGHTER: Ah,
   finished!

6. FRIEND #1: Uh-uh, forgot
   a glass. DAUGHTER: You
   forgot it. You wash it.
   FRIEND: After that greasy
   pan?

7. DAUGHTER: Try it.
   Dawn'll handle it.

8. FRIEND #1: The water
   doesn't feel greasy...and
   neither do my hands.

9. And this glass looks as good
   as the first one <u>you</u> washed.

10. ANNCR: (VO) Look. Add
    a half cup of grease to
    Dawn dishwater.

11. Dawn breaks up grease,
    takes it out of your way.
    Helps keep it away.

12. So dishes come out clean.

13. FRIEND: Dawn's great!

14. MOM: So, if lasagna's
    breakfast, what's dinner?
    DAUGHTER: Corn flakes.
    (GIRLS LAUGH)

15. ANNCR: (VO) Dawn takes
    grease

16. (SFX) out of your way.

EXHIBIT 14 Current Product Usage (%)

	Ivory	Joy	Dawn
Usual brand	23%	13%	25%
Past 12-month trial	35	30	29
Ever tried	58	43	54

NOTE: An estimated 60–80 percent of total brand volume was consumed by usual brand users for each brand.

SOURCE: Company research.

EXHIBIT 15 1981 Joy Advertising Storyboard

Radio TV Reports

41 East 42nd Street New York N.Y. 10017
(212) 697-5100

PRODUCT: JOY DISHWASHING LIQUID   758077
PROGRAM: AS THE WORLD TURNS   60 SEC.
WCBS-TV   1:35PM

1. MAN: Sam. MAN: Joe. It's been too long.

2. MAN: It sure has. Come on in. Honey, Sam's here. WOMAN: How do you do Captain Randall.

3. MAN: Major Randall now I hope my phone call didn't catch you two off guard. But Joe said, Sam if you're ever in town --

4. WOMAN: Well of course. And I hope you stay for dinner Major Randall. That is if you don't mind pot luck.

5. MAN: Oh, don't apologize. MAN: Sam. Make yourself at home. Honey, shouldn't we get out the good dishes?

6. WOMAN: Never mind the dishes. Ours here look fine. What about my dress? MAN: It's just fine.

7. ANNCR: When unexpected guests drop in one thing you don't have to worry about is the way your table looks when you use Joy.

8. Joy cleans every day dishes clear down to the shine. And smells fresh like lemons.

9. Keeps dishes ready for company, even if you're not.

10. MAN: Sure is nice to get home cooking.

11. And look at that shine. Looks like you were expecting company all the time.

12. ANNCR: Lemon fresh Joy cleans down to the shine.

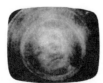

13. And that's a nice reflection on you.

EXHIBIT 16 **Shipment and Share Data for LDL Brands**

	Factory Shipments (millions of cases)			Market Share (% of LDL category)		
	Ivory	*Dawn*	*Joy*	*Ivory*	*Dawn*	*Joy*
Actual						
1977	9.1	6.7	6.7	16.3%	11.9%	11.9%
1978	9.0	7.3	6.7	15.5	12.7	11.6
1979	9.1	7.5	6.8	16.0	13.2	12.0
1980	9.1	8.2	6.9	15.5	14.0	11.7
1981	9.1	8.3	7.1	15.5	14.1	12.1
Estimated						
1982	9.2	8.7	7.2	15.5%	14.7%	12.2%
1983	9.3	9.0	7.4	15.5	15.0	12.3
1984	9.3	9.3	7.5	15.5	15.5	12.4
1985	9.4	9.7	7.6	15.5	15.9	12.5
1986	9.5	10.1	7.8	15.5	16.5	12.7

NOTE: Projections are based on each brand manager's judgment.
SOURCE: Company records.

Exhibit 16 reports factory shipments and market shares for each of the three brands over the previous five years, as well as the brands' estimates for the next five years. Exhibit 17 provides a demographic profile of users of each of the three P&G brands, illustrating how each brand appeals to a different consumer segment.

New Growth Opportunities

In evaluating the opportunities for further volume growth on P&G LDLs, Wright considered the following three options:

New-Brand Introduction
The success of Dawn led Wright to wonder if another new brand with a distinctive benefit could further increase P&G's LDL volume. Based on the impact of Dawn's introduction and the current strength of P&G's LDL brands, he estimated that a well-positioned new brand could capture at least 60 percent of its share from competitive brands. However, after talking with manufacturing and PDD, he estimated that a new brand would require $20 million in capital investment to cover additional production capacity and bottle molds.[16] Further, based on input from the

---

[16] This capital investment per case of estimated LDL volume was lower than the average for new P&G products, since substantial LDL manufacturing facilities already existed.

EXHIBIT 17   LDL-User Demographic Profile (% of total responding households)

	Total LDL Households	Heavy LDL Users*	Ivory Liquid	Joy	Dawn	Palmolive	No Name/ Plain Label
			Usual Brand				
ADW Usage—Past 7 Days							
Yes	36%	9%	48%	49%	51%	48%	47%
No	64	90	51	51	49	42	53
Yearly Income							
Under $15,000	32	46	28	32	35	30	36
$15,000–25,000	27	29	27	26	29	27	29
Over $25,000	41	25	45	42	36	43	35
Population Density (000/sq. mile)							
Under 50	32	39	30	33	38	28	20
50–1,999	45	40	45	44	43	46	48
2,000 and over	23	21	25	23	19	26	32
Geographic Area							
Northeast	22	26	22	23	19	24	36
North Central	28	28	26	27	31	27	31
South	33	35	34	37	35	33	16
West	17	11	18	13	15	16	17
Employment†							
Employed	48	37	48	50	49	49	55
Not employed	52	63	52	59	51	51	45
Age†							
Under 35	33	39	31	34	38	39	35
35–50	30	25	29	31	30	30	37
51–59	16	15	17	16	15	16	12
60+	21	30‡	23	19	17	24	16
Number in Family							
1–2	40	41	43	38	38	42	28
3–4	44	41	42	45	46	44	50
5+	16	18	15	17	16	14	22

NOTE: To be read, for example: 48 percent of respondents who claimed Ivory Liquid as their usual brand had used an automatic dishwasher in the past seven days.

* Defined as +15 sinksful per week.

† Female head of household.

‡ The heavy LDL-user skew toward older respondents may be misleading. P&G management believed that, though users washed a large number of small sinkloads, they used a lesser amount of product per sinkload because they tended to live in smaller households.

SOURCE: Company research.

Dawn brand manager, he estimated that a new LDL brand would need at least $60 million for first-year introductory marketing expenditures.[17]

Wright saw new-product potential in all three market segments. First, PDD had invented a new technology for a high-performance product. The formula, called H-80, combined suspended nonabrasive scrubbers[18] with a highly effective detergent system to provide superior cleaning compared with other LDLs when used full strength on tough, baked-on foods, and parity cleaning compared with other LDLs when diluted with water for general dishwashing. Wright believed that such a product could fulfill a clear consumer need, based on consumer research. Since market research indicated that 80 percent of US households scour and scrub their dishes at least once a week, with an average household scouring four times a week, he believed that this product would be valued by a significant percentage of consumers.[19] In addition, the results of blind, in-home-use tests, reported in Exhibit 18, were positive.

Second, Wright wondered if he could capitalize on P&G's expertise in the mildness segment to introduce another mildness brand. While the segment was currently declining, he believed there might be potential for a new brand if the mildness benefit could be further differentiated—just as had been done in the performance segment. As Exhibit 19 shows, research indicated that when consumers were asked what improvement they wanted most in their current LDL, more stated "milder to hands" than any other product benefit.

Third, P&G could introduce a price brand. PDD and manufacturing had told Wright that they could produce a brand with parity performance benefits to existing price brand competition at a cost that would allow PS&D to maintain a reasonable profit. Specifically, the percentage of sales available for marketing expenditures and profit would fall to 14 percent of sales versus the 32 percent of sales available from P&G's current LDL brands. Wright noted that P&G did not currently have an LDL entry in this fragmented segment of the market, characterized by low-share brands with little brand loyalty and substantially lower product quality than the LDL brands P&G currently marketed. He wondered if P&G's marketing expertise could enable the company to capture a significant portion of the price segment with a parity product.

---

[17] This estimate was based on Dawn's 12-month introductory marketing plan. Using updated costs, a new brand would require $18 million for media support, $37 million for consumer and trade promotion support, and $5 million for miscellaneous marketing expenses.

[18] The scrubbers were made from the biodegradable shells of microscopic sea organisms.

[19] Many consumers used soap-filled scouring pads such as Purex Industries' Brillo pads and Miles Laboratories' SOS pads. Retail sales of such pads approached $100 million in 1980.

EXHIBIT 18   **LDL Category Assessment (4-week blind in-home-use test of H-80 in 425 households)**

	H-80 with Scrubbing Instructions*	Established Competitive LDL with Scrubbing Instructions*
Attribute Ratings (%)		
Overall	77%	71%
Cleaning	79	73
Removing baked/burnt/dried-on food	73	61
Grease removal	77	72
Amount of suds made	73	69
Mildness	55	63
Odor of product	70	68
Color of product	72	69
Favorable Comments (%)		
Unduplicated cleaning	73	65
Cleans well	36	29
Cleans hard-to-remove food	25	15
Cuts grease	34	32
Unduplicated sudsing	49	45
Product color	6	5
Mildness	25	34
Unduplicated odor	45	40
Unduplicated cap/container	8	2
Unduplicated consistency	12	2
Like scrubbing particles/abrasives	12	—
Unfavorable Comments (%)		
Unduplicated cleaning	4	9
Not clean well	—	1
Not clean hard-to-remove food	1	5
Not cut grease	3	8
Unduplicated sudsing	9	17
Product color	1	3
Mildness	16	14
Unduplicated odor	10	9
Unduplicated cap/container	2	2
Unduplicated consistency	12	1
Not like abrasive/gritty feel	11	1
Dishwashing Information		
Used product full strength for scrubbing	61	52
Used scrubbing implement for tough jobs	79	85

NOTE: To be read, for example: 77 percent of the 425 households that used H-80 rated it as 4 or above on a 5-point scale on overall performance.

* Unmarked bottles of H-80 were given to one of two representative samples of LDL users. The other sample group received unmarked bottles of an established competitive brand. Both brands were accompanied by instructions suggesting the product be diluted for general dishwashing but used full strength for tough dishwashing jobs.

SOURCE: Company research.

EXHIBIT 19   Selected Research Data: Personal
Feelings Concerning Dishwashing

	Percent of Consumers
1. What is the worst thing about doing dishes?	
The time it takes	24%
Having to do them	22
Cleaning pots and pans	15
Scrubbing/scouring	14
Cleaning greasy items	6
Hard on hands	4
2. What is the toughest dishwashing job?	
Removal of baked/burnt/fried/cooked foods	39
Removal of greasy foods	32
Cleaning of pots and pans	22
Cleaning of skillets	16
Cleaning of casseroles	7
Cleaning of dishes	3
3. What is most disappointing about your current dishwashing liquid?	
Nothing	51
Suds disappear	12
Leaves grease	8
Odor	6
Hard on hands	2
Price/expensive	4
Have to use too much	4
4. What improvement do you want the most in a dishwashing liquid?	
Milder to hands	11
Do it by magic/itself	10
Eliminate scouring or soaking	9
Cut grease	9
Soak dishes clean	9
Suds never vanish	6
Nothing/satisfied	9

SOURCE: Company research.

Product Improvement on an Existing Brand

A product improvement on a current brand represented considerably less investment than a new brand, and Wright wondered if he would be wiser to introduce the H-80 formula as a product improvement to one of the current LDL brands. While he estimated that the capital costs associated with a product improvement would be about the same as introducing a new product ($20 million), incremental marketing expenditures over and above the existing brand budget would be only $10 million. He wondered which, if any, of his brands would benefit most from this change.

Separately, the Joy brand group was eager to restage the brand with a new "no-spot" formula. The formula, considered a technological breakthrough, caused water to "sheet" off dishes when they were air-dried, leaving fewer spots than other brands. In addition, the formula reduced Joy's cost of goods sold by about $3 million per year. The brand estimated this relaunch would cost $10 million in marketing expenses, but would require no capital investment.

Increase Marketing Expenditures on the Existing Brands

Finally, given the low-growth potential of the LDL category, Wright wondered if his overall profits might be higher if he avoided the capital investment and introductory marketing expenses of a new brand or product improvement and simply increased the marketing expenditures behind the existing brands in an effort to build volume. In particular, the brand manager for Ivory Liquid had submitted a request for an additional $4 million to support extra advertising and promotion. Half of the funds were to be used to achieve leadership media levels for Ivory by increasing its current media level from 300 GRPs[20]—which was the average level for major advertised LDL brands—to 365 GRPs. The remaining funds would be used to finance an incremental 20¢-off price-pack promotion on the 32-oz. size.

Conclusion

As Wright considered the various options available, he wondered about the time frame for implementation of each option. He knew that he could gain approval for increased marketing expenditures almost immediately if the plan was financially attractive—unless a test market was required, which would delay national approval by 6 to 12 months. Implementing a product improvement on an existing brand would take about a year (two years if a test market was necessary), and the introduction of a new brand would require two years plus a year in a test market before it could be expanded nationally. Could he undertake more than one option? What effect would each option have on each of the existing LDL brands? What competitive response could he expect? What were the long- and short-term profit and volume implications of each of the options?

---

[20] A GRP (gross rating point) is a measure of media delivery. Gross rating points equal the percentage of viewers reached over a specific period of time (usually four weeks) times the average number of occasions on which they are reached.

The Black & Decker Corporation Household Products Group: Brand Transition

In April 1984, Black & Decker Corp. (B&D) acquired the Housewares Division of General Electric Co. (GE), combining the GE small-appliance product line with its own household product line to form the Household Products Group. The terms of the acquisition set the stage for a unique marketing challenge. B&D was permitted to manufacture and market appliances carrying the GE name, but only until April 1987. During the intervening three years, B&D would have to replace the GE name on all the acquired models with its own brand name.

Immediately after the acquisition, Kenneth Homa, B&D's vice president of marketing, was assigned responsibility for the brand transition. Homa had to design a marketing program to transfer the B&D name to the GE small-appliance lines without losing market share. Specifically, he had to determine the timing for the transition of the various GE product lines and the roles that advertising and promotion should play in the transition. Homa had been asked to have the proposal for the brand transition completed by June 1—only a week away. Before he began to formulate the proposal, Homa reviewed the acquisition and the challenges it presented.

The Acquisition

With 1983 sales of $1,167 million, B&D was the leading worldwide manufacturer of professional and consumer hand-held power tools. Over 100 products were produced in 21 factories around the world. By the late 1970s, B&D was confronting two important problems—a slower growth

Research Assistant Cynthia Bates prepared this case under the supervision of Professor John A. Quelch as the basis for class discussion rather than to illustrate effective or ineffective handling of an administrative situation. Professor Minette E. Drumwright prepared this version of the case. Proprietary data have been disguised. Copyright © 1987 by the President and Fellows of Harvard College. Harvard Business School case 9–588–015.

rate for the power tool market worldwide together with increasing foreign competition. At the same time, management realized that the American housewares market presented a significant opportunity. Capitalizing on its expertise in small-motor production[1] and cordless appliance technology, B&D introduced the Dustbuster® in 1979, a rechargeable hand-held vacuum cleaner. The Dustbuster Vac "moved B&D from the garage into the house"; 60 percent of Dustbuster purchases were made by women. The Dustbuster's success prompted the launch of two other rechargeable products, the Spotliter™ rechargeable flashlight and the Scrub Brusher™ cordless scrubber. In 1983, these three products generated revenues of over $100 million, almost one-third of B&D's US consumer product sales. Pretax profit margins on these products were estimated at a healthy 10 percent. Sales of the three products were expected to increase by 30 percent annually between 1983 and 1985.

Consumer demand for these three innovative products led B&D executives to conclude that further penetration of the housewares market could generate substantial sales and profits for the company. They resolved to develop a family of products that could address consumer needs "everywhere in the house, not just in the basement or garage." However, a significant impediment to growth was B&D's limited access to housewares buyers in the major retail chains. B&D's three housewares products were sold along with B&D's power tools through hardware distributors to hardware buyers and were typically stocked in the hardware sections of retail stores. B&D sought to gain access to housewares buyers through the acquisition of a competitor, the GE Housewares Division.

With 1983 sales of $500 million (GE's total sales in 1983 were $26.79 billion), GE's Housewares Division was the largest competitor in the US electric housewares or small-appliance market. (GE sales of small appliances outside the United States were limited. By contrast, 40 percent of B&D's total sales were made in Europe.) GE sold almost 150 models of products in 14 categories covering food preparation, ovening, garment care, personal care, and home security. (The categories were food processors, portable mixers, electric knives, can openers, drip coffee makers, toaster ovens, toasters, electric skillets, grills and griddles, irons, hair dryers, curling brushes/irons, scales, and security alarms.) In all the appliance categories in which it competed—except food processors, hair care products, and toasters—GE ranked first or second in market share. GE's success largely resulted from continuing attention to product innovation. For example, the GE product line included the recently introduced Spacemaker™ series of premium-priced under-the-cabinet kitchen appliances. The division's 150-person sales force called on housewares buyers in all channels of distribution.

---

[1] In 1983, B&D produced 20 million small motors, four times as many as its closest competitor.

Discussions between GE and B&D culminated in an agreement, announced in February 1984, whereby B&D would acquire the GE Housewares Division for $300 million, comprising $110 million in cash, a $32 million three-year note, and 6 percent of B&D stock. In return, B&D acquired seven plants in the United States, Mexico, Brazil, and Singapore; five distribution centers; 16 service centers; and the Housewares Division's sales and management team. GE retained rights to the accounts receivable at the time of the transfer. Finally, B&D negotiated the right to continue to use the GE name on appliances in the Housewares Division product line for three years from the signing of the acquisition papers in April 1984. However, B&D could not use the GE name on any new appliances introduced after the acquisition. At a stroke, the acquisition transformed B&D from a specialist housewares manufacturer into the dominant full-line player in the housewares market.

The Housewares Market

Product Lines and Pricing

After acquiring the GE division, B&D participated in five more broad housewares categories with aggregate industry sales of $1.4 billion divided as follows:

Food preparation	$275 million
Beverage makers	$325 million
Ovening	$250 million
Garment care	$200 million
Personal care	$350 million

The housewares market was mature and fragmented. Industry growth depended primarily on the rate of household formation and the pace of new product development. About one-tenth of all small appliances in use were replaced each year. The timing of replacement purchases could be accelerated if manufacturers could persuade consumers to trade up to more highly featured, higher-priced, higher-margin models of a particular appliance.

The new B&D offered one of the broadest lines of any manufacturer, competing in 17 product groups. Market performance data for the principal product lines are summarized in Exhibit 1. In all these groups, B&D marketed multiple models that covered almost all price points and product feature configurations. For example, the B&D line included 18 different irons with suggested retail prices from $14.76 to $25.89. The range included promotional, step-up, and premium models. Proctor-Silex, B&D's closest competitor in this category, offered 12 models.

EXHIBIT 1   Market Performance Summary for Selected Product Lines

Product	Year	GE/B&D Unit Share (%)	Feature Ad Share (%)	Average Retail Price ($)	GE/B&D Share Rank in 1984	Major Competitors (share and rank)		
Food processors	1983	16%	9%	$55.00	3	Cuisinart	25%	(1)
	1984	13	7	72.00		Hamilton Beach	21	(2)
	1985*	15	8	NA		Moulinex	11	(4)
						Sunbeam	7	(5)
Mixers	1983	31	22	16.00	2	Sunbeam	28	(1)
	1984	26	20	15.40		Hamilton Beach	21	(3)
	1985*	35	16	NA				
Can openers	1983	28	25	17.65	1	Rival	30	(2)
	1984	34	23	20.52		Sunbeam	8	(3)
	1985*	30	26	NA		Hamilton Beach	6	(4)
Toasters	1983	13	16	16.63	3	Toastmaster	32	(1)
	1984	12	10	21.01		Proctor-Silex	30	(2)
	1985*	11	10	NA				
Toaster ovens	1983	56	49	45.51	1	Toastmaster	25	(2)
	1984	52	39	47.85		Proctor-Silex	8	(3)
	1985*	50	40	NA		Norelco	4	(4)
Drip coffee makers	1983	17	13	34.48	2	Mr. Coffee	19	(1)
	1984	18	15	37.63		Norelco	17	(3)
	1985*	17	16	NA		Hamilton Beach	9	(4)
						Proctor-Silex	8	(5)
Electric knives	1983	39	NA	13.54	2	Hamilton Beach	47	(1)
	1984	37	NA	17.28		Moulinex	8	(3)
	1985*	39	NA	17.65				
Irons	1983	52	39	20.44	1	Proctor-Silex	18	(2)
	1984	46	29	21.83		Sunbeam	13	(3)
	1985*	45	29	NA		Hamilton Beach	11	(4)
Hair care	1983	8	8	17.74	4	Conair	22	(1)
	1984	6	4	15.37		Clairol	12	(2)
	1985*	5	3	NA		Sassoon	8	(3)
Cordless vacuums	1983	NA	NA	NA		Douglas	8	(2)
	1984	NA	38	NA	1	Sears	8	(2)
	1985*	NA	38	25.70		Norelco	7	(4)
Lighting products	1983	65	NA	NA	1	First Alert	25	(2)
	1984	57	44	NA		Sunspot	5	(3)
	1985*	38	36	21.10		Norelco	4	(4)

NOTE: NA means not available.

* Figures for 1985 are estimated.

230

B&D's models were priced competitively within each price/feature segment but, overall, B&D's share tended to be stronger in the medium and upper rather than the lower price ranges. In the fall of 1984, the average retail price of a B&D small appliance was 16 percent higher than the average retail price of its competitors' appliances. The B&D retail price premium varied across product categories as follows:

Food preparation	8%	Cleaning (Dustbuster, Scrub Brusher)	10%
Ovening	26	Lighting (Spotliter)	6
Garment care	5	Smoke alarms	9
Personal care	16		

Some B&D executives were concerned that the price premium in certain categories left B&D vulnerable to lower-priced competition. They advocated price decreases on some models for 1985. Other executives, noting that B&D/GE housewares prices had increased on average by only 10 percent between 1980 and 1984, believed that price increases were necessary to maintain margins. (The contribution margin on B&D small appliances, after variable costs, averaged 40 percent. The percentage margin was higher on premium models such as the Spacemaker products.) However, all agreed that, despite B&D's share leadership position, competitive brands did not appear to set their prices in relation to B&D's prices.

B&D's price premium in the food preparation category was largely due to the premium-priced Spacemaker line of under-the-cabinet kitchen appliances. Launched in 1982 with a can opener, the Spacemaker line was expanded in 1983 to include a toaster oven, drip coffee maker, mixer, and electric knife. The Spacemaker line attracted some first-time purchasers into these five categories but, more important, persuaded current owners to trade up. Although the Spacemaker line at first reversed GE's share erosion in these categories, lower-priced imitations soon appeared. GE's standard countertop version of the Spacemaker appliances lost share as GE's competitors slashed prices to maintain their sales volumes in countertop models. Nevertheless, Spacemaker models were expected to account for about 40 percent of B&D's 1984 unit sales in the five product categories in which they competed.

Competition

B&D's principal competitors in the housewares market were Sunbeam (a subsidiary of Allegheny International), Proctor-Silex (Westray), Hamilton Beach (Scovill), and Norelco (Philips). Few offered as broad a line as B&D, but all four competed with B&D in at least six categories. In addition, B&D had to contend with specialist competitors in each product category. For example, Cuisinart was the market share leader in food processors as was Mr. Coffee in drip coffee makers. European manufacturers, such as Krups, were increasingly penetrating and helping to expand the premium price segment in some categories. Their higher-margin products were welcomed by department stores that sought to continue to compete with mass merchandisers in housewares. Japanese manufacturers were not a factor in the US small-appliance market except for dual-voltage travel irons.

Following the acquisition announcement, B&D's housewares competitors saw the imminent demise of the strongest brand name in the housewares market (i.e., GE) as an opportunity to increase their market shares. Hence, prices on some existing models were reduced; price increases announced for 1985 were minimal, and promotional and merchandising allowances escalated. The timing of new product introductions accelerated and, in some instances, manufacturers decided to enter new product categories. Norelco and West Bend, for example, both announced that they would launch a line of irons.

Sunbeam was especially aggressive and heavily advertised two new products in the fall of 1984: the Monitor automatic shut-off iron and the Oskar compact food processor. Both were introduced at premium rather than penetration price levels. In addition, Sunbeam announced a $43 million marketing budget for 1985, including $25 million for national advertising, $10 million for cooperative advertising, and $8 million for sales promotion. The 1985 budget was more than Sunbeam had spent in the previous five years combined. Some analysts doubted that Sunbeam would follow through with this level of spending, however.

Besides GE's long-standing competitors, B&D also had to contend with imitators of its cordless vacuums and lights. Believing that the newly acquired product lines would divert B&D's management attention and resources, these imitators redoubled their efforts to capture more market share.

Distribution

Small electric appliances were distributed through various channels. Table A shows the percentages of industry dollar sales accounted for by each of seven channels.

Mass merchandisers, such as Montgomery Ward, and discount stores, such as Kmart, had gained share in recent years, mainly at the expense of department stores. Catalog showrooms, such as Service Merchandise, carried the broadest line of small appliances, whereas other channels tended to cherrypick the faster-moving items. GE had built a disproportionately strong share position with volume retailers, notably catalog showrooms and mass merchandisers. B&D was traditionally strong in hardware stores. In the fall of 1984, B&D accounts carried, on average, 30 B&D stockkeeping units (SKUs). (An SKU is an individual model or item in the product line.)

TABLE A	Breakdown of Industry Dollar Sales by Channel (%)
Catalog showrooms	15%
Mass merchandisers	28
Department stores	9
Drug stores	6
Hardware stores	5
Discount stores	8
Other*	29
Total	100%

* Includes sales through stamp and incentive programs, premiums, and military sales.

Most retailers did not view small appliances as especially profitable. Retail margins averaged 15 percent to 20 percent, though promotional merchandise was typically sold near cost. Hence, the space allocated to housewares by most chains remained stable, despite an increasing proliferation of new products. As a result, manufacturers were under more pressure than ever to secure shelf space through merchandising and promotion incentives.

Housewares and hardware buyers at B&D's major accounts determined twice a year which models they would specify as "basics." These selected models were carried in distribution for the following six months, usually in all the stores of a chain. Other models not specified as basics might occasionally be stocked but only in response to temporary promotion offers.

Basics were typically specified in January and May. Retail sales of small appliances peaked before Mother's Day and Christmas. Twenty-one percent of retail sales occurred in the first calendar quarter, 21 percent in the second, 17 percent in the third, and 41 percent in the fourth. Manufacturers and retailers scheduled their advertising and promotion efforts accordingly.

Consumer Behavior

Consumers shopping for small appliances were often characterized as having low information needs, low perceived interbrand differentiation, and high price sensitivity. A 1984 B&D survey drew the following conclusions:

- Two out of three consumers bought their last housewares appliance on sale and/or with a rebate. The highest percentages bought on sale were the countertop drip coffee makers, mixers, and can openers.

- Two out of three consumers compared the prices of different brands and checked to see which brands were on sale.
- Fewer than one out of three consumers would wait until a specific brand went on sale.
- Almost three out of four consumers were willing to switch from their current brands when they purchased replacements.
  However, fewer than one out of four consumers were indifferent to brand names.

A follow-up study of buying behavior for irons found that most consumers, when they needed a replacement, would not wait for a sale but would check to see if a store was having a sale. Fifty percent bought a replacement within seven days. Only 10 percent of the irons were bought as gifts. Forty-two percent of the purchasers had a specific brand in mind when they set off for the store, and 85% ended up buying that brand. Thirty-eight percent were attracted to a particular store by its advertisement, and most bought at the first store in which they shopped. Half of all purchasers bought their irons on sale and/or with a rebate.

Planning the Brand Transition

Consumer Research

To aid transition planning, B&D surveyed 600 men and women 18 to 49 years old in four geographically representative cities during July 1984. The survey first probed consumers' awareness of 10 housewares manufacturers, their ownership of small appliances by each manufacturer, and

EXHIBIT 2   Consumer Research on Major Housewares Manufacturers

	Aided Corporate Awareness (%)	*Product Ownership (%)*	**Corporate Image Ranking**	
			Men	*Women*
General Electric	100%	91%	2	1
Black & Decker	99	67	1	2
Mr. Coffee	99	51	4	5
Conair	79	43	9	8
Hamilton Beach	93	43	5	6
Norelco	98	54	3	4
Proctor-Silex	80	28	8	7
Rival	56	19	10	10
Sunbeam	96	48	6	3
Toastmaster	92	41	7	9

TABLE B   B&D's Strengths and Weaknesses

	B&D Advantage vs. Closest Competitor*	B&D (Dis)Advantage vs. GE
B&D Strengths		
Has high-quality workmanship	+24	+5
Makes durable products	+23	+4
Makes reliable products	+20	+1
Leader in making innovative products	+18	(7)
B&D Vulnerabilities		
Makes products that can be easily serviced	+7	(17)
Makes products most people would consider buying	+7	(12)
Makes attractive, good-looking products	+6	(8)
Makes products that are generally priced lower	+5	(9)
Makes products that are easily found	+2	(9)

* Other than GE.

the degree to which their overall image ratings of each manufacturer were favorable or unfavorable. These results are summarized in Exhibit 2.

Next, respondents were asked to rate each manufacturer on various attributes using a 100-point scale. Averaging all responses, the researchers identified B&D's strengths and weaknesses compared with its main housewares competitors (GE excluded) and then with GE (see Table B).

The survey asked respondents whether they currently perceived B&D favorably or unfavorably as a manufacturer of each of 16 products. The percentages answering "very favorably" on a four-point scale were as follows:

Smoke alarms	62%
Flashlights	60
Vacuums	48
Grills/griddles	29
Electric knives	25
Can openers	24
Scales	22
Toaster ovens	21
Irons	18
Portable mixers	17
Toasters	17
Food processors	16
Coffee makers	13
Skillets	12
Curling irons	11
Hair dryers	9

Qualitative research indicated that consumers considered B&D a suitable manufacturer of these products but were largely unaware that B&D already made them.

Product Plans

Homa knew that B&D executives disagreed concerning both the timing and the manner in which the B&D name should be transferred to the GE small-appliance line. In talking with other executives, he had identified five points of view.

One group of executives argued that the name change should be executed across the entire product line as soon as possible to demonstrate B&D's commitment to the trade. At the other extreme, a second group, skeptical about the likely pulling power of the B&D brand in housewares, proposed that B&D delay the name transfer until the end of the three-year period.

A third group of executives supported a gradual transition whereby all the items in one or two product categories would be reintroduced under the B&D name in successive six-month periods. A fourth group wanted to execute the name change first on the premium quality items in several product categories to be followed later by the remaining lower-priced items in each product line. A fifth group argued that the transition schedule should be linked to a new product development program. Through such a program, the name change would be implemented in a product category only after the product line and packaging had been redesigned and/or when B&D could offer a new product with enhanced features.

As he planned the transition program, Homa also had to consider proposals for new or revised products that B&D product managers had submitted. The proposals included the following:

- The Spacemaker line of under-the-cabinet appliances, which had been acquired from GE, could be redesigned by B&D to look sturdier and more compact. The edges could be rounded for additional safety.
- B&D could develop Black Tie™, a line of "men's grooming tools," which would be priced at a 15 percent premium over the hair care line acquired from GE.
- Plans had been developed for the Stowaway line of dual-voltage travel appliances. The line would include a folding iron, hair dryer, and curling irons.
- The Handymixer cordless beater, the first extension of B&D's cordless technology into the kitchen, had been proposed.
- An automatic shut-off iron had been designed by B&D. Unlike the Sunbeam model, the B&D iron would beep to let the consumer know that it had been left on.

Communications

An effective communications plan would be integral to the brand transition. Historically, B&D and GE had implemented communications programs with fundamental differences. Specifically, GE had emphasized push programs (e.g., volume rebates, purchase allowances), which were aimed at the trade, while B&D had emphasized pull program (e.g., advertising, consumer rebates), which targeted consumers. These differences are reflected in Exhibits 3 and 4, which summarize the advertising and promotion expenditures for GE and B&D before the acquisition. Homa's tentative recommendations for 1985 communications expenditures also are included in Exhibit 3 and 4.

EXHIBIT 3   Advertising and Merchandising Expenditures for GE Housewares (in millions of dollars and percentage of net sales billed)

	1983		1984		1985*	
	$ million	*% of Sales*	*$ million*	*% of Sales*	*$ million*	*% of Sales*
Push Programs						
Purchase allowances	$17.5	3.5%	$22.5	4.5%	—	—
Volume rebates	14.0	2.8	14.5	2.9	$ 12.5	2.5%
Cash discounts	—	—	—	—	—	—
Subtotal	31.5	6.3	37.0	7.4	12.5	2.5
Pull Programs						
National advertising	$ 8.5	1.7%	$16.5	3.3%	$ 34.0	6.8%
Co-op advertising	26.0	5.2	25.5	5.1	32.0	6.4
Consumer rebates	13.0	2.6	9.5	1.9	15.0	3.0
Consumer promotions	1.5	0.3	1.0	0.2	0.5	0.1
Sales promotion materials	3.0	0.6	1.5	0.3	3.5	0.7
Press relations	1.0	0.2	1.0	0.2	1.0	0.2
Exhibits	1.0	0.2	1.0	0.2	1.0	0.2
Functional support expenses	1.5	0.3	1.5	0.3	2.0	0.4
Corporate promotion assessment	—	—	—	—	—	—
In-store merchandising	—	—	—	—	3.5	0.7
Subtotal	55.5	11.1	57.5	11.5	92.5	18.5
Total merchandising expenditures	$87.0	17.4%	$94.5	18.9%	$105.0	21.0%

NOTE: 1984 and 1985 figures continue to separate the former GE housewares line from the former B&D household products line for ease of comparison. Total 1985 B&D Household Products Group expenditures can be calculated by summing the last columns in Exhibits 3 and 4.

* Estimated.

EXHIBIT 4 Advertising and Merchandising Expenditures for Black & Decker Household Products (in millions of dollars and percentage of net sales billed)

	1983		1984		1985*	
	$ million	% of Sales	$ million	% of Sales	$ million	% of Sales
Push Programs						
Flexible funds (off-invoice)	—	—	—	—	—	—
Retail incentive plan	—	—	—	—	$ 1.0	0.6%
Cash discounts	$ 0.9	0.9%	$ 1.2	0.9%	1.5	0.9
Subtotal	0.9	0.9	1.2	0.9	2.5	1.5
Pull Programs						
National advertising	$ 8.9	8.9%	$12.0	9.2%	$18.6	11.0%
Co-op advertising	2.0	2.0	3.1	2.4	7.3	4.3
Consumer rebates	—	—	2.2	1.7	11.7	6.9
Consumer promotions	—	—	—	—	—	—
Sales promotion materials	0.5	0.5	1.6	1.2	1.4	0.8
Press relations	—	—	—	—	—	—
Exhibits	—	—	0.1	0.1	0.3	0.2
Functional support expenses	—	—	0.1	0.1	0.3	0.2
Corporate promotion assessment	—	—	1.0	0.8	2.0	1.2
In-store merchandising	—	—	—	—	—	—
Subtotal	11.4	11.4	20.1	15.5	41.6	24.6
Total merchandising expenditures	$12.3	12.3%	$21.3	16.4%	$44.1	26.1%

NOTE: B&D household products: Dustbuster Vac, Spotliter, and Scrub Brusher.
* Estimated.

Advertising

Increased advertising expenditures would be necessary to bolster consumer brand loyalties in the face of more aggressive competition. Homa estimated that media expenditures of $100 million would be needed for the brand transition.

The issue of how to handle the brand transition in advertising was much debated. Some executives believed that explicit references to GE in B&D's advertising were necessary to maintain market share during the transition, especially in categories where GE's brand name equity was strong. These executives wanted a transition statement such as "designed by GE, built by B&D" to be included in advertising. They also wanted hang tags on B&D products at the point of sale to indicate that the products had formerly been made by GE. Critics of this dual-branding approach, which included B&D's advertising agency, argued that it would confuse consumers and simply sustain the GE franchise. Exhibits 5 and 6

EXHIBIT 5   Proposed 1985 Spacemaker Advertisement

(SFX: TRAFFIC)
ANNCR: (VO) One of the most densely populated places on earth

is your kitchen counter. So crowded, the only place to go is up.

Presenting Black & Decker Spacemaker Appliances.

Coffeemaker,

mixer,

toaster oven,

electric knife

and can opener. The only completely coordinated line of under-the-cabinet appliances.

(SFX: BIRDS CHIRPING)
They return your counter

to a more natural state.

The Spacemaker line

from Black & Decker. Ideas at work.

---

present television advertisements proposed by B&D's advertising agency.

Promotional Programs

Homa had to determine whether or not to maintain GE's more generous support of promotional programs. Some trade accounts already had expressed concern about potential cutbacks that B&D might implement.

EXHIBIT 6   Proposed 1985 Spotliter Advertisement

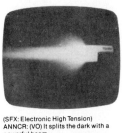

(SFX: Electronic High Tension)
ANNCR: (VO) It splits the dark with a powerful beam.

Spotliter rechargeable light from Black & Decker.

A light built so strong

it can survive a drop of 6 feet.

Spotliter stores all the power you need in its own recharging base.

So on a moment's notice

it gives you light.

Light for your safety...and peace of mind.

It's one utility light that does more than just shine.

Spotliter.

One of the many lights

in the lighting series. From Black & Decker. Ideas at work.

Competitive housewares manufacturers did all they could to cultivate this concern in an effort to secure additional basics listings and shelf space for their own products.

At the time of the acquisition, GE's promotional programs for the trade included purchase allowances, volume rebates, dating discounts, and cooperative advertising. Promotional programs for consumers focused on consumer rebates.

Purchase Allowances

During the 1970s, GE initiated purchase allowances (PAs) on selected models against orders paid for during the first two months after Christmas and Mother's Day, the peak retail selling periods. Over time, PAs came to be offered on orders placed beyond these two-month periods. By 1983, 90 percent of shipments included an off-invoice PA.

Volume Rebates

GE operated a volume rebate program that offered trade accounts a year-end refund of up to 4½ percent of their net purchases during the year. Accounts qualified for various percentage rebates according to the degree to which their purchases increased over those of the previous year. There were two other features of the program. First, the rebates were computed on an account's total purchases rather than separately for each shipping point. Second, the program attempted to maintain the total number of SKUs by requiring a dealer to have incremental sales in four of six defined product categories to earn the minimum rebate.

Dating Discounts

Dating allowed customers to pay for goods after they were shipped and received. Dating encouraged trade accounts to place early orders for goods that they did not have to pay for immediately. The seasonality of retail sales and the desire of trade accounts to avoid holding high bulk-to-value small appliances in their own warehouses made dating programs a necessity in the small-appliance industry. Production planning and scheduling could become more efficient if a trade account placed early orders at the same time that it decided which SKUs to specify for its basics lineup.

GE Housewares Division's standard terms required full payment by the tenth of the month following an order, plus 45 days. The dating program permitted an account to place an order in May and June for shipment before September 1 and payment by December 10. A second dating program required payment by May 10 on orders placed in December and January. A schedule of early-payment allowances rewarded accounts for payment of invoices before the dating program due date. GE's purchase allowance and dating programs together permitted accounts to pay less and pay later.

Cooperative Advertising

GE's Housewares Division had long offered trade accounts a cooperative advertising program. Accounts accrued 3 percent of their net purchases in a rolling 12-month cooperative advertising fund. (Allowances accrued more than 12 months previously that had not been spent were forfeited.) Accounts could draw on these accruals to subsidize the cost of retail advertising that featured GE products. GE paid the full cost of qualifying advertising but sometimes only partially charged accounts' accrual funds if they featured particularly profitable premium-priced products such as items in the Spacemaker line, if they ran advertisements featuring multiple GE items, or if they timed their advertising to coincide with flights of GE national advertising.

Consumer Rebates

Initiated in the 1970s to help sell slower-moving models, consumer rebates had become endemic to the housewares category by the early 1980s. By 1983, almost all list price increases were cushioned with rebates, and three-quarters of all feature advertisements for GE housewares included references to manufacturer rebate offers. The average value of housewares manufacturers' consumer rebates escalated as each tried to outdo the other. In an effort to lead the industry toward more realistic list pricing, GE in 1983 curtailed rebates on irons and toaster ovens, two categories in which it was the market share leader. Far from following GE's lead, competitors increased their rebate offers. As a result, GE's share declined six points in both categories within six months.

Conclusion

Homa had two main concerns. How could the B&D brand name be transferred most effectively to the GE small-appliance line? What kind of communications program would facilitate the transfer?

MEM Company, Inc.

In December 1980, Gay Mayer, president of MEM Company, Inc., was considering how to increase sales of the company's line of men's toiletries, which included the English Leather brand.[1] Sales had risen 10 percent in 1979 over the previous year but had flattened in 1980. Several options to improve sales growth existed, but the two that interested Mayer the most were expansion of distribution into food stores and introduction of a new brand.

Company Background

In 1883 Mark Edward Mayer opened a first-class women's perfume and soap store in Vienna. Exports to the United States began in 1920. Sales were so strong that the company moved to the United States in 1935. It began to shift emphasis to men's fragrances after one of its department store accounts accidentally displayed MEM cologne for women in the men's department, where it rapidly sold out. The company developed a more masculine-looking package, changed the fragrance formula slightly, and introduced a men's cologne under the generic name Russian Leather. In 1947 the name was changed to English Leather in response to the cold war and a Fifth Avenue buyer's desire to merchandise MEM products in conjunction with high-quality English clothing.

Sales growth accelerated after the company went public in 1966, approaching $60 million in 1979. Approximately one-third of these sales were derived from two subsidiaries, Tom Fields Ltd. (which manufactured the Tinkerbell line of children's toiletries) and Lebanon Packaging Company, acquired in 1969. Sixty percent of MEM sales were accounted for by six lines of men's toiletries: English Leather (introduced in 1947); Lime (1968); Timberline (1970); Wind Drift (1972); Musk (1975); and Racquet Club (1978). Lime and Musk had been developed in response to similar competitive fragrances. Timberline and Wind Drift appealed to

---

Professor John A. Quelch wrote this case as the basis for class discussion rather than to illustrate effective or ineffective handling of an administrative situation. Certain company data have been disguised. Copyright © 1981 by the President and Fellows of Harvard College. Harvard Business School case 581–154.

[1] Blondit, English Leather, Timberline, Tinkerbell, and Wind Drift were registered trademarks of MEM Company, Inc.

men who enjoyed the outdoors and the sea; Racquet Club had been introduced to capitalize on the growing popularity of tennis and other racquet sports.

All six lines carried the English Leather name on product labels, and all were sold in similar packages. They covered three broad product categories: (1) face savers, including all-purpose lotion, after-shave, and shaving cream; (2) headliners, including shampoo and hair tonic; and (3) body guards, including cologne, deodorants, bath soaps, and talc. A breakdown of MEM men's toiletries by line and product category is shown in Table A.

TABLE A   MEM's Toiletries for Men

	Face Savers	*Headliners*	*Body Guards*	*Gift Sets*	*Total*
English Leather	20	3	11	19	53
Lime	3	0	2	4	9
Musk	7	0	2	3	12
Timberline	5	0	2	4	11
Wind Drift	5	0	2	4	11
Racquet Club	6	0	3	5	14
Total	46	3	22	39	110

During 1979, 39 percent of English Leather dollar sales were in face savers, 1 percent in headliners, and 14 percent in body guards. Of the remainder, 37 percent were accounted for by gift sets and 9 percent by mixed prepacks.[2] The breakdown was similar for the other five lines, except that gift sets accounted for, on average, only 20 percent of sales. Although individual slow-selling items were sometimes dropped, MEM had never discontinued an entire line.

The MEM company distributed under license the expensive John Weitz designer and Acqua di Selva lines of men's toiletries to about 1,000 department store and men's specialty store accounts. It also sold the Embracing line of lower-priced women's spray and splash colognes, Blondit creme bleach for facial and body hair, and a variety of novelty and boutique soaps. In aggregate these products accounted for 5 percent of MEM sales in 1979.

Production Process

After-shaves and colognes are fragrances blended with varying quantities of other raw materials, principally water and alcohol. After-shaves con-

---

[2] A mixed prepack was a set of merchandise sold to the trade, sometimes at a discount, which included items from several MEM lines.

tain more water, less alcohol, and less fragrance than colognes. Once packaged, both remain chemically stable unless exposed to heat or light. When applied to the skin, evaporation releases the fragrance. It is important to ensure that the ingredients evaporate simultaneously and that the chemistry of the reaction is constant among consumers despite differences in body metabolisms.

Like its major competitors, MEM did not develop or manufacture most of the fragrances in its toiletries; these were supplied by about 30 international companies including Roure-Dupont, Givaudan, and International Flavors and Fragrances. Development of a fragrance involved skilled compounding by specialist chemists of as many as 50 raw materials, both natural and synthetic. Fragrance formulas were not usually divulged, in order to ensure the loyalty of buyers to their original suppliers.

Typically MEM would invite about six manufacturers to submit fragrance samples on a speculative basis. The company would specify a price range and target consumer group. Samples would be evaluated on a range of attitudinal dimensions by MEM employees, after which one or two would be chosen for testing in selected markets. Such research often proved inconclusive, so the judgment of senior management was usually paramount in the final selection of new fragrances.

The MEM company subcontracted manufacture of its shaving creams and some deodorant sticks. It compounded and packaged most of its products at its 205,000-square-foot Northvale, New Jersey, plant. Production efficiency was limited by the breadth of the product line, frequent need for short production runs, and seasonality of sales. Packaging, particularly of gift sets, remained labor intensive and largely unautomated. And although floor space was not fully utilized, much had to be devoted to storing over 200 lots of individual plastic, wood, paper, and glass packages and containers.

The Men's Toiletries Market

Data on the men's toiletries market were sparse, partly because of the fragmentation of the industry, partly because substantial male use of products targeted at women was believed to occur. Some 60 companies and 200 brands competed for consumer purchases of men's cologne and after-shave. Retail sales of those products through all classes of trade during 1979 were estimated at $224 million and $189 million respectively, up 10 percent and 4 percent over 1978 and six times greater than in 1965 (see Exhibit 1). Retail sales of men's deodorants, shaving creams, and hairdressings were estimated at $330 million, $135 million, and $150 million, respectively.

Mayer divided the men's toiletries market into three groups, based on price point (see Exhibit 2). The *exclusive* group included designer-name

EXHIBIT 1   Men's Toiletries for Three Classes of Trade, 1979 (dollars and unit sales in millions)

	Retail Dollar Sales				Unit Sales	
	After-shave	Cologne	Total	Percent Increase over 1978	Total	Percent Increase over 1978
Chain and independent drugstores	$ 78	$ 71	$149	15%	43	5%
Mass merchandisers and discount stores	38	26	64	15	23	5
Food stores	29	4	33	10	16	0
	$145	$101	$246	13%	82	3%

NOTE: Data for department stores and men's specialty stores were not available in this study.
SOURCE: Rosenfeld, Sirowitz & Lawson, Inc.

EXHIBIT 2   Retail Price Points for MEM Men's Toiletries and Competitive Brands, July 1980

	After-shave 2 oz.	Cologne 2 oz.	After-shave 4 oz.	Cologne 4 oz.	After-shave 8 oz.	Cologne 8 oz.
English Leather	$2.50	$3.00	$4.00	$6.00	$5.50	$8.00
Lime	2.50	3.00	3.50	5.50	5.00	7.50
Musk	3.00	3.50		6.00		
Timberline	2.50	3.00	3.50	5.50	5.00	7.50
Wind Drift	2.50	3.00	3.50	5.50	5.00	7.50
Racquet Club	3.00	4.50	5.00	6.50		
Acqua di Selva	7.50	8.40	11.00	13.50		21.00
	(1.75)	(1.75)	(3.50)	(3.50)		(7.00)
Aramis		8.50	9.00	12.50	15.00	22.00
British Sterling	3.50	4.00	7.00	7.00	7.50	9.50
Brut		4.50		9.00		15.00
		(1.50)		(3.20)		(6.40)
Brut 33			2.50	2.50		4.15
			(3.50)	(3.50)		(6.00)
Brut 33 Musk				4.15		
				(3.50)		
Cardin	6.00	8.00	8.50	12.50	15.00	22.50
Chaps		6.50	8.50	9.50	12.50	14.50
Denim	3.00		5.00	7.50		
Monsieur Jovan		3.50	7.00	7.50	10.50	11.00
Old Spice			3.00	4.50	4.75	6.50
			(4.25)	(4.25)	(8.50)	(8.50)
Oleg Cassini		7.00		11.50		

NOTE: Numbers in parentheses indicate different ounce-size package from that shown in column heading.
SOURCE: Company records.

brands, such as Pierre Cardin and Oleg Cassini, with retail selling prices over $10 for a 4-ounce bottle of cologne. These were distributed primarily through department stores and men's specialty stores and were advertised in men's, women's, and dual-audience magazines.

The MEM products competed principally in the *medium-priced* group, in which a 4-ounce bottle of cologne typically sold for between $4 and $10. English Leather's principal competitors were Old Spice, manufactured by the Shulton division of American Cyanamid; British Sterling, manufactured by the Spiedel division of Textron; Jovan, manufactured by Beecham, a major British pharmaceutical company; and Brut, manufactured by Fabergé, a public company with annual sales estimated at $250 million. Next to Old Spice, MEM had the broadest product line among these competitors. Mayer believed that English Leather users were typically somewhat younger than users of either British Sterling or Old Spice.

The third, *mass* group of brands, selling below $4, included Aqua Velva (manufactured by J. B. Williams Co.), Mennen Skin Bracer, and Brut 33. These brands were also thought to appeal to an older age group than English Leather. They were distributed primarily through food stores, drugstores, and mass merchandisers and discount stores such as Kmart.

Several trends were evident in the market during the late 1970s. Many independent manufacturers were acquired by large corporations attracted by their high profit margins. Further, many manufacturers were active in more than one segment. Shulton marketed both the Old Spice and the exclusive Pierre Cardin brands. Fabergé marketed Brut in the medium-priced segment and Brut 33 in the mass segment. Mennen marketed Mennen Skin Bracer in the mass segment and had recently introduced Millionaire in the medium-priced segment.

Many new products were introduced during the late 1970s. In the exclusive market segment, new brands with designer names were frequently launched, partly because national distribution and heavy advertising were not considered essential to success. More surprising to MEM executives was the number of new products in the medium-priced segment backed by substantial advertising expenditures. In 1979, for example, the Ralph Lauren division of Warner Communications introduced Chaps, Jovan introduced Oleg Cassini, and Lever Bros. introduced Denim. Combined advertising expenditures on these three brands approached $7 million in 1979.

Media advertising expenditures on men's after-shave and cologne in 1979 totaled $45 million, of which 80 percent was spent on television and 18 percent in consumer magazines. These represented a 30 percent increase over 1978, although media costs had increased only 15 percent. The top 12 brands accounted for 62 percent of expenditures in 1979, up from 52 percent in 1978. Shulton spent 50 percent more to advertise Old Spice than MEM spent on all six of its lines in 1979. In 1980 it appeared that English Leather would be outspent by Brut as well, as MEM's share of industry advertising declined. A consumer survey showed English Leather ranking second only to Brut in unaided advertising awareness (see Exhibit 3).

Sales and Distribution

MEM men's toiletries were distributed through a variety of channels representing about 24,000 retail outlets (see Exhibit 4). The percentages of sales by line and class of trade for 1979 and 1980 are reported in Exhibit 5. Although MEM's distribution penetration was less than that achieved by Old Spice, company executives believed that their current general merchandise, mass merchandise, and drug accounts were responsible for at least 80 percent of men's fragrance sales through these classes of trade. All shipments were made direct to retail stores or to the regional warehouses of retail chains. Wholesalers were not significantly involved in MEM's distribution.

In 1960 MEM products had been distributed primarily through department stores and men's specialty stores. However, changes in consumer shopping patterns, the broadening popularity of MEM products, and the

EXHIBIT 3   **Results of 1980 Consumer Survey (percent of respondents)**

	Brand Awareness*		Advertising Awareness		Correct Slogan Identification	Brands Ever Used	Brands Now Used	Brand Used Most Often
	Unaided	Total	Unaided	Total				
Aqua Velva	13%	94%	2%	86%	na	4%	na	na
Aramis	40	83	3	52	9%	28	22%	22%
British Sterling	na	na	na	na	na	4	4	na
Brut	52	96	28	84	80	24	8	6
Canoe	na	na	na	na	na	22	14	10
Denim	9	62	4	57	21	4	2	na
English Leather	41	96	27	85	45	30	12	4
Jovan	12	72	6	68	na	8	4	4
Mennen Skin Bracer	19	88	1	77	na	16	12	8
Old Spice	48	93	24	83	74	30	20	20
Pierre Cardin	na	na	na	na	na	6	4	na
Royal Copenhagen	15	50	4	43	na	10	8	6

NOTE: Percent of respondents is based on telephone interviews with men and women purchasers of men's cologne and after-shave conducted in New York and Chicago during December 1980.

* To qualify as having unaided awareness of a brand or its advertising, a consumer had to name it in response to questions such as "What brands of men's after-shave or cologne can you name?" and "What brands of men's after-shave or cologne have you seen advertised?" Total awareness measures also included consumers with aided awareness who replied affirmatively to questions such as "Have you heard of brand X?" or "Have you seen advertising for brand X?" Correct slogan identification required a consumer to name the associated brand correctly when presented with a particular slogan.

SOURCE: Rosenfeld, Sirowitz & Lawson, Inc.

EXHIBIT 4   Account Penetration by Class of Trade, 1980

	Number of Headquarters' Accounts Sold	Number of Retail Outlets Penetrated	Estimated Total Number of Retail Outlets
Department stores	17	900	3,000
General merchandise chains*	12	3,600	4,000
Chain drugstores†	56	6,000	9,500
Independent drugstores	na	6,500	40,000
Mail-order catalogs	8	50	
Mass merchandisers and discount stores‡	35	6,000	10,000
Armed forces stores	na	700	
Men's specialty stores and other stores§	na	1,000	
Export	na	na	na

* Includes Sears, Roebuck & Co., J. C. Penney Co., and Montgomery Ward.
† Includes drug accounts with more than five retail outlets, such as Osco Drug and Medi Mart.
‡ Includes Woolco-Woolworth, Kmart, Zayre, and Service Merchandise.
§ Includes college bookstores, gift shops, food stores, and so on.
SOURCE: Company records.

EXHIBIT 5   Percentages of Dollar Sales by Product Line and Class of Trade, 1979 and 1980

		English Leather	Lime	Musk	Timber-line	Wind Drift	Racquet Club	Mixed Prepacks	Other	Total‡
Department stores	1979	2.6%*	0.1%	0.3%	0.1%	0.2%	0.3%	0.3%	†	3.9%
	1980	2.0	0.1	0.2	0.1	0.1	0.2	0.1	†	2.8
General merchandise chains	1979	8.2	0.3	1.1	0.5	0.5	1.1	1.0	0.1%	12.8
	1980	7.4	0.2	1.1	0.4	0.4	1.1	1.0	0.1	11.7
Chain drugstores	1979	21.3	1.0	3.2	1.6	1.1	2.0	2.9	0.1	33.2
	1980	22.5	1.0	3.4	1.5	1.1	1.4	2.7	0.1	33.7
Independent drugstores	1979	5.3	0.3	0.7	0.4	0.4	0.9	0.6	0.1	8.7
	1980	5.3	0.2	0.7	0.3	0.4	0.8	0.4	0.1	8.2
Mail-order catalogs	1979	0.9	†	†	†	†	0.1	†	†	1.0
	1980	0.4	†	†	†	†	†	†	†	0.4
Mass merchandisers and discount stores	1979	16.2	0.4	2.0	0.6	0.6	1.7	1.2	0.1	22.8
	1980	18.3	0.4	2.2	0.5	0.5	2.3	0.9	0.1	25.2
Armed forces stores	1979	3.6	†	0.6	†	†	0.4	0.1	†	4.7
	1980	4.0	†	0.7	†	†	0.3	0.2	†	5.2
Men's specialty/other stores	1979	4.8	0.2	0.3	0.2	0.1	0.4	0.9	0.1	7.0
	1980	5.4	0.2	0.4	0.2	0.1	0.3	1.0	0.1	7.7
Export	1979	3.7	0.3	0.3	0.3	0.1	0.3	0.5	0.1	5.6
	1980	3.0	0.2	0.3	0.3	0.1	0.5	0.5	0.2	5.1
Total†	1979	66.6	2.6	8.5	3.7	3.0	7.2	7.5	0.6	100.0
	1980	68.3	2.3	9.0	3.3	2.7	6.9	6.8	0.7	100.0

* I.e., "2.6 percent of 1979 dollar sales of MEM men's toiletries were of English Leather sold to department stores."
† Sales volume less than 0.1 percent.
‡ Final columns and rows may not total 100 percent because of rounding.
SOURCE: Company records.

substantial merchandising support required by department stores caused the company to expand distribution. By 1980 English Leather was the highest-selling line of men's toiletries carried by general merchandise chains such as Sears, Roebuck & Co. and J. C. Penney. Nevertheless, as indicated in Exhibit 6, English Leather placed second to Old Spice in dollar market share in drugstores and mass merchandise outlets. Distribution through food stores accounted for less than 2 percent of sales in 1980; however, MEM executives were receiving an increasing number of inquiries from food chains about carrying a limited selection of their faster-moving items.

The company's accounts were classified by sales revenue potential. Frequency of calls by MEM salespeople varied accordingly. Buyers at important headquarters accounts of major chains would be visited six times a year. Several thousand accounts bought in quantities too small to justify any sales call and were serviced through the mail. The MEM sales force of 50 was one of the largest in the industry. Each salesperson was responsible for all accounts in a geographic territory. Some salespeople were required not to call on the outlets of certain national accounts located in their territories. (For example, Kmart allowed no supplier salespeople in its retail stores.) Because the sales force was able to visit and provide merchandising assistance to 14,000 retail outlets three times a year on average, MEM had achieved better distribution penetration than most of its competitors, particularly in independent drugstores.

The average salesperson compensation package of over $30,000 included 70 percent salary and 30 percent commission. (Most manufacturers of men's toiletries did not offer such a high commission component but, unlike MEM, they typically reimbursed expenses.) Partly as a result, MEM's sales force turnover was low and MEM salespeople were considered above the industry average in both quality and experience. They had

EXHIBIT 6   Market Shares of Major Men's Toiletries Brands for Three Classes of Trade, 1979

	Independent and Chain Drugstores	Mass Merchandisers and Discount Stores	Food Stores
English Leather	14.5%*	12.7%	na
Old Spice	16.4	20.5	20.8%
Mennen Skin Bracer	7.5	10.6	27.9
Brut	10.7	12.4	14.9
Four-brand share total	49.1%	56.2%	63.6%

NOTE: Data for general merchandise chains were not reported in this study.

* I.e., "14.5 percent of dollar sales of after-shaves and colognes through independent and chain drugstores in 1979 were of English Leather brands."

SOURCE: Rosenfeld, Sirowitz & Lawson, Inc.

to be versatile to sell in several classes of trade, which differed widely in merchandising objectives and practices.

Retail sales were concentrated around the Father's Day, graduation, and Christmas gift-giving periods. Over 40 percent of annual retail sales of MEM men's toiletries occurred during November and December, and three-quarters of these were believed to be gift purchases. Because of this seasonality, MEM commonly held a cash surplus during the first half of each year, but had to borrow during the second half to finance its dating program. Under this program, the trade was not required to pay invoices on midyear orders for Christmas shipments until year-end. A sliding scale of discounts for prepayment of invoices before the dating deadline was also offered.

Pricing Policy

Products were shipped by MEM with freight prepaid and typically allowed the trade a 40 percent margin. Suggested retail prices were maintained in most outlets. Rapid increases in the cost of raw materials for fragrance compounding and packaging caused retail prices of men's toiletries to rise dramatically during the 1970s, and the industry became concerned that competitiveness of their products in the gift marketplace might be jeopardized. The MEM company had not raised its prices as fast as the industry, and, partly as a result, its line had become increasingly acceptable to more price-oriented classes of trade.

An income statement outlining the cost structure for MEM men's toiletries is presented in Exhibit 7. The contribution margin varied widely

---

EXHIBIT 7 1979 Income Statement for Men's Toiletries (percent)

Gross sales	100.00%
Raw materials	37.55
Direct labor	7.17
Contribution margin	55.28
Manufacturing overhead	2.34
Real estate, taxes, insurance, utilities, depreciation	2.02
Shipping*	8.09
Advertising and promotion	20.52
Field sales force	7.52
General and administrative	7.17
Net pretax income from operations	7.62
Other income†	1.47

NOTE: Income statement does not include Lebanon Packaging Co., Tom Fields Ltd., and the Acqua di Selva and John Weitz lines.

* Company prices include prepaid freight charges.

† Net interest income on seasonal cash flows.

SOURCE: Company records.

item by item; it was highest on colognes packaged in plastic containers. (Executives believed that the significant cost difference between glass and plastic packaging would not be credible to consumers if fully reflected in a retail price differential.) Margins were lower on more frequently used products, including after-shaves, deodorants, and shaving creams, and also on gift sets. Gift sets were priced as the sum of the prices of the component items, but because of incremental packaging and labor costs their percentage margins were lower than the average on the component items.

The MEM company sometimes offered its products to the trade at promotional prices. During 1980 about 10 percent of its men's toiletries were sold at prices that allowed 45 percent or 50 percent margins as opposed to the usual 40 percent. Trade interest was maintained through frequent prepacks shipped with counter or shelf display units and

---

EXHIBIT 8   Summary of 1980 Promotions and Trade Deals

1. Prepack containing 24 English Leather Power Foam for the price of 22 (2 free with 22), providing the trade a 45 percent margin at suggested retail price of $2.00.
2. Prepack of 12 four-piece gift sets containing cologne and after-shave in both English Leather and Musk. Tied into a SuperShooter consumer sweepstakes promotion, each package flagged "Regular $8.75 value, now $6.00."
3. Prepack containing 12 16 oz.-size English Leather Shampoo for the price of 11 of the regular 9-oz. size (1 free with 11), providing the trade a 45 percent margin at suggested retail price of $2.50 each.
4. Basket display prepack containing 1-oz. sizes of English Leather Cologne (72), Wind Drift and Musk (24 of each), and Lime and Timberline (12 of each), each priced at $1.00. Profit margin to trade—40 percent.
5. Prepack containing 12 English Leather Special Formula Deodorant Sticks for the price of 11 (1 free with 11), providing the trade a 45 percent margin at suggested retail price of $2.50 each.
6. Prepack containing 48 ½-oz. trial-size Musk Cologne for Men, priced at $1.50 each for impulse purchases. Profit margin to trade—40 percent.
7. Prepack containing 36 Pocket Mist-ers in six fragrances, priced at $2.50 each. Profit margin to trade—40 percent.
8. Prepack containing 36 1-oz. travel-size Racquet Club Cologne, priced at $1.50 each. Profit margin to trade—40 percent.
9. Prepack containing six 4-oz. English Leather Cologne and six 5-oz. Musk Cologne with new pump spray caps. Profit margin to trade—40 percent.
10. Prepack containing 12 5-oz. Musk Cologne for Men. Each package is flagged "Save $1.50, Regularly $6.50—Now Only $5.00." Profit margin to trade—40 percent.
11. A $6.00 value men's nail-care set offered for $3.00 with any $6.00 purchase of English Leather toiletries.
12. A $3.00 value English Leather gift set (containing after-shave, shave cream, and shampoo travel sizes) free with any $6.00 purchase of English Leather toiletries.
13. An executive briefcase plus a travel set of 1-oz.-size colognes in English Leather, Lime, Wind Drift, and Timberline, valued at $29.00, priced at $10.00.

SOURCE: Company records.

through gift-with-purchase, purchase-with-purchase, and self-liquidating premium consumer promotions.[3]

Less-expensive brands of men's toiletries typically offered more price-oriented consumer promotions, such as coupons and refunds. Promotions for MEM men's toiletries during 1980 are summarized in Exhibit 8. A merchandising tear sheet for one of these promotions is reproduced in Figure A.

Marketing Communications

As indicated in Exhibit 9, 20 percent of MEM men's toiletries sales dollars were spent on marketing communications, principally advertising and promotion. The vice president of finance hoped to maintain this ratio in 1981 even if the company introduced a new line.

Advertising for MEM men's toiletries was aimed at males and females, aged 18 to 34, in households with annual incomes over $10,000. Men in this age group were believed to be the heaviest users of men's toiletries and the most likely to switch brands. Since 1967 MEM had employed the theme "All my men wear English Leather, or they wear nothing at all." Some MEM executives believed this theme was becoming "tired," and "a less provocative approach might be better suited for the 1980s." Slogans used by competitive brands tended to emphasize either a macho or a success theme (see Exhibit 10).

Measured media advertising expenditures, summarized in Exhibit 11, emphasized national television and consumer magazines with support from network radio. Some MEM executives believed that the budget should be concentrated entirely in television. Advertising on television was devoted exclusively to English Leather and was aired primarily during prime time, late fringe, and late night.[4] Magazine advertising in 1980 covered all six lines of MEM men's toiletries and was placed primarily during June and the fourth quarter in a diverse group of 25 magazines such as *People, Playboy,* and *Cosmopolitan.* Radio was used as a supportive medium immediately before the Christmas holiday; it afforded scheduling and copy flexibility and added to the frequency with which the advertising message was delivered. About 20 percent of advertisements in all media promoted gift sets.

---

[3] Gift-with-purchase (GWP) and purchase-with-purchase (PWP) promotions offered consumers either a free gift or a second item at a discounted price as incentives to purchase the promoted product at the regular price. A self-liquidating premium was an item offered at a price substantially below normal retail (usually 30 percent to 50 percent lower) in return for one or more proofs of purchase from the sponsoring manufacturer's products.

[4] Prime time is divided into early prime (7:30–9:00 PM) and late prime (9:00–11:00 PM); late fringe is 11:00–11:30 PM and late night, 11:30 PM–1:00 AM.

FIGURE A   Merchandising Tear Sheet for 1980 Promotion

EXHIBIT 9 Men's Toiletries Communications Budgets, 1977–1980 (dollars in thousands)

	1977	1978	1979	1980 Budget*
Media advertising, advertising production costs, and trade promotions:†				
English Leather	$2,135	$2,753	$2,755	$2,750
Lime	132	0	0	0
Musk	308	310	350	350
Timberline	300	220	250	150
Wind Drift	300	230	250	150
Racquet Club	na	370	610	750
Subtotal	3,175	3,883	4,215	4,150
Co-op advertising	819	937	1,392	1,350
Sponsorships‡	292	568	441	380
Point-of-sale samples, display fixtures	889	862	1,134	1,100
Sales sheets, flyers, brochures	107	133	140	150
Gift-with-purchase, purchase-with-purchase promotions	47	30	44	50
Public relations	40	50	46	50
Subtotal	2,194	2,580	3,197	3,080
Total	$5,369	$6,463	$7,412	$7,230
As percent of sales	18.5%	19.5%	20.6%	20.0%

NOTE: These figures exclude advertising and promotion expenditures for Acqua di Selva and John Weitz.

* As of December 1980, it appeared that actual expenditures would be close to budget.

† Figures for each line include cost of promotions and trade deals as well as cost of measured media advertising and production. Promotion costs allocated among lines on a prorated basis for cross-line events. Media advertising expenditures are reported in Exhibit 11.

‡ 1980 budget includes approximately $150,000 in media advertising to promote sponsored events.

SOURCE: Company records.

EXHIBIT 10 Advertising Slogans of Men's Toiletries Brands

English Leather:	"All my men wear English Leather, or they wear nothing at all."
Old Spice:	"Put a little spice in your life with Old Spice."
Paco Rabanne:	"A cologne for men. What is remembered is up to you."
Denim:	"For men who don't have to try."
Chaps:	"It's the West. The West you feel inside of yourself."
Aqua Velva:	"It makes a man feel like a man."
Brut:	"Make every day your Brut day."
Pierre Cardin:	"For the man who gets the most out of life."
Aramis:	"The Aramis man. He expects everything."
Mennen Skin Bracer:	"For the man who takes care of himself."
Millionaire:	"Whatever you wear it with, you feel like a million bucks."

SOURCE: Rosenfeld, Sirowitz & Lawson, Inc.

EXHIBIT 11 Measured Media Advertising Expenditures, 1979 and 1980 ($000)

	Total	*National TV*	*Network Radio*	*Consumer Magazines*	*Other**
1979 Actual	$2,036	$1,554†	$126	$318	$38
1980 Budget‡	2,470§	1,816	266	369	19
Quarter 2	561	290	133	128	10
Quarter 4	$1,909	$1,526‖	$133	$241	$ 9

NOTE: These figures exclude expenditures of Tom Fields Ltd., Lebanon Packaging Co., and minimal advertising expenditures for Acqua di Selva and John Weitz.

* Includes spot TV and advertising in military publications.

† Comprises $1,064,000 advertising on network TV and $489,000 on syndicated sports programs.

‡ No advertising budgeted for the first or third quarters of 1980.

§ Measured media advertising costs rose 15 percent in 1980 over 1979.

‖ Scheduled to deliver 640 household gross rating points (calculated as reach × frequency) during the five weeks before Christmas. During any four-week period, 92 percent of all US households would be reached an average of 5.9 times.

SOURCE: Company records.

In addition to national advertising, there were three other major areas of expenditure in the MEM communications budget. First, the company offered the trade a cooperative advertising program under which it contributed toward the cost of store advertisements that prominently featured MEM merchandise (contribution was up to 5 percent of the value of store purchases from MEM). Second, MEM was a prominent and frequent sponsor, under the English Leather name, of championship sports events in tennis, skiing, and auto racing. The company also jointly promoted local events with retailers who carried MEM merchandise. Finally, MEM, like other manufacturers of men's toiletries, made substantial use of both free samples to be distributed by sales clerks, and testers to be used by customers at the point of purchase.

Sales Growth

Mayer and other MEM executives believed that periodic new product introductions were essential in the men's toiletries market to maintain consumer and trade interest and to sustain sales growth. It had been over two years since Racquet Club had been introduced.

A new brand, tentatively named Cambridge,[5] was under consideration for introduction in 1981. A fragrance had been selected and focus

---

[5] The MEM company had acquired a trademark on the name *Cambridge* for toiletries. The Philip Morris Co. held a similar trademark for cigarettes and had recently spent $4 million launching its low-tar Cambridge brand.

EXHIBIT 12   1980 Focus Group Session: Summary of Findings

During April 1979 in New York City 12 women (average age 25) participated in a focus group session conducted by one of the company's advertising agencies, Chalk, Nissen, Hanft, Inc. Key findings included the following:

- Respondents preferred clean, natural fragrances for men. Strong fragrances for men were disliked; they were associated with a woman reeking of perfume.
- Men favorably remembered English Leather as the fragrance of their youth—the brand "all the guys wore in college." Other fragrances were now perceived as more sophisticated.
- Old Spice was typically remembered as "the fragrance my father used."
- Respondents agreed that men lack knowledge of fragrances. When buying men's fragrances as gifts, some respondents stated that they would follow their own preferences; others would follow the perceived preferences of the recipient.
- Designer fragrances were expected to reflect the fashion images of the designers.
- Respondents were skeptical that a dual set of fragrances such as Jovan Man and Jovan Woman could succeed in satisfying the fragrance needs of the male and the female.
- The name *Cambridge* in association with a men's fragrance was seen as classic, understated, and dignified. Respondents would expect the package design to reflect the traditional quality of the name.

group interviews with target consumers had been conducted[6] (see Exhibit 12). Reaction to the Cambridge name in association with a line of men's toiletries was favorable, so a preliminary marketing program was developed (see summary in Exhibit 13). It called for Cambridge to be targeted at men aged 18 to 34 and to sell at $10 retail for a 4-ounce bottle of cologne. Mayer believed Cambridge would gain sales primarily at the expense of British Sterling and other brands in the $7 to $10 range.

Yet, the level of advertising expenditures which would support a Cambridge introduction was still unresolved. The company's advertising agency had been asked to develop three media plans for high, medium, and low expenditure (see Exhibit 14). Mayer believed that the lowest expenditure level represented the minimum necessary to achieve his 1981 target of $3 million in factory sales.

Not all MEM executives were enthusiastic about the Cambridge program. Some argued that even the lowest of the media budgets was unaffordable and that the level of advertising needed to launch the new brand could be greatly reduced if the well-known English Leather name was included both on the package and in the advertising. These executives wished to call the brand "Cambridge by English Leather."

Others believed that the potential of Racquet Club had not yet been exhausted and that another new product in the medium-price range would

---

[6] In a focus group, a trained interviewer typically spends one to two hours with 6 to 10 consumers probing product and brand meanings or seeking reactions to specific new product or advertising concepts.

EXHIBIT 13   Proposed New Product Introduction Program

Brand name:	Cambridge
Target customer:	Men, aged 18 to 34
Product line:	After-shave, cologne, bath soap, deodorant stick, shaving stick, gift sets
Retail price point:	$10 for 4-oz. cologne; variable cost structure similar to other MEM men's toiletries
Trade margin:	40 percent
Introductory deals:	5 and 10 percent off-invoice allowances on small- and large-size prepacks; sales of each prepack were expected to account for one-third of 1981 Cambridge sales
Sampling:	Production of one million ⅛-oz. samples to be distributed free at the point of sale at a cost of $200,000
Merchandising aids:	Counter display materials, brochures, and testers at a cost in 1981 of $50,000
Timing of launch:	First orders accepted in April 1981; first shipments in September 1981
Sales target:	Gross factory sales of $3 million in 1981

SOURCE: Company records.

EXHIBIT 14   Three Media Plans for Cambridge Introduction

	Plan 1	*Plan 2*	*Plan 3*
Network television	$249,180	$ 570,480	$1,140,960
Spot television	384,000	411,116	1,016,070
Consumer magazines	286,058	379,213	609,925
Trade magazines	9,900	13,000	26,000
Production	70,052	70,174	100,000
Reserve	—	56,017	107,045
	$999,190	$1,500,000	$3,000,000

NOTE: Reserve funds were used to finance one-time tie-in advertising efforts with individual retail accounts independent of co-op advertising.
SOURCE: Chalk, Nissen, Hanft, Inc.

---

be wasteful. They pointed out that Racquet Club's initial sales were made largely at the expense of Lime, Musk, Timberline, and Wind Drift, because many retailers, especially chain drug buyers, had not been willing to provide additional shelf facings for MEM products.

Some of those who favored a product launch believed that MEM should give first priority to a low-priced brand to penetrate food stores. Although food stores had long carried men's toiletries, MEM had been reluctant to sell through this channel. The men's toiletries sections in many food stores had traditionally been serviced by rack jobbers.[7] The MEM company preferred to sell only direct to retail accounts to maintain consistent product margins. During the 1970s, however, many major food chains merged with or established their own drugstore chains. (For example, Medi Mart drugstores and Stop & Shop supermarkets were owned by the same company.) As a result, their direct buying from men's toiletries manufacturers increased. Mayer knew that food chains typically stocked only the high-turnover items in a product line and that they pressed for frequent trade deals and year-round national television advertising. He wondered, however, whether the MEM sales force should now attempt to sell to the major food chains, particularly those that emphasized assortment and service rather than low prices. If he proceeded in this direction Mayer wondered which, if any, items in the six existing lines should be offered to the food chains or whether a new brand would be more acceptable.

Conclusion

On December 20, 1980, Mayer learned that Shulton was planning to launch its first new brand of men's toiletries since the introduction of Old Spice in 1936. Under the brand name Blue Stratos, an after-shave and cologne would be available for shipment to the trade in March 1981, to be followed by a bath soap, stick deodorant, shave cream, and body talc. The 4-ounce bottle of cologne would carry a suggested retail price of around $10. The trade press reported that advertising would feature the slogan "Unleash the spirit" and use a hang-gliding motif to symbolize the freedom and adventure of the sky. Shulton announced that the Blue Stratos national rollout would be supported by a $12-million communications budget. In addition to network television and full-page advertisements in *Playboy, People,* and *Sports Illustrated,* Shulton planned to mail 10.3 million samples of three-pack product wipes to reach one-third of all men aged 18 to 34. Recognizing that Blue Stratos was targeted at the same market as Cambridge, Mayer wondered whether he should cancel or delay the Cambridge introduction and commit his entire 1981 communications budget to reinforcing the six existing lines.

---

[7] Rack jobbers are compensated on a percentage margin basis for stocking the shelves in retail outlets. They do not take title to the merchandise they handle.

Nissan Motor Co., Ltd.: Marketing Strategy for the European Market

In February 1989, in anticipation of the European Community (EC) market integration in 1992, Kiyoshi Sekiguchi, general manager, and Shu Gomi, deputy general manager, European sales group of Nissan Motor Co., Ltd., were discussing how to expand Nissan's market penetration in three principal southern European countries: France, Italy, and Spain.

Japanese carmakers had voluntarily limited their total exports to Europe to a ceiling of about 10 percent of the EC market, which accounted for 90 percent of the total Western European market. In addition, France, Italy, and Spain had imposed severe restrictions on Japanese imports, resulting in quite small sales of Nissan in these countries. However, because Nissan started to export the Bluebird (equivalent to its Stanza model in the United States), which was manufactured in its UK factory, to the European continent in late 1988 and because the restrictions by individual EC countries on Japanese car imports were likely to be relieved at the advent of EC integration, Nissan believed that full-scale penetration into these three European countries would become possible.

Although Sekiguchi and Gomi needed to develop a marketing strategy for the entire European market in light of the tougher competition expected after 1992, the more immediate decision was how much marketing effort to allocate to two models, the 1800-cc upper-medium-sized Bluebird and a supermini car like the Micra (hereafter New Micra). Nissan manufactured the Bluebird in its UK factory, but it planned to manufacture the New Micra there as well until 1992. Of course, to serve the markets adequately, it needed to market a complete product line of five or six models, including exports from Japan. Among them, the models that were especially important strategically were the Bluebird and the New

Professor Kyoichi Ikeo of Keio University, Japan, prepared this case in association with Professor John A. Quelch as the basis for class discussion rather than to illustrate either effective or ineffective handling of an administrative situation. Certain company data have been disguised. Copyright © 1989 by the President and Fellows of Harvard College. Harvard Business School case 9–590–018.

EXHIBIT 1   Nissan Bluebird and Nissan Micra

Micra. Because resources—especially for advertising—that could be allocated to France, Italy, and Spain were limited, Sekiguchi and Gomi had to decide which model to emphasize and how to promote both of them in those countries and then recommend their decision to Yoshikazu Kawana, director of the European sales group. Exhibit 1 shows the current Bluebird and Micra models.

Company Background

In 1935, Nissan Motor Co., Ltd., which had been established in 1933 by Gisuke Ayukawa, started the mass production of automobiles in Japan with a small 750-cc car. It eventually grew to include a full-sized 3670-cc car in its product line, expanding its production volume and becoming, along with Toyota and Isuzu, one of the leading companies in the Japanese automobile industry. However, due to shortage of material during World War II, Nissan was obliged to focus on truck production and to decrease its car output. The end of the war brought its production to a standstill.

Nissan's growth in truck and car production after World War II was due to the special procurement needs of the Korean War and the increased household penetration of cars in Japan beginning in the late 1950s. In particular, the enormous success of the new small-sized cars in the 1960s, when a major portion of vehicle demand moved from trucks and medium-sized cars for business use to small-sized cars for personal use, gave Nissan a firm footing in the Japanese automobile industry.

Exports of Nissan cars started in 1958 and increased from 10,000 units in 1960 to 400,000 in 1970. During the 1970s, partly because of the rise in gasoline prices, high-quality, fuel-efficient Japanese cars dramatically increased their share of the North American market. Nissan exported 1.46 million units in 1980.

By the 1988 fiscal year, Nissan sales totaled 3,400 billion yen. It manufactured 2.16 million units in domestic factories and 0.52 million units in foreign factories, and it exported 1.14 million units from Japan. Exhibit 2 presents Nissan income statements for 1984 to 1988, and Exhibit 3 summarizes total sales, in yen, of Japanese automobile manufacturers for 1983 to 1988.

Penetrating the European Market

Nissan's European market penetration began with exports to Finland in 1959. The company concentrated first on the northern European countries, not entering the EC countries until the late 1960s. Its exports to Europe increased from 3,600 vehicles in 1964 to 163,000 in 1973 and reached 240,000 in 1978.

EXHIBIT 2   Nonconsolidated Statements of Income: 1984–1988*
(in millions of yen)

	1984	1985	1986	1987	1988
Net sales	3,460,124	3,618,076	3,754,172	3,429,317	3,418,671
Cost of sales	2,811,052	2,943,384	3,099,243	2,948,127	2,882,252
Gross profit	649,072	674,692	654,928	481,190	536,418
Selling, general, and administrative expenses	572,947	585,155	584,870	475,691	470,779
Operating income	76,124	89,537	70,057	5,499	65,639
Other income (expense)					
Interest income	67,559	72,325	70,494	58,989	50,548
Interest expense	(46,012)	(46,190)	(42,237)	(38,428)	(36,594)
Other, net†	30,377	43,385	10,084	83,652	59,971
	51,925	69,519	38,343	104,214	73,924
Income before income taxes	128,049	159,056	108,400	109,711	139,562
Income taxes	57,517	84,780	43,648	63,105	100,978
Net income	70,532	74,276	64,752	46,606	38,584

* Years ended March 31, 1984–1988.

† *Other, net* consists of dividend income, net realized gain on sales of securities, and other sources.

EXHIBIT 3   Total Sales of Japanese Car Manufacturers: 1983–1988
(in millions of yen)

	1983	1984	1985	1986	1987	1988
Nissan	3,187,722	3,460,124	3,618,076	3,754,172	3,429,317	3,418,671
Toyota	4,892,663	5,472,681	6,064,420	6,304,858	6,024,909	6,691,299
Honda	1,746,919	1,846,028	1,929,519	2,245,743	2,334,597	2,650,077*
Mazda	1,364,229	1,431,815	1,569,553	1,626,187	1,602,293	1,844,300
Mitsubishi	1,061,375	1,173,631	1,408,307	1,578,823	1,558,670	1,752,697
Isuzu	684,624	769,071	1,016,250	1,013,434	909,915	1,023,300
Suzuki	542,319	524,259	580,841	722,336	744,854	759,550
Subaru	580,052	602,735	672,071	768,424	715,717	686,238
Daihatsu	425,909	469,950	515,911	535,645	557,627	445,665†

* Thirteen months, due to alteration of settlement term.

† Nine months, due to alteration of settlement term.

SOURCE: Company records.

However, protectionist sentiment against increased car exports from Japan began appearing in several countries in the late 1970s, resulting in the 1981 voluntary ceiling on exports to the United States and various restrictions and surveillances in European countries. Management expected this protectionist atmosphere to continue and decided in 1980 to begin to move local production overseas. In Europe, it acquired Motor Iberica, S.A., to make commercial vehicles in Spain and founded Nissan Motor Manufacturing UK, Ltd., to make passenger cars in the United Kingdom. These decisive steps were in stark contrast to Toyota's strategy, which placed much less emphasis on local production.

Nissan Motor Iberica, S.A. (NMISA)

In 1980 Nissan acquired a 35.85 percent equity stake in Motor Iberica, the largest commercial vehicle manufacturer in Spain, participated in its administration, and helped make it a more efficient manufacturer. In 1983, it started to manufacture vehicles under its own brand, gradually increasing its share holdings to 68 percent by 1989.

In 1988, NMISA manufactured 76,000 commercial vehicles, of which 66 percent were Nissan's and the rest Motor Iberica's. Of all the commercial vehicles NMISA manufactured, 32 percent were exported, mainly to other European countries. NMISA's performance was favorable, and its cumulative losses were covered by profits in fiscal year 1988.

Nissan Motor Manufacturing UK Ltd. (NMUK)

To manufacture passenger cars, Nissan founded NMUK as a local subsidiary in 1984 and began constructing a factory in Sunderland, near Newcastle, in northeast England. Completed in 1986, the factory produced an upper-medium-sized car called the Bluebird. Because Nissan volunteered to manufacture with 60 percent value-based local content rising to 80 percent by 1991, the British government in January 1988 authorized the Bluebird as a UK–made car.[1] The EC Commission supported the UK position. However, the French government insisted that local content had to reach 80 percent for EC approval and threatened to count UK–built Bluebirds against its 3 percent Japanese import ceiling until they reached 80 percent local content. The UK–made Bluebird began to be exported to other EC member countries in late 1988; by then it had reached 70 percent local content. In 1988, the Sunderland factory purchased components from 113 European companies. The French government finally conceded that the Bluebird could be exported to France without any restriction or duty, though the possibility of reducing quotas on car imports from Japan to France remained.

Although it would be some time before NMUK would be operating in the black because of the huge initial investment,[2] production volume grew smoothly: 5,079 in 1986, 28,797 in 1987, and 56,744 in 1988. Nissan planned to expand production even further, to 100,000 a year in 1990, when it would introduce a new version of the Bluebird, and to 200,000 by

---

[1] Value-based local content was calculated by subtracting from the factory price of the car the value of components and materials imported from outside the EC. Some protectionists advocated the use of cost-based local content which took into account the full production cost including all overheads as well as design and engineering costs. However, this approach was much harder to monitor and police. Others demanded local manufacturing of specific components such as engines, transmissions, axles, and electronic components. To achieve 80 percent local content, it was, however, necessary for either engines or transmissions to be locally sourced.

[2] £125 million of the investment was contributed by the UK government, motivated by the additional employment opportunities the plant would bring to the northeast.

EXHIBIT 4   Cost Structure of Nissan for Selling in the Netherlands (%)*

	Nissan's UK–made Cars		Nissan's Japan-Made Cars (average)
	Bluebird†	*New Micra*‡	
Retail price	100	100	100
Dealer margin	18	18	18
Distributor selling price	82	82	82
Distributor margin	12	12	12
Nissan selling price	70	70	70
Transportation cost	3.5	4	8
Duty	0	0	10
Labor cost	8	10	12
Parts and material cost	39	40	32
Overhead and selling cost	12	10	3

* Percent of retail price, excluding taxes other than duty.

† 1988 figures.

‡ Estimated figures for the year production began.

1992, when it would add the New Micra. By 1988, NMUK had invested 50 billion yen and planned to invest an additional 80 billion yen before full production was reached in 1992. Although Nissan's UK cost structure was not publicly available, Exhibit 4, which shows Nissan's cost structure for selling in the Netherlands, can be treated as an approximation.

Market Integration of the EC

A major impact on Nissan's European operations was the planned market integration of the EC in 1992. An integrated EC would liberate the movement of products, services, people, and capital within the Community and consolidate technical standards that hitherto had been determined by individual member countries. Much progress had already been achieved toward harmonization of technical standards for cars. By 1988, 41 of 44 voluntary technical directives proposed in 1970 had been adopted by all EC–member states. The remaining three—on tires, windshields, and towing weights—were expected to be tabled soon by the European Commission, and all were expected to be made mandatory by 1990, permitting single-type approval for the entire EC market.

Thanks to a more efficient allocation of production facilities, and concentration and reduction of inventories, production and logistics costs were expected by industry analysts to decrease as a result of the 1992 program. According to the EC Commission, such cost reductions were valued at 853 billion yen. If all these cost savings were passed through as lower prices, average retail auto prices would be lowered by 5.7 percent, and consequently, the market would expand by more than 6 percent. Market expansion would be especially strong in countries such as Spain and the UK where harmonization of value-added taxes and excise taxes on cars would substantially reduce retail prices.

At the same time, market integration was expected by analysts to intensify competition in the automobile industry and, thereby, to magnify the differences among companies. Therefore, in preparing for 1992, European auto companies made great efforts to expand, modernize, or reallocate their production resources.

Market integration promised to affect import restrictions on Japanese automobiles. Although the voluntary EC–wide ceiling on all Japanese imports was expected to remain, the bilateral import quotas on Japanese cars imposed by France, Italy, and Spain had to cease. French officials, in particular, pressed for maintenance of the EC–wide ceiling on Japanese imports, for an 80 percent EC–wide local content requirement, and for higher exports of EC–made cars to Japan. They were also sensitive to the possibility of Japanese companies shipping US–made cars to Europe to circumvent the EC–wide quota. Realistic observers foresaw a transition period whereby restrictions on Japanese automobile imports would be phased out gradually to give national producers such as Fiat and Renault time to improve the efficiency of their operations before they had to face open Japanese competition.

In addition, the possibility of cost reductions made local production more attractive for the Japanese. In this respect, Nissan had an advantage over other Japanese companies—a proven record in Spain and the United Kingdom. However, the other Japanese automobile companies, such as Toyota and Mazda, were moving toward local production in Europe. Exhibit 5 summarizes these endeavors. Some executives of European automobile companies worried that Japanese local production would bring overcapacity and price erosion to the European market. But countries with no automotive industry, such as Greece and Ireland, welcomed the Japanese as a means of increasing price competition in their markets. In addition, certain EC countries, particularly the UK, actively sought additional Japanese investment in car production following the decline of their domestic manufacturers.

Middle-Range Plan for the European Market

Although Japanese automobile sales in Europe were small when compared with domestic or North American counterparts, there was large potential for growth if their plans for local production were put into practice and EC market integration were carried out. In particular, Nissan, which trailed Toyota and was closely followed by Honda in share of the domestic and North American markets, had capitalized on its competitive advantage in the European market where it had the largest market share among the Japanese companies, thanks in part to its early establishment of local production facilities. Exhibit 6 shows the overall market

---

EXHIBIT 5   Movements of Major Japanese Automobile Companies toward Local Production in Europe*

Company	Country	Outline
Nissan	Spain	Manufacturing 76,000 commercial vehicles a year (in 1988)
Nissan	UK	Manufacturing 57,000 upper-medium-sized cars a year (in 1988)
Toyota	West Germany	Planning to manufacture 15,000 small trucks a year (from 1989) in a Volkswagen factory in Hanover
Toyota	UK	Planning to manufacture 200,000 upper-medium-sized cars a year (from 1992)
Honda	UK	Manufacturing 84,000 medium-sized cars a year (in 1987) jointly with the Rover Group
Mazda	Spain	Considering the manufacture of 25,000 commercial vehicles a year
Mazda	Undecided	Considering the manufacture of 200,000 upper-medium-sized cars a year (from 1992) in a Ford factory with which Mazda is affiliated
Isuzu	UK	Manufacturing 5,400 commercial vehicles a year (in 1987) in a joint venture with General Motors
Suzuki	Spain	Manufacturing 25,000 small four-wheel-drive off-road vehicles a year (in 1987) jointly with Land-Rover Santana
Subaru	France	Considering the manufacture of 30,000 vehicles a year in northwestern France

* Excluding knockdown productions.

shares of Japanese and major European companies in the Western European car market.

Given the importance and rapid growth of the European market (car registrations increased 5 percent in 1988), Nissan management formulated a plan in the fall of 1988 to strengthen its competitive position until 1992. The main goals to be achieved by 1992 were as follows:

1. Raise Nissan's market share in the European car market to 4.5 percent by 1992 and increase car production in the United Kingdom to 200,000 and truck production in Spain to 100,000.

2. Improve Nissan's brand image by reinforcing the quality of its sales and service organizations in Europe.

3. Further decentralize Nissan's responsibility for European operations, including product design, production, marketing, and sales.

EXHIBIT 6   Western Europe—Overall Market Share in Car Market 1983–1988 (%)

	1983	1984	1985	1986	1987	1988 (estimated)
VW group*	13.02	13.56	14.37	14.70	14.95	14.44
Ford Europe	12.47	12.80	11.90	11.67	11.93	11.45
Fiat group†	13.78	14.48	13.74	14.01	14.20	15.35
Peugeot group‡	11.71	11.50	11.52	11.38	12.12	12.83
GM Europe§	11.07	11.04	11.36	10.95	10.55	10.29
Renault group	12.63	10.90	10.65	10.61	10.62	10.34
Total Japanese:	10.06	10.27	10.77	11.71	11.38	11.00
Nissan	2.79	2.83	2.89	3.00	2.93	2.84
Toyota	2.25	2.24	2.58	2.88	2.81	2.66
Honda	1.02	1.14	1.11	1.17	1.03	1.11
Mazda	2.01	1.97	1.91	2.05	1.90	1.88
Mitsubishi	0.98	1.09	1.10	1.21	1.22	1.10
Suzuki	0.42	0.43	0.47	0.58	0.65	0.66
Subaru	0.29	0.30	0.38	0.44	0.45	0.40
Daihatsu	0.27	0.24	0.28	0.32	0.30	0.25

* VW group consisted of Volkswagen and Audi until 1985; in 1986, SEAT joined the VW group.

† Fiat group consisted of Fiat, Autobianchi, Lancia, and Ferrari until 1986; in 1987, Alfa Romeo joined the Fiat group.

‡ Peugeot group includes Peugeot, Citroen, and Talbot.

§ GM Europe includes Opel and Vauxhall.

SOURCE: DRI World Automotive Forecast Report.

According to the plan, Nissan's sales increase in Europe would be accomplished mainly through its UK–made cars, because exports from Japan had to contend with trade restrictions, political friction, and a decrease in per-unit contribution and price competitiveness due to appreciation of the yen. Reinforcing the sales and service organization and localizing overall European operations were measures to achieve the market penetration needed to justify increased production, achieve further scale economies, and increase productivity.

To coordinate European operations, Nissan established a European Technical Center (NETC) in the United Kingdom in 1988 and planned to start the operation of Nissan Europe N.V. in the Netherlands in 1990. Whereas Nissan had previously developed all of its products in Japan, NETC would, through the combined efforts of Japanese and European staff, produce new cars to meet European consumer needs. Moreover, because models for local production, which were designed in Japan, often required special orders from European parts suppliers, materials costs increased. NETC's objective was to design cars that incorporated standard parts available in Europe at lower costs, for example, a new Bluebird model to be launched in 1990, the New Micra to be launched by 1992, and any new commercial vehicles that would be manufactured in Spain.

Nissan Europe N.V. would be responsible for coordinating all development, production, logistics, and marketing in Europe, most of which had been done in Tokyo. And it would formulate overall marketing strategy for Europe, in place of the Europe Sales Group in Tokyo. Distributors in each country would continue to draft national marketing plans that were integrated with the regional plan.

Furthermore, Nissan Europe would play a key role in consolidating logistics under EC integration, which would facilitate the free flow of goods within the EC community and unify the technical standards. Nissan's plan was to gather orders from local distributors in each country and to relay them to the United Kingdom, Spain, and Tokyo. Also, Nissan Europe would totally oversee the transportation from each factory to each dealer via the large-scale collection and delivery center and predelivery inspection facility, which were under construction in Amsterdam. Therefore, transportation and inventory functions for cars and commercial vehicles, which had been shared by Nissan and local distributors, would be performed by Nissan Europe and its subsidiary logistics company. The only logistics function left to distributors would be that for parts.

Trends in the European Market

The European car market in 1987 comprised 12.4 million units, one-third of the total world market, and 10 million of these sales were accounted for by five countries: West Germany, the United Kingdom, France, Italy, and Spain. Exhibit 7 shows new car sales in European countries and other major markets. Exhibits 8 and 9 provide new car sales data for European countries in 1987 and 1988. Exhibits 10 and 11 provide market segmentation data for each major European country. Exhibit 12 shows profiles of European countries. Exhibit 13 profiles Nissan's distributors, and Exhibit 14 lists the car models Nissan marketed in Europe and their retail list price ranges.

To catch up to the Japanese, European car makers needed to improve productivity by one-third; it took Japanese workers 20 hours to assemble a car, whereas the European average was 36 hours and the US, 26½ hours. While local content restrictions were designed to make Japanese assembly in Europe more costly, industry analysts believed that, even with a 90 percent requirement, Japanese plants in Europe would be more efficient than those run by the European manufacturers.

West Germany

West Germany had the largest car market in Europe, with sales of about three million units a year and no restrictions imposed on imports; therefore, Japanese companies were able to achieve a considerable number of car sales. However, with highly competitive companies like Volkswagen,

EXHIBIT 7 New Car Sales—Overall World Market: 1983–1989 (000s of units)

	1983	1984	1985	1986	1987	1988 (est.)	1989 (est.)
West Germany	2,427	2,394	2,379	2,829	2,916	2,730	2,660
France	2,018	1,758	2,766	1,912	2,105	2,217	2,146
United Kingdom	1,792	1,750	1,832	1,882	2,014	2,195	1,939
Italy	1,581	1,636	1,746	1,825	1,977	2,131	2,002
Spain	547	520	572	686	925	1,039	1,089
Netherlands	459	461	496	561	556	485	550
Belgium	339	352	360	395	406	435	426
Other EC countries	329	342	388	402	353	388	531
EC total	9,492	9,212	9,540	10,492	11,251	11,620	11,343
Sweden	217	231	263	270	316	331	352
Switzerland	274	267	265	300	303	322	327
Other Western European countries	486	450	540	572	509	505	599
Western European total	10,494	10,161	10,608	11,635	12,380	12,779	12,622
United States	9,181	10,393	11,043	11,452	10,227	10,699	10,623
Canada	842	964	1,137	1,089	1,057	1,013	1,196
North American total	10,023	11,357	12,180	12,541	11,284	11,711	11,819
Japan	3,136	3,096	3,104	3,146	3,275	3,609	3,497
World total	29,151	30,289	31,821	33,049	32,657	34,277	35,528

Source: DRI World Automotive Forecast Report.

EXHIBIT 8 New Car Sales in Major European Countries: 1987 (000s of units)

	West Germany	France	United Kingdom	Italy	Spain	Netherlands	Belgium	Sweden	Switzerland
Total	2,915.7	2,105.2	2,013.7	1,976.5	924.8	555.7	406.2	316.0	303.3
By Manufacturer:									
VW group	872.2	159.3	116.2	225.8	161.2	63.0	65.6	37.7	50.0
Ford Europe	300.8	143.4	580.1	78.4	142.1	56.0	39.5	34.3	21.2
Fiat group	132.8	151.8	74.3	1,179.9	69.6	35.3	18.5	8.2	29.5
Peugeot group	123.3	703.5	147.3	148.8	154.2	65.0	57.3	11.0	25.1
GM Europe	453.3	96.8	270.8	57.3	130.1	88.6	46.8	31.1	37.6
Renault group	89.6	641.7	78.7	154.2	209.4	22.6	35.3	5.1	16.6
Total Japanese*	441.4	63.1	225.4	13.7	6.8	144.0	83.5	68.5	87.6
Nissan	84.5	17.8	114.2	0.0	2.1	31.3	19.4	18.1	13.7
Toyota	93.3	14.3	38.3	2.0	2.1	31.2	26.8	22.8	26.6
Honda	41.5	10.2	24.7	0.2	0.5	11.9	8.5	4.1	7.6
Mazda	91.0	16.6	18.8	0.0	0.5	24.5	10.6	13.9	8.1
Mitsubishi	68.6	3.3	11.8	0.7	1.0	15.3	9.6	3.6	11.1
Suzuki	27.1	0.9	5.6	9.9	0.4	18.0	3.3	2.4	4.1
Subaru	16.7	0.0	5.0	0.4	0.1	4.7	3.0	1.8	14.3
Daihatsu	13.0	0.0	4.6	0.5	0.0	7.1	2.3	1.7	1.4

* Total Japanese sales in Italy and Spain exceed the quotas on car imports from Japan because some parts of commercial vehicles, manufactured by Nissan and Suzuki in Spain and knocked down by Toyota and Mitsubishi in Portugal, are counted as passenger cars. Furthermore, in the case of Italy, indirect imports via other European countries boost the sales of Japanese cars.

SOURCE: DRI World Automotive Forecast Report.

EXHIBIT 9 Estimated New Car Sales in Major European Countries: 1988 (000s of units)

	West Germany	France	United Kingdom	Italy	Spain	Netherlands	Belgium	Sweden	Switzerland
Total	2,730.2	2,216.8	2,195.4	2,030.9	1,039.2	484.8	435.0	331.3	322.1
By Manufacturer:									
VW group	797.0	168.8	125.4	220.3	196.5	54.7	70.7	36.8	50.9
Ford Europe	269.9	139.2	582.2	79.6	152.9	50.6	44.5	34.0	21.5
Fiat group	138.8	217.1	86.6	1,211.7	85.4	29.4	16.3	7.6	31.0
Peugeot group	108.4	740.2	187.1	165.1	197.4	60.6	65.6	14.7	23.9
GM Europe	418.4	104.1	302.2	71.6	136.6	69.0	50.4	28.7	38.4
Renault group	84.8	639.4	84.4	148.0	217.7	21.3	38.9	4.7	16.6
Total Japanese	390.0	65.0	247.5	10.7	8.3	127.5	88.4	81.4	100.0
Nissan	71.9	18.7	132.6	0.2	2.8	23.9	20.5	19.8	13.5
Toyota	77.2	14.9	39.2	0.6	2.2	23.3	29.1	25.5	31.0
Honda	45.7	10.6	25.9	0.5	0.6	12.0	9.0	5.5	8.3
Mazda	82.6	17.2	20.4	0.1	0.6	24.5	9.8	18.3	12.3
Mitsubishi	55.0	3.0	12.4	0.8	1.0	13.1	9.4	6.0	13.1
Suzuki	26.7	0.6	5.9	7.8	1.0	18.2	3.8	3.3	4.7
Subaru	13.7	0.0	4.5	0.2	0.1	5.1	3.3	1.6	14.1
Daihatsu	10.7	0.0	3.4	0.5	0.0	7.3	3.2	1.2	1.7

SOURCE: DRI World Automotive Forecast Report.

EXHIBIT 10   New Car Sales by Segment: 1987 (000s of units)

	West Germany	France	United Kingdom	Italy	Spain
Total sales	2,915.7	2,105.2	2,013.7	1,976.6	924.8
By segment (%)					
Utility	2.22	4.06	2.30	18.50 ⎫	43.0*
Supermini	14.46	40.31	25.51	38.94 ⎭	
Lower-medium	35.62	23.03	34.41	25.37	37.1
Upper-medium	22.92	22.25	25.48	8.06	13.9
Executive	24.76	10.35	12.31	9.14	6.0†

NOTE: Typical models included in each segment are the following:

Utility	Fiat 126, Renault R4, Suzuki Cervo
Supermini	Fiat Uno, Ford Fiesta, Nissan New Micra, Peugeot 104, Toyota Starlet, VW Polo
Lower-medium	Fiat Tipo, Ford Escort, Honda Civic, Nissan Sunny, Nissan Violet, Toyota Corolla, Toyota Tercel, VW Golf
Upper-medium	Audi 80/90, Ford Capri, Honda Accord, Nissan Bluebird, Nissan Prairie, Renault Fuego, Toyota Camry, Toyota Carina
Executive	Audi 100/200, BMW (all models), Honda Legend, Mazda RX7, Nissan Cedric/Laurel, Nissan 280/300ZX, Nissan Silvia, Toyota Celica, Toyota Crown, Toyota Supra

* Includes utility and supermini.

† Includes sports cars such as the Nissan 300ZX. In other countries, sports cars are included in each segment according to vehicle size.

SOURCE: DRI World Automotive Forecast Report and company records.

EXHIBIT 11   New Car Sales of Japanese Companies by Segment: 1987 (000s of units)

	West Germany	France	United Kingdom	Italy
Nissan				
Supermini	21.8	5.1	38.9	0.0
Lower-medium	31.6	6.2	36.7	0.0
Upper-medium	25.0	4.8	35.3	0.0
Executive	6.2	1.7	3.3	0.0
Toyota				
Supermini	16.6	0.0	1.2	0.0
Lower-medium	39.0	7.9	17.1	0.0
Upper-medium	28.7	3.1	9.8	0.0
Executive	9.0	3.3	10.1	2.0
Honda				
Supermini	0.1	0.0	0.0	0.0
Lower-medium	19.3	5.2	5.8	0.0
Upper-medium	21.9	4.8	18.2	0.2
Executive	0.2	0.2	0.8	0.0
Mazda				
Supermini	0.0	0.0	0.0	0.0
Lower-medium	47.9	9.7	11.9	0.0
Upper-medium	40.0	5.6	6.2	0.0
Executive	3.0	1.2	0.7	0.0

SOURCE: DRI World Automotive Forecast Report.

EXHIBIT 12 Profiles of Major European Countries: 1987

	West Germany	France	United Kingdom	Italy	Spain	Netherlands	Belgium	Sweden	Switzerland
Car sales (000s)	2,915.7	2,105.2	2,013.7	1,976.5	924.8	555.7	406.2	316.0	303.3
Commercial vehicle sales (000s)	113.7	369.4	252.8	163.0	170.0	69.6	28.8	29.5	24.3
Nissan's commercial vehicle sales (000s)	2.9	3.1	10.5	4.0	33.7	3.1	1.5	2.8	1.3
Total sales (000s)	3,029.4	2,474.6	2,266.5	2,139.5	1,094.8	625.3	435.0	345.5	327.6
Car production (000s)	4,374	3,052	1,143	1,713	1,403	125	277	432	0
Car exports (000s)	2,451	1,681	226	641	707	112	228	340	0
Car imports (000s)	1,012	760	1,041	780	188	535	NA	226	NA
Number of cars per 1,000 people	468	385	360	392	264	340	351	400	423
Car price index* (exclusive of tax)	128	128	144	129	151	122	121	NA	NA
Car price index* (inclusive of tax)	105	124	129	112	139	135	109	NA	NA

* The EC market with the lowest price is indexed at 100 in both cases.

SOURCE: DRI World Automotive Forecast Report, BEUC Car Report, company records.

EXHIBIT 13   Profiles of Nissan's Distributors in Major European Countries

Country	Name of Distributor	Percent of Shares Held by Nissan	Number of Dealers	Number of Nissan Employees
West Germany	Nissan Motor Deutschland	100	734	4
France	Richard-Nissan	9.6	203	1
United Kingdom	Nissan UK	0	450	0
Italy	Nissan Italia	64.2	160	2
Spain	Nissan Motor Iberica	68	148	19
Netherlands	Nissan Motor Nederland	100	170	3
Belgium	N.V. Nissan Belgium	0	345	0
Sweden	Philipson Bil	0	50	0
Switzerland	Nissan Motor Schweiz	100	284	3

SOURCE: Company records.

TABLE A   Relative Importance of Product Attributes by Country*

	West Germany	United Kingdom	France	Italy	Spain
Performance	•	•			
Fuel economy					•
Price		•	•	•	•
Styling			•		
Quality	•				
Accessories				•	
Maintenance	•				

* A bullet (·) indicates a particularly important attribute. Its absence does not mean a lack of importance.
SOURCE: Estimate of Mr. Shu Gomi, deputy general manager.

the West German market was regarded as having the stiffest competition in Europe. Generally, West German consumers, known as serious readers of car magazines, were knowledgeable about cars and were apt to consider numerous data before purchasing. Table A shows the relative importance of product attributes in major European countries. Regarding vehicle size, models larger than the Supermini had a large market share, especially when compared with their share in the southern European countries.

Among Japanese competitors, Mazda focused on West Germany, where it had a relatively high market share, followed by Toyota and then Nissan. Although Nissan hoped to increase its market share in West Germany as production volume in its UK factory increased, it was thought that the market could absorb only a limited quantity.

EXHIBIT 14 Marketed Car Models and their Retail List Price Ranges in Major European Countries (thousands of yen)

European Model / US Model / Japanese Model	300ZX / 300ZX / Fairlady	Laurel / Laurel / Laurel	Maxima / Maxima / Bluebird	Bluebird / Stanza / Auster	Silvia / 200SX / Silvia	Sunny / Sentra / Sunny	New Micra / New Micra / March	Prairie / Stanza-Wagon / Prairie	Sunny-Wagon / Sentra-Wagon / Sunny-California
West Germany	4,088	2,023–2,138	2,861–3,035	1,613–1,873	2,791–2,962	1,315–1,912	962–1,179	2,093–2,512	
France	4,386–5,256			1,675–2,360	2,670*	1,364–2,308	972–1,262	2,027	
United Kingdom	4,533–5,394	3,339	Undecided	2,110–2,965	3,440*	1,721–2,645	1,246–1,588	2,369–2,743*	1,453
Italy				Undecided	3,689		Undecided		
Spain	7,095			2,543–2,917	Undecided	2,668	Undecided	Undecided	
Netherlands	5,493	2,872		1,788–2,257		1,260–2,347	1,086		1,046
Belgium	3,974–5,072	2,110–2,474		1,527–1,764	2,722–3,171	1,266–1,752	825–1,106	1,589	1,172
Sweden				2,056–2,144	2,826	1,645–2,215	1,373–1,416	2,661	
Switzerland	4,323			1,643–2,108	2,705–2,870	1,346–1,931	984–1,206	1,890–2,545	

* Old model is being marketed.

SOURCE: Company records.

West Germany took the most liberal view toward Japanese competition in the automobile industry because its car companies dominated other EC car manufacturers in the Japanese market, holding a 2 percent market share (80,000 units) by 1988. In addition, an open EC car market with the French, Spanish, and Italian bilateral quotas removed would mean that the bulk of imported Japanese cars would no longer be forced on the northern EC countries as was currently the case.

United Kingdom

A unique feature of the UK market was that fleet sales, purchases by companies for use by their employees, accounted for more than half of the total car sales. Because most of the fleet sales were of upper-medium-sized 1600-cc to 2000-cc cars, this class held about a 25 percent unit share of the total car market. The UK–made Bluebird was an upper-medium-sized car suitable for fleet sales.

In addition to the voluntary ceiling on all Japanese imports to EC countries, Japanese car imports in the United Kingdom were limited to 11 percent of the total market by a gentlemen's agreement between each country's associations of automobile manufacturers. But, because Nissan's sales were so high when this casual agreement was made, it obtained a very favorable import quota, gaining 6 percent of the market, the largest share of all the Japanese imports, and vying with Volkswagen for fourth position in the market, following Ford, GM, and Peugeot. Owing to the growth of the UK market, Nissan sales reached more than 100,000, representing 35 percent of its European unit sales. Also, the UK–made Bluebird was sold mostly in the UK market from 1986 to 1988, partly because until 1987 the EC had treated it as a Japanese import.

On January 27, 1989, Toyota announced that it would construct a factory in the United Kingdom to manufacture, beginning in 1992, 200,000 units a year of an upper-medium-sized 1800-cc car. The local content was set to start at 60 percent and reach 80 percent as soon as possible. Local production by Toyota would inevitably make competition more severe because a considerable portion of Toyota's UK–made cars had to be sold in the UK market. Therefore, the extent to which Nissan could depend on the UK market was more circumscribed; when it increased UK production, it needed to depend more heavily on exports to the European continent.

The local distributor was Nissan UK, which was 100 percent owned by a local businessman and had 450 dealers. Nissan UK was an excellent distributor, as shown by its market share in the United Kingdom; however, Nissan wished to increase its own influence over marketing in the United Kingdom and to coordinate it under a single strategy for Europe, and therefore planned to acquire the distributor. But negotiations between the two had not been successful so far, and it was somewhat uncertain that Nissan could control the marketing and logistics in the United Kingdom as they did in other countries.

France

Although France had a large car market, with about 2.2 million units a year, total imports of Japanese cars were limited to five manufacturers: Toyota, Nissan, Mitsubishi, Honda, and Mazda, which shared 3 percent of the market. The supermini class was the largest segment, followed by the lower- and upper-medium-sized cars. French consumers were thought to be price conscious and less sensitive to quality than consumers in West Germany and the Netherlands.

The French automobile companies, Peugeot and Renault, held more than a 60 percent market share, and the total share of imported cars was only one-third. Despite having the largest market share, Peugeot had not achieved productivity as high as had the Japanese manufacturers and, therefore, attempted to enlarge and modernize its production facilities in preparation for 1992. However, Renault was heavily in debt and lacked the capital to make substantial investments to raise productivity.

Nissan's marketing organization in France was weak because sales had been restricted. The exclusive distributor, Richard-Nissan SA, of which Nissan owned 9.6 percent, was limited in management and marketing capability. Thus, Nissan was making efforts to strengthen the capability of Richard-Nissan. Richard-Nissan served 203 dealers in France, most of which sold only Japanese-made cars and Nissan's Spanish-made commercial vehicles. However, these dealers were relatively small in size, varying from family-run shops with 3 to 4 employees to companies with about 20 employees.

Italy

The Italian car market, highly restricted since 1957, represented about 2 million units a year; however, in 1988, Japanese car imports were restricted to only 3,300 units, of which 750 were off-road vehicles. Fiat, which was the largest automobile company in Italy, held the highest market share not only in Italy (60 percent) but in all of Europe (15.5 percent), due in part to its dominance of the domestic market and the launch of a successful new lower-medium-sized car. However, 54 percent of its sales were in Italy. Expecting an end to the Italian market's restrictive quota on Japanese imports by 1992, Fiat aggressively increased its investment in production facilities and R&D, shortened the time to develop new products, and improved productivity.

A unique characteristic of the Italian car market was the large market share of the utility-class car. Italian consumers, like the French and Spanish, but unlike the other Europeans, tended to be price rather than quality sensitive.

Nissan sold through 160 dealerships organized under Nissan Italia S.p.A., a joint ventury of Nissan (64.2 percent) and NMISA (35.8 percent). However, because the company's car imports had been so restricted, these dealers were experienced mainly in selling Spanish-manufactured commercial vehicles, which accounted for 6,200 units in 1988. Therefore, because the average dealership had fewer than 10 employees and sold other companies' vehicles as well as Nissan's, sales performance was not strong. Nissan Italia planned to recruit or establish larger dealerships that were expected to stock Nissan vehicles only.

Spain

The car market in Spain expanded rapidly from a plateau of 500,000 units in 1985 to more than one million units in 1988. However, in 1988, the total Japanese quota was still only 3,200 units, including imports via other EC countries. This quota was slated to increase to about 7,000 in 1990 and, eventually, be integrated into the voluntary ceiling on total Japanese imports into EC countries.

Spanish market characteristics were similar to those in France and Italy; car demand concentrated on utility, supermini, and lower-medium classes, and price tended to be more important than quality.

Although Spain's car market was the fifth-largest in Europe in unit sales, it had outstripped the United Kingdom in production to become the fourth-largest since 1984, because of heavy investment by foreign companies attracted by lower labor costs and Spain's entry into the EC. However, all Spanish car manufacturers were controlled by foreign companies. Among them, SEAT, an affiliate of Volkswagen, was positioned as a base for manufacturing smaller cars for southern Europe and considered fairly competitive.

Japanese companies had little business presence in passenger cars. However, regarding commercial vehicles, Nissan carried out local production through NMISA and held about a 20 percent market share in 1987. Also, Suzuki bought 17 percent of a local commercial vehicle manufacturer, Land-Rover Santana S.A., which made a small four-wheel-drive off-road vehicle in Spain.

Although NMISA had 143 dealers for selling its commercial vehicles, it served also as a local distributor of Nissan's passenger cars. With 70 to 80 employees, the dealerships were on average relatively larger than those in other European countries. But, because they handled mostly commercial vehicles, they had very limited experience in selling passenger cars. Recognizing the need to alter the dealerships, Nissan asked them to meet appropriate standards as to space, appearance, capital, organization, and other qualities conducive to selling passenger cars.

Other Countries

In addition to the "Big Five," the Japanese held more than a 30 percent market share in countries such as Ireland, Denmark, Finland, Norway, and Austria, which had no automobile industry and no restrictions on car imports. Even in other European countries, such as the Netherlands, Belgium, Sweden, and Switzerland, the Japanese held more than a 20 percent market share, except in Portugal, where quotas were enforced. Consequently, room for raising market share was limited. Also, because individual market sizes were small, Nissan could not depend much on additional sales in these countries as it expanded production in the United Kingdom.

However, the three major southern European markets, France, Italy, and Spain, were large in size and underexploited due to import restrictions. And in Italy and Spain, the UK–made Bluebird was expected to be approved for import as an EC–made car. Even in France, importation was close to being conceded, though some uncertainties remained. Therefore, it was mostly agreed within Nissan that to increase sales in Europe on a large scale, exploiting these three markets would be critical.

Promotion Strategy

Sekiguchi and Gomi consulted with their colleagues on Nissan's marketing strategy for southern Europe. All agreed that the European market was important and that the three southern countries needed to be exploited in order to retain the competitive advantage in Europe. And they agreed to market five or six car models, including the Bluebird and the New Micra, in the three countries. The major issue was how to allocate marketing resources between the two UK–made models, because both the cars were strategically important, yet available marketing funds for the three countries were limited.

The most significant constraint was on the advertising budget. Nissan advertising in Europe was placed by Nissan itself, by national distributors, and by local dealers. Nissan's advertising copy was created first in English, translated into the appropriate language, and exposed to all European countries at the same time with the same message. Consequently, it was not that easy to stress a particular model for a particular country.

Advertising by each local distributor was prepared separately, though guided by Nissan's total marketing strategy for Europe. Distributor advertisements were paid for mostly out of their 12 percent margins and placed mainly in print media. The importance of television advertising was increasing though its role was still relatively limited compared with that in North America or Japan. Recently, the West German distributor, planning to run a large-scale TV campaign, had asked Nissan to bear some part of the cost. In France, Italy, and Spain the distributors' small sales volumes restricted the level of their advertising budgets. Any mass media advertising in these markets would therefore have to focus on either the Bluebird or the New Micra, even if Nissan or Nissan Europe provided supplemental funds.

Dealer advertisements, which were placed mostly in print media, were often funded by local distributors—so long as the advertising met certain content criteria—usually up to 50 percent of their cost. These allowances to dealers reduced correspondingly the size of distributor advertising budgets.

Bluebird vs. New Micra

Executives supporting the New Micra pointed to the relatively faster growth in sales of small cars and emphasized that a higher percentage of consumers in the southern European countries purchased smaller cars. They asserted that these markets where more potential demand existed should be targeted. And, to establish strong distribution channels, Nissan needed a rapid sales increase, which was more likely to be accomplished by the New Micra than the Bluebird.

That the New Micra would not face direct competition with other Japanese companies was another important factor in its favor. Nissan felt uneasy about competitors of similar background and image, though it would also have to compete with local European companies. But the only other Japanese car company currently engaged in local production was Honda, which jointly manufactured medium-sized cars with the Rover group in the United Kingdom. Although Toyota decided to start local production in the United Kingdom in 1992 and needed to exploit the French, Italian, and Spanish markets for the same reasons as Nissan, the model to be manufactured in the Toyota UK factory was an upper-medium-sized car. Moreover, Nissan executives were confident that no other Japanese car company could manufacture in Europe a supermini-class car like the New Micra, at least not before 1992. Therefore, the New Micra would be insulated from direct Japanese competition for a while.

One of the major reasons for supporting the Bluebird was that its profit margin per unit was higher than that for the New Micra. Also emphasizing the Bluebird would generate further increases in unit profit contribution because of experience curve and scale economy effects in the UK factory. If the New Micra were emphasized, reaching break-even on Bluebird production in the UK factory would be delayed.

Another reason for supporting the Bluebird was the probability that the New Micra would attract more attention among Nissan's European competitors. Major southern European car companies like Fiat, Peugeot, and Renault, which were very influential in automobile-related policy making in their respective countries, focused mainly on the small-size-car market, especially in southern Europe. Accordingly, stressing the New Micra meant head-on competition with these companies and, in the long term, could cause further trade friction, which in turn might result in regulations detrimental to Japanese car companies.

Furthermore, Nissan's image in Europe had to be considered. Formerly, European countries had been in advance of Japan in developing the medium- or small-size car; therefore, Japanese car designers had some yearning for the European car. Then, Japanese car companies became competitive in the North American and European markets by improving production technology and manufacturing efficiencies. However, differing from North America, where the Japanese had earlier faced no direct local competition for medium- or small-size cars, Europe had had several competitive local manufacturers in those classes of car. Thus, in Europe, the Japanese car had long been regarded as low-priced, and higher-priced Japanese cars had tended to sell poorly. But the image of Japanese cars was improving and they were now regarded as superior in quality to French and Italian cars, though still inferior to the West German cars.

At the same time, each Japanese company tried to create its own unique image. For example, Toyota featured high performance, Honda emphasized upgraded value-added cars, and Mazda focused on building market share in sophisticated, performance-oriented West Germany, making special efforts to develop cars tailored to the European market. Among these competitors, Nissan was seen as an average Japanese car maker. Hence, it sometimes happened that Nissan perpetuated the low-priced car image of the Japanese car, and focusing on the New Micra would reinforce this view.

However, in the three southern European countries, Nissan was not a well-known name, except in Spain, thanks to its locally produced commercial vehicles. Because sales were currently low due to import restrictions, Nissan executives believed it would be important to raise awareness immediately upon the lifting of the restrictions in order to obtain a favorable competitive position in these countries. The New Micra, with its broader appeal and promise of higher unit sales volume, seemed to be the model to emphasize.

Advertising and Promotion Management

Beecham Products U.S.A. (A)

In October 1984, Susan Edwards, director of brand management, and Chris Weglarz, brand manager for Aqua-fresh toothpaste, were preparing for a brand group meeting on the 1985–86 media and promotion plans. Because Beecham's fiscal year began on April 1, the date of November 30, 1984, was set for completion of the plan.

Edwards noted that increased levels of media and promotion spending had been required in recent years to maintain an Aqua-fresh market share of approximately 12 percent, the level achieved in 1980, one year after the Aqua-fresh product introduction. The major factor in the rise of promotional expenditures was ever-increasing competitive spending on trade deals. Some members of the brand group questioned the level of trade promotion expenditures and argued that reallocating some trade promotion funds to consumer promotions would result in market share increases.

New information to assist in formulating the 1985–86 plan was available to the brand group. Using consumer toothpaste purchase data provided by scanner panels, the effectiveness of various promotional vehicles had been evaluated by Information Resources, Inc. (IRI).

Company Background

Thomas Beecham's study of the medicinal properties of herbs began in 1828 at the age of 8 when he started work as a shepherd to augment his family's income. By the age of 20, Beecham was selling his herbal remedies throughout England. He became firmly established in the early 1850s as a "Chemist, Druggist, and Tea Dealer." Among Beecham's accomplishments was the formulation of Beecham's Pills, a remedy for the common cold. This medicine became increasingly well known as Beecham first distributed the pills through mail order, then developed a

This case was prepared by Research Associate Melanie D. Spencer under the direction of Professor John A. Quelch as the basis for class discussion rather than to illustrate either effective or ineffective handling of an administrative situation. Proprietary data have been disguised. Promotion plans provided are not actual plans. Copyright © 1986 by the President and Fellows of Harvard College. Harvard Business School case 1–587–012.

national marketing program. By 1859, the product was sold from Africa to Australia.

Beecham was committed to customer satisfaction through product quality. This commitment was evident in his reservations about the power of advertising:

> It is possible, by plausible advertising, set forth in an attractive style, to temporarily arrest the attention of a certain number of readers, and induce them to purchase a particular article. But it is a more difficult matter to ensure their continued patronage. Unless the advertised article proves to be all that is claimed for it, not only do the purchasers discontinue its use, but warn others against it as a thing to be avoided.

Beecham believed in tailoring his products to the markets in which they were being sold. For example, when the company introduced Beecham's Pills in the US, they were sweetened to appeal to American tastes. This philosophy also applied to the sales force. Beecham required that export salespersons speak the languages of their customers.

Growth continued through acquisition as well as international market expansion. Early acquisitions included Macleans, makers of a popular brand of toothpaste, and County Perfumery, which produced Brylcreem, the leading men's hairdressing in the United Kingdom. Brylcreem later spearheaded Beecham's expansion into the United States, becoming the best-selling men's hairdressing in the US by 1960.

Encouraged by Brylcreem's success, Beecham made further acquisitions including S. E. Massengill (1971), a Tennessee-based producer of pharmaceuticals and feminine hygiene products, and the Calgon consumer products business (1977), which marketed well-known brands such as Cling-Free fabric softener, Sucrets sore throat lozenges, and Calgon water conditioner. The Calgon acquisition tripled the size of Beecham's US consumer products business. In 1982, Beecham acquired the J. B. Williams division of Nabisco Brands, which marketed the leading US iron supplement, Geritol.

By 1984, the Beecham Group, Ltd., had become a $2.5 billion consumer products and pharmaceutical company with headquarters in the United Kingdom. Beecham Products U.S.A., the US consumer packaged goods division of Beecham Group, Ltd., manufactured and marketed 17 brands, including Aqua-fresh, Massengill, Cling-Free, Calgon, Geritol, and Sucrets. The division's sales were $400 million in 1984.

Marketing within the division was organized around the classic product management system. Directors of brand management reported to the vice president of marketing. Each director of brand management was responsible for two to four brand management groups. The marketing vice president reported directly to the president of the division, making the chain of command relatively short and facilitating quick decision making.

Product Category History

Tooth powder was introduced in the US in 1899. Similar in consistency to baking soda, tooth powder had to be combined with water before use, either by dipping a wet toothbrush into the powder or by forming a paste which could then be applied to the teeth. The procedure tended to be time-consuming and messy.

In 1936, three brands of toothpaste were introduced: Squibb, Colgate, and Pepsodent. The next milestone occurred in 1955 when fluoride was incorporated into toothpaste formulas to aid in tooth decay prevention. Crest, introduced by Procter & Gamble Co. in 1955, was the first toothpaste to include fluoride. The therapeutic value of brushing with a fluoride toothpaste earned Crest the first American Dental Association (ADA) seal of approval.

Brands such as Crest and Colgate, which emphasized fluoride content and cavity prevention, were targeted at families with young children. These products developed strong brand loyalty. Many children, whose parents had purchased a particular product for its decay prevention, continued to use the same brand as adults.

During the late 1960s and early 1970s, many new toothpaste brands were introduced, some of which emphasized cosmetic rather than therapeutic benefits. Ultra-Brite (1967), manufactured by Colgate-Palmolive, and Close-Up (1970), made by Lever Brothers, for example, focused on the whitening and breath-freshening properties of toothpaste. Advertising for these brands targeted a new audience, the teenager and young adult, who were beginning to make their own purchasing decisions, and emphasized the "sex appeal" of white teeth and fresh breath. Next came Aim, which was introduced by Lever Brothers in 1973. Like Close-Up, Aim was a gel, but since it contained fluoride, it was positioned as a therapeutic brand.

Through the late 1970s, the toothpaste category averaged volume growth of only 2 percent per year.

The Aqua-fresh Introduction

Prior to introducing Aqua-fresh nationally, Beecham conducted a test market in four cities. Aqua-fresh's market share objectives ranged from 8–9 percent. The product was positioned as a cosmetic brand with advertising emphasizing breath-freshening benefits with the tag line "Oceans of Freshness." The results were disappointing, with the product achieving only a 4 percent market share during the test period.

Research in the late 1970s had shown that two-thirds of US households purchased both cosmetic and therapeutic brands, with different members of the household using different brands. Beecham, therefore, repositioned the brand as Double Protection Aqua-fresh, offering both breath-freshening and cavity prevention benefits to the consumer. To communicate visually these dual attributes, the toothpaste combined a white paste component and an aqua gel component which gave the product a striped appearance. The toothpaste was awarded the American Dental Association (ADA) seal of approval because of its proven ability to fight cavities. Only five dentifrice brands were allowed to carry ADA seals on their cartons and in their advertising at that time: Aqua-fresh, Crest, Colgate, Aim, and Macleans. Beecham tested Aqua-fresh's new positioning in two markets in New York and Texas, with market share objectives of 10 percent and 12 percent, respectively. The achievement of their market share objectives resulted in a decision to launch Aqua-fresh nationally.

In January 1979, Beecham began a regional roll-out of Aqua-fresh in the western third of the US. Aqua-fresh was the first major new brand in the product category since Aim.

To stimulate trial of Aqua-fresh, Beecham undertook one of the largest sampling programs ever implemented in the industry. The weight of Aqua-fresh advertising during the introduction was also unprecedented. Mothers of teenagers were selected as the primary target market because management believed that teens, more than other consumers, faced the conflict between cosmetic and therapeutic benefits. Double Protection Aqua-fresh was believed especially appropriate for families with mothers concerned about cavity protection and with teens who insisted on a toothpaste that freshened breath. Advertising and promotion expenditures in the year following the introduction were $21.7 million and $23.1 million, respectively. Crest, the market leader, and Aim, the number three brand, substantially increased promotions and advertising in response to the Aqua-fresh introduction, while Colgate, the number two brand, showed little reaction.

By the end of 1979, Aqua-fresh had established a nationwide market share of 12 percent, drawn proportionately to market share from the three major competitors, Crest, Colgate, and Aim. Aqua-fresh achieved the number three share position in the category, with a higher share than Aim. Exhibit 1 shows Nielsen and SAMI[1] market share trends for the years following the Aqua-fresh introduction.

Aqua-fresh, like its major competitors, was packaged in five tube sizes: 1.4 oz., 2.7 oz., 4.6 oz., 6.4 oz., and 8.2 oz. Each size of each brand was considered an item. The percent of Aqua-fresh's 1984 volume by size was as follows:

---

[1] The A. C. Nielsen Company monitored retail sales by brand/size in a sample of retail outlets nationwide. Selling Areas Marketing Inc. (SAMI), a division of Time Inc., monitored the rate of product withdrawals from trade warehouses.

	1.4 oz.	*2.7 oz.*	*4.6 oz.*	*6.4 oz.*	*8.2 oz.*
Percent volume distribution by size	7%	13%	20%	35%	25%

The percent of volume by item was similar for the other major brands, except that Crest and Colgate tended to sell a greater proportion of their volume in the smaller sizes. Manufacturers' list prices of all the major brands were comparable.

The Aqua-fresh launch began a new era in dentifrice marketing. What historically had been a stable, predictable product category became increasingly volatile and competitive. When Aqua-fresh was introduced, 25 items accounted for 80 percent of sales volume in the category. By 1984, 40 items accounted for 80 percent of toothpaste sales volume following introductions of several new flavors and gels by the market leaders.

Product Category Development after the Aqua-fresh Introduction

The first new product introduction after Aqua-fresh occurred in January 1981, when Procter & Gamble launched Advanced Formula Crest. Advertising implied that Advanced Formula's new fluoride gave consumers

EXHIBIT 1 Toothpaste Market Size and Competitive Brand Shares

A. C. Nielsen Retail Sales Data: 1980–1984*					
	1980	*1981*	*1982*	*1983*	*1984*
Aqua-fresh	12.9%	11.9%	11.6%	11.5%	11.4%
Crest	35.4	36.2	35.1	35.2	32.9
Colgate	17.8	18.4	22.5	22.4	23.6
Aim	10.2	9.5	9.5	9.7	9.1
Total market (thousands of dozen cases)	60,464	63,082	65,886	71,848	73,793
Retail $MM	$868	$974	$1,055	$1,130	$1,177

SAMI Warehouse Withdrawal Data: 1982–1984†					
Aqua-fresh			12.1%	12.0%	12.2%
Crest			35.2	35.8	43.1
Colgate			22.9	22.8	23.3
Aim			10.0	9.0	8.6
Total market (thousands of dozen cases)			39,749	42,697	41,586

* A. C. Nielsen numbers included sales of food stores, drug stores, and mass merchandisers.

† SAMI measured product withdrawals from food chain warehouses only.

therapeutic benefits superior to those of its competitive brands. The product was presented to the trade as a one-for-one substitution for original Crest, at the same price. The number of items in the category remained the same.

In the fall of 1981, Procter & Gamble, Colgate, and Lever Brothers all introduced new flavors. Crest Gel was the third flavor of Crest toothpaste (Crest Mint had been introduced in 1955) and increased the number of Crest items from 10 to 15. Colgate Gel and Aim Mint flavors doubled the number of items for each brand from 5 to 10. The gel introductions were the result of research showing that sweeter gels appealed to a younger audience. Colgate had identified that its users were older and, therefore, developed the gel to appeal to a younger market segment. Crest already had an image as a therapeutic brand for children. In the heavy advertising and promotion war that followed these introductions, Colgate gained market share as its new gel attracted younger users. Crest, however, lost share; its new gel simply cannibalized sales of its other two formulas.

To carry the ADA seal of acceptance, toothpaste manufacturers had to have their advertising claims cleared by the ADA. During 1981, the Aqua-fresh brand attempted to clear a plaque[2] claim with the ADA. Beecham research had shown that the three most important therapeutic attributes to consumers were: "Helps prevent cavities," "Contains fluoride," and "Helps remove plaque." The research also indicated that Aqua-fresh had not yet established the reputation for therapy that Crest, Colgate, and Aim had. Despite the dual benefit positioning, Aqua-fresh users often liked the brand for its taste and breath freshening rather than for its fluoride/cavity prevention properties. Given the results, the brand group believed the plaque claim would improve Aqua-fresh's therapeutic image. However, the claim was refused by the ADA. The ADA refused to allow any dentifrice manufacturers to make the plaque claim at that time. They later established guidelines for clinical testing that would allow manufacturers to test and clear plaque claims.

Nevertheless, with the Crest Gel, Colgate Gel, and Aim Mint introductions in the fall of 1981, the brand group felt it had to reposition Aqua-fresh to address more consumer needs. Hence, in November of 1981, Beecham began shipments of new "Triple Protection Aqua-fresh" with an "even cleans stained film" claim added to the cavity prevention and breath-freshening attributes. At that time, this was as close as the ADA would allow to a plaque claim. Consumer research had indicated that stain removal was important to consumers, and clinical research proved that Triple Protection Aqua-fresh was effective at cleaning stains. Triple Protection Aqua-fresh had three stripes, red, aqua, and white.

---

[2] Plaque is a sticky film on the teeth and can lead to gum disease and cavities if not removed.

EXHIBIT 2   Six-Month Promotion Activity for 1981–1982 Toothpaste Introductions

Crest Gel 11/81–4/82	Colgate Gel 11/81–4/82	Aim Mint 10/81–3/82	Triple Protection Aqua-fresh 1/82–6/82
$.25 mailed coupon, 12/81	$.10 FSI* coupon, 11/81	$.25 FSI coupon, 10/81	Trial floor stand, 2/82
Trial floor stand, 1/82	$.25 FSI coupon, 1/82	$.15 magazine coupon, 11/81	$.15 FSI coupon, 2/82
$.25 on-pack coupon, 3/82	Mailed samples and $.10 coupon, 1/82	$.15 FSI coupon, 12/81	$.12 mailed coupon, 4/82
	$.25 FSI coupon, 2/82	2-$.15 mailed coupon, 1/82	3-$.12 BFD coupon, 5/82
	$.20 mailed coupon, 3/82	Trial floor stand, 1/82	Trial floor stand, 6/82
	1.4 oz. trial floor stand, 3/82	$.15 FSI coupon, 2/82	
	$.15 FSI/BFD† coupon, 4/82	$.25 FSI coupon, 3/82	
	$.25 in-store coupon		

* FSI = Free standing insert.
† BFD = Best Food Day.

The new product was presented to the trade as a one-for-one substitution for the existing line. Because of the Crest Gel, Colgate Gel, and Aim Mint (15 items) introductions, Aqua-fresh's share of total shelf space declined. Nevertheless, after an initial share decline in January and February of 1982, the new formula helped Aqua-fresh regain and maintain market share at 11.5 percent, despite heavy competitive promotion and advertising support. Exhibit 2 lists the trial-generating consumer promotions fielded for each of the new brand items during their first six months.

Distribution

Beecham Products U.S.A. employed a direct sales force which was responsible for achieving sales volume targets and implementing promotions in specific geographical regions.

Aqua-fresh was sold primarily through three channels: food stores, drugstores, and mass merchandisers. Table 1 shows Aqua-fresh and product category sales and Aqua-fresh distribution penetration by channel from 1981 to 1984 in millions of dozens.[3] Exhibit 3 shows

---

[3] In 1983–84, the average number of ounces of toothpaste per unit sold through channels was 6.04 (total), 5.84 (food), 6.0 (drug), and 6.65 (mass merchandiser).

TABLE 1   Toothpaste Sales—Millions of Dozens

Aqua-fresh	1981/82	1982/83	1983/84
Food	4.8	4.8	5.2
Drug	1.6	1.6	1.8
Mass merchandiser	1.1	1.4	1.3
Total	7.5	7.8	8.3
Category	1981/82	1982/83	1983/84
Food	40.0	42.2	43.6
Drug	14.8	13.5	15.0
Mass merchandiser	9.0	11.7	13.7
Total	63.8	67.4	72.3

Beecham fiscal year 1983/84 percentage ACV distribution by size for each channel.[4]

Food stores accounted for 60 percent of category dollar sales in 1984. Historically, health and beauty aid (HBA) products had been a small part of most food stores' business; however, a trend toward larger HBA sections in food stores developed in the early 1980s as they sought to emphasize higher margin merchandise. Food stores began to treat toothpaste as a loss leader to generate consumer traffic. As a result, food stores became more demanding regarding promotional offers from manufacturers. Most food stores tended to stock three sizes of each major brand flavor. Reflecting the number of items pressing for limited shelf space, many food stores did not carry weaker brands.

Drug stores, on the other hand, relied on HBA products as a major source of sales. For this reason, drug stores stocked most brands and sizes of toothpaste. However, they were also pressing for promotional offers to give them an edge in competing with the food stores. Drug stores considered toothpaste an important traffic builder, which could lead to the sale of other higher margin products. They, therefore, gave brands feature advertising support, maintained an average of four items per brand flavor, and realized lower margins on toothpaste than food stores, passing promotional savings through to the consumer. Drug stores accounted for 20 percent of category sales.

Mass merchandisers accounted for 20 percent of category sales volume and carried an average of four items per brand flavor. Because they typically offered the consumer an "everyday low price," trade promotions were not as important for mass merchandisers. Mass merchandisers featured toothpaste less frequently than food or drugstores, but when a feature was run, it usually generated greater percentage sales increases than a feature in either of the other two channels.

---

[4] An item with 70 percent ACV (all commodity volume) in grocery stores was distributed in stores that accounted for 70 percent of the sales through all grocery stores.

EXHIBIT 3   **Distribution of Four Toothpaste Brands—Fiscal Year 1983/84**

Food—Percent ACV

	Tubes				
	1.4 oz.	*2.7 oz.*	*4.6 oz.*	*6.4 oz.*	*8.2 oz.*
Aqua-fresh	36.3	80.9	81.4	82.8	63.9
Crest	38.0	83.4	85.8	87.2	71.3
Colgate	41.4	80.9	83.8	85.6	64.7
Aim	15.2	67.7	78.2	81.6	52.5

Drug—Percent ACV

	Tubes				
	1.4 oz.	*2.7 oz.*	*4.6 oz.*	*6.4 oz.*	*8.2 oz.*
Aqua-fresh	67.7	71.1	84.8	80.5	59.1
Crest	83.0	73.1	89.1	93.9	68.7
Colgate	79.5	69.4	88.6	90.7	67.2
Aim	49.7	57.4	81.5	85.7	52.4

Mass Merchandiser—Percent of Stores

	Tubes				
	1.4 oz.	*2.7 oz.*	*4.6 oz.*	*6.4 oz.*	*8.2 oz.*
Aqua-fresh	53.3	69.3	80.7	97.0	82.3
Crest	44.0	73.0	74.7	99.3	96.3
Colgate	48.7	66.3	82.7	98.7	83.3
Aim	26.3	62.3	74.7	98.3	76.3

Beecham's sales force was smaller than those of the category leaders, Procter & Gamble and Colgate-Palmolive. Therefore, Aqua-fresh distribution was better in the larger chains and in regions of the country where such chains were predominant. Sales to the trade in New York City, for example, were complicated by the high number of small, independent supermarkets. The sales force was also too small to devote much time to setting up displays. Therefore, the Aqua-fresh brand team relied heavily on prepacked display pieces that could be handled easily by retailers.

As competition in the toothpaste category became fiercer and item proliferation put pressure on the shelf space available to any single brand in the category, the salesperson's job became more challenging. The sales force had to handle complex Aqua-fresh promotional calendars and monitor multiple competitive trade promotions at any one time. Adding shelf space for Aqua-fresh became increasingly difficult. Sales management developed new sales pitches to defend Aqua-fresh's shelf space. For example, the organizer, shown in Exhibit 4, focused on Aqua-fresh's contribution per item compared to the contribution per item of competitive brands with broader product lines.

EXHIBIT 4   Aqua-fresh Trade Organizer

A Category that Draws the Consumer
Dentifrice Dollar Volume

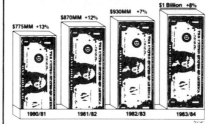

- Over last four years category has grown dramatically.
  Dollar Volume up 30% = 5.5 million cases.
- Aqua-fresh, Colgate, and Crest have accounted for nearly all of the category's growth.
- 7 of the top 10 HBA items are toothpastes—Aqua-fresh, Colgate, and Crest draw the consumer.
- Nearly 100% household penetration—every consumer is a potential sale.

Aqua-fresh®
#1 share/SKU

	AQUA-FRESH	CREST	COLGATE	AIM
Share	12.1	35.4	22.7	8.8
SKUs	5	15	10	10
	2.42	2.36	2.27	.88

- Aqua-fresh #1 seller per SKU, outselling Crest and Colgate. Outsells Aim 3 to 1.
- By flavor, Aqua-fresh is vying for the #1 position with a 12.1% share.
- Aqua-fresh sales are about equal to Crest Regular and Colgate Regular.

Aqua-fresh®
is #1 in Inventory Turns

		Aqua-fresh turns this much faster
AQUA-FRESH—10.8 Turns/Year		
CREST—9.5		**13%**
COLGATE—9.3		**16%**
AIM—7.1		**52%**

Aqua-fresh returns your investment faster than any brand in the category—in fact, 52% faster than Aim.

Aqua-fresh inventory turns nearly 11 times a year—with 2% 30 terms, you sell Aqua-fresh before you pay for it!

Fast turns + unsurpassed terms = Best Profit Return—Aqua-fresh

Aqua-fresh®
IS #1 IN MAKING MONEY
Annual Profit Return Per Inventory Dollar Invested

AQUA-FRESH $2.48

CREST $2.19

COLGATE $2.14

AIM $1.63

REACT TO THE FACTS

- Aqua-fresh delivers more profit than Crest, Colgate and Aim.
- Aqua-fresh share of inventories is too lean in proportion to category shares.
- Aim inventories are too fat in proportion to category shares.
- Aqua-fresh out-of-stocks cost you money—
  Consumer delays purchase or
  Buys a brand with shorter terms of sale

SOLUTION: Carry all 5 Sizes
  Make Aqua-fresh share of inventory = share of sales

EXHIBIT 4   (concluded)

Aqua-fresh®

#1 with your Promotion Dollars

% Increase in Movement

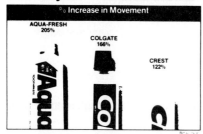

AQUA-FRESH 205%

COLGATE 166%

CREST 122%

☐ Aqua-fresh sells better on promotion than Crest or Colgate

☐ Promoting a toothpaste is a consumer draw provided the brand you use is recognized by the consumer.

☐ *Feature and display Aqua-fresh to get the most out of your promotion dollars.*

☐ It's easier and more profitable to promote Aqua-fresh

Aqua-fresh	1 SKU/size
Crest	3 SKU s/size
Colgate	2 SKU s/size
Aim	2 SKU s/size

Aqua-fresh®

Best Return Comes from Feature and Display

Based on 20¢ Price Reduction

	Increase in Movement		
		WEEKLY MOVEMENT	CS
Price Reduction	+47		CS
Price Reduction + Feature	+186		CS
Price Reduction + Feature + Display	+843		CS

Based on 30¢ Price Reduction

	Increase in Movement		
		WEEKLY MOVEMENT	CS
Price Reduction	+85		CS
Price Reduction + Feature	+260		CS
Price Reduction + Feature + Display	+1,087		CS

$ _____

Aqua-fresh®

Sells the Consumer

Advertising:

☐ Reaching 90% of all households

☐ 588 GRP's a month

☐ 16 commercials/week

Consumer Promotion:

☐ 24 million 20¢ mailed coupons week of 9/30/84

Action Plan:

Aqua-fresh TRIPLE PROTECTION

1. FIGHTS CAVITIES 2. FRESHENS BREATH 3. EVEN CLEANS STAINED FILM

BEECHAM PRODUCTS Pittsburgh PA 15230

Aqua-fresh Marketing

Brand management relied on advertising, trade promotion, and consumer promotion to market Aqua-fresh. Exhibit 5 shows media and promotion spending in dollars and as a percentage of sales for Aqua-fresh and the other major brands for 1979/80 through 1983/84. Brand management estimated that 70 percent of Aqua-fresh, Aim, and Colgate sales volume was shipped to the trade on deal; the corresponding figure for Crest was 60 percent.

Advertising

Aqua-fresh spent its advertising dollars primarily in television. Television spots focused on the brand's attributes physically represented by the toothpaste's stripes. Exhibit 6 presents a storyboard from a typical triple protection Aqua-fresh commercial. The major objectives of Aqua-fresh advertising were to promote awareness of the brand, communicate product benefits, and emphasize ADA approval. In 1984, brand management estimated that a 17 percent share of voice was necessary to maintain Aqua-fresh market share. They projected 1984–85 advertising expenditures of $21.6 million on sales of $134 million or 8.4 million dozens.

Trade Promotions

Manufacturers often offered a trade promotion or temporary price discount on a product for a specified period of time to boost short-term sales. The allowance was often dependent on the retailer providing merchandising support (retail price cut, feature advertisement, and/or special display) for the product during the promotion period. Although increased short-term sales and consumer trial might be generated, trade promotions rarely resulted in sustained sales volume and market share increases. Manufacturers encouraged the trade to accept promoted product packed in displays or floor stands to maximize sales.

In 1980, trade promotion expenditures by packaged goods manufacturers in the United States were estimated at $6.5 billion, with health and beauty aids trade promotions alone accounting for $3.3 billion of this total.[5] Trade allowances for toothpastes since 1980 had increased in step with manufacturer price increases, keeping the dead net, the unit cost to the trade after all allowances, at roughly the same level.[6] The result was more money for retailers and escalating trade promotion expenditures by manufacturers.

---

[5] Reported in Paul W. Farris and John A. Quelch, *Advertising and Promotion Management* (Radnor, Pennsylvania: Chilton Book Company, 1983).

[6] The dead net cost was the cost of an item to the retailer after all allowances had been subtracted from the manufacturer's price.

EXHIBIT 5 Estimated Advertising and Promotion Expenditures by Brand

Category Media Spending
(millions of dollars)

	1979/80		1980/81		1981/82		1982/83		1983/84		1984/85	
	$MM	*Percent Sales*	*$MM*	*Percent Sales*	*$MM*	*Percent Sales*	*$MM*	*Percent Sales*	*$MM*	*Percent Sales*	*$MM*	*Percent Sales*
Aqua-fresh	$21.7	27%	$20.7	25%	$19.5	23%	$24.5	21%	$22.9	18%	$21.6	16%
Crest	25.8	9	29.4	13	48.4	18	36.9	11	37.0	10	31.0	10
Colgate	18.1	13	17.0	15	27.7	20	26.1	12	30.0	13	28.0	12
Aim	15.7	19	15.5	25	21.3	33	17.6	19	19.5	18	18.0	20

Category Promotion Spending
(millions of dollars)

	1979/80		1980/81		1981/82		1982/83		1983/84		1984/85	
	$MM	*Percent Sales*	*$MM*	*Percent Sales*	*$MM*	*Percent Sales*	*$MM*	*Percent Sales*	*$MM*	*Percent Sales*	*$MM*	*Percent Sales*
Aqua-fresh	$23.1	28%	$13.9	17%	$17.4	21%	$20.6	18%	$29.9	24%	$30.8	23%
Crest	28.1	10	31.8	14	31.1	12	36.1	11	65.1	17	55.4	14
Colgate	19.4	14	24.8	22	41.0	29	40.6	19	44.3	18	52.1	18
Aim	10.5	13	12.9	21	19.1	29	15.4	17	24.8	23	16.9	17

Aqua-fresh Promotion Spending
(thousands of dollars)

	1980/81	1981/82	1982/83	1983/84	1984/85
Price pack	$ 7,278	$ 4,642	$ 9,349	$12,512	$12,829
Other trade merchandising	4,088	8,984	8,273	9,590	10,353
Trial events	2,569	3,731	3,009	7,787	7,620
Total	$13,935	$17,357	$20,631	$29,889	$30,802

EXHIBIT 6   Aqua-fresh Television Advertisement

FATHER: What's this . . .

a space age toothpaste!

MOTHER: No! It's our Aqua-fresh with a brand new see-through top.
TEEN: I can see its Triple Protection Formula!
MOTHER: Only Aqua-fresh has it.

(VO): The maximum fluoride protection of the leading paste . . .

all the breath freshener of the leading gel . . .

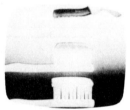

and gentle cleaners that even remove stained film . . .

SFX: SWOOSH
concentrated in one complete toothpaste.

MOTHER: And tests prove mothers prefer Aqua-fresh to the other leading brands

ANNCR (VO): Triple Protection Aqua-fresh. A complete toothpaste.

Aqua-fresh trade promotions frequently included allowances with merchandising requirements. Trade promotion was considered so important to the brand that one manager characterized the marketing planning process as follows: "First we figure the trade promotion spending required to be competitive; then, we add the media cost; then, whatever is left goes for trial events." The amount of the allowance and therefore the dead net cost varied depending on the size of the item on deal, and the brand group's projections of expected competitive offers. The objective was to offer dead nets which were comparable to those of its major competitors. Proof of merchandising performance, such as an advertising tear sheet or a picture of a display, was necessary before Beecham paid a merchandising allowance.

Aggressive promotion was necessary to ensure merchandising support for the brand and to retain distribution of as many stockkeeping units (SKUs) as possible. During periods of competitive introductions of new items, promotional expenditures to the trade were critical to sustaining shelf space. The 1983/84 shares of retailer feature advertising in the toothpaste category obtained by Aqua-fresh and the other major brands by type of distribution channel are shown in Table 2.

The Crest brand was supported by regular trade promotions on key sizes plus Procter & Gamble's Cooperative Merchandising Agreement (CMA). The CMA enabled retailers to accrue a $.10–$.50 allowance per statistical case on Procter & Gamble products. A retailer could receive these allowances if it provided special merchandising support. Allowances earned on one product could be applied to the merchandising of any other product sold by Procter & Gamble's Health and Personal Care Division. The CMA helped to ensure Procter & Gamble of distribution of its weaker products. A further benefit was that Procter & Gamble did not have to sell Crest consistently at a high discount to gain merchandising support for the brand. Colgate offered a similar program. Beecham did not offer a CMA. Instead, Beecham offered the trade more lucrative bonus allowances tied to specific promotions. This gave Beecham tighter control over expenditures and greater assurance of extra merchandising performance for specific events.

Consumer Promotions

Consumer promotions typically aimed either to switch users of competitive brands to the promoted product or, secondarily, to reward current users. Aqua-fresh brand management used three types of consumer promotion, price packs, coupons, and trial sizes, to generate trial of Aqua-fresh. Trial was viewed as an important objective as the brand was relatively new, and consumer research showed that most consumers who tried Aqua-fresh preferred it to the other leading brands.

Price packs, with a standard price reduction (for example, "20 cents off") printed on the package were frequently run on the 4.6-, 6.4-, and 8.2-ounce sizes of Aqua-fresh, Colgate, and Aim. Retailers were paid the

TABLE 2   Shares of Retailer Feature Advertising of Toothpaste

	Food	Drug/ Mass Merchandiser
Aqua-fresh	14%	11%
Crest	17	17
Colgate	24	24
Aim	13	13

amount of the price reduction and were therefore obligated to pass the reduction on to the consumer. Promotions on the 8.2-ounce size offered the advantage of taking purchasers out of the market for a longer period. In 1984, Aqua-fresh price pack values on the 8.2-ounce size were $.35, while Aim and Colgate offered $.40 and $.30 respectively. Twin packs or "buy-two-get-one-free" offers were often fielded on the 6.4-ounce size to take the consumer out of the market for even longer. Crest combined a banded pack with an on-pack premium, offering two packs banded together with free Lego building blocks to stimulate sales to families with small children. All manufacturers fielded trade promotion offers in conjunction with price packs to ensure maximum retail merchandising support.

Price packs were known to generate heavier-than-normal retail sales especially when supported by extra merchandising effort by the trade in the form of end-aisle displays and feature advertisements. Price packs were preferred over trade promotions alone since the value of the promotion was typically passed through to the consumer in the form of a lower price rather than pocketed by the retailer. Some retailers, however, especially those that pursued an everyday low price strategy,[7] were resistant to price packs. Price packs typically required special handling. A new UPC number had to be coded into store computer systems. Trade resistance prompted Procter & Gamble to curtail Crest price pack promotions in the spring of 1983, apparently in an effort to improve the company's relations with the trade. The other manufacturers offered trade accounts off-invoice allowances as alternatives to price packs. These allowances were less attractive than price pack offers and, therefore, accounted for a small portion of promoted volume.

While price packs permitted regular users to stock up on inventory during a price pack promotion, coupon promotions required a consumer to have a separate coupon for each unit purchased. Price packs were considered by some to detract more than coupons from a brand's image, and to make consumers less willing to purchase a product at its regular price. On the other hand, a coupon was physically separated from the package. The timing and duration of a price pack promotion were critical to its impact. If a nonuser were in the middle of a purchase cycle during the short (usually one week) period of a store's price pack promotion, the price incentive would be less likely to motivate trial and the consumer would be missed. Coupons, on the other hand, permitted the consumer to choose the timing of the purchases, but were not always effective in generating special merchandising support from retailers because of the extended period of the offer.

Aqua-fresh offered some coupons to stimulate trial. Consumer trial was particularly important to the brand as blind home-use tests had

---

[7] "Everyday low price" retailers used their promotion allowances to offer consistently low prices on the same items from one week to the next, as opposed to advertising very low sale prices on a different set of "hot specials" each week.

shown that consumers significantly preferred Aqua-fresh to the other major brands. Aqua-fresh coupons were distributed either through the mail, in the "Best Food Day" (BFD) sections of newspapers, or as a part of a "free standing insert" (FSI) in Sunday newspapers. Research had demonstrated that direct mail couponing generated higher redemption rates among triers; however, this method was almost more expensive in terms of cost per thousand coupons distributed. Exhibit 7 shows planned coupon costs for the 1984–85 fiscal year.

A trial size offer of 1.4-ounce tubes prepriced at $.39 was also used to stimulate brand trial. Retail inventory turnover for the trial size was high versus the normal rate. Retailers could achieve higher than normal mar-

---

EXHIBIT 7   1984–85 Aqua-fresh Coupons*

1. 20¢ free standing insert:
Distribution (43MM × $2.25/M)	$ 98M
Printing	30
Redemption (43MM × 3.1% × 30¢)†	400
Total cost	$ 528
Circulation	30MM
Cost per thousand delivered	$17.60

2. 20¢ Best Food Day coupon
Distribution (45MM × $1.95/M)	$ 88M
Redemption (45 × 2.8% × 30¢)	378
Total cost	$ 466M
Circulation	45MM
Cost per thousand delivered	$10.36

3. 20¢ mailed coupon
Distribution (23.9MM × $6.00/M)	$ 143M
Printing	12
20¢ redemption (23.9MM × 5.5% × 30¢)	395
Total cost	$ 550M
Circulation	23.9MM
Cost per thousand delivered	$23.02

4. 20¢ mailed coupon
Distribution (30MM × $9.75/M)	$ 293M
20¢ redemption (30 MM × 8.0% × 30¢)	720
Total cost	$1,013M
Circulation	30MM
Cost per thousand delivered	$33.77

    Total year: 4 coupons
Cost: $528M + $466M + $550M + 1,013M =	$2,557M
Coupons delivered: 30MM + 45MM + 23.9MM + 30MM	128.9MM
Weighted average cost per thousand delivered	$19.84

* National coupons drops only. Some regional coupons were also fielded in defense against regional competitive activity.
† Handling each redeemed coupon, regardless of value, cost 10 cents.

gins on trial sizes. They were shipped in prepacked displays that required little special handling. Because of the high margins, the high turn, and the minimal handling requirements, retailers found this type of promotion particularly attractive. In addition, regular brand users were unlikely to purchase trial sizes because they were too small.

As the toothpaste product category became increasingly competitive, trade and consumer promotion grew in importance. As one manager said:

> Since Aqua-fresh is the third-leading brand, trade promotion expenditures are important to ensure that the trade will continue to stock our product. But Aqua-fresh can't afford to escalate trade promotions to get additional merchandising support because the competition will meet the increase and we will have accomplished nothing.

Market Research

A market research study was conducted to measure the effect of the introduction of Triple Protection Aqua-fresh on consumer attitudes and usage. The study, conducted in February 1983, had the additional objectives of measuring the effect of the Triple Protection introduction on the brand's therapeutic image and the impact of the Crest Gel and the Colgate Gel introductions.

Brand management concluded that the introduction of Triple Protection Aqua-fresh and the competitive gels had not substantially changed the unaided awareness, past four-week usage, or retention levels of the major brands. There were, however, modest improvements in the therapeutic image of Aqua-fresh and in the Aqua-fresh trial rate. While brand management believed that changes in advertising to emphasize Aqua-fresh's ADA seal of approval and therapeutic attributes could further improve the brand's therapeutic image, there was no agreement as to the best way to stimulate additional trial of the brand. Some managers believed that a nationwide sampling program would produce the best results, but others thought that trial sizes would be more cost effective. One manager was convinced that in-store displays were key to stimulating new trial of Aqua-fresh and advocated increased spending for trade promotions. However, none of the managers could prove that one method was more effective than another.

BehaviorScan Research

Beecham executives decided to use BehaviorScan® research from Information Resources, Inc. (IRI)[8] to evaluate the effectiveness of various types of promotion. IRI had developed a system of tracking consumer

---

[8] See "Information Resources, Inc. (A)," Harvard Business School case 9–583–053.

purchasing behavior for most products sold through grocery and drug stores. This system used Universal Product Code (UPC) scanners to record information on the purchases of selected panels of about 2,500 households in eight US markets.

The households in the eight consumer panels were randomly selected. Each was given an ID card to present to the store cashier upon checkout. This ID card signaled the computer to record the purchase data in the file of the appropriate panel member. IRI randomly selected members of each panel to receive prizes as an incentive for continued cooperation. Because of the minimal work required of panel members, about 70 percent of consumers who were asked to be on a panel accepted, giving IRI a representative sample of consumers in each market.

IRI's eight markets were selected on the following criteria:

1. Each market had to be large enough to provide meaningful results but small enough to be manageable since IRI had to arrange to provide UPC scanners to retailers in the area.
2. Residents had to do at least 95 percent of their grocery shopping in the market area.
3. Markets in which a large proportion of all commodity volume was accounted for by a few major chains rather than a variety of small independent stores were preferred.
4. Each market had to be served by a newspaper with high readership so that newspaper advertising could be controlled and monitored.
5. Markets had to have cable television to permit control and monitoring of television advertising.
6. Markets had to be demographically similar to the US average.
7. The boundaries of the market had to be clear and spillover of media from adjacent markets had to be minimal.

Because of these restrictions, some critics claimed that the BehaviorScan results were not representative of purchasing patterns in the United States. They cited the size and isolation of the markets as problems for products whose strongest markets tended to be urban areas. Most BehaviorScan markets were also located in "C" counties, or counties with lower measured buying power that, consequently, had lower coupon distribution. Consequently, to test coupons in BehaviorScan markets, distribution levels to those markets had to be increased.

In addition to tracking consumer purchases, IRI also monitored consumer and trade promotion activity and in-store merchandising for each brand. This allowed IRI to report information on competitive activity. The effectiveness of different types of promotions and merchandising could also be assessed by relating this information to consumer purchasing patterns.

By using BehaviorScan research, Aqua-fresh brand management hoped to resolve the following issues:

1. What was the relative value of trade and consumer promotions in increasing sales, market share, and consumer brand loyalty?
2. Should promotion dollars be shifted from price packs to couponing or other trial events?
3. Which consumer promotions were most effective in stimulating trial?

Given these objectives, Beecham first purchased toothpaste data from IRI's *Marketing Fact Book*. This book, compiled quarterly and annually, summarized BehaviorScan data for over 150 product categories. The book reported brand sales, market shares, volume per purchase occasion, number of purchases in a specified period, average retail prices, and the percentage of volume purchased on deal by the trade. The *Marketing Fact Book* also provided information on competitive brand purchases by households purchasing Aqua-fresh and the percentage of volume purchased by consumers on promotion. This information is reported in Exhibit 8, while Exhibit 9 shows the *Marketing Fact Book* report on trade promotions in the toothpaste category.

IRI was commissioned by Beecham's market research department to conduct three customized studies for Aqua-fresh brand management. These measured brand loyalty, the effectiveness of different types of consumer promotions on trial and repurchase, and the effect of merchandising allowances on brand sales. Four BehaviorScan markets were included in the analysis: Pittsfield, Massachusetts; Marion, Indiana; Eau Claire, Wisconsin; and Midland, Texas.

Data used in the brand loyalty analysis were collected from February 1, 1981, to October 31, 1982. Households purchasing each of the four main toothpaste brands were divided into three groups: (1) low loyalty (the brand accounts for 40 percent or less of the household's total toothpaste consumption); (2) medium loyalty (the brand accounts for 40 to 70 percent of the household's total toothpaste consumption); (3) high loyalty (the brand accounts for more than 70 percent of the household's total toothpaste consumption). Detailed findings of the research are presented in Exhibit 10. Based on the results, Aqua-fresh brand management concluded:

- Aqua-fresh and Aim, the newer major brands, enjoyed less loyalty than Crest and Colgate, the older, larger-share brands.
- Households with low brand loyalty were more likely than households with high brand loyalty to purchase toothpaste on deal and/or with a coupon.
- Households with low brand loyalty tended to be "loyal" to a set of brands rather than to a single brand. They purchased

EXHIBIT 8 Competitive Sets among Buyers of Selected Products (percent of category volume and ranking)

| | Total Households | | Aqua-fresh | | Colgate | | | | Crest | | | | Aim | |
| | | | | | Gel | | Paste | | Gel | | Paste | | | |
	Rank	Percent	Rank	Percent	Rank	Percent	Rank	Percent	Rank	Percent	Rank	Percent	Rank	Percent
Crest paste	1	27.8%	2	17.5%	3	14.6%	2	16.2%	2	25.2%	1	46.8%	2	17.3%
Colgate paste	2	13.6	4	8.8	2	16.5	1	40.2	4	6.9	3	9.0	5	8.0
Crest gel	3	12.9	3	9.4	4	9.4	5	6.3	1	32.9	2	12.0	4	8.6
Aqua-fresh	4	10.0	1	29.5	5	8.4	4	6.4	3	7.9	4	7.2	3	10.7
Colgate gel	5	7.9	6	7.7	1	27.7	3	10.4	6	6.5	6	5.3	6	7.8
Aim	6	7.7	5	8.6	6	6.4	6	5.1	5	6.3	5	5.7	1	28.1

NOTE: Read as follows—In the case of the Aqua-fresh column, of those households who purchased Aqua-fresh, 17.5 percent of their annual toothpaste volume purchased was Crest paste, which ranked as the second-highest brand volume purchased. Among total households, Aqua-fresh had a 10 percent volume share.

Percent of Volume Purchased via Price Deal*
(index vs. total category purchases)

| | Total Households | | Aqua-fresh | | Colgate | | | | Crest | | | | Aim | |
| | | | | | Gel | | Paste | | Gel | | Paste | | | |
	Deal	Index	Deal	Index	Deal	Index	Deal	Index	Deal	Index	Deal	Index	Deal	Index
Total category	26.8%	100	30.9%	100	31.1%	100	31.2%	100	28.6%	100	29.0%	100	32.8%	100
Aqua-fresh	28.3	106	28.3	92	38.6	124	40.7	130	31.3	109	32.9	113	35.5	108
Aim	26.8	100	33.2	107	36.7	118	39.0	125	28.4	99	32.0	110	26.8	82
Colgate Total	28.5	106	36.8	119	28.6	92	28.1	90	31.7	111	32.1	111	39.3	120
Gel	28.6	107	37.2	120	28.6	92	26.7	86	33.6	117	32.9	113	39.4	120
Paste	28.5	106	36.5	118	28.7	92	28.5	91	29.8	104	31.6	109	39.2	120
Crest Total	28.8	107	34.1	110	32.8	105	35.1	113	28.5	100	28.6	99	37.5	114
Gel	28.6	107	31.5	102	30.7	99	32.2	103	28.6	100	27.2	94	36.4	111
Paste	28.9	108	35.6	115	34.1	110	36.3	116	28.4	99	28.9	100	38.1	116

* Price deals included store coupons, manufacturer coupons, price packs, and/or features.

NOTE: Read as follows—In the case of the Aqua-fresh column, of those households who purchased Aqua-fresh, 30.9 percent of their annual toothpaste volume was purchased on price deal, 28.3 percent of their Aqua-fresh volume was purchased on deal, 33.2 percent of their Aim volume was purchased on deal, etc.

SOURCE: Information Resources, Inc., *Marketing Fact Book*.

EXHIBIT 9 IRI Marketing Fact Book Toothpaste Results: 1984

Base Measures for Response to 10 Percent Price Change

	Percent Volume Change	*Rank**
Price increase	−14.5%	39
Price reduction	18.7	62
Price reduction with ad feature only	54.6	91
Price reduction with store display only	52.8	109
Price reduction with both ad and display	95.1	108
Synergy for ad and display combined†	6.4	90

Summary of Model

	Share	
Brands Included in the Analysis‡	*Minimum*	*Maximum*
Total Aqua-fresh toothpaste	9.4	15.0
Total Colgate Gel toothpaste	5.6	9.6
Total Colgate Regular toothpaste	10.2	19.7
Total Ultra-Brite toothpaste	2.2	4.8
Total Aim toothpaste	6.0	10.4
Total Close-Up toothpaste	3.3	11.7
Total Check	0.8	2.1
Total Crest Gel toothpaste	9.6	17.0
Total Crest Mint toothpaste	9.3	13.0
Total Crest Regular toothpaste	11.0	15.8

Derived Measures for Response to 10 Percent Price Reduction

Difference with:	*Percent Volume Change*	*Rank*
Ad feature vs. price reduction only	35.9%	91
Store display vs. price reduction only	34.1	111
Ad and display vs. price reduction only	76.4	110

Ratio measures:	*Ratio*	*Rank*	*Data Summary by Promotion Type*	Percentages		*Average Percent Price Reduction*
				Volume	*Observa-tions*	
Ad feature to price reduction only	2.92	90	No ad feature or display	71.0	82.2	6.8
Display only to price reduction only	2.82	110				
Ad and display to price reduction only	5.08	104	Ad feature only	10.9	7.4	12.5
			Store display only	11.8	7.9	11.9
Feature only to display only	1.03	16	Ad feature and store display	6.4	2.5	17.7
Feature and display to feature only	1.74	104				
Feature and display only	1.80	70				

* Indicates toothpaste's rank out of the 116 product categories reported in the *Marketing Fact Book*. For example, in the case of a 10 percent price increase, there were 38 product categories where the price increase would have resulted in less than a 14.5 percent decrease in volume.
† To measure the synergy between ad and display in combination, the "feature only" and "display only" effects were subtracted from the combination of "ad and display" (95.1 − 52.8 − 54.6 = −12.3). The price effect, 18.7, was then added back to arrive at a synergy of 6.4.
‡ These brands accounted for 88.3 percent of category volume. There were 35,444 observations in the analysis. The average brand share was 8.9 percent.

whichever brand in the set was on deal at the time they were in the market.

The analysis of trial promotion effectiveness covered a mailed sample, a $.12 free-standing insert coupon (FSI), three $.12 Best Food Day (BFD) coupons (fielded and analyzed as one event), price packs, and a

EXHIBIT 10   Brand Loyalty in Toothpaste Category

	1983*			
	Aqua-fresh	Colgate	Aim	Crest
Percent of households buying brand one or more times	18.6%	25.6%	12.9%	40.8%
Share of category	11.3	21.3	7.3	39.4
Total number of oz. of toothpaste purchased per year per household	36.3	36.9	39.7	34.0
Total number of oz. of brand purchased per year per household	12.0	16.7	11.4	19.4
Brand loyalty (percent of total oz. purchased that were specific brand)	34.1	45.3	28.7	51.0
Distribution of Loyalty among Purchasers				
A) Percent of brand buyers				
Low loyalty (40% or less of cat. req.)	57.1%	44.2%	59.1%	27.5%
Medium loyalty (40 to 70% of cat. req.)	17.1	21.3	19.1	19.9
High loyalty (70%+ of cat. req.)	25.8	34.5	21.8	52.6
	100.0	100.0	100.0	100.0
B) Percent of brand volume				
Low loyalty (40% or less of cat. req.)	39.9	23.7	43.8	14.6
Medium loyalty (40 to 70% of cat. req.)	23.7	24.7	25.6	18.1
High loyalty (70%+ of cat. req.)	36.4	51.6	30.6	67.3
	100.0	100.0	100.0	100.0
C) Percent of brand bought on deal (by each group)				
Low loyalty (40% or less of cat. req.)	37.4	37.0	31.2	33.6
Medium loyalty (40 to 70% of cat. req.)	30.4	33.6	20.8	32.1
High loyalty (70%+ of cat. req.)	25.4	25.0	15.7	22.5
	31.9	29.9	23.8	25.8

* Timing: 1983 = 11/1/82–10/30/83.

$.39 prepriced 1.4-ounce trial size. The study focused on trial among new users, defined as those households who had not purchased Aqua-fresh within the 24 weeks preceding each promotion, and repurchase among both new users and current users. Exhibit 11 summarizes the results of the analysis. The major conclusions were:

- Trial size and coupon events reached a greater percentage of new users, at 60 percent and 47 percent respectively, than did price pack promotions, at 36–41 percent. For perspective, 35 percent of nonpromoted open stock purchases were made by new users. (Even with the high level of trials on open stock, brand management believed that promotions to stimulate trials were necessary for Aqua-fresh because of competitive promotions and Aqua-fresh's relatively low level of brand loyalty.)
- Price packs were the most cost-efficient trial events, generating revenues of $.13 to $.39 (depending on the size of the promoted

---

EXHIBIT 11   BehaviorScan Trial Promotion Effectiveness Analysis

1. Promotion Efficiency by Type of Promotion

	1.4-oz. *Trial* *Size*	*$.12 Coupons** *FSI + BFD*	**Price Packs**		
			4.6 oz.	*6.4 oz.*	*8.2 oz.*
Average number of households purchasing	4,162M	1,867M	1,192M	2,518M	1,842M
Percent of new users†	60%	47%	41%	39%	36%
Average number of new users	2,497M	877M	488M	982M	663M
Revenue from equivalent events‡	$245M	$355M	$1,212M	$997M	$1,516M
Less cost of equivalent events	$206M	$328M	$1,149M	$820M	$1,258M
Net revenues:					
Total	$ 39M	$ 27M	$ 63M	$177M	$ 258M
Per purchase	$0.009	$0.014	$ 0.053	$0.070	$ 0.140
Per new user purchase	$0.016	$0.031	$ 0.129	$0.180	$ 0.389

* FSI = free standing insert in newspaper; BFD = Best Food Day section of newspaper.

† New users were defined as those households who had not purchased Aqua-fresh within the 24 weeks preceding the promotion.

‡ Equivalent events indicate that revenues and costs were calculated as if the same promotion had been national in scope.

2. Net Revenue from Aqua-fresh Coupons

	$.12 FSI	*$.12 BFD*	*$.20 FSI*	*$.20 BFD*	*$.20 Mailed*
Average number of households purchasing	1,281M	2,453M	2,155M	1,296M	2,870
Percent of new users	49%	46%	55%	54%	57%
Average number of new users	628M	1,128M	1,185M	700M	1,636M
Revenue from equivalent events	$395M	$315M	$580M	$622M	$1,202M
Less cost of equivalent events	$356M	$300M	$528M	$619M	$1,143M
Redemption rate	2.7%	2.4%	3.1%	2.8%	8.0%
Net revenue:					
Total ($000s)	$ 39M	$ 15	$ 52	$ 3	$ 59
Per purchase	$0.030	$0.006	$0.024	$0.002	$ 0.021
Per new user purchase	$0.062	$0.013	$0.044	$0.004	$ 0.036

3. Aqua-fresh New User Repeat Purchase*

Among New Buyers *Percent Repeat Within*	*$.12* *FSI* *10–81*	*$.12* *BFD* *5–82*	*1.4-oz.* *Trial* *4–83*	*$.30 PP* *6.4 oz.* *4–83*	*$.15 PP* *4.6 oz.* *5–83*	*$.35 PP* *8.2 oz.* *5–83*	*$.30 PP* *6.4 oz.* *7–83*	*$.15 PP* *4.6 oz.* *9–83*
12 weeks	13%	19%	33%	24%	15%	21%	17%	17%
24 weeks	19	43	36	29	31	30	23	25

*NOTE: Read as follows: Among new buyers who first purchased Aqua-fresh with the $.12 FSI coupon delivered 10–81, 13 percent purchased Aqua-fresh again within 12 weeks and 19 percent within 24 weeks.

item) per new user generated versus $.016 for the trial size event and $.03 for coupons. (These values did not take account of repeat business and the strength of the revenue stream generated by a given event.)

• The 1.4-ounce trial size produced the highest level of new user repurchase within 12 weeks, and, along with the $.12 BFD coupon, generated higher levels of repurchase within 24 weeks than did the FSI coupon or the price packs. However, because the BFD coupons were fielded over a four-week period, many of the coupon repurchases might have been made with a second coupon.

• Aqua-fresh purchases tended to be limited to a single tube. Consumers did not typically make multiple purchases of Aqua-fresh when it was on promotion.

The third study by IRI analyzed the impact of price changes and retailer merchandising on the sales of Aqua-fresh, Crest, Colgate, and Aim during the 78-week period from July 26, 1982, to January 22, 1984. Findings from the research are presented in Exhibit 12. Brand management concluded the following:

• The degree of consumer loyalty exhibited by a brand was inversely proportional to the brand's promotion sensitivity. Aqua-fresh and Aim displayed a higher level of sensitivity to trade merchandising than Crest or Colgate.

• Given that Aqua-fresh fielded 10 promotion events annually and that an average trade account featured and/or displayed Aqua-fresh during 10.3% of the weeks, the average trade account appeared to be providing merchandising support for half of the promotion events.

• All types of trade merchandising increased Aqua-fresh sales, with the combination of feature advertising, special off-shelf displays, and price reductions generating tremendous increases over normal retail sales during weeks when there was no special merchandising support.

• The more generous price packs appeared to be very effective in increasing short-term sales volume for Aqua-fresh.

Conclusion

When the Aqua-fresh brand group met to discuss the 1985–86 media and promotion plan, there was disagreement on what actions were indicated by the BehaviorScan research. The brand manager believed the findings indicated that the combination of price packs and trade promotion should continue to be the major component of the plan. Another manager felt that the research supported couponing as the principal method of stimulating consumer trial. Still others favored sampling and argued that price packs did not reach sufficient new users and gave current users an unnecessary price break. Edwards asked each team member to review the promotion plans for 1983–84 and 1984–85 (see Exhibits 13 and 14) and develop a 1985–86 promotion spending plan for their next meeting the following week.

EXHIBIT 12   BehaviorScan Price and Promotion Sensitivity Analysis

---

1. Increase in Total Brand Sales by Type of Promotion

	20% Price Cut	20% Price Cut + Display	20% Price Cut + Feature Ad	20% Price Cut Display + Feature Ad
Aqua-fresh	50%	122%	113%	152%
Crest	45	91	70	122
Colgate	52	105	106	166
Aim	45	154	155	198

2. Effect on Sales of a Competitive 20 Percent Price Reduction

	Percent Change in Volume			
20% Price Reduction	*Aqua-fresh*	*Crest*	*Colgate*	*Aim*
Aqua-fresh	—	−3%	−3%	−7%
Crest	−9%	—	−5	−18
Colgate	−5	−5	—	−6
Aim	−5	−2	−6	—

3. Toothpaste Promotion Sensitivity

	Percent of Weeks with Feature or Display	Percent of Brand Volume Moved by Feature and Display	Index of Percent of Volume Moved to Percent of Weeks with Feature and Display	Percent of Brand Volume Purchased by Households with Low Brand Loyalty
Aqua-fresh	10.3%	17.9%	174%	30.9%
Crest	21.4	27.4	128	14.6
Colgate	12.9	20.7	160	23.7
Aim	8.2	16.8	205	43.8

NOTE: Read as follows: For Aqua-fresh, 17.9% of brand volume was sold when brand was featured or displayed. Aqua-fresh had feature or display support during 10.3% of the weeks measured.

4. Increase in Aqua-fresh Sales by Promotion Type

Price Change	No Feature or Display	Price Pack Only	Display	Feature	Feature and Display
—	—	—	41%	48%	210%
−10%	24%	28%	50	59	336
−15	40	51	102	128	590
−20	47	71	186	186	843

NOTE: Read as follows: For a 10% price reduction, sales of the 6.4 oz. regular size increased 24% with no feature or display, 28% if the 10% reduction was delivered via a price pack, 50% with display support, 59% with feature support, and 336% with feature and display support.

5. Effect of Aqua-fresh Price Pack on Sales

	4.6 oz.	*6.4 oz.*	*8.2 oz.*
Price pack value	$0.15	$0.30	$0.35
Percent price reduction	9%	16%	15%
"On-shelf" price cut only	18	61	45
Price pack with same price cut	20	76	75

EXHIBIT 13   Aqua-fresh 1983–1984 National Promotion Plan*

Period	Event	Merchandising Allowance	Handling Allowance	Dead Net Unit Price	Total Cost ($000)
I	8.2-oz. 35¢ price pack† ($4.20/dozen)	$3.55	$.25	$1.40	$2,003
II	6.4-oz. 30¢ price pack ($3.60/dozen)	4.40	.25	.99	3,840
	20¢ mailed coupon	—	—	—	550
III	4.6-oz. 15¢ price pack ($1.80/dozen)	1.00	.25	.96	1,237
IV	2.7-oz. 10¢ price pack ($1.20/dozen)	.20	.25	.75	572
V	8.2-oz. 35¢ price pack ($4.20/dozen)	3.00	.25	1.43	1,894
	20¢ FSI coupon	—	—	—	528
	Mail-in umbrella premium (free with 4 proofs of purchase)	—	—	—	576
VI	2.7-oz. 10¢ price pack ($1.20/dozen)	.20	.25	.75	650
VII	6.4-oz. 30¢ price pack ($3.60/dozen)	1.00	.25	1.10	3,134
VIII	8.2-oz. 35¢ price pack ($4.20/dozen)	4.45	.25	1.35	2,186
	1.4-oz. prepriced trial-size floor stand	2.70	.25	.27	1,655
IX	4.6-oz. 15¢ price pack ($1.80/dozen)	.65	.25	.99	686
	20¢ mailed coupon	—	—	—	1,092
X	6.4-oz. 30¢ price pack ($3.60/dozen)	1.05	.25	1.20	2,495

* Does not include $3,000M in consumer sampling efforts such as programs like Gift Pax, which samples to college students and newlyweds, $1,000M in miscellaneous trade promotion expenditures, including allowances for military sales and nontraditional channels of distribution, and $2,800M in regional defensive promotions for Aqua-fresh. These factors explain differences in total promotion costs between Exhibits 5 and 13.

† Merchandising and handling allowances are included here in the calculation of total Aqua-fresh price pack costs, but were excluded from the price pack cost data in Exhibit 5, which covered only the actual value of the price packs.

EXHIBIT 14   Aqua-fresh 1984–1985 Promotion Plan*

Period	Event	Merchandising and Handling Allowance	Dead Net Unit Price	Total Cost ($000)
I	6.4-oz. 30¢ price pack ($3.60 dozen)	$1.35	$1.10	$2,946
II	8.2-oz. 35¢ price pack ($4.20/dozen)	3.40	1.43	1,970
	20¢ FSI coupon	—	—	528
III	4.6-oz. 15¢ price pack ($1.80/dozen)	.90	.99	1,221
	Inflatable raft premium ($4.50 + 2 proofs)	—	—	203
IV	2.7-oz. 10% price pack ($1.20/dozen)	.10	.71	715
V	6.4-oz. $1.00 price pack–twin pack ($6.00/half dozen)	.80	1.04	4,325
	20¢ mailed coupon	—	—	550
VI	1.4-oz. prepriced trial-size floor stand	2.95	.26	1,103
VII	4.6-oz. 15¢ price pack ($1.80/dozen)	.90	.99	1,067
	Shower massage premium ($9.95 + 3 proofs)	—	—	94
	20¢ mailed coupon	—	—	1,013
VIII	8.2-oz. 35¢ price pack ($4.20/dozen)	4.00	1.40	2,069
IX	6.4-oz. 30¢ price pack ($3.60/dozen)	4.80	.99	4,205
	20¢ BFD coupon	—	—	466
X	2.7-oz. 10¢ price pack ($1.20/dozen)	.12	.75	630

* Does not include sampling, tests of new promotions, or promotions which were regional only.

General Electric Company: Consumer Incandescent Lighting

In December 1982, William Frago, general manager of the Consumer Marketing and Sales Department within General Electric (GE) Company's Lamp Products Division (LPD) was preparing to meet with Gary Rogers, LPD vice president and general manager, to discuss the 1983 operating plan for GE's consumer incandescent lighting (light bulb) business. Both Frago and Rogers had recently assumed their positions.

The discussion was to review three strategic alternatives proposed by different constituencies within the LPD to deal with GE's long-term share decline. First, the marketing programs section argued for an increased advertising program and shift in trade spending from off-invoice purchase allowances to bill-back advertising performance allowances. This plan had been tested in late 1981 and had begun to be implemented in early 1982. However, increased advertising spending and some promotion events were opposed by Consumer Sales and the Incandescent Lamp Department (ILD) and were on hold pending review by Frago and Rogers. Second, the Consumer Sales force believed LPD should attempt to gain more new distribution in the rapidly expanding channels such as mass merchandisers and discount chains. Third, ILD strongly believed LPD should invest resources to improve its cost position and utilize excess capacity to manufacture private label light bulbs. There was a strong feeling in ILD that light bulbs were a commodity and that a more favorable cost and price position was the secret to long-term success. There was a great deal of internal dissent among each of these groups as to which course of action should be pursued.

Despite improved performance in 1982, several issues were still debated by LPD executives. Some believed that the light bulb was a push product and that increasing national advertising expenditures at the expense of promotion allowances was risky. They argued that GE would have to narrow further its price premium over competitive light bulbs if it

---

This case was prepared by Professor John A. Quelch as the basis for class discussion rather than to illustrate either effective or ineffective handling of an administrative situation. Proprietary data have been disguised. Copyright © 1986 by the President and Fellows of Harvard College. Harvard Business School case 587–014.

was to gain market share. Others argued that the current price premium could be sustained by a strong national advertising campaign to build preference for GE light bulbs. Some members of this group did not support LPD's decision to make private label product.

The Lamp Products Division

GE achieved a record $26.5 billion in outside sales in 1982. John F. Welch, Jr., GE's CEO, summarized his views on GE's strategic direction in a letter to shareholders in the 1982 annual report:

> Whether it's bringing new technologies and services to the marketplace or revitalizing our strong core businesses, we want GE to be a place where the bias is toward action—a high-spirited world-class enterprise that uses the resources of a large company and that moves with the agility of the youngest and smallest. The last decade has seen a dramatic shift in our business mix—from the old to the new, from relatively mature businesses to those in their high-growth stages . . .
>
> While our shift to high technology has been significant, we have also been upgrading our core businesses. During 1982, there were strong cost improvement efforts and major plant and equipment expenditures to increase productivity and assure the competitiveness of these important traditional businesses.

In 1982, GE's businesses were grouped into product sectors. The Consumer Products Sector, which included the Lighting Business Group (LBG), accounted for 22 percent and 13 percent of GE's 1982 revenues and net earnings, down from 25 percent and 21 percent respectively in 1980. LBG's sales were 15 percent of the sector total in 1982 but LBG's return on investment had slipped 7 percent from 1979. The LBG comprised three divisions, one of which, the Lamp Products Division, was principally responsible for the manufacture and sale of lighting products to end consumers. Commercial, industrial, and OEM sales were handled by the other divisions. The LPD accounted for 48 percent and 52 percent of LBG's revenues and earnings in 1982.

The LPD manufactured and sold eight distinct product lines to consumers: consumer incandescent, consumer fluorescent, automotive, holiday, photographic, battery, wiring devices, and outdoor. Consumer incandescent products accounted for 54 percent of LPD sales in 1982. The GE consumer incandescent line included 1,300 stockkeeping units (SKUs) manufactured in six plants.

As shown in the organization chart (Exhibit 1), responsibility for the consumer incandescent business was shared between the general managers of the Incandescent Lamp Department and the Consumer Marketing and Sales Department. Product line managers in the Lamp Department were primarily responsible for cost analysis, sales forecasting,

EXHIBIT 1   Lamp Products Division: 1982 Organization Chart

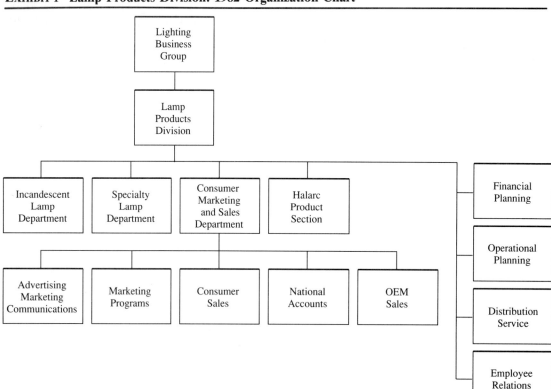

production scheduling, capacity planning, and working with Research and Development on new products. Product marketing managers in the Marketing Department were primarily responsible for developing advertising and promotion programs and exploring product improvements and line extensions. The two departments shared profit and loss responsibility for consumer incandescent lighting. Pricing strategies were discussed by both departments and approved by the LPD general manager.

The Consumer Incandescent Lighting Market

Consumer incandescent lamps were invented by Thomas Edison in 1880. During the next 60 years, a series of technical improvements increased the light intensity or lumens delivered per watt. However, since 1940, no major breakthroughs had occurred until 1982 when GE launched the Miser® line of energy-efficient lamps.

In 1982, manufacturers sold 1.19 billion consumer incandescent lamps in the US valued at $445 million. Market demand for light bulbs was directly related to the size of the private housing stock and the size of the average housing unit. Industry sales typically correlated with the number of household light bulb sockets. During the 1970s and 1980s, sales were flat due to heightened consumer interest in energy conservation following the oil price increases of 1973 and 1979 and due to periodic decreases in housing starts. The average annual growth rate in consumer incandescent lamp unit sales was 0.4 percent between 1970 and 1980. Most recently, unit sales had declined 1 percent between 1980 and 1982. Exhibit 2 graphs industry dollar and unit sales, and GE dollar and unit market shares, since 1973. GE's dollar and unit market shares both rose 1 percent during 1982.

Consumer incandescent lamps were generally divided into five product categories: soft white, inside frost, three-way, PAR and R, and decorative. Soft white bulbs had whitened glass that helped diffuse light and reduced harshness and glare. Inside frost bulbs, which represented an older technology than soft white, contained an inside frosting, did not diffuse light as effectively as soft white, but were lower priced and less

EXHIBIT 2   Consumer Incandescent Industry Sales and GE Market Share Trends*

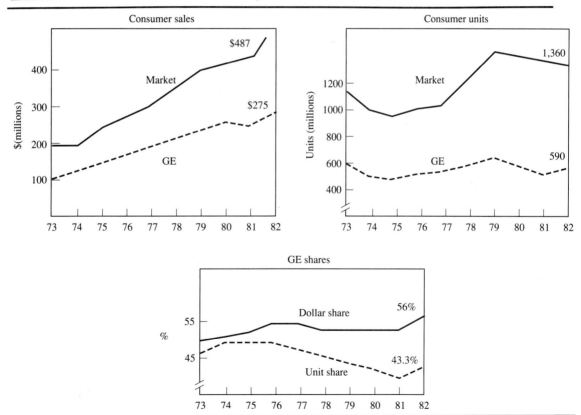

* These figures (in millions) are for all consumer sales, branded, private label, and generic.

EXHIBIT 3   Consumer Incandescent Dollar and Unit Sales and Shares by Product Category, 1982*

	Product Category's Share of Industry $ Sales	*Product Category's Share of Unit Sales*	*Product Category's Share of GE $ Sales*
Soft white	33%	38%	43%
Inside frost	38	46	28
Three-way	9	5	13
Parabolic reflectors and reflectors	13	2	10
Decorative	7	9	6

* These figures include branded, private label, and generic consumer incandescent lamp sales, both for the industry and GE. Unit sales of nonbranded GE lamps amounted to 20 million units in 1982.

costly to manufacture. Three-way bulbs, in conjunction with three-way lamps, allowed the user to select three different levels of brightness—such as 50, 100, and 150 watt. PAR lamps (parabolic reflectors) were for outdoor spot lighting. Reflector lamps (Rs) were primarily used as indoor flood lights. Decorative bulbs, the fastest-growing category, were used in chandeliers and in concealed or specialty lighting fixtures. Exhibit 3 shows each product category's share of 1982 dollar and unit sales.

Distribution

Consumer incandescent lamps were sold through four principal channels: food stores, discount stores, hardware stores, and drug stores. A 1981 consumer survey showed that consumers were most likely to purchase incandescent bulbs in food stores, but that there were different channel patronage patterns for heavy versus light users.

Outlets for Purchase of Incandescent Bulbs in Past Two Years	*Total Households (100%)*	*Low (29%)*	*Medium (44%)*	*High* (26%)*
Food store	70%	69%	72%	69%
Discount store	52	47	52	59
Hardware store	32	26	34	38
Drug store	20	19	20	24
Department store	17	16	16	21
Home improvement center	14	9	13	21
Electric supply company	14	8	11	27
Other	6	1	7	8

* 26 percent of households purchased 50 percent of consumer incandescent lamps in 1981.

Food stores were still the most important channel in 1982 though they had lost a point of share since 1980. An average food store carried 50 SKUs of light bulbs and turned its inventory six times a year. Most food stores carried a single branded line of bulbs, but many had recently added a private label line. For many years, light bulbs had been an important source of profit for food stores. Compared to their average gross margin of 22 percent, food stores earned a gross margin of 56 percent on light bulbs. A 1980 GE study indicated that light bulbs alone accounted for 11 percent of the profits of one major food store chain.

Discount stores and mass merchandisers increasingly used light bulbs as traffic builders, promoting them as often as six times a year. They typically carried as many as 100 SKUs including both a branded line and private label line, but they often emphasized the latter. As many as 75 percent of the bulbs sold by some major discount chains were private label. Inventory turned six times each year. More bulbs were bought per purchase occasion in discount stores than in food stores. Discount store gross margins on light bulbs averaged 41 percent compared to the channel's overall average gross margin of 35 percent.

Hardware stores carried a broad line of lamp SKUs. They were more likely to carry new items and specialty lamps. To hold their share of lamp sales, hardware stores increasingly promoted inside frost bulbs. Their gross margin on sales of lamps averaged 45 percent compared to an overall average gross margin of 21 percent. The corresponding figures for drug stores, which typically carried one branded line of bulbs, were 45 percent and 28 percent. Exhibit 4 breaks down the 1982 sales of consumer incandescent lamps by class of trade.

Within LPD's Consumer Marketing and Sales Department, sales to the major national discount store chains, hardware co-ops, and national drug chains were handled by a national accounts group, separate from the field sales force which dealt with regional food, drug, and hardware accounts.

EXHIBIT 4   Channel Growth Trends and Manufacturer Unit Market Share by Channel, 1982

	Food	Discount	Hardware and All Other	Drug	Total
Channel unit share	45%	25%	23%	7%	100%
Change in channel unit share (1980–1981)*	(1%)	—	1%	—	—
Industry annual unit growth rate (1980–1982)	(3%)	(1%)	5%	(2%)	(1%)
GE annual unit growth rate (1980–82)	(6%)	4%	(1%)	7%	(3%)

* ( ) Signifies negative growth rates.

GE's Competitive Position

GE's two main competitors in the consumer lighting business in 1982 were Westinghouse and Sylvania. Both had several decades of experience in the market and, like GE, they had invested heavily in automated assembly processes for consumer incandescent lamps. Their unit costs of production were believed to be comparable. The fourth national brand was Norelco, manufactured by the US subsidiary of Philips, the $16 billion Dutch electrical equipment manufacturer which dominated the consumer incandescent lamp market in Europe.

All of the major manufacturers not only sold their own brands but also contracted for private label business. GE, the last to begin private label manufacture, generated $4.0 million in consumer incandescent private label lamp sales in 1981. Private label unit market share was 15 percent in 1981, 17 percent in 1982. Many of the imported lamps, which accounted for 10 percent of units sold in 1982, were for private label. The largest imported brand, Action, was made in Hungary and distributed in the US by Action Industries. It was often used by hardware stores as an "in and out promotional item."[1]

The competitive structure of the consumer incandescent market in 1982 had evolved over the previous decade. At the end of 1973, GE held a 46.5 percent unit share of the consumer incandescent market and sold its bulbs at a 4 percent price premium over domestic competition and a 53 percent premium over imports which then accounted for only 3 percent of the US market.

GE bulbs were distributed to retailers on consignment. In other words, GE retained ownership until they were sold. Until 1973, GE operated on the "agency" system, a form of fair trading established during the 1930s. Consignment continued after 1973 but the resale price of GE bulbs was no longer maintained.

Between 1974 and 1977, GE's price premium over domestic competition increased to 12 percent and its premium over imports to 63 percent due, in large part, to product mix changes. Moreover, a number of industry experts felt that imports of light bulbs from Eastern bloc countries were being "dumped" into the US market at prices below cost. However, GE's unit share remained stable and GE maintained its position as the single supplier of light bulbs in 78 percent of its accounts. The GE sales force concentrated on selling the trade a profitability story. Imports during these three years captured 5 percent of the market, primarily in mass merchandise discount stores. Indeed, during this period, both the dis-

---

[1] The brand was not maintained by an account in continuous distribution, but was stocked temporarily on special display when an especially attractive promotional deal could be arranged.

count stores and the price brands secured their footholds. As one LPD executive explained:

> We were not encouraging the trade to put any special merchandising effort behind bulbs, although the category had a lot of potential as a traffic builder, a point that the discount stores recognized. Using private labels and generics, the discount stores began promoting light bulbs aggressively as traffic builders. Those that carried branded light bulbs often did so just as a comparison to drive their private label sales.[2] As a result, the discount stores captured an increasing share of light bulb volume at the expense of the food and hardware channels where we were strong.
>
> Pretty soon, the food and hardware channels that had traditionally valued light bulbs for their good margins rather than as traffic builders started carrying private label and generic bulbs to stay competitive with the discount stores. The food and drug chains couldn't stand the embarrassment of promoting light bulbs at higher prices than discount stores in the free-standing inserts of the Sunday newspapers. At the same time, our branded competitors, faced with volume and share losses to private labels and generics, started pressing food stores for feature advertising support and offered deeper allowances to the trade to maintain their distribution. The price premium of GE bulbs over its branded competitors' increased.

Between 1977 and 1979, the GE price premium grew to 19 percent over domestic competition. More discount chains began to market their own private label bulbs. The import share of the market climbed to 8 percent. Norelco aggressively pursued food store distribution, offering substantial promotion allowances and arguing that food stores were collectively losing share to discount stores because of higher prices on GE bulbs. Westinghouse also was attempting to gain share by offering steeper discounts and competitive buyouts to the trade. To new accounts, Westinghouse offered payments for the existing inventory that would be displaced, free display racks, minimal order size requirements, a progressive annual volume rebate program, and deeper than normal off-invoice promotional allowances on its inside frost bulbs. Westinghouse's strategy was, apparently, to use an attractive price on inside frost bulbs to gain access to an account and to earn its margin on its other consumer incandescent lines. During 1979, the trade's acquisition cost, net of trade promotion, for a Westinghouse inside frost bulb was 25 cents a unit compared to 32 cents for a GE bulb. Many food chains appeared to pass through the Norelco and Westinghouse allowances to the consumer in the form of lower retail prices, at the same time maintaining their unit profit margins on these lines.

Between 1975 and 1979, LPD recovered inflation with consumer incandescent price increases. LBG's return on investment peaked at an

---

[2] A simultaneous promotion of both a branded and a private label line with a "compare and save" message over the private label display was known as a promotion split.

impressive 25 percent in 1979. However, two problems arose. First, as shown in Exhibit 5, GE's market share fell as its price premium over competition increased. Second, not all of GE's price increases were realized as LPD found it necessary to deal back some of the increases in additional trade promotion allowances. As one LPD executive explained:

> As discount store competition eroded the food chains' share of sales, they focused more on their acquisition costs. We had to devise a strategy that would let us maintain our share in our traditional channels but get a piece of the volume going through discount stores. Our first reaction was to secure distribution and offer our customers promotional packages that enabled them to lower their acquisition costs on both GE soft white and inside frost bulbs. The problem was that many of our food accounts did not pass these discounts through to the consumer. The food stores' prices on GE lamps remained as high as ever and our market share continued to erode. At the same time, consumer price sensitivity was increased. I remember a March 1981 survey showing 35 percent of consumers bought light bulbs on sale. That figure was 6 percent in 1979.

The pattern continued into 1981. GE's dollar sales and unit volume in consumer incandescent lamps declined. For the first time, LPD experienced a net distribution loss of $1.5 million worth of business. In addition, the sales mix deteriorated. Inside frost sales increased at the expense of

EXHIBIT 5   Relationship between GE Unit Share and Price Premium, 1960–1981

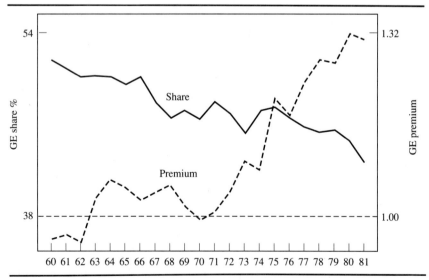

higher-margin soft white sales when LPD tried to respond to the price premium by running a strong price promotion on inside frost bulbs.

Market Segmentation

The average consumer bought light bulbs five times each year. Some consumers bought them as needed, others kept an inventory on hand in their homes. Sixty percent of bulbs were bought for general room lighting. Other uses were reading and writing (9 percent), work aid (6 percent), decoration (7 percent), personal care (7 percent), security (5 percent), and outdoor lighting (4 percent).

As competitive pressures increased during the 1970s, LPD executives increasingly explored the segmentation of the consumer incandescent market. Their objective was to identify segments that might be interested in distinct product benefits and be willing to pay a price premium for them. To this end, five studies were conducted, four of them during 1980 and 1981:

- A 1974 study clustered respondents according to the importance they attached to different lighting benefits. However, no single advertisable benefit stood out among those appealing to consumers in each of the five segments. In addition, GE's market share was similar across the segments (Exhibit 6).
- A 1980 Yankelovich, Skelly and White (YSW) study identified six segments based on consumer attitudes rather than a rank ordering of lighting benefits (Exhibit 7).
- A 1980 HTI study identified six segments based on consumer rankings of different lighting benefits. GE's market share again varied only modestly from one segment to another (Exhibit 8).
- A 1980 Opinion Research Corporation study aimed to identify the relative importance of energy efficiency, price, package shape, bulb type, and light quality. A segment of consumers especially interested in energy efficiency was identified. GE's share of this segment was relatively low (Exhibit 9).
- A second YSW study in 1981 identified three segments based on level of involvement in lighting. Exhibits 10–12 profile these three segments.

LPD executives were especially interested in YSW's two benefit segments. They believed that GE soft white could be positioned to appeal to the quality-of-light segment while GE's new Miser line of energy-efficient

EXHIBIT 6   1974 Hale Consumer Attitude Segmentation Study

Objective: Identify consumer attitude segments and the benefits motivating each.

Methodology: 1,016 self-administered questionnaires to households representing all income levels.

Segment	Highest-Ranking Interests	Percent of Total Market*	GE Share of Segment
1. Vision-value buyers	Reasonable price Long lasting Good value Easy to read by Eliminates eye strain	18%	50%
2. Quality-product value buyers	Economical to burn Reasonable price Long lasting	12	58
3. Quality-vision buyers	Eliminates eye strain Reasonable price Long lasting	21	58
4. Practical (price) buyers	Ready availability Glare-free light Easy to read by Good value	21	65
5. Aesthetic buyers	Wide selection Attractive bulbs/good packaging Well-known manufacturer Guaranteed/pre-tested	28	58

Conclusions: Could not identify segments where GE share was significantly higher or lower. Analysis of key interests of segments could not isolate advertisable consumer benefit.

* Percent of light bulbs purchased by consumers falling into each segment rather than percent of consumers.

bulbs, due to be launched in 1982, could be targeted at the utility/energy segment.

The 1981 Test Market

Based in part on the results of the market segmentation studies, LPD marketing executives decided to test the impact of an advertising and promotion program designed to pull volume through the retail channel. Believing that LPD should develop more tailored programs for different products in the line, they fixed on quality of light as the differentiating benefit to build preference for GE soft white bulbs. To address consumers

---
EXHIBIT 7   Yankelovich, Skelly and White (YSW) Attitude Segment Study, 1980

Objective: Isolate benefit segments and describe the attitudes and motivations of each.

Methodology: 770 in-home personal interviews with consumers in households with annual incomes of $15,000 and above.

Segment	*Description of Segment Motivation*	*Percent of Total Market*
1. Cost conscious	Lowest level of interest in light bulbs No reason to spend more than minimum No added value can be communicated Decide on price	12.3%
2. Convenience oriented	Wants to save time and effort in changing or buying bulbs and will pay extra to achieve this Share some characteristics of cost-conscious segment	12.3
3. Technology	High motivation level Always searching for a better way to do things Early adopters . . . new means better But "new" quickly becomes "not new"	5.0
4. Energy conscious	Highest motivation level Need is to save energy Socially responsible Very important to buy the very best bulb Will respond to new products	17.7
5. Undecided buyers	Low level of motivation Want to reduce risk, avoid mistakes Tend to buy leading established brands Followers, not innovators	20.2
6. Home enhancers	Seek better light to improve personal/home environment Extrinsic reasons for choice—other-directed behavior Choose "quality" product to match peer group standards Brand loyal	32.5

NOTE: GE share by segment not available in this study.

EXHIBIT 8   1980 HTI Consumer Attitude Segmentation Study

Objective: Develop market segments based on consumer rankings of different light bulb benefits/interests.

Methodology: 1,387 self-administered mail questionnaires to consumers of all income levels.

Segment	*Highest-Ranking Interests*	*Percent of Total Market*	*GE Share of Segment*
1. Vision/construction of light bulb	Bulb is guaranteed Highest overall quality Bulb is attractive Is pretested Bulb doesn't overheat	12%	45.5%
2. Value/vision	Energy saved pays for bulb Efficient like fluorescent Economical Natural-looking light Lasts as long as supposed to Good value for money	15	42.0
3. Positive attitudes	No harsh shadows Helps eliminate eye strain Glare-free light Pleasing lighted appearance Easy to read by Makes things look nice Doesn't grow dim with age Natural-looking light	16	54.5
4. Reputable manufacturer	Readily available Well-known manufacturer Wide selection Screws easily in and out Is pretested Makes things look nice Pleasing lighted appearance	18	50.2
5. Value/reliability	Reasonably priced Good value for money Lasts as long as supposed to Base doesn't twist off Durable, not easily broken Screws easily in and out Economical	19	54.8
6. No interest in lighting	Light level adjustable Durable, not easily broken Bulb is attractive	20	52.5

Conclusions: Interpretation hampered because the items ranked included usage needs, product attributes, and general attitudes. A key advertisable consumer benefit for each segment was hard to identify.

EXHIBIT 9   1981 O.R.C. Study

Objective: Determine the key additional benefit(s) by segment to support the basic long-life position of a new line of long-lasting GE bulbs.

Methodology: 502 mall interviews with consumers of all income levels.

Segment	Highest-Ranking Interests	Percent of Total Market	GE Share of Segment
1. Energy conscious	Energy saving	16%	48.3%
2. Aesthetic	Price	30	67.0
	Package quantity		
3. Convenience	Package quantity	21	63.4
	Bulb shape/type		
	Price		
4. Equal sensitivity	Equal sensitivity for	33	55.5
	Price		
	Light quality		
	Life		
	Not energy conscious		

Conclusion: Segments were identified among which GE's share does differ significantly.

---

interested in eye comfort and decor enhancement, a television advertisement was developed showing a painter fashioning a family portrait with the aid of GE soft white bulbs (see Exhibit 13).

Between October and December 1981, LPD conducted a field experiment. In four control markets, LPD continued its two current merchandising programs. These were a $1.00 on-pack rebate offer to consumers who submitted purchase proofs for three packs of four bulbs and a cooperative advertising allowance of up to 6 percent of an account's purchases with the entire cost of advertisements paid for by LPD. In the four test markets (which accounted for 10 percent of US consumer light bulb sales), 160 GRPs of advertising were aired per week at a national expenditure rate of $8 million, equivalent to the estimated cost of the rebate program. In addition, the trade received a 3 cents per unit off-invoice allowance on soft white bulbs, plus an additional 4 or 5 cents bill-back allowance if one or two feature advertisements were run. The test program limited trade allowances to one order per feature advertisement whereas the existing cooperative advertising program allowed the trade to accrue allowances on all its purchases. One LPD marketing executive explained the rationale for the so-called 3, 4, 5 program:

> Because consumers buy bulbs in food and drug channels for convenience, our consumer rebate offer only had impact in discount stores where consumers are more likely to purchase bulbs in volume. On the other hand, consumer advertising was thought likely to benefit sales in all channels.

EXHIBIT 10   **Yankelovich, Skelly and White Consumer Involvement Segments***

Involved (35% of market)	*Uninvolved* (10%)	*Latent* (55%)
Seeking special lighting benefits Atmosphere Aesthetics Modern, unique	Low attention to special benefits	Low attention to special benefits
Highest interest in function	Lowest interest in function	High interest in function
Into lighting	*Not* into lighting	Into lighting
Needs/wants vary most on room-by-room basis	Least variation by room	Some variation by room
Price sensitive	Less price sensitive	Price sensitive
More problems in achieving end results	Fewer end-result problems	Fewer end-result problems
Satisfied with lighting effects in major living areas	Not necessarily satisfied	Satisfied with lighting in specific rooms
Concern with illumination Effectiveness Avoiding glare Interest in color	Less concern with illumination	Concern with illumination Effectiveness Avoiding harshness
Greatest attention to nearly all bulb attributes	Lower concern with bulb attributes	High concern with bulb attributes
Highest use of lamps/sockets/bulbs	Moderate use	Lowest use
More women	More men	More women
All ages—especially 30–64	Younger	Older
Average education	Most educated	Least educated
Most homeowners (largest homes)	Fewer homeowners (medium homes)	Fewer homeowners (smallest homes)

* These segments were based on respondents' importance and dissatisfaction rankings.

The change in the allowance structure was designed to increase the feature advertising support given by the trade and turn the trade into a proactive marketing partner. The gap between an account's promotion acquisition cost and LPD's regular price remained at about 8 cents per soft white bulb, but now 5 cents of the discount was contingent on feature advertising support.

The highlights of the test results are summarized in Exhibit 14. GE gained share, increased its average selling price per lamp, and narrowed the price premium over competition. In addition to sales and share data,

---

EXHIBIT 11   YSW Study: Consumer Choice of Outlet for Lighting Products

Rated "Major Consideration" in Choice of Outlet for Lighting Products	Total Purchasers	Segments		
		Involved	*Uninvolved*	*Latent*
Convenience				
Convenient location	56%	55%	48%	58%
Shop at for other items	41	44	39	38
Light bulbs easy to locate	33	34	19	36
Outlet Economy				
Lower prices regularly	51	50	39	55
Frequent sales/bargains	48	50	34	50
Full-Line Outlet				
Offers variety in bulbs—selection to choose from	33	40	19	30
Offers preferred brands	29	33	12	29
Offers best quality lighting	29	33	17	27
Offers "specialty" lighting	26	32	19	23
Offers full range of lighting products	26	30	11	25

LPD executives had the survey results from two waves of interviews conducted before and after the experiment in both test and control markets.

Both surveys included comparative questions on perceived value for money of soft white lamp brands at fixed price points for each brand and type. The GE soft white brand price was given as either 69¢, 79¢, 89¢, or 99¢ on each questionnaire on a four-way split sample basis. All competitive soft white lamps were priced at 79¢. Respondents were asked to indicate their perception of value for money (on a four-point scale) for the brands listed at the prices shown.

As the price of the GE soft white increased from cell to cell, the proportion of consumers indicating that GE soft white was a "very good value" (the top of the scale) went down, and the proportion indicating the same for other soft white lamps went up.

However, the rate of loss of relative demand for GE was not matched by gains in demand by competitive brands at higher GE price points. Before exposure to the advertising (Pre), every 10¢ increase in the GE soft white price led to a loss of 8 percent of the respondent base but a gain of only 7 percent for each competitive soft white brand. After exposure to the advertising campaign (Post), competitive gains in demand were only 2–3 percent per 10¢ increment. And at parity pricing the perceived "very

---

EXHIBIT 12   YSW Study: Elements of Purchase That Were Planned and Unplanned on Last Light Bulb Purchase Occasion

	Total Purchasers (percent)	Segments		
		Involved (percent)	Uninvolved (percent)	Latent (percent)
Wattage				
Planned	84%	85%	86%	84%
Unplanned	15	13	18	15
Type of Bulb				
Planned	83	83	80	83
Unplanned	16	16	19	16
Outlet				
Planned	83	83	85	83
Unplanned	16	15	15	15
Bulb Quantity				
Planned	71	74	67	67
Unplanned	27	23	32	30
Brand Purchase				
Planned	49	55	40	48
Unplanned	48	43	57	49

YSW Study: Light Bulb Brand and Type Preferences by Segment

Segment	Involved	Uninvolved	Latent
Believe GE is "best for regular bulbs"	56%	47%	46%
Believe GE is "best for soft white bulbs"	46	37	37
Believe GE is "best for long life"	44	33	26
Bought a soft white bulb on last purchase occasion	53	55	41
Bought a GE bulb on last purchase occasion	57	50	43

good value" rating of GE soft white increased 8 percentage points (48–56 percent) while competitive brands increased 3 to 4 percentage points:

	"Very Good Value" (percent)					
	GE		Sylvania		Westinghouse	
GE Soft White Test Prices	*Pre*	*Post*	*Pre*	*Post*	*Pre*	*Post*
@69¢	61%	65%	21%	28%	25%	27%
@79¢ (competitive price point)	48	56	34	37	33	37
@89¢	41	42	38	36	39	34
@99¢	38	34	42	38	45	36
Slope	−.8	−1.1	.7	.3	.7	.2

EXHIBIT 13 Soft White Television Commercial Storyboard

This is the soft pure light of the GE Soft White bulb.	It creates a soft warm glow	that's beautiful to see by
and bright enough to work by,	with less glare and no harsh shadows.	Because its high-diffusion coating makes light that's soft, warm, glowing.
So you can see the world	the way you want to see it.	The Soft White by GE.
It puts your life in a better light.	GE	We bring good things to life.

From these and other test data, many LPD marketing executives believed that the power of a national consumer advertising campaign had been proven. Others were more skeptical. According to one LPD sales manager:

> In my opinion, 90 percent of the share gain was due to the feature advertising prices and 10 percent due to the national advertising. The quality and share of GE's feature advertisements did improve in the food and drug channels but not in the discount chains. These price features did close the gap between our

---

EXHIBIT 14   Selected Results of 1981 Test Market

- In test markets, GE soft white's unit market share increased during the experiment by 8 more points than it did in control markets. The point spread ranged from plus 23 points in drug channels to plus 1 point in food channels.
- In test markets, the unit market share of other GE bulbs increased during the experiment by 2 more points than it did in control markets. The net market share gain for all GE bulbs in test markets was plus 4 points, representing about 50 million annual unit sales.
- Partly as a result of shifting some purchasers to the higher unit margin soft white bulb from inside frost, the average manufacturer selling price of GE bulbs purchased in the test markets was 6 cents higher than in control markets.
- In test markets, 36 percent of respondents reported seeing the GE soft white advertising, and 60 percent of them were able to recall key points of the advertising unaided.
- Of those consumers who saw the GE soft white advertising:
  - 68 percent agreed that light bulbs are very or somewhat different from each other (48 percent control markets).
  - 73 percent agreed that GE soft white is different from other soft white brands (68 percent control markets). Those who valued lighting for reading and for making a room more attractive were more likely to agree that GE soft white is different.
  - 79 percent named GE as their favorite brand of light bulb (71 percent control markets).
  - 15 percent stated that they would go to another store if GE soft white bulbs were not available in their usual store (12 percent in control markets). The corresponding figures for GE inside frost bulbs were 14 percent and 9 percent.
- 72 percent of consumers choose a type of bulb (e.g., inside frost, soft white) first before deciding among brand alternatives within a type.
- 42 percent of respondents who reported buying GE soft white when they last **purchased** were not certain of the price they paid. Corresponding figures for Sylvania **and** Westinghouse were 31 percent and 30 percent.

---

soft white and the competition. The trade recovered the lost margin resulting from the more frequent features by increasing prices on nonpromoted GE and competitive bulbs.

The 1982 Marketing Program

LPD executives set out in 1982 to revitalize the consumer incandescent lighting business. Their program involved a reallocation of marketing expenditures, a new product launch, and the pursuit of new distribution opportunities.

New Marketing Mix

In 1981, LPD had spent 10 percent of its marketing funds on advertising, 9 percent on consumer rebates, 63 percent on off-invoice allowances, 5 percent on bill-back allowances for feature advertisements, and 13 percent on merchandising aids. Based on the test results, funds were shifted from off-invoice allowances and consumer rebates into national advertising, consumer coupons and bill-back allowances. In particular:

- National advertising, principally for GE soft white bulbs, was increased by 40 percent. Some executives believed that it should have been more than doubled. However, GE's share of total category advertising was over 90 percent in 1982.
- The 3, 4, 5 program was implemented on GE soft white and 3-way bulbs, but not on inside frost. To qualify for bill-back allowances, the trade had to run feature advertisements of specified size during specified time periods which coincided with LPD's flights of national advertising.
- GE inside frost was offered at a special price once each quarter. The trade could place one order during each promotion event.
- The remaining smaller-volume consumer incandescent products were grouped together each quarter in a dealer's choice promotion. A 10 percent bill-back allowance could be earned on one order of any item after a feature advertisement was run.
- Consumer rebates were curtailed. Coupons (usually 25 cent values) were used as an alternative consumer promotion on soft white and 3-way bulbs.

New Products

LPD planned to take its new Miser energy-efficient lamps national by the end of 1982. Miser lamps delivered 5 percent more lumens per watt than ordinary lamps. Sixty percent of in-home use testers had rated Miser lamps better than those they replaced. The Miser product group expected to sell 20 million Miser lamps by the end of 1982. A Miser product line manager commented:

> There are three advantages to new products. First, if they change consumer preferences and expectations, they can put pressure on our competitors. Second, new products broaden our line, making it easier for us to fill all the slots on a trade account's promotion calendar. Third, new products give us something worth advertising. In my view, soft white bulbs are old hat. Most of our national advertising should be put behind the Miser line.

New Distribution

LPD executives had initiated private label sales in 1981 and had generated $4 million worth of business. In 1982, they decided to pursue more private label business in order to both maintain their position in existing accounts and open up new accounts. The LPD national accounts manager explained the approach:

Large trade accounts could acquire private label bulbs at about half the price of GE bulbs. They could sell private label bulbs at retail prices well below GE and make more money per unit. Private label volume grew 30 percent in 1981. Given we were using only about 65 percent of our capacity for consumer incandescent bulbs, we decided in 1981 to go into private label. In order not to further commoditize the category, we decided to do this only under certain conditions. First, the customer had to be a GE account and second, had to already stock or be committed to stocking private label. Finally, we decided to supply only inside frost and not soft white on a private label basis.

Early in 1982, our national accounts group solicited several discount chains, particularly those that were less price oriented. First, we'd try to persuade the account to test, substituting the GE line for private label in some of its stores. Failing this, we would make both branded and private label bulbs for them. Even chains which took on both typically moved as much volume as before without trading all of its consumers down to private label. Profits have improved for us and for the chain, so much so that in one or two cases, we've been able to persuade trade accounts that used to carry only private label to subsequently delete the GE-made private label product and sell only GE brand bulbs. In addition, by servicing both an account's private label and its brand name requirements, we thought we could better help manage the account's promotion calendar. Overall, what we've discovered is that by being involved in the private label end of the business, we've gained a more complete market perspective and we're better able to deal with the growth of private label.

1982 Results

The performance of GE's consumer incandescent lighting business in 1982 suggested that some of the initiatives which had been taken were working:

- GE consumer incandescent lamp revenues increased from $205 million in 1981 to $227 million in 1982 and operating profits increased 24 percent.
- GE's unit share of the consumer incandescent lamp market increased from 43.0 percent in 1981 to 44.5 percent in 1982 while its share of branded light bulbs rose from 45 percent to 47 percent. Sales of GE brand lamps increased from 488 million to 508 million.
- GE's average factory price per branded lamp rose from 41¢ in 1981 to 44¢ in 1982, yet GE was able to maintain its price premium at 30 percent, the 1981 level.
- In 1982, trade feature advertisements for GE soft white and/or Miser bulbs increased over 1981 by 60 percent in food stores, 47 percent in drug stores, and 19 percent in discount stores.
- GE sold $6.8 million worth of private label consumer incandescent lamps in 1982, 10 percent of all private label units

sold, and a 70 percent increase over GE's 1981 private label sales.

- GE secured $10 million worth of consumer incandescent lamp sales to new accounts.

Planning for 1983

As Frago reviewed the 1982 results and his department's marketing plans for 1983, he was primarily concerned about which overall strategy his business should pursue. He debated the relative merits of first, a plan to increase private label penetration, increase capacity utilization, reduce costs, and then reduce the price premium; second, a plan to secure increased distribution in emerging channels by increasing "push-oriented" off-invoice allowances; and third, a plan to reinstitute consumer advertising and merchandising performance allowances which had been cut back in mid–1982.

Price Premium

Several LPD executives believed that GE's share of the consumer incandescent market would never increase significantly until GE's price premium was reduced. According to one:

> The way to correct the price premium is to increase promotion allowances, take a list price cut, or at least to take price increases less than the inflation rate. If we become more price competitive, we'll gain distribution, sell more volume, and so maintain or even increase our total margin dollars. We could also improve our margins by investing in productivity improvements to increase our machine speeds and lower unit costs.

Frago believed that the price premium should be maintained at 30% but he asked for estimates of pretax income from the consumer incandescent business under the following three scenarios:

	Raise Premium *Scenario 1*	*Hold Premium* *Scenario 2*	*Lower Premium* *Scenario 3*
GE price premium in Year 7	43%	30%	25%
GE unit share in Year 7	32	45	52

The scenario analysis assumed a flat market, fixed marketing and sales expenses, steady changes in the price premium and unit share over the seven-year period, and an additional 0.5 percent annual productivity gain on increasing volume. The results of the scenario analysis, presented in Exhibit 15, seemed to support Frago's conclusion.

EXHIBIT 15   Pro Forma Projections: Three Scenarios for Annual Pretax Income over Seven Years

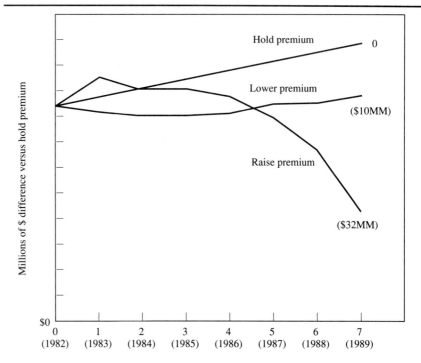

To be read: "The lower premium approach resulted in $10MM less annual pretax income than the hold premium approach."

Promotion Allowances

Few doubted that bill-back allowances had been effective in encouraging the trade to merchandise GE bulbs more aggressively to the consumer. However, some problems were evident. According to one LPD sales manager:

> Checking performance on these allowances is an administrative nightmare and can lead to disputes with some of our most important accounts. We're rapidly overcomplicating our allowance structure. Our salespeople are too busy explaining conditions on our allowances to do any real selling. We should give the trade these allowances up front on the basis of an affidavit or letter of intent that they'll run the feature ads.

National Advertising

Several LPD marketing executives were arguing to reinstitute national advertising in 1983 to support GE's soft white and Miser lines. The incremental funds were to come out of the budget for off-invoice allowances. The LPD sales force opposed this proposed shift of expenditures. Many LPD salespeople continued to be skeptical about the ability of national advertising to build the business. The following exchange took place between an LPD regional sales manager and a product marketing manager:

> *Sales manager:* A light bulb is a light bulb. There's no brand differentiation. When consumers want to improve their lighting, they think of adding a lamp or a fixture rather than changing the bulb they use. What's more, demand for light bulbs is not price-elastic. Consumers don't burn them up any faster if you give them away. In short, this is a push business. Your market share depends on your share of distribution.
>
> *Product manager:* We should be selling light, not light bulbs. We have a story to tell the consumer. Soft white stands for quality light. Miser stands for energy efficiency. There's so little light bulb advertising that a strong LPD national advertising campaign will not go unnoticed. Our share of voice will be high, so I'd expect our advertising to have impact. In addition, think what it will mean to sales force morale to be able to present a really strong national advertising campaign to the trade.
>
> *Sales manager:* I don't agree. Heavy national advertising will make us an even more attractive traffic builder to the trade. They'll give us more advertising features and lower their retail prices further. They'll make even less money on GE bulbs than they're making now, so they'll just continue using us as a traffic builder and then emphasize private label bulbs in their store displays because they'll make more unit margin on those than they will on GE bulbs.
>
> *Product manager:* But if we run a strong benefit-oriented national advertising program, we'll build our consumer franchise. More consumers will insist on the GE brand and be willing to pay a price premium over private label if we educate them in advertising as to why they should pay more. Our realized unit margins will improve. Yes, feature advertisements at discount prices can cause further commoditization, but only on brands which are not strongly advertised.

5-3 Procter & Gamble Company (B)

It was June 1982, and Mr. Charles Garner had been brand assistant on H-80 for six months. H-80 was the code name for a new light-duty liquid detergent[1] (LDL), scheduled for introduction into test market at the end of 1982 by the Packaged Soap and Detergent Division (PS&D) of the Procter & Gamble Co. (P&G). The H-80 Brand Group had been hard at work developing the H-80 first-year marketing plan. Under the guidance of Ms. Kate Jones, the brand manager, overall volume objectives and marketing support levels had been determined, and marketing support had been appropriately divided between introductory advertising and promotion. As brand assistant, Mr. Garner had responsibility for developing all promotion plans for H-80. His task over the next few weeks was to formulate a detailed Year 1 national sales promotion plan from which a test market plan for a limited geographical area could be derived.

Company Background

By 1981, the Procter & Gamble Company operated in 26 countries. As indicated in Exhibit 1, sales totaled $11.4 billion, of which 70 percent were made in the US. P&G manufactured 90 consumer and industrial products in the United States, including three of the leading LDL brands, Ivory Liquid, Dawn, and Joy. The company also sold the leading brands in 14 of the other 24 consumer product categories in which it competed.

The company comprised nine major operating divisions organized by type of product: Packaged Soap and Detergents, Bar Soap and Household Cleaning Products, Toilet Goods, Paper Products, Food Products, Coffee, Food Service and Lodging Products, and Special Products. Each division had its own brand management (called Advertising), Sales, Finance, Manufacturing, and Product Development line management groups. These groups reported to a division manager who had overall

This case was prepared by Alice MacDonald Court, Research Associate, under the direction of Professor John A. Quelch as the basis for class discussion rather than to illustrate effective or ineffective handling of an administrative situation. Names and proprietary data have been disguised but all essential relationships have been preserved. Copyright © 1983 by the President and Fellows of Harvard College. Harvard Business School case 9–584–048.

[1] LDLs are defined as all mild liquid soaps and detergents designed primarily for washing dishes.

EXHIBIT 1   Consolidated Statement of Earnings ($ millions except per-share amounts)

	Fiscal Year Ending June 30	
	1981	*1980*
Income:		
Net sales	$11,416	$10,772
Interest and other income	83	52
	11,499	10,824
Costs and expenses:		
Cost of products sold	7,854	7,471
Marketing, administrative, and other expenses	2,361	2,178
Interest expense	98	97
	10,313	9,746
Earnings from operations before income taxes	1,186	1,078
Income taxes	518	438
Net earnings from operations (before extraordinary charge)	668	640
Extraordinary charge: costs associated with the suspension of sale of Rely tampons (less applicable tax relief of $58)	(75)	—
Net earnings	$ 593	$ 640
Per common share:		
Net earnings from operations	$8.08	$7.74
Extraordinary charge	(.91)	—
Net earnings	$7.17	$7.74
Average shares outstanding:		
1981—82,720,858		
1980—82,659,861		
Dividends	$3.80	$3.40

SOURCE: Company records.

profit and loss responsibility. The divisions used centralized corporate staff groups for advertising services,[2] distribution, and purchasing.

The Advertising Department was organized on the brand management system. The responsibility for planning and directing the marketing effort for each brand was assigned to a brand group which typically included a brand manager, an assistant brand manager, and one or two

---

[2] Advertising services include the following specialized staff departments: TV Commercial Production, Media, Copy Services, Art and Package Design, Market Research, Field Advertising, Market Systems and Computer Services, Promotion and Marketing Services, and Advertising Personnel.

brand assistants. This group planned, developed, and directed the total marketing effort for its brand. In developing its marketing plans, the brand group worked closely with other departments within their division, with specialists in the advertising services staff groups, and with the advertising agency[3] assigned to their brand. Exhibit 2 presents the PS&D Division Advertising Department's organizational chart.

Light-Duty Liquid Detergents

The LDL industry recorded factory sales of $850 million and a volume of 59 million cases in 1981.[4] The average US consumer had 1.5 LDL brands at home at any one time, used 0.6 fluid ounces of product per sinkful of dishes, and washed an average of 12 sinksful each week. The average purchase cycle was 3–4 weeks. LDL consumption increases resulting from the growing number of US households[5] were partly offset by the increased penetration of automatic dishwashers (ADWs) as ADW households used one-half less LDL than non-ADW households.[6] Based on these trends, P&G executives projected category volume growth of 1 percent per year over the next five years.

The market could be conceptually divided into three major segments on the basis of product benefit. The performance segment, accounting for 35 percent of category volume, included brands providing primarily a cleaning benefit; the mildness segment, accounting for 37 percent of category volume, included brands providing primarily the benefit of mildness to hands; and the price segment, accounting for 28 percent of category volume, included brands whose primary benefit was low cost.[7] Three companies sold almost 75 percent of LDLs, with P&G holding a 42 percent share[8] of the market, Colgate-Palmolive Company a 24 percent share, and Lever Brothers, the US subsidiary of Unilever, a 7 percent share.[9] The remaining 27 percent of the market consisted mainly of generic and private label brands. A higher proportion of the marketing budgets of P&G LDLs was allocated to advertising and a lower percentage to

---

[3] P&G retained 10 leading advertising agencies to work with the brand groups on the development and execution of advertising strategy.

[4] Volume is measured in P&G statistical cases, each containing 310 ounces.

[5] Household growth was a better indicator of LDL volume than population growth, as research indicated LDL household consumption varied only slightly with the number of people in the household.

[6] ADW households still used LDL for pots and pans and small cleanups.

[7] Price brands were sold to retailers for an average of $7.50 per statistical case versus $17.00 per statistical case for the premium-priced mildness and performance brands.

[8] Share of the market is defined as share of statistical case volume.

[9] In 1981, US sales of Colgate-Palmolive Company were $5.3 billion and US sales of Lever Brothers were $2.1 billion.

EXHIBIT 2 PS&D Division Partial Organization Chart, Fall 1981

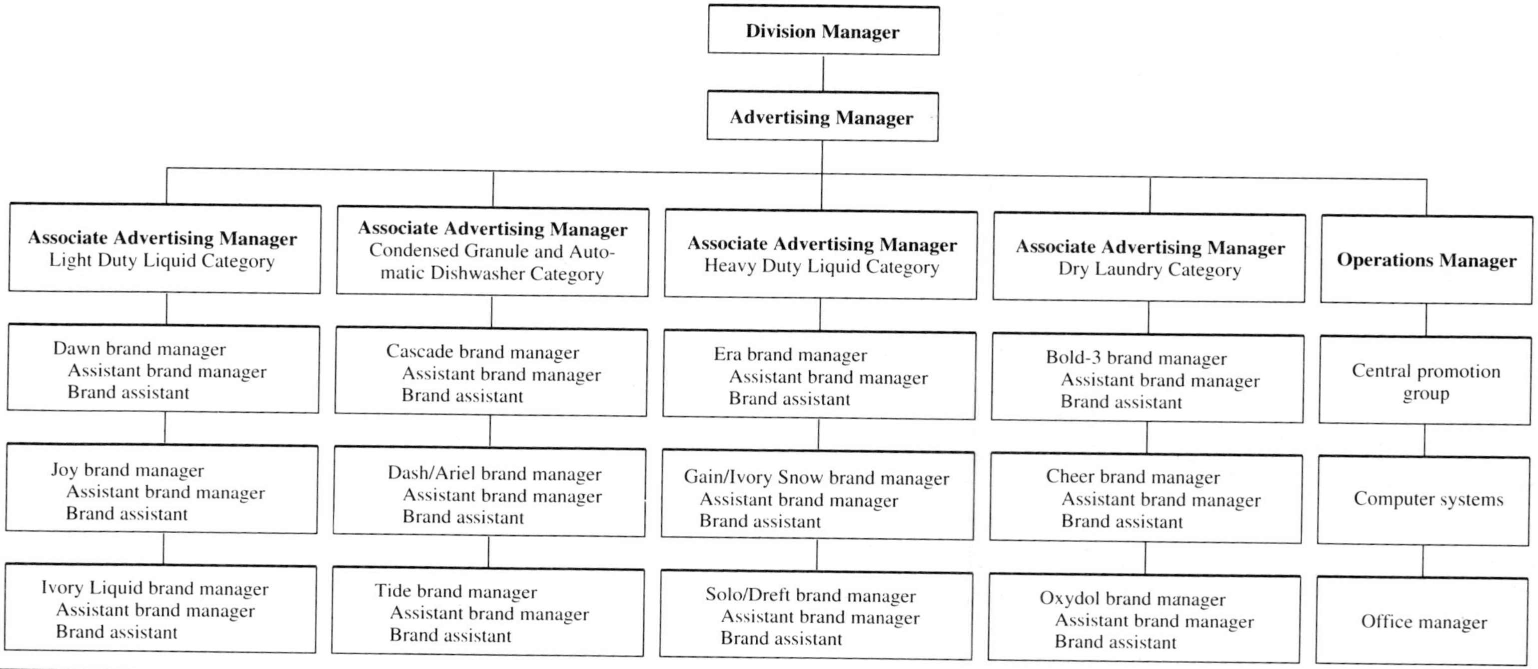

```
                              Division Manager
                                    │
                            Advertising Manager
                                    │
     ┌──────────────────┬──────────────────┬──────────────────┬──────────────────┐
```

Associate Advertising Manager Light Duty Liquid Category	Associate Advertising Manager Condensed Granule and Auto-matic Dishwasher Category	Associate Advertising Manager Heavy Duty Liquid Category	Associate Advertising Manager Dry Laundry Category	Operations Manager
Dawn brand manager Assistant brand manager Brand assistant	Cascade brand manager Assistant brand manager Brand assistant	Era brand manager Assistant brand manager Brand assistant	Bold-3 brand manager Assistant brand manager Brand assistant	Central promotion group
Joy brand manager Assistant brand manager Brand assistant	Dash/Ariel brand manager Assistant brand manager Brand assistant	Gain/Ivory Snow brand manager Assistant brand manager Brand assistant	Cheer brand manager Assistant brand manager Brand assistant	Computer systems
Ivory Liquid brand manager Assistant brand manager Brand assistant	Tide brand manager Assistant brand manager Brand assistant	Solo/Dreft brand manager Assistant brand manager Brand assistant	Oxydol brand manager Assistant brand manager Brand assistant	Office manager

promotion than was the case for either Colgate or Lever LDLs. Colgate and Lever sold an estimated 75 percent of their LDL volume to the trade on deal compared to about half for P&G.

Promotion of P&G's Established LDL Brands

P&G's three brands in the LDL category, Joy, Ivory Liquid, and Dawn, together accounted for 30 percent of the dollar sales volume and profit of the PS&D Division. While each of the three brands was a different formulation which offered a distinct benefit to appeal to separate consumer needs, they were all marketed similarly. The percentage breakdown of marketing expenditures between advertising and promotion for the three brands is indicated in Table 1.

In general, the brand managers spent about half of each LDL's marketing budget in advertising, with the balance in promotion. Competitive brands allocated about 40 percent of their marketing budgets to advertising.

Ivory Liquid was the leading brand in 1981 with a 15.5 percent share of the LDL category. Because Ivory had the highest trial levels in the category, the brand's primary sales promotion strategy was continuity of purchase combined with a secondary objective of stimulating trial among younger women and heavy LDL users.[10] Ivory had reduced its promotion frequency from eight 4-week events in 1972 to six events in 1982. Only 20 percent of Ivory's promotion budget was allocated to trade allowances. Despite merchandising performance requirements tied to these allowances, it was difficult to ensure that the funds were passed through to the consumer in the form of retail price cuts.

The remaining 80 percent of Ivory's promotion budget was allocated to consumer promotion. About two-thirds of Ivory's promotion events

TABLE 1   Advertising/Consumer Promotion/Trade Promotion Dollar Splits for P&G's LDL Brands

	1977	1978	1979	1980	1981	1982
Ivory Liquid	48/42/10	54/38/8	54/36/10	54/35/11	50/40/10	55/37/8
Dawn	NA	NA	58/31/11	51/39/10	46/42/12	51/40/9
Joy	55/36/9	51/41/8	48/42/10	55/34/11	50/39/11	60/30/10

[10] Ivory Liquid's current customers tended to be both slightly older than the average and lighter LDL users (defined as consumers who washed eight sinksful of dishes or less per week).

were price packs,[11] which were intended to encourage continuity of purchase by current brand users. Such price packs accounted for 30 percent of Ivory's total yearly volume. The remaining one-third of consumer promotions were coupon offers supported by trade allowances. The brand used couponing to stimulate trial. Exhibit 3 summarizes Ivory Liquid's 1981 and 1982 promotion plans, as well as the plans proposed for 1983.

Dawn was introduced nationally in 1976 as a performance brand. In two years Dawn rose to the no. 2 position in the LDL category, and by 1981 held a 14.1 percent market share. Dawn had captured about 70 percent of its volume from non-P&G brands, with the remaining 30 percent cannibalized equally from Ivory and Joy. Dawn's rapid growth was attributed to its unique benefit as the superior grease-cutting LDL in the category. Dawn's sales promotion strategy was trial oriented with two-thirds of Dawn's promotion events being trial-oriented coupon events supported by trade allowances, while the remaining one-third were price packs. Exhibit 4 summarizes Dawn's 1981, 1982, and 1983 promotion plans. The brand manager believed that Dawn's success was due to its distinctive grease-cutting benefit. He therefore tried to design consumer promotion events which emphasized this benefit at the same time as they provided an economic incentive to the consumer.

Joy ranked third in the LDL category with a 12.1 percent share in 1981. Its product benefit was to deliver "shiny dishes." Joy had the lowest trial level of P&G's three LDLs. To strengthen Joy's appeal, an improved "no-spot" formula was scheduled for national distribution by September 1982. The new formula caused water to "sheet" off dishes when they were air drying, leaving fewer spots than other brands. In addition, the improved formula reduced the cost of goods sold by about $3 million per year. The brand manager hoped to increase Joy's volume by 10 percent with the introduction of Joy's improved product. Marketing expenditures were to be increased modestly with emphasis on trial-oriented consumer promotion events. Approximately half of Joy's promotions were trial-oriented couponing events supported by trade allowances, and prepriced events.[12] The balance of events were price packs. Exhibit 5 summarizes Joy's 1981, 1982, and 1983 promotion plans.

The PS&D promotion planning calendar comprised 13 four-week promotion events. Each LDL participated in at least five events annually.

---

[11] A price pack was defined as a specially produced retail package announcing a temporary reduction from the standard retail price—for example, "30¢ off the regular retail price." The average percent reduction to the consumer was 10–20%.

[12] A prepriced pack was defined as a specially produced retail package that had the retail price marked on the label before it was delivered to the retail store. P&G generally used prepriced packs to promote smaller LDL sizes to stimulate trial. The average percent reduction to the consumer was 30–50%.

EXHIBIT 3   Ivory Liquid Promotion Calendars, 1981–1983

	January	*February*	*March*	*April*	*May*	*June*
1981	20¢-off mailed coupon *plus* $1.30 per case trade allowance	48 oz. 30¢-off price pack *plus* 22 oz. $1.30 per case trade allowance			32 oz. 20¢-off price pack	22 oz. $1.30 per case trade allowance
1982	48 oz. Harlequin Romance book on-pack premium *plus* $1.30 per case trade allowance	32 oz. 20¢-off price pack			22 oz. 13¢-off price pack	32 oz. 20¢-off price pack
Proposed 1983	20¢-off BFD coupon on any size *plus* $1.80 per case trade allowance	22 oz. 20¢-off price pack			32 oz. 27¢-off price pack	

NOTES: Coupons were redeemable on any package size. Per case allowances are quoted in terms of statistical cases.

EXHIBIT 4   Dawn Promotion Calendars, 1981–1983

	January	*February*	*March*	*April*	*May*	*June*
1981	32 oz. 20¢-off price pack		22 oz. 13¢-off price pack		32 oz. $1.30 per case trade allowance	
1982	20¢-off PCH* coupon *plus* $1.30 per case trade allowance		32 oz. 20¢-off price pack		22 oz. 13¢-off price pack	
Proposed 1983	20¢-off PCH coupon *plus* $1.80 per case trade allowance		32 oz. 27¢-off price pack		20¢-off free-standing insert coupon *plus* $1.80 per case trade allowance	

* Coupon distributed along with Publisher's Clearing House mailing.

July	August	September	October	November	December
	32 oz. 20¢-off price pack *plus* 20¢-off BFD coupon on any size		20¢-off free-standing insert coupon *plus* $1.30 per case trade allowance		
		20¢-off free-standing insert coupon *plus* $1.30 per case trade allowance			32 oz. 27¢-off price pack
22-oz. 20¢-off price pack		20¢-off free-standing insert coupon *plus* $1.80 per case trade allowance		48 oz. 40¢-off price pack	

July	August	September	October	November	December
22 oz. 13¢-off price pack		48 oz. 30¢-off price pack	32 oz. 20¢-off price pack		
48-oz. 30¢-off price pack			22 oz. 20¢-off price pack	$1.30 per case 32 oz. trade allowance	
20¢-off free-standing insert coupon *plus* $1.80 per case trade allowance			22 oz. 20¢-off price pack		20¢-off free-standing insert coupon *plus* $1.80 per case trade allowance

---

EXHIBIT 5   Joy Promotion Calendars, 1981–1983

	January	February	March	April	May	June
1981		32 oz. 20¢-off price pack		22 oz. 13¢-off price pack		20¢-free-standing insert coupon *plus* $1.30 per case trade allowance
1982		48 oz. two 40¢ cross-ruff* coupons distributed in 171 oz. Cheer laundry detergent *plus* 22 oz. 13¢-off price pack		32 oz. 20¢-off price pack		22 oz. 13¢-off price pack
Proposed 1983	32 oz. 27¢-off price pack	20¢-off free-standing coupon insert *plus* $1.80 per case trade allowance		22 oz. 20¢-off price pack		12 oz. 49¢ prepriced pack

* Two coupons good on the next purchase of Joy, distributed in specially marked boxes of Cheer laundry detergent.

While the brand groups occasionally planned regional promotion variations to facilitate testing of a new promotion idea or strengthen promotion support in a weak performance area, they generally planned national sales promotions. The brands generally avoided the simultaneous promotion of two or more of the company's LDLs whenever possible, in order to avoid fragmenting the attention of the sales force and the trade. In addition, there was concern that some trade buyers might respond by promoting only one of P&G's LDLs and ignoring the others. However, some sales managers believed that promoting all three LDLs together would lessen cannibalization among the brands by minimizing the consumer switching resulting from promotion, and argued that such line promotions would be attractive to the trade since such promotions would include high-volume brands. The PS&D Division organized one or two divisional promotion events each year involving 3 to 10 brands, often including one or more LDLs.[13]

---

[13] Such divisional promotion events typically included a sweepstakes or contest combined with cash refund offers and coupons.

July	August	September	October	November	December
	22 oz. 13¢-off price pack	20¢-off free-standing insert coupon *plus* $1.30 per case trade allowance		32 oz. 20¢-off price pack	
	20¢-off free-standing insert coupon *plus* $1.30 per case trade allowance		48 oz. 40¢-off price pack	20¢-off mailed coupon *plus* $1.30 per case trade allowance	
		22 oz. 20¢-off price pack		20¢-off mailed coupon *plus* $1.80 per case trade allowance	

The Development of H-80

H-80 was a high-performance LDL that combined suspended nonabrasive scrubbers[14] with a highly effective detergent system to provide superior cleaning versus other LDLs when used full strength on tough, baked-on foods and parity cleaning versus other LDLs when diluted with water for general dishwashing. The scrubber system represented a distinctive new product benefit, and was the first major technological innovation in the category since the introduction of Ivory Liquid.[15] The H-80 formula was completely homogenous and did not require shaking.

The PS&D Division began work on this innovation in response to a 1980 Dishwashing Habits and Practices Study which revealed that 80 percent of US households scour and scrub their dishes at least once a

---

[14] The scrubbers were made from the biodegradable shells of microscopic sea organisms.

[15] Ivory Liquid's formula included a detergent with a patented molecular structure that prevented the roughness and cracking that exposure to other detergents caused to human skin.

TABLE 2 **H-80 Projected Sales**

Year	LDL Market Projections (000,000 cases)	H-80 Estimated Market Share (%)	H-80 Estimated Market Volume (000,000 cases)	H-80 Estimated Sales* ($000,000)
1982	59.4	—	—	—
1983	59.8	7%	4.2	$ 71.4
1984	60.1	11	6.6	112.2
1985	60.8	11	6.7	113.9

* H-80 carload cost of a statistical case was $17.00. See Table 3.

week, with an average household scouring four times a week. This research also revealed that the removal of burnt or baked-on foods was considered the toughest cleaning job by more consumers than any other dishwashing task, and that most consumers did not view their current LDL as sufficiently effective for such tough cleaning jobs. Based on this research, the Advertising Department concluded that a consumer need existed for a high-performance LDL.

The Product Development Department (PDD) began work on this project in early 1981. An H-80 brand group was established to guide the development process and test marketing of the brand. By mid-1981, they had developed a technological breakthrough and a formula that they believed would fulfill the existing consumer need. Successful laboratory and in-home use testing was completed by the end of 1981.

H-80 emerged from the development process as a rich green opalescent liquid that felt slightly gritty to the touch. The liquid was thicker than that of other LDLs, and H-80's herbal fragrance was completely unique within the category. The package was bright green and shaped like an arrowhead. The label carried an endorsement from the American Fine China Guild that read, "Safe for all fine china."

Based on the results of pretest market research[16] conducted to project H-80's potential market share, the brand had recommended a market share objective of 11 percent. The pretest market research projected H-80's market share to reach 13 percent by the end of Year 1. However, given the aggressive competitive environment of the LDL market, the brand group had thought it prudent to set a conservative objective for H-80. The brand group projected H-80's national volume and share as indicated in Table 2.

Planned capital investment of $20 million for H-80 was below the average for a new P&G product. The cost structure of P&G's existing LDL brands, summarized in Exhibit 6, was applicable to H-80. The brand

---

[16] P&G uses a proprietary technique for simulating test markets and predicting market shares.

EXHIBIT 6   Cost Structure for an Established LDL Brand (percent)

Cost	51%
Distribution	7
Selling and general administration	10
Marketing expenditures	20*
Profit	12
Total	100

* Includes advertising, trade, and consumer promotion expenditures.
SOURCE: Company records.

EXHIBIT 7   H-80 Marketing Payout Schedule

	Year 1	Year 2	Year 3	Year 4
Revenue (millions of dollars)	$ 71.4	$112.2	$113.9	$113.9
Expenses:				
Marketing (20% of sales after Year 1)	60.0	22.4	22.8	22.8
Cost of goods, distribution, and				
SG&A (68% of sales)	45.2	76.2	77.5	77.5
Total	105.2	98.6	100.3	100.3
Profit/(loss)	(33.8)	13.6	13.6	13.6
Cumulative profit/(loss)	(33.8)	(20.2)	(6.6)	7.0

---

group estimated that P&G would have to spend at least $60 million on a 12-month introductory marketing plan for H-80. While this did not meet the 36-month marketing payout objective generally sought by a new PS&D product (see Exhibit 7), the brand believed a longer payout was justified because of the low capital investment required. However, the payout picture was further clouded because of the likelihood that some of H-80's volume would be cannibalized from current P&G LDLs. Based on current market shares, only about 60 percent of H-80's volume would be net extra for the PS&D Division. If this occurred, it would lengthen payout for the division considerably.

P&G management was fully aware that H-80 was a risky venture. P&G's current market share of over 40 percent made cannibalization a virtual certainty and suggested a limited marketing investment to generate an attractive payout. Conversely, establishment in the increasingly competitive LDL category suggested the need for substantial marketing investment. An added element of risk was the revolutionary nature of the H-80 product, which contained a mild abrasive. Acceptance of this would require that consumers be educated and persuaded to modify current

EXHIBIT 8   LDL Market Share Projections (1982–1989)

	Percent of LDL Market Volume						
	Without H-80			With H-80			
Year	Ivory Liquid	Dawn	Joy	Ivory Liquid	Dawn	Joy	H-80
1982	15.5%	14.7%	12.2%	15.5%	14.7%	12.2%	—
1983	15.5	15.0	12.3	14.7	14.0	11.4	7.0%
1984	15.5	15.5	12.4	14.2	13.9	11.1	11.0
1985	15.5	15.9	12.5	14.2	14.3	11.2	11.0
1986	15.5	16.5	12.7	14.2	14.9	11.4	11.0

usage habits, a formidable task. Nevertheless, company management supported H-80 because it was an innovative product which met a real consumer need. The company had had outstanding successes with similar risky innovations in the past such as Pampers, Crest, and Bounce, although some other innovations had failed. P&G attempted to limit risk by test marketing new products and only expanding distribution of those which proved to have high consumer appeal in the marketplace, and thus a high likelihood of success. Further, initial test market failures were frequently modified, retested successfully, and later expanded to national distribution.

The brand managers on P&G's established LDLs also expected some cannibalization, but projected that their brands' losses would be less than proportional to their market shares. As shown in Exhibit 8, Ivory Liquid and Joy expected to lose only 75 percent and 80 percent, respectively, of their proportionate losses, since their benefits would not compete directly with those of H-80.[17]

When the brand managers on Ivory, Dawn, and Joy were asked how they might change their brand marketing plans in light of the introduction of H-80, all three indicated that they would not increase their spending, but that they would formulate their promotion plans more defensively. Specifically, all three said they would plan to run strong offers designed to encourage consumers to stock up before H-80's introduction, then trial-oriented couponing events following H-80's introduction to regain lost users.

Based on P&G LDL category experience, the brand group expected the following distribution by size two months after H-80's introduction: 70 percent distribution in stores representing 90 percent of total grocery volume on 48 oz., 85 percent on 32 oz., 90 percent on 22 oz., and 75

---

[17] Proportionate loss is defined as a loss of sales proportionate to market share. For example, Ivory's 1983 share was expected to be 15.5 percent. If Ivory lost its fair share of H-80's 11 percent of the market, it would lose 15.5 percent × 11% = 1.7 share points.

percent on 12 oz.[18] To maintain these distribution levels, Garner believed the brand had to promote all sizes of H-80 in the first year.

P&G did not advertise a new brand until it had achieved 70 percent distribuution, which the brand group expected H-80 to achieve six weeks after introduction. H-80's media plan would give the brand LDL category leadership media weights for the first six months of its introductory advertising campaign. The average media weight for the major advertised LDL brands was 300 gross rating points (GRPs)[19] every four weeks. H-80 planned 450 GRPs during weeks 6–18, 375 GRPs during weeks 19–31, and 300 GRPs during weeks 32–52. The Brand and Advertising Agency expected this media campaign would achieve a 65 percent consumer awareness of H-80's advertising by three months after introduction.

The H-80 advertising strategy aimed to convince consumers that H-80 was an outstanding dishwashing liquid for cleaning tough-to-remove foods from dishes. Advertising would be targeted at female heads of larger households aged 18–35. Consumer research had revealed that H-80 had the most well-defined target audience of any of the LDLs. The research also suggested that H-80's target audience should be the heavy LDL user.[20]

Total cost for the 12-month media plan would be $18 million. In addition, promotion costs were expected to be $37 million, and miscellaneous marketing expenses $5 million (including point-of-sale display material and $500,000 to produce television commercials).

H-80's introductory year advertising/promotion split would be 40 percent/60 percent, similar to the company average for a new brand. Thereafter, the brand manager's objective was to have at least 50 percent of marketing support in advertising.

H-80 would be available in four sizes and at prices equivalent to those of P&G's established LDL brands, as indicated in Table 3.

Promotion Issues for H-80

P&G's introduction of Dawn in 1976 was considered very successful. Dawn's introductory promotion plan, outlined in Table 4 with 1982 updated costs, helped Dawn achieve a market share equivalent to that required by H-80.

With this introductory promotion program, Dawn had achieved the market share growth detailed in Table 5.

---

[18] While the PS&D sales force only serviced 27 percent of grocery stores accounting for 75 percent of grocery sales volume, additional distribution could be achieved through grocery wholesale distributors which serviced smaller grocery stores.

[19] One gross rating point is achieved when one advertising exposure reaches 1 percent of the advertiser's potential audience. Gross rating points can be calculated as the product of media reach times exposure frequency.

[20] A heavy LDL user washes 12 or more sinksful of dishes per week.

TABLE 3   **H-80 Sizing and Pricing**

Size	Number of Items per Actual Case	Number of Items per Statistical Case*	Manufacturer's Carload Item Price	Estimated Average Retail Price	Estimated Percent of Volume per Size†
48 oz.	9	6.5	$2.53	$2.99	10%
32 oz.	12	9.7	1.70	2.04	30
22 oz.	16	14.0	1.21	1.46	45
12 oz.	24	25.8	0.70	0.84	15

* A statistical case equals 310 ounces.

† Statistical cases.

TABLE 4   **Dawn's Year 1 Introductory Promotion Plan**

Month	Event	Cost in 1982 ($000,000)	Number of Average Weeks of Year 1 Volume per Promotion Event*
2 and 3	$2.70/statistical case trade allowances on all sizes	1.8	8
	6-oz. sample mailed to 50% of households	30.3	—
4	22-oz./13¢-off price pack	1.2	10
6	32-oz./20¢-off price pack	1.0	10
8	48-oz./30¢-off price pack	0.3	13
10	22-oz./13¢-off price pack	1.2	10

* For example, 8 weeks' worth of total Year 1 volume of all sizes would be sold with the initial trade allowance, and 10 weeks' worth of total Year 1 volume on the 22-oz. size would be sold with the second event (13¢-off price pack).

TABLE 5   **Dawn's Year 1 Market Share Growth**

	Month						Total Year 1
	1–2	3–4	5–6	7–8	9–10	11–12	
Percent of total Year 1 share	30	80	100	120	130	140	100

Garner realized that he would probably not be able to achieve the same results for H-80 if he simply copied the Dawn plan. When Dawn was introduced, there was little couponing in the LDL category. However, by 1982, most major LDL brands distributed coupons frequently, and as Exhibit 9 shows, research indicated that coupons were widely used by consumers. Also, the LDL competitive environment was becoming more

---

EXHIBIT 9 **Consumer Use of Manufacturers' Coupons**

Question: How often do you use a manufacturer's coupon when you purchase a dishwashing liquid?

| | By Year | | | By 1981 Usage Patterns | | |
				Heavy *(+12 sinkfuls per week)*	*Medium* *(7–14 sinkfuls per week)*	*Light* *(1–7 sinkfuls per week)*
	1979	*1980*	*1981*			
Almost always	22%	25%	28%	28%	26%	24%
About half the time	17	18	18	18	19	18
Just occasionally	44	42	40	40	43	44
Never	16	14	13	13	12	13
No answer	1	1	1	1	—	1

NOTE: To be read, for example: In 1979, 22 percent of all respondents who had washed some dishes by hand in the past seven days claimed that they used a manufacturer's coupon almost always when they purchased a dishwashing liquid.
SOURCE: Company research.

intense with the expansion of Sunlight by Lever Brothers in 1982. While it was still too early to tell how successful Sunlight would be with its national expansion, Sunlight had achieved an 11 percent share in the test market after only 12 months.

Sunlight's introductory promotion plan had been much more aggressive than the Dawn plan. It involved 10 promotion events, including a $2.70/statistical case trade allowance for months 1–3 in support of a free 5-oz. sample size plus 15¢ coupon mailed to 50 percent of all households, three coupon events (one 20¢ free-standing insert coupon,[21] one 20¢ magazine coupon, and one 25¢ Best Food Day coupon),[22] three preprice events (on 12-oz., 22-oz., and 32-oz. sizes), a 6-oz. trial size, and two trade allowance promotions (one on the 48-oz. size and one on the 22-oz. size). The cost of Sunlight's Year 1 promotion plan was estimated at $75 million on a national equivalent basis.

Another key issue Garner faced was how to minimize H-80's cannibalization of P&G's other LDLs. As Garner examined the 1981, 1982, and 1983 promotion schedules for Ivory, Dawn, and Joy, he pondered when and how often H-80 should be promoted. He wanted to avoid the simultaneous promotion of two or more of the company's LDLs. However, given the limitation of 13 promotion periods, H-80 would have to be promoted alongside another LDL on at least some occasions.

Garner also wondered what promotion mix would be most effective for the H-80 introduction. Price packs and coupons seemed to be the most

---

[21] A free-standing insert coupon was a coupon and ad preprinted on heavy paper and inserted loose into a newspaper or magazine.

[22] A Best Food Day coupon was a coupon run in a newspaper on the day that paper ran editorial material on food. This was also the edition in which most retail grocers placed their retail advertisements and hence, the most advantageous day for grocers and manufacturers to run coupons.

commonly used promotion vehicles in the category and recent P&G research, summarized in Table 6, indicated that these vehicles were liked and used by consumers.

However, the same research also indicated that a trial size represented the best purchase incentive for a consumer who had never tried a brand.

Garner wondered if the less frequently used types of consumer promotion in the LDL category, such as premiums, mail-in refunds, or sweepstakes, could enable H-80 to attract the trade's attention and cut through the clutter of competitive promotions. He was particularly interested in the ability of free mail-in offers to achieve sampling of new users as reported in the independent industry research study presented in Exhibit 10.

Independent of the types of promotion event scheduled, Garner believed on the basis of LDL category experience that the following percentages of incremental trial would be achieved with each subsequent promotion.

Event I	All reach is incremental trial.
Event II	Assume ½ of reach is incremental trial.
Event III	Assume ¼ of reach is incremental trial.
Event IV	Assume ¼ of reach is incremental trial.
Event V	Assume ¼ of reach is incremental trial.

TABLE 6   1981 Consumer Ratings and Use of Promotion Devices (index: highest rated/used device = 100)

	Coupons		Price Pack	Premiums		Refund/ Rebate	Trial Size	Bonus Pack	Sweepstakes
	Manufacturer	*Store*		*Pack*	*Mail*				
Percent liking very much/fairly well	95%	85%	100%	75%	46%	74%	90%	90%	46%
Percent used past 3 months	97	87	100	51	30	56	61	74	44

NOTE: These ratings were based on general consumer preferences rather than preferences within the LDL category.
SOURCE: Company research.

TABLE 7   1981 Consumer Ratings and Use of Promotion Devices (index: highest rated/used device = 100)

	Coupons		Price Pack	Premiums		Refund/ Rebate	Trial Size	Bonus Pack	Sweepstakes
	Manufacturer	*Store*		*Pack*	*Mail*				
Brand never used	46%	37%	29%	37%	17%	27%	100%	35%	13%

EXHIBIT 10 Effectiveness Ratings of Premiums and Sweepstakes by Manufacturers Who Sell through Supermarkets

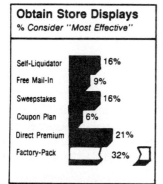

Obtain Store Displays
% Consider "Most Effective"

Self-Liquidator	16%
Free Mail-In	9%
Sweepstakes	16%
Coupon Plan	6%
Direct Premium	21%
Factory-Pack	32%

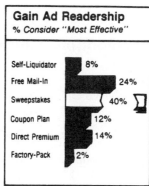

Gain Ad Readership
% Consider "Most Effective"

Self-Liquidator	8%
Free Mail-In	24%
Sweepstakes	40%
Coupon Plan	12%
Direct Premium	14%
Factory-Pack	2%

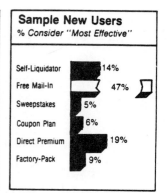

Sample New Users
% Consider "Most Effective"

Self-Liquidator	14%
Free Mail-In	47%
Sweepstakes	5%
Coupon Plan	6%
Direct Premium	19%
Factory-Pack	9%

Good Will, Old Users
% Consider "Most Effective"

Self-Liquidator	20%
Free Mail-In	22%
Sweepstakes	7%
Coupon Plan	15%
Direct Premium	22%
Factory-Pack	14%

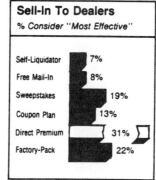

Sell-In To Dealers
% Consider "Most Effective"

Self-Liquidator	7%
Free Mail-In	8%
Sweepstakes	19%
Coupon Plan	13%
Direct Premium	31%
Factory-Pack	22%

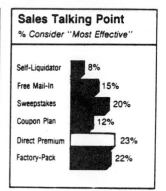

Sales Talking Point
% Consider "Most Effective"

Self-Liquidator	8%
Free Mail-In	15%
Sweepstakes	20%
Coupon Plan	12%
Direct Premium	23%
Factory-Pack	22%

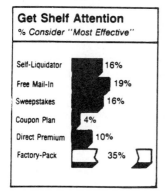

Get Shelf Attention
% Consider "Most Effective"

Self-Liquidator	16%
Free Mail-In	19%
Sweepstakes	16%
Coupon Plan	4%
Direct Premium	10%
Factory-Pack	35%

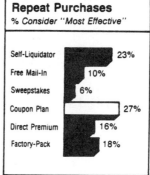

Repeat Purchases
% Consider "Most Effective"

Self-Liquidator	23%
Free Mail-In	10%
Sweepstakes	6%
Coupon Plan	27%
Direct Premium	16%
Factory-Pack	18%

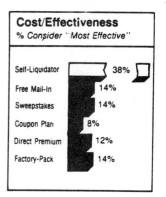

Cost/Effectiveness
% Consider "Most Effective"

Self-Liquidator	38%
Free Mail-In	14%
Sweepstakes	14%
Coupon Plan	8%
Direct Premium	12%
Factory-Pack	14%

Source: *Incentive Marketing*, December 1981.

Garner predicted that he would have to achieve about a 40 percent trial level to support an 11 percent share based on results of previous introductions of products with similar usage profiles.

Sales Promotion Alternatives

Trade Allowances

Sales had advised Garner that a $2.70/statistical case trade allowance on all sizes in months 1–3 was necessary to stimulate initial stocking, in-store displays, and feature advertising by the trade. Garner also wondered whether a second trade promotion allowance event was necessary because of the competitive environment. He believed it would be most effective as a fourth event. Sales had informed him that an allowance below the current $1.80/statistical case used on the other P&G LDLs would be insufficient to generate trade support.

Sampling

Sampling was considered by P&G as the most effective trial-producing promotion device. Garner considered only mailed samples, as door-to-door delivery of samples by specially recruited crews was more expensive.

Garner worked with the Manufacturing Department to develop mailed sample costs for various sizes, as shown in Exhibit 11. He was aware of P&G research indicating that too small a sample might not permit sufficient use to develop consumer interest in the product. He wondered which size would generate the most efficient and effective trial levels for H-80.

Couponing

While Dawn's introductory plan had not included any couponing, Garner felt that he should consider this promotion vehicle given its broad usage

EXHIBIT 11   Mailed Sampling Costs per Sample Unit for H-80

Sample Size	Delivered* Cost per Unit	Percent Usage†	Percent of Consumers That Use Sample Who Repurchase
6-oz. miniature bottles	$.75	85	50
3-oz. miniature bottles	.53	75	40
1.5-oz. miniature bottles	.41	65	35
Two .75-oz. foil packets	.31	40	30

* Includes mailing costs as well as manufacturing costs.

† Usage and repurchase rates vary by size.

within the current LDL category and apparent appeal to consumers. He examined the costs and redemption estimates by distribution vehicle (see Exhibit 12) and by coupon value (see Exhibit 13) for five types of coupon programs:

- Coupons for H-80 alone could be mailed selectively to members of the target audience. The impact and redemption rate would be high because there would be no coupons for other brands in the mailing which might reduce consumer attention to H-80. However, this couponing method was expensive.
- Coupons for H-80 could be co-op mailed with other product coupons. Co-op couponing had slightly less impact but was considerably less expensive since delivery costs were shared with other brands. Such co-op mailings were organized by outside agencies. As a result, the timing of deliveries was fixed in advance and only one LDL brand could participate in any one coupon drop. The only available delivery times open to H-80 in the test market were three months and seven months following introduction.
- Free-standing newspaper insert (FSI) coupons offered Garner more flexibility in timing. The redemption rates for FSI coupons were strong but coupon theft and misredemption could also be high (particularly if the FSI was inserted in newsstand issues).
- Coupons distributed through the Best Food Day editions of local newspapers offered both low-cost delivery and flexibility in timing and in geographical coverage. There was, however, a greater potential for a new brand like H-80 to be lost among the many coupons run in newspapers. Also, the redemption rate was low and misredemption was high.
- Magazine coupons also offered low delivery costs and could be targeted at specific consumer groups. However, the potential to tie in with specific retailer feature dates did not exist. In addition, the redemption rate was low.

Special Pack Promotions

Garner considered four types of special packs: trial-size packs, prepriced packs, price packs, and bonus packs. Sales had advised that special packs should not be run until at least the second half of Year 1, since the trade was reluctant to buy a special pack until a new brand was established to avoid carrying dual inventories of regular pack and special pack. However, if a new brand were introduced with a special pack, the trade would not need to carry dual inventories. A cost comparison by value/size and vehicle is shown in Exhibit 14.

EXHIBIT 12 Theoretical Couponing Economics—20¢ Coupon Good on Any Size*

	Mail			Free Standing Insert				Magazine (on page)
	Single Brand	Basic Co-op†	Extended Co-op‡	Single Brand	Full-Page Co-op	2/5 Page Co-op	Best Food Day	
No. of coupons distributed (millions)	40	24	45	44	38	38	58	58
Distribution cost/M$	$110.00	$16.45	$14.00	$37.50	$12.05	$5.05	$9.20	$5.70
Total distribution cost	$4,400,000	$395,000	$630,000	$1,650,000	$458,000	$182,000	$478,000	$319,000
Estimated percent redemption	11.6	11.6	10.6	7.6	5.7	5.1	3.1	2.6
No. of coupons redeemed (thousands)	4,640	2,784	4,770	3,344	2,166	1,938	1,612	1,456
Total redemption costs‖ ($000)	$1,322.4	$793.4	$1,357.5	$953.0	$617.3	$552.3	$459.4	$415.0
Grand total costs ($000)	$5,722.4	$1,188.2	$1,989.5	$2,603.5	$1,075.3	$744.3	$937.4	$734.0
Estimated percent misredemption	10	10	10	25	25	25	25	10
No. of households reached with product (thousands)	4,174	2,506	4,293	2,508	1,625	1,454	1,209	1,310
Total cases moved (thousands)	422	253	434	257	167	149	124	132
Cost per household reached	$1.37	$0.47	$0.46	$1.03	$0.66	$0.51	$0.78	$0.56
Cost per case moved	$13.56	$4.70	$4.58	$10.13	$6.44	$5.00	$7.55	$5.56

* Chart based upon average redemption data. Assume a new P&G LDL brand would redeem 50 percent higher due to strong advertising, product news, and high household category penetration.

† A coupon mailing involving at least 10 noncompeting brands. Redemption rates were stable regardless of the number of brands.

‡ Extended coverage version of basic co-op coupon mailing.

§ Includes coupon production and preparation costs, as well as cost of mailing.

‖ Includes trade and clearinghouse handling fees totaling 8.5¢ per coupon as well as amount of coupon.

EXHIBIT 13   Approximate Relationship of Redemption Rate to LDL Coupon Value

Coupon Vehicle	Coupon Value					
	20¢	*25¢*	*35¢*	*50¢*	*$1.00*	*Get One Free*
Mail						
Single brand	100	110	125	150	200	250
Co-op	100	110	125	150	200	250
FSI co-op	100	110	125	150	200	250
Best Food Day	100	110	125	150	200	250
Magazine	100	110	125	150	200	250
On-pack	100	110	125	150	200	N/A
Cross-ruff*	100	110	125	150	200	N/A

NOTE: Data indexed to 20¢ value.

* Advertised on pack of another brand.

A trial size would offer the consumer a low-risk, low-cost method of trying H-80. Because the consumer paid for the trial-size package, the cost to P&G per trial was lower than a sampling program.

A prepriced pack would also offer the consumer a low-risk, low-cost method of trying H-80, similar to a trial size. Usually, a prepriced pack was offered on the smallest saleable size, in this case the 12-oz. size.

Price packs were widely used in the LDL category. Price packs were generally regarded as an effective promotion vehicle to retain current users and encourage repeat purchase. The trade often set up special displays of price packs which could stimulate impulse purchases. Garner, however, wondered if a price pack would be good at generating trial for H-80.

Bonus packs offered low-cost distribution of free product but were not regarded as a strong trial device since they did not reduce the financial risk of trial to the consumer who had never used the product. However, bonus packs were considered an excellent means of promoting continuity of usage and offered a strong purchase incentive to the consumer who had purchased and liked the product before. Garner wondered if a bonus pack promotion would be effective in the second half of the introductory year.

Refunds

P&G did not usually use refund offers on a new brand because the economic benefit to the consumer was not immediately delivered and the value of the device in stimulating trial was questionable. However, Garner wondered if a high-value refund supported by point-of-purchase display material could generate significant trade and consumer interest. He also wondered if a refund requiring multiple purchases would be an

EXHIBIT 14 LDL Special Rack Promotions

Type:	Trial Size (6-oz. product miniature)	Prepriced Size (12 oz.)	Bonus Pack (32-oz. oversize)	Price Pack Cents Off
	Consumer Price per Bottle	Consumer Price per Bottle (savings off retail price)	Percent of Free Product	Percent of Normal Retail
Value:				
High	$.19	$.39 (50%)	25% (8 oz.)	30%
Medium	.29	.39 (40)	15 (5 oz.)	20
Low	.39	.59 (30)	10 (3 oz.)	10
Cost:				
High value	36¢ per unit	Savings off retail price times no. of units per statistical case plus 50¢ per statistical case manufacturing and trade handling	$6.10 per statistical case	Cents off times no. of units per statistical case plus 50¢ per statistical case manufacturing and trade handling
Medium value	29¢ per unit		$5.00 per statistical case	
Low value	22¢ per unit		$4.25 per statistical case	
Amount of Promoted Volume Sold per Event:	4.77M bottles	13 weeks' business for 12 oz.	10 weeks' business for 32 oz.	10 weeks' business for 22 and 32 oz.; 13 weeks for 12 and 48 oz.

NOTE: All three types of promotion would be accepted by stores representing 70 percent of all commodity volume (ACV).

effective continuity device if used in the second six months of H-80's first-year promotion plan. Garner analyzed the company's experience with refunds over the past three years (see Exhibit 15 for a refund fact sheet), and found that P&G distributed 30 percent of their refund offers through print, 27 percent through point-of-sale display material, 5 percent in- or on-pack, and 38 percent through divisional group promotions that used a combination of all three distribution methods plus television advertising.

EXHIBIT 15   Refund Facts: Industry Experience

I. Factors Which Influence Refund Response Rates

1. Method of distribution.
2. Proof-of-purchase requirement/difficulty in obtaining proofs.
3. Actual value of refund; value relative to price.
4. Length of promotion.
5. Design/appeal of offer and ad.
6. Whether store coupon used with refund offer.
7. Consumer interest in product/size of brand's consumer franchise.
8. Whether single choice or variable offer.
9. Whether refund in cash, check, or coupon.
10. Brand's retail availability.
11. Whether offer advertised via media or trade, or publicized in refund columns and newsletters.

II. Typical Response Patterns

Refund value	$1.00	$1.00	$1.00
Purchase requirements	1 22-oz. size	2 22-oz. size	3 22-oz. size
Consumer outlay for purchases	$1.50	$3.00	$4.50
Percent savings on 22-oz. size	67%	33%	22%

Estimated Response as Percent of Offers Distributed

Print	.9%	.5%	.3%
Point of sale	5.4	3.0	1.8
Direct mail	3.6	2.0	1.2
In-/on-pack other brand	8.2	4.5	2.7
In-/on-pack own brand	12.7	7.0	4.2

III. Estimated Fulfillment Costs*

	Number Distributed (millions)			
Print	44	$ 530,000	$300,000	$175,000
Point of Sale	3	220,000	120,000	75,000
Direct Mail	25	1,200,000	670,000	400,000
In-/On-Pack Other Brand	6	660,000	360,000	220,000
In-/On-Pack Own Brand	6	1,020,000	560,000	335,000

* Fulfillment costs include the $1.00 refund itself plus 34¢ return for handling. In addition to the fulfillment costs, assume $70M to $150M for display material/sales aids and/or $300M to $500M for print advertising; 3¢ per unit for in-/on-pack distribution carried by own brand, no extra package cost if carried by other brand, and $16.45/M for distributing direct mail offers via multibrand co-op.

Premiums

Premiums were believed useful in attracting attention at the point-of-sale and could offer excellent in-store display support, thereby stimulating impulse purchases. There were four major methods of premium distribution and types.

On-/in-pack premiums were attached to or packed in the product container and were offered free with the purchase of the promoted brand. These premiums made a strong impact on the shelf and often encouraged the trade to display the product off-shelf because of their irregular size. In-pack premiums were considered good trial-generating devices. However, the costs of extra packaging and of the premiums themselves could be significant. In addition, trade acceptance was estimated at only 30–50% of all commodity volume because of inventory and shelf space problems (due to irregular size) as well as the risk of pilferage.

Near-pack premiums were displayed on the shelf next to or near the promoted product. Most near-pack premiums were free with the designated purchase but in the case of saleable or price-plus near-packs the

EXHIBIT 16   Objectives and Costs of LDL Premiums

Type of Premium	Marketing Objectives				
	Trial	Repeat Purchase	Obtain In-Store Displays	Increase Advertisement Readership	Copy/Product Reinforcement
Self-liquidator			●	●	●
Partial liquidator by mail		●	●	●	
Free-in-mail for multiproofs		●	●	●	●
Free-in-mail for one proof	●		●	●	●
Near-pack—in store	●		●		●
On-/in-pack—in store	●		●		●

Type of Premium	Typical Item	Offer Structure	National Cost of Promotion
Self-liquidator	Hair dryer	$9.00 plus 1 proof of purchase	$ 200,000
Partial liquidator	Hair dryer	$2.00 plus 4 proofs of purchase	400,000
Free-in-mail	Hair dryer	Free for 6 22-oz. proofs of purchase	2,200,000
Near-pack	Coupon holder	Free with one 22 oz.	950,000
On-/in-pack	Playing cards	Free with one 22 oz.	950,000

NOTE: Cost estimates include the premium itself, display materials, and offer fulfillment. In the case of completely or partially self-liquidating premiums, they reflect offsetting revenue from consumers.

EXHIBIT 17   P&G Group Sweepstakes Promotion

 1st Prize

One (1) 13-day cruise for two on the luxury schooner Fantome PLUS $5,000 cash (approximate retail value $11,300.00).*

 2nd Prize

Five (5) 6-day cruises on the Flying Cloud (approximate retail value $3,200.00 per trip).*

*The First and Second Prizes include transportation to and from Freeport, Bahamas where the cruises originate.

3rd Prize

2,000 L.L. Bean Boat and Tote™ Bags (approximate retail value $10.00).

Name

Address

City

State

Zip Code

Telephone

OFFICIAL RULES—NO PURCHASE NECESSARY

1. Each entry you submit must be accompanied by one of the following:
   a. Any retail store ad dated between August 1, 1982 and September 30, 1982 which includes an ad for any one of these fine Procter & Gamble products:

Dash   Oxydol   Gain   Era   Bounty

White Cloud* or Charmin   Folger's Ground Roast or Flaked Coffee   Instant High Point   Ivory Liquid

*Available only in limited areas.

Circle the name of the product and its picture (if a picture is included in the ad) and circle the date printed on the ad.

OR

   b. A plain piece of 3″ x 5″ paper on which you have handprinted or typed the name of any one of these fine Procter & Gamble products: Dash, Oxydol, Gain, Era, Bounty, White Cloud, Charmin, Folger's Ground Roast or Flaked Coffee, Instant High Point, Ivory Liquid.

2. Mail one of the above along with an Official Entry Form or plain piece of 3″ x 5″ paper on which you have handprinted your name and address. Mail your entry to: Sail For Savings Sweepstakes, P.O. Box 4036, Blair, NE 68009.

3. Retail ads submitted must be dated between August 1, 1982-September 30, 1982. Any printed retailer ad is acceptable — newspaper ads, in-store circulars, etc. You do not

need to send the complete retail ad — only that portion which shows the participating brand and the date is necessary.

4. Enter the Sail For Savings sweepstakes as often as you wish, but each entry must be mailed separately in a hand addressed envelope no larger than 4⅛″ x 9½″ (#10 envelope). Entries must be postmarked between August 3, 1982-October 14, 1982, and received by October 22, 1982.

5. Winners will be determined in a random drawing conducted by D.L. Blair, an independent judging organization, whose decisions are final. All prizes will be awarded, limit one prize per name and address. Winners will be notified and prizes delivered by mail by approximately December 31, 1982.

6. One (1) First Prize of a 13-day cruise for two on the luxury schooner Fantome plus $5,000 cash (approximate retail value $11,300.00); five (5) Second Prizes of 6-day cruises for two on The Flying Cloud (approximate retail value $3,200.00 per trip) and 2,000 Third Prizes of L.L. Bean Boat and Tote™ Bags (approximate retail value $10.00) will be awarded. The First and Second Prize winners will also receive transportation to and from Freeport, Bahamas where the cruises originate. The cruise package includes meals while on board. All cruises awarded as First or Second Prizes must be completed by September 1, 1983; dates of departure are subject to availability.

7. This sweepstakes is open to residents of the United States, eighteen years or older at time of entry, except employees of Procter & Gamble and their advertising, judging, and promotion agencies, and the families of each. Void via participation at retail stores in Wisconsin and wherever prohibited by law. All federal, state, and local laws and regulations apply. Taxes, if any, are the sole responsibility of the prize winner. The odds of winning a prize will depend upon the number of entries received by October 22, 1982. Limit one prize per name and address. No substitution for prizes.

8. For a list of prize winners, send a separate, stamped, self-addressed envelope to: Sail For Savings Sweepstakes Winners' List, P.O. Box 4151, Blair, NE 68009.

Form No. 664-6172 528HXM

EXHIBIT 18   H-80 National Sales Promotion Plan

	Timing					
Event	*January*	*February*	*March*	*April*	*May*	*June*
Stocking allowance $/Physical case						
Trade allowance $/Statistical case						

Sampling
  6 oz.
  3 oz.
  1.5 oz.
  2 × 0.75 oz.						

Couponing
  Mail
    Single
    Co-op
    Extended
  FSI
    Single
    Full page co-op
    2/5 page co-op
  BFD
  Magazine						

Special pack
  Price pack
  Bonus pack
  Trial size						

Refund
  Print
  Point of sale
  Direct mail
  In-/on-pack self
    Other						

Premium
  On-/in-pack
  Near-pack
  Free-in-mail
  Self-liquidator
  Partial liquidator
Group promotion						

		Timing				Number of Average Weeks Volume	Cost
July	*August*	*September*	*October*	*November*	*December*		

consumer was asked to pay a token sum. While near packs offered more flexibility in the size of the premium a manufacturer could choose, they were hard to control, as retailers often found it difficult to ensure that consumers made the purchases necessary to qualify to receive the premium.

A free-in-mail premium was mailed to the consumer when (s)he sent the company the purchase requirements. Such offers were easily executed but did not provide an immediate benefit to the consumer. Self-liquidating premiums were delivered through the mail much like free mail-ins, but the consumer was required to send money as well as one or more proofs-of-purchase to cover the cost of the premium, handling, and mailing. The cost of such premiums to the consumer was between 30 and 50% lower than the regular retail price. Response rates were, however, quite modest. Exhibit 16 presents a company fact sheet comparing typical premium costs.

Sweepstakes/Contests

P&G was scheduled to run a group promotion four months following the introduction of H-80. Company research had revealed that smaller brands achieved good results behind group promotions because of the high distribution and display support these offers stimulated among the trade. However, Garner wondered if a new brand might get lost among P&G's established brands. See Exhibit 17 for an example of an upcoming group promotion. Garner estimated the cost of participating in a group FSI sweepstakes promotion would be about $50,000 and that it would achieve about a 2 percent response rate for H-80. Most brands participating in an offer of this type would also include a coupon in the FSI advertisement for the sweepstakes.

Conclusion

As Garner prepared to write the details of H-80's Year 1 national promotion plan in the format shown in Exhibit 18, he considered several things. How should he split his promotion dollars between trade and consumer promotions during the first year? How much of his brand should he plan to sell to the trade on deal? What promotion events should he recommend? How many times should he promote H-80 in its first year? Was the Dawn plan strong enough to work in the more competitive LDL environment H-80 faced? Would he be able to gain more leverage with the trade if he promoted H-80 with the other LDLs or would this hurt his brand? Which potential overlaps with the other LDLs should he most try to avoid?

PART VI

Managing the Augmented Product

General Electric Company: Major Appliance Business Group (A)

Consumers seem to understand and like porcelain. Maybe we're foolish to think we can educate them to prefer our plastic. Besides, who's going to convince them? Our dealers?

Mr. Don Jones, manager of the General Electric (GE) Major Appliance Business Group's (MABG) Dishwasher and Disposal Marketing Department, was commenting in February 1980 on the Project C proposal.

This proposal, developed by a 13-member cross-functional team, called for a $28 million investment to overhaul GE's Louisville dishwasher assembly plant. A modern, robot-equipped, computer-controlled factory and a redesigned built-in dishwasher product line would be the most visible results of this investment. GE's existing midline and low-end built-in dishwashers with tub and door liners made of plastisol-coated steel would be replaced by a new design incorporating a proprietary plastic material known as PermaTuf.[1]

Jones and his department had been asked to evaluate the Project C proposal. He was expected to give a recommendation to the MABG Dishwasher and Disposal general manager in one week.

The MABG Organization

MAGB was the leading US manufacturer of major kitchen appliances. It produced GE and Hotpoint refrigerators, ranges, microwave ovens, and home laundry appliances as well as dishwashers and disposal units.

This case was prepared by Research Associate Neil Collins, under the supervision of Professor John A. Quelch, as a basis for class discussion rather than to illustrate either effective or ineffective handling of an administrative situation. Proprietary data have been disguised. Copyright © 1985 by the President and Fellows of Harvard College. Harvard Business School case 9–585–053.

[1] PermaTuf® and Potscrubber® are registered trademarks of General Electric Company.

MABG was headquartered in Louisville, Kentucky, a strong union town. Other MABG facilities included a plastics plant in Frankfort, Kentucky, and a dishwasher plant in Milwaukee, Wisconsin, which produced Hotpoint brand dishwashers with porcelain-coated metal interiors.

During the 1960s, GE overlaid a strategic business unit (SBU) structure on its existing hierarchy of groups, divisions, and departments. MABG was designated an SBU because its products all used similar raw materials and manufacturing processes, shared common distribution channels, and were affected by the same environmental trends. In 1977, GE's many SBUs were grouped into six industry sectors, each led by a sector executive. MABG became part of the Consumer Products Sector (CPS). In 1979, CPS contributed 23 percent of GE's $22 billion revenues and 28 percent of its earnings. With factory sales approaching $2 billion, MABG contributed approximately one-third of CPS revenues.

EXHIBIT 1   MABG Line Organization: 1979

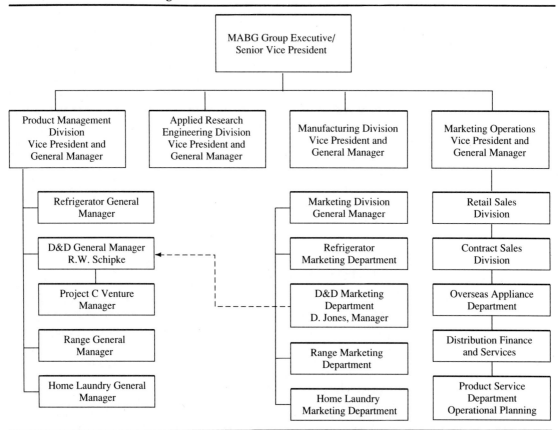

The MABG organization (Exhibit 1) comprised three major line functions: Applied Research and Engineering, Manufacturing, and Marketing Operations. Within each function, there were four general managers, each responsible for one of MABG's major product lines—refrigerators, dishwashers, ranges, and home laundry products. Each general manager reported in a matrix structure both to a functional vice president and to a general manager within the Product Management Division who had overall responsibility for his product line's business results.

The Product Management Division developed long-range (two years and beyond) strategies and priorities for each product category. Its managers were responsible for deciding which models should be in the product line. Performance evaluations were based on their achievement of sales, market share, and profit goals.

The Marketing Division within the Marketing Operations function, on the other hand, dealt with marketing issues that were more short term, implementation oriented, sales related, and local or regional in scope. The Marketing Division executives priced the product line, planned a national calendar of co-op advertising, and designed promotional programs to be implemented by the field sales force. They also assisted sales offices on specific problems. A secondary responsibility was to give Product Management their recommendations on the structure of the product line. The Marketing Operations function also included the MABG Sales Divisions, which handled all MABG products as well as GE's line of video products. The sales force was divided into two groups; the majority of salespeople dealt exclusively with retailers and the remainder with contractors. In 1979, GE estimated that 18,000 dealers in the US representing 25,000 outlets carried either the GE or Hotpoint product lines.[2]

MABG products were marketed under two brand names, GE and Hotpoint; Hotpoint had been acquired by GE in the 1920s. In recent years planning for the two brands had been entirely integrated. Hotpoint was viewed as the company's "value" brand while the GE brand served as the "quality" line. Price points overlapped, but the Hotpoint line was more strongly represented at lower- and middle-price points. Although differences between the two brands had become blurred over the years and Hotpoint models were sometimes featured lavishly, major feature innovations such as automatic icemaking for refrigerators were still introduced to the GE line a year or two before the Hotpoint line. In 1979, 72 percent of MABG built-in dishwasher unit sales were GE brand, 27 percent were Hotpoint, and 1 percent were private label (J. C. Penney). Retail sales of GE and Hotpoint dishwashers were distributed as follows:

---

[2] MABG sales executives estimated that this 25,000 amounted to 90 percent of US appliance outlets, excluding Sears Roebuck, which carried no GE appliances.

	GE	Hotpoint
	(Units %)	*(Units %)*
General merchandise chains	0%	0%
Appliance specialty stores	46	56
Department stores	9	6
Discount stores	25	15
Kitchen remodelers	13	8
Furniture stores	5	5
Home improvement centers	2	10

MABG limited retailers, most of whom stocked several brands, to carrying only one of the two MABG brands. Recently, however, this policy had been questioned by some MABG managers on the grounds that a second brand would permit MABG to command a greater share of its dealers' floor space.

The MABG Dishwasher Business in the 1970s

MABG management viewed its dishwasher business as a problem in the early 1970s, despite market shares exceeding 20 percent in the retail channel and 30 percent in the contract channel, and generally strong financial performance. While GE was producing refrigerators and ranges of premium quality, management believed that consumers viewed its dishwashers as merely adequate machines of medium quality. Survey research with consumers and dealers conducted during this period confirmed this belief.

Many GE dishwashers were built differently from most competitive models during the 1970s. Whereas most dishwasher tubs and door liners were constructed of a porcelain-coated steel composite, many GE tubs and door liners were built of steel coated with a thin layer of plastic compound known as plastisol. Plastisol, unlike other coatings, was susceptible to scrapes and scratches from dropped cutlery, and surface lesions were aggravated by dishwasher detergents. Once scratched, the exposed steel tended to rust. Rust was unsightly and shortened the life of the machine. While porcelain-coated tubs were not immune from rust problems, the incidence was lower.

A further problem with GE's dishwashers was that they were excessively noisy. Finally, GE dishwashers were criticized as heavy water users. This translated into excessive energy use, an increasingly sensitive issue in 1973 when fuel costs doubled.

At the same time, GE shared the cost leadership position among dishwasher producers, along with Design & Manufacturing, Inc. (D&M),

a large supplier of private label dishwashers. GE's cost advantage over most competitors in dishwashers, coupled with its cost parity on other kitchen appliances, enabled GE to compete effectively in supplying full-line kitchen appliance packages to contractors. Partly because of its importance to GE's continued success in the contract market, MABG managers resolved to upgrade GE's dishwasher line.

This commitment was also due to the sales growth forecast for dishwashers. In the late 1960s, over 70 percent of dishwashers were sold through the contract channel. As dishwasher household penetration increased, a growing percentage was sold through the retail channel and replacement buyers accounted for an increasing percentage of retail sales. With the benefit of product knowledge, these consumers often held strong brand preferences and specific ideas about features to be sought or avoided.

MABG executives were not optimistic about their ability to serve the growing replacement market with products perceived as noisier, costlier to operate, and less durable than those of competitors.

PermaTuf A

In 1971, MABG design engineers proposed a new tub and door liner made of a GE proprietary plastic compound of unusual strength, named Perma-Tuf. This A design provided several benefits. First, the use of all-plastic tubs and door liners completely eliminated rust problems. Laboratory-simulated "life-cycle" testing convinced project engineers that a 10-year warranty against failure of the tub and door liner could be offered. In addition, the improved reliability of the new machines was projected to save $2 per unit in the cost of covering the existing standard one-year parts and labor warranty. Second, tests showed that the plastic tub reduced operating noise by 10–15 percent relative to plastisol models. Third, the full cost of a PermaTuf dishwasher was less than a similarly featured plastisol machine. Accounting for these savings were lower labor, material, transportation (PermaTuf models weighed less), scrap and rework, and first-year warranty costs. These savings were only partially offset by higher equipment depreciation costs and the cost of covering the proposed 10-year tub warranty.

In December 1971, the GE board of directors authorized a $17 million investment to convert a major portion of the Louisville dishwasher plant to manufacture all GE brand dishwashers with PermaTuf. The scheduled completion date was September 1975. Projected annual volume of Perma-Tuf dishwashers was 750,000 units.

Unfortunately, technical difficulties combined with reduced sales during the 1974 recession resulted in a decision to reduce the scope of the project. Actual investment, principally in molds, was $13.5 million.

The scaled-down project focused on developing a top-of-the-line model. This model, the General Electric GSD 1050, was introduced in October 1976 under pressure to deliver good fourth-quarter sales figures. The usual in-home test phase was omitted. The sales force was instructed to achieve a strong sell-in of the new model. Brochures explaining the tub and its benefits to both dealers and consumers were created and distributed.

The sell-in was a success; 28,000 GSD 1050s were ordered by dealers during the fourth quarter. Unfortunately, problems developed once these new models were installed in consumer homes. These problems would have been detected if the usual in-home test procedures had been followed. As a result of the problems, sales of the GSD 1050 were halted.

The PermaTuf B Project

Once the problems of the A design were understood, an additional $4 million in funds was approved for the development of new, redesigned PermaTuf dishwasher models. The PermaTuf B design effort focused from the start on the upper end of the dishwasher market. The unit cost target, improved durability, and reduced noise were again achieved.

New features were added to the PermaTuf B models to appeal to the replacement buyer. First, wash performance was improved by introducing a self-cleaning bypass filter and a wash arm (called a multiorbit spray arm), which changed the water spray pattern with each revolution. A new upper rack with increased capacity and improved appearance was added. Finally, a redesigned tub bottom contour permitted a significant reduction in water and energy usage.

This B design was applied to the three top models in the GE brand line (GSD 1200, GSD 1000, and GSD 900). Extensive performance and reliability testing made the project design team confident of the new models' superiority over previous GE models and current competition. However, after the problems with the A model, neither GE salespeople nor dealers were eager to push three new models using the same radical tub and door material and similar design principles. Many salespeople also questioned whether GE ought to be trying to place so many models in the upper price band. They believed that most dealers were satisfied with the KitchenAid and Maytag models they already carried in that price range.

As a result of sales force and trade resistance, sales of the new B models during 1978 were 40 percent below projections. PermaTuf models accounted for 20 percent of the mix of GE built-in dishwasher models sold through the retail channel in 1978. This percentage rose to 31 percent in 1979, but B model unit sales were still 30 percent below plan. Sales of other GE models were 17 percent below plan.

EXHIBIT 2   **MABG Dishwasher Performance Data**

	1975	1976	1977	1978	1979
Market share ($ basis)	24%	24%	25%	25%	26%
Sales (000s)	$138,726	$168,190	$194,168	$220,407	$235,078
Price index	87.9	92.2	95.8	100.0	103.5
Net income (000)	$2,913	$3,700	$4,466	$6,171	$7,522
Return on sales	2.1%	2.2%	2.3%	2.8%	3.2%
Return on investment	6.1%	7.9%	8.0%*	12.5%	15.5%

* An increase in dollar investment in 1977 was partly due to LIFO accounting adjustments and partly due to a $4 million investment in the PermaTuf B design.

SOURCE: Company records.

The GE Brand Dishwasher Business: 1979

During 1979, MABG dishwasher sales and market share were higher than at any time in the 1970s (Exhibit 2). The 1979 GE line of built-in dishwashers consisted of seven models. Exhibit 3 summarizes these models' features, costs, prices, sales by channel, and strategic roles within the line.

The three PermaTuf B models, the GSD 1200, GSD 1000, and GSD 900, were prominently labeled Potscrubber III, while the GSD 750, GSD 650, and GSD 551 carried the name Potscrubber in addition to the GE brand name and their model numbers.[3] The Potscrubber name had been applied to GE dishwashers since 1972 when a new cycle was developed with an extended main wash period and water temperature booster. Laboratory tests showed this cycle to be effective at cleaning pots and pans with baked-on food. Fifty-two percent of respondents to a 1979 telephone survey showed aided awareness of the Potscrubber name. Thirty percent of respondents linked the Potscrubber name to GE, 15 percent linked it to other brands, and 55 percent did not know. Thirty-two percent expressed the belief that Potscrubber dishwashers were above average in quality, and 35 percent considered them technologically advanced. Because of these findings, MABG management believed the Potscrubber name augmented the quality image of GE dishwashers, and decided to retain it on all models incorporating that cycle for the foreseeable future.

---

[3] Potscrubber III and Potscrubber dishwashers incorporated the same Potscrubber cycle. The Potscrubber III name was simply reserved for PermaTuf design models.

EXHIBIT 3 General Electric 1979 Dishwasher Line

				Models			
Attributes	GSD 1200	GSD 1000	GSD 900	GSD 650 (750)	GSD 551	GSD 400	GSD 390
Approximate retail price	$479	$419	$349	$319	$299	$269	$249
GE net realized factory prices:							
Retail	$360	$325	$281	$237	$220	$195	$185
Contract	368	346	310	253	205	174	172
Full production cost	$194	$174	$168	$143	$134	$127	$117
1979 units sold (000s)							
Retail	12.0	17.5	33.9	56.2	44.4	19.4	22.3
Contract (90% of total units)	4.9	8.0	6.5	0.5	68.6	122.6	140.8
Design	PermaTuf B	PermaTuf B	PermaTuf B	Plastisol	Plastisol	Plastisol	Plastisol
Features:							
No. of cycles	12	9	5	8	6	4	2
Power scrub	0	0	0	0	0		
Normal–heavy soil	0	0					
Normal–reg. soil	0	0	0	0			
Hot water usage in gallons	(10.3)	(10.3)	(10.3)	(11.4)	(11.4)	(11.4)	(11.4)
Normal–energy saver wash	0						
China and crystal	0						
Short wash				0			
Plate warmer				0			
Cancel reset	0						
Rinse and hold	0	0	0	0			
Energy-saver drying	0	0	0	0	0	0	
Wash levels	3	3	3	3	2	2	2
Hi-performance wash system (self-cleaning filter and multiorbit spray arm)	0	0	0	3	2	2	2
Rinse aid dispenser	0	0	0	0	0		
Racks	Super	Super	Deep	Deep	Standard	Standard	Standard
Reversible color door panels	5 color	5 color	5 color	4 color			
Strategic position in GE line	High-end	High-end	Midline	Midline	Contract step up	Low-end	Contract volume

SOURCE: GE company records.

In 1979, GE attempted to maintain higher dealer margins than its competitors on dishwashers at comparable retail price points, particularly in the premium quality segment where GE's market share was traditionally weakest. MABG strategists believed the dealer had to be motivated to invest the extra effort needed to convince a customer to buy GE rather than KitchenAid. Due to its strong premium image, KitchenAid was usually an easier sale. GE dealer margins on PermaTuf models were believed to average 25–30 percent, while KitchenAid's were believed to average 15–18 percent.

GE offered its dealers a strategy for selling the line. It recommended that the dealer first show dishwasher prospects the top-of-line GSD 1200 model to educate them about GE's high quality and technical leadership. If price resistance was communicated by the customer, the salesperson was to show progressively lower priced GE models. As each successive model was shown, GE recommended that the salesperson point out exactly which features from the prior model had to be sacrificed to gain the price savings. By following this orderly approach, GE argued that salespeople would avoid confusing their prospects. Feeling more confident about his or her understanding of product features and options, the prospect was thought to be more likely to make a purchase.

In 1979 GE decided to deemphasize its line of portable dishwashers because portables represented a declining share of the dishwasher category. Accordingly, it raised prices on portables more aggressively, recognizing this would result in a loss of dealer floor space and market share.

GE dishwasher manufacturing capacity for 1980 was unchanged from 1979. In both years capacity figures were:

Louisville	700,000 units (GE brand)
Milwaukee	215,000 units (Hotpoint and private label)
	915,000

Portable capacity and built-in unit capacity were interchangeable. Capacity estimates were based on a two-shift, five-day work week and 45.5 effective production weeks per year.

Consumer Research

Given the work being done on the PermaTuf B design, Mr. Roger Schipke, the Dishwasher and Disposal general manager, decided to evaluate consumer attitudes toward alternative tub and door liner materials. MABG's market research team conducted a mall intercept survey with 458 female heads of household who owned dishwashers. The sample was drawn in roughly equal numbers from Detroit, Los Angeles, and northern New Jersey. The specific objectives of the study were to assess:

1. Consumer preferences for five types of tub materials, with and without retail price information.
2. The price premiums (if any) that consumers were willing to pay for their preferred tub material.
3. The influence of a possible 10-year PermaTuf warranty on consumer preferences.

The five tub materials compared were plastisol (plastic-coated steel), PermaTuf plastic, porcelain-coated steel, stainless steel, and epoxy-coated steel. Exhibit 4 presents key findings from this study.

The Project C Proposal

In the fall of 1979, after two years of dedicated effort, the 13-member Project C team, including representatives from MABG's manufacturing, marketing, engineering, and finance functions, finalized a proposal calling for fundamental changes to the GE built-in dishwasher line and a new state-of-art, robot-equipped production process.

EXHIBIT 4   Consumer Dishwasher Tub Material Attitude Survey

1. Current Brand Ownership within Sample Group (N = 458)

Brand	Ownership (%)
GE	22%
KitchenAid	18
Sears	19
Hotpoint	8
Waste King	7
Whirlpool	6
Frigidaire	4
Other brands	16
Total	100%

2. Current Tub Material × Current Brand*

Tub Material**	Total	GE	KitchenAid	Sears	Other
Base	(458)	(100)	(84)	(85)	(189)
Vinyl-coated steel	10%	16%	6%	8%	9%
Solid plastic	12	26	2	8	10
Porcelain	55	40	76	58	51
Stainless steel	5	1	1	4	10
Don't recall	19	17	14	22	21
Total	100%	100%	100%	100%	100%

* Responses are based on recall and are not always accurate. For example, 51% of those reporting they had solid plastic tubs said they owned brands other than GE, despite the fact that GE was the only manufacturer employing them.
** Vinyl-coated steel was the same as plastisol. Only GE Permatuf models had solid plastic tubs. Only the Thermidor brand used stainless steel tubs.

EXHIBIT 4 *continued*

3. Percent of Sample Reporting Tub/Door Material Problems

By Material:

Current Tub Material	Number Reporting That They Owned This Type of Tub Material	Percent with This Material Reporting Problem
All materials	(458)	16%
Vinyl-coated steel	(44)	30
Solid plastic	(53)	15
Porcelain	(250)	14
Stainless steel	(24)	4
Don't recall	(87)	20

By Brand:

Current Brand	Number Having Each Brand	Percent with This Brand Reporting Problem
All brands	(458)	16%
GE	(100)	19
Sears	(85)	11
KitchenAid	(84)	8
Hotpoint	(37)	19
Waste King	(32)	12
Whirlpool	(26)	15
Frigidaire	(18)	11
Other brands	(64)	22

4. Features in Current Dishwashers vs. Features Sought in Next Dishwasher Purchase

Features	Current Dishwasher	Expect to Buy on Next Dishwasher
	(458)	(458)
Sound insulation for quiet operation	37%	80%
Power saver for natural drying	21	76
Long wash for baked-on food	47	74
Adjustable upper rack	31	71
Rinse and hold	75	69
Short wash for light soil	63	66
High temperature (sanitizing)	56	63
China and crystal cycle	26	51

5. Intended Brand of Next Dishwasher Purchase vs. Current Brand Owned

Brand Would Buy Next	Total	Current Brand GE	KitchenAid	Sears	Other
GE	13%	47%	—	6%	3%
KitchenAid	38	21	85	26	32
Sears	11	3	—	42	6
Maytag	6	6	4	6	8
Whirlpool	6	5	1	1	10
All other	10	6	—	2	21
Don't know	16	12	11	17	20
	100%	100%	100%	100%	100%

EXHIBIT 4 *continued*

6. Consumers Unaided Preferences for Five Alternative Tub Materials

Tub Material Ratings—Unaided

	Plastisol (458)	PermaTuf (458)	Porcelain (458)	Epoxy (458)	Stainless (458)
5 (most likely to buy)	11%	5%	24%	17%	42%
4	22	10	33	25	11
3	22	18	19	30	10
2	25	28	15	22	10
1 (least likely to buy)	20	39	8	6	28
	100%	100%	100%	100%	100%

7. Aided Consumer Preferences for the Same Five Tub Materials*

Tub Material Ratings—Aided

	Plastisol ($260)	PermaTuf ($260)	PermaTuf +10 Yr. Warranty ($270)	Porcelain ($260)	Epoxy ($260)	Stainless ($335)
6 (most likely to buy)	7%	3%	47%	16%	4%	24%
5	9	37	20	12	9	12
4	24	19	11	13	24	10
3	21	13	12	18	32	5
2	15	18	8	30	23	6
1 (least likely to buy)	25	10	2	11	8	43
	101%	100%	100%	100%	100%	100%

* Aided: After consumers were briefed with information on relative prices and specific material strengths and weaknesses. Responses reflect the same base of 458 consumers.

8. Aided Consumer Preferences for Other Materials over Plastisol

Plastisol Is $260— Other Material is:	PermaTuf over Plastisol	PermaTuf +10-Year Warranty over Plastisol	Porcelain over Plastisol	Epoxy over Plastisol	Stainless Steel over Plastisol
	(458)	(458)	(458)	(458)	(458)
Same Price	71%	78%	54%	48%	53%
$10 more	69	75	52	43	NT*
$20 more	63	68	45	36	NT
$25 more	NT	NT	NT	NT	48
$30 more	48	56	37	29	NT
$40 more	43	50	31	24	NT
$50 more	NT	NT	NT	NT	37
$75 more	NT	NT	NT	NT	26
$100 more	NT	NT	NT	NT	20

* NT = Not tested.

EXHIBIT 4 *concluded*

---

9. Attitudes Toward Plastic by Current Brand Ownership (%)

	Total	GE	KitchenAid	Sears	Other
Plastic materials and parts in a product mean "cheap" to me and I am more careful before I buy.	36%	29%	45%	38%	35%
Plastics have improved tremendously over the past 10–15 years. I am exposed to so many plastic products and parts that I don't even pay attention.	25	44	16	24	21
I depend on the reputation of the manufacturers and their integrity. When they use plastic, I assume it is an acceptable substitute for a higher-cost material.	47	46	38	47	52
I resist buying products—particularly higher-priced ones—that are made from plastic or have a high percentage of plastic parts in them.	41	32	54	37	43

The plan was to use a third-generation PermaTuf-based design in new models which would replace GE brand's current medium- and lower-priced dishwashers. The design objectives of the plan were:

1. To replace plastisol tubs with PermaTuf tubs throughout the GE line and to offer thereby a more durable product which would increase the actual and perceived quality of GE dishwashers.

2. To implement a quality improvement program in concert with product line and manufacturing process changes. Improved quality was to be derived primarily from gains in assembly uniformity through automation, through requiring closer tolerances on both externally supplied components and internal assembly/fabrication work, and through raising concern for quality among management and workers.

3. To achieve cost reductions in the following areas:

Per Unit Savings over the Plastisol Design

a. Product costs including $8.52
  - Material costs
  - Labor costs (achieved through automation and less material handling)
  - Scrap and rework (due to improved production quality)

   • Energy (more efficient new
    assembly equipment)
  b. Outbound transportation (finished   .91
    unit would weigh 12 lbs. less than
    current plastisol models)
  c. Service call reduction (3.5 fewer   2.00
    calls per 100 machines installed
    during first year of ownership)
    and reduced concessions to
    owners (result of quality
    improvements)

These reductions, totaling $11.43, would be offset, in part, by the additional cost of providing a 10-year tub and door-liner warranty on all PermaTuf models, leaving $9.43 in net savings per unit.

The PermaTuf C design did not incorporate the B design's advanced wash system features, the multiorbit spray arm, and self-cleaning filter. These omissions saved $11 per unit relative to the B design.

Under the proposal, the PermaTuf C models would be introduced in phases during 1983. By 1985, the upper-end PermaTuf B models would be converted to the C design but their advanced wash system features would be retained. Production of portable units would be moved in 1982 to the MABG Milwaukee plant where the porcelain-based Hotpoint line would continue to be produced. There was a $7 per unit production cost penalty associated with moving portable production to Milwaukee.

The required investment to implement Project C was estimated at $28 million, of which $1.9 million had already been spent on the development of prototype models and experimentation with advanced assembly techniques. This new investment was similar to the depreciated value of the existing dishwasher plant.

EXHIBIT 5   Project C Market Share Impact

Year	Retail Market Size Units (000s)	Incremental Retail Market Share (%)	Incremental GE Unit Volume (000s)	Average GE Unit Contribution Margin plus Project C Mfg. Cost Reduction	Incremental Contribution ($000s)
1983	1,525	0.4%	6.1	$115.73	$ 706
1984	1,650	0.8	13.2	131.82	1,740
1985	1,810	1.1	19.9	145.54	2,896
1986	2,000	1.2	24.0	161.37	3,873
1987	2,000	1.2	24.0	178.37	4,281
1988	2,000	1.2	24.0	198.01	4,752
1989	2,000	1.2	24.0	219.16	5,260
Total					$23,508

SOURCE: Company records.

The Project C team believed that the change to a full PermaTuf line would result in incremental retail market share for GE from 1983 on. The team projected a 1983 incremental retail market share of 0.4 percent rising to 2.0 percent by 1989. Due to the capacity limits of the proposed facility projected at 1.02 million units in 1985, the incremental market share would be capped at 1.2 percent in 1986. In forecasting industry sales, the team assumed incremental household penetration resulting in a 5 percent average annual unit growth from 1973. The US built-in dishwasher market size was, therefore, projected to be 4.7 million units in 1986, 47 percent sold at retail and 53 percent sold through the contract channel. The incremental contribution from the additional retail market share was calculated at $23.5 million through 1989, as indicated in Exhibit 5.

According to the team's most probable scenario, the project promised product cost savings of $75 million by 1989 and an internal rate of return (IRR) of 25 percent. Supporting cost savings and cash flow analyses are shown in Exhibits 6 and 7.

The proposal also included low- and high-side risk analyses. The low-side scenario assumed 10 percent higher investment, tooling, and expense (ITE) outlays, 10 percent lower cost savings, and no incremental market share impact. The result was an IRR of 15 percent. The high-side analysis assumed 10 percent lower ITE expenditures and 10 percent greater product cost savings. Incremental market share was the same as in the most probable case. This scenario resulted in a 30 percent IRR.

Concerns about Project C

Despite the enthusiasm and hard work of the Project C team, MABG managers in the Marketing Operations, Retail Sales, and Contract Sales divisions had several outstanding concerns about the plan:

1. Some argued that it was fruitless to promote as premium products dishwashers which were not built with porcelain tubs and door liners, the industry standard. Research indicated that consumer and dealer confidence in porcelain was too solidly entrenched. These managers argued that GE ought to offer porcelain tubs in its high-end models. Differentiation from KitchenAid could be achieved through better washability, better energy conservation, or additional features. This group also pointed to the problems with GE's PermaTuf A model as an important obstacle to educating consumers about PermaTuf C's premium qualities. Further, competitor sales forces could be counted on to try to discredit PermaTuf.

2. Other MABG managers held that PermaTuf was "too good" to use throughout the entire product line. They argued that GE's

existing line of three high-end PermaTuf models and four lower-priced plastisol models helped retailers to trade up consumers to one of the more expensive models. On the other hand, bringing the main benefit of GE's premium models—its innovative, durable, scratch-resistant, rust-free tub material—to the rest of the line would encourage consumers to trade down. The consequent lost contribution might more than offset all of the project's forecasted financial benefits.

3. Some contended that tub material was irrelevant to consumers and that substantial improvements in product quality could be achieved at one-quarter the cost of Project C with the existing mix of tub designs.

4. Some MABG managers were reluctant to stake the future of the entire GE line on PermaTuf out of fear that a competitor might source off-shore cheap plastic tubs which would crack and leak in use. The result would then be word-of-mouth disparagement of all dishwashers with plastic tubs including GE's superior product.

5. Because of the petroleum price rises of 1973 and 1979, there were concerns about the advisability of shifting to plastic raw materials. Project C planners estimated that it would take a 60 percent increase in petroleum prices to offset the $2 per unit material cost savings of the PermaTuf C dishwasher compared to the plastisol design.

6. Many objected to the idea of investing $28 million in incremental funds for a modern computer-run plant in Louisville. The loss of jobs associated with moving portable production to Milwaukee and automating the Louisville plant was thought unlikely to be accepted readily by the Louisville unions. Some argued that the $28 million would be better spent in a location less tightly controlled by labor unions such as MABG's production facility in Columbia, Maryland.

7. Some MABG managers believed that the dishwasher market was too small and its growth prospects too poor to justify a $28 million investment. One manager suggested that this money could be better invested in MABG's refrigerator factory. Proponents of Project C countered by arguing that successful implementation of this dishwasher improvement program would demonstrate to GE's corporate office the financial benefit of investing in appliance facility modernization generally, and thereby pave the way for a future refrigerator project.

With all of these issues competing for his attention, Jones sat down to consider again the recommendation he would make on Project C.

EXHIBIT 6 **Project C Most Probable Case Product Cost Savings Summary**

	1982	1983	1984	1985	1986	1987	1988	1989	Total
Volume (000s)									
Plastisol to PermaTuf C	—	300	690	761	866	866	866	866	5215
PermaTuf B to PermaTuf C	—	—	—	80	173	173	173	173	772
Portables to Milwaukee	50	50	50	50	50	50	50	50	400
Cost Improvement per Unit: PermaTuf C vs. Plastisol									
Material, scrap and rework	—	$5.22	$5.63	$6.08	$6.57	$7.10	$7.66	$8.28	
Labor, other	—	3.30	3.56	3.84	4.15	4.48	4.84	5.23	
Outbound transportation*	—	.91	.98	1.06	1.14	1.23	1.33	1.44	
Ten-year tub and door warranty**	—	(2.00)	(2.00)	(2.00)	(2.00)	(2.00)	(2.00)	(2.00)	
Service call reduction, concessions	—	2.00	2.16	2.33	2.52	2.72	2.93	3.17	
Total	—	9.43	10.33	11.31	12.38	13.53	14.76	16.12	
Cost Improvement per Unit PermaTuf C vs. B									
Material, scrap and rework	—	—	—	$5.30	$5.73	$6.19	$6.68	$7.22	
Labor	—	—	—	2.51	2.71	2.93	3.16	3.42	
Overhead, other	—	—	—	1.31	1.42	1.53	1.65	1.78	
Outbound transportation*	—	—	—	2.64	2.86	3.08	3.33	3.60	
Total	—	—	—	11.76	12.72	13.73	14.82	16.02	
Portable Cost Penalty	$(7.00)	$(7.00)	$(7.00)	$(7.00)	$(7.00)	$(7.00)	$(7.00)	$(7.00)	
Savings (000s)									
Material, scrap and rework	—	$1,566	$3,885	$5,051	$ 6,681	$ 7,219	$ 7,789	$ 8,420	$40,611
Labor, other	—	990	2,456	3,123	4,063	4,387	4,738	5,121	24,878
Overhead, other	—	—	—	105	246	265	285	308	1,209
Outbound transportation	—	273	676	1,018	1,482	1,598	1,728	1,870	8,645
Warranty	—	(600)	(1,380)	(1,522)	(1,732)	(1,732)	(1,732)	(1,732)	(10,430)
Service call reduction, concessions	—	600	1,490	1,773	2,182	2,356	2,537	2,745	13,683
Portable cost penalty	(350)	(350)	(350)	(350)	(350)	(350)	(350)	(350)	(2,800)
Total	$(350)	$2,479	$6,777	$9,198	$12,572	$13,743	$14,995	$16,382	$75,796

NOTE: A factor of 8% per year has been used to escalate product cost savings per unit.

* PermaTuf C weighs 8 pounds less than the plastisol unit and 20 pounds less than PermaTuf B.

** Represents same accrual now in effect on all PermaTuf B dishwashers.

SOURCE: Company records.

EXHIBIT 7 Project C Most Probable Case—Income and Cash Flow Analysis ($ in 000s), Favorable/(Unfavorable)

Incremental Net Income	1979	1980	1981	1982	1983	1984	1985	1986	1987	1988	1989	Total
Market share impact	$—	$—	$—	$—	$706	$1,740	$2,896	$3,873	$4,281	$4,752	$5,260	$23,508
Product cost savings	—	—	—	(350)	2,479	6,777	9,198	12,572	13,743	14,995	16,382	75,796
Implementation costs												
Investment related expense	(21)	(232)	(324)	(4,412)	(1,261)	(701)	(39)	—	—	—	—	(6,990)
Depreciation	—	(1)	(2)	(839)	(2,071)	(2,183)	(2,022)	(1,999)	(1,800)	(1,780)	(1,776)	(14,473)
Start-up	—	—	(10)	(170)	(490)	(330)	—	—	—	—	—	(1,000)
Maintenance of equipment	—	—	—	—	50	50	50	50	50	50	50	350
Total	(21)	(233)	(336)	(5,421)	(3,772)	(3,164)	(2,011)	(1,949)	(1,750)	(1,730)	(1,726)	(22,113)
Income/(loss) before tax	(21)	(233)	(336)	(5,771)	(587)	5,353	10,083	14,496	16,274	18,017	19,916	77,191
Federal tax (46%)	10	107	155	2,655	270	(2,462)	(4,638)	(6,668)	(7,486)	(8,288)	(9,161)	(35,506)
Investment credit (10%)	1	—	16	1,972	195	36	0	0	0	0	0	2,220
Net income/(loss)	$(10)	$(126)	$(165)	$(1,144)	$(122)	$2,927	$5,445	$7,828	$8,788	$9,729	$10,755	$43,905
Cash Flow—Current Year												
Net income/(loss)	$(10)	$(126)	$(165)	$(1,144)	$(122)	$2,927	$5,445	$7,828	$8,788	$9,729	$10,755	$43,905
Depreciation	—	1	2	839	2,071	2,183	2,022	1,999	1,800	1,780	1,776	14,473
Plant and equipment	(10)	(4)	(163)	(19,719)	(1,950)	(354)	—	—	—	—	—	(22,200)
Finished goods/WIP inventory	—	—	—	—	60	750	190	50	50	50	50	1,200
Warranty reserve	—	—	—	—	172	535	754	736	694	566	430	3,887
Deferred taxes on reserve	—	—	—	—	(79)	(246)	(347)	(339)	(319)	(260)	(198)	(1,788)
Total	$(20)	$(129)	$(326)	(20,024)	$152	$5,795	$8,064	$10,274	$11,013	$11,865	$12,813	$39,477
Cumulative Cash Flow	$(20)	$(149)	$(475)	$(20,499)	$(20,347)	$(14,552)	$(6,488)	$3,789	$14,802	$26,667	$39,477	$39,477

SOURCE: Company records.

Ford Motor Company: The Product Warranty Program (A)

On Friday, January 23, 1987, Ford Motor Company executives, in a special meeting, held a lengthy discussion about warranty program alternatives. The meeting was organized to identify the best possible response to General Motors' (GM) change in its warranty policy. At a press conference the previous day, GM had announced improved warranty coverage to back its contention that the quality of its cars had reached an unprecedented high. Industry analysts expected the new warranty to increase GM's market share.

The Ford executives—from various departments such as marketing, sales, manufacturing, product quality assurance, engineering, after-sales service, parts, warranty, and extended service plans—considered several warranty program alternatives and had to make recommendations to Donald E. Petersen, Ford's chairman of the board and chief executive officer.

The US Car Market

Two important external events—the oil shocks of the 1970s and the US economic recession—had both sent the US car market into a sharp depression in the early 1980s. New-car sales declined dramatically, from 11.3 million units in 1978 to 8 million in 1982. In addition, foreign competitors were rapidly gaining market share (see Exhibit 1). Profitability of the four US manufacturers—Ford, GM, Chrysler Corporation, and American Motors Corporation (AMC)—had also fallen sharply to an aggregate loss of $1.8 billion per year during 1980–1982.

In 1983, however, the industry began a swift recovery that industry analysts attributed to increased efficiency, quality, and commitment. By 1986, sales of new cars had reached a record level, and the aggregate

Professor Melvyn A. J. Menezes prepared this case as the basis for class discussion rather than to illustrate either effective or ineffective handling of an administrative situation. Certain information has been disguised. Copyright © 1988 by the President and Fellows of Harvard College. Harvard Business School case 9–589–001.

EXHIBIT 1   US New-Car Production, Sales, and Market Shares (millions of units)

| | | Retail Sales | | | | |
| | | Domestic | | Imports | | |
Year	*Domestic Production Units*	*Units*	*% of Total*	*Units*	*% of Total*	*Total Units*
1973	9.7	9.7	85.1%	1.7	14.9%	11.4
1974	7.3	7.4	84.1	1.4	15.9	8.8
1975	6.7	7.0	81.4	1.6	18.6	8.6
1976	8.5	8.6	85.1	1.5	14.9	10.1
1977	9.2	9.1	81.3	2.1	18.7	11.2
1978	9.2	9.3	82.3	2.0	17.7	11.3
1979	8.4	8.3	78.3	2.3	21.7	10.6
1980	6.4	6.6	73.3	2.4	26.7	9.0
1981	6.3	6.2	72.9	2.3	27.1	8.5
1982	5.1	5.8	72.5	2.2	27.5	8.0
1983	6.8	6.8	73.9	2.4	26.1	9.2
1984	7.8	8.0	76.9	2.4	23.1	10.4
1985	8.2	8.2	74.5	2.8	25.5	11.0
1986	7.8	8.2	71.3%	3.3	28.7%	11.5

SOURCE: Ward's Automotive Yearbook, various years.

profit of the four US automakers was $7.5 billion. The domestic share of the US car market, however, reached an all-time low, while imported car sales and market share were both at record high levels in 1986 (see Exhibit 1).[1] Japanese import sales remained strong, despite Japan's continuation of voluntary restraints and the rise in the yen's value vis-à-vis the US dollar. The Japanese automakers had moved up into the middle of the market with new, more upscale models that sold well. New models from Korea and Eastern Europe also helped to bolster import sales.

The US car market was mature, global, high-technology, intensely competitive, and largely a replacement market. It was divided into five broad categories based on car size (see Exhibit 2). Stabilized fuel prices and the popularity of Ford's new Taurus and Sable models accounted for the intermediate category's success.

Outlook

For 1987, the forecast for new-car sales in the United States was 10.4 million units, 9 percent below the 1986 sales level. The predicted drop in sales was partly a result of the 1986 year-end sales boost, as buyers hurried to take advantage of sales-tax deductions that were to be phased

---

[1] Domestic cars refers to cars built in the United States by the four US automakers and three non-US manufacturers (Honda Motor Company, Nissan Motor Corporation, and Volkswagen of America). Imported cars refers to cars sold in the United States but built elsewhere.

EXHIBIT 2   US Domestic Car Sales and Market Share by Size Category

	Subcompact	Compact	Intermediate	Full-Size	Luxury	Overall
1985 unit sales	1,296,701	2,562,588	2,463,556	1,077,308	804,389	8,204,542
1985 share of industry	15.8%	31.2%	30.0%	13.2%	9.8%	100.0%
1986 unit sales	1,325,325	2,461,192	2,540,491	1,115,789	772,091	8,214,888
1986 share of industry	16.1%	30.0%	30.9%	13.6%	9.4%	100.0%
1987 unit sales*	1,150,000	2,300,000	2,200,000	940,000	650,000	7,240,000
1987 share of industry*	15.9%	31.7%	30.4%	13.0%	9.0%	100.0%
Breakdown of 1987 Sales by Competitor						
Ford	35.7%	20.9%	25.9%	23.1%	23.0%	25.3%
General Motors	25.0	51.8	64.0	62.7	77.0	55.1
Chrysler	22.5	18.7	9.8	14.2	—	14.2
American Motors	5.0	—	0.3	—	—	0.9
Volkswagen	5.5	—	—	—	—	0.9
Nissan	4.0	—	—	—	—	0.6
Honda	2.3	8.6	—	—	—	3.0
	100.0%	100.0%	100.0%	100.0%	100.0%	100.0%

* Expected.

out in 1987. The domestic automakers' sales were expected to decline by 12 percent, while the market share of imported cars was expected to rise. The challenges facing US automakers included:

1. Increased competition from cars produced in countries new to the US market (e.g., Korea and Yugoslavia).
2. The growing array of higher-priced imported models.
3. Intensified price competition as new entrants sought their share of a mature market.
4. The anticipated increased production of cars produced in the United States by foreign companies.
5. Substantial overcapacity, both in the United States and abroad.

In addition, US domestic car production was coming under increased pressure. In 1986, domestic production declined 4.8 percent from its 1985 level, even though sales increased 4.5 percent; record sales did not mean record production. Several foreign automobile manufacturers announced plans to build new production capacity in the United States, and output from these plants was projected to grow from 400,000 units in 1986 to between 1.5 and 2 million by 1990.

Domestic manufacturers prepared by increasing their efforts to achieve a slimmer work force, higher productivity, more efficiency, and leaner managerial staffs. They instituted massive capital expenditure programs for upgrading and building new plants as well as installing robots and other state-of-the-art, labor-saving equipment. Computer-aided design of new models contributed to parts standardization and cost control. The increased adoption of just-in-time delivery systems for components and supplies reduced inventory and operating expenses.

Company Background

Founded by Henry Ford in 1903 and headquartered at Dearborn, Michigan, Ford Motor Company grew rapidly into a worldwide leader in automotive and automotive-related products and services. By 1986, Ford was one of the world's largest manufacturing enterprises, was the world's second-largest automaker, and was America's third-largest industrial corporation with 382,300 employees. In 1986, both sales ($62.7 billion) and net income ($3.3 billion) were the highest in the company's history, and Ford's profits topped GM's for the first time since 1924. In the US market, Ford's 1986 sales and net income were $50 billion and $2.5 billion, respectively—up 14.9 percent and 23.6 percent, respectively, from the previous year. This was a spectacular turnaround from its poor 1980–1982 performance, when cumulative net losses amounted to $3.5 billion.

Ford had two major lines of business—automotive and nonautomotive. The automotive line, which accounted for 93 percent of the company's revenue and 105 percent of the company's operating income, had two main operations:

- The North American Automotive Operations (NAAO) designed, engineered, developed, produced, and marketed cars, trucks, industrial engines, vehicle components, and replacement parts in the United States and Canada.
- The International Automotive Operations (IAO) handled the same functions as NAAO on six continents in nearly 200 countries and territories.

Management Philosophy

Ford's mission was "to improve continually our products and services to meet our customers' needs, allowing us to prosper as a business and to provide a reasonable return for our stockholders, the owners of our business." In 1980, management established six guiding principles to accomplish this mission. "Quality comes first" was the first principle. The company emphasized quality in every aspect of its functioning, and "Quality is Job One" was much more than an advertising slogan; it was a way of life. As one Ford executive stated, "Quality drives everything we do—more so than profitability does. It's because we believe that better quality leads to greater productivity, reduces the cost base, and results in higher profitability."

The importance given to quality and customers throughout the organization was strongly influenced by top management. As chairman and chief executive officer, Petersen stressed quality and commitment to customers in every aspect of the business. This philosophy guided Ford executives during 1980–1982, when they faced increasing losses and declining market share. Management's short list of priorities included quality, investing in new products and research and development, and bringing costs into line. Between 1980 and 1984, Ford spent almost $14 billion on new products, processes, machinery, and equipment, and another $9 billion on research and engineering development. The 1985 and 1986 results seemed to indicate that these priorities had paid off.

North American Automotive Operations (NAAO)

Ford's performance was linked strongly to that of NAAO, which had three major US divisions—the Ford Division, the Lincoln–Mercury Division, and the Ford Parts and Service Division (FPSD). In 1986, NAAO sold 2.28 million cars and 1.53 million trucks, and the gross contributions per unit (after considering warranty costs) were $500 for subcompact and compact cars; $1,000 for intermediate and full-size cars; $2,000 for luxury cars; and $1,500 for trucks.

During 1986, Ford stressed quality and productivity, not market share; in fact, the company's car market share declined slightly from 18.8 percent in 1985 to 18.2 percent in 1986. With high industry sales volumes, capacity constraint was an important factor in the decline of Ford's car market share. By the end of 1986, the company had been producing at maximum capacity for 29 consecutive months.

Main Competitors

The automobile industry comprised four major US manufacturers and several foreign competitors (see Exhibit 3). Ford management believed that its principal competitors were GM, Chrysler, and more recently, the Japanese manufacturers as well.

GM dominated new-car sales. During 1979–1985, GM invested $41.5 billion in reconstruction and expected it to pay off in the long run with greater profitability, quality, and productivity. GM's share of the US car market declined, however, from 44.3 percent in 1984 to 41 percent in 1986. This decline caused several new high-tech assembly plants to run below capacity, slashing profitability.

Chrysler's share of the US car market had improved for the sixth consecutive year, and its divisions were the fastest growing in the US auto industry. Chrysler's strategy, starting in 1986, was to introduce a proliferation of models which included small sedans (Dodge Shadow and Plymouth Sundance) and a midsize pickup truck (Dodge Dakota).

EXHIBIT 3 Competition in the US Car Market

	Sales* ($ billions)		Net Income* ($ billions)		US Car Sales (000s of units)		Share of US Car Market (%)		Advertising Expenses ($ millions)	Number of Dealers	Customer Profile, 1986		
											Loyalty Levels† (%)	Mean Family Income ($ thousands)	Female Buyers (%)
	1985	1986	1985	1986	1985	1986	1985	1986	1986	1986			
Ford	$52.77	$62.71	$2.51	$3.33	2,079	2,081	18.8%	18.2%	$648.5	5,460	46%	$30.7	41%
General Motors	96.37	102.81	4.00	2.93	4,692	4,693	42.5	41.0	839.0	9,680	61	34.6	41
Chrysler	21.26	22.59	1.64	1.40	1,245	1,309	11.3	11.4	426.0	4,023	45	30.6	43
AMC	4.04	3.46	(0.13)	(0.09)	131	77	1.2	0.7	116.2	1,349	NA	NA	NA
Toyota	24.35	38.21	1.24	1.55	620	634	5.6	5.5	208.8	1,079	35	36.3	50
Nissan	14.47	22.75	0.30	0.39	575	546	5.2	4.8	180.1	1,113	29	33.6	47
Volvo	13.58	13.24	1.02	1.02	104	113	0.9	1.0	NA	407	18	53.4	39
Honda	10.59	16.36	0.52	0.82	552	694	5.0	6.1	205.1	862	44	34.2	48
Mazda	6.28	9.85	0.13	0.49	211	222	1.9	1.9	156.8	764	27	34.9	48
Hyundai	—	NA	—	NA	—	169	—	1.5	NA	75	NA	NA	NA
Volkswagen	21.01	30.75	0.31	0.36	218	215	2.0	1.9	152.2	878	21	41.3	34
BMW	6.16	7.81	0.13	0.18	88	97	0.8	0.8	NA	422	27	55.3	32
Mercedes-Benz	22.68	34.11	0.73	NA	87	99	0.8	0.8	NA	417	42	80.0	33
Subaru	2.69	4.74	0.60	0.76	178	183	1.6	1.6	NA	809	NA	NA	NA
Others	NA	NA	NA	NA	258	319	2.4	2.8	NA	NA	NA	NA	NA
Total					11,038	11,451	100.0%	100.0%			NA	$33.8	43%

NOTE: NA means not available.

* Sales and net income have been converted to US dollars at the following rates:

	1985	1986
Toyota, Nissan, Honda, Mazda, Subaru	Y250 = $1	Y165 = $1
Volkswagen, BMW, Mercedes-Benz	DM 2.31 = $1	DM 1.92 = $1
Volvo	SEK 6.35 = $1	SEK 6.35 = $1

† Percentage of owners who repurchase a new car from the same corporation.

The Automobile Consumer

In the United States, an automobile was considered a necessity, and there was at least one vehicle on the road for every adult. In 1986, of the 88.5 million US households, 53 percent owned two or more cars, and over 33 percent owned one car. Over 70 percent of all work-related commutes and over 80 percent of all travel from city to city were by car.

Ford conducted continuous market research on new-car buyers' shopping habits, buying processes, and ownership experiences. (Some general demographic and psychographic data on new-car buyers appear in Exhibit 4.) The research also indicated that consumers had become increasingly deliberate about the shopping process. On average, consumers visited five dealers before purchasing a car, and approximately half of those visits were to dealers selling the make that the consumer bought.

Ford tracked customers' purchase reasons, using a list of over 20 criteria. The most important criterion for buyers of all car categories was quality, measured by reliability and customers' perceptions of how well a car was made. The importance of all other purchase criteria varied substantially by car category. For example, warranty coverage was more important to buyers of compact and subcompact cars than to luxury-car buyers (see Table A).

TABLE A   Ranking of Top 12 Purchase Criteria after Quality

	Overall	Subcompact	Compact	Intermediate	Full-Size	Luxury
Value for money	1	2	1	2	4	7
Ease of handling	2	5	3	1	2	2
Price/deal offered	3	3	4	4	6	12
Riding comfort	4	9	6	3	1	1
Warranty coverage	5	4	5	5	7	8
Fuel economy	6	1	2	9	16	18
Safety features	7	7	7	6	5	3
Dealer service	8	6	8	8	8	6
Quietness	9	10	10	7	3	4
Cost of service/repair	10	8	9	10	11	17
Exterior styling	11	13	11	11	13	5
Interior styling	12	14	13	12	14	10

NOTE: Other criteria included future resale/trade-in value, power and pickup, fun to drive, technical innovations, large trunk/cargo area, passenger seating capacity, prestige, and dealer-assisted financing.

In 1986, research on the buying process indicated the following:

• The new-car ownership cycle (i.e., the average age of the car that is replaced by the original owner when buying another new car) had increased steadily from 3.7 years in 1975 to 5.4 years.

Availability of extended-length financing was a significant
contributing factor.

· Of the 72 percent of buyers who financed their car purchases, the
vast majority (80 percent) bought on a four- to five-year loan
period.

· Loyalty among Ford owners (i.e., the percentage of Ford owners
who purchased another new Ford) was 46 percent. This was the
highest level Ford had achieved in the 1980s, approaching the
level attained in the 1970s.

· The percentage of competitive-make owners who switched to
Ford had increased in the 1980s. For example, 12 percent of the

EXHIBIT 4   New-Car Buyer Profile, 1986

	Domestic Cars	Imported Cars	All Cars
Purchasing Characteristics			
Replaced previous car	85.0%	76.5%	82.5%
Plan to keep new car:			
0–1 years	3.9%	2.2%	3.4%
2–3 years	28.1	20.1	25.8
4–5 years	41.3	39.3	40.7
6–9 years	14.3	17.0	15.1
10 + years	12.4%	21.4%	15.0%
Median time	5.2 yrs.	5.5 yrs.	5.4 yrs.
Average price of car	$12,459	$12,978	$12,608
Demographic Characteristics			
Gender: Male	59.0%	57.2%	58.5%
Female	41.0	42.8	41.5
Age			
Under 24	9.8%	14.0%	11.0%
25–34	21.0	38.1	25.9
35–44	19.1	22.2	20.0
45–54	15.9	11.1	14.5
55–64	16.9	9.1	14.7
65 and over	17.3%	5.5%	13.9%
Median age	45.7 yrs.	34.2 yrs.	43.0 yrs.
Median family income	$33,500	$37,000	$34,000

Vehicle Ownership by Household Income

Number of Vehicles	Under $10,000	$10,000– $19,999	$20,000– $29,999	$30,000– $39,999	$40,000 and over	All Households
0	39.5%	8.8%	2.3%	1.5%	1.1%	13.5%
1	42.8	46.2	30.4	17.7	12.2	33.7
2	13.6	31.6	44.8	49.7	43.8	33.6
3	3.1	10.2	15.2	20.5	25.5	12.8
4 or more	1.0	3.2	7.3	10.6	17.4	6.4
Total	100.0%	100.0%	100.0%	100.0%	100.0%	100.0%

EXHIBIT 4 *(concluded)*

	1981	1985
Psychographic Categories		
Driving enthusiast	10%	15%
Loves cars	15	18
Conspicuous consumer	12	12
Socially aware	13	7
Value conscious	19	18
Economy-minded	16	10
"America First"	15	20
	100%	100%

NOTE: The psychographic categories and the attitudes of the people they comprise are as follows:

Driving enthusiast: Enjoys cars, especially the driving experience. Thinks imports have good quality and would not go out of his or her way to "Buy American." Has the strongest import orientation, particularly toward European cars, of any psychographic group.

Loves cars: Regards his or her car as a possession to take pride in rather than as a driving experience. Considers car's styling extremely important. Tends to be outgoing.

Conspicuous consumer: Engages in frequent trade-ins and brand switching. Likes to be the first to try new things and have all the latest options. Tends to like big, roomy, comfortable cars.

Socially aware: Considers social issues important, tends to be politically liberal. Desires fuel-efficient cars and has no empathy for big Detroit cars. Favors inexpensive cars and believes imports are good.

Value conscious: Tends not to be involved emotionally with cars or interested in them functionally. Appreciates a good value and favors Japanese cars.

Economy-minded: Is interested in inexpensive and economical transportation. Tends to have conservative life-style.

"America First": Says he or she will keep buying big, roomy cars as long as Detroit keeps making them. "Buys American" whenever possible. Does not think Japanese and German cars have better quality than US cars. Has great interest in comfort and little interest in sports cars.

EXHIBIT 5 Buying Process, 1986

	Subcompact	Compact	Intermediate	Full-Size	Luxury	Overall
Ownership cycle (years)	5.0	5.3	5.7	6.3	4.8	5.4
Median income ($000)	$30	$34	$34	$39	$58	$34
Median age (years)	32	42	60	61	59	43
Ford's loyalty rates	47	36	40	64	56	46
Major other brand(s) bought by Ford owners	Japanese (28%) Chrysler (13%)	GM (32%) Japanese (18%)	GM (43%) Chrysler (9%)	GM (30%) —	GM (30%) European (14%)	GM (25%) Japanese (15%)
Owners of Other Makes Switching to Ford (%)						
GM	19*	10	8	10	10	12
Chrysler	13	11	16	22	18	14
Japanese	10	9	7	18	5	9
European	7	11	4	27	2	9

* To be read: "Of GM owners buying a subcompact in 1986, 19 percent bought a Ford."

GM owners purchasing a new car in 1986 bought a Ford, compared with 8 percent in 1980.

· Ford's gain/loss ratio (the ratio of new buyers gained through switching sales to sales lost through disloyalty) had increased substantially, from 0.6 in 1980 to 1.1 in 1985. Corresponding competitive figures were as follows: GM, 1.3 and 0.8; Chrysler, 0.8 and 1.5; and imports, 3.6 and 2.1

Exhibit 5 shows how the various aspects of the buying process differed by category.

An owner's satisfaction with a new car was strongly influenced by the car's quality, for example, its driveability, engine, and transmission. Satisfaction was critical because it affected customer loyalty to the company (see Table B).

TABLE B   Impact of Owner Satisfaction on Loyalty

Satisfaction with Prior Ford Car	Loyalty Rate
Completely satisfied	55%
Very satisfied	51
Fairly satisfied	43
Somewhat dissatisfied	37
Very dissatisfied	31
Overall average	46%

Product Policy

Ford's product policy had changed from its early focus on standardization and a narrow product line to challenging GM in the 1950s through several new product introductions. Throughout the 1960s, Ford had proliferated and upgraded its models so that, in 1970, it offered 88 variations of basic models, compared with 44 in 1960 and 15 in 1946.

Introducing successful new models had become a key to success in the industry. The total investment in a truly new product, however, was becoming extremely high, exceeding $500 million. The lengthy production process involved three main stages—design and development, manufacture of parts and subassemblies, and assembly. The design phase typically began five to seven years before product introduction and involved developing general product concepts, sketches of concepts, full-size models, and production cost targets.

Product quality at Ford was a corporate philosophy. As one executive said, "Quality includes every aspect of the vehicle that determines customer satisfaction and provides fundamental values. This means how well the vehicle is made, how well it performs, how well it lasts, and how well the customer is treated by both the company and the dealer." The importance of product quality was expected to become even greater in the years ahead, because the market was growing more competitive, and customers were increasingly emphasizing quality. To pursue the quality philosophy, Ford implemented several changes with its suppliers, dealers, and employees.

Ford set tougher standards for suppliers, assisted them to achieve those higher standards, made quality considerations a critical factor in every supplier selection decision, and established awards for suppliers that contributed to an improvement in Ford's quality performance. Award winners received preferential consideration for new business and for long-term contracts. In 1985, customer service introduced Quality Care, a joint program with Ford dealers, to improve predelivery and delivery procedures. Besides the Quality Care program, dealers offered customers a lifetime service guarantee with no recharge for repairs. For its internal operations, Ford established Quality Responsible Teams, linking their formal performance evaluation and bonuses to quality that was measured by customer reports of "things gone wrong" (TGW) per 100 cars. A TGW was whatever caused a customer to complain to the dealer—anything from a blemish in the paint to a broken transmission.

Customer research showed that the quality of Ford's 1986 cars, measured by TGW, was over 50 percent better than that of its 1980 models. For six consecutive years (1981–1986), nationwide respondents to Ford's surveys judged it to be the best American manufacturer of high-quality cars and trucks. The quality ratings, which were supported by surveys conducted by independent firms, narrowed the gap with Japanese manufacturers.

Product Warranty

Most new cars in the United States were covered by four different types of warranty coverage:

1. Basic warranty (covering most parts except tires and maintenance items such as filters and spark plugs).
2. Powertrain warranty (covering the engine, transmission, front- or rear-wheel drive shaft).
3. Corrosion warranty (generally applying to outer body rust-through).

4. Emissions warranty (by federal law, every car manufacturer
    had to provide a warranty on the emission control system for
    at least 5 years/50,000 miles, whichever occurred first).[2]

Both American and Japanese manufacturers tended to offer "partitioned" warranties, with separate coverage assigned to specific parts of the car. Most European manufacturers covered nearly all components of a car for a specified time or mileage (see Exhibit 6).

Over the past two decades, the role of warranties and the coverage they provided had varied considerably. Until 1960, Ford and the other auto manufacturers had offered a basic warranty of 3 months/4,000 miles, primarily to limit their liability. In 1960, this was increased to 1 year/ 12,000 miles.

Ford first used warranties as a marketing variable in the mid-1960s, when it offered a longer warranty on its Lincoln cars. This move met with great success, and Lincoln sales increased substantially. As a result of that success and the then-growing emphasis on consumerism, the Mercury and Ford divisions also offered longer warranties. By 1967, the basic warranty was 2 years/24,000 miles, and the powertrain warranty was 5 years/50,000 miles.

The auto industry's downturn in 1969–1970 led to intense efforts at cost reduction. Analyses revealed that warranty costs had become extremely high because of both the high frequency of product failure and the longer warranty period. Consequently, the basic warranty was reduced in 1970 to 1 year/12,000 miles, and the additional powertrain warranty was made optional. By 1980, the improvement in quality permitted Ford executives (in marketing, manufacturing, and quality assurance) to convince top management and members of the board that the costs of increasing the powertrain warranty to 2 years/24,000 miles would be significantly lower than in the late 1960s.

Ford, GM, and Chrysler were usually fiercely competitive on warranties. Through the 1980s, however, Chrysler had been the most aggressive warranty marketer in the industry. Chrysler placed enormous marketing emphasis on product warranty, and in 1981, the company increased the powertrain warranty on all its domestic cars from 2 years/24,000 miles to 5 years/50,000 miles. Chrysler used its chairman, Lee Iacocca, as the pitchman in national television commercials, proclaiming that Chrysler had improved its car quality and was prepared to stand behind it and that the company's powertrain coverage was the best in the industry. Chrysler began to gain market share. Industry analysts estimated that the automak-

---

[2] The warranty period is usually defined in time and mileage and restricted to whichever occurs first. Throughout the rest of the case, the phrase "whichever occurs first" will be implied (unless otherwise stated) whenever the warranty period is mentioned.

EXHIBIT 6 1987 New-Car Warranties as of January 21, 1987 (time in years/miles in thousands)

	Basic	Powertrain	Corrosion	Emissions Defect
		Type of Warranty		
Nonluxury Cars				
Ford*	1/12	3/U† ($100)‡	3/U	5/50
GM	1/12	3/U ($100)	3/U	5/50
Chrysler	1/12	5/50§ ($100)	5/50	5/50
AMC	1/12	3/36 ($100)	3/U	5/50
Toyota	1/12.5	3/36	5/U	5/50
Nissan	1/12.5	3/36	3/U	5/50
Hyundai	1/12	3/36	3/U	5/50
Honda	1/12	2/24	3/U	5/50
Mazda	1/U	2/24	3/U	5/50
Volkswagen	2/U	2/U	6/U	5/50
Luxury Cars				
Ford	1/12	5/50 ($100)	5/100	5/50
GM	1/12	5/50 ($100)	5/100	5/50
Chrysler	1/12	5/50‖ ($100)	5/50	5/50
Mercedes	4/50	4/50	4/50	5/50
BMW	3/36	3/36	6/U	5/50
Volvo	3/U	3/U	8/U	5/50

* Of the 2.081 million Ford cars sold in the United States in 1986, 1.903 million (91%) were nonluxury cars.

† U signifies unlimited.

‡ $100-deductible charge for each repair visit.

§ Limited to first retail owner; subsequent owners received 2/24.

‖ Limited to first retail owner. Second owner could obtain coverage for $25; otherwise, coverage reverted to 2/24.

er's superior warranty coverage accounted for at least one of the approximately three percentage points that Chrysler gained in market share between 1980 and 1985. Ford and GM had lost 0.5 percent market share each. Consequently, they increased their powertrain warranties on non-luxury cars to 3 years/unlimited miles in January 1986 (see Exhibit 6 for various manufacturers' warranty coverage).

To invoke a warranty, a customer had to take the car to a dealer, who carried out the repair at no charge if the part or component that failed was still under warranty. Although most Ford dealers would honor the warranty, most customers returned to the dealer from whom they had purchased the car because they expected to receive preferential treatment from that dealer.

Ford dealers fulfilled an important role concerning warranties. They were required to explain the warranty coverage to a buyer at the time of sale, and they had to provide warranty repair service, whenever needed, according to the provisions of a sales and service agreement and Ford's warranty policy. On average, dealers were reimbursed for warranty work 26 days after they informed Ford.

Many dealers were concerned that their gross margins on warranty repairs were only 35 percent compared with 50 percent on customer-paid repairs. This happened because of the automakers' reimbursement policies, which had two components—parts and labor. For parts, dealers generally charged dealer price plus 50 percent for customer-paid work but received only dealer price plus 30 percent from manufacturers for warranty work. Reimbursement of labor costs for any given repair was based on the dealer's approved labor rate multiplied by the manufacturers' standard labor time allowed for that particular repair job. Many dealers believed that the commercially available labor time standards (used for customer-paid work) exceeded the manufacturer's recommended time standards (used for warranty work) by about 30 percent.

The total cost of Ford's warranty program, approximately $1 billion in 1986, had three components. The first and largest was claims—parts and labor. This cost was related to product repair frequency as well as labor rates and parts costs. Over the past few years, repair frequency had declined, but labor rates and parts costs had increased. The claims costs associated with each type of coverage are shown in Exhibit 7. A second

---

EXHIBIT 7 Estimated Claims Costs of Warranties

Warranty Terms (years/miles)	Basic*		Powertrain†		Corrosion†		Emissions Effect	
	N‡	L§	N	L	N	L	N	L
1/12,000	$157	$229						
2/24,000	325	445						
3/36,000	407	564						
3/Unlimited	435	609	$33		$1	$1		
4/50,000	467	653	49		2	2		
5/50,000	508	716	51	$62	2	3‖	$93	$93
6/60,000	598	829	66	96	2	4	107	117
6/100,000	650	890	77	117	3	5	118	129
6/Unlimited	661	905	79	120	3	5	120	142
7/70,000	695	940	86	135	4	6	130	157
7/Unlimited	$760	$1,018	$100	$160	$5	$7	$145	$183

NOTE: Figures in boxes are values as of January 23, 1987.

* The figures under basic correspond to all warranty costs (except emissions effect). For example, for nonluxury cars, $157 is the cost of the warranty for basic, powertrain, and corrosion for one year.

† The figures under powertrain and corrosion correspond to the warranty costs associated with them after the 1 year/12,000 miles basic coverage expires.

‡ N signifies nonluxury.

§ L signifies luxury.

‖ Corresponds to 5 years/100,000 miles.

component was the cost incurred on the warranty payment and administration department, which had 94 people in five sections: (1) warranty and policy, (2) parts return and inspection, (3) claims review, (4) dealer claims and supplier accounting, and (5) special processing. The final component—communication expenses—was minor because most of it was accounted for under Ford's advertising expenses.

Some Ford managers believed that Iacocca's punchy "best-built, best-backed" Chrysler television commercials, which attracted much attention, may have goaded GM into increasing its warranty. GM's new warranty policy, announced on January 22, 1987, upgraded the powertrain warranty from 3 years/unlimited miles to 6 years/60,000 miles, and the corrosion warranty from 3 years/unlimited miles to 6 years/100,000 miles. The new warranty program, which applied retroactively to all GM's 1987 cars built in North America, covered the first buyer only. The second owner could buy the new warranty terms from GM for $100. Third and any successive owners would be entitled to a powertrain warranty of 2 years/24,000 miles. GM's new warranty policy, like Chrysler's, marked a change in philosophy. The focus shifted from the vehicle to the owner.

To remain competitive, Ford's marketing and sales executives believed that they had to respond quickly to GM's new warranty policy. For various alternative Ford powertrain warranty terms, industry experts' estimates of the effect of GM's powertrain warranty of 6 years/60,000 miles on Ford's luxury and nonluxury domestic car market share (ms) points are shown in Table C.

Ford usually made its product warranty and pricing decisions in the summer for the following year's models, which were normally introduced in the fall. The warranty decision-making process was complex because

TABLE C   Estimated Effect of Alternative on Ford's Market Share (ms) Points

Ford's Powertrain Warranty Alternatives	**Estimated Effect on Ford's Market Share Points**	
	Nonluxury Cars	*Luxury Cars*
3 years/36,000 miles	1.75% ms loss	—
4 years/50,000 miles	1.5% ms loss	—
5 years/50,000 miles	1.0% ms loss	0.5% ms loss
6 years/60,000 miles	No change	No change
7 years/70,000 miles	0.75% ms gain	0.25% ms gain
Cover all parts ("European")		
3 years/36,000 miles	1.5% ms gain	1.0% ms gain
4 years/50,000 miles	2.0% ms gain	1.5% ms gain

the warranty program affected various departments with differing perspectives and often conflicting interests, and because the decisions were made at the highest levels. Changes in the warranty program needed to be approved by Chairman of the Board and CEO Donald Petersen; President and COO Harold Poling; and the Policy and Strategy Committee. The departments that recommended and influenced changes in the warranty program were sales, marketing, parts and service, product development, manufacturing, quality assurance, and extended service plans. Because of the warranty program's high financial implications, the controller's office scrutinized warranty costs.

Extended Service Plans

A program closely related to product warranties was the Extended Service Plans (ESP) program. Sold as a separate stand-alone product, an extended service plan provided for long-term protection against certain unexpected repairs beyond the warranty period.

In the 10 years since its introduction in 1977, ESP had grown rapidly and increased in complexity. Various plans had been added, and support for ESP had grown substantially. By the end of 1986, 84 people worked full-time on ESP, and 350 service representatives spent approximately 8 percent of their time on ESP. The rest of their time was spent on other activities: 50 percent on owner relations, 25 percent on warranty administration, and 17 percent on equipment and technical administration.

Nearly 45 percent of Ford's new-car retail buyers bought a service contract. Approximately 60 percent of these bought a Ford service contract, and the others bought one from the over 200 companies operating in the automobile service contract industry. Most service contracts were purchased with the new vehicle (80 percent) or when the basic warranty of 1 year/12,000 miles expired (20 percent).

In January 1987, to meet different customer needs, Ford offered four different types of service plans: ESP BASE, ESP PLUS, ESP TOTAL, and ESP CARE (see Exhibit 8). Ford had over 100 different plans, because each of these four types of contracts was available in a variety of time (3, 4, 5, or 6 years) and mileage (36,000, 48,000, 60,000, 100,000, or unlimited miles) combinations, and for different types of vehicles (nonluxury car, luxury car, light truck, or heavy truck). The consumer prices of these plans ranged from $200 to $1,250 and averaged $415. Repairs covered by ESP were carried out on about 35 percent of the cars that had an ESP, and Ford's expense averaged $330 per car that needed repair. On each plan, Ford and the dealers got gross margins of $100 and $200, respectively. Although dealers sold ESP for new and used Fords as well

---

EXHIBIT 8   Types of Extended Service Plans (ESPs), 1987

Features	ESP	ESP PLUS	ESP TOTAL	ESP CARE
Number of major components covered	81	113	All*	113
High-tech coverage	No	Yes	Yes	Yes
Scheduled maintenance	No	No	No	Yes
Wear-item coverage	No	No	No	Yes
Protection while traveling	Yes	Yes	Yes	Yes
Deductible per repair visit	$50	$25	$25	None
Prior approval	No	No	No	No
Transportation reimbursement	No	$20/day†	$20/day†	$20/day‡
Towing reimbursement	No	$45 max.	$45 max.	$45 max.

* With a few exceptions.
† Maximum of 5 days.
‡ Maximum of 10 days.

---

as other makes, their margins on ESP were lower than those on competitors' service contracts.

The ESP department focused its communication on two broad target markets, trade and consumer. The strategy for the trade market (dealers) was to use the credibility of dealer testimonials to communicate the benefits of ESP. Ads were placed in leading automotive trade publications. The strategy for the consumer market (all potential purchasers of new Ford cars) was to create an awareness of Ford's ESP and a consumer predisposition to purchase ESP by emphasizing peace of mind and the avoidance of expensive repairs with ESP coverage. Ads were placed in prominent national weekly news magazines, especially in the spring and fall.

Ford management believed that the ESP program was successful because 80 percent of Ford's dealers sold ESP—a higher percentage than that of any other domestic manufacturer (GM, 66 percent; Chrysler, 67 percent; and AMC, 71 percent). More important, ESP contributed significantly to Ford's profits (see Exhibit 9), resulting in additional parts profits of $3.6 million and a cumulative cash flow from 1976 through 1986 of about $300 million. As one Ford executive noted, "ESP by itself would equal or exceed the profitability of many consistently profitable company activities."

ESP managers worried that an increase in the warranty period would reduce ESP's attractiveness and consequently would cut into the department's sales and profits. Ford dealers disagreed on the salability of service contracts with longer warranties. A majority of the dealers believed that longer warranties would lower ESP sales; a few dealers felt that ESP sales would be unaffected.

EXHIBIT 9   Extended Service Plans (ESPs): Sales and Profits ($ millions)

	1984	*1985*	*1986*
Gross sales	$140.2	$195.0	$265.4
Lifetime profit before taxes	47.8	82.0	117.5
Added parts profits	$ 1.6	$ 2.5	$ 3.6
Contract volume (000s)			
New			
Ford	417	540	669
Competitors	5	7	12
Used			
Ford	120	160	210
Competitors	63	83	110
Others	209	239	214
Total	814	1,029	1,215

TABLE D   Sales and Profits of Average Dealership by Department, 1986 ($000s)

	Sales	*Gross Profit*
New-car department	$ 7,325.7	$ 720.4
Used-car department	2,242.7	223.9
Service and parts	1,442.5	551.1
Finance and insurance	258.8	103.8
Total	$11,269.7	$1,599.2

Distribution

In the United States, cars were sold through an elaborate network of franchised dealers. The franchise agreement detailed clearly both the manufacturer's and the dealer's sales and service responsibilities. Over the years, the number of new-car dealerships had declined steadily; the average size of the dealerships had increased (due primarily to the closing of smaller-volume dealers), and there was a growing trend toward one dealer principal operating more than one dealership. In 1950, there were 50,000 retail outlets or dealerships, each run primarily by a different dealer principal. In 1986, however, there were 25,156 dealerships, with only 17,000 dealer principals. Another change was the increased concentration of the dealer network: in 1986, 20 percent of the dealerships (5,155) accounted for 80 percent of the sales. As the size of the dealerships grew, the balance of power began to shift from the manufacturers to the dealers. In 1986, the average dealership's sales and gross profit were $11.27 million and $1.6 million, respectively (see Table D).

Service and parts (S&P) comprised warranty work (18 percent of S&P sales), customer-paid work (43 percent), and wholesale and counter sales (39 percent). Four successive years of strong new-car sales led to substantial increases in warranty work—an 18 percent increase in 1986. However, car owners typically abandoned dealers after the warranty period. Dealerships' share of customer-paid (nonwarranty) work dropped from 40 percent during the warranty period to 15 percent after the warranty period for those without an ESP, and to about 30 percent for those with an ESP. Overall, dealerships accounted for only 33 percent of the total warranty and customer-paid automobile service and parts business.

Advertising and Promotion

The automobile industry was one of the most heavily advertised in the United States. In 1986, nine auto manufacturers were among the nation's 100 leading advertisers, with GM (fifth) and Ford (sixth) in the top 10.

From 1986 onward, Ford's ads emphasized warranties. Corporate ads stressed warranties, and all the divisional ads ended with a warranty message. Ford's advertising appeared primarily on television (49 percent), although newspapers (16 percent) and magazines (25 percent) were also used extensively. To develop distinctive brand identities, Ford and other automakers created ad themes by brand. For example, Ford Division ads used the theme "Have you driven a Ford . . . lately?"; Lincoln ads had the "What a luxury car should be" theme; and Mercury ads used "The shape you want to be in" theme. GM's Pontiac division used "We build excitement," and its Chevrolet division proclaimed the "Heartbeat of America" theme.

Auto marketers also offered consumer promotions through cash rebates and low finance rates. In 1986, Ford spent over $100 million on consumer promotions. Industry analysts attributed the record 1986 car sales partly to the biggest consumer incentive promotion in automotive history. In the fall of 1986, GM announced a low financing rate of 2.9 percent. Ford matched that offer; Chrysler announced a 2.4 percent rate, and AMC introduced 0 percent financing. All these promotions lured unprecedented numbers of buyers into the marketplace. Some industry analysts believed that, despite their impact on sales, such consumer promotions were not good for the manufacturers in the long run because competitors easily matched them and because many consumers would not buy cars without them.

The Decision

During the discussions at the January 23 meeting, managers from various departments expressed different views on Ford's warranty position, and they proposed and supported several courses of action. Five alternatives were identified and discussed:

1. Do not respond. Maintain the existing warranty terms.
2. Match GM's terms. Offer a powertrain warranty of 6 years/60,000 miles, a corrosion warranty of 6 years/100,000 miles, and change from a vehicle warranty to an owner warranty. Have a $100 deductible and a transfer fee, but do not advertise those restrictions.
3. Exceed GM's terms. Offer a powertrain warranty of 7 years/70,000 miles. Also offer a corrosion warranty of 7 years/unlimited miles for all coastal states and 6 years/100,000 for inland states.
4. Offer less than GM but equal to Chrysler's coverage—5 years/50,000 miles.
5. Adopt a "European" approach. Offer a basic warranty (including powertrain) of 3 years/36,000 miles (for nonluxury cars) or 4 years/50,000 miles (for luxury cars) and a corrosion warranty of 6 years/100,000 miles.

One executive urged that the five options be compared in terms of expected market share, sales, contribution per unit, and total contributions. The executive wondered what would have happened if all manufacturers (including GM) had retained the warranty terms that existed on January 21.

When to implement the warranty policy change was also discussed. Some managers felt that a new warranty policy should be retroactive to all 1987 Ford cars; others felt that it should be effective immediately, and a few felt that the change should be announced and implemented for 1988 models.

Considerable debate arose over whether the warranty terms ought to be the same for all cars. Some managers argued for better warranty terms for nonluxury cars; other managers felt that luxury cars ought to have the best warranties. Yet others felt that all Ford cars should have the same warranty terms. This last group argued that different warranty terms for different categories of cars would confuse everyone. Some managers expressed strong concern about the impact that an increase in the warranty coverage would have on ESP profits and dealer profitability.

Despite the disagreement on the best response to GM's new warranty policy, the executives at this meeting realized that they had to decide on a course of action to recommend to Petersen.

Loctite Corporation: Industrial Products Group

The first place a marketing person has to sell is on the inside—and that's the hardest of all.

Jeffrey Fox, vice president for marketing of Loctite Corporation's Industrial Products Group (IPG), was commenting on the concerns of some Loctite executives regarding the proposed introduction of a simple adhesive dispensing system, tentatively named the Bond-A-Matic 2000.[1]

The system was designed to dispense instant adhesive to bond metals, plastics, rubber, and other materials in manufacturing operations. In September 1978 Fox had to decide whether to recommend full-scale launch of the Bond-A-Matic in early 1979 and, if launched, what marketing strategy to employ.

Company Background

With a product line of over 300 items, Loctite Corporation, headquartered in Newington, Connecticut, was a leader in the development and marketing of high-performance adhesives and sealants for industrial and consumer applications. One of the company's principal objectives was to become the premiere worldwide marketer of instant adhesives for industrial use by 1985.

The company had three major profit centers:

1. IPG was responsible for sales of adhesives to industrial customers in the United States and Canada, both original equipment manufacturers (OEMs) and companies in the business

---

Professor John A. Quelch prepared this case as a basis for class discussion rather than to illustrate either effective or ineffective handling of an administrative situation. Certain industry and proprietary data have been disguised. Copyright © 1980 by the President and Fellows of Harvard College. Harvard Business School case 581–066.

[1] Permatex, Quick Set, SuperBonder, and Super Glue are registered ® trademarks, and Bond-A-Matic, Duro, Front Line, Gluematic, Tak Pak, and Vari-Drop are ™ trademarks of Loctite Corporation.

of maintenance, repair, and overhaul (MROs). IPG accounted for about 25 percent of Loctite's sales in FY 1978 and was responsible for most of the company's research and development.

2. The Woodhill Permatex Group, accounting for 34 percent of sales, reached the North American do-it-yourself market through 75,000 retail outlets with its Duro product line and Super Glue, which held the second-highest market share among consumer instant adhesives. In addition, it sold the Permatex line of gasketing and adhesive products designed for the automotive aftermarket through 20,000 wholesalers and jobbers to 800,000 professional mechanics.

3. Loctite International, for 41 percent of sales, serviced industrial and consumer markets outside North America.

IPG sales had been growing 25 percent each year and in FY 1978 had reached $32 million.[2] IPG's two principal business units, both of which had profit responsibility, were General Industrial Business (GIB) and Selected Industrial Business (SIB). They accounted for 60 percent and 30 percent of IPG sales respectively. GIB sold to industrial distributors who resold to medium and small OEMs and the MRO market. SIB sold direct to large OEMs, such as automobile and farm equipment manufacturers. Over half of SIB's FY 1978 sales were generated by the Systems Division, which manufactured and sold equipment for applying adhesives, both direct to OEMs and through distributors.

The Market for Adhesives

A variety of technologies competed in the industrial adhesive market. They included mature technologies, such as solvent cements and epoxies, and newer technologies, such as anaerobics and cyanoacrylates (CAs). The mature technologies presented numerous problems. For example, solvent cements were often toxic, flammable, and subject to shrinkage after being applied. Epoxies were toxic and inconvenient. Furthermore, they required high-temperature ovens, energy, and significant operator training. On the other hand, 70 percent of IPG's revenues were from anaerobics and CAs.

Anaerobic Adhesives

Anaerobic adhesives were colorless and nontoxic, required no mixing, cured at room temperature, and hardened within a few minutes of application. They were intended to bond cylindrical metal parts (such as a bolt to a nut), a limited application. Increasingly, however, they were viewed as

---

[2] FY 1978 ran from July 1, 1977, through June 30, 1978.

an attractive alternative to traditional mechanical locking devices, such as lock washers and crimped nuts. Through improved locking, sealing, and retaining of mechanical parts subject to stress, anaerobics could prevent leakage, loosening, wear, and corrosion; cut repair and replacement costs; improve energy efficiency; and reduce equipment downtime. Although mechanical locking devices could be easily disassembled for service and inspection, they were often more cumbersome and costly to maintain. Adhesives, however, distributed loads more evenly than mechanical joints, and so permitted more flexibility in product design.

Despite the apparent advantages of anaerobics, North American industry in 1978 still spent almost $4 on mechanical locking devices for every $1 on adhesives. One explanation was that, although metalworking firms could easily be located, considerable sales effort was required to convince mechanical engineers that adhesives could be as effective as metal lock washers. They were skeptical about a chemical solution to a mechanical problem.

As the original patent holder on anaerobic technology, Loctite held an 85 percent share of the North American anaerobic market in 1978. Low capital barriers to entry and expiration of some patents in 1978 had attracted several small European and Japanese competitors, but Loctite believed these companies lacked adequate selling expertise. A more serious threat was 3M Company, whose highly trained sales force had begun to promote anaerobics and CAs aggressively under the Scotch Weld brand name.

Cyanoacrylates

CAs, popularly known as instant adhesives, set faster than anaerobics, but were less tough and durable. CAs could be used to bond a broad range of materials, including rubber, plastic, and metal. The first CA was introduced by a division of Eastman Kodak in 1958. During the 1960s, Eastman sold CAs to Loctite for repackaging under the brand name Loctite Quick Set 404. After developing its own manufacturing technology in 1971, IPG introduced its SuperBonder line of CAs. By FY 1978 Loctite was believed to have exceeded Eastman's share of the North American industrial CA market. Eastman sold a line of four CAs through its own sales force and was a particularly important supplier to the electronics industry. Loctite's other significant competitor was the Permabond Division of National Starch and Chemical, Inc., a Unilever subsidiary. Loctite, Eastman, and Permabond collectively accounted for about 75 percent of the industrial CA market, and all were manufactured in the United States. Other competitors sold CAs made in Japan under their own brand names.

Unlike anaerobics, CAs were also sold to consumers. Of the 890,000 pounds of CAs sold in North America during FY 1978, about 625,000 pounds were sold to consumers under brand names such as Krazy Glue (manufactured by Toagosei in Japan), Super Glue (manufactured by Loctite and sold through its Woodhill Permatex subsidiary), and Elmer's Wonder Bond (marketed by Borden Chemical). The remaining 265,000 pounds were sold to industrial users. Convenience, however, prompted many industrial users who required only small quantities of CAs to purchase an additional 25,000 pounds from retailers serving the consumer market.

The total adhesives market was growing at about 10 percent, but CA sales were increasing twice as fast. Industrial usage was expected to outpace consumer market growth significantly, although the industrial market was more vulnerable to economic downturns. Sales of 335,000 pounds were forecast for the industrial market in 1979. CA management was determined to participate in this growth.

Information about the identity of CA's industrial users was sparse. Estimates of actual and potential use of CAs by SIC[3] industry groups during FY 1978 are presented in Exhibit 1. The market for CAs was much broader and more fragmented than that for anaerobics. The principal purchasers of anaerobics were large, easily identifiable firms concentrated in metalworking. Firm size was a poor predictor of CA demand. Small firms (with fewer employees) in such diverse products as electronic circuits, sneakers, and lipstick could be relatively heavy CA users.

SuperBonder Adhesives

In 1976 there were 11 products in Loctite's SuperBonder line of CAs. They differed in viscosity, curing time, and the materials they were best suited to bond. (Exhibit 2 shows a 1976 sales force data sheet illustrating the line.) Beginning in 1977 IPG executives made efforts both to increase the number of SuperBonder users and to expand the volume purchased by existing users. To this end, several SuperBonder kits were developed for specific industries. The Front Line Tool Box was targeted at mechanics and engineers concerned with sealing pipes and gaskets, and the Tak Pak, a wiretacking kit, was introduced to appeal to the electronics industry. Executives hoped trial of the SuperBonder kits would stimulate brand loyalty and repeat purchases.

During 1977 IPG commissioned a market research study of CA buyer behavior (see Exhibit 3). Partly as a result, it attempted in FY 1978 to give a stronger identity to the SuperBonder brand and to link it more closely to the well-known Loctite name. Packaging was redesigned to distinguish items in the line. The number of SuperBonder adhesives was reduced to five to minimize confusion among end users and distributor salespeople, and to make it easier for distributors to stock the full line (see Exhibit 4).

---

[3] Standard Industrial Classification (SIC) codes denote groups of related industries.

EXHIBIT 1 Actual and Potential Usage of Instant Adhesives in the Industrial Market, FY 1978

SIC Code	Industry	Number of Establishments	Instant Adhesives Usage (lbs.)	Percent of User Establishments	Additional Percent of Potential User Establishments
20–24	Food, textile, wood products	92,874 ⎫	4,700	5.0%	7.6%
26–27	Paper and printing	62,872 ⎭		14.3	6.4
25	Furniture	13,845	9,500	12.0	20.2
28–29	Chemicals, petroleum products	20,167	15,850	12.5	6.0
33–35	Metal products, machinery	102,523	48,200	14.7	7.8
36	Electrical and electronic equipment	19,610	42,000	26.7	18.3
38	Scientific instruments, photo equipment, watches	10,143	10,650	27.6	20.1
30–31	Rubber, plastic, leather products	16,332 ⎫		15.3	9.7
32	Stone, clay, glass products	19,190 ⎬	27,350	15.1	3.8
37	Transportation equipment	11,771 ⎪		17.3	15.2
39	Jewelry, toys, sporting goods	23,904 ⎭		24.6	18.7
40–49	Transportation, communications, utilities	135,657	16,000	11.8	7.1
70, 72, 73	Personal, tourist, business services	282,239	8,450	8.3	6.2
75	Motor vehicle services	89,257	58,900	36.1	10.1
76	Appliance repair	85,838	13,500	30.8	4.1
78–80	Entertainment and health services	42,001	9,900	10.1%	5.6%

SOURCE: Company records.

A cap with a built-in applicator allowing greater dispensing control was also introduced on the standard one-ounce bottles. An advertising and promotion budget of $175,000 for FY 1978 was spent primarily on trade magazine advertisements targeted at particular industry segments. The ads (see Exhibits 5 and 6) aimed to give visibility to instant adhesives, to increase SuperBonder brand awareness, to compare SuperBonder performance with those of competing adhesive technologies, and to highlight Loctite's ability to develop formulations customized for particular industry segments. During FY 1978 SuperBonder advertising expenditures exceeded those of all competing CAs combined.

EXHIBIT 2   1976 SuperBonder Line Sales Force Data Sheet

LOCTITE®
SUPERBONDER®
Adhesives for
Product Assembly

Loctite SuperBonders are rapid setting (fixturing in 1-30 seconds) adhesives, engineered to meet varied product assembly needs, providing advantages over conventional assembly techniques...

**SuperBonder Adhesives
Reduce Direct Costs**
• Save labor and time
• Waiting periods can be reduced between on-line assembly operations
• Mechanical fastening techniques (fasteners, keys, retaining rings, etc.) can be replaced with rapid setting bonds
• Part tolerances can be reduced
• Weight of final assembly can be reduced by eliminating mechanical components

**SuperBonder Adhesives
Reduce Indirect Costs**
• Capital investment in assembly tooling is eliminated
• Inventory carrying costs are minimized
• Handling and secondary processing costs for mechanical fastenings are eliminated.

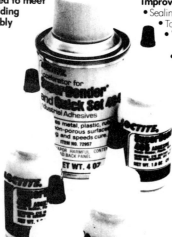

**SuperBonder Adhesives
Improve Product Reliability**
• Sealing components as they are joined
   • Tamper proofing
      • "Unitizing" assembly, increasing vibration-resistance
      • Distributing working stresses more evenly than mechanical fastening techniques

**SuperBonder Adhesives
Increase Finished
Product Value**
• Aesthetic advantage of colorless bonding
• Performance advantage of improved reliability

EXHIBIT 3   Selected Findings of Instant Adhesive Industrial Market Research Study

---

- 16% of all firms used instant adhesives. In only 16 SIC industry groups did more than 10% of the firms use instant adhesives.
- 55% of volume was accounted for by small firms with fewer than 20 employees.
- 71% of purchasers used the product in only one application.
- 64% of volume was used by OEMs, 36% was used by MROs. Many firms used instant adhesives in OEM applications alone.
- 62% of users purchased their instant adhesives through distributors; 3% purchased direct from manufacturers; and 35% purchased from retail stores.
- 81% of users stated that all instant adhesives were about the same price; 67% of purchasers from distributors and manufacturers and 75% of retail purchasers stated that price was not very important in instant adhesive purchase decisions.
- 72% of purchasers from distributors and manufacturers and 45% of retail purchasers stated that technical service was important in their choice of an instant adhesive supplier.
- 67% of brand purchases from distributors and manufacturers and 84% of retail purchases were specified by production, quality control, design, and plant engineers in larger firms, and by company presidents in firms with fewer than 20 employees. Employees and users specified brands on 18% and 9% of purchase occasions, and purchasing agents on 12% and 6% of purchase occasions respectively.
- 11% of firms using instant adhesives purchased 10 or more pounds annually; 29% purchased between one and nine pounds; 60% purchased less than a pound. Many purchasers were uncertain about the exact volume and cost of instant adhesives they used.
- 26% of current users expected to increase their usage of instant adhesives; 51% expressed interest in improving dispensing technology.
- 64% of instant adhesive users did not have a preferred brand, though 97% were satisfied with the products they used; 21% of users could recall the SuperBonder brand name.
- 72% of nonusers of instant adhesives stated that price was not a barrier to their use; 19% stated they had an assembling/fastening operation where instant adhesives might be used; 15% had received sales calls regarding instant adhesives. Among nonusers, there was a low knowledge of instant adhesives and their capabilities.

SOURCE: Company records.

Industrial sales of SuperBonder adhesives increased from 62,150 pounds in FY 1977 to 91,800 pounds in FY 1978. Their average sales price was $37.45 per pound during FY 1978, of which 52 percent was variable cost. Marketing and selling expenses ordinarily amounted to 30 percent of dollar sales. The rest was available for other overheads, including research and development expenditures, and profit. During FY 1978, 14,200 pounds of Quick Set 404 (Loctite's other CA) were sold at $129.40 per pound. Quick Set 404 had built substantial brand loyalty, so it commanded a premium price. SuperBonder adhesives were priced to attract new users of CAs rather than current users of Quick Set 404, but they

EXHIBIT 4   SuperBonder Adhesives' Benefits, Characteristics, and Typical Applications

Product Benefits

Speed assembly and test
- Bonds most material in less than 30 seconds without pressure—simplifies fixturing and clamping

Easy to use
- Single component—no mixing
- No surface preparation normally required
- Bonds materials to each other or in any combination

Improve product reliability
- Bonds have high strength—up to 5000 psi
- Bonds have good solvent and weather resistance

Speed production
- Loctite SuperBonder adhesives can be automatically dispensed in as small a volume as .001cc at a rate of 60 cycles per minute

Economical to use
- Eliminate need for costly heat and curing ovens—Loctite SuperBonder adhesives cure at room temperature
- Low cost-per-unit application—one pound contains 40,000 drops at an approximate cost of 1/7 cent per drop

Preserve product attractiveness
- Bond is colorless and transparent
- Negligible shrinkage—no solvent to evaporate
- Automatic application virtually eliminates clean-up problems

Product Characteristics

SuperBonder 420 Adhesive
- Low viscosity
- Very fast setting
- Bonds rubber, plastics, or in combination with metals
- Penetrating action
- Parts should be closely matched

SuperBonder 495 (IS04E) Adhesive
- Medium-to-low viscosity
- Fast setting
- Bonds rubbers and plastics or in combination with metals
- Parts should be closely matched

SuperBonder 430 (IS06) Adhesive
- Medium viscosity
- Fast setting
- Bonds metal and plastic
- Parts should be well matched

SuperBonder 414 Adhesive
- Medium viscosity
- Fast setting
- Excellent for metal and plastic bonding or in combination to themselves
- Moderate strength on hard-to-bond plastics such as polyethylene and polypropylene

SuperBonder 416 Adhesive
- High viscosity
- Bonds irregular or porous surfaces
- Excellent for bonding rubber and plastic parts

EXHIBIT 5   1978 SuperBonder Magazine Advertisement

SuperBonder® Instant Adhesive assembly cost: 6¢

Mechanical fastener assembly cost: 30¢

Loctite® SuperBonder® Instant Adhesives cut your assembly costs. They cost less to buy than mechanical fasteners. And take less time to use. Because they reduce or eliminate the clamping, drilling, tapping, screwing, countersinking and torquing that make mechanical fasteners so time consuming, and expensive.

SuperBonder Instant Adhesives are instant setting. Instant curing. Bond almost any material in 1 to 30 seconds with a continuous, stress resistant bond.

Loctite will give you the right SuperBonder Instant Adhesive for the job, get it on line, and service what we sell better than any other adhesive manufacturer in the world.

The #1 threadlocking company is also the #1 engineering adhesive company.

For further information or a free demonstration call your local Loctite distributor. For his name and number, call 1-800-243-8810. In CT call 1-800-842-8684. In Canada call (416) 625-6511.

LOCTITE. SuperBonder® Instant Adhesives

© 1979 Loctite Corporation, Newington, CT 06111
Loctite Canada, Inc., Mississauga, Ontario L4W 2S3

EXHIBIT 6 1978 SuperBonder Magazine Advertisement

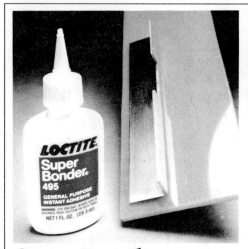
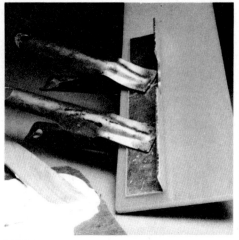

SuperBonder Instant Adhesive assembly time: 3 seconds.

Epoxy assembly time: 45 minutes.

Loctite' SuperBonder Instant Adhesives are faster than epoxies. And super strong.

SuperBonder adhesives are instant setting. Instant curing. SuperBonder adhesives eliminate critical two part mixing. Clamping. Heating equipment. Messy cleanup. And no waiting for parts to cure.

Bond almost any material in 1 to 30 seconds, depending on your needs.

We'll give you the right SuperBonder Instant Adhesive. Get it on line. And service what we sell better than any other adhesive manufacturer in the world.

Free sample and valuable demonstration. Call your local distributor. Or toll free, 1-800-243-8810 (CT 1-800-842-8684).

SuperBonder Instant Adhesives
LOCTITE

© Loctite Corporation. Newington. CT 06111

SOURCE: *Assembly Engineering, Design News, Production Engineering, Appliance Manufacturer,* and *Modern Machine Shop* magazines.

were priced above competitive industrial CAs, which sold at an average of $33 per pound in FY 1978. In FY 1978 Loctite Corp. sold $3.44 million of SuperBonder, $1.84 million of Quick Set 404, and $17.12 million of anaerobics.

The SuperBonder marketing plan for FY 1979 would continue the FY 1978 strategy with similar advertising and promotion efforts. Objectives included an increase in sales to $4.5 million, a market share of at least 35 percent across SICs 20 through 39, and a substantial increase in awareness and trial. To broaden the reach of SuperBonder advertising, the FY 1979 media schedule more heavily emphasized general engineering rather than industry-specific magazines. The principal innovation for FY 1979 was the introduction of the Gluematic Pen—a handheld plastic disposable tube of SuperBonder adhesive connected to a spring valve designed to open when applied to a firm surface and close instantly when removed. The valve, called the Gluematic tip applicator, was to facilitate precise placement of the adhesive and prevent clogging inside the pen. The pen was expected to reduce waste, protect users' fingers, and eliminate mess. It was scheduled to be introduced in January 1979 by Woodhill Permatex in a 3-gram size for both industrial and consumer markets.

Distribution and Sales Organization

In 1978 Loctite sold selectively through 285 distributors with 1,400 outlets. Although there were about 10,000 distributors nationwide through which Loctite products could have been distributed, executives believed that their distributors provided good market coverage and superior service. Sixty percent of Loctite's distributors were bearing distributors (who supplied to machinery and equipment manufacturers a diverse range of products costing between $1 and $10,000); 25 percent were general-line distributors; and 15 percent were specialty distributors for a particular market segment, such as the electrical and electronics industry.

Over 50 percent of SuperBonder adhesive sales were made through Loctite's distributors. A higher percentage of Loctite CAs than anaerobics was sold to industrial users through distributors, who typically expected a 25 percent margin on adhesives. They stocked products with established demand. Most distributors avoided stocking equipment that required servicing; however, a distributor might arrange a direct or drop shipment from factory to end user, in which case Loctite would usually pay the distributor 10 percent of the price to the end user.

Relationships with distributors were highly valued. The efforts of IPG salespeople were considered critical to maintaining and developing these relationships. In 1978, 20 IPG salespeople specializing by industry sold CAs and other Loctite products direct to SIB accounts, while 80 GIB salespeople, each with a geographic territory, sold the same product line to distributors. IPG salespeople earned a base salary plus commission on incremental sales over the previous year. The commission percentage was lower on equipment than on adhesives.

Most IPG salespeople were qualified engineers and highly regarded as experts in their field. They were viewed by management as problem solvers who would work with end users, demonstrating, testing, and recommending the most appropriate adhesive for specific applications. They frequently called on end users with distributor salespeople who were also usually compensated on a commission basis, complementing the latter's account knowledge with their technical expertise. The Loctite sales force also helped distributors plan their inventories of instant adhesives to maximize return on investment.

In addition, Loctite training programs for distributor and end-user personnel were highly regarded. During 1978 IPG trained 75,000 people in its five technical service and training facilities and its six "labmobiles," which traveled to end users' plants. IPG also held annual distributor advisory council meetings and published a newsletter which distributors could deliver to their customers under their own names. Together with consistently high product quality, these services enabled Loctite to command premium prices among both distributors and end users. Distributors were expected to carry a full line of Loctite adhesives, to list Loctite products in their catalogs, and to use Loctite's promotional literature and display materials.

Some IPG executives believed the company should move toward more extensive distribution. They argued that many existing or potential users of Loctite CAs were not reached by existing distributors. In addition, distributor salespeople often called on only one person at a particular firm, and this person might not be the most appropriate or indeed the only person to approach regarding CAs.

The Bond-A-Matic 2000 Dispenser

In FY 1979 IPG was also considering introduction of a unique low-cost adhesive dispensing system using the Gluematic tip. The IPG Systems Division developed the product at the request of the marketing group following the 1977 Sales Leadership Conference, in which several salespeople highlighted the difficulties of assembly line workers in dispensing CA from the standard one-ounce and smaller bottles. Because these bottles were cumbersome, the adhesive frequently clogged in the nozzle. The Systems Division developed a device which could precisely dispense dots, dashes, or lines of adhesive. (The prototype, tentatively named the Bond-A-Matic 2000 dispenser, and the Gluematic tip are shown in Exhibit 7.) When the reservoir of the Bond-A-Matic dispenser, which held a 1-lb. container of adhesive, was pressurized, air would force the adhesive

EXHIBIT 7   Prototype Bond-A-Matic 2000 Dispenser and Gluematic Tip Applicator

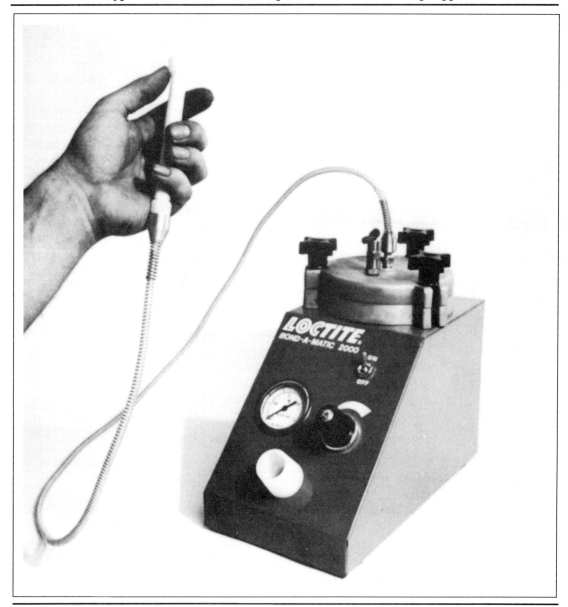

through a feed tube to the Gluematic tip.

After extensive testing, two Bond-A-Matic dispenser models were developed: a high-pressure model with an aluminum reservoir to dispense the more viscous adhesives, and a low-pressure model with a plastic reservoir to dispense less viscous adhesives.[4] Material costs were estimated at $105 for the high-pressure model and $75 for the low-pressure model, assuming annual production of at least 250 units each. Variable labor costs for in-house assembly would be $17.50 per unit for both models, or parts assembly could be subcontracted to an outside supplier at $15.75 per unit. By September 1978 prototype development costs had been $18,000 and capital investment had been $30,000. Significant additional capital investment was not anticipated.

The Gluematic tip was especially suited to dispensing adhesives onto hard surfaces. The Vari-Drop applicator was designed for soft surfaces. It dispensed adhesive through a detachable needle which could be replaced when worn. The needle could also deliver free-falling drops where the applicator tip could not touch the part. Variable costs of each Gluematic tip and each Vari-Drop needle were 25 cents and 15 cents, respectively. Preliminary tests indicated that an operator using the Bond-A-Matic dispenser and Gluematic tip could apply a dot of adhesive every three seconds. Speed of application and durability of the tip depended on the surface and adhesive; however, tests suggested that a tip, if used properly, would be good for at least 12,000 dot applications. An ounce of SuperBonder adhesive could provide at least 850 such applications.

Fox believed the Bond-A-Matic offered many advantages to the end user, though some might view it as nothing more than an interesting gadget (see Exhibit 8); however, he was not sure how large a market might exist for it. He wondered what level of usage would be sufficient to warrant purchase of the Bond-A-Matic. A related issue was whether its anticlogging feature would stimulate increased sales of instant adhesives or merely highlight to potential users one of their principal problems.

Internal Reaction to the Bond-A-Matic

Before planning the details of a Bond-A-Matic market introduction, Fox had to consider the likely response of the Systems Division, the IPG sales force, and Loctite's distributors.

During FY 1978 the Systems Division estimated that it secured half the dollar market for instant adhesive applicator control consoles and dispensing heads in North America. Equipment valued at $750,000, much of it customized, was sold direct to SIB customers. Standard models valued at $450,000 were sold direct to GIB customers, with an additional $250,000 worth reaching GIB customers through distributors or drop shipment. The Systems Division had built a reputation for high-quality equip-

---

[4] The high-pressure model was designed for SuperBonder 430, 414, and 416. The low-pressure model was designed for SuperBonder 420 and 495, though SuperBonder 430 and 414 could also be used. (About half of existing sales were of SuperBonder 420 and 495.)

EXHIBIT 8   Features of the Bond-A-Matic 2000 Dispensing System

---

- Anticlog application using the Gluematic tip.
- No mess or waste.
- Simple, inexpensive maintenance.
- Short start-up and shutdown time (2 minutes each).
- Average operator training time of 15 minutes.
- Easy loading of 1-lb. or 150-ml containers.
- Portable; weighs less than 10 lbs.
- Only one cubic foot of space required.
- Hand-activated; shuts off automatically when pressure is released.
- No electrical connection requirement.
- Adjustable pressure range, handling most Loctite adhesives with varying viscosities.
- Faster parts assembly.
- Decreased assembly error, increased product reliability, and reduced scrap and rework costs.
- More accurate control of labor and material costs.

SOURCE: Company records.

ment. Exhibit 9 shows two consoles and a patented pencil-type applicator dispensing head typical of the product line, together with cost and price information. The Model 200 could dispense a variety of adhesives; the more sophisticated and durable Model 205 had been specifically designed to dispense CAs. Both were more precisely engineered than the Bond-A-Matic and included adjustable pressure regulators. The cheapest system (200 console plus applicator) was priced at $725 to end users. Comparable competing equipment was priced as much as one-third lower. Competitors were generally small with limited resources, serving either regional markets or particular industries. None manufactured instant adhesives. They usually sold through independent manufacturers' representatives rather than direct to users.

Automatic adhesive dispensing equipment was generally purchased by large firms that manufactured products not subject to frequent design changes. Although plant and production engineers often had discretionary purchasing authority on capital equipment of up to $250, the size of the dispensing equipment purchase usually meant that design engineers and the purchasing staff also became involved in the decision-making process.

The Systems Division had designed both Bond-A-Matic models to dispense a broad range of adhesives including CAs and anaerobics, but the IPG marketing group argued that the Bond-A-Matic should be positioned primarily as a CA dispenser. Systems Division executives wondered how the new dispenser might affect the image of their existing product line, particularly if it carried the Loctite name. They were uncertain as to whether the Bond-A-Matic would stimulate or cannibalize sales.

EXHIBIT 9   Systems Division Applicator Control Consoles and Dispensing Heads

Model 200 Control Console
End-user price: $450
Drop shipment price: $405
Total manufacturing cost: $300
Variable cost: $255

Model 27A Pencil Applicator
End-user price: $275
Drop shipment price: $247.50
Total manufacturing cost: $186
Variable cost: $160

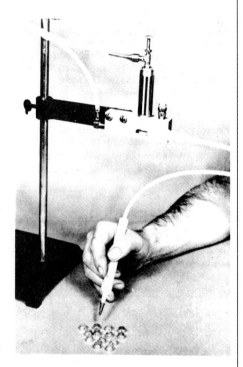

Model 205 Control Console
End-user price: $995
Drop shipment price: $895.50
Total manufacturing cost: $670
Variable cost: $570

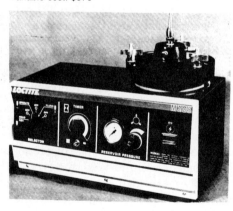

SOURCE: Company records.

They doubted that they could rapidly manufacture large quantities of a standard product, and feared being inundated with customer service calls from end users inexperienced with adhesive dispensing equipment. Existing Systems Division equipment sales already required heavy account maintenance. Finally, further Systems Division tests had uncovered two problems with the Vari-Drop applicator: SuperBonder tended to clog in the needle, and the pressure required to dispense adhesive comfortably differed between men and women operators.

The Loctite sales force had not traditionally focused on selling equipment. Fox wondered whether they would be interested in learning to demonstrate the Bond-A-Matic and to determine which model and tip best fit each intended application. There was also a risk that, given the limited time of any sales call, salespeople would either ignore the new dispenser or push it at the expense of Loctite's basic products. The cost of a sales call, estimated at $120, would probably preclude visiting a distributor or end user solely to sell the Bond-A-Matic.

Fox also suspected that sales force reaction would depend on the willingness of Loctite's distributors to stock the Bond-A-Matic dispenser and necessary accessories. Distributors would have a stake in its success only if they could be persuaded to stock it.

Developing a Marketing Plan

Product, Pricing, and Quality Assurance

If the Bond-A-Matic dispenser was introduced, Fox first had to decide which customers to pursue. Only then could he develop a detailed marketing plan and decide whether both models should be made available and whether the Vari-Drop needle as well as the Gluematic tip should be included with each unit. He also had to determine a pricing schedule for the dispenser and accessories. (Exhibit 10 presents one schedule being considered.) Some executives argued that a $175 price might jeopardize Loctite's quality image without encouraging multiple purchases for several work stations in an assembly line.

A further question was whether the Loctite name should appear prominently on each unit. Some executives argued that the Loctite name was associated with high-quality adhesives, not low-cost dispensing equipment, and questioned linking the name with the unproven Bond-A-Matic. They also suggested that the similarity between the names Bond-A-Matic and SuperBonder might jeopardize the favorable brand name recognition recent advertising had built up for SuperBonder should the Bond-A-Matic prove unsuccessful.

Fox was considering two approaches to assure potential end users and distributors of the new dispenser's quality. A 30-day free trial could

---

EXHIBIT 10   Proposed Distributor and End-User Price Schedule for Bond-A-Matic 2000 Dispenser and Replacement Parts

	Suggested Price to End User	*Loctite Price to Distributor*
Bond-A-Matic 2000 (both low- and high-pressure models)	$175.00	$140.00
Gluematic tip	1.00	0.75
Vari-Drop dispensing needle	0.50	0.28
Vari-Drop applicator	22.00	15.00
Feed line replacement kit	27.00	18.75
Airline filter replacement kit	14.25	9.95

NOTE: Loctite would receive $157.50 ($175.00 less a 10 percent drop shipment allowance to the local distributor) on a direct sale to an end user.

SOURCE: Company records.

---

be introduced, with the purchaser being invoiced at the end of the trial period if the dispenser was not returned. Or, a one-year limited warranty, valid only so long as Loctite adhesives were used in the dispenser, could be offered. A warranty registration card to be returned to Loctite's head office would be included with each unit. This would also allow Loctite to inform purchasers of future product improvements or additions. The Systems division, however, questioned whether the costs of returned equipment and service repairs associated with these offers would be treated as a marketing or a manufacturing expense.

Advertising

Fox was uncertain whether to use advertising to assist the product launch since he could not forecast its impact. An advertising campaign might fail; but it also might be too successful, stimulating unmanageable inquiries and orders. But Fox doubted whether advertisements for the Bond-A-Matic dispenser, even if placed in magazines directed at specific industries, could convey a message sufficiently tailored to stimulate purchase. Nevertheless, Loctite's advertising agency had developed the media schedule in Exhibit 11 on the assumption that the dispenser would be introduced early in 1979. Magazines were selected to maximize reach to production and packaging engineers of firms in SICs 35 through 39. Insertions were timed to complement the projected editorial emphasis and SuperBonder advertising in each issue. The agency also recommended that brochures on the Bond-A-Matic be included with all 1 lb.-packages of SuperBonder adhesives and with 10-packs of 1-oz. SuperBonder bottles during the launch period.

Concerns about the content of any advertising centered on whether the price of the dispenser should be included and what degree of emphasis

EXHIBIT 11   Proposed Media Schedule for Bond-A-Matic and SuperBonder: First Half of 1979

Magazine	Circulation	January	February	March	April	May	June	Cost of BAM Advertising
Assembly Engineering	74,570		SB		BAM	BAM	BAM	$ 9,375
Design News	149,307		SB	SB	SB	SB	SB	
Electronic Products	93,196				BAM	BAM	BAM	8,190
Industrial Equipment News	186,796		SB	SB	SB	SB	SB	
					BAM	BAM	BAM	13,320
Production Engineering	92,660				BAM	BAM	BAM	11,130
Production	80,063				BAM	BAM	BAM	9,801
								$51,816

NOTE: All four-color, full-page advertisements. BAM denotes an advertisement for the Bond-A-Matic, SB an advertisement for SuperBonder.
SOURCE: Mintz & Hoke, Inc.

should be placed on the Loctite name. Fox also wondered whether the advertising should be used merely to develop awareness or whether it should actively solicit inquiries and orders. In the latter case, ads could simply include the company's address or incorporate a reply coupon in the body of the advertisement, or the Bond-A-Matic could be included on the multicompany "Bingogram" information request cards included in most industrial magazines. Any inquiries could be followed up with a telephone sales call by Loctite headquarters staff, company salespeople, or an outside telephone sales organization, which would charge $12 per call. Telephone orders might be credited to the salesperson managing the territory from which they originated. If an order came from a firm already using a Loctite distributor, the distributor might receive Loctite's standard 10 percent drop shipment allowance.

Direct-Mail Program

Because of uncertainty that all potential Bond-A-Matic purchasers could be effectively reached through advertising, Fox was considering direct mail as an alternative or supplement to the advertising campaign. Three mailing lists could be purchased from different sources containing the names and addresses of production and packaging engineers working for firms in SIC categories 35 through 39. The lists would cost as follows: $225 (containing 2,678 names), $675 (14,740 names), and $305 (5,177 names). At a unit cost of $3, a package could be produced and mailed to each individual; this would contain a letter tailored to the recipient's business, a brochure describing the Bond-A-Matic, a reply card, and a Gluematic Pen which could highlight the dispenser's unique anticlogging feature. Fox hoped that at least 10 percent of the recipients would return the reply cards. Each might then receive a telephone sales call.

ROLM: The SIGMA Introduction

In January 1987, Bob Lundy was sizing up the progress he and the SIGMA team had made on the new PBX development at ROLM Corporation. Lundy had joined ROLM late in 1984, a few months before International Business Machines Corporation acquired 100 percent of the 15-year-old company's stock. On arriving at ROLM, Lundy had taken charge of a system development project that was intended to improve ROLM's cost competitiveness. After two years of effort, Lundy was pleased that his project, which had been given the code name SIGMA, had become the centerpiece of ROLM's future product line.

In many ways the SIGMA system promised significant improvements over the company's existing product line. It would be less costly to build and less costly for customers to operate. But SIGMA also presented problems because it would be technologically incompatible with ROLM's earlier PBX systems. Essentially, for the first time in the company's history, ROLM was planning to introduce a next generation product that could not be integrated with any of the 20,000 installed systems of its customer base. ROLM's share of the installed base was about 12–15 percent.

By 1987, ROLM was committed to introducing SIGMA, but controversy remained concerning the introduction strategy and implementation. Lundy's task was to propose solutions for several critical implementation issues associated with the SIGMA introduction. And, because senior management had widely differing views about SIGMA, he had to build a consensus for how the SIGMA introduction would be managed.

Professor V. Kasturi Rangan of the Harvard Business School prepared this revised case as the basis for class discussion rather than to illustrate either effective or ineffective handling of an administrative situation. Cliff Fitzgerald prepared the original case under the supervision of Jay Misra, Lecturer in Decision Sciences at Stanford Graduate School of Business. Copyright © 1990 by the Board of Trustees of the Leland Stanford Junior University, and Copyright © 1990 by the President and Fellows of Harvard College. Harvard Business School case 9–590–082.

Company Background

ROLM Corporation was founded in June 1969 by four electrical engineers who had recently graduated from Rice University.[1] Sharing an entrepreneurial interest, the founders started ROLM with the goal of developing a military specification, or mil-spec, computer. By using newly available minicomputer technology, ROLM's founders believed they could design a computer that would cost 80 percent less to build than the mainframe systems that dominated the mil-spec market. After nine months of development, the company shipped the first units of its new mil-spec computer, priced approximately 50 percent below the closest competitor.

In those early years, ROLM was committed to maintaining its technical leadership in the mil-spec business and to building responsive service and support capabilities. By combining technical leadership, superior service, and unrivaled price/performance, ROLM quickly earned a reputation as a leading mil-spec supplier. By 1973, however, Ken Oshman, ROLM's president, became concerned about the prospects for future growth at ROLM. Oshman predicted the mil-spec computer market would be nearly saturated by the time ROLM reached $10–$20 million in sales. Driven by higher ambition, Oshman and his fellow founders decided to investigate other markets where the company's computer expertise could be applied.

After considering several alternatives, ROLM became interested in private branch exchanges (PBX) as a promising market to diversify into. A PBX is a customer-oriented telephone switching system that connects telephone extensions within an organization to the local telephone company's switching office or directly to other extensions within the organization. A simple PBX system would consist of desktop telephones, wires that link the telephone to the PBX cabinet, and the cabinet itself. By owning a PBX rather than paying the local telephone company for individual telephone lines for each extension, a company could reduce the costs of using and maintaining its telephones. A PBX also provided a company with greater flexibility and management control of its telecommunications systems.

Business users that did not own a PBX had to access a central office switching service (Centrex) offered by the local telephone companies. Central office switches were premised at the telephone company. The customer did not pay for the equipment, or its maintenance, but a line fee every time the switch was used. PBX, on the other hand, was premised at the customer site. Though customers paid for the equipment, they did not pay a fee for intra-office use, because the switching was done internally.

---

[1] The name ROLM is an acronym for the founders' last names: Gene Richeson, Ken Oshman, Walter Lowenstern, and Bob Maxfield.

In 1973, an estimated 40,000 PBX systems were installed in the United States, supporting approximately 10 million telephone lines. Most of these systems had been supplied by AT&T and were based on analog technology that had been developed in the 1960s or earlier. ROLM's project assessment team identified several shortcomings of analog PBX systems that they believed could be remedied by a digital, or computer-controlled, PBX. They also believed a computer-controlled PBX would become a necessity for supporting the technology-leading PBX applications of the future. Finally, they believed that developing such a system would be an easier job for ROLM than it would be for AT&T. Weighing the advantage of being first to market, Oshman decided to commit his company to developing a computer-controlled PBX. In April 1975, after little more than a year of development, ROLM introduced its first "CBX" (computer-controlled private branch exchange) with a capability of serving customers' installations requiring up to 800 extensions.

Growth Years: 1975–1982

Between 1975 and 1982 ROLM's revenues grew from $11 million to $380 million, 85 percent of which was contributed by sales of the CBX product line. During this period of rapid growth, ROLM spent aggressively to expand and enhance the CBX product line. The company added software releases every year that provided customers with a succession of innovative, industry-leading features. ROLM also adapted the CBX hardware "platform" to serve a broader range of customer installation sizes. See Exhibit 1 for ROLM product lines and launch data.

Because of rapid changes in technology during this period, telecommunications managers were uneasy about the possibility of their PBX equipment becoming obsolete as soon as a new and better system was announced. An investment in a single PBX system installation could amount to as much as $15 million for a large organization, and a minimum useful life for the asset was generally expected to be five years. In response to this concern about obsolescence, ROLM designed its new products so that any customer could easily upgrade to the company's latest, full-feature system. Therefore, customers were able to incorporate the currently available state-of-the-art technology without losing their present investment in an installed CBX. This capability became a hallmark of the company and was emphasized by ROLM executives and salespeople. Exhibit 2 illustrates how this theme was used in ROLM's advertising.

Several trends were shaping the competitive environment in the PBX market during the 1970s and 1980s. First, deregulation in the telecommunications industry was dissolving the legal monopoly AT&T had enjoyed since the 1930s. This trend had facilitated ROLM's entry to the PBX market, but it also made the business increasingly attractive to new competition. Second, increased reliance by businesses on information sys-

EXHIBIT 1   ROLM Product Lines

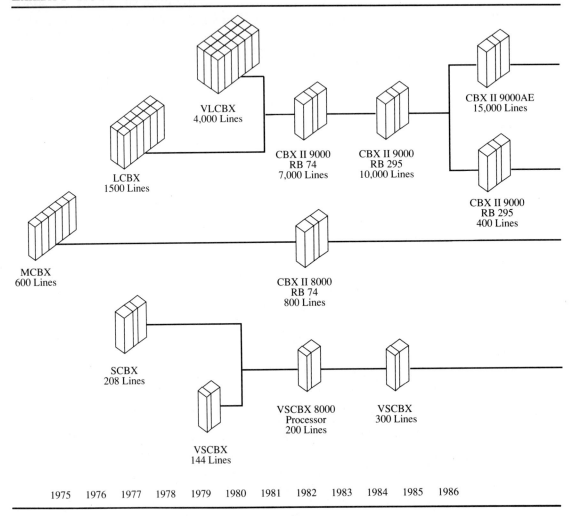

tems was creating a need for accessing and moving data within the organization. Many people considered the PBX to be the most promising system for tying information together, particularly because of its already installed wiring and access to public network. This potential opportunity also increased competitive interest in the PBX market.

As a consequence, Northern Telecom, a Canadian start-up, and several other companies had become active in marketing digital PBX systems that were increasingly competitive with ROLM's CBX. AT&T introduced

EXHIBIT 2   ROLM Advertising

DON'T LET THE STEPS KILL YOU.

Take The Ramp. ROLM has perfected a breakthrough communications controller: The CBX II.

It's the centerpiece for a spectacular new ROLM' business telephone system — the fastest, most advanced way to manage voice and data in the world.

Instead of the typical stops, starts, steps and plateaus of expansion, CBX II lets you grow smoothly, easily and very, very cost-effectively.

You can move up The Ramp from sixteen phones to more than ten thousand phones, terminals and personal computers. You can store and forward messages. You can monitor costs. You can have the least expensive long distance routes automatically, instantly. You can even network networks, from Dow Jones to the IBM Infonet. And we're plugged into IBM and HP and DEC and Data General and the other movers and shakers to guarantee that we can take their new products and new systems in stride.

The CBX II is just the latest reason why ROLM is the choice of more than two-thirds of the *Fortune 500* companies, why more than fourteen thousand ROLM systems are up and running today.

When it's all said and done, the best thing about The Ramp is that it ends that recurring nightmare that you may be buying a business communications system that can't grow, can't change or has a big, gee whiz capability missing.

Make your life a lot simpler. Just skip the steps and take The Ramp. **ROLM**

a series of new PBX systems in the 1970s, but these systems were based on outdated analog technology, and AT&T's share of the PBX market slid from 50 percent in 1976 to 27 percent in 1982. Lacking a competitive digital offering, AT&T was beginning to show signs that it would fight its loss of market share through aggressive pricing.

Technological Concerns

By 1982, a significant technology concern had developed at ROLM due to the prevalent use by the company's principal competitors of a sampling rate difference from the one used in the CBX product line. Sampling rate refers to the number of times per second a digital PBX converts voice (analog) signals into a digital form or vice versa. The electronic "chip" that performs this operation is known as a coder-decoder, or codec for short. When ROLM introduced the CBX in 1975, it used a sampling rate of 12,000 samples per second (also called 12 kilohertz, or 12 khz), which was then the standard for the industry. Later, when ROLM's competitors were developing their own digital PBX technology, 8 khz emerged as the preferred sampling rate and became the de facto industry standard.

ROLM's use of nonstandard 12 khz sampling was increasingly perceived as a technical liability of the CBX line. Some customers began to view ROLM as offering old and obsolete technology that was poorly positioned for the future of telecommunications. While ROLM was in fact able to modify its CBX systems to convert between 12 khz and 8 khz samplings, and therefore could support any current and future 8 khz applications, doing so required extra circuitry and development expense.[2] Furthermore, 12 khz codec chips were not only less plentiful and more expensive then 8 khz codec, but 8 khz codec prices were continuing to fall while 12 khz codec prices had leveled off.

A second technological problem at ROLM concerned the aging of CBX technology. Much of ROLM's R&D effort through 1982 had been directed at developing software and hardware enhancements that would maintain the company's product leadership while remaining compatible with existing CBX technology. Over the years, the company's competitors were building entirely new systems that incorporated latest available technologies. As a result, competitive PBX offerings were smaller and required less power and air-conditioning than the CBX, making them less expensive for customers to operate. Also using newer technologies often meant that competitors experienced lower manufacturing and service

---

[2] Several new telecommunications technology standards, including ISDN (Integrated Services Digital Network) and T-1 bypass, incorporated 8 khz sampling. ROLM could accommodate these emerging standards with extra circuits, but customers were increasingly skeptical of ROLM's position for the future.

costs. ROLM's disadvantage in hardware technology had become a serious drawback in competitive bidding situations, resulting in lost business and wasted effort on the part of account people who had to explain ROLM's position to customers.

Late in 1983, ROLM announced it would introduce a new version of the CBX, dubbed the CBX II, which would consolidate its product line and offer advance performance. However, the CBX II would not address either the concerns about aging technology or ROLM's use of 12 khz sampling. Nevertheless, the CBX II would remain technologically compatible with earlier CBX systems.

Competitive Considerations

Prior to 1981, AT&T was the monopoly provider of both long-distance telephone service through its long lines division as well as local area service through its 22 Bell operating companies. Judge Harold Greene's 1984 Modified Final Judgment decreed that the Bell operating companies be spun off into seven regional holding companies (RHC) that would be independently operated. As a result, the local telephone companies were no longer obliged to buy AT&T equipment. (AT&T's Western Electric division manufactured central office switching, as well as PBX equipment.) By 1985, while several manufacturers offered keen competition in the PBX market, the central office switching market was still dominated by AT&T and Northern Telecom with market shares of 45 percent and 40 percent respectively. ROLM did not manufacture central office switching equipment.

After the 1984 divestiture, initially the local telephone companies aggressively pushed PBX technology (by acting as distributors for PBX manufacturers), but by 1985 had realized that more revenues and profits could be made by pushing Centrex services. There was little distribution margin left because of aggressive price competition among PBX manufacturers. The RHCs began to pressure AT&T and Northern Telecom to upgrade their installed central office switching equipment's business features. This involved mainly software, and some hardware upgrades. Both AT&T and Northern Telecom were able to respond quite quickly to this need, forcing end users to wonder about the economics of owning PBX equipment, instead of renting Centrex (central office switching) services from the local telephone companies. This move further hurt the PBX market development and sharpened the competition in the PBX market.

SIGMA

Late in 1984 IBM acquired ROLM in order to accelerate the development of PBXs that could interact with IBM computers. The end of 1984 also marked Bob Lundy's arrival at ROLM. Lundy, an electrical engineer and a Stanford MBA, joined ROLM from Hewlett-Packard to manage a product development and introduction program that was in early concept phase. See Exhibit 3 for an organization chart. The principal goal of Lundy's new program was to reduce the life cycle cost of the CBX. (Life cycle cost refers to the total of the customer's cost of owning and ROLM's cost of manufacturing, maintaining, and servicing the CBX.)

As product manager, Lundy led a product development team consisting of managers from hardware and software engineering, reliability and maintainability engineering, planning, and manufacturing. In four months of all-out effort, this tightly focused group completed a new product definition and set a development schedule. As proposed, the new product would be an entirely new system that would preserve the best of the CBX technology. Most important, it would be able to run the same software applications that CBX customers already knew how to use.

However, the new system would utilize the industry standard 8 khz sampling rate rather than the 12 khz sample rate used in the current CBX product line. Although 8 khz sampling would reduce hardware costs and facilitate product development, the resulting system would be incompatible with the 20,000 CBXs currently installed. To upgrade from the CBX to the new system, ROLM's customers would need to replace their CBX controllers with new controllers, an operation that was known as a "forklift upgrade." To preserve security over these plans, Lundy adopted the code name SIGMA for his program.

Not all of the CBX system components would be incompatible with the SIGMA system, however. The telephone lines themselves and the wiring that connected the controller to the individual telephone extensions could be used with the SIGMA system. For small installations, the

---

EXHIBIT 3 ROLM Organization Chart

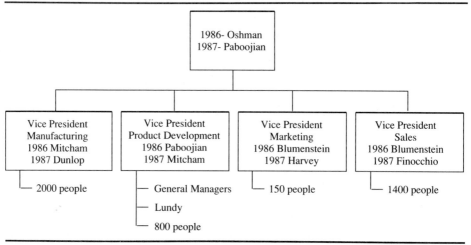

cost of purchasing and installing these components amounted to 40 percent of the hardware system cost while for installation of 10,000 or more lines that accounted for 60 percent of the bill.

The development team believed the SIGMA system would deliver the following improvements compared to the CBX:

Switching capacity	70% higher
Reliability	100% higher
Service cost	55% lower
Power requirements	50% lower
Physical space requirements	50% lower

Lundy felt strongly that these improvements would answer the criticisms that had been directed at the CBX. Concerns about obsolete technology, air-conditioning requirements, and physical bulk would be resolved. Moreover, Lundy believed that SIGMA's increased performance would enable ROLM to capture a higher win ratio in the market and would provide an excellent foundation for developing future industry-leading applications. See Exhibit 4 for management's assessment of SIGMA's strengths with respect to competition.

By late 1985, SIGMA had emerged as ROLM's best bet for the future. The new design would save manufacturing costs, and potentially improve current gross margins by as much as 50–75 percent. The SIGMA team had completed the specifications for the new system and Ken Oshman

EXHIBIT 4   SIGMA versus Competition

	<600 Lines Segment	
Factors	*SIGMA*	*"Best of Breed"*
Reliability	=	A
Cost of ownership	−	A
System coverage	+	SIGMA
Function/feature	=	A/SIGMA
Connectivity/data support	+	SIGMA
	>600 Lines Segment	
Factors	*SIGMA*	*"Best of Breed"*
Reliability	=	A/SIGMA
Cost of ownership	+	SIGMA
System coverage	+	B/SIGMA
Function/feature	=	C/SIGMA
Connectivity/data support	+	SIGMA

SOURCE: Company records.

had made the decision to go ahead with further development. Oshman also decided that the target market for SIGMA should be extended across the entire range of the current CBX line, covering installations from 600 to 20,000 lines. The SIGMA team had reason to be pleased with the importance that their program had taken on. Moving ahead, Lundy prepared for the next management checkpoint meeting, scheduled for January 1986 with the VP of systems development.

Implementation Issues

At the management checkpoint meeting of January 1986 Lundy presented his team's specifications and product development plans for SIGMA. During the presentation, Lundy stressed that the general goal of the SIGMA program was to increase revenue and profitability at ROLM, and he listed the following specific objectives of the program:

1. Increase ROLM's win ratio in competitive bidding situations.
2. Increase margins.
3. Avert any decline in orders and revenue during the introduction period.
4. Minimize value erosion of ROLM's installed base of CBX.
5. Maximize customer confidence.
6. Avoid confusion in the marketplace.

After listening to the presentation, ROLM's VP of systems development, Dennis Paboojian, was very concerned about how the introduction of SIGMA would be managed. He believed the SIGMA introduction was vastly more difficult than any previous new product introduction at ROLM. This stemmed from two principal facts: (1) SIGMA was technologically incompatible with ROLM's installed base; and (2) the SIGMA rollout would span the entire range of the CBX II product line, which provided the majority of ROLM's revenues. Paboojian believed an introduction that was anything less than superbly orchestrated would place ROLM's entire business at risk. See Exhibit 5 for ROLM-installed systems as of 1987.

With development work continuing on the SIGMA system, Lundy and his team spent much of the next 12 months addressing the concerns Paboojian had raised. By January 1987, Lundy believed his team had enough information to fully characterize these issues and he knew that engineering and manufacturing had committed to rolling out production units of SIGMA in December. Lundy framed the following five critical implementation issues.

1. *Security*. ROLM managers were apprehensive about how customers would react when they learned that SIGMA was incompatible with the CBX line. Most thought that a premature leak of information

EXHIBIT 5   ROLM—Installed Base (1987)

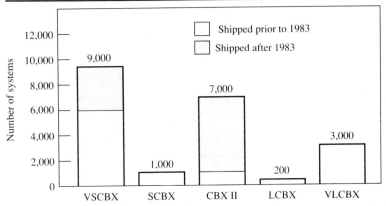

- Systems of greater than 400 lines represented 30 percent of unit systems sales but 70 percent of revenue.
- Shipments of approximately 200 systems per month were planned for 1987.

SOURCE: Company records.

about SIGMA would result in a significant reduction of revenue. Customers would be afraid that the new system would signal a reduction in ROLM's efforts to support the CBX. Customers bought systems from ROLM not only for their current capabilities but also with the expectation of adding future system expansions and software updates as was done on a yearly basis to enhance mainframe computers.

Until 1986, knowledge about SIGMA had been kept to a small number of inside people. Maintaining security would become increasingly difficult, however. For example, during 1987 SIGMA would be installed for testing at ROLM and at eight different IBM locations; thus an increasing number of inside staff would have to know about the new system. Also, 20 demonstration sites, requiring six weeks of installation time, would need to be in place throughout the United States prior to announcement day. Third, a number of market-leading large system contracts were being vied for at this time—installations that SIGMA would be capable of handling but the CBX II would not. On these contracts, ROLM could either decline to bid, or bid and risk broad disclosure about the new system. Fourth, account managers at IBM, whose primary interest was to secure IBM computer sales, were being asked by their clients to reveal the ROLM subsidiary's new product plans. Finally, ROLM managers thought that divulgence of product plans, even to major existing customers, would inevitably constitute a general announcement.

Despite tight security measures, Lundy was aware that rumors about SIGMA had already appeared in trade journals (see Exhibit 6). These rumors were being used by ROLM's competitors to undermine the company's sales efforts. Prompted by the rumors, major customers were requesting ROLM to allow guarantees in purchase contracts providing assurance that their CBX II systems would not become obsolete.

2. *Announcement.* Lundy faced three basic issues concerning the SIGMA announcement: whether to announce quietly or with a "splash"; and what information to emphasize in the announcement. Lundy surveyed several senior managers on these issues and received differing views, as indicated in the following excerpts:

> Dennis says don't splash. Thinks we would lose control, and believes big splash announcements lead to a very complex situation for the sales force to handle. For example, maybe we wouldn't be able to deal with customers who are in the process of installing a CBX II system but who want to convert their orders to a SIGMA system.
>
> From interview with Dennis Paboojian, vice president of Systems Development

---

EXHIBIT 6   News Reports

IS ROLM READYING CBX III?

Switch Maker Denies CBX II Successor in Beta Test

Despite ROLM Corp.'s staunch contention that the rumored successor to its CBX II private branch exchange is a figment of the industry's imagination, observers close to the company insist the IBM subsidiary is on the verge of making a significant announcement, possibly involving a new generation PBX.

According to one anonymous source, ROLM is already beta testing a CBX III architecture that will be introduced soon. Other analysts believe pending announcements will simply involve enhancements to the existing CBX II.

All observers, however, voiced strong opinions regarding ROLM's CBX II failings noting that an upgrade or new switch would serve to strengthen the company's position in the PBX market.

ROLM's introduction of the low-end Redwood PBX in June represented a departure from the company's proprietary architecture, rekindling speculation that ROLM would eventually shift its larger, mainstream switch products to industry standards. Rumors of a CBX III have dogged ROLM ever since, although the company has never indi-

cated such a product was slated for introduction.

ROLM's current PBX architecture samples analog voice signals 12,000 times per second and represents each sample with a 12-bit digital word. Industry-standard pulse-code modulation samples analog signals 8,000 times per second and represents each sample with an 8-bit byte. Some analysts contend ROLM's break with the industry standard is creating compatibility problems with the data processing products of parent company IBM and bodes ill for ROLM's compatibility with Integrated Services Digital Network environments.

According to Jerry Eisen, president of Office Sciences International, Inc., of Iselin, NJ, ROLM has been aware for some time that the CBX II architecture had to change. Eisen, who has been in discussions with ROLM over the last four months, said, "We told ROLM, and they agreed, that the switch has to support 64K bit/sec ISDN, the footprint has to change, and the power requirements have to change."

ROLM's admission of architectural shortcomings, he said, would probably

---

EXHIBIT 6 *concluded*

---

result in a new architecture with the same digital interface, enabling users to retain CBX II station equipment but requiring new racks and cards. Eisen said he would be surprised not to hear an announcement in the immediate future. "ROLM is overdue as far as the market is concerned."

Donald Dittberner, president of Dittberner Associates, Inc., a consultancy located in Bethesda, MD, said he, too, is expecting an announcement. "I see ROLM having serious problems in competition from ISDN Centrex," he said. "I would think that IBM, which has never supported ISDN, now sees the handwriting on the wall. If something isn't announced by spring, I think ROLM will be in very difficult straits." A new switch should support local-area network capabilities and IBM protocols and be ISDN-compatible, he said.

Doane Perry, senior telecommunications analyst with International Data Corp., said he believes ROLM is poised to make an announcement. "On the inside of the switch, it will have to be more IBM Systems Network Architecture compatible, and on the outside, more ISDN- and T-1-compati-

ble. ROLM has had problems achieving T-1 compatibility," he added.

Lee Goeller, president of Communication Resources, Inc., of Haddonfield, Conn., elaborated on the T-1 point. "Everybody else who had a chance made a T-carrier-compatible PBX," he said. "To not do this is foolish: all ROLM has to do is change the switching matrix."

If Goeller's assertion is correct, ROLM might accomplish the necessary enhancements by introducing a new processor for the CBX II in lieu of a completely new machine.

That, said Joaquin Gonzalez, service director of Enterprise Networking Strategies at Gartner Group, Inc., in Stamford, Conn., is the far more likely scenario. "ROLM has taken great pains to talk about the CBX II as its only high-end PBX now and forever," Gonzalez said. He refuted the possibility of a CBX III introduction, but said. "I think Rolm will come out with more powerful processors under the existing architecture, with enhancements enabling network management of voice."

SOURCE: By Pam Powers. Copyright November 1986 by Network World, Inc., Framingham, MA. Reprinted from *Network World*.

*   *   *   *

ROLM held a press conference in New York in early 1986 to squelch speculation about a CBX III development program. The delegation was lead by Vice President Jack Blumenstein, who emphasized the following point: ROLM would be foolish to develop any new PBX that was

SOURCE: *MIS Week*, January 13, 1986.

incompatible with or would obsolete the company's installed base of some 20,000 CBX systems. "Our customer base was one reason IBM bought us; the guy who bought the first CBX 10 years ago will still be able to get everything," insisted Blumenstein.

Dick thinks we have to prepare to announce but seems to imply that we may end up with something less than a major splash. After discussion, he pointed out that a splash had better have a lot of content, and we need to assess what the promotable value of SIGMA really is. At first he did not think a splash announcement would help in increasing the win ratio.

From interview with Dick Moley, vice president of Marketing

> Ken thinks it would be a major mistake to announce at all. Very
> concerned about the installed base. Suggests making the announcement a
> year late. Proposes that we highlight what we've got in the new product,
> but recognize that good release materials (sales and support
> documentation) without a big splash announcement accomplishes the same
> thing. After all, we win deals across the desk, talking with customers.
>
> From interview with Ken Oshman, president and founder

By comparison, Lundy felt very strongly that SIGMA should be announced as an exciting new hardware platform for the future. A further
question Lundy faced was whether to portray SIGMA in an announcement as an entirely new system or simply as an upgrade in the cabinet and
hardware. Here, again, he favored the more aggressive story.

3. *Timing.* To study the question of when to announce, Lundy considered a number of scenarios. The first scenario he considered assumed
an announcement three months ahead of general availability. This scenario had the advantage of putting ROLM in the running for certain large
contracts that were in the bidding process at the end of the year.

The second scenario Lundy considered also assumed announcement
three months in advance of product availability, but in this case he assumed a gradual ramping up of production over three months after
SIGMA introduction.

The third scenario assumed an announcement timed to coincide with
general product availability. Lundy wondered about the pros and cons of
each scenario with respect to the goals and objectives of the program.

Lundy also began to consider how an announcement might work in
December. On close examination, he became discouraged about announcing in December because of problems with doing business at the end of the
year. December was the end of the accounting year for both IBM and
ROLM, and usually there was frenzied business activity at that time,
though it was difficult to get anything done in the last 10 days because of
the holidays. At the same time, pressure was building to push the announcement forward to October. An October announcement would coincide with the announcement of a new European CBX system that would
also be based on 8 khz sampling technology. This schedule would leave
less than nine months for planning and would require manufacturing to
push forward their commitment date.[3]

In contemplating when to announce, Lundy was aware that SIGMA
had already missed its original introduction date of January 1987.

4. *Backlog.* A major issue for Lundy's team was how to manage
ROLM's backlog of orders in the months leading up to the announcement. Orders in the pipeline could be categorized according to four
stages: ordered but not shipped, shipped but not installed, installed but

---

[3] Manufacturing planning faced six month lead times for procuring certain parts.

not paid, and paid. The amount of time the average order spent in each of the first three stages was 90 days, 40 days, and 60 days, respectively. ROLM typically would begin production on an order as soon as the order was received.

Lundy already had a general idea about what the backlog would look like during the middle of the year. He knew, however, that he would need better information about the types of installations and customers if his team was going to be able to manage the backlog effectively. To collect this information and to manage the various accounts he formed the Backlog Management Team (BMT). Its goals were as follows:

- Plan to convert 95 percent of the backlogged orders from the CBX II system that was ordered to an equivalent SIGMA installation.
- Ensure complete secrecy about SIGMA before announcement.
- Take all steps necessary to avoid customer confusion.

The BMT believed many customers in the backlog could be convinced to accept a SIGMA system in lieu of a CBX because SIGMA would cost the same at purchase but would be less expensive to operate over the product's life. Also, while SIGMA would require less floor space and air-conditioning than customers had installed for the CBX, SIGMA's applications were functionally equivalent to the CBX. Generally, therefore, a customer could accept a SIGMA installation as a direct replacement of a CBX, and the primary impact would be that in some cases less than half of the area that was allocated for the system would be utilized.

However, Lundy's team did not expect all customers to willingly convert to a SIGMA system. Customers would be reluctant to buy a new system that might have glitches in it. In fact, most buyers rated system reliability as the most important criterion for selecting a PBX. As a result, a major question for Lundy was whether or not ROLM should continue marketing and/or shipping its widely accepted CBX II line after the SIGMA announcement. Continuing to market the CBX II would help safeguard ROLM's backlog of orders, but it would also complicate ROLM's manufacturing efforts and would confuse customers. Lundy favored the higher-risk solution of stopping active marketing of the CBX II. Under Lundy's plan, the company would continue to ship CBX II system expansions to its installed base and new CBX II systems on a special request basis only.

Perhaps a larger problem was how to keep sales and installation activity going through the summer. While ROLM was making every attempt to contain information about SIGMA within the company, there was widespread speculation in the industry that a new ROLM product was coming on line. Customers were becoming wary and demanding assurances that their investments would not become obsolete by a new ROLM product.

EXHIBIT 7   Investment Protection Plan

Customer Economics

In a system purchase scenario, a customer accepts a CBX II in July 1987 for a total cost of $2 million. The chart below indicates the proportions of component cost.

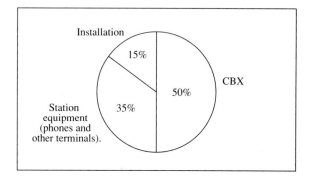

In December, 1987 the customer decides to trade in the CBX II controller for a SIGMA controller costing an additional $500,000 (without IPP discount). The component costs are as follows:

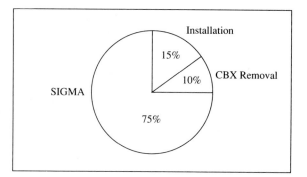

To buy an equivalent new system in December 1987 from one of ROLM's competitors would cost:

Competitor	Cost
X	$2.8 million
Y	$2.0 million
Z	$1.8 million

In the worst case, Lundy's team worried about the reactions (and careers) of telecommunications managers whose CBX systems would be installed and paid for just before SIGMA was announced.

ROLM's regional sales managers, who took the brunt of customers' concerns, demanded the ability to disclose ROLM's product plans to key clients and to offer some form of financial incentive to keep sales rolling. Lundy and the team members began to work on a program that would guarantee a trade-in allowance on any recently installed CBX system. Such a program would take the sting out of the SIGMA announcement, but it would also negatively impact ROLM's bottom line.

To better appraise the economic effects of such a program, Lundy devised a preliminary investment protection plan (IPP) that would provide a discount option to current customers of 55 percent off the incremental cost of upgrading to SIGMA (see Exhibit 7). Lundy was not certain how successful he would be in selling a 55 percent discount program to senior management considering ROLM's sales executives wanted a discount of 80–100 percent while IBM executives, who had never before provided this kind of benefit, wanted a discount of not more than 10–15 percent. There were also several questions of timing: namely, how many months prior to announcement should the IPP be grandfathered, and how many months after announcement should the option expire? Another issue was whether to compute the discount on the cost of the controller only or on total system cost including installation.

Lundy knew his team would face tremendous challenges in persuading backlogged customers to convert to SIGMA once the new system was announced. To accomplish its goals, the backlog management team would need to actively manage each account, learning as much as possible about each account's circumstances and gauging the likelihood of conversion without divulging ROLM's plans about the new product. If the team was not thoroughly prepared to manage this challenge, Lundy expected the resulting confusion would seriously injure ROLM's standing in the market and result in losses and deferrals in orders and revenues.

5. *Installed Base*. ROLM's installed base of 20,000 CBX systems presented another major problem to Lundy's group. Because of ROLM's historic high growth rate, most of the company's installed systems had not yet been fully depreciated by its customers. These customers expected that ROLM would continue its policy of protecting their investment by providing an easy and relatively inexpensive means of incorporating ROLM's latest-available technologies. The SIGMA announcement, however, would be perceived by these customers as a signal that ROLM was ending its commitment to enhance the CBX II line, and they would expect that future developments would only be available on the SIGMA platform. Lundy's team had to find ways to minimize this perception of value erosion among existing customers.

ROLM would continue to ship and support system expansions to its installed base. This activity was projected to account for 25 percent of revenue in 1987. ROLM was committed to providing the same level of service to these customers as it had done before. But ROLM did in fact plan to reduce development efforts on the CBX II in favor of developing future capabilities for SIGMA. This meant that installed base customers would have no other option than a "forklift upgrade" if they wanted to utilize the capabilities ROLM was developing for the future. This promised to add considerably to the expense of staying up-to-date with PBX technology.

To soften the blow to installed base customers, Lundy's team worked on a migration incentive plan that would provide some value to customers who wanted to trade in their CBX II systems for SIGMA systems. The preliminary plan called for a 20 percent allowance, although Lundy thought older systems should receive less of an allowance than newer systems. While he hadn't yet decided how to structure the allowance schedule, he did conclude that only CBX systems installed after 1984 would qualify for any benefit under this program.

Next Steps

In recent months, AT&T and Northern Telecom each had announced extremely competitive products in the 100–600 line range. In particular, the new AT&T System 75 family had earned the "best of breed" status in the low-end segment by offering compact digital systems that had low power requirements. Furthermore, these competitors had announced that their new products would support ISDN.[4] As a result, competition in the low-end segment was expected to be severe if not brutal. See Exhibit 8 for PBX market statistics from 1982–86. Nevertheless, Lundy felt SIGMA would still lead the industry on the following key attributes:

- Seamless architecture—through SIGMA, ROLM had the unique capability of covering the entire line range with a single product.
- Superior performance—SIGMA's advanced processor offered 70 percent more traffic capacity than the competition.
- Voice and data integration—SIGMA offered superior solutions and support for voice and data standards.
- Desktop devices—SIGMA would be compatible with ROLM's industry-leading product line of digital phone sets and terminals.

---

[4] Although SIGMA would not ship with ISDN capability, ROLM planned to issue a statement of direction.

Although the SIGMA team had made considerable progress in framing the five critical issues, Lundy still had to set a clear direction for each one. Once his choices were set, he would need to actively campaign to win approval from senior management.

EXHIBIT 8 PBX Market Statistics

	1982	1983	1984	1985	1986
Market size (000 lines shipped)	3,200	3,700	4,400	4,800	5,000
Market size ($ billions)	2.90	3.30	3.50	3.50	3.50
ROLM PBX revenue ($ millions)	380	500	560	540	550
ROLM gross margin after sales and marketing expense ($ millions)*	60	75	78	72	65

* Gross margin before sales and marketing expenses was 45 percent to 50 percent of sales.

Market Share of Top Eight Competitors

	1982	1983	1984	1985	1986
AT&T	27	23	19	23	22
Northern Telecom	13	17	22	23	23
ROLM	13	15	17	15	16
MITEL	12	12	10	9	9
NEC	4	5	6	7	8
GTE	5	4	4	4	4
Siemens	4	4	4	3	4
Intecom	1	2	3	3	2

NOTE: This exhibit has been constructed from the following sources:
- Roger G. Noll and Bruce M. Owen, "United States *vs.* AT&T: An Interim Assessment," in Stephen Bradley and Jerry Hausman, eds., *Future Competition in Telecommunications* (Cambridge, MA: HBS Press, 1989).
- *Business Week,* section on Information Processing, July 10, 1989.

Goodyear: The Aquatred Launch

In August 1992, Barry Robbins, Goodyear's vice president of Marketing for North American tires, was contemplating whether and how to launch the Aquatred, a new tire providing improved driving traction under wet conditions. The Aquatred would be positioned in the US market as a replacement tire for passenger cars. Over recent years, the replacement tire market had matured and new channels had gained share, so Robbins needed to make sure Goodyear had the right product and the right timing to generate support from the company's traditional base of independent dealers. Despite a long and close relationship with those independent dealers, Goodyear was also weighing the risks and benefits of expanding the company's distribution channels. If new outlets were added, Robbins would also have to assess whether the new channel would sell the Aquatred. To launch the Aquatred, Robbins would have to plan for a new product launch as well as for the future of the company's distribution system.

The Tire Industry in the United States

From the early 1900s through the early 1970s, the US tire industry was dominated by five companies: Goodyear, Firestone, Uniroyal, BF Goodrich, and General Tire. All five were based in Akron, Ohio, and were run by executives who socialized together at the same country club. The five companies had competed in a US market characterized by consistent growth in revenues and profits, and a complete absence of foreign competition. In the 1970s and 1980s, the US tire industry experienced three important changes. The first was the emergence of the radial tire to replace the older "bias" and "bias-belted" tire constructions.[1] Compared to the older constructions, radials offered superior tread-wear, handling, and gas mileage, but had a stiffer ride. While bias and bias-belted tires

---

Doctoral Candidate Bruce Isaacson prepared this case under the supervision of Professor John A. Quelch as the basis for class discussion rather than to illustrate either effective or ineffective handling of an administrative situation. Copyright © 1993 by the President and Fellows of Harvard College. Harvard Business School case 9–594–106.

[1] In the radial tire, layers of rubberized material extended from side to side across the tire, perpendicular to the direction of travel. An additional layer or "belt," typically steel, was placed underneath the tread.

EXHIBIT 2   Goodyear Tire Lines with Typical Suggested per Tire Retail Prices

Performance Radials		All Season Radials		Light Truck Tires	
Eagle GS-C	$280	Aquatred	$90	Wrangler	$120
Eagle VR/ZR	255	Invicta GS	80	Workhorse RIB	70
Eagle GT+4	140	Invicta GL	65	Workhorse M&S	80
Eagle GA	120	Arriva	60		
Eagle ST	100	Tiempo	50		
Eagle M&S	215	Corsa GT	40		

SOURCE: Company records.
NOTE: All tires varied in price according to tire size.

the substantial price differential between them. Exhibit 3 shows the differences among Goodyear's broad-line tires. In the US passenger tire market, performance tires represented 25 percent of Goodyear's unit sales, 30 percent of dollar sales, and an even higher percentage of profits.

The market could also be segmented based on replacement and OEM tires. Replacement tires were sold to individual consumers, while OEM tires were sold to car manufacturers. Car makers used volume purchases to negotiate substantial discounts on tires. In 1991, US replacement tire sales were estimated at $8.6 billion (see Table D). In the United States, Goodyear's passenger tire division derived 65 percent of its revenues from replacement tires, and 35 percent from OEM tires. Division revenues were $1.98 billion, on sales of 39.1 million tires.

TABLE D   The US Market for Passenger Tires, 1991

	Dollars (in millions)			Units (in millions)		
	Replacement	*OEM*	*Total*	*Replacement*	*OEM*	*Total*
Industry	$8,600	NA*	N/A	152.0	43.0	195.0
Goodyear	1,290	$695	$1,985	22.8	16.3	39.1

* Indicates data were not available.
SOURCE: *Modern Tire Dealer*

A third segmentation scheme was along brand classifications, which included major brands, minor brands, and private label. Major brands, which carried the name of a major tire manufacturer, accounted for 36 percent of unit sales in the replacement passenger tire market. Major brands had the highest recognition among consumers and included Good-

EXHIBIT 3   Goodyear's Broad-Line Tires

AQUATRED
Improved Wet Road Stopping, Quiet All-Season Performance.

Aquachannel, deep connecting grooves pump water out of the way fast

Exclusive new compound gives road-hugging traction and longer life

Careful tread placement offers a smoother, quieter ride

Sleek sidewall design to complement today's automotive designs

INVICTA GS
Luxury Handling, Smooth, Quiet Ride, All-Season Performance

A smooth, quiet ride enhances the pleasure of driving a vehicle

Unique crisscross tread elements plus deep, effective shoulder grooves produce outstanding year-round traction

A noticeable dexterity in cornering, braking, and handling, the result of carefully selected tread rubber compounds

Impressive long term mileage capability for both front and rear wheel drive vehicles

ARRIVA
Great Traction In Any Weather

All season tread design for year round traction

Aggressive tread design features more gripping edges for improved snow traction

Easy rolling, long wearing tread compound

Dependable wet/dry traction for year-round performance

INVICTA GL
Advanced Rib, All Season Tread Design

All season traction from segmented tread lugs and open shoulder grooves

Long, even wear, quiet ride, excellent fuel economy from advanced tread rib pattern

Precision handling from natural molded shape

TIEMPO
Steel Belted Strength, All Season Traction

Flexible sidewalls deliver a smooth, comfortable ride

Steel belted radial construction delivers strength, tread wear, and fuel efficiency

Tread designed to dissipate heat for tire durability

CORSA GT
Great Handling And Mileage For Small Cars

All season traction designed tread

Center rib tread design and special tread rubber compound deliver long, even tread wear

Wraparound shoulder and tread lug design produce outstanding year-round traction

year, Firestone, Michelin, Bridgestone, Pirelli, and Goodrich. Minor brands represented 24 percent of unit sales and included tires made by smaller manufacturers as well as tires made by major manufacturers but sold under a different name. Minor brands included Sears, Dunlop, General, Kelly (a Goodyear subsidiary), Uniroyal, Cooper, Yokohama, and Toyo. Although minor, these brands were often well recognized by consumers and included high-priced niche brands.

Sales of private label tires constituted the remaining 40 percent of the market. Many small manufacturers specialized in private label tires, while some larger manufacturers used excess capacity to service the private label market. Most private label tires carried names exclusive to a particular retailer, but others were available to any retailer. Private label manufacturers typically had only one distributor per territory, which gave the distributor some flexibility in pricing. In 1991, private label tires constituted 80 percent of the sales of Goodyear's wholly owned Kelly-Springfield subsidiary; the remaining 20 percent were sold under the Kelly brand.

The average retail selling price of a private label tire was 18 percent lower than the price of a comparable branded tire. Although sales of private label tires had grown, their average life remained lower than the life of a branded tire (see Table E).

TABLE E   Average Tire Life (miles)

	All Tires	Branded Tires	Private Label
1991	38,600	39,700	37,000
1986	33,100	34,500	30,900
1981	28,600	29,100	28,500

SOURCE: Company records.

Many of the attributes important to consumers when purchasing a tire were not apparent upon visual inspection. To certify product quality, some retailers added warranties to their tires. These warranties were paid for by the retailer and would typically guarantee the tire for 60,000 miles, with the value of the guarantee decreasing on a pro-rata basis over the life of the tire. Retailer warranties were particularly common on sales of private label tires.

In past years, Goodyear had produced two lines of private label tires, the All American and the Concorde. The Goodyear brand was not placed on these tires, providing Goodyear's independent dealers with low-priced lines to compete with other types of outlets. In 1991, Robbins replaced the

All American and the Concorde with Goodyear-branded tires at comparable prices because market research showed that the nonbranded lines cannibalized sales of branded tires. Although the sales of these two lines were relatively small, some analysts felt that discontinuing the All American and Concorde increased incentives for Goodyear's independent dealers to sell tires made by other manufacturers. Some independent dealers believed that consumers wanted to choose from a range of tires, and favored offering private brands to provide consumers with a reference point, which they argued would increase the sales of Goodyear tires.

Consumers in the Replacement Passenger Tire Market

Consumer Behavior

Most consumers viewed tires as a "grudge purchase"—an expensive necessity to keep a vehicle in driving condition. The average time between purchases of tires was 2.5 years, but over half of all tire-buying consumers made their purchase the same day they became aware of their need for tires. Most tires were bought in pairs: 42 percent of consumer purchases involved two tires, 40 percent involved four tires, 16 percent involved one tire, and only 2 percent involved three tires.

Goodyear regularly surveyed car owners, asking about performance attributes considered when purchasing tires. The five most important tire attributes, in order from higher to lesser importance, were: tread life, wet traction, handling, snow traction, and dry traction. Goodyear also regularly surveyed car owners concerning the criteria they used to select a tire retailer. The seven most important criteria, again in order from higher to lesser importance, were as follows:

1. Price.
2. Offers fast service.
3. Can trust personnel.
4. Store is attractive.
5. Offers mileage warranty.
6. Brand selection.
7. Maintains convenient hours.

A 1989 Goodyear survey had shown that with no other information available, consumers expected Goodyear's broad-line tires to be priced within a six-dollar range from the most expensive to the least expensive. The research also demonstrated that Goodyear's point-of-sale display did little to alter consumers' expectations of retail prices.

Consumer Segments

Goodyear used research about consumers' shopping behavior to segment tire buyers into four categories (see Exhibit 4):

1. Price-constrained buyers   Price-constrained buyers bought the best brand they could afford within their budget. They had little loyalty to any specific outlet or brand, and tended to shop for tires for a long time before purchasing.

2. Value-oriented buyers   Value-oriented buyers searched for their preferred brand at the best price. They were predisposed to major brands, shopped around extensively, and had little loyalty to any specific outlet.

3. Quality buyers   Consumers in this segment were loyal to outlet and brand, tended to be upscale, and shopped for only a brief time before purchasing. The segment could be divided into two subsegments. *Prestige buyers* wanted to own the best tires on the market, while *comfortable conservatives* tended to develop a strong, lasting relationship with a specific outlet. Comfortable conservatives would often buy the brand recommended by their favorite outlet; major brands accounted for 38 percent of their purchases, versus 65 percent of purchases made by prestige buyers.

4. Commodity buyers   Commodity buyers valued price and outlet, and could be divided into two sub-segments. Typically, *bargain hunters* were young, with little brand preference, low retailer loyalty, and a tendency to shop around extensively. *Trusting patrons* viewed brand as unimportant, and tended to buy lower-priced tires at a preferred retailer. Trusting patrons made their purchase decision relatively quickly, without extensive shopping.

In 1992, 45 percent of tire buyers were price oriented when shopping for tires; 22 percent were brand oriented, and 33 percent believed the outlet was most important. By contrast, in 1985, 48 percent were price oriented, 26 percent were brand oriented, and 26 percent were outlet oriented. Over the past four years, the percent of consumers classified as

---

EXHIBIT 4   Major Consumer Segments for Replacement Passenger Tires

		Percent of Sales Represented by		
	Percent of Consumers	*Major Brands*	*Minor Brands*	*Private Brands*
Price-constrained buyers	22%	30%	35%	35%
Value-oriented buyers	18	54	29	17
Quality buyers	23	51	28	21
Commodity buyers	37	18	37	45
All tire buyers	100	33	33	34

SOURCE: Company records.

quality oriented declined by four percent, while commodity buyers increased four percent.

Wholesale and Retail Channels for Replacement Tires

Tire manufacturers sold replacement tires to wholesalers. Wholesalers resold the tires to a variety of retailers and dealers, who then sold the tires to consumers. This section describes both wholesale and retail distribution channels for replacement passenger tires.

Wholesale Distribution Channels

The US replacement passenger tire market depended on the four wholesale channels listed in Table F.

TABLE F   **Wholesale Distribution Channels (percent of all tires wholesaled, US passenger tire replacement market)**

Type of Outlet	1976	1981	1986	1991
Oil companies	9%	5%	3%	2%
Large retailers	24	20	16	19
Manufacturer-owned outlets	11	10	13	12
Independent dealers	56	65	68	67

SOURCE: *Modern Tire Dealer.*

The majority of tires wholesaled to oil companies were resold through franchised or company-owned gas stations or service stations. Wholesaling by oil companies had declined in recent years, reflecting increased competition at the retail level.

Large retailers, including mass merchandisers and warehouse clubs, bought tires directly from the manufacturers to resell in their stores. Smaller retailers bought tires from independent dealers. Tires wholesaled through manufacturer-owned outlets were resold in outlets owned and operated by tire producers.

Independent dealers had increased their share of wholesale distribution in recent years. Like other tire makers, Goodyear sold passenger tires to three kinds of independent dealers. Dealers who were strictly wholesalers, with no retail operations, accounted for 10 percent of Goodyear's factory sales to independent dealers and resold their tires to car dealers, service stations, small independent dealers, and other secondary outlets. Another 40 percent went to dealers who both sold tires at retail and resold tires to other dealers or to secondary outlets. The remaining 50 percent went to dealers who bought tires to resell in their own retail outlets and did not resell to other outlets. This breakdown was typical of the industry.

Retail Distribution Channels

Six major retail channels competed for market share in the US replacement passenger tire market. Exhibit 5 shows each channel's market share, relative prices, and reliance on private label tires. The six channels can be described as follows:

1. Garages/service stations   These were typically small, neighborhood outlets offering gasoline, tires, and auto services. Their share of the tire market had declined in recent years in favor of lower-cost, higher-volume outlets. Garages and service stations sold private label tires to combat price pressure from larger outlets.

EXHIBIT 5   Retail Sales of Replacement Passenger Tires by Channel (US market only)

Channel Share of Retail Sales	1976	1981	1986	1991
Garages/service stations	18%	11%	18%	6%
Warehouse clubs	0	0	2	6
Mass merchandisers	28	24	16	12
Manufacturer-owned outlets	11	11	11	9
Small independent tire dealers	36	47	46	39
Large independent tire chains	4	2	12	23
Other	4	6	5	4
Total	100%	100%	100%	100%

	Relative Price Index, 1991	Sales of Private Label Tires as a Percent of Retail Sales Dollars, 1991
Garages/service stations	110%	57%
Warehouse clubs	80	8
Mass merchandisers	97	34
Manufacturer-owned outlets	107	16
Small independent tire dealers	100	36
Large independent tire chains	90	54
Other	NA	59

NOTE: Relative price index indicates typical retail prices for the same tire in each channel. Retail prices in "other" category varied according to the specific outlet.
SOURCE: Company records.

2. Warehouse clubs   Warehouse clubs operated large stores carrying a wide assortment in categories as diverse as food, clothing, electronics, tires, and hardware. Sam's, the largest of the warehouse clubs, had 208 outlets, while PACE had 87 outlets, Price Club had 77 outlets, and Costco had 75 outlets. Warehouse clubs offered a limited brand selection, with the selection changing according to the deals their buyers could strike with vendors. Also, warehouse clubs offered minimal in-store service. For example, in some warehouse clubs, consumers had to select tires from sales floor racks, cart the tires to the cash register, and bring the tires outside to service bays for installation. Although warehouse clubs were a relatively new retail format, they were growing quickly due to their low prices. Some independent dealers felt that warehouse clubs offered tires at cost to increase store traffic, generating profits from tire installation and sales of other merchandise.

3. Mass merchandisers   Mass merchandisers were retail chains that sold tires, performed auto services, and carried other types of merchandise. The largest mass merchandisers had many outlets. Kmart sold tires in 991 outlets, Sears in 850 outlets, Wal-Mart in 425 outlets, and Montgomery Ward in 335 outlets. Mass merchandisers typically maintained a very wide brand selection. For example, Sears sold Michelin, Goodrich, Pirelli, Bridgestone, Yokohama, and its own Roadhandler brand; while Montgomery Ward sold Kelly, Goodrich, Michelin, Bridgestone, General, and its own RoadTamer brand.

4. Manufacturer-owned outlets   These outlets, owned and operated by the tire manufacturers, typically sold only one brand of tires and offered a range of auto services.

5. Small independent tire dealers   Small independent tire dealers operated one or two outlets, where they sold and installed tires and also offered auto services. Many small independent tire dealers started as single-brand outlets but over time added additional brands. Both small dealers and large independent tire chains derived an increasing portion of their revenues from private label tires.

6. Large independent tire chains   Also known as "multibrand discounters," large independent tire chains typically had 30–100 outlets concentrated within a geographic region. Examples of this type of outlet included Tire America, National Tire Warehouse, and Discount Tire. These chains carried major brands of tires as well as private label, and tended to be low-priced, high-volume operations. In recent years, there was increasing concentration of independent tire outlets as large independent tire chains gained share, often by acquiring smaller independent dealers.

7. Other   Half the sales in the "other" category were accounted for by full-service auto supply stores such as Western Auto, Auto Palace, or Pep Boys. These stores sold tires at low prices as traffic builders and were resented by independent dealers as a consistent source of low-priced competition.

In most markets, consumers could choose among these types of channels. As one independent dealer noted, ''The tire manufacturer is not only our supplier, but also our competitor through manufacturer-owned outlets. On top of that, we compete with the warehouse clubs, mass merchandisers, corner station, and who knows who else.''

Goodyear's Distribution Structure

Goodyear did not sell tires in garages/service stations, warehouse clubs, or mass merchandisers; instead, the company relied on three types of outlets. Goodyear's 4,400 *independent dealers* accounted for 50 percent of sales revenues, while the 1,047 *manufacturer-owned outlets* generated 27 percent of sales and the 600 *franchised dealers* accounted for another 8 percent of sales. (The remaining 15 percent of sales were primarily to government agencies.)

Manufacturer-owned outlets provided control over retail operations and could be opened or closed at the discretion of the manufacturer. During the 1970s, Goodyear opened as many as 200 outlets per year. By 1983, the company owned 1,300 outlets in the United States, but became concerned about the associated demands for capital and management attention and turned to franchising of new outlets. Over time, Goodyear also converted some company-owned outlets to franchised status, eventually selling those outlets to independent dealers.

New owners were franchised by Goodyear for three years and then became independent. During the three years, Goodyear provided training in operations, finance, and other aspects of the business. The number of franchised dealers was kept at 600 by adding new outlets as older franchisees became independent.

Goodyear had 4,400 independent dealers, but only about 2,500 were considered active dealers in that they generated a consistent level of sales, maintained the major Goodyear retail displays, and offered the full line of Goodyear tires. A typical independent outlet required the owner to invest $100,000 and generated annual revenues of $1,000,000. Goodyear's independent outlets sold an average of 15.5 tires/day, including both Goodyear and other brands of tires, although most Goodyear dealers derived the majority of their sales from Goodyear tires. The average selling price of all tires sold by Goodyear's independent dealers was $75 per tire. Retail margins for independent dealers averaged 28 percent on Goodyear tires, 25 percent for dealers carrying other major brands, and 20 percent for private label tires. Average wholesale margins were 18 percent for private label tires and 14 percent for Goodyear tires.[3]

---

[3] These margins are estimated from several sources and may vary by region or time period.

Although Goodyear claimed not to want its tires sold in low-priced outlets such as warehouse clubs, mass merchandisers, and auto supply stores, those outlets sporadically obtained Goodyear tires. The price-based ads and frequent discounting from those outlets angered Goodyear's independent dealers. One owner of two independent tire outlets said: "The mass merchandisers are eating up the distribution of our product. It could drive me out of the tire business."[4] Industry observers felt that tires were diverted to those outlets by the large independent dealers who acted solely as wholesalers. As one analyst said, "There's a lot of big wholesalers who will sell to anybody."

Goodyear's options to stop the diversion were limited by legal restrictions which prohibited manufacturers from dictating either retail selling prices or to whom their tires could be resold. However, in December of 1990, Goodyear sued two automotive chains: Tire America and Western Auto Supply. Both were owned by Sears, and neither was an authorized Goodyear dealer. The suits charged that the Sears units were advertising Goodyear tires without maintaining enough inventory to meet demand. Consumers drawn to the store were allegedly switched to other brands in a "bait and switch" tactic. Goodyear also maintained that the chains were not authorized to use the Goodyear trademark in their advertising.

Just Tires was a new format under test by Goodyear. Modeled after "quick lube" stores, which offered fast oil changes without an appointment, *Just Tires* stores sold and installed tires but did not offer any other products or services. *Just Tires* stores' focused capabilities were backed with guarantees covering speed and quality.

Although there was some overlap, most outlets that sold Goodyear tires did not sell Kelly-Springfield tires. Kelly-Springfield had no company-owned outlets, and sold primarily through mass merchandisers, independent tire dealers, and gas/service stations.

Promotions

It was estimated that three-fourths of all Goodyear tires sold in independent or company-owned outlets were sold on promotion, at an average discount of 25 percent. This discount was offered to the consumer in a number of ways, such as one free tire with the purchase of three tires, one tire for half price with the purchase of another tire at full price, or 25 percent off the price of selected tires. For both independent and company-owned dealers, promotions were organized around "core events"— six three-week periods spread throughout the year during which Goodyear dealers could buy merchandise at a discount. Goodyear supported core events with radio, television, and print advertising announcing special prices on specific tire lines. Every spring, Goodyear offered dealers

---

[4] *Wall Street Journal*, June 24, 1991, p. B1.

"spring dating," which provided extended financing on tire orders. Experiments with everyday low pricing in the tire industry had been unsuccessful because price competition among dealers undermined attempts to set consistently low but fair prices. As one dealer explained, "Consumers expect to buy their tires on sale. We have created a price-conscious monster."

Goodyear's Independent Dealers

Goodyear operated separate sales organizations to service company-owned outlets and independent dealers. The company-owned outlets were grouped into 42 districts, each with 20 to 23 stores. There was one district manager per district, plus one store manager per store. Another sales organization called on independent dealers and was organized into 28 districts, each with a district manager and an average of three area sales managers.

Besides providing tires, Goodyear supported its independent dealers with a variety of services, including the following:

- *Expertise and training* on issues such as financing, architecture, wholesaling, operations, and merchandising.
- *Certified Auto Service,* which allowed dealers to attend training classes and become certified in auto services.
- *The Goodyear Business Management System,* a computer system to help dealers with inventory and accounting.
- *National and regional advertising* to support dealer sales.
- *Research on market trends,* such as information on the popularity of each tire, by size, in a given market.
- *Assistance in outlet location,* either in selling company-owned outlets to independent dealers or in avoiding locations for company-owned outlets that would compete with dealers.

Goodyear serviced independent dealers through the area sales manager, who made sure that dealer orders were placed properly, provided information about market trends, offered advice on operations, and handled complaints. Visits from area sales managers were very important to dealers. As one area sales manager noted, "You never get to the dealer enough. You could spend all day there and then the next day the guy would say, 'Gee, I have this problem today. Too bad you weren't around.' "

Most dealer complaints involved relatively minor billing problems, although complaints about competition from other channels or the location of company-owned outlets were also common. Issues that could not be handled by the area sales manager were referred to the district manager. Complaints common to many dealers were taken up by the dealer council.

Each of 10 regional councils elected one dealer to Goodyear's national dealer council for passenger tires. Goodyear's top marketing and sales executives attended council meetings to answer questions, address complaints, or hear suggestions. Council meetings typically covered issues such as market trends in a region or city, new product development, advertising schedules, the availability of particular tires, or Goodyear's overall strategy. Due to antitrust laws, the council could not discuss the selling practices of specific dealers, the brands sold by specific dealers, competition from Goodyear-owned outlets, or retail prices.

The services Goodyear provided its dealers were not free. The cost of these services was built into Goodyear's list prices, but discounts were available for dealers who paid upon receipt of merchandise, ordered in full trailer loads, or purchased under occasional promotional programs. Also, various allowances applied. A *wholesale allowance* applied on all approved wholesale sales to any authorized Goodyear dealer within a specific territory. (The wholesale allowance helped Goodyear limit competition among wholesalers.) A *merchandising allowance* of 1.5 percent was credited on all dealer sales; these credits could be used to obtain point-of-sale materials such as brochures, signs, and displays. Independent dealers also earned *advertising accruals* equal to 4 percent of tire purchases. The accruals could be used for local advertising, which Goodyear split evenly with the dealers provided no other brands were mentioned in the ad and the ad focused on tires rather than auto services.

Not all of these services were popular with every dealer. For example, some of Goodyear's largest dealers would have preferred to buy their tires at the lowest possible "net" price and develop their own advertising and promotion programs. However, smaller dealers had neither the staff nor the expertise to develop their own programs, and Goodyear was concerned that without coordinated programs, some dealers would stop advertising and simply reap the benefits of other dealers' efforts.

Independent Dealers in the Tire Industry

In the 1970s, most major tire companies had maintained networks of company-owned dealers. By 1991, tire manufacturers owned fewer of their distribution outlets, as independent dealers typically offered more choice than the single-brand selection offered at most company-owned stores, and required less capital and attention from the manufacturer. Some tire companies believed that independent distribution systems could grow faster than company-owned distribution systems, with the expectation that increasing outlet density and brand availability would increase market share. During the 1980s, both Uniroyal and General Tire sold or closed all of their company-owned outlets.

In 1992, Michelin had fewer than 125 company-owned outlets, but Michelin tires were available through 7,000 independent dealers. Most of Michelin's independent dealers were multibrand outlets and sold Michelin as the prestige brand in their product offerings. Michelin tires were also available in 95 percent of the 600 warehouse clubs in the United States, mass merchandisers such as Montgomery Ward and Sears, and a variety of gas and service stations. Michelin, Uniroyal, and Goodrich had recently combined their sales forces to allow their salespeople to sell all three brands.

Firestone was an exception to the trend toward independent distribution. During the mid-1980s, many of Firestone's independent dealers switched to other manufacturers; some felt that the company had stopped supporting its dealers and its products in order maximize short-term financial results. In 1991, there were 1,550 company-owned Firestone outlets, which also carried Bridgestone tires. Firestone's presence in independent dealers, mass merchandisers, and warehouse clubs was minimal. Also in 1991, General Tire decided to exit the retail store business entirely and instead rely on independent dealers.

While manufacturer-owned outlets were part of the manufacturer's management hierarchy, independent dealers had more autonomy. For example, tire manufacturers could suggest retail prices, but by law independent dealers were free to set their own prices. Some manufacturers felt that independent dealers' focus on price had contributed to the decline in retail tire prices.

Independent dealers also set their own inventory policies. For many years Goodyear had protected its dealers by not selling Goodyear-branded tires in other outlets; in exchange, Goodyear dealers did not carry other brands. In 1989, 70 percent of Goodyear's independent dealers carried only Goodyear tires, while 30 percent stocked other brands. Typically, the other brands were not aggressively merchandised but used only as lower-priced alternatives to Goodyear. By 1991, estimates suggested that 50 percent of Goodyear's independent dealers sold only Goodyear tires, while the other 50 percent stocked at least one other brand. However, Goodyear tires generated 90 percent of the revenues for dealers who stocked but did not aggressively merchandise other brands.

Independent dealers' concern for protecting their interests led the National Tire Dealers and Retreaders Association (NTDRA) to pass a bill of rights in 1992 (see Exhibit 6). NTDRA president Robert Gatzke said that "[T]his bill of rights clearly identifies certain rights which independent tire dealers have a right to expect from their tire suppliers."[5] The bill

---

[5] *Tire Business*, June 1992.

Exhibit 6   Tire Dealers' Bill of Rights

Tire dealers as independent business people have earned the right to the respect of all other facets of the tire, retreading, and auto service industries since it has long been established that they fulfill the role as the most important channel of tire distribution . . .

Tire dealers expect to give loyalty to, and receive loyalty from, their manufacturers; to be treated like valued customers; and to be encouraged to sell to end users without direct competition from their manufacturers. Independent tire dealers have a right to the uninhibited exercise of their ability to increase their market share with the cooperation of their manufacturers . . .

Tire dealers have a right to expect reasonable and timely communications from, and where appropriate, consultation with their manufacturers on actions taken by the manufacturers which directly affect independent tire dealers and their customers . . .

Independent tire dealers have the right to expect their manufacturers to pay careful attention to supply and demand, pursuing neither to excess, and to keep the dealer supplied in a timely fashion with high quality products which will allow the dealer to sell and serve the customer properly . . .

Independent dealers have a right to a level playing field including the availability of tire lines, pricing, terms, and programs equal to those offered to wholesale clubs, discounters, company-owned stores, mass merchandisers, chains, and other forms of competition . . .

Tire manufacturers should recognize the need for profits, not only for themselves, but also for the independent tire dealer who performs the major distribution function for them . . .

Independent tire dealers have a right to the timely, proper, and uniform issuance of credits for advertising, national account sales, return goods, adjustments, and any other money due . . .

Independent tire dealers . . . have a right to expect that the manufacturer will use the network of independent tire dealers as the first step for expansion, increasing the dealers' market share; and that commitments made are commitments kept.

Source: *Tire Business,* June 1992.

---

demanded that manufacturers respect the independent dealers' importance, consult independent dealers on key decisions, avoid placing company-owned outlets in competition with independent dealers, supply tires to independent dealers in a timely manner, and grant dealers the same pricing and programs given to high-volume outlets such as wholesale clubs and multibrand discounters.

Auto Services

Auto services were a $50 billion market in 1991. Auto services included jobs such as oil changes, tune-ups, and front-end alignments, as well as repairs to parts such as brakes or transmissions. Revenues from auto services included parts and labor, and were differentiated from tire sales. The price of services varied by outlet and job, but $60 was typical. Garages and service stations had a 40 percent share of auto service revenues, while new car dealers had a 29 percent share. Specialty outlets focusing on parts such as mufflers or brakes had a 15 percent share, followed by tire dealers with an 8 percent share, and mass merchandisers with an 8 percent share.

Monthly auto service sales for independent tire dealers averaged $38,100 per outlet. Most tire dealers changed oil, performed alignments, replaced shocks, fixed exhaust systems, and did minor engine work. Independent dealers received 48 percent of their revenues and 49 percent of their earnings from auto service; in 1980, auto service represented 26% of revenues. Margins for independent dealers were 50 percent on service labor and 20–25% on parts installed; 70 percent of service revenues were earned from labor, with the remaining 30 percent earned from parts. Revenues from tire installation were considered auto services and included the following:

Mount and balance new tires:	$8.00 per tire
Place valve on new tires:	$2.50 per tire
Scrap charge to dispose of old tires:	$2.00 per tire

The average number of tires installed per day at a typical independent dealer increased 13 percent from 1983 to 1991, but the average service dollars per outlet grew 92 percent during the same period. Not all dealers were pleased with their reliance on service revenues. As one dealer said, "To me it's an indictment of the industry that we cannot support ourselves on tire sales. We have to have that service to survive." Tires were an expensive purchase for most consumers, and independent dealers worried about the "sticker shock" resulting from service charges increasing the bill to the consumer.

Competition

Goodyear regularly surveyed car owners to monitor their image of the major tire brands (see Exhibit 7). In 1991, Goodyear and Michelin were virtually even, but Michelin's image was stronger among value-oriented and quality buyers, while Goodyear had a stronger image among price-constrained buyers and commodity buyers. The percent of consumers who did not know what brand of tire they planned to buy next rose to 53 percent in 1992 from 36 percent in 1982.

Exhibit 8 presents a brand-switching matrix, showing loyalty by brand among consumers replacing passenger tires. Michelin owners were the most loyal, followed by Goodyear owners, but significant proportions of consumers who owned major brands replaced their tires with private label brands. Goodyear typically spent 9–11 percent of sales on advertising and promotion; Goodyear's share of voice in television and magazine advertising was about 60 percent.

Goodyear's competitors were planning a wide range of campaigns for 1992. Both Bridgestone and Michelin were planning to introduce new tires with 80,000-mile warranties, while Uniroyal was introducing a new tire for light trucks. Under Michelin's ownership, BF Goodrich was focusing on the high-performance market, while Goodyear's Kelly-Springfield subsidiary used advertising primarily to announce the low price of its tires.

EXHIBIT 7 Brand Image of Major Tire Manufacturers

In a survey of broad-line tire owners during the first quarter of 1992, Goodyear had asked what brand of tires the owners intended to buy the next time they needed tires. Results are reported below for the five major brands and for the four major consumer segments.

Intent to Buy for Major Consumer Segments

	All Buyers	Price-Constrained Buyers	Value-Oriented Buyers	Quality Buyers	Commodity Buyers
Goodyear	13%	16%	17%	18%	10%
Michelin	13	9	24	22	6
Other	19	18	20	25	16
Uncommitted	53	57	39	35	68

SOURCE: Company records.

EXHIBIT 8 Switching among Tire Brands, 1991

	Brand Bought						
Brand Replaced	*Bridgestone*	*Firestone*	*Goodyear*	*Michelin*	*Minor Brands*	*Private Label*	*Total*
Bridgestone	29%	4%	8%	8%	7%	43%	100%
Firestone	2	27	11	6	7	45	100
Goodyear	2	5	39	5	9	38	100
Michelin	3	3	7	44	6	36	100
Minor brands	2	4	10	7	32	42	100
Private label	2	5	8	5	7	7	100

NOTE: The above chart can be read as follows: 4 percent of car owners with Bridgestone tires bought Firestone tires to replace the Bridgestones.
SOURCE: Company records.

The Aquatred Tire

In 1989, Goodyear started the NEWEX project, to develop a new and exciting replacement market tire that would have a tangible, perceptible difference over existing models. Howard MacDonald, marketing manager for Passenger Tires, said that "we were looking for something that appearancewise was different—something that a customer would walk into a showroom and tell from a distance that it was different."[6] The Aquatred was developed after comparing 10 different designs on performance and consumer preference. The deep groove down the center of the tire was dubbed the "Aquachannel." According to Goodyear, the Aquatred's

---

[6] *Modern Tire Dealer*, March 1992.

tread design channelled water out from under the tire, reducing hydro-planing and improving traction in wet conditions.[7] Performance tests showed that in wet conditions, cars equipped with Aquatreds traveling at 55 miles per hour stopped in as much as two car lengths' less distance than similar cars equipped with conventional all-season radials. When 50 percent worn, the Aquatred maintained the same wet traction as a new all season tire.

Goodyear planned to sell the Aquatred with a 60,000-mile warranty, and to position the tire at the top of the broad-line segment. The last tire to promise increased wet traction to the broad-line segment was the Uniroyal Rain Tire, introduced in the early 1970s. The Aquatred was patented, but patent protection on tread designs was difficult to enforce. Continental Tire was known to be working on its own antihydroplaning tire, to be called the Aqua Contact, which could be launched in early 1993.

The Aquatred was test marketed in a large, representative, metropolitan area. A Goodyear survey from the test market compared purchase behavior for Aquatred buyers with purchase behavior for buyers of the Invicta GS, Goodyear's most expensive broad-line tire (see Exhibit 9). Compared to buyers of the Invicta GS, Aquatred buyers were more likely to replace competitors' tires, searched more extensively for information prior to purchase, were more likely to drive imported cars, and more often came to Goodyear outlets specifically for the Aquatred. Exhibit 10 presents data gathered by a "mystery shopper," a Goodyear employee who shopped for tires at independent dealers without identifying his affiliation with Goodyear. Despite the uniformity of the company's literature and policies, there was variation in the presentation and pricing of the Aquatred.

In another survey, Goodyear asked drivers of cars equipped with either the Aquatred or the Invicta GS to rate their tire's traction on wet roads. Owners of each tire responded as follows:

Response	Aquatred Drivers	Invicta GS Drivers
1. (Poor traction)	5	3
2.	5	5
3. (Average)	30	27
4.	80	81
5. (Excellent)	180	184
Total responses:	300	300

---

[7] Hydroplaning occurs in wet conditions due to a layer of water forming between the tire and road, causing a momentary loss of traction.

EXHIBIT 9   Aquatred Test Market Data

	Buyers of	
	Aquatred	*Invicta GS*
What brand of tire was replaced?		
Goodyear	38%	51%
Michelin	17	15
Other	25	16
Don't know	20	18
Steps in information search:		
Checked newspaper ads	33%	23%
Telephoned outlets	21	14
Shopped other dealers	20	12
Primary shopping orientation:		
Store	36%	44%
Brand	56	47
Price	8	9
Purchase decision segments:		
Price-constrained buyers	6%	6%
Value-oriented buyers	23	13
Quality buyers	61	64
Commodity buyers	10	17
Bought four tires	91%	54%
Reasons for buying tires at Goodyear:		
(multiple answers allowed)		
Past experience	36%	49%
Want Goodyear brand	33	33
Want Aquatreds	25	NA
Convenience	11	18
Familiar with personnel	11	12
Advertising	9	NA
On sale/good price	8	13
Recommended by a friend	4	4
Always go to that dealer	4	9
Other	26	20
Vehicle make:		
Domestic	74%	94%
Import	26	6
What features or benefits did the salesperson tell you about the Aquatred? (multiple answers allowed)		
Has 60,000 mile warranty	41%	10%
Great wet traction	33	38
Didn't tell me about them	13	42
Won't hydroplane	16	9
Other	29	18

SOURCE: Company records.

EXHIBIT 10   Results of Mystery Shopping in Aquatred Test Market

---

A male mystery shopper visited nine independent Goodyear outlets in the Aquatred test market during October 1991. The mystery shopper told the staff in each outlet that his wife needed tires for her Plymouth Voyager. In the sales presentations that followed:

- Eight of the nine salespersons mentioned the Aquatred during their presentations. Of those eight, five began their presentation with the Aquatred and three finished with the Aquatred.
- Three salespeople made specific claims concerning the Aquatred's superior performance in wet traction. One claimed the Aquatred was 15 percent better than other tires, another claimed 20–25 percent, and a third claimed up to 35 percent better traction with the Aquatred.
- Goodyear's suggested retail prices for the Aquatred were $89.95 with a black sidewall, and $93.95 with a white sidewall. Prices quoted by six outlets were as follows:

Store Number	Price with Black Sidewall	Price with White Sidewall
1	$ 79.95	$ 79.95
2	81.95	81.95
3	80.00	83.00
4	85.00	85.00
5	85.00	88.00
6	100.00	100.00

SOURCE: Company records.

The Launch of the Aquatred

A storyboard for a proposed Aquatred television advertisement is presented in Exhibit 11. Due to the long buying cycles of auto manufacturers, the Aquatred would not be available as original equipment, so all sales of the Aquatred would come through the replacement market. It was estimated that a full-scale launch would cost Goodyear about $21 million.

Managers at Goodyear still had two concerns about the launch. First, did Goodyear have the right product for the dealers and for the consumer? Michelin and Bridgestone both planned high-profile launches of tires with 80,000-mile warranties in 1992. Would Goodyear's dealers be receptive to a high-priced tire when the industry seemed to be turning toward long-life warranties and low-cost private labels? One dealer had said,

> I would be much more interested in a tire that went 80,000 miles than one that channels the rain out of the way. Even a 35,000-mile tire at a decent price point would be better. The Aquatred is a boutique tire, but where do we make our money as a dealer? Middle-of-the-road products.

Second was the channel itself. Goodyear management debated whether distribution should be expanded, and if so, what specific chan-

EXHIBIT 11   **Proposed Aquatred Advertisement**

GOODYEAR

"TIRES OF THE FUTURE" :30

AQUATRED

GTBM 8863

(MUSIC UNDER)
ANNCR. (VO) Yo 're about to see

how Goodyear is changing all-season driving

right before your eyes

Introducing Aquatred

only from Goodyear.

(MUSIC)

Aquatred's advanced design

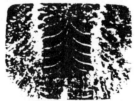

channels water out of your way

for dependable

all-season traction.

especially in the rain

when you may need it most

Aquatred

The newest reason why we say the best tires in the world.

have Goodyear written all over them

nels or retailers should be added. Expanding distribution could boost sales and prevent Goodyear OEM tires from being replaced by other brands in the replacement market. However, selling tires in lower-service outlets could erode the value of the Goodyear brand, cannibalize sales of existing outlets, and might cause dealers to take on additional lines of tires. Stanley Gault, Goodyear's new chairman, had expanded distribution at Rubbermaid, and many Goodyear dealers were concerned that he would do the same at Goodyear. As one dealer said, "Today, you can go to any store and get a Rubbermaid product, and the prices on Rubbermaid have dropped accordingly. We feel that Goodyear tires should not be that way."

If the decision was made to launch the Aquatred, there would be a variety of launch-related issues to settle. For example, Robbins was concerned about the timing. Goodyear had made commitments for commercial time during the Winter Olympics in January of 1992 and could use this time to introduce the Aquatred. Launching during the Olympics might spark sales of the Aquatred, but the initial inventory of Aquatreds had been made to fit domestic cars, as opposed to the smaller sizes for imported cars. Molds to produce other sizes would not be available until several months after the Olympics.

Also, given the wide range of tires sold by Goodyear, dealers would need advice regarding which customers would be likely to switch to Aquatreds. In the test markets, some dealers had tried to sell Aquatreds only to customers who drove newer cars or looked affluent. And if distribution was expanded, Goodyear would need to decide whether the new channel would receive the Aquatred.

Finally, Goodyear would need pricing and promotional policies for the Aquatred. Goodyear hoped to price the Aquatred at a 10 percent premium over the Invicta GA, but the successful launch of the Tiempo in 1977 was partly attributed to a low retail price. Independent dealers in test markets had consistently asked for price promotions on the Aquatred. Robbins had turned down all such requests, but given the growing problem of tires diverted to unauthorized dealers, it was not clear that the tire could be kept out of channels that were prone to discounting and promotions.

Plans for the launch were proceeding during an important period in Goodyear's history. Any change in distribution strategy would affect the launch, but the launch and the associated marketing programs would affect Goodyear's dealers. Stanley Gault was upbeat, and saw the Aquatred as a product to revitalize Goodyear. Robbins, armed with consumer research, wanted to be sure that the consumer and the channel would agree.

H.J. Heinz Co.: Plastic Bottle Ketchup (C)

It's been a roller coaster ride during the past year. I knew we hit the jackpot after the introduction of the 28-oz. plastic bottle in the southern region. We had a solid marketing support program, and the sales force did a splendid job selling-in to the trade. Within six weeks, we reached our target retail distribution level of 80 percent ACV. The squeezable bottle really took the wind out of the sails of Hunt's product reformulation. Then, gradually, our product shortage problem surfaced. Our accounts are clamoring for product, but we simply don't know when we can fix our capacity problem. We don't have a set format for dealing with this problem—it has never happened to us before.

Barbara Johnson, product manager on Heinz Ketchup, was describing her predicament in early July 1984 involving the introduction of the 28-oz. plastic bottle ketchup. She was in the midst of a national rollout, and she did not have sufficient product to ship. Johnson had to decide on a course of action for handling the product shortage problem.

The Introductory Program

Heinz introduced the 28-oz. plastic bottle in the southern region in August 1983, and put the 64-oz. into test market in November 1983. Management accepted Barbara Johnson's recommended marketing program for the 28-oz. introduction using a national equivalent spending plan of $6.1 million. The program included a new 30-second television commercial that focused on the new package—a first for Heinz Ketchup. (See Exhibit 1 for a photoboard of the 28-oz. commercial.) The media plan included prime time, daytime, and late night schedules that reached 95 percent of the target audience over nine times during the first 12 weeks of advertising. Trial-generating consumer promotions were run, including a 25¢ October free-standing insert (FSI) coupon and a follow-up 20¢ FSI coupon

This case was written by Research Assistant John L. Teopaco, under the direction of Professor John A. Quelch, as the basis for class discussion rather than to illustrate either effective or ineffective handling of an administrative situation. Copyright © 1985 by the President and Fellows of Harvard College. Harvard Business School case 9–586–067.

EXHIBIT 1   Heinz 28-oz. Plastic Bottle Television Commercial

(Anncr VO): Now you can take Heinz, America's thickest, best-tasting ketchup...

and give it a squeeze!

MUSIC: UP
SFX: SNAP!

SING: GIVE HEINZ A SQUEEZE...

ANY TIME THAT YOU PLEASE...

JUST A LITTLE OR A LOT...

RIGHT ON THE SPOT...

GIVE HEINZ A SQUEEZE...

ON A BURGER WITH CHEESE.

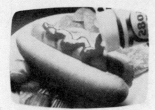

ON A HOT DOG, OR A FEW OF THESE. NOW POURING'S A BREEEEEZE!

SFX: SNAP

(Anncr VO): Introducing Heinz in the squeezable, portable, shatter-proof bottle. Go ahead...
SING: GIVE HEINZ A SQUEEZE!

EXHIBIT 2   Heinz 28-oz. Plastic Bottle FSI Advertisement

distributed in February 1984. (See Exhibit 2 for a copy of the FSI ad.) A "buy-two-get-one-free" neckhanger refund offer was employed to generate repurchase. Trade promotion consisted of a two-month introductory allowance of 9 percent of the base price plus a $1 per-case stocking allowance. Heinz gave a special incentive to its brokers (the South was all broker sales) of one-half percent of all ketchup sales the first two months after the 28-oz. launch if they achieved 100 percent account headquarters authorization to stock the plastic bottle, 80 percent ACV retail distribution, and no loss of 24-oz. authorizations.[1]

Heinz priced the 28-oz. plastic to the trade at $1.30 per bottle—two cents below the Heinz 32-oz. base price—and suggested a retail price of $1.59. The trade took the full 18 percent gross margin, which meant that the 28-oz. sold at retail for 25 cents more than the Heinz 32-oz. everyday price of $1.34, and up to 40 cents more than the deal price of $1.09–$1.19. It was the single most profitable item for the trade in the ketchup category.

The 28-oz. plastic bottle achieved a 6 percent unit market share in the South within two months after its introduction. Heinz management considered this performance to be very successful. The sales department, however, was concerned that the Heinz 32-oz. business was down 10 percent as a result of 28-oz. plastic cannibalization. On the other hand, they had expected to lose all their 24-oz. business, yet this size had held 60 percent of its volume level prior to the plastic introduction. In total, the 28-oz. plastic volume came from the following sources: 27 percent from increased category consumption, 20 percent from Hunt's, 18 percent from Del Monte and all others, and 35 percent from cannibalization.

After the successful introduction in the South, Heinz management decided in October 1983 to extend the roll-out of 28-oz. plastic to the West, Heinz's other low development region. Product shipments to the West began in January 1984. The roll-out to the Northeast, followed by North central, was scheduled for May 1984 after the installation of a new plastic line that month. It would have a capacity of producing 167,000 cases per month. The existing converted line would continue producing plastic if necessary.

Competitive Reaction

Following the Heinz plastic bottle introduction, Hunt's, in collaboration with Owens-Illinois, aggressively pursued its own plastic bottle development. In February 1984, the Hunt's sales force started selling-in a 32-oz. squeezable plastic bottle in the South, where Heinz was test marketing its 64-oz. plastic, to replace its 32-oz. glass. Hunt's could not justify another

---

[1] Performance against these criteria was measured using A. C. Nielsen audit data.

new size to the trade as Heinz could. Hunt's advertised their plastic bottle specifically, and they priced it identically to their 32-oz. glass. In order to gauge the competitive threat posed by Hunt's 32-oz. plastic, Heinz commissioned monadic, unbranded home-use tests of the Heinz 28-oz. (January 1984) and Hunt's 32-oz. (March 1984) squeezable bottles, both filled with Heinz ketchup. On the key purchase intent measure, the Hunt's bottle scored higher than the Heinz bottle:

Purchase Intent (unpriced)	*Hunt's 32-oz. Plastic* *(N = 200)*	*Heinz 28-oz. Plastic* *(N = 300)*
Definitely buy	48%	43%
Probably buy	46	48
Probably not buy	3	7
Definitely not buy	2	2

NOTE: Respondents were female heads of household, aged 20–59, who had purchased ketchup during the past 30 days.

Capacity Problems

Heinz conducted a follow-up promotion in the South in February 1984, at the same time as the western expansion, which resulted in an "oversell" of the plastic bottle. Demand was greater than expected, and Heinz began facing a capacity problem. As a result, in March 1984, Heinz management delayed the northern roll-out one month (to early June 1984). Management faced more problems upon roll-out. As Johnson explained:

> We projected plastic's market share in our strong Northeast market (8 percent) to be greater than what we had seen in the South (6 percent) and West (7 percent), but our adjustments were conservative. The sell-in indicated an 11 percent market share in the Northeast. Accounts planned to feature 28-oz. plastic aggressively going into the summer, and ordered large inventories on the introductory deal, creating greater demand than we anticipated.

In addition, management did not anticipate production start-up problems. The converted line's output was only half of what had been projected during May. Through June, orders were averaging 50,000 cases per week, versus production of 30,000 cases. Parts for the new second line that was specially designed for plastic bottle production were late arriving, which delayed the second line by one month. In July, the factory had to shut down for the first two weeks for unexpected maintenance. Johnson also learned that the plastic bottle and cap suppliers could not deliver the increased requirements until they installed new lines in September and November, respectively.

Instead of delivering the planned 90,000 cases per week in July, production was zero during the first two weeks. Assuming three shifts a day and seven days a week on both lines, Heinz engineers were projecting production rates of 45,000 cases in the third week and 50,000 in the fourth week of July, gradually increasing to 100,000 cases per week in late September. Orders in early July had jumped to 60,000 cases per week, and the sales force was projecting a buy-in of 225,000–300,000 cases during the last week of the 60-day introductory deal. After a brief post-promotion dip, orders were expected to stabilize at 25,000–30,000 cases per week.

Alternative Actions

"By late June, we figured out that the product shortage problem was of major magnitude. But we still couldn't tell the trade when we'd be up to speed with demand." Barbara Johnson had to act quickly in conjunction with the Production Planning and Inventory Control Manager and the Sales Planning Manager at headquarters. The Sales Planning Manager, who liaised between the brand groups and field sales, commented:

> Our salespeople are concerned and confused. Their bonuses depend on meeting volume targets we set three months ago. Some are encouraging their trade accounts to double their 28-oz. orders so that they can get the product volume they need. Others are suggesting that we ease off pushing 28 oz. to ensure strong summer promotions on 32 oz. and 44 oz. They want to discourage accounts from substituting 28-oz. features for features on these established items. The only thing going for us is that the trade experienced this same inventory shortage problem when Welch's went to plastic jelly containers four months ago.

One option was to withdraw the plastic bottle from the Northeast region where it was now being rolled-out. However, the sales force already had announced the introduction to the trade in February, and introductory orders had been shipped to two accounts. Heinz could cut off certain accounts, and give priority to building the 28-oz. business in the South and West, turning to the rest of the country later. Another option was to cut all trade orders in half. Another was to refuse truckload orders, which accounted for 75 percent of the volume of orders received so far. A fifth alternative was to cancel the introductory deal scheduled to last through the end of July, which would mean withdrawing advertising and couponing programs. However, Johnson knew several trade accounts had already committed to newspaper advertisements prominently featuring the 28-oz. bottle.

Heinz could cancel the deal with the promise of running a make-up deal on the same terms later when production and inventories were up to speed. At this time, Johnson could not promise when that would be. She did know that, without a deal, it would be three months before Heinz could have reserve factory inventory representing four weeks of normal supply. Johnson believed that she needed 16 weeks' normal supply in inventory before a deal could be reoffered.

Another option was for Heinz to extend the deal to reduce inventory loading by the trade. Or, Heinz could allocate to trade accounts either a weekly quota of the 28-oz. size, or an estimate of normal shelf-turn volume (one-sixth of deal volume) rather than deal volume. Barbara Johnson knew that in choosing a course of action, she had to consider the impact on Heinz's future relations with the trade. She also had to be careful on how much information to divulge to the trade for fear of helping competition. In addition, she was considering the following executional issues:

- Should she try to cancel the late July FSI coupon drop scheduled as part of the introductory program in the Northeast? A three-month lead time was normally needed for cancellation, but Johnson could try to substitute ads and coupons for other Heinz products.
- Should she substitute other Heinz commercials for 28-oz. introductory spots in the Northeast and/or in other regions?
- Should she cancel a 28-oz. trade promotion scheduled for September in the South and West? If so, should she substitute another size?
- Should she run a print ad in trade publications highlighting the success of the 28 oz. and apologizing for the product shortage problem?

Johnson had to act fast because she was in the middle of a crisis, and all senior marketing and sales managers were in the Southern and Western regions announcing to the trade a new line of Heinz instant baby foods.

Black & Decker Corporation: Spacemaker Plus[1] Coffeemaker (A)

"My Black & Decker Spacemaker Plus coffeemaker has just set itself on fire," said the California caller to Black & Decker's customer service "800" number on December 1, 1988. Fortunately, as the caller calmly explained, the fire had been confined to the unit and was quickly extinguished. As he was preparing to paint his kitchen, he was not concerned about the smoke damage, though he did want a replacement coffeemaker. Black & Decker's concern was to get the unit back to the Household Product Group's (HPG) Shelton, Connecticut, headquarters as soon as possible to establish the cause of the fire in its new "Cadillac product."

With sales exceeding the same period in 1987 by more than 20 percent, 1988 Christmas orders were strong for HPG. By December, it had succeeded in shipping all it could produce of the Spacemaker Plus line, including over 80,000 coffeemakers, in time for the peak holiday buying period. Launched mid-1988, the Spacemaker Plus line was a "key introduction" for HPG in the United States, illustrating Black & Decker's commitment to innovation and the development of quality new products with design appeal. A product recall would be a big professional and personal disappointment to HPG president Dennis Heiner. It could not automatically be assumed that a product involved in a fire would need to be recalled; it would need to be established whether the product was the cause or the victim of a fire. However, customers had already reported steaming problems with the Spacemaker Plus coffeemaker prior to the December 1 fire call. One of HPG's main competitors had recently settled out of court a product liability suit involving a fire hazard in one of its coffeemakers, at a figure around $40 million. But the prospect of litiga-

Professor N. Craig Smith prepared this case as the basis for class discussion rather than to illustrate either effective or ineffective handling of an administrative situation. Certain nonpublic data have been disguised. Copyright © 1990 by the President and Fellows of Harvard College. Harvard Business School case 9–590–099.

[1] Spacemaker Plus is a trademark of the General Electric Company, U.S.A.

tion was only one of many considerations likely to influence Heiner's decision about a recall.

Black & Decker Corporation

In 1910, Duncan Black and Alonzo Decker started their Baltimore machine shop. The name Black & Decker was soon to become synonymous with power tools after the company obtained a patent, in 1917, on the world's first portable power drill with pistol grip and trigger switch, virtually inventing an industry. Seventy years later, Black & Decker was "a global marketer and manufacturer of quality products used in and around the home and for commercial applications." It was the world's largest producer of power tools but had also become a leading supplier of household products, such as irons and toaster ovens. Marketing its products in over 100 countries, there was worldwide recognition of its brand name and a strong reputation for quality, value, and innovation. In fiscal 1988[2] Black & Decker sales were $2.28 billion, generating net earnings of $97 million and a return on equity of 14.1 percent. These figures constituted a turnaround after some years of poor performance and were a credit to the leadership of Nolan Archibald, CEO since 1985, and his management team. In 1987, Alonzo Decker, Jr., the 80-year-old son of the company's cofounder, was able to say to Archibald: "Noland, I want you to know this is the best Christmas I've had in 10 years."

Much of the success of the turnaround was attributed to a transformation in the corporate culture, with a customer orientation replacing a complacent manufacturing mentality such that "being market driven is more than a catchphrase; it defines [the] entire organization." This was a vital part of Black & Decker's efforts to reverse a persistent decline in market share to foreign competition, such as Makita of Japan and Bosch of West Germany. There was also a major restructuring, involving a $215 million write-off in 1985, five plant closures and downsizing of others, streamlining of the distribution system, and a 10 percent reduction in the number of employees to 20,800 by 1988. Under this "cut and build" strategy, globalization in manufacturing and marketing also came to be emphasized. With many of its products based around small electric motors, Black & Decker had been using 100 different motors worldwide. Rationalization and globalization reduced that number to less than 20. A global product strategy allowed Black & Decker to have common products worldwide that were customized to suit individual markets.

By 1988, Black & Decker had also digested its 1984 acquisition of the General Electric (GE) Housewares Division. Under the terms of the acquisition, Black & Decker had been permitted to manufacture and market

---

[2] The Black & Decker fiscal year end was September 30. A calendar fiscal year was adopted as of 1990.

appliances under the GE name until 1987. A marketing program was developed which successfully transferred the Black & Decker name to the GE small appliance lines, increasing market share from 27 percent to over 30 percent by 1988. The slower growth rate of the power tool market and increased foreign competition, as well as the success of its Dustbuster[3] rechargeable hand-held vacuum cleaner, had prompted Black & Decker to significantly increase its presence in the housewares market, with the GE acquisition providing greater access to housewares buyers. Further acquisitions were likely, to expand the earnings base and exploit a substantial tax loss carryforward. A hostile bid for American Standard, attractive to Black & Decker because it included a plumbing products business, had proven unsuccessful in 1987.[4]

In 1988, 52 percent of Black & Decker sales were in the United States, 33 percent European, and 15 percent in other countries. Following the GE acquisition, Black & Decker had been formed into two key business units: power tools and small household appliances. The Power Tools Group was responsible for power tools (42 percent of worldwide sales), accessories (11 percent) and outdoor products (8 percent). Power tools included portable electric and cordless electric drills, screwdrivers, saws, sanders, and grinders; car care products; Workmate[5] Workcenters (a workbench with vises), and stationary woodworking tools. Accessories included power tool accessories and fastening products. Outdoor products included hedge and lawn trimmers, electric mowers, cordless brooms, and chain saws. The Household Products Group (33 percent of worldwide sales) was responsible for products used inside the home: cordless vacuums, irons, food preparation products (such as mixers), coffeemakers, toasters, toaster ovens, lighting, heating, and fire safety products. HPG sales grew by 14 percent in fiscal 1988. Supporting both groups was Black & Decker's service operation (6 percent worldwide sales), comprising 244 company-owned service centers (120 in the United States) and several hundred authorized independent outlets.

Spacemaker Plus

Industry analysts described the flow of new products as probably the single most critical factor in Black & Decker's growth equation. In 1988, 40 percent of HPG sales came from products three years old or less. At

---

[3] Dustbuster is a registered trademark of Black & Decker Corporation.

[4] In April 1989, Black & Decker acquired the larger Emhart Corporation, a diversified multinational producer of industrial and consumer products, including fastening products, and information and electronic systems. Annual revenues would be doubled but industry analysts had doubts about the acquisition, with the more favorable commenting that this would be ''an interesting story in the long term.'' A bid to acquire Sunbeam/Oster from the bankrupt Allegheny International had fallen through earlier in 1989.

[5] Workmate is a registered trademark of Black & Decker Corporation.

the housewares trade exhibition in January 1989, Black & Decker planned to display 12 new small appliance lines. Archibald had said, "There are no mature markets, only mature managements." Heiner believed the way to sell a product as mature as an iron was to add something like an automatic shut-off feature; similarly blenders became cordless and Dustbuster vacuum cleaners became more powerful. Average industry returns on sales were low, at 3–4 percent, in the price-sensitive domestic appliance market. (It had yet to attract much interest from Japanese competition.) Some companies serving narrow niches in the market realized 8 percent; HPG had done better still, realizing an operating income in excess of 10 percent of sales in 1987 and 1988. But achieving growth and high levels of profitability through innovation was certainly a challenge for HPG.

Black & Decker's household product sales were $749 million worldwide in 1988, the majority of which were in the United States. Heiner aimed to significantly increase US sales over the next five years by concentrating on the five core business areas where Black & Decker felt it had sustainable competitive advantage: irons, vacuum cleaners, toaster ovens, coffeemakers, and toasters. While some of this growth would probably be through acquisitions, much of it would need to be internally generated. In keeping with Black & Decker's market-driven philosophy, HPG's mission was "to provide superior customer satisfaction as the dominant brand of high-quality, innovative household products." Heiner was striving to develop a total quality culture with a commitment to customer care within HPG. He believed this approach would enable the group to realize its ambitious sales targets.

In a composite market share estimation, Black & Decker dominated the US small domestic appliance market in 1988, with around a 30 percent share by volume and value, compared to the roughly 10 percent share held by each of its nearest rivals, Proctor Silex and Sunbeam. Exhibit 1 shows Black & Decker and competitor composite quarterly market shares 1987–1988. Exhibit 2 shows Black & Decker and leading competitor market shares by product category for July–September 1987 and 1988. Exhibit 3 shows Black & Decker and competitor quarterly market shares for drip coffeemakers 1987–1988.

The new Spacemaker Plus line was described in the annual report as a "major product highlight of 1988." As well as offering new products, this line was able to command the better profit margins HPG was keen to secure: its "contribution margin" (effectively gross profit) was substantially higher than the 40 percent average of all HPG lines. Black & Decker had inherited the Spacemaker concept from GE. An under-the-cabinet electric can opener had been launched in 1982, followed in 1983 by the addition of a toaster oven, a drip coffeemaker, a mixer, and an electric knife to the Spacemaker line. However, while off the countertop, these products remained bulky and saved little space in their vertical configuration. Lower-priced competitive imitations had also appeared.

EXHIBIT 1 Composite Quarterly Market Shares by Volume and Value: Small Domestic Appliances, 1987–1988

Core Categories*	By Volume 1987				1988				By Value	
	January–March	April–June	July–September	October–December	January–March	April–June	July–September	October–December (E)	July–September	October–December (E)
Black & Decker	25.0%	25.9%	26.1%	27.4%	27.3%	29.0%	29.0%	32.2%	28.6%	31.1%
Hamilton Beach	7.8	7.8	7.4	8.1	7.8	7.9	7.4	7.1	6.1	5.3
Proctor Silex	9.5	10.3	10.7	9.5	11.4	10.4	11.2	9.0	8.3	6.6
Sunbeam	10.7	10.1	10.5	10.7	10.0	9.8	10.2	9.4	9.4	8.4
Norelco	8.0	7.1	6.6	5.0	5.1	4.1	3.5	2.8	2.6	2.2
Toastmaster	5.5	5.2	5.5	5.3	5.4	5.4	5.3	4.6	4.5	3.7
Other	33.5	33.6	33.2	34.0	33.0	33.4	33.4	34.9	40.6	42.6

NOTES: E = Estimated.

Columns may not total 100% due to rounding error.

* Core categories are irons, rechargeable hand-held vacuum cleaners, rechargeable stick vacuum cleaners, toaster ovens, toasters, drip coffeemakers, food processors, food choppers, portable mixers, can openers, electric knives, and blenders.

SOURCE: Black & Decker Corporation.

EXHIBIT 2   Volume Market Shares by Product Category, 1987 and 1988

Product Category	Company (rank ordered)	Percent of Market Share by Volume	
		July–September 1987	July–September 1988
Irons	Black & Decker	47.4%	47.7%
	Proctor Silex	13.6	18.3
	Sunbeam	18.9	18.0
Can openers	Rival	30.6	29.2
	Black & Decker	22.6	23.3
	Sunbeam	11.2	11.3
Rechargeable hand-held vacuum cleaners	Black & Decker	79.8	74.4
	Hoover	2.1	15.0
	Eureka	8.6	5.6
Toaster ovens	Black & Decker	45.7	59.7
	Toastmaster	16.0	13.8
	Proctor Silex	19.9	13.4
Portable mixers	Black & Decker	27.2	35.0
	Sunbeam	28.7	23.0
	Hamilton Beach	7.9	10.0
Food choppers	Black & Decker	14.5	27.0
	Sunbeam	13.9	23.9
	Cuisinart	21.2	16.2
Food processors	Sunbeam	30.5	22.4
	Hamilton Beach	15.1	12.5
	Black & Decker	8.2	9.5
Drip coffeemakers	Mr. Coffee	21.3	21.6
	Black & Decker	11.3	16.4
	Proctor Silex	13.6	15.3
Toasters	Toastmaster	32.8	30.7
	Proctor Silex	25.7	25.9
	Black & Decker	12.0	12.6
Rechargeable stick vacuum cleaners	Black & Decker	NA	37.6
	Eureka	32.6	32.7
	Regina	62.4	29.7
Rechargeable "lites"	First Alert	35.2	31.3
	Black & Decker	34.7	24.7
	Houseworks	5.0	20.4
Smoke alarms	First Alert	38.2	38.4
	Southwest Labs	2.1	20.0
	Family Gard	23.0	17.6
	Black & Decker	7.1	11.6
Stand mixers	Sunbeam	50.0	45.7
	Kitchen Aid	15.3	34.3
	Hamilton Beach	10.6	7.1
	Waring	13.5	5.2
	Krups	8.5	5.2
	Black & Decker	0.0	0.5
Electric knives	Hamilton Beach	34.2	37.0
	Black & Decker	30.7	31.4
	Regal/Moulinex	16.9	11.1
Regular blenders (excluding hand blenders)	Oster	44.6	45.7
	Hamilton Beach	37.5	34.0
	Waring	16.0	10.4
	Black & Decker	2.0	7.1
Hot air corn poppers	West Bend	36.8	32.1
	Presto	36.4	31.3
	Wearever	22.0	19.9
	Hamilton Beach	3.4	8.5
	Black & Decker	1.4	6.5

SOURCE: Black & Decker Corporation.

EXHIBIT 3 Drip Coffeemakers: US Market Shares by Volume and Value, 1987–88

Company (ranked order)	January–March 1987		April–June 1987		July–September 1987		October–December 1987		January–March 1988		April–June 1988		July–September 1988		October–December 1988 (E)	
	By Volume	By Value	By Volume	By Value	By Volume	By Value	By Volume	By Value	By Volume	By Value	By Volume	By Value	By Volume	By Value	By Volume	By Value
Black & Decker	12.0	(14.9)	12.8	(15.1)	11.3	(12.8)	14.3	(14.8)	12.8	(13.6)	16.7	(16.8)	16.4	(16.2)	22.0	(23.3)
Mr. Coffee	21.9	(17.6)	19.4	(15.5)	21.3	(16.9)	21.6	(17.6)	19.0	(15.2)	19.3	(15.4)	21.6	(16.3)	20.8	(15.2)
Braun	7.8	(9.6)	9.2	(11.6)	10.5	(13.9)	12.0	(15.5)	11.7	(15.7)	11.6	(15.8)	12.2	(16.5)	13.0	(17.4)
Proctor Silex	11.4	(7.5)	13.3	(8.8)	13.6	(9.4)	14.0	(9.5)	17.7	(12.6)	16.6	(11.6)	15.3	(10.0)	11.9	(7.4)
Krups	8.3	(13.6)	9.7	(15.2)	9.4	(14.4)	6.8	(10.0)	7.1	(11.5)	8.1	(13.2)	9.3	(15.6)	9.4	(15.0)
Norelco	18.3	(14.3)	15.6	(12.2)	15.0	(11.8)	13.3	(10.7)	12.6	(10.1)	8.9	(7.1)	7.3	(5.7)	7.2	(5.8)
All other	20.3	(22.5)	20.0	(21.6)	18.9	(20.8)	18.0	(20.0)	19.1	(21.4)	18.8	(20.3)	17.9	(19.6)	15.7	(15.7)

NOTES: E = Estimated.

Columns may not total 100% due to rounding error.

SOURCE: Black & Decker Corporation.

In the product line evaluation after the GE acquisition, Black & Decker decided the Spacemaker line needed to be completely redesigned. An integrated development team, comprising former GE and Black & Decker designers, engineers, and manufacturing experts, was responsible for the project from conception to production. Focusing on the coffeemaker, the product development team sought to reduce its size and bulk, making it as horizontal as possible and a genuine spacesaver. A new "book-shaped" water reservoir that inserted like a video cassette was developed and much of the volume of the housing of the coffeemaker was kept to the rear of the cabinet, significantly reducing actual and, from a standing position, perceived size. An innovation stemming from consumer research, the use of a thermal carafe eliminated the requirement for a "keep-warm plate," reducing space and size but also manufacturing and assembly costs. Design featured strongly in Black & Decker's strategy of leveraging low-cost manufacturing with aggressive marketing.

Launched to praise from many quarters in June 1988, the Spacemaker Plus line comprised five models: the PDC403 coffeemaker, with digital clock for preset brewing (suggested retail price $112); the PDC401 coffeemaker, without clock ($80); the PEC90 can opener, with knife sharpener ($37); the PEC60 can opener, without knife sharpener ($32); and the PLA100 kitchen accessory light ($24). In contrast to the dark colors of the original Spacemaker line, these products were in white and together made up a cohesive visual scheme, encouraging consumers to combine units, as shown in Exhibit 4. Said to resemble a Danish stereo, Spacemaker Plus met with the approval of the Industrial Designers Society of America, winning in August 1988 its Design Excellence award; the "design's elegant restraint is exquisite" said the jurors. In October 1988, *Appliance Manufacturer* magazine named Spacemaker Plus the first-place winner in its annual award competition for appliance products, based on its aesthetic appeal, functionality, ease of use and engineering execution. Spacemaker Plus was soon "making inroads in a market that swooned over Krups and Braun," commented the *New York Times*. Until December 1988, at least, it was a Black & Decker success story.

The Fire Investigation

When the fire call came in, David Wildman, manager of the HPG Product Safety and Liability Group, had been immediately alerted. This group was responsible for safety. It had reviewed the design and initial prototype of the coffeemaker and arranged for its testing in Black & Decker's laboratories when approval had been given for the production of larger numbers of prototypes. A Failure Mode Effect Analysis had not indicated a safety problem arising from any of the three primary causes of injury: fire, shock, or cut hazard. However, the coffeemaker's new design meant there were no established standards. The normal industry practice for

EXHIBIT 4 **Spacemaker Plus Coffeemaker, Can Opener, and Accessory Light**

  BLACK & DECKER®

Spacemaker Plus™* Appliances

THE ULTIMATE IN SPACESAVING CONVENIENCE AND CONTEMPORARY STYLING!

- **Kitchen Accessory Light** brightens up your kitchen counter, and features a handy, hidden electric outlet. PLA100
- **Can Opener and Knife Sharpener.** Opens cans — hands free — then shuts itself off. Plus, provides fail-safe sharpening of even your finest cutlery. PEC90
- **Thermal Carafe Drip Coffeemaker with Electronic Clock/Timer** offers an unique convenience feature — coffee brews THRU lid, locks in freshness, flavor. Clock/Timer lets you set brewing time in advance. Automatic Shut-Off for safety. PDC403.

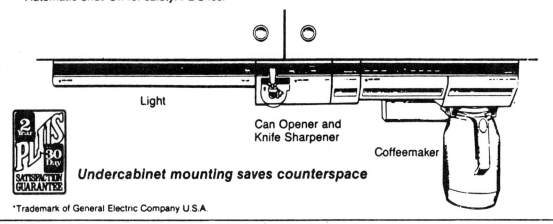

Light

Can Opener and
Knife Sharpener

Coffeemaker

Undercabinet mounting saves counterspace

*Trademark of General Electric Company U.S.A.

Spacemaker Classic Line

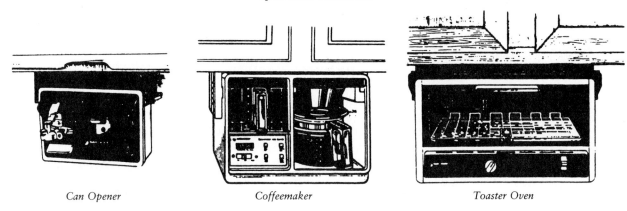

Can Opener   *Coffeemaker*   *Toaster Oven*

SOURCE: Black & Decker Corporation.

small appliances was to have them certified as safe by Underwriters' Laboratory (UL), an independent testing service. This was not mandatory, but it was required for manufacturers by many retailers. It was Black & Decker company policy not to sell a product unless it met, if not exceeded, UL requirements. The Spacemaker Plus exceeded the UL requirement for coffeemakers of a single temperature cut-off (TCO), which shuts the unit off in the event of overheating. Black & Decker fitted two TCOs to all its coffeemakers, believing that the fire and consequent liability problems experienced by a competitor with one of its coffeemakers might have been avoided if a second cut-off had been included in the unit. The PDC401 and PDC403 coffeemakers were both fitted with two TCOs.

Wildman spoke with the California customer about possible causes of the fire and arranged for the immediate collection of the coffeemaker by a courier service. Within 24 hours the damaged coffeemaker was in Shelton and investigations began immediately. Working round the clock, it was concluded on December 3, less than 48 hours after the fire had been reported, that the unit was responsible and external sources or misuse could be ruled out. The precise cause of the fire had yet to be established. However, a laboratory test, which involved clamping the feed from the reservoir to the heater element, starving the unit of water, had produced overheating and fires in new units, despite the TCOs. Accordingly, all units could be considered potentially faulty and therefore fire hazards. Wildman informed Heiner, who was then in Australia and promptly curtailed his trip to return to Shelton.

A manufacturer was obligated under the United States Consumer Product Safety Act to recall a product where there was knowledge of a substantial product hazard. Although telephone calls to California had led Wildman to suspect the fire had something to do with the customer not fully inserting the water reservoir drawer, he did believe there was some prospect of a legal requirement to recall the coffeemaker. In the event any product liability claims emerged, these would have to be met by the company because Black & Decker was self-insured.

Product Recalls

Product recalls were not uncommon, with the Consumer Product Safety Commission (CPSC) overseeing more than 100 product recalls annually, involving millions of individual items. Other federal agencies with recall authority were the Food and Drug Administration (FDA), the National Highway Traffic Safety Administration (NHTSA), the Environmental Protection Agency (EPA), and the Federal Trade Commission (FTC). The agencies relied primarily on self-reported voluntary recalls, which manufacturers had strong incentives to organize, but NHTSA could mandate recalls and had forced automobile manufacturers to undertake major recall programs. Recalls could result from poor design or manufacturing, although many arose from faults that developed in unanticipated ways. Product tampering (e.g., Tylenol case) or legal action by a competitor (e.g., in response to a breach of trademark) could also prompt recalls. As well as the costs of obtaining recalled goods and possible harm to the company's reputation, recalls could increase the prospect of product liability litigation. However, delays to a necessary recall, by not acting quickly when a problem was apparent or not responding to a federal agency request for a voluntary recall, could have severe legal consequences.

The CPSC, created in 1972, was responsible for all goods used by final consumers except those covered by the FDA, NHTSA, and EPA. The agency relied upon the legal requirement of firms to report safety problems. It would then negotiate a recall plan with the firm if needed. The firm then had to provide monthly reports on progress of the recall. Black & Decker believed CPSC could mandate a recall if necessary. According to CPSC, a dangerous defect could result from

1. A fault, flaw, or irregularity that causes weakness, failure, or inadequacy in form or function.
2. Manufacturing or production error.
3. A product's design or materials.
4. A product's contents, construction, finish, packaging, warnings, and/or instructions.

Guidelines also helped determine whether the safety problem was substantial:

1. The nature of the risk of injury the product presents and the severity of the risk (i.e., the seriousness of the possible injury and the likelihood that an injury could occur).
2. The necessity for the product, its utility, and the ways it can be used or misused.
3. The number of defective products, and the population group exposed to the products.
4. The physical environment within which the defect manifests itself.
5. Case law involving health, safety, and product liability.
6. The CPSC's own experience and expertise as well as other relevant factors.

Recall return rates varied greatly. NHTSA recalls for automobiles reportedly achieved correction rates of 15–70 percent. Many CPSC recalls achieved return rates under 10 percent, particularly with the difficulty in contacting owners of inexpensive but harmful products. A study of CPSC recalls,[6] obtained by HPG, had examined factors influencing the three conditions necessary for a successful recall:

- Product availability—in the distribution channel or at least still in the possession of consumers (determined by the average age of the product and its average useful life).
- Distributor and consumer awareness of the recall.
- Benefits of compliance with the recall exceeding perceived costs of time, effort, and lost product services.

The CPSC study outlined a model for predicting likely recall return rates, highlighting these variables:

- The number of months separating end of distribution and the start of the recall.
- The percentage of products owned by consumers who are notified of the recall directly by mail.
- The percentage of items (produced) in retail inventory. (Distributors and retailers had strong incentives to comply with recalls, because of concern for their reputations and the prospect of liability suits; their costs of compliance were usually relatively low and they could be relatively easily reached.)
- The percentage of items (produced) in the hands of consumers. (Return rates are typically lower for products with consumers than those in the distribution channel. Factors said to influence consumer compliance include the severity of the safety hazard, the value of the product—higher benefit of compliance with more expensive products—and the type of remedy provided.)
- Whether a repair at home is offered to the consumer (relative to more inconvenient alternatives).

While the CPSC study reported an average correction/return rate of 54.4 percent over the sample of 128 recalls between 1978 and 1983, there was considerable variance, largely explained by the above variables. In the experience of Black & Decker personnel, return rates of products distributed to consumers were historically low, with a domestic appliance industry average said to be around 5 percent and anything over 22 percent "doing excellent." HPG had not previously recalled a product, though the GE Housewares Division had recalled an electric fan some years ago and Black & Decker had recalled some of its power tool products in the past. The GE fan recall had also involved a fire hazard. The low response rate of 6 percent was attributed to the late announcement of the recall; negotiations with the CPSC had delayed the announcement to November,

---

[6] R. Dennis Murphy and Paul H. Rubin, "Determinants of Recall Success Rates," *Journal of Products Liability* 11 (1988), pp. 17–28.

when few consumers were thinking about fans. Return rates on Black & Decker outdoor products had been as low as 3 percent.

In the opinion of Ken Homa, vice president of marketing at HPG, most manufacturers would try to avoid recalls but, should they arise, had few incentives to pursue high return rates. The conventional wisdom was that recalls were difficult to do effectively, they increased the possibility of product liability litigation, the regulatory agencies were cumbersome to deal with, and a high return rate would set a precedent for future recalls. The cost of recalls and the potential damage to the company's brand name were also considerations. As a consequence, established procedures were limited and, as Gael Simonson, director of brand marketing and strategy development, put it: "There was a precedent to be passive."

Heiner's Decision

On December 5, Wildman informed the CPSC that there had been a fire in a Spacemaker Plus coffeemaker, which was being investigated, and that shipments of the product had stopped. He also advised the corporate legal department. The next day at a meeting with Heiner, Homa, and other senior management, Wildman reported his investigations. While not certain of the cause of the starvation problem, he suspected it was due to incomplete closure of the reservoir drawer. "You'd have to try hard to get the reservoir in the wrong way" was one exasperated reaction at the meeting.

Heiner was told that about 25,000 units were with consumers in virtually any of the 90 million households in the United States. About 10 percent of these owners were believed to have returned warranty cards, supplying their names and addresses. Black & Decker had distributed 88,400 Spacemaker Plus coffeemakers, the majority through major retailing chains such as Sears, Penney's, Best Products, and Service Merchandise, with the remainder through small local appliance and department stores and some within Black & Decker. The precise number of units sold through to consumers could not be ascertained, but was believed to be about 30–35 percent of units distributed. In some recalls consumers were provided with a similar or superior model to replace the faulty product, but HPG did not have a suitable replacement for the Spacemaker Plus coffeemaker. Most worrisome for the HPG management team was the likelihood of the safety problem arising when the product was unattended. Both versions of the coffeemaker operated automatically; the PDC403 had a 24-hour digital clock/timer so that consumers could preset the machine at night to start at a selected time, in order to wake in the morning to fresh-brewed coffee. Around 40 percent of HPG sales were during the pre-Christmas season and many of these units were therefore wrapped up as gifts.

EXHIBIT 5   Recall Cost Estimates

Consumer Recall	*Approximate $ millions*

25,000 units sold @ 25% response = 6,250 units returned.

Option 1. Replacement of coffeemaker when available at (current) manufactured cost of $40 (PDC403) and $30 (PDC401). PDC403 sales were approximately twice those of PDC401.

PDC403 $6{,}250 \times \frac{2}{3} \times 40 = \$166{,}667$

PDC401 $6{,}250 \times \frac{1}{3} \times 30 = \underline{62{,}500}$

 $229{,}167$ $ .230

Option 2. Cash refund at suggested retail prices.

PDC403 $6{,}250 \times \frac{2}{3} \times 112 = \$466{,}667$

PDC401 $6{,}250 \times \frac{1}{3} \times 80 = \underline{166{,}667}$

 $633{,}334$ $ .635

Freight, labels, administration
Approximately $100/unit returned $ .625

Retail Recall

Return of 63,400 units for refund (and to be reworked).
Lost margin, at an average of $30/unit
 $63{,}400 \times 30 = \$1{,}902{,}000$ $1.900
Freight, refunds on joint promotions, administration, etc.
 Estimated at $500,000 $ .500
Rework of returned units for later sale
 Best estimate, unless major work required, of $10/unit
 $63{,}400 \times 10 = \$634{,}000$ $ .635

Total cost $4.3M
approximately
with cash refund
to consumers)

NOTE: Cost and margin data have been disguised, but estimates provided here are useful for analysis.

HPG was facing increased pressure on margins, with rising costs of raw materials. The corporate safety manager from Black & Decker's Towson, Maryland, headquarters had suggested a 15–20 percent return of units with consumers would probably meet the letter of the law. It had been estimated that with a 25 percent consumer return rate the recall would cost around $4 million (excluding opportunity costs of lost sales). Exhibit 5 shows recall cost estimates. The corporate safety manager explained that the normal procedure, in the event of a recall, was to notify CPSC and develop a recall program. This usually took four to six weeks, but the process could be accelerated if Heiner wished.

Heiner had informed Archibald of the safety problem, but it was Heiner's decision as to what HPG should do next.

Product Management Organization

General Foods Corporation: The Product Management System

In February 1985, senior marketing executives from General Foods (GF) Desserts Division (DD) met over lunch to discuss the trimming of the marketing organization that had been implemented during the previous two years under the leadership of Roger Smith, general manager. The discussion turned to the broader issue of the future of the product management system in use at GF since the company was founded in the 1920s. Differences of opinion about the product manager's tasks and responsibilities were evident in the comments of two senior DD managers:

> Our product managers must have profit responsibility. Only then will they act to add to stockholder value, to manage our assets effectively, and to deliver an ROI that exceeds the cost of capital. As for advertising, that is just one aspect of their job.
>
> Product managers should not be general business managers. They should be the advertising and promotion specialists on their products, responsible for building the franchise in terms of sales volume and share. With no growth in the volume of food consumed in the US, franchise building depends upon regional marketing and rifling more finely defined target segments. This takes time.

As Roger Smith looked at the current DD organization chart (see Exhibit 1), he wondered about the effectiveness of the product management system and what, if anything, he and his colleagues could do to improve it.

This case was prepared by Harvard Business School Professor John A. Quelch and Professor Paul W. Farris, Colgate-Darden Graduate School of Business Administration, University of Virginia, as the basis for class discussion rather than to illustrate either effective or ineffective handling of an administrative situation. Names have been disguised. Copyright © 1985 by the President and Fellows of Harvard College. Harvard Business School case 9–586–057.

EXHIBIT 1 Desserts Division Organization Chart

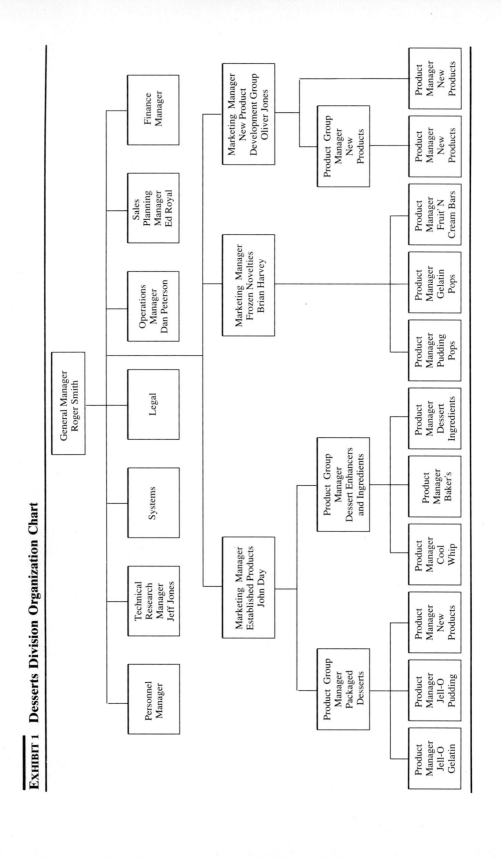

Company Background

Product Lines

Since its formation in the 1920s, GF had been a leading US producer of processed food products. In 1984, with sales of $8.9 billion and operating profits of $768 million, up 12 percent from 1983, GF was still the largest US company operating solely in the food business. Beatrice Foods and Dart & Kraft were larger, but only as a result of revenues from their nonfood businesses. GF marketed over 1,200 items in the US and held the first or second market share position in three-quarters of the product categories in which it competed.

GF was organized into the following sectors, each representing a specific menu segment:

- Basic Foods and Baked Goods included Entenmann's Inc. and the Breakfast Foods division, which marketed Post cereals and Log Cabin syrup.

- The Oscar Mayer sector manufactured and sold processed meats, and was also responsible for the manufacture of Louis Rich turkeys and Claussen pickles.

- Coffee and Food Service included the Maxwell House division and the Food Service Products division which sold coffee and other GF products to institutional buyers.

- The Packaged Convenience Foods sector included three divisions organized by menu segment. Each division sold products that used a variety of manufacturing processes and distribution systems:

    The Beverage division sold powdered soft drinks including Tang, Kool-Aid, Country Time, and Crystal Light.

    The Meals division produced Bird's Eye frozen products, and dry products such as Minute Rice, Stove Top stuffing , Shake'n Bake seasoned coating mixes, and Ronzoni pasta.

    The Desserts division manufactured Jell-O gelatin, Jell-O pudding, D-Zerta, and frozen toppings like Cool Whip. In addition, DD had recently expanded into the frozen novelty category with Jell-O pudding pops and Jell-O gelatin pops. Most DD brands were share leaders in their respective subcategories. In FY 1984, the division delivered $110 million in operating profits on more than $600 million in revenues.

- International Operations. Organized into five geographical groups and accounting for a quarter of GF sales, the international division had subsidiaries or joint ventures in 20 countries and exported GF products to 100 more. As well as marketing products paralleling GF's US lines, GF subsidiaries, as a result of acquisition, also marketed the leading ice cream in Brazil, the leading chewing gum in France, and the leading snack product line in Canada.

Evolution of Strategy

During the 1970s, the rate of US population growth flattened, and volume growth in the food industry declined to 1–2 percent per year. In addition, many of the product categories which GF dominated had matured. For example, per capita consumption of coffee, which accounted for a third of GF's sales, peaked in 1962. Consumption of Jell-O gelatin topped out in 1969. As these products matured, GF had to identify new avenues for future growth.

Nevertheless, during this period, GF's financial results were strong. Earnings per share doubled between 1973 and 1979. By FY 1981, GF's return on equity and return on invested capital were among the highest in the food industry. CEO James Ferguson commented, however, that "the predominant part of the growth we've achieved has been a function of our good control of costs. What we were not doing was broadening the base of the business."

Hence, in 1981, GF shifted strategy from earnings and margin protection to volume and franchise building. Under the leadership of a new president, Philip Smith, GF managers were instructed to strive for 3–5 percent annual volume growth instead of 1 percent, and to achieve 15 percent return on capital instead of the 13.2 percent achieved in the previous year.

GF management responded in three ways. First, there was renewed emphasis on new product development to identify and develop new items that would appeal to a more convenience-oriented consumer. Second, continued attention was paid to achieving cost reductions on established products in order to build margins that could be used to fund new product development. Third, GF engaged in a selective acquisition strategy to acquire food companies that would fill gaps in GF's product menu as well as add new manufacturing processes, technologies, or distribution systems. Oscar Mayer, Entenmann's, and Ronzoni were all acquired as part of this strategy. Unlike competitors such as Quaker Oats and General Mills, which acquired nonfood businesses that made products with high margins and fast growth, GF maintained its focus on food and beverages. At the same time, the emphasis on volume growth led GF to divest operations that continued to experience volume declines, notably the pet foods division, which was sold to Anderson Clayton Foods in 1984.

Top management realized that volume growth could not be achieved without investment. Capital investment in 1984 exceeded $200 million; and advertising close to $500 million made GF the second-largest national advertiser after Procter & Gamble.

Philip Smith espoused three principles to guide GF's mission through the 1980s:

- GF aims to be the premier food and beverage company in the world *through providing superior customer satisfaction.*
- GF believes that *ideas* are what build business.
- GF affirms that it will reward well the people who come up with business-building ideas and *carry them successfully into action.*

The Product Management Function

Overview

Within each operating division dealing with a particular menu segment, GF used a product management system to manage its businesses. The strength of the system was that it identified specific individuals responsible for the well-being of each business. As a result, the system encouraged individuals to develop a sense of ownership for their businesses, within the framework of a larger organization.

While the operation of the product management function varied somewhat from one division or business to another, there were elements common to all brands. Brian Harvey, DD marketing manager for frozen novelties, explained the basic organizational structure and career path:

> The product management system is like a pyramid in which individuals take on more responsibilities and brands with increased experience. At the base of the pyramid is the assistant product manager, the entry-level position for recent MBA graduates. At the top of the pyramid is the marketing manager. Along the way, an individual progresses from assistant product manager to associate product manager, product manager, product group manager or category manager, before being appointed marketing manager. Beyond this level, individuals leave the product management function to take on general management responsibilities.

The broad-based training and exposure individuals received as they progressed through the product management career path were regarded as excellent preparation for general management. All but one of GF's domestic division general managers had risen through the product management function.

Assistant Product Manager

Recruitment and Training

Recent business graduates entered GF as assistant product managers (assistants). Occasionally, assistants were drawn from other functions. A GF recruiting brochure profiled candidates for a product management career as people who

- Can figure out what needs to be done and get it done without substantial supervision.

- Have leadership qualities and the ability to guide others to reach an objective.
- Have an entrepreneurial spirit, like to maintain a degree of ownership for their ideas and translate them into reality.
- Possess good instincts for the marketplace—feel empathy with consumers—and show the vision and creativity that lead to new ideas of worth and value to consumers.
- Are able to apply their intelligence in an analytic framework.
- Can demonstrate administrative skills.
- Have the potential to develop into candidates for general management.

According to one DD marketing manager:

We want people who are at one and the same time leaders and team players; people who have an enormous amount of drive and self-confidence and are able to innovate rather than just be the stewards of others' ideas.

Training and development began as soon as a new assistant joined GF. Training was considered fundamental to the effectiveness of the product management system. As a result, senior marketing executives were evaluated not only on their business results but also on the training of individuals within their organizations. According to Denise Rodriguez, DD product group manager for packaged desserts:

The sound development of assistant and associate product managers is key to GF's longer-term success. After all, the product management system is our major source of candidates for general management. There is so much to be done and so few people to do it, it's critical to have everyone contributing at a maximum degree of effectiveness.

Ninety percent of a new assistant's training was on the job. In addition, GF's line management and marketing staff groups offered in-house seminars throughout the year. These seminars focused on topics such as product positioning, sales promotion, consumer research, and advertising copy development. The seminars enabled individuals to discuss their businesses with their peers who were facing similar challenges.

All new DD assistants also completed a 13-week sales training program shortly after arrival. This program was designed to improve their understanding of the changing retail environment and of how products are actually sold and distributed as well as to give them a feel for the sales representative's job. This exposure was considered essential, given the importance of sales and its role in developing longer-term brand strategies. During the 13 weeks, individuals called on accounts, observed retail and key account representatives, and undertook special projects for field personnel.

Tasks and Responsibilities

The tasks and responsibilities of assistants were defined to provide as broad an exposure to an entire business in as short a time as possible. Initially, assistants were responsible for volume planning (market and share forecasting), financial budget control, production planning coordination, promotion execution, coordination with legal and purchasing functions, and business analysis. A conscious effort was made to expose new assistants to the nonmarketing functions. In addition, the assistant often assumed responsibility for national promotion strategy, planning, and execution, as well as packaging strategy and execution.

When asked about the assistant's responsibilities, one product manager commented:

> A good assistant will come in, learn the fundamentals of the business during the first few months, and then generate new ideas and programs which will yield results. The most successful assistants define their job far more broadly than volume planning or forecasting.

Comments from several DD assistants reflected varying attitudes toward the nature of the job:

> The scope of the assistant's job depends on the size of the brand. The larger the brand, the more likely that the assistant will specialize. On the other hand, a new assistant assigned to a smaller brand would be part of a smaller team so would be exposed to a broader array of issues.
> * * * * *
> I felt important from day one. But it was six months before I knew what I was doing. The next six months I spent turning my ideas into actions and making something happen in the marketplace.
> * * * * *
> I found volume planning to be great fun. Some people thought that projecting a brand's sales would mean spending all day at a computer. What it really involved was talking to people, interpreting data, and making judgments about what was going on. In fact, I felt enormous power because I was the one person in the organization with the most knowledge of what was happening in the marketplace.
> * * * * *
> I liked being given projects for which I was responsible from day one. I was able to watch my ideas take shape and, with the guidance of my product manager, see the plan executed. In many ways, my first experiences were a microcosm of what the product manager was doing for the brand as a whole.

The need to ensure that assistants maintained a broad business perspective and did not become bogged down in numbers was a concern of some senior managers. The corporate vice president of Marketing Services commented:

> Our MBA hires are very numbers-oriented when they come here. I feel that we reinforce that bias by putting them to work on volume planning and regional marketing analyses. Assistants spend more time on the personal

computer than any other level of management. True, an assistant can understand the business better by running the numbers, but there's always a temptation to rely too much on the numbers. You must develop a strategy without the numbers first. It's important that the job of the assistant is not so detailed and numbers-oriented that we end up merely developing detail and numbers-oriented product managers.

Typically, assistants would work on their initial brand assignment for a year or more. This provided sufficient time to enable an assistant to become familiar with a brand and make significant contributions to its growth. One assistant noted:

> It was six months before I felt in control enough to take charge of programs and to direct the organization in implementing the programs I felt were right. Had I left my initial assignment too soon, I would have had to start up the learning curve again.

Associate Product Manager

Assistants who performed well could expect promotion to associate product manager (associate) within 18–20 months of arrival. However, GF managers stressed that promotion was based on performance rather than according to a timetable. Promotion was not automatic. According to Roger Smith:

> Every new brand assistant has the intellectual ability needed to do a good job. Those that succeed derive enjoyment from building the business. We quickly separate out people who merely play the system and do formula business management from those who have ideas and initiative, seize opportunities and show an ability to lead and manage.

Associates were given the autonomy to make things happen in a business by identifying business-building ideas, convincing others they were worthwhile, and taking them from concept to execution. Associates were often given responsibility for substantial projects on a large brand or total responsibility for managing a small brand. In addition, associates maintained day-to-day contact with personnel in operations, technical research, and market research, as well as executives at the advertising agency, particularly regarding media and copy execution.

Several DD associates commented on the position as follows:

> I've been an associate for seven months now. I've worked on a project to add Jell-O to chocolate chip cookies. It didn't work out but it was a memorable project. Many associates spend some time working on secondary line extensions for their brands. This gives an associate responsibility for a tangible product with minimal financial risk.

* * * * *

> I've been an associate for eighteen months on sugar-free Jell-O. I've had three product managers during that time. I know more about the brand than my boss so my recommendations carry a lot of weight. I'm also effectively

the product manager on D-Zerta and report directly to the category manager on issues relating to this brand.

* * * * *

An associate might not do a better job than an assistant would but, as a result of greater experience, would get it done faster. Another difference is that an associate would never go to his or her product manager with a problem without a suggested solution.

* * * * *

I've learned a lot beyond marketing at this level. In developing and introducing a line extension, I have worked on business proposals, facility plans, cost programs, and product formulations in addition to advertising and promotions. It has broadened my knowledge and exposure as I prepare to run my own brand.

Product Manager

The GF product manager (PM) was responsible for the day-to-day health of his or her franchise. This responsibility involved the development of annual plans, and once approved, ensuring their excellent execution. Since the plans were related to functions beyond marketing, PMs were responsible for leading all functional resource efforts affecting their products. The scope of the PM's responsibilities was often discussed by senior DD managers, some of whom supported a broader definition of the PM's role:

> We no longer want PMs to be just advertising and promotion managers. We want each PM to be the hub of the interfunctional decisions and activities that affect the product. PMs must provide leadership, not just coordination. They must lead and encourage the other functions in developing business-building ideas.
>
> We are moving to a business manager view of product management, pushing the concept of general management further down the organization. When GF had multiple SBUs and matrix management, too many decisions were made at too high a level.

Gail Turner was product manager on Pudding Pops. She described how she spent her time:

> I've worked on all three parts of the business—packaged desserts, toppings, and now frozen novelties. They're at different life-cycle stages and use different distribution systems. I've also had assignments on both new and established products. There's a conscious effort in DD to plan an individual's career path to develop breadth and depth, while also permitting you to get to know the same team of professionals in Marketing and other functions. Also, there's so much new product activity in DD that career progress can be fast.
>
> Right now, about 10 percent of my time is spent touching base with my boss, Brian Harvey, the marketing manager on frozen novelties. About 20 percent of my time is spent coaching and directing the associates and assistants in my brand group. A third of my time is spent working with our advertising agency and with other functions such as MRD and Sales Planning. Daily fire fighting takes about 10 percent of my time, probably a higher

percentage in the summer when Pudding Pops sales peak and retail stock-outs are more frequent. The rest of the time, I'm thinking and working on plans for the product.

Increasingly, PMs in the DD are being evaluated on their ability to lead the other functions. The marketing manager is also looking to me for longer-term planning because, on a growing business, the cost and timing of incremental capacity investment is important. A good PM should have a portfolio of business-building projects at various stages of development in his/her operating plan. For me, the fun of the job is selling ideas to management and building the business by making them happen.

I have only one reservation. I think there should be bonuses for performance at the PM level to reflect the increased responsibility that management is claiming the PM should assume.

To illustrate the broadening nature of the PM job, Brian Harvey summarized several of Turner's contributions to the business in the past year:

She initiated a major review of the Pudding Pops advertising strategy, which culminated in a presentation we made to Roger Smith. She managed the technical development, marketing research, and introduction of a subline of the Pudding Pops brand. She and her team have reassessed the sales promotion strategy for Pudding Pops. Finally, she has worked with Technical Research to develop a research program for Pudding Pops for the next three years.

Transfers of individuals from one division to another did not typically occur before the product manager level. Management believed that each division could provide a sufficient breadth of experience during the first few years of an individual's product management career. Because DD's product line included frozen as well as dry distribution systems, and new businesses like Pudding Pops alongside old ones like Jell-O gelatin, there was a wide diversity of assignments. One DD product manager who had been in another division commented on the differences:

I found some differences when I moved to DD. The products here have high unit margins so tend to be driven by marketing ideas and marketing spending. The previous product I worked on was more sales driven, but it gave me a different perspective. I've had fun in both assignments. In fact, now I feel I could move anywhere in GF and manage any kind of business.

Beyond Product Manager

Product Group Manager and Category Manager

Following the product manager level, individuals were placed in charge of a series of businesses. The product group managers (PGMs) and category managers (CMs) were responsible for the overall strategic direction and long-term financial health of the businesses they supervised. They focused on overall business management and the quality of execution of their brands' annual plans. When necessary, they were responsible for making resource trade-offs among their businesses. Typically, a PGM or CM would supervise two or more PMs and would be responsible for sales of over $200 million.

According to PGM Denise Rodriguez:

> The PM focuses on brand volume, brand share and the marketing expenditure details of the P&L. The PGM worries more about nonmarketing issues such as capacity planning and asset management.
>
> PGMs differ in the closeness with which they supervise their PMs, often as a function of how experienced the PMs are. If a PGM is consistently supervising too closely, that means either that the PGM is not doing his/her job or that the PM is having real problems.

In addition to his/her specific responsibilities, a PGM or CM might also be given divisionwide responsibility for coordinating training, recruiting, or the development of the divisional five-year plan. PGMs and CMs could organize their management teams as they saw fit and also frequently headed multifunctional task forces within DD.

Marketing Manager

The DD marketing manager (MM) was responsible for the direction of marketing activities, both staff and line, across the division's entire menu segment. The MM was the prime mover in shaping long-term strategies for the segment and was the ultimate determinant of the quality of near-term marketing activities. As a member of the DD general manager's (GM) staff, the MM participated in developing financial strategies to improve the overall profitability of the division's franchises.

John Day, DD MM for established products, commented on the thrust of his position and on his role in the approval process:

> Idea generation and strategy are the key elements of my job. My responsibility is to have a vision of where the DD businesses under my direction should be going and then to secure the organization's commitment to that vision. I spend about 60 percent of my time on marketing-related issues, giving advice and approving the proposals of my direct reports. As is typical in a consumer-driven business, my role as marketing manager goes beyond marketing since I'm really responsible for the overall health and value of DD businesses. So I spend a good portion of my time with nonmarketing functions, especially finance and operations on capital investment planning.
>
> As marketing manager, I oversee the development of and approve each product's annual marketing plan. I deliver synopses of all the plans to the GM. Any major changes in a brand's strategic direction reflected in the plan have to be approved by him. He also reviews each product's five-year strategic plan. While this sounds primarily like an approval and refinement role, a big part of this responsibility is shaping an environment in which the organization is encouraged to generate new ideas.

In the advertising area, a new execution of an existing campaign would be shown to the GM as a courtesy but any new copy proposal would be shown to the GM at the storyboard stage. A major shift in the media budget from radio to print would need the GM's approval but not a reallocation of television dayparts.

Approvals for price changes go beyond the division general manager. On many GF products, the price-value relationship got out of line in recent years. Annual price increases on our brands, therefore, have to be approved by the group vice president for Packaged Convenience Foods.

General Manager

The DD general manager was responsible for the performance of the division and oversaw staff in all functional areas. According to Roger Smith:

> My job is to prioritize business opportunities and allocate resources to ensure that the necessary long-term commitments are made to development projects and that resources are properly allocated to achieve our quantitative division goals. I have to bring home the plan.

Retention

GF's product management pyramid was such that almost all appointments and promotions occurred from within. Attrition occurred at all levels and for a variety of reasons. According to John Day, marketing manager, the ability to be a strong leader was the key skill where product management personnel were most likely to run into difficulty. Day recalled what happened to the twelve assistants who joined GF with him in 1974:

> Three left before the PM level, one to start his own company, another went to an advertising agency. Seven left at the PM and PGM levels. Three went into management consulting and one transferred to our corporate marketing services department. Three others left for smaller companies to gain what they hoped would be more general management responsibility faster than they thought they could get it at GF.
>
> One of the other two survivors apart from me is the marketing manager for new product development in the beverage division. His previous assignment was as GF marketing manager in Puerto Rico. The other is a category manager in the Maxwell House division. He took a two-year stint as a district sales manager in the course of his career. This kind of cross-functional experience is being encouraged more and more.

There was concern among senior managers that GF sometimes lost marketing personnel it would rather have retained, but there was little agreement on how such losses could be prevented. One subject, however, on which there was agreement was the importance of superior-subordinate coaching, and the need to ensure that product management personnel not only had the skills to do a good job in this area, but also practiced them. According to one PGM:

> It's easy to know if a product manager isn't paying enough attention to some aspect of his business. Results will either be unacceptable, or the situation will be brought to my attention. Sometimes, this isn't the case with training. We need to make sure people aren't short-changed here.

Product Management's Relations with Other Functions

As in other packaged goods companies, the product management organization at GF had traditionally been the lead function in initiating and executing product policies and programs. The other functions—such as Technical Research, Operations, and Sales—had often been viewed merely as support groups that put into effect what Marketing wanted to happen.

This put a substantial burden of responsibility for the company's success on Marketing. As one GF general manager put it:

> As the lead function, Marketing personnel must realize that they are ultimately responsible for the well-being of the thousands of people who work for GF in the other functional areas.

By 1985, the GF product manager was being encouraged to act more as a team leader than a ringmaster. According to a DD product group manager who had begun his career in market research:

> Our product management personnel should not just approach the other functions with requests for executional and fire-fighting assistance. They should approach them with *questions* on how to grow the business and involve them in strategic as well as tactical decision making. This would enhance the morale of the people in these functional areas, ensure that GF continues to attract top quality personnel to serve in them, and add to the overall climate of creativity in the division. The world has become increasingly complex. Marketing needs the help of our functional specialists now more than ever.

As shown in Exhibit 1, the divisional heads of all non-Marketing functions in the DD organization, such as Technical Research, Operations, and Sales, reported to the DD general manager. They also reported on a dotted-line basis to the corporate vice presidents responsible for their respective functions. Two marketing service groups, the Consumer Promotion Group and the Marketing Research Department, reported to the DD marketing manager.

Technical Research

GF prided itself on the quality of its Technical Research staff, numbering 400 in Central Research and 1,200 in the divisions. Research spending was twice that of GF's nearest food industry competitor. A Technical Strategy board, which included Phil Smith, decided and directed activity on GF's technical research priorities. Central Research personnel focused on long-term basic research to address these priorities, though half their time was spent on research commissioned and paid for by the GF divisions. Applied research was conducted by the Technical Research staff of each division. Jeff Jones, who held a PhD in organic chemistry, was the DD Technical Research manager. He described his organization and responsibilities:

> Our organization structure mirrors that of product management. We have food technologists, project leaders, group leaders, laboratory managers, and a senior laboratory manager who work with different levels of the product management organization. For example, an associate product manager who needed specific ingredient or package cost information would ask the appropriate project leader.
>
> My team comprises 100 people working in three groups that each focus on a category of products—frozen novelties, frozen whipped emulsions, and ready-to-eat desserts. The rationale here is that each group deals with a different technical process. Coincidentally, this breakdown matches the way Marketing splits the category managers' responsibilities, which makes cross-functional communications easier.
>
> My primary responsibilities are to guide product and process development for new and established products, to specify all raw materials, and to ensure the technical validity of any claims Marketing may wish to make about our products.
>
> I take a special interest in new product development—moving products from the laboratory benchtop through a pilot plant to full-scale production. Once a new product hits the market, the development work will often focus on achieving cost reductions while maintaining the product quality. On Pudding Pops frozen novelties, we are currently looking at cost reductions and line extensions such as the development of different products for each season. On Jell-O, we are investigating ways to make the product more convenient.
>
> Each year, I oversee the development of our operating plan and budget. Technical Research personnel will interface with their Marketing counterparts to develop a research wish list. Then we'll screen out proposals that are technically unfeasible or require too much capital investment relative to potential profit. Next we'll estimate the man-years required to execute each of the remaining projects, allocate our limited resources, and request any additional help we need from Central Research. The cost of each project is charged against the budget of the relevant product.
>
> Although Marketing takes the lead, we in Technical Research in no way feel like second-class citizens. There is a feeling of mutual dependency.

However, I do sometimes wish that our marketers were more knowledgeable about the technical characteristics and manufacturing of their products. If product managers visited the laboratories and plants more often, they'd be less likely to make ill-informed suggestions that would require major capital investment to be implemented. In addition, young product managers who want to make their mark will invariably suggest a new flavor or formulation for an established product. Our experience at Technical Research is that relative to the time and money required to implement such suggestions, the incremental profits are minimal.

Operations

The DD operations manager, Dan Peterson, was responsible for operating within budget the plants that made GF desserts, meeting productivity improvement targets, delivering sufficient product to meet weeks-of-supply targets, and adhering to quality specifications. Reporting to Peterson were four plant managers, three operations service managers responsible for packaged desserts, frozen novelties, and ready-to-eat products, plus managers responsible for logistics, inventory control, scheduling and deployment, engineering, and quality assurance. These five managers also reported on a dotted-line basis to the corporate directors for their respective functions.

The operations service managers and their assistants were a key link between Operations, Marketing, and Technical Research. They were responsible for reviewing cost and quality trends for their assigned products, managing cost reduction programs, overseeing the implementation of capital projects and providing volume and promotion planning input to the logistics manager to ensure consistent delivery of product to trade accounts.

Peterson commented on the relationships between Marketing and Operations:

There was a time when Marketing totally dominated the other functions. That's not to say that the Marketing people didn't pay attention to Operations or that Operations people were second-class citizens. But recently, I've seen a change, particularly with the increased focus on business management and on identifying our sources of competitive leverage. Our production processes are highly complex and product managers need to fully understand them because, often, our source of advantage is in operations. Marketing people are waking up to this. As a result, there is more career path interchange across functions. For example, we recently had a product manager spend time in one of our plants and he is now much more sensitive to the operations implications of his marketing decisions. Sometimes, product managers don't think of the plant layoffs involved with some decisions or forget that an organization can't always turn on a dime!

Sales

A dry grocery sales organization of 700 salespeople represented the products of the Desserts, Breakfast Foods, and Main Meal divisions. GF maintained separate sales forces for coffee (460 salespeople), refrigerated meats (470), and baked goods (250). Both GF soft drinks and frozen foods were sold primarily through brokers.

The organization of GF's separate sales forces partly reflected the different delivery systems used to distribute the products they represented. Distribution costs including transportation and warehousing were about 4 percent of sales for dry foods and 11 percent for frozen foods. Items with less than a 60-day shelf life, including Oscar Mayer and Entenmann's products, were store-door delivered rather than distributed through warehouses. In FY 1984, GF field sales costs totalled 3.3 percent of net revenues, 3.7 percent when broker commissions were included.

A GF recruiting brochure described the qualities sought in candidates for a career in sales as

- Professionalism—either previous professional knowledge or the frame of mind to absorb quickly the basics of professional sales.
- Good judgment.
- The ambition to perform in increasingly responsible positions.
- An orientation towards achieving results.
- Creative problem-solving ability.

Each DD sales representative covered about 50 grocery stores. DD salespeople were responsible for using market research data to develop each account; relating national advertising campaigns, shelving plans, and merchandising programs to the advertising and promotion programs of each account; gaining placement and shelf space allocation for each brand to ensure product availability in proper proportions; and maintaining regular contact with warehousing accounts on delivery schedules, promotions, and new products.

New salespeople developed their knowledge through on-the-job experience, working with their supervisors, and seminars on selling skills and account management. They could advance through a series of account, district, and regional management positions to eventually become division national sales managers. Promising individuals were often assigned to the headquarters sales planning function to expose them to product management perspectives before they were promoted to a higher level in the field sales organization.

Mr. Ed Royal was in charge of sales planning at DD headquarters. He supervised 15 executives including two sales planning managers assigned to dry and frozen desserts who each led a team of four region franchise managers (RFMs). The latter spent half their time in the field. Each RFM had responsibility both for the merchandising of all DD products in a specific region and for the merchandising of one group of products across all regions. Royal explained the tasks of his group:

> Broadly, our role is to serve as a link between Sales and Marketing. Marketing looks to us for advice on how to deal with the trade. Sales looks to us, as former salespeople, to represent their views to product management. For example, if a sales district needed an additional deal on a product to match unexpected competitive deal rates, the district manager would send a request to product management through the appropriate RFM.
>
> In addition to communicating information back and forth between headquarters and the field, we have four key functions. First, we evaluate the operating plans developed by each product group. As early as July, we would be in discussions with each group about the merchandising support needed to achieve its volume projections for the fiscal year starting the following March.
>
> Second, we play a very important role in trade promotion planning. We assess the promotion events proposed by the product groups, help prioritize them, and then propose a promotion calendar. Sometimes the small brands justifiably feel short-changed. Since our sales force also serves two other GF divisions, the DD's preferred calendar may be subject to negotiation. Partly to reduce the burden on the sales force, we have been trying to focus our promotion dollars behind fewer, more powerful events. Once the promotion budget for each product is approved, we develop detailed allowance allocations by calendar quarter and sales district.
>
> Third, we develop specific annual objectives by product in the areas of distribution, shelf facings, merchandising performance, and retail pricing. With the help of syndicated research data and for our own sales force, we measure our performance against these objectives.
>
> Fourth, we provide assistance to our sales force. We recently developed a software program that uses checkout scanner information to calculate the profitability of different shelf arrangements. Salespeople can use this program in their presentations to key accounts.

Royal commented on the relations between Sales and Marketing:

> There's a cultural difference between the field and headquarters. Most assistants have MBAs. Few sales trainees do, though many now take part-time MBA [programs]. I wish there was more career interchange between Sales and Marketing. The problem is that the Marketing career path moves faster than the Sales career path so that a product manager moving into Sales as a district manager might have to make a short-term career sacrifice for a longer-term benefit. Also, with only 23 sales districts, how could we assign product managers to these positions—it would be demoralizing for our salespeople.

Consumer Promotion Group

A similar review process to that conducted by the sales planning function for each product's trade promotions was conducted by a four-person Consumer Promotion Group (CPG) that reported to the DD marketing manager. It jointly reviewed the consumer promotion component of each product's operating plan and developed promotion objectives with each product group that supported the product's marketing strategy. Detailed program development and execution was to be left to the CPG with the product group operating in an approval capacity. According to Tony Taylor, a former salesperson who was now the DD consumer promotion manager:

> As promotion experts, our role is to help execute innovative promotion ideas in the marketplace. The product management function used to execute promotions, but we found this cumbersome and were constantly reinventing the wheel. Now, with experts handling the task, we have freed up some of their time.

Marketing Research Department

GF had one of the largest marketing research departments of any corporation, numbering over 100 executives throughout the company. Henry Katz, DD market research manager, supervised nine executives. Four associate managers serviced each of the four product category groups. Three other executives worked on forecasting and planning. Katz reported to the DD marketing manager and, on a dotted-line basis, to the corporate director of marketing research who, in turn, reported to the corporate vice president for information management.

MRD played an important role in the development of DD marketing strategy. According to John Day, marketing manager:

> Analysis of market research data is central to our success. We have developed many new products not through brilliant creativity but by really understanding the marketplace.

Henry Katz commented on MRD's level of involvement in DD marketing decision making:

> We are the business's eyes and ears for the consumer. We share responsibility with Marketing for the development of a product line that delivers superior consumer satisfaction. Three-quarters of my bonus depends upon the division's overall performance, and only one-quarter on MRD's performance against its specific objectives.
>
> MRD analyzes data for the product group that, at other companies, the groups would analyze for themselves. To my mind, the second approach is like putting Morris the cat in charge of a tuna fish sandwich. We in MRD provide objectivity and a sophistication that's extremely important as market research techniques become more complex. In addition, the desserts' marketplace is pretty complicated, so our help is in demand among the product groups even though their budgets are charged for the services we deliver.

According to Katz, MRD's principal function was the management of market and consumer information within DD. MRD was responsible for the quality, quantity, and prioritization of information used by the division. Specifically, MRD was charged with:

- Monitoring, measuring, and projecting the results of marketing programs, changes in the environment, and competitive factors.
- Helping to identify consumer and marketplace issues and opportunities critical to short- and long-range planning.
- Conducting appropriate and cost-effective research to support strategic as well as tactical planning.
- Providing objective business counsel to Marketing from a consumer perspective.

Under Katz's leadership, the MRD within DD was heavily involved in forecasting the impact of alternative advertising and pricing programs, counseling line marketing managers on the use of new marketing research techniques, and providing advice on the positioning of new and established brands. As Katz pointed out:

> Brand personnel change frequently. We provide continuity and can offer a historical perspective to a new product manager. We are the knowledge leaders in this division. My one problem is that our market research staff often do not exercise the leadership that they could or should in making recommendations to push the business forward. It's very rare for a market research executive to transfer from product management. In DD, though, we are lucky to have two people in product management who started their careers in marketing research. That helps relations considerably.

New Product Development

GF had a long and proud history of new product development. Kool-Aid, Jell-O gelatin, and Bird's Eye frozen foods were all dramatic innovations. Between 1978 and 1983, GF introduced six new food products that each earned at least $40 million in annual sales. Only 25 other grocery products introduced in the US during that period met this criterion. According to Chairman and CEO James L. Ferguson:

> When we enter new categories, we are careful to select those where we see major opportunities to improve margins by taking costs out of our business or improving production capacity. Sugar-Free Kool-Aid and Crystal Light are expected to generate $300 million in annual sales. Another fifteen new products in various stages of development should add almost $600 million in annual revenues when they reach national distribution.[1]

---

[1] Duane L. Taylor, "New Product Analyses," *Food Engineering,* October 1984, p. 94.

Line Extensions versus Innovations

How to encourage the generation of new product ideas and, more importantly, their translation into commercial successes, was a subject of frequent debate at GF. Line extensions presented no problem. Product management personnel were constantly looking for new ideas that would build established businesses. Opportunities of this nature were, however, decreasing. According to the DD Technical Research manager:

> Our traditional research approach has been to look for flavor improvements. But our flavor delivery system is now of such excellent quality that only minor improvements can be expected. We are increasingly taking a longer-term perspective, asking, "What can we do that's different?" and "How can we add value to the consumer?"

An increasing concern was how to ensure that dramatic new product concepts were explored and commercialized. Technical Research personnel were in their jobs longer than product management personnel, enjoyed working on challenging projects, and provided a measure of continuity to longer-term new product development. They typically assumed a more important role, the more radical the product innovation. On the other hand, securing the long-term commitment of Marketing personnel to a new product development project could be more difficult. A DD product group manager commented:

> Our product management people are very career oriented. They aren't prepared to commit three or four years without a promotion to a high-risk, new product project. Even if the product proved successful, at the end of the day their peers would have passed them by on the career ladder. In addition, when you're working on an established product, both you and your boss can assess your performance versus your predecessor's. This isn't as easy on a new product.

Managing New versus Established Products

Almost all newly hired assistant product managers worked on established brands for their two initial assignments. They, therefore, were trained in a style of management that was not necessarily applicable to new products. Two DD product managers who had worked on both new and established brands commented on the differences:

> The world won't come to an end if the product manager on an established business is away for a day. His task is to manage the information flow, massage and analyze the data, and develop business-building programs. The product manager on a new product has a lonelier existence. He has to be more self-motivated and set his own time line and deadlines. He has to collect information, not merely manage it. He has to persuade the other functions to give him their attention and buy into the product. This is especially challeng-

ing because the other functions have been involved with so many new product concepts that have never been successfully commercialized.

I started as an assistant on Jell-O gelatin, our flagship business. I used to receive lots of notes from senior managers who had worked on the business themselves. The tasks—and the deadlines—were clearly defined. Now, working on a new product, I have more freedom. I am the expert. If Phil Smith wanted a presentation on my product, I'd probably do it because I'm the only one who could field the questions.

Organizing for New Product Development

The DD tried in several ways to ensure a high level of successful, new product development activity, both in the established business groups as well as in a separate development organization. First, development of DD's established businesses focused on extending existing trademarks and building on existing strengths, through the introduction, for example, of new forms of packaged desserts or different types of frozen novelties. New product introductions within the established businesses were important in creating excitement in the marketplace and could usually be developed and implemented within one to two years. One product group manager noted:

> It's important for the growth of the existing brands to develop and implement new product ideas. The prospect of new products and line extensions also excites the top agency people who are assigned to our major established brands.

Second, the DD organization included a group dedicated exclusively to new product development which was headed by a marketing manager, Oliver Jones. Jones supervised six marketing executives working on product areas new to DD. The group had worked on the frozen novelty category prior to GF's entry into this market and was currently developing and test marketing an in-house soft ice cream similar to Dairy Queen. Typically, Jones' group developed a product to the point of expansion beyond test market and then turned it over to an established brand group. It was not unusual for the person who had managed the product in test market to continue to manage it once it was rolled out.

The new product development group included individuals who had previously worked on established products and were now broadening their experience, as well as others who wished to make a career in new product development. One such manager, Dave Feldman, had guided Pudding Pops from concept development to national expansion. He commented:

> For me new product development is the core of marketing. It's exciting to figure out what the consumer wants and how we can deliver that in a way which will have long-term impact on GF profits. It's fun to nurture your

project to reality and then to apply the marketing muscle to make an impact in the marketplace.

Third, DD was experimenting with a seven-member multifunctional venture team working on a major new product development project. Reporting to Jones and led by a product group manager, the team included representatives from each of the key promotional areas who were all working solely on the project. Team leader Diana Morgan described the venture team concept:

> We are all making a three- to four-year commitment to seeing this project through to completion. In return for putting our career paths on hold, all team members have been offered a very attractive bonus if the product succeeds commercially. The result is that we have more senior people involved in our group than would normally work on a new product. The finance representative, for example, has 15 years' experience with GF.
>
> New products that use the existing asset base don't require venture teams. But this one does, for three reasons. First, it involves a new technology that GF is not currently involved in. Second, because it is a short-shelf-life, fast-turn product, it requires a new distribution system. Third, this product will, we hope, be the basis for an entirely new product category which GF will dominate. Even though our venture team draws staff from existing product groups, we believe it's very important to the division long term.

Two Examples

DD managers provided two examples of effective product development—the revitalization of Jell-O gelatin and the successful launch of Jell-O Pudding Pops, GF's first entry in the frozen novelties category.

Sales volume on Jell-O gelatin peaked in 1969, then declined consistently so that, by 1983, volume was 35 percent less than in 1969. Not only did GF's market share dip below 70 percent but the entire category declined as increasingly health-conscious Americans cut down on sweets in general. Second, demographic shifts left fewer children in the Jell-O target group. A third problem was the fact that Jell-O took at least three hours to set and was therefore increasingly perceived as inconvenient by working mothers. Fourth, at a time when snacking was on the increase, 80 percent of gelatin consumption occasions were associated with traditional meals.

John Day, marketing manager, described the inadequacies of the initial response:

> All our functional resources were used initially to justify why the business was declining and why we couldn't really do much about it. Then we said, "Let's stop wringing our hands! Let's fix it!"

What followed was a turnaround. Technical Research developed a patented low-cost starch that delivered product quality superior to competition.[2] Manufacturing resources were focused to ensure that GF could become the low-cost producer. Marketing developed new advertising to counter Jell-O's association with traditional life-styles and stimulate faster household usage. No price increases were taken for three consecutive years. Finally, Technical Research tapped into a corporate commitment to subsidize new products using aspartame to develop a newsworthy line extension, Sugar-Free Jell-O gelatin.[3] As a result, in 1983, Jell-O volume grew for the first time in 15 years.

The maturation of the Jell-O gelatin business also stimulated interest in new product development. Attention focused on frozen novelties which were single prepackaged frozen desserts or snacks including ice cream cones, cups, bars and sandwiches, and ice milk bars and fudgsicles. The concept of a frozen Jell-O pudding had been aired as early as 1965 and a prototype product had been developed. However, no further development had been undertaken, partly because the product was viewed more as a snack than a dessert. Then, in 1975, a marketing research analyst, Dave Feldman, became enthusiastic about the product:

> Retail sales of frozen novelties were only $400 million in 1975 and volume growth was only 1 percent a year. But I believed the category was undermarketed. Most frozen novelties were produced by regional dairies, often under license from the Popsicle division of Consolidated Foods. The challenge was to develop an appealing product that could capitalize on the Jell-O name and GF's refrigerated distribution system. The eventual result was Jell-O Pudding Pops, individual servings of frozen pudding on a stick.
>
> In 1975, I was working in marketing research and had previously analyzed several other new product opportunities which I knew were losers. Then I looked at Pudding Pops, saw a potential winner and decided that I wanted to manage its development. I made a presentation to the DD general manager and was appointed associate, then product manager, on Pudding Pops.
>
> I was a brand champion in the old sense. The way you sell an idea to management is what distinguishes a good product manager from a poor one. You gain authority here by what you recommend rather than by what you decide.
>
> Technical Research was enthusiastic about Pudding Pops from the start. They developed a product that would melt at zero degrees rather than twenty below like ice cream and that could, therefore, be shipped along with Bird's Eye frozen vegetables. However, it wasn't all plain sailing. Operations and Sales were not supportive. To get the attention of Operations, I signed a $45,000 contract with a copacker. I didn't know or care whether I was breaking any rules. I didn't want control. I just wanted the product to happen.
>
> Sales was also lukewarm. I wanted to capitalize on GF's frozen food distribution network rather than use the store-door distribution approach

---

[2] Nabisco Brands' Royal line was GF's main competitor in this category.

[3] GF's corporate priority system provided corporate subsidies to the divisions for new product development in specific areas.

employed by the regional dairies. But Sales said such a distribution system would not be effective, that Pudding Pops would be buried at the bottom of the grocer's freezer. I therefore had a consultant survey 200 dairies to show that GF could achieve the required distribution at lower cost with my proposed system. I then had the data to go head-on-head with the national sales manager—and win.

Feldman took Pudding Pops to test market in 1979. Because the manufacturing process required a $75 million plant investment, the national launch did not occur until April 1982. In that month, three flavors were launched in three package sizes, backed by a $25 million advertising campaign featuring Bill Cosby. Pudding Pops was positioned as a wholesome lower calorie alternative to frozen ice cream novelties.

Sales reached $100 million in the first year. Pudding Pops expanded the frozen novelty category by 25 percent. Market research showed, unexpectedly, that half of all Pudding Pops were eaten by adults. GF's only challenges were to ensure that Pudding Pops were placed in the ice cream rather than the frozen food section of the grocer's freezer and that the shelves were restocked often enough—since Pudding Pops turned much faster than other frozen novelties.

By 1985 GF was researching and test marketing additional frozen novelties such as Gelatin Pops, whipped frozen gelatin on a stick, and a soft-serve product called Soft-Swirl.

A Leaner Organization

Partly as a result of increasing pressure for cost control, the DD Marketing Department in 1985 comprised 30 executives compared to 50 in 1980, even though the number of products had increased and the pace of new product development was greater than ever before.

Roger Smith commented on the change:

> Until last year, the Marketing function was overstaffed. We bent over to give good people career and salary advancement, and in the Desserts division, we could afford to do so. Our margins are so good that relatively small new product ideas can seem profitable enough to justify the expense of a separate product group.
>
> The problem was, however, that we had too many people chasing a finite level of decision-making responsibility. You distinguished yourself as an assistant by coming up with the big new promotion idea for the eastern region. Now, there is more work and task diversity for each person. More than ever before, you have to be a juggler and have a general business perspective, even at the assistant and associate levels.
>
> With fewer people, the atmosphere is less bureaucratic. There is less emphasis on formal written reports. Our annual product marketing plans are much shorter now than they used to be. The depth of analysis may not be as

great but the speed of decision making is faster. Our five advertising agencies appreciate not having to make presentations to as many levels of management and the specialist support of our staff functions such as MRD is more highly valued by the product groups.

A leaner organization is more flexible. There are fewer turf issues. My philosophy is that the people who do the work present it, no matter what level of management it goes to. In addition, I maintain an open-door policy. Last week, for example, about three-quarters of our product managers were in to see me, not for approvals but for advice.

Smith's enthusiasm for the leaner organization did have some side effects. Two product managers noted:

The breadth of tasks in this job is great. But I wish I had more time to think and to get out in the field to talk to consumers.

True, a leaner organization has advantages. It forces you to focus on the actions and programs that will generate the most impact. But the world is becoming more complicated—the grocery trade is increasingly sophisticated, more precise target segmentation is needed, and there's growing interest in regional marketing. We need more people, more specialists, not less.

As Roger Smith evaluated the results of trimming the Marketing organization within DD, his thoughts turned to the effectiveness of the product management system and what he could do to improve it. He jotted down some of the key questions that came to mind:

- Should our product managers have responsibility for profits as well as for volume, share, and marketing expenditures?
- Should our product managers be general business managers rather than advertising and promotion experts? Can they be both?
- Should we have the same product management system and the same types of product manager working on new as well as established products?
- Was the traditional product management system still appropriate for GF and DD in 1985? Or would product management through formal business teams, led by Marketing, but including representatives of all functions, be more effective?

As he pondered these issues, Smith recalled a comment made by his former boss:

The strength of the product management system is that it puts one person in charge of making a business plan work for each product.

8-2 General Foods Corporation: Local Marketing

In August 1988, Tom Hoeppner, group vice president of General Foods USA (GF USA), met with several of the company's senior sales executives to discuss whether and how General Foods Corporation (GF) should expand local marketing throughout its sales organization. A major test of local marketing had been conducted in Denver since February 1987, and several other local marketing experiments were under way. Although difficult to quantify, most executives agreed that sales effectiveness had improved due to local marketing.

In addition, between December 1986 and August 1988, one local marketing tool, a personal computer-based system of computer programs from Market Metrics, known as Supermarket Solutions, had been installed in 17 of GF USA's 22 district sales offices. National rollout was to be completed by the end of October 1988. Several sales successes could be attributed directly to use of the Supermarket Solutions software. However, both headquarters and field salespeople agreed that the software was not yet being used to its full potential.

Grocery Marketing in the 1980s

Traditionally, manufacturers of national brands of consumer packaged goods depended on mass marketing as the primary vehicle to sell their products to both their trade customers and end consumers. Local marketing, the tailoring of a brand's marketing plans to respond to customer, consumer, and competitive variations by market, was viewed largely as a necessary inconvenience. It was undertaken for defensive reasons to combat especially competitive regional brands or to boost brand trial in markets with low category development indices (CDI) or brand development indices (BDI).

Research Assistant Tammy Bunn Hiller prepared this case under the supervision of Professor John A. Quelch as the basis for class discussion rather than to illustrate either effective or ineffective handling of an administrative situation. Certain nonpublic data have been disguised. Copyright © 1988 by the President and Fellows of Harvard College. Harvard Business School case 9–589–029.

By the late 1980s, environmental changes and trends in the grocery industry raised both manufacturers' and retailers' interest in local marketing as a potential source of competitive advantage. First, consumer heterogeneity was increasingly evident. The majority of consumers were no longer members of "traditional" families; indeed households comprising a father, nonworking mother, and two children at home were only 8 percent of the total. Between 1960 and 1988, average household size dropped almost 25 percent from 3.3 to 2.5 members per household. One- and two-person households grew from 46 percent of all US households in 1970 to 55 percent in 1988. During that time, the number of households grew at a faster rate than the approximate one percent annual population growth rate. The mix of households became more diverse as a result of high divorce rates, later marriages resulting in more people living alone, the postponement of childbearing by many working women, and the aging of the population.

The white majority of the United States declined from 84 percent of the population in 1970 to 69 percent in 1988. During the same period, the percentage of Hispanics increased from 4 percent to 15 percent while the black population remained stable at 10 percent. Specific racial groups were of more importance in some markets than others; seventy-five percent of Hispanics, for example, were concentrated in six states.

Greater diversity of race and household types implied that the mass market had given way to a large number of distinct demographic, geographic, and life-style segments. Both product needs and buying motivations differed among these segments. This fact argued for grocery manufacturers to customize their marketing programs to target specific segments of consumers.

Grocery product brand loyalty among all consumer groups other than Hispanics had decreased significantly, especially for brands in mature product categories. Many consumers perceived national, regional, and private label brands of mature items to be of equal quality and chose among them on the basis of price. Some executives believed that matching brand benefits with specific consumer target group needs through local marketing could help to reverse this trend.

In response to the demographic trends mentioned above, retailers had developed new retail store formats such as warehouse stores and club stores that offered narrow assortments of fast turnover merchandise at rock-bottom prices with minimum service, and hypermarkets that offered the convenience of a vast assortment of merchandise under one roof. These multiple store formats were designed to serve the needs of the increasingly segmented consumer population. Retailers pressured manufacturers to tailor marketing programs to the needs of individual store formats.

In addition to demographic changes, the balance of power in the grocery industry was shifting from the manufacturers to the trade.

Through the early 1980s, grocery manufacturers controlled almost all the marketing research information and the high-powered marketing talent. They were able to force retailers to stock and promote items by spending millions of dollars advertising and promoting them to consumers. In order to satisfy their customers, retailers were forced to accept manufacturers' marketing plans and served merely as a distribution conduit for manufacturers' products.

By 1988, that situation had changed. Retailers were successfully competing with manufacturers for top marketing talent. The quality and professionalism of their buyers and managers had improved. Many retailers had built state-of-the-art information systems. Scanners had been installed in stores accounting for 60 percent of all grocery volume. Retailers had begun to exploit the information power inherent in sales data collected by scanners at the point-of-sale. Many retailers were using sophisticated computer models to optimize shelf space allocation and direct product profitability (DPP).[1] They were attempting to tailor their product assortments, shelving, and merchandising to the needs of the consumers in their own trading areas.

Although national market shares of individual retailers had not changed significantly, the trade had become more concentrated. Within a given market, combined market shares held by the top two or more chains had increased substantially, thereby giving retailers more bargaining power with manufacturers.

As trade power grew, retailers had become increasingly marketing and merchandising oriented. They no longer just accepted manufacturers' plans. In addition to developing and merchandising their own private label products, they often developed their own localized promotion programs and offered participation opportunities to manufacturers. Moreover, some retailers were beginning to decentralize merchandising decisions by allowing individual store managers to make distribution, shelving, display, and/or pricing decisions for their stores.

At the same time that the trade was demanding more localized marketing, mass marketing was becoming increasingly less effective and more expensive. Traditionally, grocery manufacturers used network television and women's magazines as their primary advertising media. The cost of each television flight and magazine insertion had risen steadily during the 1980s, but each flight and insertion reached fewer people. Between 1979 and 1988, the prime-time television audience that the three network stations could command dropped from 92 percent to 77 percent

---

[1] DPP calculations attempted to determine the *true* profitability of individual items by assigning to each item the total costs of buying, transporting, warehousing, and shelving the item. The size, shape, and weight of an item figured into its DPP calculation, as did the manner in which it was delivered to retail stores and the amount of labor its shelving involved.

in the face of an ever-expanding array of cable channel and videotape alternatives. Similarly, the number of magazines being published had exploded over the 1980s. In the 1970s, manufacturers could reach most grocery shoppers by advertising in 30 women's magazines. By 1988, they had to advertise in up to 300 magazines, most of which were special interest ones, to reach the same percentage of shoppers.

Grocery manufacturers responded to pressures for local marketing by increasing the percentage of their media budgets spent on local spot advertising versus national advertising and by increasing the percentage of sales promotion versus advertising in their marketing budgets. In addition, many companies set aside a percentage of their trade dollars for their district or regional sales managers to allocate equitably among their trade customers based on local opportunities. One manufacturer, Campbell Soup Company, reorganized its sales and marketing functions in 1986 to create 22 regional brand sales manager positions.

General Foods Corporation Company Background

GF had been a leading US grocery manufacturer since its formation in the 1920s. In 1987 it had revenues of almost $10 billion and operating income of $722 million. It was the largest company in the United States which operated solely in the food business. Over three-quarters of its products held first- or second-place market shares in the categories in which they competed.

In November 1985, GF was acquired by Philip Morris Companies Inc., the world's largest tobacco company, and run as a wholly owned subsidiary. Through July of 1987, GF was organized as it had been before its acquisition, into three sectors and 10 operating divisions, each representing a specific menu segment. Then, in August of 1987, the company was reorganized into three separate operating companies: Oscar Mayer Foods (OMF), General Foods Worldwide Coffee & International (GFWCI), and GF USA.

OMF manufactured and sold Claussen pickles and processed red meats, poultry, and seafood under the Oscar Mayer, Louis Rich, Louis Kemp, and other brands. GFWCI manufactured and sold Maxwell House, Sanka, Brim, Yuban, and other brand coffees worldwide, sold all General Foods products to food service and other institutional buyers in the United States, and sold all General Foods products in non-US markets. GF USA manufactured all General Foods products other than coffee and meats and sold them in the United States.

Products marketed by GF USA were grouped into five categories managed by 12 business units. Dessert products included all Jell-O brand packaged desserts and frozen novelty desserts, Baker's coconut and chocolate, and Cool Whip and Dream Whip toppings. Beverage products included Kool-Aid, Crystal Light, Tang, and Country Time brands of powdered and aseptically packaged soft drinks. Breakfast products included Post cereals and Log Cabin syrups. Meals products included Bird's Eye frozen vegetables, Stove Top stuffing mixes, Minute Rice, Shake 'n Bake and Oven Fry coating mixes, and Ronzoni pasta. Bakery products included Entenmann's, Oroweat, Freihofer, and Boboli.

GF Sales Force Organization

The restructuring of GF led to numerous changes in headquarters staff and executive positions. A substantial number of staff positions were eliminated and decision making was moved closer to the marketplace. The field sales forces, however, were not restructured. Before and after the August 1987 reorganization, GF employed approximately 2,000 field salespeople in the United States divided into eight separate sales forces. The total cost of GF field sales was approximately 3.5 percent of net revenues.

OMF had a direct sales force of approximately 450 people who sold refrigerated products. Domestically, GFWCI had two direct sales forces, Maxwell House Sales with 450 salespeople who sold all GF coffee brands, and Food Service Sales with 100 salespeople who sold all GF products to institutional buyers. GF USA had three direct sales forces and two brokered ones.[2] The direct sales forces included the 700-person Grocery Sales Organization (GSO) which sold all dry grocery products, the 50-person Military Sales force which sold all GF products to US military bases in the United States and overseas, and the Bakery division sales forces which sold baked goods through a store–door delivery distribution system. The two brokered sales forces in GF USA were Frozen Food Sales which sold all frozen desserts and meals products, and Beverage Sales which sold all beverage products. GF USA employed brokers to sell its beverage products because demand for products such as Kool-Aid was highly seasonal and required intensive retail point-of-sale management during the peak season. A direct sales force would have been too large in the winter and too small in the summer. Frozen Food Sales were brokered because of size and the fact that most retailers had limited freezer space and frequent sales calls were therefore needed to ensure a brand's proper presentation.

[2] Brokers were independent sales organizations which sold products of many grocery manufacturers. They were paid commissions based on volume sold. Most manufacturers prohibited brokers from representing competing products.

GF USA Sales Organization

Ervin Shames was president and CEO of GF USA. Tom Hoeppner reported to him and was responsible for customer support, marketing, and administrative services, which included sales, distribution, logistics, purchasing and information systems, market research, consumer affairs, marketing services (including media buying and consumer promotion development), internal and external communications, government affairs, and two supply businesses. John Mann, vice president of sales, reported to Hoeppner. As shown in Exhibit 1, he had direct responsibility for all sales divisions within GF USA except the Bakery and Beverage sales forces. Bakery operated as a subsidiary of GF USA and its president reported directly to Shames. The Beverage division controlled its focused sales force. In addition to Mann's direct reports, the US national sales directors of Maxwell House Sales and Beverage Sales sat on his expanded staff.

Each sales force within GF USA was headed by a national sales director.(NSD) who was assisted by a sales planning and development manager. Also reporting to the NSDs were regional sales managers (RSM) whose responsibilities included both national account management of those national accounts headquartered in their areas and management of several district sales managers (DSM). National account responsibilities involved meeting with senior management of the largest US grocery chains to improve customer relations as well as to sell chainwide promotions. All RSMs worked out of GF USA's headquarters in White Plains, New York.

GF USA divided the country into 22 sales districts. DSMs for each of its sales forces, excluding Entenmann's, worked out of common district offices. Maxwell House and Food Service DSMs were located in these district offices as well. In GF USA's brokered sales forces, the DSMs managed the sales efforts of brokers who sold their products to grocery retailers and wholesalers. The Military Sales DSMs managed salespeople who sold directly to military bases in the US and abroad. GSO DSMs managed both key account executives (KAE) and district retail managers (DRM). All DSMs were held accountable for meeting district sales volume objectives and for managing district sales expense budgets. They were not accountable for profits.

KAEs managed grocery chain and grocery wholesaler accounts. Most KAEs managed two or three major accounts. They were responsible for reaching quarterly volume targets at each account. Their duties included selling new items into distribution and influencing their placement on retail store shelves, convincing buyers to merchandise GSO products in conjunction with GF USA's national advertising events via chainwide advertisement, displays, or reduced shelf prices, and ensuring

EXHIBIT 1   General Foods USA Sales Organization Chart

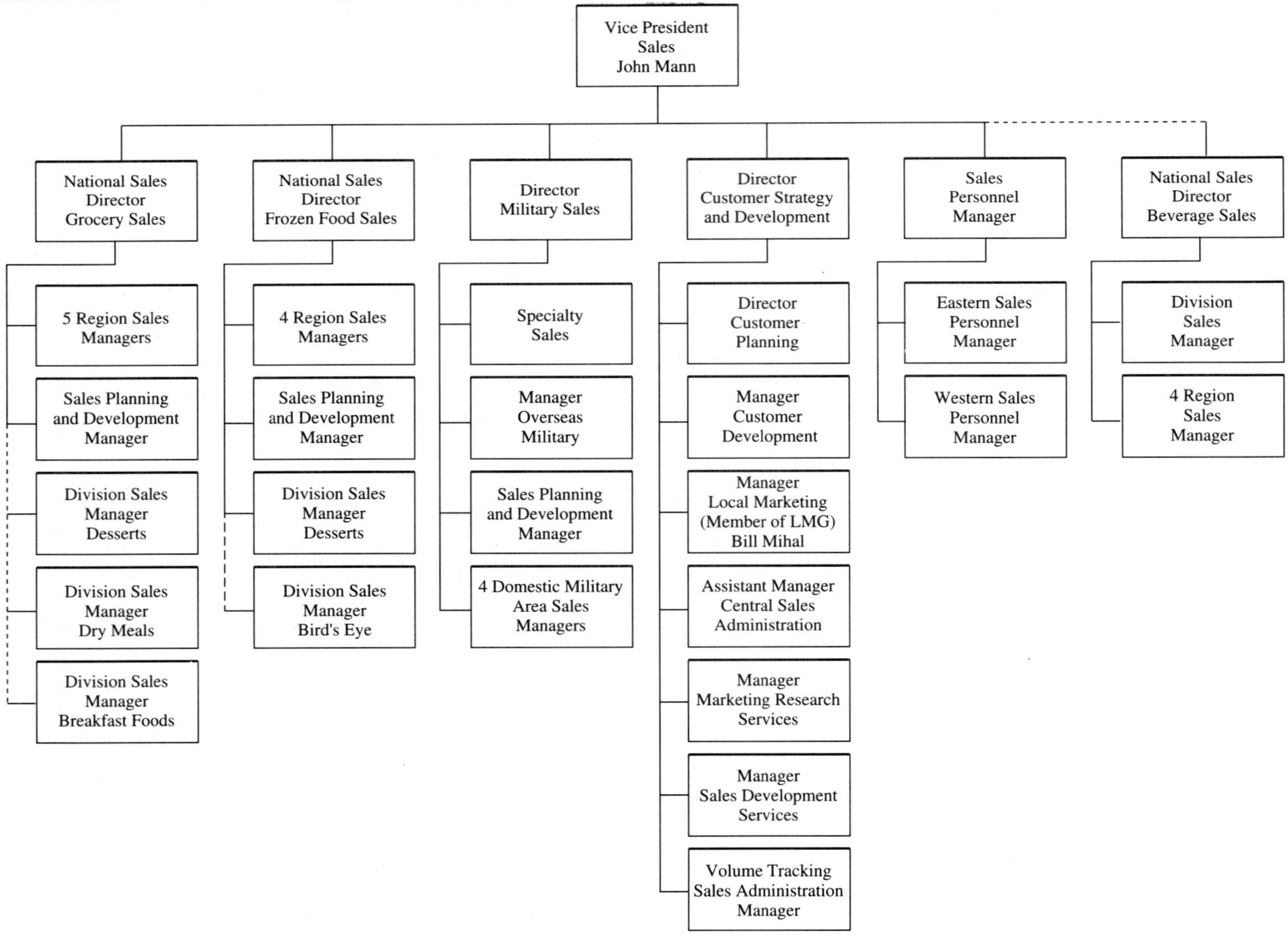

Vice President Sales
John Mann

- **National Sales Director Grocery Sales**
  - 5 Region Sales Managers
  - Sales Planning and Development Manager
  - Division Sales Manager Desserts
  - Division Sales Manager Dry Meals
  - Division Sales Manager Breakfast Foods

- **National Sales Director Frozen Food Sales**
  - 4 Region Sales Managers
  - Sales Planning and Development Manager
  - Division Sales Manager Desserts
  - Division Sales Manager Bird's Eye

- **Director Military Sales**
  - Specialty Sales
  - Manager Overseas Military
  - Sales Planning and Development Manager
  - 4 Domestic Military Area Sales Managers

- **Director Customer Strategy and Development**
  - Director Customer Planning
  - Manager Customer Development
  - Manager Local Marketing (Member of LMG) Bill Mihal
  - Assistant Manager Central Sales Administration
  - Manager Marketing Research Services
  - Manager Sales Development Services
  - Volume Tracking Sales Administration Manager

- **Sales Personnel Manager**
  - Eastern Sales Personnel Manager
  - Western Sales Personnel Manager

- **National Sales Director Beverage Sales**
  - Division Sales Manager
  - 4 Region Sales Manager

that the chain priced GSO products competitively. KAEs were expected to "be GF" to their customers. They were charged with creating excellent working relationships with their several buyers at each account as well as with buying department heads.[3] DSMs worked closely with their KAEs to develop customer-specific merchandising, distribution, and account relationship objectives targeted at achieving volume goals.

DRMs managed an average of 8 to 10 sales representatives (SR) and field merchandisers (FM). They recruited and trained new SRs and FMs. They worked with all of their salespeople regularly in order to help them refine their skills. They helped SRs develop account strategies for the customers whom they managed. DRMs answered their salespeople's questions and were sounding boards for their ideas and their frustrations. They were accountable for achieving volume targets through their salespeople and for coaching them for promotion.

SRs' jobs varied. Some called only on retail stores. Others were responsible for one grocery chain or wholesaler as well as a trip list of retail stores. An average trip list consisted of approximately 80 chain and independent retail stores. In chain stores, SRs were responsible for selling displays in conjunction with the retailer's or GF's advertising, ensuring that each store carried all GSO products authorized by its headquarters point, ensuring that the shelf position and space allocation of all GSO products met GSO standards or chain plan-o-grams,[4] and ensuring that pricing was accurate. In independent stores, in addition to the above duties, SRs sold ads and had greater influence on shelving and pricing than in chain stores because most independent store managers had more decision-making authority than chain store managers. Most SRs also participated in store sets, which involved major shelving changes and usually required a full day per store. They also performed "housekeeping" duties such as rotating products on the shelves and picking up damaged merchandise. SRs decided their own weekly store coverage plans, but were responsible for calling on each store according to assigned frequencies, which varied by a store's volume and merchandising potential.

FMs were part-time employees who did the "nonselling" part of the SR job. They were used primarily in districts which required numerous

---

[3] Most accounts had several grocery buyers, each of whom made routine buying and merchandising decisions for his/her assigned categories of grocery products. New item distribution and major merchandising decisions were usually made by a committee of all the grocery buyers, the head buyer, and merchandising and pricing managers. In addition to the grocery buyers, most accounts had at least one health and beauty aids buyer, produce buyer, and meat buyer. These buyers were sometimes included on the grocery buying committee. Salespeople rarely addressed the entire buying committee. Normally, they presented their products or merchandising ideas to one or two buyers who then had to sell the product/idea to the full buying committee.

[4] A plan-o-gram was a document which indicated how items were to be arranged in a particular section of a specific chain's grocery stores.

store sets. They spent their time doing store sets or calling on chain stores. Only half of the districts used FMs.

Exhibit 2 provides a demographic breakdown of GF USA's direct sales forces. It shows the average age and salary of each sales position from SR to NSD. With the exception of FMs, who were hourly employees, all direct field salespeople were salaried. In addition, they were eligible for quarterly sales incentive plan bonuses (SIP). SIP was awarded to each salesperson as a percentage of the average quarterly salary for his/her salary grade level. It was based totally on meeting/exceeding districtwide volume objectives. Either the total district for a given sales force earned SIP, or no one did. Everyone in the district received the same percentage SIP.

Every year each salesperson entered into a performance agreement with his or her manager. For SRs and KAEs, agreements contained specific volume, distribution, shelving, pricing, merchandising, and account relationship goals. In addition to goals on those dimensions, DRM, DSM, and RSM agreements had hiring and people development goals and DSM and RSM had expense management goals. Managers used the agreements to evaluate their salespeople's actual performance and to determine salary increases, the timing and amount of which were based on merit.

The majority of sales training was on-the-job training by a salesperson's manager. In addition, each SR attended a three-day basic selling skills seminar after his/her first few months on the job. A key account management seminar and a people management seminar were also offered periodically to new or potential KAEs and DRMs.

Prior to 1980, SRs were recruited from a wide variety of backgrounds. In 1980 approximately 75 percent of SRs had college educations and 18 percent had been hired away from the retail grocery trade. In 1981, GF instituted a policy of hiring recently graduated college students, preferably business majors, as SRs. By 1988, 96 percent of SRs were college

EXHIBIT 2   General Foods USA Sales Force Demographics: 1988

Job Title	Average Age*	Average Annual Base Salary	Average Annual SIP Bonus (%)
Sales representative (SR)	26	$ 27,000†	12%
Key account executive (KAE)	30	38,000	12
District retail manager (DRM)	30	38,000	12
District sales manager (DSM)	38	52,000	12
Regional sales manager (RSM)	44	90,000	25
National sales director (NSD)	47	115,000	25

* SRs ranged from 21-year-old recruits to 60-year-old career SRs.

† Entry-level SR salary is $22,000.

graduates, fewer than 10 percent had a retail grocery background, and a growing percentage were women and minorities.

Almost all promotions in GF USA's sales organization were from within or from other GF sales forces. Historically, there was very little transfer of people from sales to other functions such as marketing; however, most product management personnel received sales training.

Sales' Relations with Other Functions

GF's marketing function was built around a product management system. Product managers were responsible for developing and ensuring execution of the national strategies for their brands. They had profit and loss responsibility. Traditionally, the product management organization had been the lead function in GF. Other functions, including Sales, had been viewed as support groups that put into effect what Marketing wanted to happen. Many product management positions were consolidated in the August 1987 restructuring, and the culture began to more broadly recognize the potential of salespeople to become marketers and general managers.

GF had one of the largest market research departments (MRD) of any corporation, although significant staff reductions were made in the 1987 reorganization. Traditionally, MRD viewed Marketing, not Sales, as its client. MRD conducted research to support Marketing's strategic and tactical planning, identified consumer and marketplace issues and opportunities, and monitored, measured, and projected the results of marketing programs, changes in the environment, and competitive factors. Until recently, Marketing shared with Sales consumer and market knowledge generated by MRD only when Marketing perceived a specific need to do so, most often when a new item was being introduced.

Division sales managers reported directly to division general managers and reported on a dotted-line basis to the NSDs. They worked with a staff of region franchise managers (RFM), all of whom were former salespeople. RFMs served as a link between Sales and Marketing. They evaluated the operating plans developed by each product group and assisted Marketing in developing a coordinated trade promotion plan covering all products. When DSMs wanted to add to or change the trade deals planned for their districts, they usually worked through the RFMs to secure product management agreement.

The distribution and customer service function worked closely with Sales. Distribution costs, including transportation and warehousing, varied from a low of 4 percent of sales for dry grocery to a high of 11 percent of sales for frozen foods. GF shipped most of its products from a network of 16 distribution centers, all located at the sites of district sales offices. The DSMs worked with the Distribution (DSSD) managers to ensure that all customers received their products on time, undamaged, and in the manner most convenient to the customer. DSSD managers supervised both the operation of the warehouses and staffs of customer service representatives (CSR). They were also responsible for coordinating distribution with production, a job made difficult due to uncertain retail demand in response to trade and consumer promotions and due to trends toward forward buying and diverting.[5]

GF created the CSR position in 1982. It was the first grocery manufacturer to use the CSR position and, in 1988, was one of few companies offering the service to its customers. Customers called in their orders to the CSRs. The CSRs checked the orders to ensure that the trade deals which the customers were requesting were correct. Then they handled all of the logistics required to ensure the orders' prompt delivery. Salespeople worked closely with the CSRs to keep them up-to-date on the trade deals for which each customer had qualified. CSRs often helped salespeople by convincing customers to order more merchandise when they called in less-than-truckload orders.

The information systems group also worked closely with Sales. All district offices were equipped with personal computers. In addition the KAEs and DRMs in 50 percent of the districts had individual laptop computers. Eventually all KAEs and DRMs would have them. The information systems group trained the salespeople to use their computers and worked with them to develop and disseminate useful analytical sales tools and programs designed to decrease the administrative reporting burden on Sales by improving information management.

GF's Experience with Local Marketing

For years GF had a reputation as a premier mass marketer. By 1985, many GF executives recognized that GF's traditional marketing strengths were becoming less potent due to environmental changes favoring local marketing. They also believed that the sales and distribution functions were becoming much more critical than in the past. Consequently, the position of group vice president of customer support services was established in order to group under one executive all the functions which were

---

[5] Forward buying occurred when a grocery retailer or wholesaler bought multiple weeks' supply during the last week of a manufacturer's trade deal. After the deal ended, the account would sell this product at its regular shelf price. Some accounts had sophisticated computer programs which determined the optimal number of weeks of supply to buy at the end of a given deal period by balancing the deal dollars earned against the costs of inventorying the product. Diverting occurred when a grocery retailer or wholesaler bought product in one market in which a trade deal rate was high and resold the product in another market where there was either no promotion or a lower deal rate.

important to the sales force in making a sale and to the customer in buying.

Hoeppner placed high priority on developing new and exploiting existing value-added services which would help GF salespeople to be regarded by their customers as preferred partners in the categories in which they competed. These value-added services included assigning a CSR to each account, offering GF computer-to-computer customer ordering capability (UCS), offering a menu of product delivery choices from the 16 distribution centers including backhaul,[6] common carrier, rail, and direct store delivery, and offering custom-made palletized display modules. GF concentrated on developing services which benefited both parties, ones which allowed both GF and its customers to operate more efficiently.

Market Metrics' Supermarket Solutions

In early 1985, Tom Morgan, chairman of both a Philadelphia food brokerage and a new start-up company called Market Metrics (MM), approached GF with a concept for a new database/computer system which would have the ability to analyze the demographic composition of an individual supermarket's consumers and trading area. Morgan offered GF a voice in the development of the system and exclusive use of the system among its competitors through December 31, 1988, in exchange for $300,000 in start-up capital.

From the outset, GF's information systems group (IS) recognized the potential of MM. In December 1985, IS provided MM with $100,000. Eventually Corporate Sales agreed to fund the remaining $200,000. Top Sales management was unsure whether or not the system would add real value to the business, but did see some value in the "sizzle" of being the leader in a new local marketing technology.

In October 1986, MM delivered the software and databases for its first three markets. In December 1986, the system was installed in GF's Chicago and Los Angeles district sales offices and in February 1987, in GF's Philadelphia district sales office. When GF was restructured in mid-1987, the new senior Sales managers, including John Mann and his NSDs, were strong advocates of the use of the MM system to achieve real business results, not just "sizzle."

Description of Supermarket Solutions

Supermarket Solutions (SS) was the name of MM's system of computer programs. The system had two databases: a retail store directory which

---

[6] A customer backhauled his GF products when he sent one of his own trucks to pick up the merchandise from a GF distribution center. The customer negotiated a backhaul allowance for doing so.

listed 70 physical attributes of every supermarket with weekly dollar volume of $35,000 or more, and a comprehensive list of 295 demographic facts about each store's trading area prepared from the 1986 US Census. The store directory information was gathered on a market-by-market basis through a network of 39 food brokers. Exhibit 3 shows the survey sheet which broker representatives used to collect the data. Brokers were responsible for updating the store directory as stores closed or new stores opened and for resurveying each store once a year.

Once store data was gathered, a trade area, i.e., a demographic description of a store's *potential* shoppers, was calculated for each store by SS's Trade Area software. Each store's weekly dollar sales volume was divided by $19.75, the 1986 national per capita weekly grocery expenditure. This calculation determined the number of people being shopped for in the store each week and became the store's trade area target population.

Stores were plotted on topographical maps. Road networks and the local topography were examined to determine from which directions shoppers were likely to come. The strength of the draw of consumers along eight compass points was assessed based on population density, size of store, competition, traffic patterns, and physical barriers such as rivers. Census tracts were then used to build each store's trade area. The system aggregated census tracts up to the store's trade area target population, taking into account the prior directional flow assessments. It then weighted the demographics from each census tract, added them together, and built a composite demographic description of the store's trade area.

MM designed the SS system to be sold to both manufacturers and retailers. The 10 menu-driven computer programs included in the SS system could be used to:

- Create reports showing detailed information on every store in the system.
- Compare and contrast stores by specific characteristics. Any store fact (or combination) could be used as a criterion to group stores for analysis.
- Rank any group of stores by the presence of a single or multiple demographic attribute(s).
- Identify groups of stores with similar characteristics in order to target promotions or other special programs.
- Describe the trade area(s) of any single store, group of stores, or markets.
- Rank a group of stores based on the match between the demographic profile of a given product's consumer target and the demographics of each store's customer base (trade area), thereby revealing "targets of opportunity" for distribution and product promotion.

EXHIBIT 3 Supermarket Solution's Store Survey Sheet

Market Metrics, Inc.
Store Survey Sheet

Broker ID_____
Broker's store ID #_____
Survey coordinator_____

Date of Survey __/__/__

Salesman name_____

Basic Data

Store name_____
Address_____
Shopping center_____
City/state/zip_____
County_____
Phone_____

Average weekly volume ($000)_____
Employees, part-time_____
Employees, full-time_____
Manager's name_____
Sq. ft. selling space _____
No. of checkouts_____ Scanners   Y   N

Store classification (circle one):   1. chain   2. independent   3. indirect chain

Format	**Measurements**	**Features**
(circle choice)		(circle Y or N)

Format
(circle choice)

1. Limited assortment
2. Supermarket
3. Warehouse
4. Super store
5. Super warehouse

Measurements

Nonfood open_____ft.
Nonfood shelves_____ft.
HaBA shelves_____ft.
HaBA open_____ft.
Frozen upright_____ft.
Frozen coffin_____ft.
Frozen cabinet_____ft.
No. of frozen end caps_____
No. of frozen spot
    merchandisers_____
No. of end aisle displays_____
_____
_____
_____
_____

Features
(circle Y or N)

Fresh ground coffee_____   Y   N
Bulk food_____   Y   N
Restaurant_____   Y   N
Scratch bakery_____   Y   N
HaBA racks_____   Y   N
Service fish_____   Y   N
Gourmet center_____   Y   N
Service deli_____   Y   N
Pharmacy_____   Y   N
Salad bar_____   Y   N
Books, magazines_____   Y   N
Greeting cards_____   Y   N
Lawn/garden_____   Y   N
Video rental_____   Y   N

Total Hours Open

Per week: _____ hours

Years since Last Remodeling
(circle choice)

1. New store
2. 1 to 5 years
3. 6 or more

PSD (powdered drinks)_____ft.
Sec. left of PSD:_____ft.
    Describe:_____
    _____
Sec. right of PSD:_____ft.
    Describe:_____
    _____

Clothing_____   Y   N
Sporting_____   Y   N
Auto supplies_____   Y   N
Beer/wine_____   Y   N
Liquor_____   Y   N
Floral center_____   Y   N
Jhooks, clip strip_____   Y   N
Deli display space_____   Y   N

Advertising (circle Y or N)

Controls own ads   Y   N
If yes, then:

Newspapers	Y	N	Double coupon	Y	N
Television	Y	N	Circular	Y	N
Direct mail	Y	N	Radio	Y	N

Store Setting (circle choice)

1. Major regional shopping mall
2. Shopping mall
3. Uncovered shopping center
4. Strip shopping center
5. Stand alone, suburban and rural
6. Stand alone, urban

Supplier ID Code by Department (for completion by broker home office only):

Grocery_____
Frozen food_____
Dairy/deli/perishables_____
Food service_____

Confection_____
HaBA_____
General merchandise_____

- Distribute a user-defined target number of cases across a group of stores based on a combination of each store's demographic potential and weekly all-commodity sales volume (ACV).
- Determine stores with the highest demographic presence of consumer targets and compare them to competitors, the market, or other reference bases.
- Explore "What if?" scenarios based on a change in ACV, merchandising methods, or market environment.
- Compare new store site selection choices demographically.

SS Installation and Training in GF

MM maintained a master national database of over 30,000 stores and their trade area demographics. In contrast, GF had separate databases for each of its district sales offices. SS was installed in each district office on a personal computer which was specially equipped to run the system. All GF sales forces which worked out of an SS-installed district office had access to the SS system.

Jay Lurch, a development manager in IS, and Leslie Liss, an associate systems analyst, were responsible for installing and implementing the SS system within GF. When the system was first installed in a district, DSMs, KAEs, and DRMs were trained to use it by Lurch, Liss, and Marcia Slaw, a sales trainer. Over time, the focus of the training sessions evolved from how to use the software and "which buttons to press" to how to use the system to solve district-specific business problems. In addition, a leave-behind SS reference manual written in sales language, not "computerese," was completed in April 1988 and sent to every district.

Lurch's ultimate goal was sales force self-sufficiency in using the SS system. In mid-1988, Lurch and Liss were still receiving many calls for help from the sales force. These calls were encouraging because they indicated that the system was being used in the field. However, the volume of calls implied that an information resource was needed at a local level. Two markets, Chicago and Denver, were chosen to test a new staff position, field sales information support specialist. The two people assigned to the new position were charged with assisting all the district's DSMs and their sales forces in accessing and using information, including SS and all other computer programs which GF salespeople were currently using or could be taught to use.

GF Sales Experience with SS

By August 1988, salespeople in GF's Chicago district had been using SS for slightly over a year and one-half. They described how the system had been used, the successes they had achieved with it, and its limitations.

John Biltgen, GSO RSM, explained:

Before using the SS system to try to sell more cases to our customers, we had to ensure the system was credible to them. Therefore, we first held informational meetings with our major customers. We invited everyone from the president to the buyers to attend. Jay or Leslie made many of the initial contacts with us. We explained the system and its applications to our customers in a nonselling situation. We gained access to senior managers in the accounts whom we had never been able to reach before.

Some of our more sophisticated customers had store demographics computer systems of their own. We were able to show them that the output from the SS system was consistent with their own data. That gave us enormous credibility.

Dan Kathol, GSO DSM, added:

This has been a learning experience for both our customers and ourselves. The customers are excited by the potential, but many of them are not yet equipped to market on a store-by-store basis. We can present store-specific shelving, pricing, and promotion plans, but their internal control and distribution systems sometimes force them to reaggregate the plans to a chain or zone level. At first our recommendations didn't always fit our customers' capabilities, but we have now learned what each customer can and cannot do and we tailor our recommendations to each customer's capabilities.

We have had a lot of successes which are directly attributable to use of the SS system. For example, one account which had never purchased module displays[7] from us bought 40 modules of Post Crispy Critters cereal for use in stores which the system identified as having high sales potential for children's cereals. The modules sold through to consumers in one week. The customer was delighted. Another customer authorized distribution of all four flavors of new Stove Top Select when we showed him that the Stove Top Stuffing consumer demographic profile closely matched that of the consumers in his stores' trade areas. In addition to buying the product, the account decided to display and sample the product in the 60 stores identified by SS as having the highest sales potential. In the first week of distribution, the customer experienced 300 percent incremental volume in its Stove Top sales.

The system has helped us close several long-standing distribution voids. It has also helped us to identify key Hispanic stores in which to target in-store displays/promotions behind those of our products which are especially popular with Hispanics. SS has also allowed us to identify nontrip-list stores

---

[7] A module display was a multi-case configuration of a GF product which was assembled in a GF distribution center. Several cases of product were cut open, packages were priced as desired by the customer, and stacked into a display. The entire display was then shrink-wrapped in plastic. When the module display reached a retail store, the store manager simply had the plastic removed and set up the display.

which have high sales potential for GF products. We sold 3,000 incremental cases of Open Pit barbecue sauce last season by targeting high potential stores on whom we normally do not call.

The system has also helped us put together more accurate and productive trip lists. As a result we are more efficient with our selling time and travel time.

Bottom line, use of the system has broken down barriers with our customers. I also feel better as a DSM knowing that my people are selling more professionally now than they were a year ago.

Chris Gardier, a GSO DRM, commented:

Overall, I believe that using the system has improved our relationships with our customers. We have moved closer to becoming their truly preferred partners. Even so, we have to be careful when we present our SS-based conclusions and recommendations to our buyers. They can take offense at our going in and telling them who their customers are. They think they know that better than we do. Also, some of the buyers, like some of the salespeople, feel threatened by the new technology. You have to know how to use a computer to use the system.

The system's capabilities are great. When I was a KAE I used it often as the basis of recommendations to my accounts. Unfortunately, my salespeople have not used the system much. Their opportunity to use it is very limited because they don't have the time to drive to the district office. In November 1988 our district will test the use of laptop computers for selling at retail. All my salespeople will then have computers. If they could tap into the system via modem, I think they'd begin to use the system more.

Louis Schuhler, a GSO KAE, added:

My biggest problem is finding time to sit down and use the system creatively. The lead time on most of our programs is so short that I find myself using the system reactively rather than proactively.

Also, the system can sell against you. We strive to gain distribution and promotional support on all of our items in every store. The system can indicate that some items shouldn't be carried or displayed in a particular store. Our main accountability has always been and always will be volume. We have to be careful we don't use the system to unsell a product or a display.

Jack Brown, director of Customer Planning, summed up:

It is difficult to quantify the total cost to GF for the development of the SS capability. The best estimate includes the salaries and benefits for the two people who worked on this project for the past three and a half years ($400,000), plus the initial outlay ($300,000) to fund the start-up of the Market Metrics company.

The benefits to GF are threefold. First is the extra profit associated with the incremental sales resulting from increased product distribution authorizations by grocery stores and faster shelf turnover. While it is impossible to separate out the volume impact of the use of SS from the overall quality of our sales presentations, logs monitoring results suggest a 1 percent volume growth. The resulting profit impact pays back the investment in less than two years.

Second, SS has increased our salespeople's ability to think as "local marketers." Their ability to develop programs for our trade accounts that attract consumers is an important strategic benefit and source of competitive advantage. We have not measured the incremental number of trade programs or the improvement in selling effectiveness resulting from having SS.

A third benefit is that GF has become recognized as a leader in local marketing. The influence of GF's sales force has grown as the trade begins to use local marketing information.

Denver Local Marketing Test

While GF had conducted a number of local marketing tests over time, GF executives decided in February 1987 to test a comprehensive, multifunctional approach to local marketing. They assembled a task force, the Local Marketing Group (LMG), whose goal was to determine the potential and mechanics of local marketing. The LMG consisted of representatives from Sales, Marketing, Consumer Promotion, MRD, DSSD, IS, and Finance.

The task force chose Denver, Colorado, as the area in which to test local marketing because it was a relatively self-contained market. There was little trade-flow[8] or media spillover from outside the Denver market area. Although the area was large geographically, it had a population of only 500,000, and three chains accounted for 74 percent of the ACV. Denver was, however, a highly competitive market with old, established chains battling newcomers such as club stores and Cub Foods, a 70,000-square-foot upscale warehouse store, and competing heavily on price. Also important for the test, GF had a distribution center located in Denver.

The objective of the test was to build profitable, incremental consumption through local marketing activities which encouraged leading customers to aggressively merchandise GF products. Strategies included:

- Tailoring national consumer promotion and trade programs to appeal to the interests, tastes, and imaginations of Denver customers and consumers.
- Developing and executing innovative consumer promotion and

---

[8] Trade-flow meant that merchandise acquired in one market area was sold at retail in another market area. Trade-flow occurred when a chain had stores located in several market areas.

trade programs that incorporated Denver customers' strategies and supported their merchandising practices.

· Combining individual brand events to create tailored group promotions whose aggregate impact on consumption could be greater than the sum of the individual events.

· Making GF brands an integral part of the community fabric by association with major local events.

· Developing and executing, by customer, tailored distribution services that provided both GF and the customer with a competitive advantage.

· Providing opportunities for customers to improve their positions in the community through their participation in GF local marketing activities.

· Using information technology and market research as strategic assets to support customer planning and local marketing activities.

The role of the LMG was to initiate the local marketing test in Denver and to act as a consultant resource to Denver salespeople once the test was under way. The LMG's ultimate goal was to transfer to the sales force the capability to design and execute local programs.

The LMG introduced the project to field sales in February 1987. Before making any customer contacts, John Boughter, a market research manager and member of the LMG, commissioned an outside agency to conduct six focus group interviews with Denver consumers in order to learn Denver supermarket shoppers' basic food shopping habits and their attitudes and opinions about the major Denver area supermarket chains and the various ways retailers and manufacturers marketed and promoted products. In addition, Boughter sought to learn what kind of local events would motivate consumers' grocery purchases.

Beginning in March 1987, members of the LMG made joint presentations with field sales to the Denver customers. The presentations were two hours long. They were "information sharing" presentations which explained GF's future plans for local marketing, shared the results of the consumer focus groups which were pertinent to the account, and explained SS and its potential uses. Overall, the initial presentations were well received. Many customers shared strategic planning and sales data with GF which they had never before revealed.

After completing the customer "information sharing" presentations, Denver DSMs worked with the LMG to develop local trade and promotional programs. The first local marketing programs were executed in September and October 1987. By the end of 1987, local marketing programs had been executed by every GF sales organization in Denver. Exhibit 4 lists several local marketing promotions which were conducted

EXHIBIT 4   Sample Local Marketing Promotions in Denver—1988

Timing	Event/Theme	Participating Brands	Details
February	"Have breakfast on us"	Log Cabin syrup, Oroweat muffins, Post Raisin Bran and Post Grape Nuts cereal, Tang, and Oscar Mayer bacon	Customer in-ad coupon for free private label breakfast item Customized point-of-sales (POS) pieces by customer Customized ad slick Display modules
February/March	Kids ski free with Kool-Aid	Kool-Aid Koolers and Kool-Aid unsweetened	Kids ski free at local ski areas with Kool-Aid proofs-of-purchase. Newspaper ads/two Kool-Aid coupon drops Co-op radio Promotional radio (consumer sweepstakes) Customer ad slick and POS
March	Frozen food festival	Bird's Eye Farm Fresh vegetables	Newspaper coupon in co-op frozen food festival
April	Grape Nuts/bananas	Post Grape Nuts cereal	Instantly redeemable coupon good for one pound free bananas with purchase of Grape Nuts Only available in module displays with coupons affixed to Grape Nuts boxes
May/June	*What's Hot* magazines	Kool-Aid Koolers and Kool-Aid canisters	Free *What's Hot* magazine with purchase of Kool-Aid Koolers or canisters Display modules
June	Post cereals' All-Star Legends baseball game	Post cereals	Old-timers baseball game to benefit Denver Children's Hospital sponsored by Post Cereals Ties in with national Children's Miracle network promotion cosponsored by Post Cereals Free kids tickets with two Post purchase proofs POS, radio, and newspaper support
July/August	Holiday Health Club	Crystal Light beverages and Crystal Light diet bars	Free two-week membership and $100 discount to Holiday Health Club with two POPs from Crystal Light Products

continued

EXHIBIT 4 (*concluded*)

Timing	Event/Theme	Participating Brands	Details
			In-store POS
			Three weeks radio
			Radio sweepstakes
			* Trip to Jamaica (supplied by radio station)
			* Five annual health club memberships (supplied by Holiday)
			* Twenty-five Crystal Light videotapes (supplied by GF)
August	Cool Whip/Colorado peach promotion	Cool Whip whipped topping	TV co-op (peach focus)
			Co-op newspaper coupon with peach board
			Coupon for one pound free peaches with purchase of Cool Whip
			Cool Whip/peach recipe brochure
			Peach Festival tie-in in Grand Junction

EXHIBIT 5 Denver Trial Market Costs/Benefits ($000)

Costs

Consumer Promotion Costs	Total 1987	Estimated 1988
• Total expense	540	340
Percent incremental*	30%	40%
• Net program expense	162	136
• Program development/creative costs	500	200
Total promotion costs	662	336
Administrative Costs		
• Salaries and benefits	220	200
• Travel, office, miscellaneous	235	140
Total administrative costs	455	340
Total costs	1,117	676

Benefits

GF grouped sales volume into statistical units. Each incremental unit of volume produced, on average, $10 of profit contribution. Four million units were sold in Denver in 1987; 4.2 million were expected to be sold in 1988. Nationwide sales volume was expected to increase 2% in 1988.

* Percent incremental represents the degree to which consumer promotion expenditures exceeded the amounts which would have been spent in Denver on national consumer promotion programs.

in Denver in the first eight months of 1988. Exhibit 5 details the costs and potential benefits identified in Denver.

GF Salespeople's Experience with Denver Local Marketing Test

In August 1988, after one year of planning and executing local marketing programs, GF salespeople described their experiences. Bill Mihal, manager of Local Marketing and a member of the LMG, described how local marketing was funded in Denver:

> Local marketing has been occurring within GF for years. Prior to the Denver test, local marketing was done on an opportunistic basis. Whenever the DSM in a particular market area saw an opportunity for a local marketing event, he/she would propose the idea to the product manager of the relevant brand. If the brand had promotion funds available and the product manager believed the promotion was worthwhile, he/she would fund the event. This happened inconsistently.
>
> In the Denver test, total trade dollars for each brand remained the same as prior to the test. However, Sales was given a bigger voice in deciding how those trade dollars should be spent. Prior to the Denver test, all advertising and consumer promotion expenditures were controlled by the brand groups and 95 percent of all expenditures were on national events. In the Denver test, DSMs were given local advertising and promotion budgets which they were responsible for managing. Depending on the brand, these budgets represented up to 20 percent of the portion of the brand's national advertising and promotion budget allocated to the Denver area. DSMs used these local advertising and promotion budgets to pay for producing and placing ads in local media, point-of-sale material production, coupon production and redemption, and various other local consumer promotion expenses. For most local events, DSMs were required to clear their planned promotions with the brand groups to ensure consistency with national brand strategies. The tactical decisions, however, were left up to the DSMs.
>
> Ideally, as we expand local marketing nationally we will not increase the total dollars spent on advertising, trade promotion, and consumer promotion. Instead we will reallocate some of these funds to local marketing. The size of the local marketing budget for an individual brand could range up to 50 percent of total expenditures for the brand depending on local marketing's importance to the brand's sales.

Mike Victor, Denver's GSO DSM, explained how customers' participation in GF's local marketing programs had evolved over time:

> From the beginning we learned that the trade was no more ready or structured to do local marketing than we were. Several of our customers had internal communications problems which kept them from taking full advantage of our first couple of promotions. For example, our first local promotion was a tie-in with the Denver Broncos called "Team Up For Kids." Post kids' cereals and several other GF products were involved in the promotion. One of our biggest customers was excited by the event and

planned a feature ad and displays to support it. The customer's execution was a disaster. The ad ran the wrong week and the customer shipped the displays to its stores late.

When we discussed the dismal performance with the account, its executive vice president committed to outperforming all of his competitors on our next promotion. He restructured his own organization, adding a liaison between its stores and its buyers whose responsibilities included coordinating the account's execution of local promotional events. Since then, the account has been increasingly successful, selling more product with each succeeding promotion.

A year ago, GFers generated 100 percent of our ideas for local promotions. About 25 percent of them involved localizing national promotions. For example, Post cereals' sponsorship of Denver's All Star Legends Baseball Game, the proceeds of which were donated to Denver Children's Hospital, grew out of Post cereals' national sponsorship of the Children's Miracle Network. The remaining 75 percent of local promotions were Denver-specific ideas hatched by our salespeople. Over time, however, as they became more in tune with what GF was doing, the trade started coming to us with ideas for promoting our products. Today close to 40 percent of our local promotion ideas are coming from our customers.

For example, the customer I mentioned earlier came to us wanting to cross-merchandise one of our cereals with bananas. In our distribution center we put $.40 instantly redeemable coupons (IRCs) on boxes of Post Grape Nuts and built 12 case display modules of the cereal. The customer sent modules to every store and displayed them in the product section with bananas. The displays sold out quickly. Now that customer wants to sit down with us and lay out a whole year of cross-merchandising plans for our products in its produce and meat departments.

As our local marketing has evolved, the way our customers view our promotions has changed. We are now paying less in trade promotion dollars than we paid last year for the same local marketing events. Our customers are demanding fewer trade dollars because they understand that we are creating events which draw consumers into their stores to buy our products. Many of our local promotions tie the purchase of a GF product into support for a local charitable event or give consumers discounts to area ski resorts or amusement parks. We are giving the consumer a reason to buy the product other than price. Therefore, our customers can sell our products at a decent margin rather than giving them away. With local promotional events, we increase the sales of our products without having to spend as much on the programs.

Sue McLean, a Maxwell House account manager (similar to a GSO KAE), explained how local promotion ideas were generated and executed:

> Initially, we [the salespeople] executed all aspects of the local promotions, including working with local printers and public relations agencies to design local coupons and point-of-sale pieces and handle local media buys. We didn't realize what a big job we were taking on. Then, in early 1988, GF

corporate sales hired Julie Swarsen into the new position of district merchandising manager. Julie had sixteen years of experience working in Denver in promotions. Julie helps develop and execute local marketing programs and we do the selling.

About once a quarter, all the divisions have a meeting with all the DSMs, KAEs, and DRMs. Julie and Lori Snyder, our field sales information specialist, also attend. We discuss our national promotions and brainstorm how to convert them to local ones. There is a lot of emphasis on interdivisional promotions because they seem to have the biggest impact at retail. We all voice our ideas and then discuss funding them. One thing I've learned is that you can't do something just because it's nice to do. It's got to make financial sense as well. Through trial and error you learn what kinds of promotions are likely to generate enough volume to justify the cost. Ideally, we want promotions which excite our customers so that they give us retail support and also excite our consumers so that they buy the product that is on display in the retail stores.

Bob Medina, a GSO DAM, explained what it took to make local marketing succeed:

In order to make local marketing work, you have to form a partnership with each customer. You have to design local programs which not only achieve GF's corporate goals, but also help each customer achieve its individual goals. To do that, you have to listen to your accounts and customize programs to their needs. Then you have to constantly follow up with buyers, merchandisers, and store managers to make sure that your accounts are maximizing execution against the programs.

By law we must offer equivalent promotions to all competing accounts within a market area. Therefore, whenever we develop a program for one account, we offer participation to all of the accounts in the market area. If several accounts decide to back the same promotion, the KAEs have to work together to coordinate the timing of their accounts' support so as to try to make the event successful in every account.

In the past, brokers tended to have better relationships with accounts than did manufacturers because brokers' programs were often localized. Now we can best the brokers because we offer not only localized programs, but also professionalism.

The biggest thing we need to improve is corporate communications. We either need the authority to make all program and funding decisions locally, or we need faster communications from headquarters.

Mike Grabowski, a GSO KAE, explained how he felt about his job since GF became involved in local marketing:

The average KAE and SR in Denver are probably working 20 percent more time than other GF KAEs and SRs because of the time it takes to plan and execute our local marketing programs. Even so, I'd be bored in any other environment now. If you can make it in Denver, you can make it anywhere. We know we are ahead of everyone else in GF and we feel good about it.

I get a big sense of accomplishment when my customers perform well against our local programs. Unfortunately, some of our competitors are starting to copy our programs. No one has what we have though, not even close. In Denver, GF is one step ahead of our competitors and we're determined to stay that way.

Sue McLean explained how local marketing had changed her job:

We are still responsible for everything for which we were before local marketing came along. Now we have more responsibility. We have new local marketing objectives in addition to all our old objectives. Any local marketing promotion gets a great deal of focus, but when it comes to quarter end, you still better have those boxes on the truck. We can't lose sight of the fact that selling cases is the point of our jobs.

There is more of a marketing focus in the sales job now. I take more pride in my job than I did in the past. Marketing pays more attention to our ideas than ever before. In the past, marketing and sales butted heads. Now they are more happily married.

Bruce Nordstron, Frozen Foods DSM, discussed the impact of local marketing on his business:

My major products, Bird's Eye vegetables and Cool Whip, have high local market shares and have always gotten good display action and support without local marketing programs. Local marketing has given me an extra fund [local marketing budget] to administer and more opportunities to tie-in promotions with the other divisions, but I don't see any significant incremental volume generated on my products.

I know that local marketing has had substantial impact on volumes in some of the other GF divisions. My question is how far do we go with it? I'm not sure that the same level of local marketing is appropriate for every division or for every part of the country.

Bill Mihal talked about sales results and the changing costs of local marketing:

Cost/benefit analyses for the test are deceiving. One reason is that the costs changed dramatically over time. The first local promotions conducted in Denver cost approximately twice as much as later ones. Costs have been reduced by learning over time which local media and consumer promotion vendors are the most productive and what levels of local media spending are needed to generate desired sales volumes. Originally we were spending at overkill levels. It takes time and trial and error to learn the appropriate spending levels.

Sales results have been very favorable. The products promoted via local marketing in Denver have registered higher percentage increases in both factory shipments and retail sales in Denver than in the entire Western Region and nationwide. Part of this is due to the public relations effect of local marketing, including press coverage of local events.

John Mann discussed ways GF should consider structuring the company if it expands local marketing:

> With local marketing, the sales organization becomes much more important than it was in the past. Until recently, salespeople were the foot soldiers. They were told to execute programs and did. That role has changed. We're now in the process of trying to take them from being program executors to being master marketers. To be successful in creating that change, we need to bring marketing resources closer to where the rubber meets the road. Unfortunately, when you bring the resources closer to the field they become less efficient due to duplication of effort. You have to balance the trade-off between increased effectiveness and decreased efficiency.
>
> By efficiency, I mean "doing things right" as opposed to effectiveness, which is "doing the right things." GF has historically been a very efficient marketer. Centralized marketing control has allowed GF to take advantage of national economies of advertising production and media placement, for example, which have kept marketing costs down. Local marketing, while giving up some of the efficient use of resources, increases the effectiveness of our promotions by giving our customers and ultimate consumers compelling reasons to buy and consume our products. The issue boils down to spending more marketing dollars on local promotions but selling enough incremental cases to more than make up for the added marketing cost.
>
> You can't set up this new structure in a vacuum. You can't just add on human resources. You have to shift them from one place to another.
>
> The resources we need include a consumer promotion person, a marketing researcher, a person from I/S, a legal resource, and a financial resource. I see two broad options: divisional sales resource groups assigned to each region which would work with only one GF sales organization, or corporate sales resource groups assigned to each district which would work with all GF sales organizations. Both options have strengths and limitations.
>
> I think we'll probably end up with a hybrid local marketing organization which is separate from the sales organization but closely aligned with it. I envision a national local marketing manager who manages some of his resources regionally and some by district. For example, each district may have a consumer promotion manager and a market researcher assigned to it, whereas information services, legal, and financial resources would be handled on a regional basis.
>
> Today, each sales organization is given a pot of marketing funds to use for local advertising and consumer promotions. However, we DSMs must clear local promotion plans with the brands. Ideally, in the future, districts will become profit centers. We will have more flexibility in our local marketing spending in exchange for profit accountability.

Marketing's Reactions to Local Marketing

Two Marketing executives at GF headquarters who were involved in the Denver local marketing test expressed their views about the future of local marketing in GF. Jean Washington, associate director of promotion for GF USA, explained:

> It is unclear whether local marketing in Denver has generated enough incremental sales to pay back the money that was invested in Denver for the start-up of the test. Two positive results are certain, however. First, the expertise of the Sales organization has been upgraded. The salespeople now think in marketing and business terms instead of focusing just on selling cases. Second, the marketing people who were involved in the test developed a better understanding of the retail grocery trade.
>
> Certain brands can benefit from individualized programming in specific markets. Other ones cannot. We need to make that distinction. GF is now addressing the potential of local marketing on a brand-by-brand basis. Currently, people are developing programs in their own markets for which the volume results don't give payback for the management time involved. The sales organization needs clearer direction as to which brands benefit from local marketing and which ones do not.
>
> Currently, many brand managers feel that the people to whom they are transferring local marketing money and accountability (DSMs) are not equipped to make marketing decisions. They worry about possible mismanagement of brands or that confused messages will be sent to consumers. Therefore, a training program was developed to teach DSMs to be local marketers. They need to be taught general marketing principles, the strategies of each brand, and which types of promotions are likely to work with given brands. Ultimately, DSMs should have some profit as well as sales volume responsibility.
>
> As local marketing is expanded within GF, planning and direction should be maintained at GF headquarters. Each division should identify one or two brands which have local marketing potential and should communicate their strategies for local marketing to the sales force. Implementation should be through headquarters personnel and outside resources working with existing people in the field. From a corporate perspective, there should be one person who would coordinate all of GF's local marketing efforts. This person would be responsible for consolidating both costs and learning.

Steven Sadove, vice president and general manager of the Meals division, explained:

> The relevant question is no longer "Does local marketing make sense?" GF is committed to being at the forefront of local marketing as a source of competitive advantage. Today the relevant question is "What is the appropriate organizational structure for local marketing?" Three structural issues must be decided:
>
> 1. Who will control strategy development?
> 2. Who will control resource allocation among geographies?
> 3. Who will control execution of local marketing events?

The Future of Local Marketing in GF

Tom Hoeppner sat at a conference table with several sales executives. They were meeting to discuss the future of local marketing in GF.

Hoeppner opened the discussion with the following comments:

> Changes in our operating environment have led GF to experiment with local marketing. We have already committed to expand one local marketing tool, the SS system, to all of our districts. We are also expanding our customized menu approach to distribution of products to customers. That is only the beginning. How do we ensure that the system is used to its full potential? How do we make it more brand-driven and consumer- versus trade-oriented?
>
> A bigger question is: How do we move beyond our Denver local marketing test? There are many implications if we choose to conduct local marketing nationally as it is currently performed in Denver. Organizational structure changes would certainly be needed in order to market successfully both nationally and locally. In addition, changes in our sales recruiting, training, compensation, and evaluation systems would probably be necessary. I'd like to leave the room today with a clear vision of the GF sales organization and structure needed to move us successfully into the 1990s.

Cases in Product Management

Index